# Fourth Workshop on Simple and Efficient Natural Language Processing (SustaiNLP 2023)



Toronto, Canada
13 July 2023

ISBN: 978-1-7138-8235-0

**Printed from e-media with permission by:**

Curran Associates, Inc.
57 Morehouse Lane
Red Hook, NY 12571

**Some format issues inherent in the e-media version may also appear in this print version.**



Printed with permission by Curran Associates, Inc. (2024)

For permission requests, please contact the Association for Computational Linguistics at the address below.

Association for Computational Linguistics
209 N. Eighth Street
Stroudsburg, Pennsylvania 18360

Phone: 1-570-476-8006
Fax: 1-570-476-0860

acl@aclweb.org

**Additional copies of this publication are available from:**

Curran Associates, Inc.
57 Morehouse Lane
Red Hook, NY 12571 USA
Phone: 845-758-0400
Fax: 845-758-2633
Email: curran@proceedings.com
Web: www.proceedings.com

SustaiNLP 2023

# The Fourth Workshop on Simple and Efficient Natural Language Processing

## Proceedings of the Workshop

July 13, 2023

Order copies of this and other ACL proceedings from:

Association for Computational Linguistics (ACL)
209 N. Eighth Street
Stroudsburg, PA 18360
USA
Tel: +1-570-476-8006
Fax: +1-570-476-0860
acl@aclweb.org

ISBN 978-1-959429-79-1

# Introduction

It is our great pleasure to welcome you to the fourth edition of SustaiNLP: Workshop on Simple and Efficient Natural Language Processing.

The Natural Language Processing community has, in recent years, demonstrated a notable focus on improving higher scores on standard benchmarks and taking the lead on community-wide leaderboards (e.g., GLUE, SentEval). While this aspiration has led to improvements in benchmark performance of (predominantly neural) models, it has also came at a cost, i.e., increased model complexity and the evergrowing amount of computational resources required for training and using the current state-of-the-art models. Moreover, the recent research efforts have, for the most part, failed to identify sources of empirical gains in models, often failing to empirically justify the model complexity beyond benchmark performance.

Because of these easily observable trends, we organized the SustaiNLP workshop with the goal of promoting more sustainable NLP research and practices, with two main objectives: (1) encouraging development of more efficient NLP models; and (2) providing simpler architectures and empirical justification of model complexity. For both aspects, we encouraged submissions from all topical areas of NLP.

This year, we received 46 submissions, proposing a multitude of viable resource-efficient NLP methods and spanning a wide range of NLP applications. We have selected 26 submissions for presentation at the workshop, yielding an acceptance rate of 57%.

Many thanks to the SustailNLP program committee for their thorough and thoughtful reviews. We would also like to thank to our panelists and invited speakers whose discussions and talks we strongly believe will make the workshop exciting and memorable.

We are looking forward to the fourth edition of the SustaiNLP workshop!

SustaiNLP Organizers
June 2023

# Organizing Committee

**Organizers**

Nafise Sadat Moosavi, University of Sheffield
Iryna Gurevych, TU Darmstadt
Yufang Hou, IBM Research Ireland
Gyuwan Kim, UC Santa Barbara
Young Jin Kim, Microsoft Research
Tal Schuster, Google Research
Ameeta Agrawal, Portland State University

# Program Committee

**Program Committee**

Hadi Abdi Ghavidel, Bell Canada
Hend Al-khalifa, King Saud University
Ahmed Alajrami, The University of Sheffield
Abhinav Arora, Facebook
Sina Bagheri Nezhad, Portland State University
Mohaddeseh Bastan, Stony Brook University
Samuel Cahyawijaya, HKUST
Roman Grundkiewicz, Microsoft Research
Benjamin Heinzerling, RIKEN AIP and Tohoku University
Amr Hendy, Microsoft
Zhiqi Huang, Tencent AI Lab
Peter Izsak, Intel Labs
Sungho Jeon, Heidelberg Institute for Theoretical Studies
Rishabh Joshi, Google
Mihir Kale, Google
Lis Kanashiro Pereira, Ochanomizu University
Kartik Kannapur, Amazon Web Services
Md. Shahriar Karim, North South University
Constantinos Karouzos, University of Sheffield
Anne Lauscher, University of Hamburg
Ji-ung Lee, UKP, TU Darmstadt
Els Lefever, LT3, Ghent University
Florian Mai, Idiap Research Institute
Jonathan Mamou, Intel Labs
Ekata Mitra, Portland State University
Anhad Mohananey, Google
Yusuke Mori, The University of Tokyo
Marius Mosbach, Saarland University
Sergiu Nisioi, Human Language Technologies Research Center, University of Bucharest
Siddhesh Pawar, Google
Oren Pereg, Emergent AI Lab, Intel Labs
Vikas Raunak, Microsoft
Ines Rehbein, University of Mannheim
Hossein Rouhizadeh, University of Geneva
Edwin Simpson, University of Bristol
Pranaydeep Singh, LT3, University of Ghent
Marek Suppa, Comenius University in Bratislava
Danae Sánchez Villegas, University of Sheffield
Yufei Tao, Portland State University
Lovre Torbarina, doXray
Moshe Wasserblat, Intel Labs
Miles Williams, University of Sheffield
Genta Winata, Bloomberg
Tiezheng Yu, The Hong Kong University of Science and Technology

# Table of Contents

# KwikBucks: Correlation Clustering with Cheap-Weak and Expensive-Strong Signals

**Sandeep Silwal**[†1], **Sara Ahmadian**[2], **Andrew Nystrom**[2], **Andrew McCallum**[2],
**Deepak Ramachandran**[*2], **Mehran Kazemi**[* 2]
[1] MIT, [2] Google Research
silwal@mit.edu, {sahmadian, nystrom, mccallum,
ramachandrand, mehrankazemi}@google.com

## Abstract

For text clustering, there is often a dilemma: one can either first embed each examples independently and then compute pair-wise similarities based on the embeddings, or use a cross-attention model that takes a pair of examples as input and produces a similarity. The former is more scalable but the similarities often have lower quality, whereas the latter does not scale well but produces higher quality similarities. We address this dilemma by developing a clustering algorithm that leverages the best of both worlds: the scalability of former and the quality of the latter. We formulate the problem of text clustering with embedding-based and cross-attention models as a novel version of the Budgeted Correlation Clustering problem (BCC) where along with a limited number of queries to an expensive oracle (a cross-attention model in our case), we have unlimited access to a cheaper but less accurate second oracle (embedding similarities in our case). We develop a theoretically motivated algorithm that leverages the cheap oracle to judiciously query the strong oracle while maintaining high clustering quality. We empirically demonstrate gains in query minimization and clustering metrics on a variety of datasets with diverse strong and cheap oracles.

## 1 Introduction

Modern ML techniques have made incredible advances at the cost of needing resource-intensive models (Sharir et al., 2020). Many recent approaches are so resource-intensive that despite amazing accuracy, they are infeasible to be scaled as-is in practical usage. The total effect of all such deployments on energy usage is also a major sustainability concern (Wu et al., 2022).

With the increased cost in querying ML models, the cost of obtaining similarities between objects of different types (texts, images, etc.) has also substantially increased. In this paper, we aim to answer a challenging question when working with such costly similarity measure models: how can we group similar objects together when similarities of objects are obtained via expensive queries? This problem can be naturally cast as a popular and versatile clustering framework, named *Correlation Clustering (CC)*, which has been extensively studied over the past 15+ years (Bonchi et al., 2022): given similarities between arbitrary objects represented as a graph, CC minimizes a natural objective that attempts to cluster together similar vertices while simultaneously separating dissimilar ones. The high cost of querying large ML models motivates the use of the Budgeted CC (BCC) setting studied in (Bressan et al., 2019; García-Soriano et al., 2020a) where relationships between nodes are determined by making a limited number of queries to an oracle, e.g. a large ML model.

We posit that in many practical settings, coarse but efficient approximations of an expensive model can be obtained through substantially cheaper but weaker models. These weaker models can be used as a guide to spend the query budget for the expensive model more carefully. A motivating example, which heavily inspires our work, is in text clustering where one wishes to obtain similarity signals from the latest highly-accurate *cross-attention (CA)* language models (e.g., (Brown et al., 2020; Thoppilan et al., 2022)), but may be hindered by the computational burden as obtaining each pair-wise similarity between data points requires an inference call to the model, giving rise to a worse case $O(n^2)$ inference calls, where $n$ is the number of data points. *Embedding based models* (e.g., (Mikolov et al., 2013; Devlin et al., 2018) can come to the rescue as they require only $O(n)$ inference calls to obtain embedding vectors for each data point that can then be used for fast similarity computation. While embedding models typically produce substantially lower quality similarity signals than CA

*Co-advised. †Work done while interning at Google.



*Proceedings of The Fourth Workshop on Simple and Efficient Natural Language Processing (SustaiNLP)*, pages 1–31
July 13, 2023 

models (see, e.g., (Menon et al., 2022)), they can still provide a good approximation to guide where the budget for the CA model should be spent.

Inspired by the above, we introduce a variant of BCC where, along with a limited number of queries to an expensive oracle, we also have unlimited access to a cheaper but less accurate second oracle. We develop an algorithm dubbed **KwikBucks** that extends the well-known **Kwik**Cluster algorithm to **bu**dgeted CC with **c**heap-wea**k** and expensive-**s**trong signals. KwikBucks uses the weak signal as a guide to minimize the number of calls to the strong signal. Under the assumption that the weak signal returns a strict superset of the strong signal edges, our algorithm approximately matches the performance of KwikCluster, i.e., a 3-approximation, using a small number of queries to the expensive model. In our experiments, we strengthen our theoretical modelling with several well-motivated optimizations and demonstrate that KwikBucks manages to produce high quality clusterings with only a small number of queries to the expensive oracle even when there is only a weak correlation between the weak and strong signal.

We conduct extensive experiments with multiple datasets to evaluate the performance of KwikBucks over natural extensions of previous algorithms for closely-related problems. KwikBucks recovers the best clustering solution with a much smaller strong signal budget than the alternatives, and it finds asymptotically better solutions in many cases. KwikBucks is also robust to the choice of weak signal oracle across different dataset settings and obtains significant improvements over five baselines — **64%** relative improvement in clustering quality (measured in terms of F1 score) when averaging over 9 datasets, and over $>$ **3.5x** reduction in query complexity compared to the best baseline.

### 1.1 Related Work

Our paper spans correlation clustering, clustering with budget constraints, and learning from multiple annotators. For brevity, we focus on the closely related key works in these areas.

**Correlation clustering** is one of the most well studied graph clustering problems and has been actively researched over the past 15+ years (see the book (Bonchi et al., 2022)). It has numerous applications in ML and beyond, including spam detection (Ramachandran et al., 2007; Bonchi et al., 2014), social network analysis (Bonchi et al., 2015; Tang et al., 2016), entity resolution (Getoor and Machanavajjhala, 2012), and many others (Gionis et al., 2005; Hassanzadeh et al., 2009; Cohen and Richman, 2002; Kim et al., 2011). (Bansal et al., 2004) introduced and gave the first constant factor approximation for complete graphs (see Def. 1). Variants include incomplete signed graph (Bansal et al., 2004; Ailon et al., 2008), where the problem is APX-Hard (Demaine et al., 2006), and weighted graphs (Charikar et al., 2005), where it is Unique-Games hard (Chawla et al., 2006).

**Clustering under budget constraints** studies the problem of a limited number of pairwise similarity queries. In this setting, a line of work looked at spectral clustering on partially sampled matrices: Fetaya et al. (2015) in general setting, and Shamir and Tishby (2011) and Wauthier et al. (2012) for bi-partitioning. The most relevant works to our paper are those of García-Soriano et al. (2020a) and Bressan et al. (2021) who devised algorithms for correlation clustering that given a budget of $Q$ queries attain a solution whose expected number of disagreements is at most $3\cdot$ OPT $+O(\frac{n^3}{Q})$, where OPT is the optimal cost for the instance. Another closely related line of work studies "same-cluster" queries for various clustering problems including CC (Ailon et al., 2018; Saha and Subramanian, 2019). The differences between these works and ours are (1) they assume *all* $\binom{n}{2}$ similarity queries are already known in advance whereas we must query the strong signal to obtain similarities, (2) their queries give access to the *optimal* clustering, whereas we only query for edge signs.

**Learning from multiple annotators** considers cost-effective learning from multiple annotators where the cost of a labeler is proportional to its overall quality. The most relevant work to our setting is (Guha et al., 2015) as it considers hierarchical clustering which uses lightweight similarity scores to identify candidate pairs with high similarity (detailed comparison in Section $A$). Ensemble approaches (Dietterich, 2000) are also relevant, but they require knowing the similarities in advance and do not apply to our budgeted setting. Lastly we survey additional related works on learning from multiple annotators as well as algorithms with predictions in Section A.

### 1.2 Preliminaries and Notation

The input of correlation clustering is a complete undirected graph $G = (V, E^+ \cup E^-)$ on $|V| = n$

vertices. $E^+$ and $E^-$ represent the partitions of all possible $\binom{n}{2}$ edges where an edge $e = (u, v) \in E^+$ indicates that $u$ and $v$ are similar and $e = (u, v) \in E^-$ indicates that $u$ and $v$ are dissimilar. We simplify the notation to $G = (V, E = E^+)$ so any present edge is a positive edge and any missing edge is a negative edge. Additionally, we use $m$ to denote the size of $|E|$ and $\Gamma(v) = \{u \mid (v, u) \in E\}$ to denote the neighborhood of vertex $v$.

A *clustering* is a partitioning $C = \{C_1, C_2, \cdots\}$ of $V$ into disjoint subsets. Let $C_{v,u}$ denote the indicator variable if the vertices $v$ and $u$ are assigned to the same cluster. We study the min-disagreement formulation of the correlation clustering problem defined as follows (Bansal et al., 2004).

**Definition 1** (Correlation Clustering (CC))**.** *Given a graph $G = (V, E)$, the objective of correlation clustering (CC) is to output a clustering $C$ that minimizes:*

$$\sum_{e=(v,u)\notin E} C_{v,u} + \sum_{e=(v,u)\in E} (1 - C_{v,u}). \quad (1)$$

KwikCluster (Ailon et al., 2008) is a well-known CC algorithm which proceeds by successively picking a vertex $p$, called a pivot, uniformly at random from the graph and forming a cluster $\{p\} \cup \Gamma(p)$. The algorithm removes this cluster and recurses on the remaining graph until all vertices are assigned to clusters. Based on the fact that the set of pivots is a maximal *independent set* constructed from a random order of vertices, Bonchi et al. (2013) suggests an equivalent algorithm that first constructs the independent set and then assigns any non-pivot to its first neighbor in the independent set. Both algorithms yield 3-approximation in expectation, however the second algorithm is more efficient as the assignment of non-pivots can be performed in parallel.

Despite practicality and simplicity of KwikCluster (and its variants), the algorithm assumes access to the full similarity graph $G$ and is not feasible when similarity measures are expensive to acquire. We consider budget CC studied before by (García-Soriano et al., 2020b; Bressan et al., 2019) where there is a limit (budget) for the number of queries that can be made.

**Definition 2** (Expensive / Strong Oracle)**.** *Given an edge e, the query $\mathcal{O}_S(e)$ outputs whether $e \in E$, i.e., e is a positive edge.*

Following the motivations provided in Section 1, we also introduce a second weaker oracle which is cheaper to query.

**Definition 3** (Cheap / Weak Oracle)**.** *Given any vertex $v$, the query $\mathcal{O}_W(v)$ outputs a similarity score in $\mathbb{R}$ between $v$ and every other vertex in $V$, where higher values indicate higher similarity*

We frequently refer to $G$ as the *strong signal graph* and likewise a strong signal edge refers to an edge in $E$. We interchangeably use the terms signal or oracle, the terms strong and expensive signal, and also the terms weak and cheap signal.

## 2 Theoretical Modelling

We introduce an algorithm that leverages the cheap signal for strong signal query efficiency. Our goals are twofold: **(1)** Design a flexible algorithm paradigm which can adapt to incorporate constraints necessitated by practice, i.e., limited access to expensive queries, **(2)** Analyze the quality of the produced solution with respect to the CC objective (see equation 1). We first introduce a modelling assumption for the weak oracle for the purpose of theoretical analysis. While this results in a *different* but related weak oracle formulation compared to Definition 3, it lets us derive a robust algorithm design which we subsequently adapt to the more realistic setting of Definition 3.

First, we introduce a noise factor $\gamma$ that determines the usefulness of a weak signal. $\gamma = 0$ corresponds to a perfect weak signal that exactly matches the strong signal and $\gamma = n$ corresponds to a completely uninformative weak signal.

**Assumption 1.** *For a fixed noise parameter $\gamma > 0$, the query $\mathcal{O}_W^\gamma(v)$ outputs a subset of $V$ such that $\Gamma(v) \subseteq \mathcal{O}_W^\gamma(v)$ and $|\mathcal{O}_W^\gamma(v)| \leq (1+\gamma)|\Gamma(v)|$.*

The existence of such a signal with a small $\gamma$, say $O(1/n)$ or $\gamma < 1$ might seem like a strong assumption for most applications. However, our experiments show that weak signal can actually provide predictive hints about the true underlying strong signal graph. More precisely, given vertex $v$, we order $V$ with respect to the weak signal, and observe that *true* strong signal neighbors of $v$ are often ranked higher. Thus, returning the most similar vertices for an input node captures many of the true strong signal neighbors of $v$ and mimics the clean abstraction of Assumption 1 (See Appendix F.6 for further empirical justification).

Using the above characterization, we next explain the high level ideas of our algorithm KwikBucks (Algorithm 1). It is inspired by a variant of KwikCluster (Bonchi et al., 2013) adapted

**Algorithm 1** KwikBucks (Our Algorithm)

**Require:** A bound on sampled vertices, $t$, the strong signal budget, $Q$.

$P \leftarrow$ GetPivots$(t, Q)$<br>
**return** AssignToClusters$(P, V \setminus P, Q)$

**Algorithm 2** AssignToClusters$(P, U, Q)$

**Require:** List of pivots, $P$, a vertex set, $U$, remaining strong signal budget, $Q$.

$A \leftarrow \emptyset$ {the set of singletons}<br>
$C_p \leftarrow \{p\}$ {cluster for any pivot $p \in P$}<br>
**while** $Q > 0$ and $U \neq \emptyset$ **do**<br>
    $v \leftarrow$ extract first vertex of $U$<br>
    $N_v \leftarrow$ WeakFilter$(v, P)$<br>
    $p \leftarrow$ FirstNeighbor$(v, N_v, Q)$<br>
    **if** $p \neq \emptyset$ **then**<br>
        $C_p = C_p \cup \{v\}$<br>
    **else**<br>
        $A \leftarrow A \cup \{v\}$<br>
$A \leftarrow A \cup U$<br>
**return** $\cup_{p \in P} C_p \cup_{v \in A} \{v\}$

**Algorithm 3** GetPivots$(t, Q)$

**Require:** A bound on the number of sampled vertices, $t$, the remaining strong signal budget, $Q$.

$\{v_1, \ldots, v_t\} \leftarrow t$ sampled vertices<br>
$P \leftarrow \{v_1\}$<br>
**for** $i \geq 2$ **do**<br>
    $N_i \leftarrow$ WeakFilter$(v_i, P)$<br>
    **if** FirstNeighbor$(v_i, N_i, Q) = \emptyset$ **then**<br>
        $P \leftarrow P \cup \{v_i\}$<br>
**return** $P$

**Algorithm 4** FirstNeighbor$(v, N, Q)$

**Require:** Input vertex, $v$, an ordered list of vertices, $N$, the remaining strong signal budget, $Q$.

**while** $Q > 0$ and $N \neq \emptyset$ **do**<br>
    $u \leftarrow$ extract first vertex from $N$<br>
    $Q \leftarrow Q - 1$<br>
    **if** $\mathcal{O}_S(v, u) = 1$ **then**<br>
        **return** $\{u\}$<br>
**return** $\emptyset$

to our two oracle setting. In this variant, we first pick pivots by forming a maximal independent set from a random ordering of vertices, and then assign non-pivots to their first neighbor (which must exist by maximality of the independent set). A naive extension of this algorithm can result in $\Omega(n^{1.5})$ queries to the strong signal (see 1). However, one may argue that by using the weak signal, we can prune the possible neighborhood of vertices which results in fewer strong signal queries.

While the weak signal can help us make smarter queries to the strong signal, we can still show that even for a weak signal with a small error rate, i.e., $\gamma = O(1)$, we still need $\Omega(n^2)$ queries to the strong signal when forming a maximal independent set (see 2). To circumvent this difficulty, we consider another modification of KwikCluster by Bonchi et al. (2013) where instead of picking a maximal independent set, we pick $t$ vertices uniformly at random and then pick an independent set from them. The caveat of this approach is that some non-pivots may not have any neighbor in the chosen pivot set, and so these non-pivots are returned as singleton clusters. This results in an algorithm which returns a solution with cost at most $3OPT + O(n^2/t)$. We additionally modify this algorithm by incorporating the weak signal to further prune possible strong signal queries. While this algorithm has an additive error for correlation clustering cost, it helps us direct our queries to "impactful" portions of graph. We now have all the ingredients for describing our algorithm, KwikBucks.

KwikBucks first picks *all* pivots via random sampling as shown in GetPivots: each sampled vertex is added to the pivot set if it is not connected to the current subset of pivots that is trimmed down by WeakFilter (which uses the weak signal). Then, it continues to assign non-pivots to clusters, through AssignToClusters, which finds the first vertex (FirstNeighbor) in the subset of ordered pivots trimmed down by the weak signal via WeakFilter. If no such vertex exists, then the vertex is assigned to its own cluster, i.e., a singleton cluster. Note that having a small $t$ (the number of sampled vertices) helps query efficiency by functionally reducing the set of vertices that the weak signal is applied to (both when selecting pivots and when assigning to pivots) and then further queried by the strong signal. This comes at the cost of a small additive error. Our next theorem formally bounds the number of queries and the effect of $t$ (proof in Appendix B).

**Theorem 1.** *Under Assumption 1,* KwikBucks *uses* $n + t + 2\gamma tm/n + 2\gamma t^2 m/n^2$ *queries to* $\mathcal{O}_S$ *to achieve approximation* 3OPT + $O(n^2/t)$.

Our next corollary, considers the interesting case

**Algorithm 5** `WeakFilter`$(v, S)$

**Return** $\mathcal{O}_W^{\gamma}(v) \cap S$

of a constant-size pivot set, i.e., $t = 1/\epsilon$, which will incur an additive error of $\varepsilon n^2$. This can be thought as the 'right scale' as we make a mistake on only an $\varepsilon$ fraction of all edges. We complement our corollary by presenting a matching lower bound in the appendix (Lemma 3) showing that $\Omega(n+d\gamma/\varepsilon)$ strong signal queries are necessary to obtain the guarantees of Corollary 1.

**Corollary 1.** *Let $d$ be the average degree of the strong signal graph and suppose $n$ is sufficiently large ($n > 1/\varepsilon$). We can achieve approximation* $3{\cdot}\mathrm{OPT} + \varepsilon n^2$ *with $n + O(d\gamma/\varepsilon)$ queries to $\mathcal{O}_S$.*

## 3 The Final Empirical Algorithm

We now extend the algorithm for the idealized setting of Section 2 into a practical version of `KwikBucks` for general weak signals, i.e. Definition 3. While this version does not satisfy Assumption 1 and hence does not have similar approximability guarantees, it still retains some theoretical motivation (sketched below), and is empirically very successful (see Section 4).

The modifications we make for our practical algorithm are based on the following natural inductive bias: *'similar' edges according to the strong signal are likely to have a high weak signal similarity score.* At a high level, we incorporate this assumption throughout our algorithm design by ranking potential queries to the strong signal according to weak signal similarity values.

**Weak Filter by Ranking** The most noticeable change occurs for `WeakFilter`: In our theoretical modelling, it returns a subset of $S$ which intersects with the noisy neighborhood returned by the cheap oracle. For the general weak signal version (Definition 3), we update the `WeakFilter` function to instead rank the vertices in $S$ with respect to the weak signal similarity to $v$ and then output the top $k$ elements in $S$ with the highest similarities (Algorithm 6)). Intuitively, for a suitable parameter $k$, the top $k$ candidates capture many of the strong signal neighbors of $v$ in $S$. Indeed, we empirically verify this in our experiments and show that predictive weak signals usually rank true strong signal neighbors much higher compared to a random ordering. For our experiments we fix $k = 100$ and perform ablation studies on this parameter.

**Algorithm 6** `WeakFilterByRanking`$(v, S, k)$

**Require:** Input vertex $v$; set $S \subseteq V$

$w_i \leftarrow$ similarity of $(v, u_i)$ for all $u_i \in S$ as computed by weak signal

Sort elements of $S$ in decreasing $w_i$ values

**Return** First $k$ elements of new sorted order

To better understand the effect of this modification, consider `AssignClusters` where non-pivot vertices attempt to connect to a pivot. In our theoretical modeling and in the classical `KwikCluster` algorithm, each non-pivot vertex checks for a strong signal edge among the list of pivots in an ordering which is fixed for all vertices. This ordering can be thought of as the ordering inherited from `GetPivots`. In contrast, `WeakFilterByRanking` introduces a data adaptive ordering step where each non-pivot vertex can re-rank pivots based on weak signal similarities. As shown in Section 4, this has a sizeable impact on the empirical performance of our algorithm. In Section D.1, we explain these gains by introducing a natural data model that makes some well-motivated assumptions about the relationship between the strong and weak signal, as well as the inherent clusterability of the underlying graph. Under this model, we prove that the quality of the clustering after re-ranking is strictly better than for the unranked filter.

**Further optimizations.** We make three additional enhancements to `KwikBucks`. The first one simply sorts the non-pivots based on the maximum weak signal similarity to the pivots so that 'easier' non-pivots are assigned clusters first which improves query efficiency. The second one modifies the `WeakFilterByRanking` function slightly by increasing the weak signal similarity value between a non-pivot $v$ and a pivot $p$ if $p$ has 'many' nearest neighbors (in weak signal similarity) of $v$ already in its cluster. Finally, the last enhancement introduces a post-processing step where we potentially merge some clusters after our algorithm terminates. As shown in Section D.2, this optimization is motivated by a theoretical worst-case example for `KwikCluster`. The merging step proceeds by first curating a list of clusters to consider for merging based on the average weak signal value between the two clusters and we sample a small number of strong signal edges between potential clusters to merge to determine if the pair is suitable for merging. Each of these optimizations is described in detail in Section C.

## 4 Experiments

**Datasets.** We use 9 datasets, 8 publicly available and 1 proprietary internal. Each dataset exhibits different properties such as varying strong signal graph densities and diverse strong and weak signals to demonstrate the versatility of our method. We provide high-level descriptions here and refer to Section E for more details.

Four public datasets are comprised of text inputs: Stackoverflow (SOF) (Xu et al., 2017), SearchSnippets (Phan et al., 2008), Tweet (Yin and Wang, 2016) and AgNews (Rakib et al., 2020). For Stackoverflow and SearchSnippets, we use word2vec embedding similarities (Mikolov et al., 2013) as the cheap signal and a large cross-attention based language model as the strong signal. For Tweet and AgNews, BERT embedding similarities (Devlin et al., 2018) are the cheap signal; the strong signal of an input pair is the indicator variable of the two examples belonging to the same class plus a small amount of i.i.d. noise to prevent the formation of disconnected connected components, which is the 'easy' case for `KwikCluster` [1].

The other four public datasets are comprised of attributed graphs: Cora (Sen et al., 2008), Amazon Photos (Shchur et al., 2018), Citeseer (Sen et al., 2008), and Microsoft Medicine (Shchur and Günnemann, 2019). For Cora and Amazon photos, node embedding (learned using deep graph infomax (Velickovic et al., 2019)) similarities are the cheap signal; the strong signal is generated similarly to those of Tweet and AgNews. For Citeseer and Microsoft Medicine, node attribute similarities are the cheap signal and the existence/absence of edges in the graph is the strong signal.

Moreover, we report results on a large proprietary dataset based on the shopping reviews of a commercial website. We use internally developed (and finetuned) embedding based and cross-attention based language models for the cheap and expensive signals respectively; both models are based on the publicly available language models such as BERT and T5 (Raffel et al., 2020).

**Baselines.** Since our work is the first BCC algorithm which utilizes both strong and weak signals, we adapt algorithms from prior work, e.g. some which only use a strong signal, to our setting. We also propose several new algorithms as baselines.

**Baseline 1:** A variant of `KwikBucks` where we do not use the weak signal ordering computed in Algorithm 6 when checking for a strong signal edge between a node and a set of pivots. Rather we use the the order the pivots were picked.

**Baseline 2:** Algorithm presented in (García-Soriano et al., 2020b; Bressan et al., 2019). It follows the `KwikCluster` algorithm and uses the strong signal to query edges. If the query budget is depleted, the algorithm is terminated and any remaining vertices are returned as singletons.

**Baseline 3 / 4:** We compute a $k$-NN graph based on the weak signal to narrow down the set of all possible queries to a small set of relevant pairs. Each edge of the $k$-NN graph is re-weighted (either 0 or 1) based on the strong signal. Baseline 3 runs the classic spectral clustering algorithm and baseline 4 runs the vanilla `KwikCluster` algorithm to completion on this graph.

**Baseline 5:** This baseline is inspired by the baseline used in (García-Soriano et al., 2020b). We pick $k$ random vertices and query their complete neighborhood using the strong signal. $k$ is again chosen as high as possible within the allotted query budget. Instead of running an affinity propagation algorithm, which was already shown in (García-Soriano et al., 2020b) to be inferior to Baseline 2, we run the vanilla `KwikCluster` algorithm.

**Evaluation metrics.** We evaluate our algorithm and baselines based on the correlation clustering objective (equation 1). For the purpose of evaluating metrics, we use all edges of the strong signal graph in contrast to the duration of algorithm execution which we limit the access. In addition, we compute the **precision** and **recall** of edges of the strong signal graph. Given a clustering $\mathcal{C}$, its precision is defined as the ratio between the number of strong signal edges whose endpoints are together in the same cluster and the total number of pairs of vertices clustered together in $\mathcal{C}$. The recall is defined as the fraction of all strong signal edges whose vertices are clustered together in some cluster of $\mathcal{C}$; see equation 2 and 3. We combine the precision and recall into a single metric via the standard $F_1$ score

**Parameter configurations.** Our algorithm has two main parameters to select: $t$ in Algorithm 3 corresponding to the number of vertices we select uniformly at random which is then pruned to form the set of pivots, and $k$ in Algorithm 6 corresponding to the number of top vertices we select based on the weak-signal similarity for the strong signal

[1] One can easily show that in such a case the classical `KwikCluster` algorithm is able to recover OPT.

Table 1: $F_1$ values for a fixed budget of $3n$ to the expensive-strong signal, where $n$ indicates the dataset size. For Citeseer and Medicine, we use a budget of $50n$ as they have substantially sparse graphs. Winners are in bold and second winners are underlined.

| | **SOF** | **Search** | **Tweet** | **AgNews** | **Cora** | **Photos** | **Citeseer** | **Medicine** | **Internal** | **Avg.** |
|---|---|---|---|---|---|---|---|---|---|---|
| B1 | $.13_{\pm.02}$ | $.73_{\pm.15}$ | $.02_{\pm.00}$ | $\underline{.74_{\pm.01}}$ | $.57_{\pm.08}$ | $.44_{\pm.01}$ | $.07_{\pm.01}$ | $.02_{\pm.00}$ | $.00_{\pm.00}$ | .30 |
| B2 | $.28_{\pm.10}$ | $\underline{.81_{\pm.12}}$ | $.15_{\pm.07}$ | $\underline{.74_{\pm.01}}$ | $\underline{.58_{\pm.13}}$ | $.53_{\pm.13}$ | $.09_{\pm.01}$ | $.03_{\pm.01}$ | $\underline{.05_{\pm.04}}$ | $\underline{.36}$ |
| B3 | $\underline{.33_{\pm.07}}$ | $.70_{\pm.04}$ | $\underline{.21_{\pm.03}}$ | $.66_{\pm.04}$ | $.54_{\pm.02}$ | $\underline{.66_{\pm.05}}$ | $.00_{\pm.00}$ | $.00_{\pm.00}$ | - | - |
| B4 | $.01_{\pm.00}$ | $.01_{\pm.00}$ | $.03_{\pm.00}$ | $.00_{\pm.00}$ | $.01_{\pm.00}$ | $.00_{\pm.00}$ | $\mathbf{.46_{\pm.01}}$ | $\underline{.25_{\pm.00}}$ | $.00_{\pm.00}$ | .08 |
| B5 | $.00_{\pm.00}$ | $.00_{\pm.00}$ | $.00_{\pm.00}$ | $.00_{\pm.00}$ | $.00_{\pm.00}$ | $.00_{\pm.00}$ | $.04_{\pm.01}$ | $.00_{\pm.00}$ | $.00_{\pm.00}$ | .00 |
| KwikBucks | $\mathbf{.72_{\pm.05}}$ | $\mathbf{.92_{\pm.05}}$ | $\mathbf{.28_{\pm.04}}$ | $\mathbf{.87_{\pm.00}}$ | $\mathbf{.82_{\pm.02}}$ | $\mathbf{.83_{\pm.00}}$ | $\underline{.41_{\pm.01}}$ | $\mathbf{.29_{\pm.00}}$ | $\mathbf{.14_{\pm.01}}$ | **.59** |

to query. We pick both these parameters in a data-driven manner. Thorough motivation and trade-offs associated with both parameters are presented in Section F.2; ablation studies of these parameters are provided in our empirical results. Lastly, we always reserve $10\%$ of the query budget for performing the merge post processing step. If the main algorithm terminates with remaining budget, we correspondingly increase the merge post processing budget to incorporate this.

**Results.** We highlight key experimental themes and defer additional details to Appendix F.

**Superior performance over baselines:** Table 1 shows that our algorithm outperforms the baselines in terms of the $F_1$ metric: it consistently has the highest $F_1$ value for the fixed query budget result displayed in Table 1. For example for the SOF dataset, the best baseline has a **2.2x** factor smaller $F_1$ value. Figures 1(a),(b) show the CC objective and $F_1$ score as a function of the query budget for the SOF dataset. It shows that our algorithm achieves a higher $F_1$ score and a lower correlation clustering objective value with only $\approx 7 \cdot 10^3$ queries whereas the baselines require at least $25 \cdot 10^3$ queries to match KwikBucks with $7 \cdot 10^3$ queries, showing the efficacy of our algorithm with a **3.6x** reduction in query complexity. Intuitively, the weak signal allows us to make clustering progress much faster by directing the query budget to impactful strong signal queries after filtering using the weak signal. The results for other datasets are deferred to Figures 3 and 4 in the appendix which display qualitatively similar behaviour. The strong signal graphs of Citeseer and Medicine are quite sparse. Therefore for these datasets, the trivial clustering of all singletons already achieves a very low CC objective score. As argued above, in these cases the $F_1$ score is a much more meaningful measure of cluster quality. As shown in Figures 4, our algorithm achieves superior $F_1$ values compared to the baselines. Lastly we note that the performance of our algorithm stabilizes once it has exploited sufficiently many strong signal queries. We note that B3 is omitted from the CC objective value plots for clarity as it always had much higher objective value than other algorithms.

**Relative performance of baselines is dataset dependent:** As shown in Table 1, for many datasets such as Cora, Search, and AgNews, B2 is the best among our five baselines. However this does not generalize across all datasets. As shown in Figures 4, B3 is the best baseline (with respect to the $F_1$ score) for the Tweet and Photos datasets while B4 is the best baseline for the Citeseer and Medicine datasets. B4 can be a competitive baseline in the case where the strong signal graph is extremely sparse, such as in Citeseer (see Figure 4). This is because the weak signal $k$-NN graph is able to recover many relevant edges of the (sparse) graph if the weak signal is informative.

**Varying weak signal performance:** We perform addition weak signal ablation studies with the SOF and Search datasets. We replace the Word2Vec (W2V) embeddings used in our cheap oracle with tf-idf embeddings and fix all other components of the algorithm. Figure 1(c) and 7 show the performance of our algorithm on these datasets and in both cases, the algorithm's performance noticeably worsens. The intuitive answer for *why* this is the case is because the alternative weak similarities computed from tf-idf embeddings are worse than W2V embeddings at ranking strong signal neighbors. We empirically verify this claim. For every vertex $v$ in the SOF dataset, we rank all other vertices in decreasing weak signal similarities to $v$. The average rank of the true strong signal neighbors of $v$ is then computed and this value is plotted in a histogram for all vertices $v$ in Figure 1(d). A

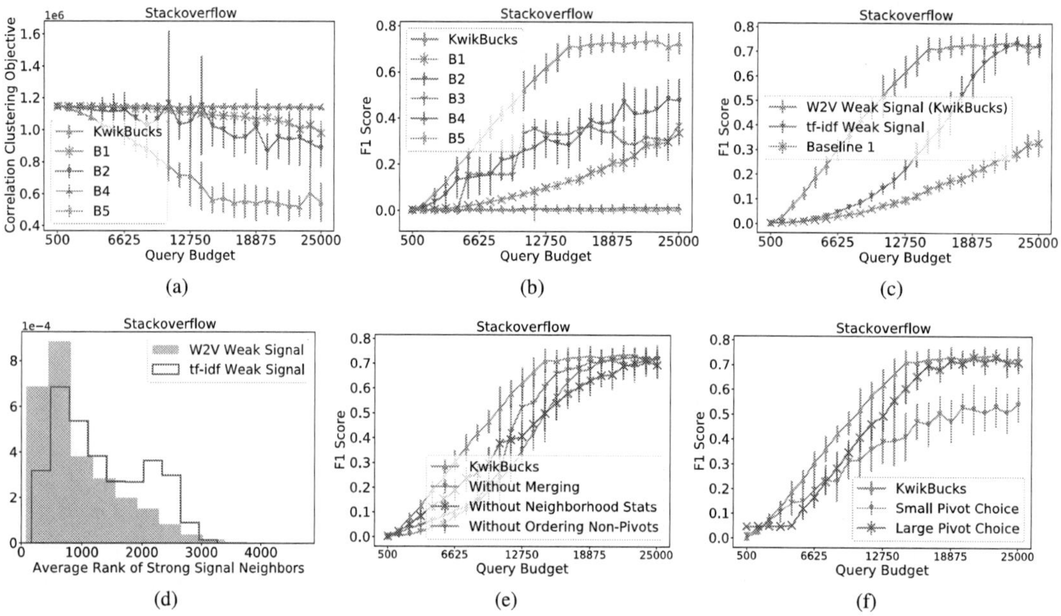


Figure 1: (a) and (b) represent the CC objective and the F1-scores for the Stackoverflow dataset across various query budgets. (c) compares performance across weak signals of various strength (Baseline 1 corresponds to a random weak signal). (d) represents a (normalized) histogram showing average rank assigned to actual strong signal neighbors by two different weak signals (lower is better). (e) represents an ablation study on some of the main components of the algorithm. (f) represents a sensitivity analysis to the parameter corresponding to the number of pivots selected.

'good' weak signal should rank actual strong signal neighbors much higher than non strong signal neighbors. Indeed we observe this to be the case for the W2V embeddings and this fact is qualitatively captured the aforementioned figures which show that W2V has superior F1 score plots. We also observe that even the weaker tf-idf embeddings still provide significant gains over not using a weak signal. Overall, these experiments along with Baseline B1 empirically verify that (1) the quality of the weak signal correlates with the performance of the algorithm, and (2) the two-oracle framework we introduced is superior than the previously studied single-oracle setting even when the cheap signal is considerably weak.

**Ablation studies.** We perform ablation studies on all tune-able parameters of our algorithm. A sample of the ablation studies for SOF is shown in Figure 1(e) and details of other results are presented in Section F.4. We observe that removing any of the main components of the algorithm (merging, ordering with respect to weak signal, and ordering with respect to the statistics of the neighboring nodes) deteriorates the performance of the algorithm, thus all the introduced components are paramount in KwikBucks. We also verify the role of the parameter $t$ corresponding to the number of pivots we select for our algorithm in Figure 1(f). We observe that both large and small choices for this parameters can be harmful, but choosing larger values is a safer option compared to smaller values as it asymptotically offers a similar performance as the optimal value.

## 5 Conclusion

We introduced and studied a novel variant of the (budgeted) correlation clustering algorithm where besides having a limited query budget to an expensive-strong oracle, one also has access to a readily available cheap-weak oracle. We developed an algorithm for this setting with strong theoretical motivations and demonstrated its strong practical performance for text clustering. We anticipate the proposed framework could become a standard building block, especially for text clustering strategies.

## References


Nir Ailon, Anup Bhattacharya, and Ragesh Jaiswal. 2018. Approximate correlation clustering using same-cluster queries. In *LATIN 2018: Theoretical Informatics - 13th Latin American Symposium, Buenos Aires, Argentina, April 16-19, 2018, Proceedings*, volume 10807 of *Lecture Notes in Computer Science*, pages 14–27. Springer.

Nir Ailon, Moses Charikar, and Alantha Newman. 2008. Aggregating inconsistent information: Ranking and clustering. *J. ACM*, 55(5):23:1–23:27.

Keerti Anand, Rong Ge, Amit Kumar, and Debmalya Panigrahi. 2022. Online algorithms with multiple predictions.

Alexandr Andoni, Piotr Indyk, and Ilya Razenshteyn. 2018. Approximate nearest neighbor search in high dimensions. In *Proceedings of the International Congress of Mathematicians: Rio de Janeiro 2018*, pages 3287–3318. World Scientific.

Antonios Antoniadis, Christian Coester, Marek Elias, Adam Polak, and Bertrand Simon. 2020a. Online metric algorithms with untrusted predictions. In *International Conference on Machine Learning*, pages 345–355. PMLR.

Antonios Antoniadis, Themis Gouleakis, Pieter Kleer, and Pavel Kolev. 2020b. Secretary and online matching problems with machine learned advice. *Advances in Neural Information Processing Systems*, 33:7933–7944.

Hassan Ashtiani, Shrinu Kushagra, and Shai Ben-David. 2016. Clustering with same-cluster queries. In *Advances in Neural Information Processing Systems 29: Annual Conference on Neural Information Processing Systems 2016, December 5-10, 2016, Barcelona, Spain*, pages 3216–3224.

Pranjal Awasthi, Avrim Blum, and Or Sheffet. 2012. Center-based clustering under perturbation stability. *Inform. Process. Lett.*, 112(1-2):49–54.

Maria Florina Balcan and Yingyu Liang. 2012. Clustering under perturbation resilience. In *International Colloquium on Automata, Languages and Programming*.

Étienne Bamas, Andreas Maggiori, Lars Rohwedder, and Ola Svensson. 2020a. Learning augmented energy minimization via speed scaling. In *Advances in Neural Information Processing Systems 33: Annual Conference on Neural Information Processing Systems, NeurIPS*.

Étienne Bamas, Andreas Maggiori, and Ola Svensson. 2020b. The primal-dual method for learning augmented algorithms. In *Advances in Neural Information Processing Systems 33: Annual Conference on Neural Information Processing Systems, NeurIPS*.

Nikhil Bansal, Avrim Blum, and Shuchi Chawla. 2004. Correlation clustering. *Machine learning*, 56(1):89–113.

Michael Barz and Daniel Sonntag. 2021. Incremental improvement of a question answering system by re-ranking answer candidates using machine learning. In *Increasing Naturalness and Flexibility in Spoken Dialogue Interaction*, pages 367–379. Springer.

Jo Bergum. 2022. Pretrained transformer language models for search.

Francesco Bonchi, David García-Soriano, and Francesco Gullo. 2022. Conclusions and open problems. *Correlation Clustering*, pages 113–114.

Francesco Bonchi, David García-Soriano, and Konstantin Kutzkov. 2013. Local correlation clustering. *CoRR*, abs/1312.5105.

Francesco Bonchi, David Garcia-Soriano, and Edo Liberty. 2014. Correlation clustering: From theory to practice. In *Proceedings of the 20th ACM SIGKDD International Conference on Knowledge Discovery and Data Mining*, KDD '14, page 1972, New York, NY, USA. Association for Computing Machinery.

Francesco Bonchi, A. Gionis, Francesco Gullo, Charalampos E. Tsourakakis, and Antti Ukkonen. 2015. Chromatic correlation clustering. *ACM Trans. Knowl. Discov. Data*, 9:34:1–34:24.

Marco Bressan, Nicolò Cesa-Bianchi, Silvio Lattanzi, and Andrea Paudice. 2021. On margin-based cluster recovery with oracle queries. *Advances in Neural Information Processing Systems*, 34:25231–25243.

Marco Bressan, Nicolò Cesa-Bianchi, Andrea Paudice, and Fabio Vitale. 2019. *Correlation Clustering with Adaptive Similarity Queries*. Curran Associates Inc., Red Hook, NY, USA.

Tom Brown, Benjamin Mann, Nick Ryder, Melanie Subbiah, Jared D Kaplan, Prafulla Dhariwal, Arvind Neelakantan, Pranav Shyam, Girish Sastry, Amanda Askell, et al. 2020. Language models are few-shot learners. *Advances in neural information processing systems*, 33:1877–1901.

Moses Charikar, Venkatesan Guruswami, and Anthony Wirth. 2005. Clustering with qualitative information. *Journal of Computer and System Sciences*, 71(3):360–383.

Moses Charikar, Samir Khuller, David M. Mount, and Giri Narasimhan. 2001. Algorithms for facility location problems with outliers. In *Proceedings of the Twelfth Annual ACM-SIAM Symposium on Discrete Algorithms*, SODA '01, page 642–651, USA. Society for Industrial and Applied Mathematics.

Shuchi Chawla, Robert Krauthgamer, Ravi Kumar, Yuval Rabani, and D Sivakumar. 2006. On the hardness of approximating multicut and sparsest-cut. *computational complexity*, 15(2):94–114.

Justin Y. Chen, Talya Eden, Piotr Indyk, Honghao Lin, Shyam Narayanan, Ronitt Rubinfeld, Sandeep Silwal, Tal Wagner, David P. Woodruff, and Michael Zhang. 2022. Triangle and four cycle counting with predictions in graph streams. In *The Tenth International Conference on Learning Representations, ICLR*.

William W Cohen and Jacob Richman. 2002. Learning to match and cluster large high-dimensional data sets for data integration. In *Proceedings of the eighth ACM SIGKDD international conference on Knowledge discovery and data mining*, pages 475–480.

Ofer Dekel, Claudio Gentile, and Karthik Sridharan. 2012. Selective sampling and active learning from single and multiple teachers. *The Journal of Machine Learning Research*, 13(1):2655–2697.

Erik D Demaine, Dotan Emanuel, Amos Fiat, and Nicole Immorlica. 2006. Correlation clustering in general weighted graphs. *Theoretical Computer Science*, 361(2-3):172–187.

Jacob Devlin, Ming-Wei Chang, Kenton Lee, and Kristina Toutanova. 2018. Bert: Pre-training of deep bidirectional transformers for language understanding. *arXiv preprint arXiv:1810.04805*.

Ilias Diakonikolas, Vasilis Kontonis, Christos Tzamos, Ali Vakilian, and Nikos Zarifis. 2021. Learning online algorithms with distributional advice. In *Proceedings of the 38th International Conference on Machine Learning, ICML*, pages 2687–2696.

Thomas G Dietterich. 2000. Ensemble methods in machine learning. multiple classifier systems. *Lecture Notes in Computer Science*, 1857:1–15.

Pinar Donmez. 2008. Proactive learning: Towards cost-sensitive active learning with multiple imperfect oracles.

Talya Eden, Piotr Indyk, Shyam Narayanan, Ronitt Rubinfeld, Sandeep Silwal, and Tal Wagner. 2021. Learning-based support estimation in sublinear time. In *9th International Conference on Learning Representations, ICLR*.

Derek Eder. 2022. [link].

Meng Fang, Xingquan Zhu, Bin Li, Wei Ding, and Xindong Wu. 2012. Self-taught active learning from crowds. In *2012 IEEE 12th international conference on data mining*, pages 858–863. IEEE.

Ethan Fetaya, Ohad Shamir, and Shimon Ullman. 2015. Graph approximation and clustering on a budget. In *Artificial Intelligence and Statistics*, pages 241–249. PMLR.

David García-Soriano, Konstantin Kutzkov, Francesco Bonchi, and Charalampos Tsourakakis. 2020a. Query-efficient correlation clustering. In *Proceedings of The Web Conference 2020*, pages 1468–1478.

David García-Soriano, Konstantin Kutzkov, Francesco Bonchi, and Charalampos Tsourakakis. 2020b. Query-efficient correlation clustering. In *Proceedings of The Web Conference 2020*, pages 1468–1478.

Lise Getoor and Ashwin Machanavajjhala. 2012. Entity resolution: Theory, practice & open challenges. *Proc. VLDB Endow.*, 5:2018–2019.

A. Gionis, Heikki Mannila, and Panayiotis Tsaparas. 2005. Clustering aggregation. *21st International Conference on Data Engineering (ICDE'05)*, pages 341–352.

Sreenivas Gollapudi and Debmalya Panigrahi. 2019. Online algorithms for rent-or-buy with expert advice. In *Proceedings of the 36th International Conference on Machine Learning, ICML*, pages 2319–2327.

Ramanathan Guha, Vineet Gupta, Vivek Raghunathan, and Ramakrishnan Srikant. 2015. User modeling for a personal assistant. In *Proceedings of the Eighth ACM International Conference on Web Search and Data Mining*, pages 275–284.

Oktie Hassanzadeh, Fei Chiang, Renée J. Miller, and Hyun Chul Lee. 2009. Framework for evaluating clustering algorithms in duplicate detection. *Proc. VLDB Endow.*, 2(1):1282–1293.

Chen-Yu Hsu, Piotr Indyk, Dina Katabi, and Ali Vakilian. 2019. Learning-based frequency estimation algorithms. In *7th International Conference on Learning Representations, ICLR*.

Sheng-Jun Huang, Jia-Lve Chen, Xin Mu, and Zhi-Hua Zhou. 2017. Cost-effective active learning from diverse labelers. In *IJCAI*, pages 1879–1885.

Panagiotis G Ipeirotis, Foster Provost, Victor S Sheng, and Jing Wang. 2014. Repeated labeling using multiple noisy labelers. *Data Mining and Knowledge Discovery*, 28(2):402–441.

Tanqiu Jiang, Yi Li, Honghao Lin, Yisong Ruan, and David P. Woodruff. 2020. Learning-augmented data stream algorithms. In *8th International Conference on Learning Representations, ICLR*.

Sungwoong Kim, Sebastian Nowozin, Pushmeet Kohli, and Chang Yoo. 2011. Higher-order correlation clustering for image segmentation. *Advances in neural information processing systems*, 24:1530–1538.

Christopher H Lin, M Mausam, and Daniel S Weld. 2015. Reactive learning: Actively trading off larger noisier training sets against smaller cleaner ones. In *Proceedings of the 32nd International Conference on Machine Learning, Lille, France (ICML)*.

Christopher H Lin, Daniel S Weld, et al. 2014. To re (label), or not to re (label). In *Second AAAI conference on human computation and crowdsourcing*.

Thodoris Lykouris and Sergei Vassilvitskii. 2018. Competitive caching with machine learned advice. In *Proceedings of the 35th International Conference on Machine Learning, ICML*, pages 3302–3311.

Luigi Malago, Nicolo Cesa-Bianchi, and J Renders. 2014. Online active learning with strong and weak annotators. In *NIPS Workshop on Learning from the Wisdom of Crowds*.

Aditya Menon, Sadeep Jayasumana, Ankit Singh Rawat, Seungyeon Kim, Sashank Reddi, and Sanjiv Kumar. 2022. In defense of dual-encoders for neural ranking. In *International Conference on Machine Learning*, pages 15376–15400. PMLR.

Tomas Mikolov, Kai Chen, Greg Corrado, and Jeffrey Dean. 2013. Efficient estimation of word representations in vector space. *arXiv preprint arXiv:1301.3781*.

Michael Mitzenmacher. 2018. A model for learned bloom filters and optimizing by sandwiching. In *Advances in Neural Information Processing Systems 31: Annual Conference on Neural Information Processing Systems, NeurIPS*, pages 462–471.

Kim Thang Nguyen and Christoph Dürr. 2021. Online primal-dual algorithms with predictions for packing problems. *CoRR*, abs/2110.00391.

Fabian Pedregosa, Gaël Varoquaux, Alexandre Gramfort, Vincent Michel, Bertrand Thirion, Olivier Grisel, Mathieu Blondel, Peter Prettenhofer, Ron Weiss, Vincent Dubourg, et al. 2011. Scikit-learn: Machine learning in python. *the Journal of machine Learning research*, 12:2825–2830.

Xuan-Hieu Phan, Le-Minh Nguyen, and Susumu Horiguchi. 2008. Learning to classify short and sparse text & web with hidden topics from large-scale data collections. In *Proceedings of the 17th international conference on World Wide Web*, pages 91–100.

Manish Purohit, Zoya Svitkina, and Ravi Kumar. 2018. Improving online algorithms via ML predictions. In *Advances in Neural Information Processing Systems 31: Annual Conference on Neural Information Processing Systems, NeurIPS*, pages 9684–9693.

Colin Raffel, Noam Shazeer, Adam Roberts, Katherine Lee, Sharan Narang, Michael Matena, Yanqi Zhou, Wei Li, Peter J Liu, et al. 2020. Exploring the limits of transfer learning with a unified text-to-text transformer. *J. Mach. Learn. Res.*, 21(140):1–67.

Md Rashadul Hasan Rakib, Norbert Zeh, Magdalena Jankowska, and Evangelos Milios. 2020. Enhancement of short text clustering by iterative classification. In *International Conference on Applications of Natural Language to Information Systems*, pages 105–117. Springer.

Anirudh Ramachandran, Nick Feamster, and Santosh S. Vempala. 2007. Filtering spam with behavioral blacklisting. In *Proceedings of the 2007 ACM Conference on Computer and Communications Security, CCS 2007, Alexandria, Virginia, USA, October 28-31, 2007*, pages 342–351. ACM.

Radim Rehurek and Petr Sojka. 2011. Gensim–python framework for vector space modelling. *NLP Centre, Faculty of Informatics, Masaryk University, Brno, Czech Republic*, 3(2).

Barna Saha and Sanjay Subramanian. 2019. Correlation clustering with same-cluster queries bounded by optimal cost. In *27th Annual European Symposium on Algorithms, ESA 2019, September 9-11, 2019, Munich/Garching, Germany*, volume 144 of *LIPIcs*, pages 81:1–81:17. Schloss Dagstuhl - Leibniz-Zentrum für Informatik.

Prithviraj Sen, Galileo Namata, Mustafa Bilgic, Lise Getoor, Brian Galligher, and Tina Eliassi-Rad. 2008. Collective classification in network data. *AI magazine*, 29(3):93–93.

Ohad Shamir and Naftali Tishby. 2011. Spectral clustering on a budget. In *Proceedings of the Fourteenth International Conference on Artificial Intelligence and Statistics*, pages 661–669. JMLR Workshop and Conference Proceedings.

Or Sharir, Barak Peleg, and Yoav Shoham. 2020. The cost of training nlp models: A concise overview. *arXiv preprint arXiv:2004.08900*.

Oleksandr Shchur and Stephan Günnemann. 2019. Overlapping community detection with graph neural networks. *arXiv preprint arXiv:1909.12201*.

Oleksandr Shchur, Maximilian Mumme, Aleksandar Bojchevski, and Stephan Günnemann. 2018. Pitfalls of graph neural network evaluation. *arXiv preprint arXiv:1811.05868*.

Jiliang Tang, Yi Chang, Charu C. Aggarwal, and Huan Liu. 2016. A survey of signed network mining in social media. *ACM Computing Surveys (CSUR)*, 49:1 – 37.

Romal Thoppilan, Daniel De Freitas, Jamie Hall, Noam Shazeer, Apoorv Kulshreshtha, Heng-Tze Cheng, Alicia Jin, Taylor Bos, Leslie Baker, Yu Du, et al. 2022. Lamda: Language models for dialog applications. *arXiv preprint arXiv:2201.08239*.

Ruth Urner, Shai Ben David, and Ohad Shamir. 2012. Learning from weak teachers. In *Artificial intelligence and statistics*, pages 1252–1260. PMLR.

Petar Velickovic, William Fedus, William L Hamilton, Pietro Liò, Yoshua Bengio, and R Devon Hjelm. 2019. Deep graph infomax. *ICLR*, 2(3):4.

Fabian L Wauthier, Nebojsa Jojic, and Michael I Jordan. 2012. Active spectral clustering via iterative uncertainty reduction. In *Proceedings of the 18th*

*ACM SIGKDD international conference on Knowledge discovery and data mining*, pages 1339–1347.

Alexander Wei and Fred Zhang. 2020. Optimal robustness-consistency trade-offs for learning-augmented online algorithms. In *Advances in Neural Information Processing Systems 33: Annual Conference on Neural Information Processing Systems 2020, NeurIPS*.

Jing Wong. 2022. Model-based candidate generation for account recommendations.

Carole-Jean Wu, Ramya Raghavendra, Udit Gupta, Bilge Acun, Newsha Ardalani, Kiwan Maeng, Gloria Chang, Fiona Aga, Jinshi Huang, Charles Bai, et al. 2022. Sustainable ai: Environmental implications, challenges and opportunities. *Proceedings of Machine Learning and Systems*, 4:795–813.

Jiaming Xu, Bo Xu, Peng Wang, Suncong Zheng, Guanhua Tian, and Jun Zhao. 2017. Self-taught convolutional neural networks for short text clustering. *Neural Networks*, 88:22–31.

Yan Yan, Romer Rosales, Glenn Fung, and Jennifer G Dy. 2011. Active learning from crowds. In *ICML*.

Yan Yan, Rómer Rosales, Glenn Fung, Faisal Farooq, Bharat Rao, and Jennifer Dy. 2012. Active learning from multiple knowledge sources. In *Artificial Intelligence and Statistics*, pages 1350–1357. PMLR.

Jianhua Yin and Jianyong Wang. 2016. A model-based approach for text clustering with outlier detection. In *2016 IEEE 32nd International Conference on Data Engineering (ICDE)*, pages 625–636. IEEE.

Taraneh Younesian, Dick Epema, and Lydia Y Chen. 2020. Active learning for noisy data streams using weak and strong labelers. *arXiv preprint arXiv:2010.14149*.

Chicheng Zhang and Kamalika Chaudhuri. 2015. Active learning from weak and strong labelers. *Advances in Neural Information Processing Systems*, 28.

Xiang Zhang and Yann LeCun. 2015. Text understanding from scratch. *arXiv preprint arXiv:1502.01710*.

Zhun Zhong, Liang Zheng, Donglin Cao, and Shaozi Li. 2017. Re-ranking person re-identification with k-reciprocal encoding. In *Proceedings of the IEEE conference on computer vision and pattern recognition*, pages 1318–1327.

## A Additional Related Works

In the realm of learning from multiple annotators, there is a long line of work studying these both empirically and theoretically. Empirical work on this can be divided into two main streams: (1) each labeler is coming from a different generative model, (2) each labeler is an expert over an unknown subset of categories, (3) different labelers with quality proportional to their cost. In the first case, the learning algorithm focuses on learning parameters of each labeler and then for each example decides which labeler to query (Yan et al., 2011, 2012; Lin et al., 2015, 2014; Fang et al., 2012). In the second case, it uses data to measure the class-wise expertise in order to optimally place label queries (Ipeirotis et al., 2014; Donmez, 2008). In the last case, empirical results comparing designed algorithms to baselines are developed: active learning from noisy data streams (Younesian et al., 2020), active learning using diverse labelers (Huang et al., 2017), and content segmentation for personal assistants (Guha et al., 2015). Theoretical work looked at the setting where the weak labeler made mistakes mostly in heterogeneous regions of space, i.e., correct in label-homogeneous regions but may deteriorate near classification boundaries. Different formulations were considered in this setting: non-parametric setting (Urner et al., 2012), fitting classifiers in a hypothesis class (Zhang and Chaudhuri, 2015), online selective sampling with applications in linear classifiers and robust regression (Malago et al., 2014; Dekel et al., 2012).

The idea of judiciously utilizing an expensive but accurate strong model with the help of cheaper but noisier methods have already been successfully used in many practical and important domains. In nearest neighbor search and information retrieval, the dominant algorithmic paradigm is to return multiple possible nearest neighbors using scalable methods and then re-rank the returned points using exact distance calculations (which is prohibitive to perform over the entire input)[2]. In recommendation systems, the "standard practice for machine learning-driven recommendations in industry" (Wong, 2022) is driven by the two-step procedure of cheaply retrieving a set of possible candidates and iterating over them using a more powerful but costlier ML models (Wong, 2022; Bergum, 2022; Eder, 2022). Similar ideas are also used in question answering and vision applications (Zhong et al., 2017; Barz and Sonntag, 2021).

There has also been extensive work in incorporating additional predictions in algorithmic design for online algorithms (Bamas et al., 2020b; Purohit et al., 2018; Lykouris and Vassilvitskii,

[2]We refer to `http://ann-benchmarks.com/` for a large collection of practical nearest neighbor search algorithms and (Andoni et al., 2018) for a overview of theoretical works.

2018; Purohit et al., 2018; Gollapudi and Panigrahi, 2019), sublinear space and time algorithms (Chen et al., 2022; Hsu et al., 2019; Eden et al., 2021), and other algorithmic and data structural problems (Mitzenmacher, 2018; Bamas et al., 2020b,a; Wei and Zhang, 2020; Jiang et al., 2020; Diakonikolas et al., 2021; Charikar et al., 2001; Antoniadis et al., 2020a,b; Anand et al., 2022; Nguyen and Dürr, 2021). We refer to the Algorithms-with-Predictions website[3] for comprehensive references. The high level motivations of these works is to apply predictions to aid in beyond worst-case analysis of algorithmic problems. The prototypical examples of predictions used in these works include algorithm parameter settings (for example 'warm starts' or 'seeds' which can be constructed from past inputs). Thus a common underlying assumption is that many similar inputs are given so that predictions are meaningful and feasible. Furthermore in many of these works, the predictions are modeled after particular problem settings in mind and the inputs are always fully specified. In contrast, our predictions are inspired by a particular application domain, e.g. text clustering, which we connect to CC, rather than motivating the predictions from a purely algorithmic problem perspective. Furthermore, our predictions (e.g. queries from the weak signal) help us learn about the true underlying input (e.g. the strong signal graph).

We also give a detailed comparision to the work of (Guha et al., 2015). While at a high level both (Guha et al., 2015) and our work aggregate information across various signals, the two works differ in terms of the generality of oracles considered, the formal guarantees given, and the problems studied. The oracles used in (Guha et al., 2015) are highly specialized to the datasets at hand; for example, the cheap oracle used in (Guha et al., 2015) is an inverted index model which heavily relies on the specifics of the datasets used. In contrast, we take a broader view of weak and strong oracles and present theoretically founded algorithms which only assume query access to the weak and strong model and not any particular model idiosyncrasies. Therefore, our algorithm has provable guarantees on both the approximation quality and the query complexity, making it broadly applicable across different oracles. In terms of problems, we study correlation clustering while the focus of (Guha et al., 2015) is not on a clustering problem. Rather, they use hierarchical clustering as an intermediate problem to perform user modeling and do not consider any specific clustering objective functions. The strong signal queries made by our algorithm are guided through formal reasoning and they exploit the structure of the clustering problem we are studying. In (Guha et al., 2015) the weak signal is used at a more intuitive level and serves the informal role of filtering possible strong signal queries with no formal reasoning.

[3]https://algorithms-with-predictions.github.io/

## B Omitted Proofs of Section 2

**Proposition 1.** *There exists a strong signal graph $G$ such that the* KwikCluster *algorithm makes $\Omega(n^{1.5})$ strong signal queries.*

*Proof.* Consider the case where the strong signal graph consists of $\sqrt{n}$ cliques, all of size $\sqrt{n}$. In this case, every time KwikCluster picks a pivot, it has to examine an existence of an edge from this pivot to all the unassigned vertices. So for at least the first $\sqrt{n}/2$ times KwikCluster picks a pivot, it has to make at least $n/2$ calls to $O_S$ , resulting in $\Omega(n^{1.5})$ calls to $O_S$. □

**Proposition 2.** *Consider a variation of* KwikCluster, *called* KwikCluster$^\gamma$, *which for a chosen pivot $p$ from uncovered vertices $V'$, only queries $V' \cap \mathcal{O}_W^\gamma(p)$ from strong signal. There exists a graph $G$ such that* KwikCluster$^\gamma$ *still makes $\Omega(n^2)$ strong signal queries in expectation even when $\gamma = O(1)$.*

*Proof.* Consider the following strong signal graph: the graph $G$ is comprised a fully connected clique on $0.9n$ nodes. The graph also has $0.1n$ nodes, called 'outside vertices' which all connect to the same $0.1n$ vertices in the fully connected clique but have no edges between them. Suppose that $\mathcal{O}_W^\gamma$ returns the correct strong signal neighborhood for vertices in the clique but for the outside vertices, it returns an additional $\Omega(n)$ arbitrary vertices among the outside vertices.

Now consider the simulation of KwikCluster$^\gamma$ on $G$. With constant probability, the first time a pivot is picked, it comes from the clique vertices which have no neighbors among the outside vertices. Condition on this event. Now the algorithm still needs to run until the outside vertices have been selected in a cluster. However, every time each such vertex is picked as a pivot, we need to check over $\Omega(n)$ erroneous vertices. Furthermore, removing an outside vertex $v$ and its neighborhood $\Gamma(v)$ does not remove any of the other outside vertices. Thus it follows that the expected number of queries made to $O_S$, while still utilizing $\mathcal{O}_W^\gamma$ in this natural variant of KwikCluster, is $\Omega(n^2)$ with constant probability since there are $\Omega(n)$ outside vertices, each which requires $\Omega(n)$ queries to $O_S$. Altogether, this natural algorithm can incur $\Omega(n^2)$ queries, a super linear amount. □

**Lemma 1.** *Let $t$ be the parameter of* GetPivots *(Algorithm 3). Algorithm 3 uses $t + 2\gamma t^2 m/n^2$ queries to $O_S$.*

*Proof.* Let $T = \{v_1, \ldots, v_t\}$ denote the set of $t$ sampled vertices in line 1 of Algorithm 3. Fix a vertex $v \in T$, we show that there are $O(\gamma t|E|/n + 1)$ queries in expectation for such vertex. Let $P_i$ denote the set of pivots right before we start scanning vertex $v_i$. When we check for the neighbors of vertex $v_i$, we immediately stop if a strong signal neighbor in $P_i$ is found. Let $A(v_i) = \mathcal{O}_W^\gamma(v_i) \setminus \Gamma(v_i)$ be the vertices which $\mathcal{O}_W^\gamma$ errs on for query $v_i$ and can result in needless calls to $O_S$. The number of expected calls to the strong signal is exactly the expected number of unnecessary calls $\mathbb{E}[|A(v_i) \cap P_i|]$ plus one call that may result in the early stoppage in line 4 of Algorithm 4. So for each $v_i$, the expected number of calls to $O_S$ can be bounded by

$$\begin{aligned}
1 + \mathbb{E}[|A(v_i) \cap P_i|] &\le 1 + \mathbb{E}[|A(v_i) \cap T|] \\
&= 1 + \mathbb{E}_{v_i}\mathbb{E}[|A(v_i) \cap T| \mid v_i] \\
&\le 1 + 2\mathbb{E}_{v_i}\mathbb{E}\left[|A| \cdot \frac{t}{n} \mid v_i\right] \\
&\le 1 + \frac{2t\gamma}{n}\mathbb{E}_{v_i}[|\Gamma(v_i)|] \\
&= 1 + \frac{2t\gamma m}{n^2}.
\end{aligned}$$

Summing over all $t$ vertices in $T$ results in the final bound. □

**Lemma 2.** *Let $P$ be the output of* GetPivots(t,Q), *then* AssignToClusters($P, V \setminus P, Q$) *makes $n + 2\gamma tm/n$ queries to $O_S$.*

*Proof.* Consider a fixed vertex $u \in V \setminus P$. We perform a similar analysis as in Lemma 1: ideally $S = \mathcal{O}_W^\gamma(u) \cap P$ informs us the pivot which $u$ should connect to. However since the cheap oracle can be noisy, we can have many vertices in $(\mathcal{O}_W^\gamma(u) \setminus \Gamma(u)) \cap P$. The number of queries to $O_S$ is at most $|(\mathcal{O}_W^\gamma(u) \setminus \Gamma(u)) \cap P| + 1$. It remains to calculate the following expected value:

$$\mathbb{E}[|(\mathcal{O}_W^\gamma(u) \setminus \Gamma(u)) \cap P|] \le \gamma\,|\Gamma(u)| \cdot \frac{t}{n}.$$

Thus the total expected number of queries for non-pivot vertices is

$$\begin{aligned}
&\sum_{u \in V \setminus P} \left(1 + \gamma\,|\Gamma(u)| \cdot \frac{t}{n}\right) = \\
&\qquad |V \setminus P| + \frac{\gamma t}{n} \sum_{u\ inV \setminus P} |\Gamma(u)| \le n + \frac{2\gamma tm}{n}.
\end{aligned}$$

□

**Theorem 2** ((Bonchi et al., 2013)). *Let $T'$ be the maximal independent set formed by scanning randomly sampled $t$ vertices of a graph $G$. Then the expected number of edges of $G$ not incident with an element of $T'$ union the neighborhood of $T'$ in $G$ is at most $n^2/2t$.*

*Proof.* The bound on the number of queries to $O_S$. There are two tasks which require calls to $O_S$: forming the set of pivots in GetPivots and assigning non-pivot vertices to a pivot in AssignClusters. The expected number of queries forGetPivots is handled by Lemma 1 and the expected number of queries for AssignClusters is handled by Lemma 2.

We now need to bound the approximation guarantee. Consider the subgraph $G'$ of the strong signal graph which is the union of the pivots returned by GetPivots and their neighborhood. Theorem 2 gives us that the number of edges not part of this subgraph is at most $O(n^2/t)$ which can be charged to the additive error incurred by our algorithm (all vertices which do not have a strong signal edge to any of the pivots are clustered as singletons). Now on this subgraph note that we are exactly mimicking the KwikCluster algorithm on $G'$. This is because the pivots of Get-Pivots are chosen from the same distribution as the KwikCluster algorithm since we ensure that all pivots chosen are not in the neighborhood of previously chosen pivots. Thus we obtain a 3· OPT guarantee on $G'$. To obtain the final guarantee on the original strong signal graph, note that the OPT clustering of $G$ restricted to $G'$ cannot be better than the OPT correlation clustering of $G'$. The result follows from considering our additive error as well. □

We now show a lower bound on the query complexity of our algorithm. First we recast the lower bound result of (García-Soriano et al., 2020b) in the language of strong and weak oracles. They show that *any* algorithm which only has access to the strong signal must make $\Omega(n^3/(\Delta c^2))$ queries to obtain a $c\cdot$ OPT $+\Delta$ correlation clustering objective guarantee. We can translate their lower bound into our setting of strong and weak oracles by essentially making the weak oracle useless through a suitable choice of $\gamma$. The lower bound shows that for constant $\varepsilon$ and $n$ large enough, Corollary 1 is optimal. First we formally state the guarantees given by (García-Soriano et al., 2020b) in our language of strong and weak signals.

**Theorem 3** ((García-Soriano et al., 2020b)). *For any $c \geq 1$ and $\Delta$ such that $8n < \Delta \leq \frac{n^2}{2048c^2}$, any algorithm finding a clustering with expected cost at most $c\cdot$ OPT $+\Delta$ must make at least $\Omega(n^3/(\Delta c^2))$ adaptive strong signal queries.*

**Lemma 3.** *Let $\varepsilon \geq \Omega(1/n)$ be sufficiently small. In the worst case input, any algorithm must use at least $\Omega(n + d\gamma)$ strong signal queries to obtain a $3\cdot$ OPT $+O(\varepsilon n^2)$ approximation to the correlation clustering objective.*

*Proof.* We recall the lower bound example of (García-Soriano et al., 2020b) (which is proved in Theorem 4.1 in (García-Soriano et al., 2020b)). Let $k = n^2/(32c\Delta)$ (note that $k < n$ by design). Their worst case strong signal graph example consists of $k$ equal sized cliques and all vertices have degree $\Theta(n/k)$. Now we consider the case where the weak oracle is completely useless and always returns the entire set of vertices on any query. This corresponds to the case where $\gamma = \Theta(k)$ (for $\gamma$ defined in Assumption 1). Now directly applying Theorem 4.1 of (García-Soriano et al., 2020b) gives us that any algorithm which only has access to the strong signal must make at least $\Omega(n^3/(\Delta c^2))$ queries to obtain a $c\cdot$ OPT $+\Delta$ correlation clustering objective guarantee. The theorem follows by noting that if $\Delta = \varepsilon n^2$ then any algorithm must make $\Omega(n/\varepsilon) = \Omega(n + k\cdot n/k) = \Omega(n + d\gamma)$ queries in this worst case example, as desired. Note that the valid range of $\varepsilon$ here follows from the restriction on $\Delta$ so $\varepsilon \geq 8/n$ and cannot be larger than some fixed constant. □

## C Additional Algorithmic Details for Empirical Algorithm.

We provide additional details on the algorithm design of Section 3.

**Algorithm 7** `SortNonPivots`$(T, V \setminus T)$

**Require:** $T$, the set of pivots; $V \setminus T$, vertices which are not pivots

**for** vertices $v \in V \setminus T$ **do**
  $w_v \leftarrow$ Maximum weak signal similarity between $v$ and any vertex in $T$
**Return** $V \setminus T$ sorted in decreasing $w_v$ values

**Optimizing non-pivot order.** Continuing on the theme of ranking, once we curate the pivots, we need to assign the non-pivots to a pivot. To do so, we sort the non-pivots based on 'easiness' to assign to a pivot. Hence we sort the non-pivots by the maximum weak similarity to some pivot. This has the effect of utilizing our query budget as efficiently as possible as 'easier' non-pivots are checked first. We re-rank the vertices $V \setminus P$ in `SortNonPivots` before calling `AssignClusters` in `KwikBucks`.

**Utilizing Weak Signal Neighborhood.** We can use strong signal queries that we have already made for vertices in the weak signal neighborhood to further optimize the sorting of the pivots in `WeakFilterByRanking`. The inductive bias we are using is that if many vertices in the immediate weak signal neighborhood of a vertex $v$ connect to the same pivot $p$, then the likelihood $v$ having a strong signal edge to $p$ is high. Thus to better utilize our expensive query budget, we should query $(v, p)$ earlier than later. To make the intuition more precise, we simply update the similarities to pivots computed by $v$ in `WeakFilterByRanking` to account for the inductive bias. The new similarity score $w'p$ of a pivot $p$ is equal to $w_p$, the similarity score between $v$ and $p$ computed by the weak signal, plus a term for the number of vertices in the $k$-weak signal neighborhood of $v$ that are already connected to $p$:

$$w'_p = w_p + \lambda(\#\text{ of vertices in } k\text{-weak signal neighborhood of } v \text{ that are already in } p\text{'s cluster})$$

This has the affect of 'boosting' some pivots to a higher ranking. See Section F.2 for further details.

### C.1 Details on Post-processing Merging

In this section we provide the details of our post-processing merging strategy outlined in Section 3.

Let $C_1, \ldots, C_r$ be the clusters outputted by our algorithm. First we curate a list of cluster pairs to consider for merging. Then we rank the pairs in terms of suitability for merging. Finally we enumerate over the pairs in the order computed (until we run out of any query budget) and determine if the pair should be merged. Each of the three steps is described in detail below.

1. **Curating pairs of clusters.** It is prohibitive to consider all pairs of clusters (which might be super linear if there are many clusters). We again appeal to the weak signal and construct a $k$-nn weak signal similarity graph on the vertices for some small $k$, such as $k = 20$. Then we only consider pairs of clusters which are edges in the graph. More precisely, we consider the pair $(C_i, C_j)$ for merging if there is some $v \in C_i$ and $u \in C_j$ such that $(v, u)$ is an edge in the $k$-nn graph. This narrows down the number of pairs considerably.

2. **Ranking pairs by suitability.** For each pair $(C_i, C_j)$ of clusters from the prior step, we compute the average weak signal value between vertices in $C_i$ and $C_j$ respectively. We then rank the pairs in decreasing order based on this value.

3. **Determining if a pair should be merged.** Finally, we enumerate over the pairs in the order computed previously. Suppose we are deciding if we want to merge the pair $(C_i, C_j)$. We must ensure the pair has a high number of strong signal edges (more than 0.5 fraction). To do so we simply sample a small number of random pairs of vertices (say 20), one vertex from each cluster, and estimate the fraction of these random edges which are strong signal edges.

## D Theoretically Motivating Practical Modifications of the Algorithm

In this section we provide theoretical justifications for the practical modifications of our algorithm.

### D.1 Theoretically motivating raking pivots by weak signal

In the classical `KwikCluster` algorithm and our query efficient variant in the two oracle model of Section 2, it is imperative that the pivots are selected in a random order to provide theoretical guarantees on the quality of the computed clustering. Specifically, the worst case theoretical guarantees dictate that vertices must connect to the *first* pivot in the random order which they have a strong signal edge to.

Nevertheless, in our data driven optimization of the algorithm, we choose an adaptive ordering of the pivots for each vertex where the order is based on the weak-signal similarity scores. We empirically observed that this ordering is superior to the random ordering and achieves a higher clustering quality while utilizing a $>$ **3.5x** factor or more less strong signal queries. The explanation behind this improvement is two fold:

1. **Increased query efficiency:** fewer strong signal queries are used when a vertex attempts to connect to a pivot.

2. **Maintaining cluster quality:** connecting to pivots with larger weak signal similarities are high quality pivots.

The positive effects of the first point are straightforward to explain. Indeed, making the natural assumption that higher weak signal similarities are more indicative of a strong signal edge, checking pivots in the weak signal ordering leads to less queries wasted when a vertex attempts to connect to a pivot. In addition to the empirical results of Section 4, this point is further expanded upon in Figure 7 and Section F.6.

Thus the main goal of this section is to provide an intuitive and theoretically motivated understanding of the second point. While it may not be true that re-ranking pivots according to the weak signal similarities maintains the worst case guarantees proved in Section 2, we study a natural data set model where such a re-ranking provably helps. We wish to capture our data driven observations that pivots with larger weak signal similarities are of high quality and larger weak signal values indicate better cluster relationships.

In our experiments, the weak signal scores are mostly computed using distances between embedding vectors. If a weak signal is useful, then it must have be predicative of the strong signal values, even if the weak signal is noisy. To mimic this, we consider the following general family of data sets:

- Each vertex $v$ has an associated vector $p_v \in \mathbb{R}^d$, representing it's 'true' embedding representation.
- The weak signal values are computed according to an appropriate distance measure $d$ on the embedding vectors (for example cosine or Euclidean distances) plus a random noise term $\xi$ (expanded upon shortly). This models the setting where the weak signals are helpful but noisy signals as they only have noisy access to the 'true' representations.
- There exists a function $f : \mathbb{R}^{\geq 0} \to [0, 1]$ which gives the probability of a strong signal edge. More precisely, let $p_v$ and $p_u$ denote the embedding of vertices $v$ and $u$. Then the probability of having the strong signal edge $(v, u)$ is given by $f(d(v, u))$. This is quite a general formulation as it includes a wide array of geometric or kernel similarity graphs for appropriate choices of $f$ and $d$.

For example, if $f = \exp(-x/\sigma)$ and $d$ is the Euclidean distance, then the true strong signal graph is the Gaussian kernel similarity graph where $\sigma$ is the scale of the kernel. Intuitively, the closer $u$ and $v$ are under the metric $d$, the higher probability $f$ assigns to the edge between $u$ and $v$.

We additionally impose the following clusterability assumptions on the data set. Our goal is to capture a natural underlying cluster structure which can be accessed via strong and weak signal queries. Vertices which are part of the same underlying cluster should have higher weak signal similarity scores, even if the scores are noisy, and the strong signal edges should be highly accurate. Our model defined below satisfies these intuitive criteria. Furthermore under our natural model, there is a 'true' pivot for a vertex $v$, even though $v$ may have strong signal edges to other pivots.

Our cluster assumptions on the data set is the following.

1. The 'true' embedding vectors $p_v \in \mathbb{R}^d$ can be partitioned into $k$ clusters such that all vectors in a cluster are within distance $R$ of each other.
2. All embedding vectors in different clusters are distance at least $2R$ from each other.
3. The probability of a strong signal edge is at least $1 - p$ for distances at most $2R$ and at most $p$ for distances at least $2R$. We think of $p < 1/2$ as a small parameter close to 0.
4. Given inputs $u, v$, the weak signal outputs $d(p_u, p_v) + \xi$ where $\xi$ is uniformly random in $[-R, R]$. Thus smaller values are interpreted as having higher weak signal similarity.

Note that we only have access to the strong and weak signal values via queries and do not know the true underlying embedding vectors $p_v$. We now argue that the above assumptions are motivated and natural.

- The assumption (1) gives a cluster structure to the data and allows us to compare the classical `KwikCluster` algorithm and our re-ranking modification under natural clusterability assumptions. The exact formulation we are employing is inspired by the works of (Awasthi et al., 2012; Balcan and Liang, 2012; Ashtiani et al., 2016) which study clustering under similar proximity assumptions. For example, it can be easily checked that the 'margin' property assumption of (Ashtiani et al., 2016) directly implies our assumptions (1) and (2).
- Our assumption (3) is a natural and necessary assumption on the function $f$ as it ensures the true strong signal graph captures the underlying cluster structure of the inputs. This also corresponds to picking an appropriate *scale* parameter if $f$ is a kernel function, for example picking $\sigma$ in the Gaussian kernel. A judicious choice of $\sigma$ ensures that the underlying kernel similarity graph, which corresponds to the strong signal, is able to capture the cluster structure of the data set. Thus our assumption that $p \ll 1$ ensures that the similarity graph has strong inter-cluster connectivity while having sparse connectivity across different clusters. Indeed in practice, the kernel scale parameter is often picked using the 'median' rule and thus $\sigma = \Theta(R)$ is a natural choice which ensures our choice of $p$.
- Our data set construction ensures that the strong signal is 'more powerful' than the weak

signal. Indeed, the weak signal only has access to the distances between the true embedding vectors up to some additive noise as stated in assumption (4). While the exact form of the random noise is not very consequential, we stick to the uniform noise model as it as several desirable properties:

1. Given vertices $v, u, w$ where $u$ is in $v$'s true cluster (according to the true embedding vectors) and $w$ is not, the weak signal can potentially output a smaller value on query $(v, w)$ compared to $(v, u)$. Thus the weak signal incorrectly states $w$ is more similar to $v$ than $u$ due to the additive noise. For example if $d(v, u) = R$ and $d(v, w) = 2R$, this happens with probability $1/8$. Therefore the weak signal accurately reflects our desired goal of an indicative but noisy signal.
2. The weak signal can be modeled by fast nearest neighbor search algorithms which return noisy nearest neighbor estimates. On the other hand, we imagine the strong signal as being expensive since it needs the true distances among the embedding vectors without any additive noise.

We believe that this natural graph model we examined for our algorithm modification helps explain and predict the strong empirical performance of our method. Thus our goal is to show that under the above data set modelling, re-ranking pivots based on weak signal similarity values provably helps. Assume that we have picked a pivot $u$ from each of the $k$ clusters of Assumption (1). We permute them randomly to form an ordering $u_1, \ldots, u_k$. This corresponds to the random ordering used by the `KwikCluster` algorithm and our theoretical algorithm of Section 2. Each non-pivot vertex $v$ re-ranks the pivots forming the ordering $u_{\pi_v(1)}, \ldots, u_{\pi_v(k)}$ where $\pi_v$ is a permutation depending on the weak signal similarities from the pivots to $v$. The weak signal similarities are calculated as detailed above: the weak signal outputs 'noisy' distances based on the true embedding vectors and smaller distances correspond to higher similarities. Note that each non-pivot vertex $v$ has a 'true' pivot $u$ corresponding to the pivot chosen from the cluster that the true embedding vector $p_v$ is part of. We say that a non-pivot vertex $v$ is correctly assigned by a clustering algorithm $C$ if $C$ assigns $v$ to its 'true' pivot. The following lemma shows that assigning vertices to pivots based on weak signal similarities strictly outperforms using a random order.

Intuitively, if another pivot $u'$ is ranked higher than $u$ in the random ordering, our proposed medication of re-ranking asked on weak signal similarities is likely to *correct* the ordering re-ranking $u$ to ahead. The lemma below provides theoretical justification of why this is sound and complements our experimental evaluation which demonstrates the empirical advantage of our re-ranking procedure.

**Lemma 4.** *Consider the setting above. Let $C$ be the clustering where every non pivot vertex picks the* first *pivot in this ordering that it has a strong signal edge to. Let $C'$ be the clustering where each non pivot vertex re-ranks the pivots using weak signal similarities then picks the first pivot that it has a strong signal edge to. Let $A$ be the number of non-pivot vertices that $C$ correctly assigns and similarly define $B$. We have $\mathbb{E}[A] < \mathbb{E}[B]$.*

*Proof.* Fix a non-pivot vertex $v$. Let $X$ denote the indicator variable for $C$ correctly assigning $v$ and define $Y$ similarly for $C'$. It suffices to show that $\mathbb{E}[X] < \mathbb{E}[Y]$. The lemma then follows by linearity of expectations and summing across all non-pivot vertices $v$. Note here that the expectation of each variable is with respect to the randomness used by the respective algorithms.

Let $u$ denote the true pivot of $v$. If $v$ does not have a strong signal edge to $u$ (according to the strong signal) then both algorithms will fail. Similarly, if $v$ only has a strong signal edge to $u$ and to no other pivots, then the performance of either clustering is the same. Now consider the case that $v$ has at least two strong signal edges to pivots, one to $u$ and rest arbitrary. Then the probability that $v$ is correctly classified by the random ordering is at most $1/2$. This is because if there is at least 1 other pivot that $v$ as a strong signal edge to, then the probability that the random ordering places $u$ ahead of it is at most $1/2$.

One the other hand, the probability that $v$ is correctly classified by the weak signal ordering is strictly larger than $1/2$. To see this, we calculate the probability that $u$ has the highest weak signal similarity. Identically, it suffices to calculate the probability that the weak signal outputs the smallest noisy distance value for $u$. Recall the modelling assumptions of the data set: we know that

$d(v,u) \leq R$ whereas $d(v,u') \geq 2R$ for all other pivots $u'$ that are not equal to $u$. The weak signal outputs $d(v,u')$ plus a uniformly random value in $[-R,R]$. Let $\xi_u$ be the random value added for $d(v,u)$. With probability $1/2$, this value is negative so the noisy distance computed by the weak signal is strictly smaller for $u$ than all other pivots $u'$ (since in the best case, their distance is at least $2R-R=R$). Furthermore, conditioning on the additive noise being positive for $u$, there is a non-zero probability that $u$ has the smallest additive noise (in absolute value) among all pivots. $u$ is again ranked the highest in this case. Altogether, the probability that $u$ is ranked the highest in terms of the weak signal similarity is strictly larger than $1/2$. It follows that $\mathbb{E}[X] < \mathbb{E}[Y]$, as desired. □

### D.2 Explaining why merging helps

We consider a particular worst case example for the `KwikCluster` algorithm which motivates why a post processing merging step helps. At a high level, it is possible to pick pivots which do not have a strong signal edge but nevertheless 'should' belong to the same cluster. Then when we a clustering algorithm is run, these two pivots can possibly lead to two disjoint clusters whereas that merging them lowers the correlation clustering objective and improves the overall clustering quality.

Concretely, consider the following example: we have a complete graph on $n$ vertices where every edge is a strong signal edge except a single edge $(u,v)$ which is not. In the classical `KwikCluster` algorithm, if $u$ is picked as a pivot then we will form two clusters, one consisting of all vertices besides $u$ and the the other cluster being the singleton $\{u\}$. The same is true if we pick $v$ to be the pivot. Thus the expected correlation clustering objective of the algorithm is

$$\frac{2}{n}\cdot(n-1)+\left(1-\frac{1}{n}\right)\cdot 1 \to 3.$$

On the other hand, clustering every vertex to be one cluster has correlation clustering objective value 1. Thus in the case where there are two clusters in the above example, a merging post-processing improves the overall cluster quality. This crisply captures our motivation.

While the above situation may not be representative, our merging post processing verifies that a possible merge is sound (after ranking possible cluster candidates to merge using the weak signal) by querying a (small) number of strong single values and merging only if the average strong single similarity is sufficiently high. Thus our post processing merge routine can only help the overall clustering.

### D.3 Inherent Trade-offs Between Precision and Recall

The goal of this section is to show that there is an inherent tradeoff between precision and recall of *any* clustering algorithm on graphs.We first restate the definitions of precision and recall as defined in our experimental section. Let $G$ be an unweighted (not necessarily complete) graph and let $\mathcal{C}$ be a clustering of its vertices. The edges of $G$ correspond to the edges in the strong signal graph (i.e., the edges are pairs of vertices the strong signal labels as 'similar.'). Correspondingly, the non-edges of $G$ represent the negative edges of the strong signal.

We first restate the definitions of precision and recall as defined in our experimental section. The recall of $\mathcal{C}$ is defined as the fraction of edges of $G$ which are together in some cluster given by $\mathcal{C}$. The precision of $\mathcal{C}$ is defined as the fraction whose numerator is the number of edges of $G$ which are together in some cluster and the denominator is the total number of pairs of vertices that are clustered together.

We state a natural (random) graph dataset such that with high probability, *any* clustering $\mathcal{C}$ has either recall or precision bounded away from 1 by a fixed constant. In particular, $G$ will be sampled from the standard $G(n,1/2)$ Erdos-Renyi graph distribution. Note the order of the quantifiers: we first generate a random graph. There is an event $E$ which $G$ satisfies with high probability. Condition on this event, *any* clustering of the vertices of $G$ will either have its precision or recall bounded away from 1, including the OPT correlation clustering.

Note that we have not made an attempt to optimize the constants in the following lemma for clarity. It is likely that one can optimize our proof and obtain a smaller constant than 0.75.

**Lemma 5.** *Let $G$ be sampled from the $G(n,1/2)$ distribution. With probability at least $1-1/poly(n)$,* ***all*** *clusterings of $G$ have recall or precision at most 0.75.*

*Proof.* Let $C>1$ be a fixed constant. We first consider the following event $E$ : for any subset $S$ of vertices of size at least $C\log n$, there are at most $1.01|S|^2/4$ and at least $0.99|S|^2/4$ edges of $G$ within $S$.

We now show that $E$ holds with probability at least $1 - 1/poly(n)$. For a fixed subset $S$ of $k$ vertices for $k \geq C \log n$, the expected number of edges within $S$ is $\binom{k}{2}/2$. Thus the probability that there are more than $1.01k^2/4$ and less than $0.99k^2/4$ edges within $S$ is at most $\exp(-ck^2)$ by a standard Chernoff bound for a fixed constant $c > 0$. There are $\binom{n}{k}$ such choices of $S$ and thus union bounding over all $S$ and all $k \geq C \log n$, we have that the probability there exists some set $S$ with $|S| \geq C \log n$ vertices violating the required number of edges is at most

$$\begin{aligned}
&\sum_{k \geq C \log n} \binom{n}{k} \exp(-ck^2) \\
&\leq \sum_{k \geq C \log n} 2 \left(\frac{ne}{k}\right)^k \exp(-\varepsilon^2 k^2/6) \\
&= \sum_{k \geq C \log n} \exp(\log 2 + k \log(ne) - k \log k - ck^2) \\
&\leq n \cdot \exp(-\Omega(k^2)) \\
&\leq \frac{1}{poly(n)}
\end{aligned}$$

for $k \geq C \log n$ for a sufficiently large constant $C$ and $n$ large enough. Thus $\mathbb{P}(E) \geq 1 - 1/poly(n)$ where we can make the polynomial arbitrarily large by increasing $C$. We also condition on the fact that $G$ itself has at least $0.999n^2/4$ edges with also happens with inverse polynomial failure probability.

Now consider an arbitrary clustering $\mathcal{C}$. If the recall of $\mathcal{C}$ is at most $0.75$ then we are done so suppose the recall is at least $0.75$. Given this, we claim that there exist a cluster within $\mathcal{C}$ of size at least $0.74n$.

To see this, let $C_1, \cdots, C_j$ be the clusters of $\mathcal{C}$. The clusters of size at most $C \log n$ have at most $n \cdot (C \log n)^2/2$ edges of $G$ inside them. All other clusters $C_i$ have at most $1.01|C_i|^2/4$ edges of $G$ inside them. Altogether, the number of edges of $G$ inside some cluster is at most

$$n \cdot (C \log n)^2/2 + \sum_{|C_i| \geq C \log n} \frac{1.01|C_i|^2}{4}$$

subject to the constraint that $|C_i| \leq 0.74n$ and $\sum_i |C_i| \leq n$. This is a convex function which is maximized at its boundary, meaning the number of edges of $G$ inside some cluster of $\mathcal{C}$ is at most

$$\begin{aligned}
n \cdot (C \log n)^2/2 + \frac{1}{0.74} \cdot \frac{1.01 \cdot 0.74^2 n^2}{4} \\
\ll 0.75 \cdot \frac{0.999n^2}{2}
\end{aligned}$$

which contradicts the fact that the recall of $\mathcal{C}$ is at least $0.75$. Thus there exists a cluster of $\mathcal{C}$ of size at least $0.74n$. Now given this, we show that the precision must be at most $0.75$.

Towards this end, let $C_i$ be the cluster of $\mathcal{C}$ of size at least $0.74n$. It has at most $1.01|C_i|^2/4$ edges of $G$ inside it and $\binom{|C_i|}{2}$ pairs of vertices. Let $A$ be the other edges of $G$ not inside $C_i$ and let $B$ be the total pairs of vertices where both of the vertices in the pair lie outside of $C_i$. Then the precision of $C_i$ is bounded by

$$\frac{1.01|C_i|^2/4 + A}{\binom{|C_i|}{2} + B}.$$

Since $|C_i| \geq 0.74n$, one can easily verify that

$$B \leq \frac{(0.26n)^2}{2} < \frac{1}{8} \cdot \binom{|C_i|}{2}$$

and thus

$$\begin{aligned}
\frac{1.01|C_i|^2/4 + A}{\binom{|C_i|}{2} + B} &\leq \frac{1.01|C_i|^2/4 + B}{\binom{|C_i|}{2} + B} \\
&\leq \frac{1.01|C_i|^2/4}{\binom{|C_i|}{2}} + \frac{B}{\binom{|C_i|}{2} + B} \\
&\leq 0.51 + \frac{B}{9B} \\
&< 0.75,
\end{aligned}$$

as desired. □

### D.4 Motivating Using Weak Signal Neighborhood Statistics.

In Figure 2, we plot the the fraction of times a vertex $v$ connects to a pivot $p$ in the `KwikBucks` algorithm as a function of the number of nearest neighbors of $v$ (in terms of the weak signal similarity) which have already connected to the same pivot $p$.. We see that the probability increases as a function of the number of nearest neighbors, empirically justifying our algorithmic design optimization of 'Utilizing Weak Signal Neighborhood' in Section C. Note that this optimization has the affect of slightly boosting such pivots $p$ (if they exist) to a higher similarity (and thus a better ranking).

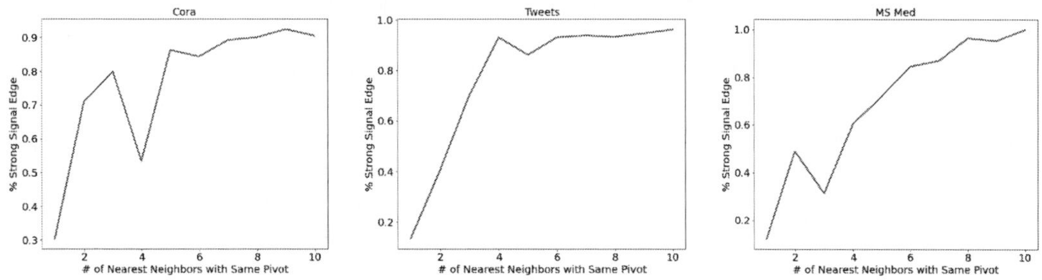


(a) (b) (c)

Figure 2: The propensity for a vertex $v$ to connect to a pivot $p$ given that $k$ of $v$'s neighbors have already connected to $p$.

## E Details for Dataset & Weak/Strong Signals

We provide a detailed description of the datasets used in the paper as well as the weak and strong signals used for each of the datasets. Table 2 provides a summary.

**Stackoverflow (SOF) and SearchSnippets:** Stackoverflow and SearchSnippets are commonly used for short-text clustering/classification. For stackoverflow, we used a subset collected by (Xu et al., 2017) consisting of of 20,000 question titles associated with 20 different categories obtained from a dataset released as part of a Kaggle challenge. For SearchSnippets, we used the dataset from (Phan et al., 2008) which consists of 12,340 snippets (extracted from web search snippets) associated with 8 groups. For these two datasets, we experimented with two different types of cheap signals: word2vec embeddings (Mikolov et al., 2013) and tf-idf embeddings. In both cases, we trained/finetuned on the training set of the datasets. We used the Gensim package (Rehurek and Sojka, 2011) for word2vec and sklearn (Pedregosa et al., 2011) for tf-idf. Word2vec provides a vector representation for each English word; to compute the embedding for a sentence/document, we average the embeddings of each of its words. For the strong signal, for each dataset we finetuned a T5-1.1 XXL model (11B parameters) (Raffel et al., 2020) on the training data where given two examples, the model was finetuned to predict if they belong to the same cluster or not. In both cases, we sampled 10K positive pairs and 50K negative pairs and finetuned the model for 10 epochs on a 4x4 DragonFish TPU architecture.

**Twitter and AgNews:** Twitter and News data are commonly used for short-text clustering/classification. From Twitter, we use the dataset created by (Yin and Wang, 2016) consisting of 2,472 tweets with 89 categories. From News, we use the data from (Rakib et al., 2020) which is a subset of the dataset from (Zhang and LeCun, 2015) containing 4 topics. For the cheap signal, we use pretrained BERT embeddings (Devlin et al., 2018) where we feed each example into the BERT model, obtain contextual token embeddings, and then average them (ignoring the [CLS] and [SEP] tokens) to obtain the embedding for each example. We use the 12-layer uncased BERT-Base model for this experiment. For the strong signal, we first created a graph by connecting two nodes if they belong to the same category, then added noise to the graph by flipping the existence/non-existence of an edge for 5% of node pairs selected uniformly at random (note that without adding noise, the problem becomes much easier as graph of the strong signal becomes composed of multiple connected components).

**Internal:** This is a vertical of a large, internal, proprietary text dataset. The weak signal is embedding similarity, and the strong is an indicator variable from a cross-attention model.

**Citeseer and Microsoft Medicine:** Citeseer (Sen et al., 2008) and Microsoft Medicine (Shchur and Günnemann, 2019) are attributed graph datasets. Citeseer is a citation network in which nodes represent papers, edges represent citations, and features are bag-of-word abstracts. Microsoft Medicine is a subset of the Microsoft Academic graph where the nodes represent authors, edges represent co-authorship, and node features are a collection of paper keywords from author's papers. For both datasets, we used the cosine similarity between the node features as the weak signal and we assume the edges of the graph correspond to the strong signal.

**Cora and Amazon Electronics Photos:** Similar to Citeseer and Microsoft Medicine, Cora and Amazon Electronics Photos are also attributed graph datasets. They are typically used for node classification but here we adapt them to our problem. Cora (Sen et al., 2008) is a citation network similar to the Citeseer dataset with the node labels corresponding to paper topics. Amazon Electronics Photos (Shchur et al., 2018) is a subgraphs of the Amazon copurchase graph where the nodes represent goods, an edge between two nodes represents that they have been frequently purchased together, node features are bag-of-word reviews, and class labels are product categories. For these two datasets, we used the deep graph infomax (DGI) model (Velickovic et al., 2019) to learn unsupervised node representations and used these representations as the cheap signal. We also used noisy labels as the strong signal similar to the Twitter dataset.

**Total cost analysis:** Our work is mostly based on the applications where the weak oracle values are computed via distances based on embeddings and the strong signal values are the output of a large cross-attention transformer model. In this case, there are three different factors that comprise the total cost of the clustering algorithm: 1- the cost of the queries to the strong signal, 2- the cost of computing embeddings from the cheap signal, and 3- the cost of geometric operations on the embeddings. So the total cost can be summarized as follows:

$$Total\ Cost = \eta_S \zeta_S + \eta_E \zeta_E + \eta_G \zeta_G$$

where $\eta_S$ represents the number of calls to the strong signal, $\zeta_S$ represents the cost of making a call to the strong signal, $\eta_E$ represents the number of calls needed to compute embeddings, $\zeta_E$ represents the cost of obtaining one embedding, $\eta_G$ represents the number of geometric operations (cosine similarity in our case) we perform on the embeddings, and $\zeta_G$ represents the cost of a single geometric operation.

The number of calls $\eta_E$ required to obtain embeddings is $n$ (i.e. the number of data points) which is smaller than $\eta_S$ (which, in our case, is typically a linear factor of $n$) and the cost $\zeta_E$ of obtaining one embedding is significantly smaller than the cost of obtaining one strong signal similarity $\zeta_S$. Therefore, $\eta_E \zeta_E$ can be subsumed in $\eta_S \zeta_S$.

When using 32 TPU v3 chips for the strong signal and a CPU for the geometric operations, each call to the strong signal was approximately $10^4$ times slower (i.e. $\zeta_S \approx 10^4 \zeta_G$). This gap becomes even more stark if we use fast geometric algorithms such as nearest neighbor search or use TPUs for geometric operations. It follows from the analysis of our algorithm that $\eta_G \in O(nk)$ where k is the parameter defined in Algorithm 6. This is comparable to $\eta_S$. Therefore, $\eta_G \zeta_G$ is negligible compared to $\eta_S \zeta_S$ in our experiments.

Following the above justifications, as well as for theoretical simplicity, in this paper we ignored the cost of querying the weak signal in our analysis (i.e. assume $\eta_E \zeta_E + \eta_G \zeta_G \approx 0$). However, if future work considers costlier operations for the cheap signal, these extra terms should also be considered in determining the total clustering cost.

## F Additional Experimental Results

### F.1 Precision and Recall

The precision and recall (with respect to a clustering $C$) definitions used in Section 4 are defined as follows:

$$\text{Precision}(C, O_S) = \frac{\sum_{e=(i,j)} C_{i,j} O_S(e)}{\sum_{e=(i,j)} C_{i,j}} \tag{2}$$

where $C_{i,j}$ is the indicator for if vertices $i, j$ are in the same cluster.

$$\text{Recall}(C, O_S) = \frac{\sum_{e=(i,j)} C_{i,j} O_S(e)}{\sum_{e=(i,j)} O_S(e)}. \tag{3}$$

As stated in (García-Soriano et al., 2020b), while our algorithm and baselines have been designed to minimize the total correlation clustering objective, it is important to consider precision and recall as they are problem independent measures of cluster quality. Furthermore in cases where the underlying strong signal graph is extremely sparse, the correlation cost objective might not be meaningful. For example in such a case, returning all vertices as singleton clusters already has low objective value (equation 1). We use the entire strong signal graph for the purposes of evaluating the experimental metrics, such as CC objective, precision, and recall.

### F.2 Parameter Selection Details

We first describe how to select the value $t$ in Algorithm 3 and $k$ in Algorithm 6, which selects the top

Table 2: Properties of datasets used in our experiments. $n$ denotes the number of vertices and Non-zero entries denotes the number of non-zero entries in the adjacency matrix of the strong signal graph (i.e. twice the number of edges), both rounded to two significant digits.

| Name | Type | Weak Signal | Strong Signal | $n$ | Non-zero entries |
|---|---|---|---|---|---|
| SOF | Text | W2V / tf-idf | Cross-attention model | $4.9 \cdot 10^3$ | $2.3 \cdot 10^6$ |
| Search | Text | W2V / tf-idf | Cross-attention model | $3.3 \cdot 10^3$ | $2.0 \cdot 10^6$ |
| Twitter | Text | BERT Embeddings | Noisy label indicator | $2.4 \cdot 10^3$ | $4.7 \cdot 10^5$ |
| AgNews | Text | BERT Embeddings | Noisy label indicator | $8.0 \cdot 10^3$ | $1.8 \cdot 10^7$ |
| Internal | Text | Embeddings | Cross-attention model | $1.0 \cdot 10^5$ | $9.5 \cdot 10^7$ |
| Cora | Attributed Graph | DGI Embeddings | Noisy label indicator | $2.7 \cdot 10^3$ | $1.5 \cdot 10^6$ |
| Photos | Attributed Graph | DGI Embeddings | Noisy label indicator | $7.7 \cdot 10^3$ | $1.2 \cdot 10^7$ |
| Citeseer | Attributed Graph | Node Features | Adjacency matrix | $3.3 \cdot 10^3$ | $10^4$ |
| Med. | Attributed Graph | Node Features | Adjacency matrix | $6.3 \cdot 10^4$ | $1.6 \cdot 10^6$ |

$k$ vertices in weak-signal similarity for the strong signal to query.

The intuition in picking $t$ is that it must be sufficiently large so that only few vertices do not have a pivot in their neighborhood (and thus contribute to the additive error of Theorem 1). This parameter naturally depends on the density of the underlying strong signal graph: for sparser graphs, one must pick a larger value of $t$ since each vertex on average has a small degree and is thus less likely to have a pivot chosen in its neighborhood than a vertex with a larger degree. We use the above intuition to design the following data-dependent method to select $t$: we first sample a sublinear number of random strong signal edges ($\sqrt{n}$ strong signal edges to be exact). This returns an estimate of the density of the graph up to small additive error (for example via standard Chernoff bounds). We then set $t$ to be 10 times the inverse of the density. If the density is extremely sparse, i.e. less than $1/1000$ fraction of possible edges exist, we simply set $t$ to be equal to $n/2$.

The second parameter we set is $k$ in `WeakFilterByRanking`. We can pick a value of $k \ll n$ because intuitively, a meaningful weak signal assigns a high similarity score to relevant pivots relative to all other pivots and thus such pivots have higher ranking. To understand the trade offs in selecting $k$, consider the most prominent place where it is used in our algorithm: when a vertex $v$ attempts to find a strong signal edge to one of the pivots by iterating through them in the weak signal ordering. The trade offs are the following: a smaller value of $k$ leads to better query efficiency as $v$ is guaranteed to only make $k$ strong signal queries in this step. However the clustering quality can suffer because the first $k$ pivots, for a small $k$, in the weak signal order might not have a strong signal edge to $v$. Conversely a larger value of $k$ leads to increased exploration from $v$ as it attempts to connect to a pivot. However in the case that $v$ is truly a singleton cluster, i.e. it has no strong signal edges to any pivot, we potentially waste many strong signal queries. To balance these trade offs, we pick an 'intermediate' value of $k = 100$ *for all our experiments*. Ablation studies for both parameters are given in Section F.

We also always set $k = 10$ when we use the "Utilizing Weak Signal Neighborhood" optimization of Section 3. We also always fix $\lambda = 1/10$ which appropriately normalizes the second term to be between 0 and 1 (note the weak signal similarity $w_p$ is between $-1$ and 1). The parameter 10 here is fairly robust and can likely be replaced by any (small) reasonable value and we also perform ablation studies on this optimization.

For spectral clustering, we always use $k = 25$ for the number of clusters. Higher values were computationally prohibitive to use.

### F.3 Results

We present additional experimental results in Figure 3 and 4 which show similar qualitative results as Figure 1: our algorithm `KwikBucks` has superior query complexity over the baselines as it achieves a higher $F_1$ value (and lower CC objective values) while utilizing fewer strong signal queries than baselines.

### F.4 Additional Ablation Results

In our ablation experiments, we fix all parameter settings except the component we are altering. We perform ablation studies on 4 representative

Table 3: CC objective values are shown for a fixed budget of $3n$. See Table 1 for the corresponding $F_1$ values. We normalize the smallest CC value to 1.0 so smaller quantities are desirable. See Figures 3 and 4 for results as a function of query budget. For the sparser graph datasets of Citeseer, Med., and Internal we use the budget of $50n$. Due to their sparsity, the CC objective value is less meaningful than $F_1$ values for these two datasets.

| | **SOF** | **Search** | **Tweet** | **AgNews** | **Cora** | **Photos** | **Citeseer** | **Medicine** | **Internal** |
|---|---|---|---|---|---|---|---|---|---|
| B1 | 1.9 | 2.5 | 1.2 | 2.0 | 2.0 | 2.5 | 1.3 | 1.1 | 1.01 |
| B2 | 1.8 | 2.0 | 1.2 | 2.0 | 2.0 | 2.4 | 1.3 | 1.1 | 1.04 |
| B3 | 6.4 | 4.0 | 6.3 | 2.5 | 2.5 | 2.2 | 745.1 | 2550.8 | - |
| B4 | 2.0 | 6.0 | 1.1 | 4.1 | 3.0 | 3.2 | 1.0 | 1.0 | 1.01 |
| B5 | 2.0 | 6.0 | 1.1 | 4.1 | 3.0 | 3.2 | 1.3 | 1.3 | 1.01 |
| `KwikBucks` | 1.0 | 1.0 | 1.0 | 1.0 | 1.0 | 1.0 | 1.1 | 1.0 | 1.0 |

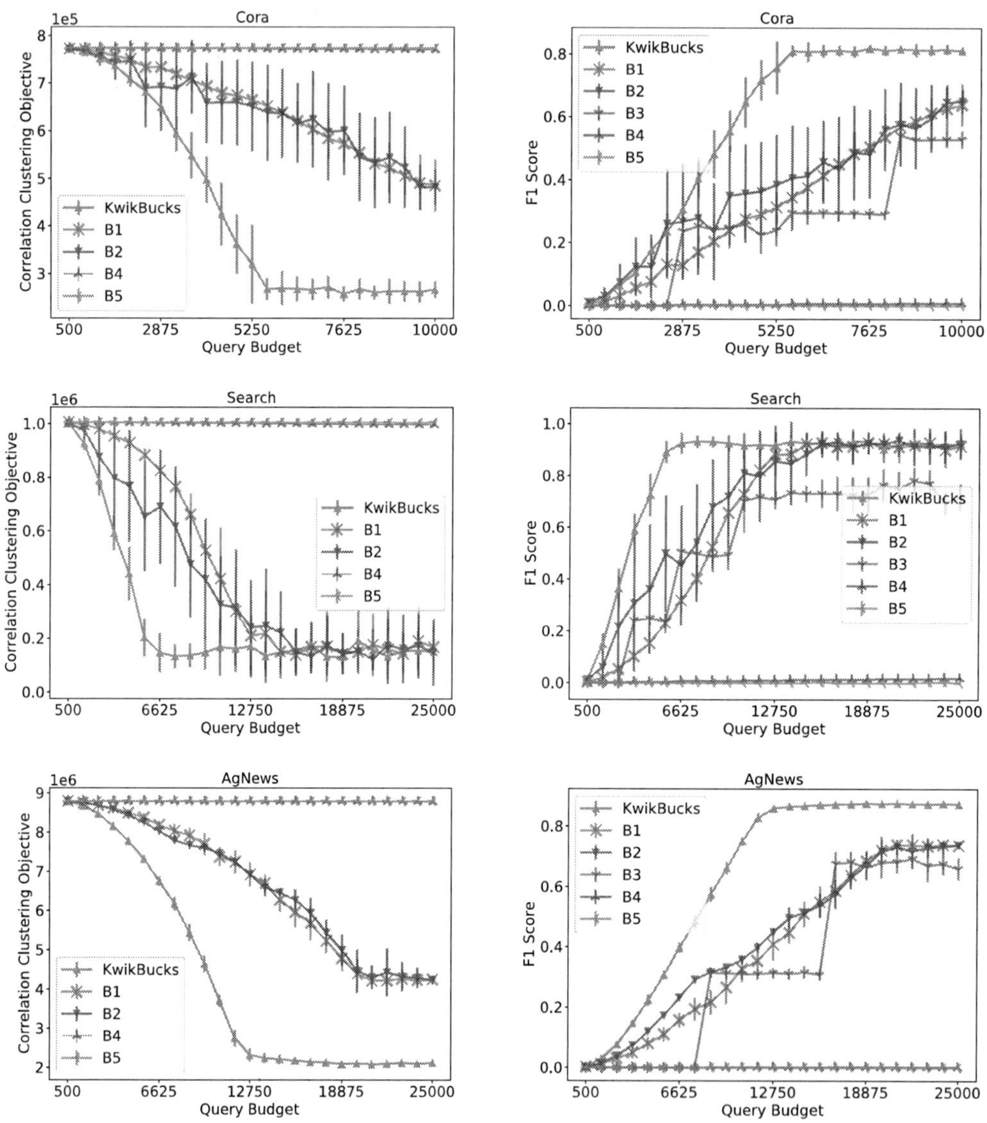


Figure 3: Empirical results for the Cora, Stackoverflow, Search, and News datasets.

datasets: Cora, Citeseer, Stackoverflow (SOF), and Search. Our first observation is that the merge post processing procedure can help return a higher quality clustering, for example for the Cora, SOF, and Citeseer datasets; see Figures 5 and 6 for details and Section D.2 for theoretical intuition of why post processing merging helps.

Next we consider removing the `SortNonPivots` step and replacing it with an using an arbitrary ordering of non pivot vertices. We see that the positive benefits of removing this component are more subdued compared to the merge post processing. However, this change never hurts the quality of the clustering. Overall, we view the different data-driven components introduced in Section 3 and C as having complementary benefits as each optimize a different part of the algorithm.

We observe that one must choose a sufficiently large value of $t$ in `GetPivots` which is the initial number of random vertices sampled which are later processed to be pivots. As argued in Section F.2, it is important to select a sufficiently large value of $t$ to limit the number of vertices which do not have a pivot in their strong signal neighborhood (as captured by the additive error term in Theorem 1). For our ablation studies, we consider two other settings of $t$, one which is a factor of 10 smaller than the choice used in our main experimental results and one which is a factor of 10 larger. They represent the 'Small' and 'Large' pivot choices respectively. We see in Figures 5 and 6 for the Cora and Citeseer datasets, that a smaller choice of $t$ can lead to a decrease in the performance of our algorithm. Nevertheless, our data driven density based approach outlined in F.2 hits the 'sweet spot' and performs comparable to the best choice of pivots in all cases as shown in Figures 5 and 6.

We also perform ablation experiments on the choice of $k$ in `WeakSignalFilterPractice` by considering $k = 10$ and $k = 1000$ (a 'small' and 'large' choice respectively as before). Our ablation experiments also show that a large choice of $k$ in `WeakSignalFilterPractice` can lead to many queries wasted as argued in Section F.2. Indeed, we see in the above figures that for the Citeseer dataset, a large value of $k$ leads to worse performance initially as we waste many strong signal queries on vertices which have no strong signal edge to any of the pivots. This is due to the sparse nature of the Citeseer dataset. However as the query budget is increased, the quality of the clustering improves. The choice of $k$ seems to have negligible impact on the other datasets we tested on and our choice of $k = 100$ (which we fixed in the main experimental results) was always competitive.

### F.5 Measuring the Quality of Weak Signals

We design a simple and informative experiment to measure the quality of weak signals. For the Stackoverflow (SO) dataset, we run `KwikBucks` where we replace the weak signal with a linear *interpolation* of the strong signal and a random matrix will all entries i.i.d. from the uniform distribution in $[-1, 1]$. The purpose of this experiment is to show a higher quality weak signal gives better clustering results than using a lower quality weak signal. Indeed, Figure 8 shows that `KwikBucks` performs the best if we replace the weak signal completely with the strong signal, as naturally expected. As we vary the amount of randomness in the weak signal, the performance degrades and the case where the weak signal is a fully random matrix performs the worst as a function of query budget. It is also interesting to consider the cases where the weak signal are given by the (stronger) W2V model versus the comparatively weaker tf-idf model: the performance of using the W2V embeddings for the weak signal lies between the 'half-random' and '$2/3$ random' case whereas the tf-idf plot lies between the '$2/3$ random' and 'fully random' cases. The random interpolated weak signal cases, while artificial, help us qualitatively access the usefulness of a particular real world weak signal instance.

### F.6 Average Rankings of Strong Signal Neighbors

In this Section we present additional experiments in the similar spirit as the right figure of the second row of Figure 1 for the Tweet, Med., and Cora datasets. For every vertex $v$ in these datasets, we rank all the other vertices in decreasing weak signal similarities to $v$. The average rank of the true strong signal neighbors of $v$ is computed and plotted as a histogram (normalized to be a distribution). Intuitively, a good weak signal should have the property that *true* strong signal neighbors have much higher weak signal similarity scores (and thus better rankings) than the an arbitrary vertex. Indeed, we see that to be the case of the datasets in Figure 9 where the distributions are much more left shifted and has a much smaller mean compared to the case if the weak signal was fully random. This validates the connection between our empirical weak signal Definition 3 and the theoretical assumption we made for the weak oracle in Assumption 1. Indeed, Figure 9 gives empirical validation to the claim that returning a top $k$ most similar vertices to a vertex $v$ in terms of weak signal similarity captures many actual *true* strong signal neighbors.

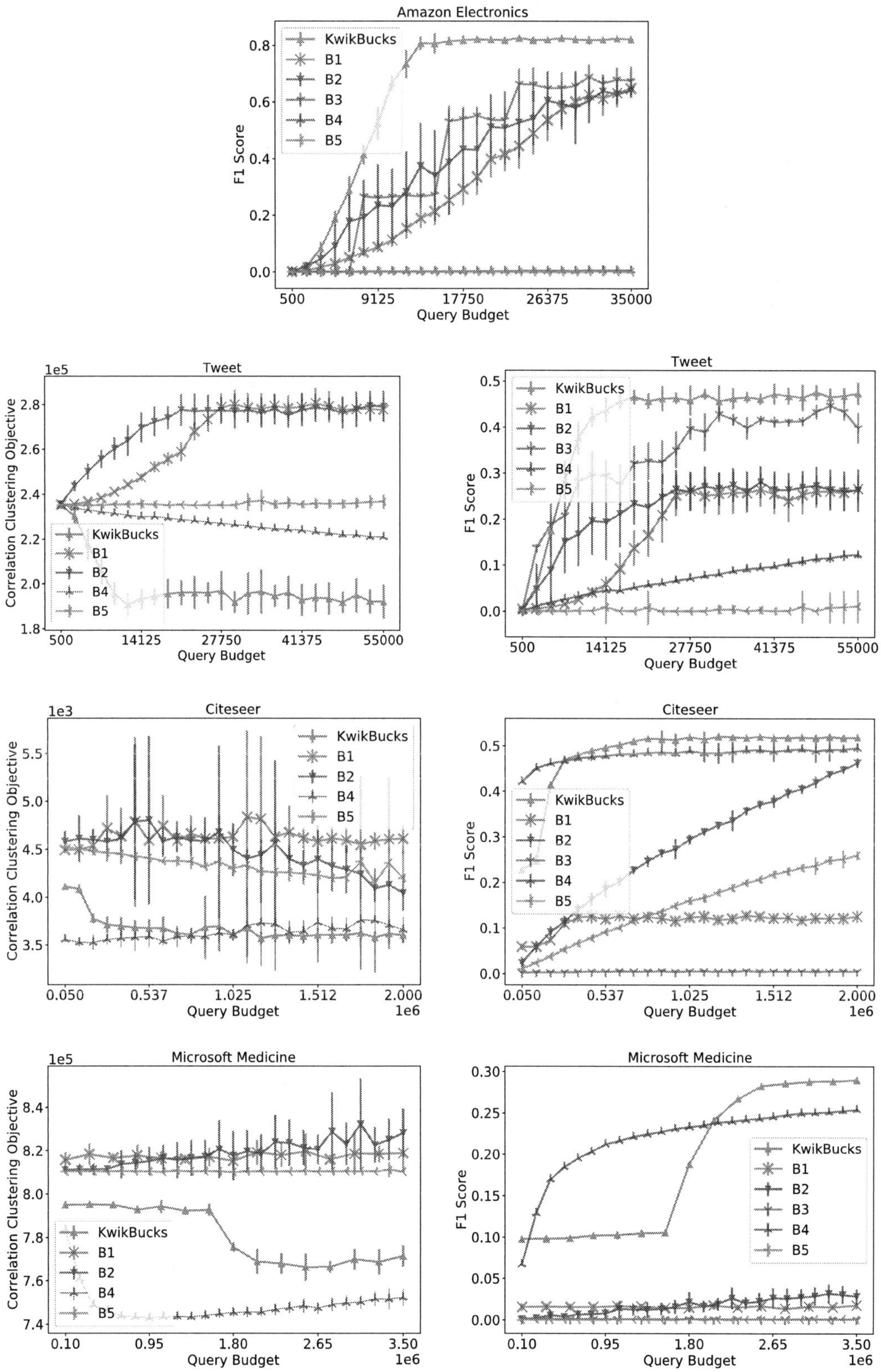


Figure 4: Empirical results on the datasets omitted from Figure 3. The results are qualitatively similar to that of Figure 3.

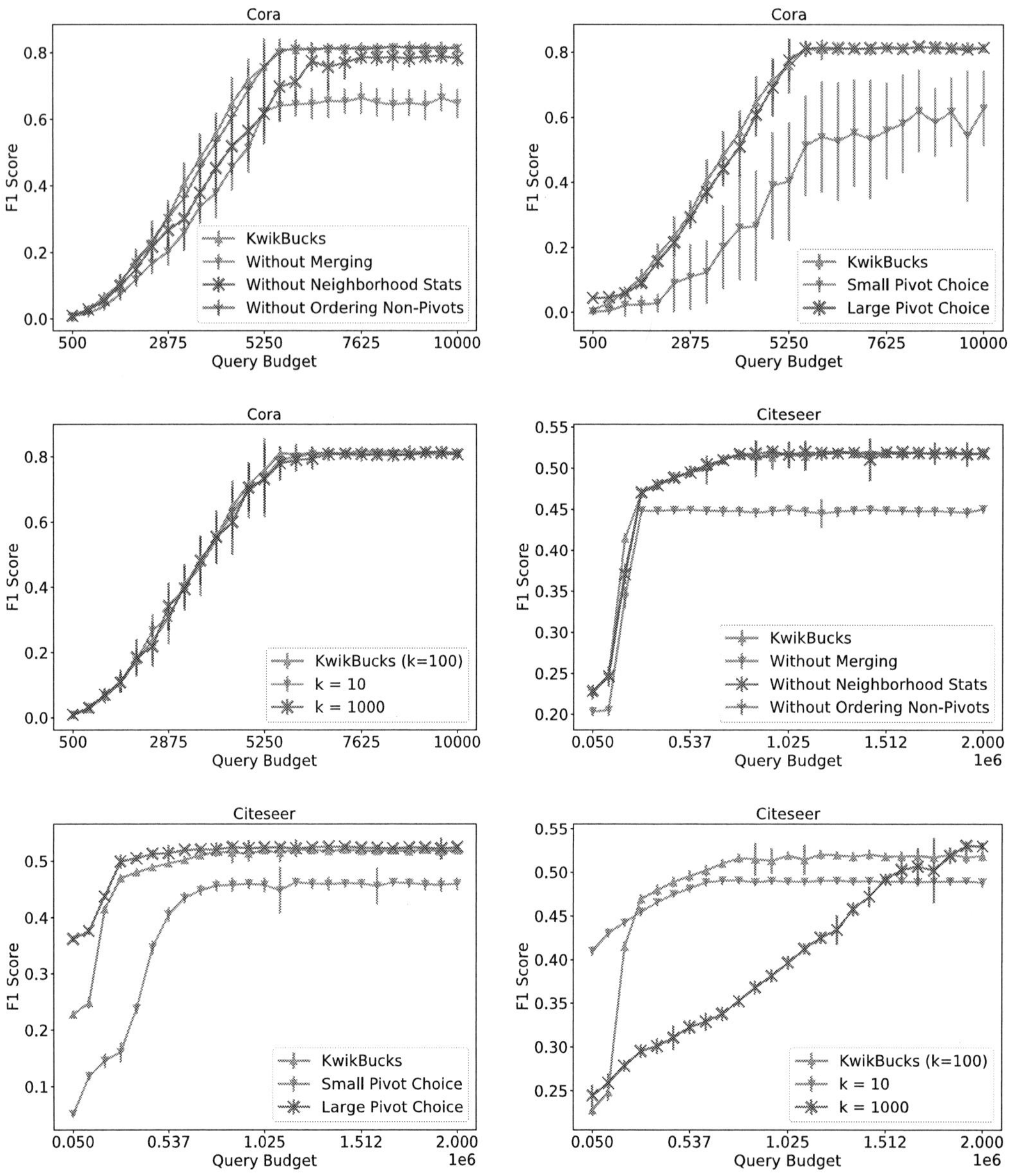


Figure 5: Figures for ablation studies for Cora and Citeseer datasets.

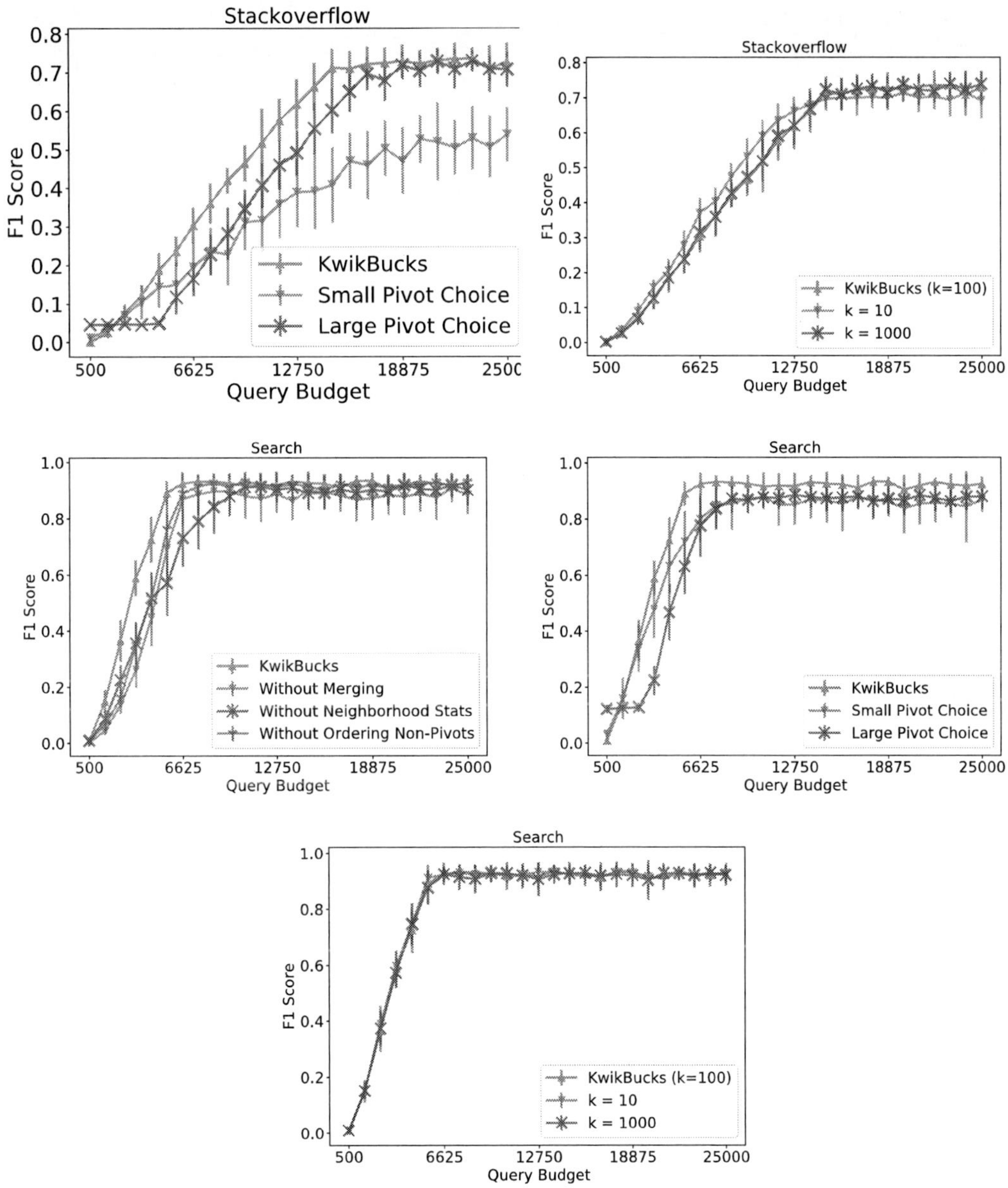


Figure 6: Figures for ablation studies for SOF and Search datasets.

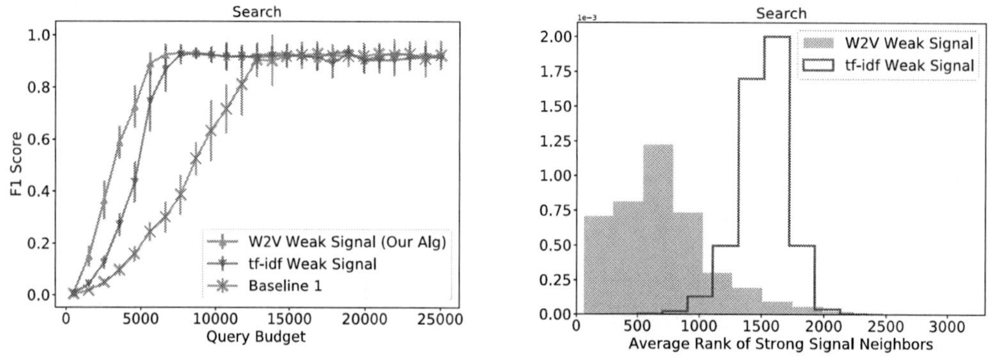


Figure 7: The figure shows a qualitatively similar result as the SOF results shown in Figure 1.

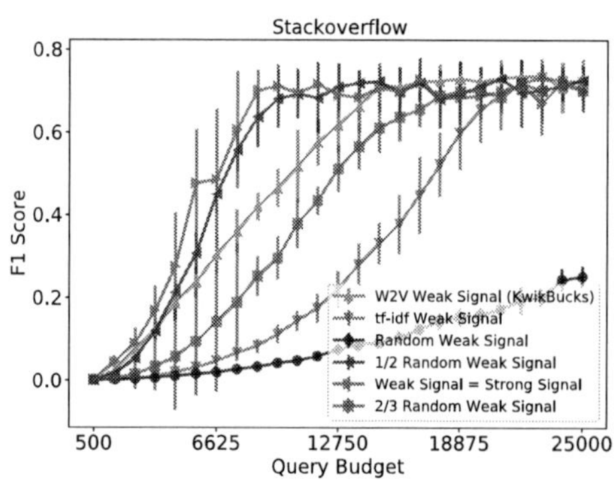


Figure 8: Interpolating the weak signal between uniformly random values and the strong signal.

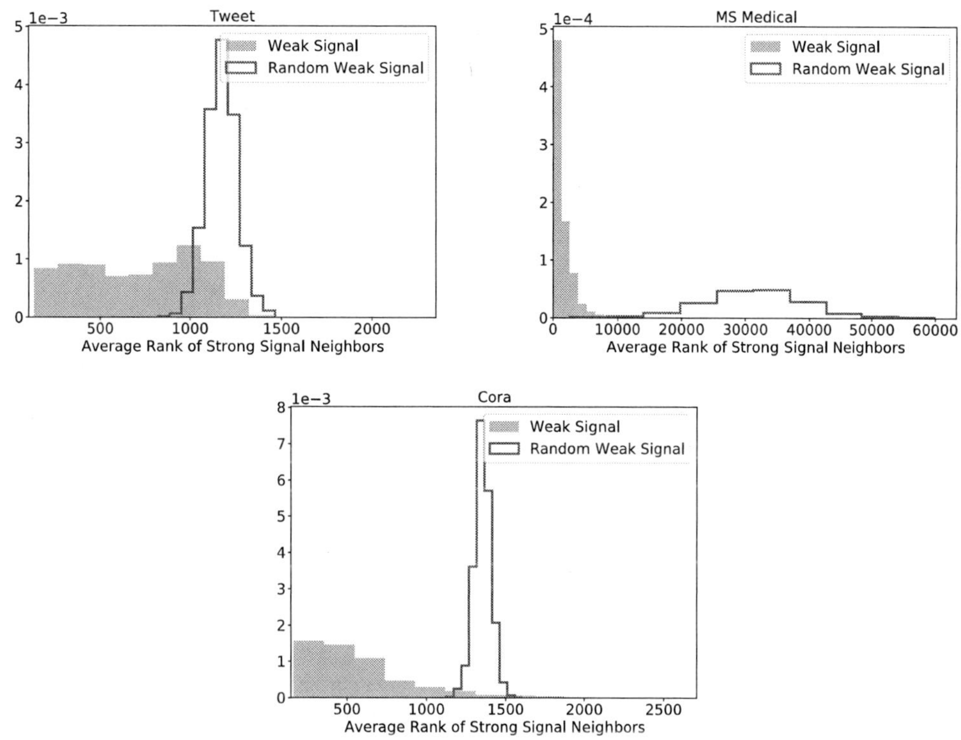


Figure 9: The average weak signal rank of actual strong signal neighbors is shown in orange. The blue curve shows the average rank if the weak signal was fully random.

# Semantic-Oriented Unlabeled Priming for Large-Scale Language Models

**Yanchen Liu**[1] **Timo Schick**[2] **Hinrich Schütze**[3]
[1]Harvard University [2]Meta AI Research [3]LMU Munich
yanchenliu@g.harvard.edu, schick@meta.com

## Abstract

Due to the high costs associated with finetuning large language models, various recent works propose to adapt them to specific tasks without any parameter updates through in-context learning. Unfortunately, for in-context learning there is currently no way to leverage unlabeled data, which is often much easier to obtain in large quantities than labeled examples. In this work, we therefore investigate ways to make use of unlabeled examples to improve the zero-shot performance of pretrained language models without any finetuning: We introduce Semantic-Oriented Unlabeled Priming (SOUP), a method that classifies examples by retrieving semantically similar unlabeled examples, assigning labels to them in a zero-shot fashion, and then using them for in-context learning. We also propose *bag-of-contexts* priming, a new priming strategy that is more suitable for our setting and enables the usage of more examples than fit into the context window.

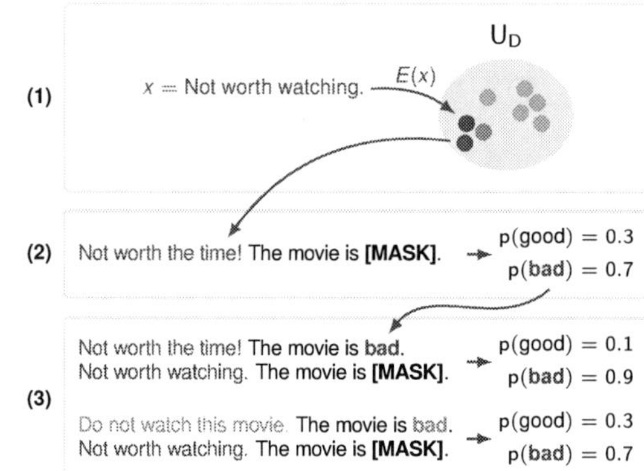


Figure 1: Schematic representation of the steps involved in SOUP for binary sentiment classification of movie reviews. (1) **Semantic Search**: For a given input $x$, we retrieve semantically similar, unlabeled examples from a set $U_D$ using a sentence encoder $E$. (2) **Self-Prediction**: We obtain zero-shot predictions for all similar examples using natural language prompts. (3) **Bag-of-Contexts Priming**: We use the retrieved examples along with their most probable labels one at a time as in-context examples to obtain predictions for $x$; the resulting distributions over possible labels are finally averaged.

## 1 Introduction

In recent years, there has been a trend in NLP towards larger and larger language models (LMs) (Radford et al., 2018, 2019; Raffel et al., 2020; Brown et al., 2020; Fedus et al., 2021). Different from prior pretrained LMs that are typically finetuned for specific downstream tasks using labeled training datasets (Devlin et al., 2019; Liu et al., 2019), recent work proposes to use such large models in zero- or few-shot settings without any finetuning (Brown et al., 2020; Sanh et al., 2021) due to the often prohibitive costs associated with training, storing and deploying large models (Strubell et al., 2019). In particular, Brown et al. (2020) propose *priming* where training examples are simply provided as additional context together with test examples; this *in-context learning* does not require updating the parameters of the model.

In prior work on in-context learning, only labeled examples are used for priming (Brown et al., 2020; Lu et al., 2021; Kumar and Talukdar, 2021; Min et al., 2021; Jiang et al., 2021). But in many settings, these are extremely scarce or even entirely unavailable, while unlabeled examples can easily be accessed. Unfortunately, there is currently no way to leverage unlabeled examples for priming. Other approaches for leveraging unlabeled data such as domain-adaptive pretraining (Gururangan et al., 2020) would again require finetuning.

Therefore, we investigate how we can make use of unlabeled examples to improve the performance of large-scale language models without requiring changes to their parameters: We propose a self-supervised method called Semantic-Oriented Unlabeled Priming (SOUP), which uses unlabeled examples for in-context learning. Following the observation that semantically similar examples are better



*Proceedings of The Fourth Workshop on Simple and Efficient Natural Language Processing (SustaiNLP)*, pages 32–38
July 13, 2023 ©2023 Association for Computational Linguistics

candidates as in-context examples than dissimilar ones (Gao et al., 2021a; Liu et al., 2021), we first retrieve the semantically most similar unlabeled examples as contexts for a given input; then, we query the language model to obtain predictions for these unlabeled examples, and finally provide them along with their most likely labels as additional context. Intuitively, this approach is particularly helpful whenever the retrieved examples are easier to classify then the actual input of interest.

Whereas in prior work, the in-context examples and test example are usually concatenated to form a single input that is provided to the LM, we propose to use one in-context example at a time and compute a weighted average of the so-obtained label distributions to obtain a final prediction. Besides resulting in much better performance, one benefit of this methods is that we are no longer constrained by the maximum sequence length of the used LM and thus, more neighbors can be used for priming than with the usual, concatenation-based approach. We also investigate an iterative variant of our approach where predictions for unlabeled examples are iteratively improved with SOUP. On four English text classification datasets, we show that SOUP improves performance of pretrained LMs.

## 2 Related Work

First proposed by Brown et al. (2020), in-context learning has been studied by many recent works (Lu et al., 2021; Kumar and Talukdar, 2021; Min et al., 2021; Jiang et al., 2021). Concurrent with our work, Min et al. (2021) also propose to perform priming with individual examples and combine the resulting predictions; however, they use a different combination technique and, similar to all prior work on in-context learning, only investigate settings with labeled examples. Our approach is also related to various approaches that leverage unlabeled data in few- or zero-shot settings (Xie et al., 2019; Gururangan et al., 2020; Schick and Schütze, 2021a), but all of them require finetuning the underlying language model.

We make use of different Transformer-based sentence encoders (Reimers and Gurevych, 2019; Gao et al., 2021b) and of textual instructions to improve model performance, an approach that was first proposed by Radford et al. (2019) and has since been investigated extensively (Schick and Schütze, 2021a,b,c; Gao et al., 2021a, i.a.).

## 3 Semantic-Oriented Unlabeled Priming

We introduce Semantic-Oriented Unlabeled Priming (SOUP), our approach for in-context learning with unlabeled examples. To this end, let $M$ be a masked language model (Devlin et al., 2019) where for some sequence of tokens $t_1, \ldots, t_k$ that contains exactly one mask token, $M(t \mid t_1, \ldots, t_k)$ denotes the probability that $M$ assigns to $t$ at the masked position.[1] Further, let $E$ be a sentence encoder where $E(x)$ denotes the representation assigned to $x$ by $E$, and $D_U$ be a set of unlabeled examples. We consider a text classification setup where for a given input $x$, a label $y$ from a set $Y$ has to be predicted.

Obtaining predictions for $x$ with SOUP consists of the following steps:

1. **Semantic Search**: We search for unlabeled examples that are semantically most similar to $x$ using the sentence encoder $E$.
2. **Self-Prediction**: We use $M$ to obtain predictions for these neighboring examples.
3. **Bag-of-Contexts Priming**: We use the neighbors and their estimated labels as additional context for priming $M$ and compute an average of the resulting label distributions to obtain a final prediction for $x$.

### 3.1 Semantic Search

Similar to prior work (Gao et al., 2021a; Liu et al., 2021), the unlabeled examples $x_u \in D_U$ are encoded to obtain vector representations $E(x_u)$; this can be done in advance for the entire set $D_U$. We also compute the representation $e(x)$ of our test example and use semantic search to find the $k$ nearest neighbors of $x$ according to a specific similarity measure (e.g., cosine similarity). We denote the set of neighbors as $N_x = \{x_1, ..., x_k\} \subseteq D_U$.

### 3.2 Self-Prediction for Unlabeled Examples

We use $M$ to predict the label distribution for each $x_i \in N_x$, which is done similar to prior work by providing a short prompt and assigning meaningful names to all labels (e.g., Radford et al., 2019; Schick and Schütze, 2021a,c). We use the same notation as Schick and Schütze (2021a,c) in that we make use of a *pattern* $P$ that converts inputs $x$ into cloze questions $P(x)$ containing a single mask,

[1] We focus on masked language models, but our approach can easily be transferred to autoregressive language models.

and a *verbalizer* $v$ that maps each label $y \in Y$ to a single token $v(y)$ representing its meaning. We define the probability of $y$ being the correct label for $x$ based on $M(v(y) \mid P(x))$, the probability that $M$ assigns to $v(y)$ at the masked position in $P(x)$. We normalize this probability and set

$$p(y \mid x) \propto \frac{M(v(y) \mid P(x))}{M(v(y) \mid P(\varepsilon))} \quad (1)$$

with $\varepsilon$ denoting an empty sequence following prior work (Brown et al., 2020).

### 3.3 Priming

Let $\hat{N}_x = \{(x_i, \hat{y}_i)\}_{i=1}^k$ be the selected in-context neighbors with their predicted labels. Based on these semantically similar examples, we want to obtain a prediction for $x$. In the following, let $\hat{P}(x_i)$ denote $P(x_i)$ with the mask token replaced by $\hat{y}_i$.

**Concatenation Priming** Previous work usually provides all in-context examples at a time to the LM. That is, all examples are concatenated followed by the test example to obtain the input $c = [\hat{P}(x_1), \hat{P}(x_2), ..., \hat{P}(x_k), P(x)]$, which is provided to the LM to get the final prediction. We refer to this variant as CONCAT priming.

**Bag-of-Contexts Priming** We propose *bag-of-contexts* (BOC) priming where instead, we only use individual examples for priming and prediction each time and then compute the average of the resulting label distributions as the final prediction. The key advantage of this method lies in the fact that it allows us to use more examples than fit in the context window of the used model.

For each in-context example $x_i \in N$, we construct a corresponding context $c_i = [\hat{P}(x_i); P(x)]$, similar to CONCAT with $k = 1$. For each $c_i$, we then use the LM to obtain a distribution $q_i(y)$ over possible labels $y \in Y$ for $x$, where we employ normalization analogous to Eq. 1. Finally, we make use of a weighting function $w(x_i) : N \to \mathbb{R}^+$ and compute

$$q_f(y) = \frac{1}{Z} \cdot \sum_{i=1}^{k} w(x_i) \cdot q_i(y) \quad (2)$$

with $Z = \sum_{i=1}^k w(x_i)$. We obtain the final prediction for $x$ as $\hat{y} = \arg\max_{y \in Y} q_f(y)$. We experiment with the following two weighting functions. *uniform*: $w(x_i) = 1$. *similarity-based*: $w(x_i)$ is the cosine similarity between $x_i$ and $x$.

### 3.4 Iterative SOUP

We also experiment with an iterative variant of SOUP where the labels for the unlabeled examples in $D_U$ are iteratively refined. To this end, we treat each example $x_u \in D_U$ as a test example: We use SOUP to reclassify $x_u$ with $D_U \setminus \{x_u\}$ as the set of unlabeled examples. This means for each example $x$, we select in-context neighbors from $D_U \setminus \{x_u\}$ as priming contexts to allow us to refine the prediction for $x$. We can repeat this process for multiple iterations.

## 4 Experiments

**Datasets** We evaluate SOUP on four English datasets: IMDb (Maas et al., 2011) and Yelp Reviews (Zhang et al., 2015) for sentiment analysis as well as AG's News and Yahoo Questions (Zhang et al., 2015) for text categorization. For each dataset, we use one of the the patterns and verbalizers introduced by Schick and Schütze (2021a); further details can be found in Appendix A. For IMDb, the unlabeled in-context examples are selected from the training set of SST-2 (Socher et al., 2013) following Liu et al. (2021). For all other datasets, the in-context examples are obtained from the respective training sets.[2]

**Experimental Setup** For our main experiments, we use *ALBERT-xlarge-v2* (Lan et al., 2020) as underlying LM and *paraphrase-MiniLM-L6-v2* (Reimers and Gurevych, 2019) as sentence encoder. As the context window of ALBERT is 512 tokens, we truncate each example to 120 tokens for CONCAT. To enable a fair comparison between both priming strategies, we also set the maximum token number for BOC to 120. We compare SOUP to zero-shot performance using only the patterns and verbalizers ("prompt only"), similar to Radford et al. (2019) and Schick et al. (2021). We do not compare to other baselines as we are not aware of other approaches that enable leveraging unlabeled data in zero-shot settings *without finetuning*. For iterative SOUP, we use 3 iterations to improve the labels assigned to unlabeled data.

**Results** As shown in Table 1, when using CONCAT with $k = 3$, our method clearly performs worse than the prompt-only baseline. However, using our proposed BOC approach consistently out-

[2]To ensure a resource-friendly evaluation, we restrict both the unlabeled sets and the test sets to a maximum of 10,000 randomly selected examples.

| | $k$ | $w(x_i)$ | AG's | Yahoo | IMDb | Yelp |
|---|---|---|---|---|---|---|
| Prompt only | – | – | 66.01 | 48.04 | 72.67 | 43.37 |
| SOUP (CONC.) | 3 | – | 43.88 | 21.96 | 54.71 | 29.56 |
| SOUP (BOC) | 3 | unif. | 68.18 | 45.64 | 68.30 | 40.43 |
| | | sim. | 68.18 | 45.57 | 68.31 | 40.43 |
| | 10 | unif. | 69.64 | 49.93 | 71.03 | 44.05 |
| | | sim. | 69.74 | 49.98 | 71.01 | 43.93 |
| | 50 | unif. | 69.70 | **52.67** | 72.97 | **46.21** |
| | | sim. | **70.00** | 52.56 | 72.95 | 46.20 |
| iSOUP (BOC) | 50 | unif. | 69.88 | 45.22 | **73.78** | 45.79 |

Table 1: Accuracy with zero-shot prompting, SOUP with CONCAT and BOC as well as iterative SOUP (iSOUP) using different numbers of neighbors ($k$) and both uniform ("unif.") and similarity-based ("sim.") weighting.

| Size | Method | AG's | Yahoo | IMDb | Yelp |
|---|---|---|---|---|---|
| xlarge | Prompt only | 66.01 | 48.04 | 72.67 | 43.37 |
| xlarge | SOUP | 69.70 | 52.67 | 72.97 | **46.21** |
| xxlarge | Prompt only | 73.51 | 57.89 | 76.67 | 45.84 |
| xxlarge | SOUP | **74.89** | **61.82** | **79.54** | 41.00 |

Table 2: Performance of a prompt-only baseline and SOUP with $k = 50$ and uniform weighting using different model sizes

performs not only priming with CONCAT by a large margin, but also leads to consistent improvements over our baseline on three out of four datasets for $k \geq 10$. Moreover, performance grows consistently with the number of in-context examples, with $k = 50$ resulting in improvements for each dataset considered. On average, similarity-based weighting leads to negligible gains over uniform weighting. For our iterative variant of SOUP, we therefore only experiment with uniform weighting; iterative SOUP leads to slight improvements for two tasks, but performs much worse than SOUP for Yahoo.

## 5 Analysis

We examine the influence of both increasing the language model's size and replacing the Sentence Transformer with different encoders on the performance of SOUP. We also briefly discuss the efficiency of our method.

**Model Size** We first focus on the impact of model size on the performance of SOUP; to this end, we also evaluate our method (with $k = 50$ and uniform weighting) and the prompt-only baseline using ALBERT-xxlarge-v2 (Lan et al., 2020), a model that is about four times as large as ALBERT-xlarge-v2. As shown in Table 2, for our prompt-only baseline performance consistently improves with model size for both methods. With exception of ALBERT-xxlarge-v2 on Yelp, for which our method surprisingly leads to worse performance, SOUP consistently outperforms the baseline method.

| Sentence Encoder | AG's | Yahoo | IMDb | Yelp |
|---|---|---|---|---|
| paraphrase-MiniLM-L6-v2 | 69.70 | 52.67 | 72.97 | **46.21** |
| msmarco-bert-base-dot-v5 | **69.93** | **53.04** | **74.47** | 45.82 |
| unsup-simcse-roberta-large | 69.76 | 52.40 | 73.90 | 45.19 |

Table 3: SOUP (ALBERT-xlarge-v2, $k = 50$, uniform weighting) is robust to choice of sentence encoder.

**Sentence Encoder** We also investigate the impact of the sentence encoder on downstream task performance. As *paraphrase-MiniLM-L6-v2* was trained on a mixture of tasks that has some overlap with the tasks we evaluate on, we additionally consider *msmarco-bert-base-dot-v5* (Reimers and Gurevych, 2019), a model that was trained exclusively on MS MARCO passages (Bajaj et al., 2018), and *unsup-simcse-roberta-large* (Gao et al., 2021b), an encoder that was trained in a fully unsupervised fashion. As can be seen in Table 3, the choice of sentence encoder has little influence on performance, illustrating that performance improvements do not come from the encoder being pretrained on downstream task data.

**Efficiency** One disadvantage of our approach is that the number of required forward passes grows linearly with $k$. After precomputing encodings and labels for $U_D$, classifying a single example with $k = 3$ took about 0.6s using a single NVIDIA GeForce GTX 1080Ti; for $k = 10$ and $k = 50$, the required times were 1.5s and 6.8s. However, performance can be improved a lot with decoder-only LMs (e.g., Radford et al., 2018, 2019; Brown et al., 2020), as this enables the precomputation of contextualized representations for each $x_u \in U_D$.

## 6 Conclusion

We have presented SOUP, a method for *unlabeled priming* that classifies inputs by retrieving semantically similar unlabeled examples, classifying these examples in a zero-shot fashion and providing them as additional contexts for in-context learning. Beyond that, we have proposed a new priming strategy that leads to much better performance and scales to more than just a few examples. We have shown that with sufficiently many retrieved examples, SOUP consistently leads to improved performance.

## References


Payal Bajaj, Daniel Campos, Nick Craswell, Li Deng, Jianfeng Gao, Xiaodong Liu, Rangan Majumder, Andrew McNamara, Bhaskar Mitra, Tri Nguyen, Mir Rosenberg, Xia Song, Alina Stoica, Saurabh Tiwary, and Tong Wang. 2018. Ms marco: A human generated machine reading comprehension dataset.

Tom Brown, Benjamin Mann, Nick Ryder, Melanie Subbiah, Jared D Kaplan, Prafulla Dhariwal, Arvind Neelakantan, Pranav Shyam, Girish Sastry, Amanda Askell, Sandhini Agarwal, Ariel Herbert-Voss, Gretchen Krueger, Tom Henighan, Rewon Child, Aditya Ramesh, Daniel Ziegler, Jeffrey Wu, Clemens Winter, Chris Hesse, Mark Chen, Eric Sigler, Mateusz Litwin, Scott Gray, Benjamin Chess, Jack Clark, Christopher Berner, Sam McCandlish, Alec Radford, Ilya Sutskever, and Dario Amodei. 2020. Language models are few-shot learners. In *Advances in Neural Information Processing Systems*, volume 33, pages 1877–1901. Curran Associates, Inc.

Jacob Devlin, Ming-Wei Chang, Kenton Lee, and Kristina Toutanova. 2019. BERT: Pre-training of deep bidirectional transformers for language understanding. In *Proceedings of the 2019 Conference of the North American Chapter of the Association for Computational Linguistics: Human Language Technologies, Volume 1 (Long and Short Papers)*, pages 4171–4186, Minneapolis, Minnesota. Association for Computational Linguistics.

William Fedus, Barret Zoph, and Noam Shazeer. 2021. Switch transformers: Scaling to trillion parameter models with simple and efficient sparsity. *Computing Research Repository*, arXiv:2101.03961.

Tianyu Gao, Adam Fisch, and Danqi Chen. 2021a. Making pre-trained language models better few-shot learners. In *Proceedings of the 59th Annual Meeting of the Association for Computational Linguistics and the 11th International Joint Conference on Natural Language Processing (Volume 1: Long Papers)*, pages 3816–3830, Online. Association for Computational Linguistics.

Tianyu Gao, Xingcheng Yao, and Danqi Chen. 2021b. Simcse: Simple contrastive learning of sentence embeddings.

Suchin Gururangan, Ana Marasović, Swabha Swayamdipta, Kyle Lo, Iz Beltagy, Doug Downey, and Noah A. Smith. 2020. Don't stop pretraining: Adapt language models to domains and tasks. In *Proceedings of the 58th Annual Meeting of the Association for Computational Linguistics*, pages 8342–8360, Online. Association for Computational Linguistics.

Zhengbao Jiang, Jun Araki, Haibo Ding, and Graham Neubig. 2021. How Can We Know When Language Models Know? On the Calibration of Language Models for Question Answering. *Transactions of the Association for Computational Linguistics*, 9:962–977.

Sawan Kumar and Partha Talukdar. 2021. Reordering examples helps during priming-based few-shot learning. In *Findings of the Association for Computational Linguistics: ACL-IJCNLP 2021*, pages 4507–4518, Online. Association for Computational Linguistics.

Zhenzhong Lan, Mingda Chen, Sebastian Goodman, Kevin Gimpel, Piyush Sharma, and Radu Soricut. 2020. ALBERT: A lite BERT for self-supervised learning of language representations. In *International Conference on Learning Representations.*

Jiachang Liu, Dinghan Shen, Yizhe Zhang, Bill Dolan, Lawrence Carin, and Weizhu Chen. 2021. What makes good in-context examples for gpt-3? *CoRR*, abs/2101.06804.

Yinhan Liu, Myle Ott, Naman Goyal, Jingfei Du, Mandar Joshi, Danqi Chen, Omer Levy, Mike Lewis, Luke Zettlemoyer, and Veselin Stoyanov. 2019. RoBERTa: A robustly optimized BERT pretraining approach. *Computing Research Repository*, arXiv:1907.11692.

Yao Lu, Max Bartolo, Alastair Moore, Sebastian Riedel, and Pontus Stenetorp. 2021. Fantastically ordered prompts and where to find them: Overcoming few-shot prompt order sensitivity. *Computing Research Repository*, arXiv:2104.08786.

Andrew L. Maas, Raymond E. Daly, Peter T. Pham, Dan Huang, Andrew Y. Ng, and Christopher Potts. 2011. Learning word vectors for sentiment analysis. In *Proceedings of the 49th Annual Meeting of the Association for Computational Linguistics: Human Language Technologies*, pages 142–150, Portland, Oregon, USA. Association for Computational Linguistics.

Sewon Min, Mike Lewis, Hannaneh Hajishirzi, and Luke Zettlemoyer. 2021. Noisy channel language model prompting for few-shot text classification. *Computing Research Repository*, arXiv:2108.04106.

Alec Radford, Karthik Narasimhan, Tim Salimans, and Ilya Sutskever. 2018. Improving language understanding by generative pre-training. Technical report, Open AI.

Alec Radford, Jeff Wu, Rewon Child, David Luan, Dario Amodei, and Ilya Sutskever. 2019. Language models are unsupervised multitask learners. Technical report, Open AI.

Colin Raffel, Noam Shazeer, Adam Roberts, Katherine Lee, Sharan Narang, Michael Matena, Yanqi Zhou, Wei Li, and Peter J. Liu. 2020. Exploring the limits of transfer learning with a unified text-to-text transformer. *Journal of Machine Learning Research*, 21(140):1–67.

Nils Reimers and Iryna Gurevych. 2019. Sentence-BERT: Sentence embeddings using Siamese BERT-networks. In *Proceedings of the 2019 Conference on Empirical Methods in Natural Language Processing and the 9th International Joint Conference on Natural Language Processing (EMNLP-IJCNLP)*, pages 3982–3992, Hong Kong, China. Association for Computational Linguistics.

Victor Sanh, Albert Webson, Colin Raffel, Stephen H. Bach, Lintang Sutawika, Zaid Alyafeai, Antoine Chaffin, Arnaud Stiegler, Teven Le Scao, Arun Raja, Manan Dey, M Saiful Bari, Canwen Xu, Urmish Thakker, Shanya Sharma Sharma, Eliza Szczechla, Taewoon Kim, Gunjan Chhablani, Nihal Nayak, Debajyoti Datta, Jonathan Chang, Mike Tian-Jian Jiang, Han Wang, Matteo Manica, Sheng Shen, Zheng Xin Yong, Harshit Pandey, Rachel Bawden, Thomas Wang, Trishala Neeraj, Jos Rozen, Abheesht Sharma, Andrea Santilli, Thibault Fevry, Jason Alan Fries, Ryan Teehan, Stella Biderman, Leo Gao, Tali Bers, Thomas Wolf, and Alexander M. Rush. 2021. Multitask prompted training enables zero-shot task generalization. *Computing Research Repository*, arXiv:2110.08207.

Timo Schick and Hinrich Schütze. 2021a. Exploiting cloze questions for few shot text classification and natural language inference. In *Proceedings of the 16th Conference of the European Chapter of the Association for Computational Linguistics*, Kyiv, Ukraine (Online). International Committee on Computational Linguistics.

Timo Schick and Hinrich Schütze. 2021b. Few-shot text generation with pattern-exploiting training. In *Proceedings of the 2021 Conference on Empirical Methods in Natural Language Processing (EMNLP)*. Association for Computational Linguistics.

Timo Schick and Hinrich Schütze. 2021c. It's not just size that matters: Small language models are also few-shot learners. In *Proceedings of the 2021 Conference of the North American Chapter of the Association for Computational Linguistics: Human Language Technologies*, pages 2339–2352, Online. Association for Computational Linguistics.

Timo Schick, Sahana Udupa, and Hinrich Schütze. 2021. Self-diagnosis and self-debiasing: A proposal for reducing corpus-based bias in NLP. *Transactions of the Association for Computational Linguistics*.

Richard Socher, Alex Perelygin, Jean Wu, Jason Chuang, Christopher D Manning, Andrew Y Ng, and Christopher Potts. 2013. Recursive deep models for semantic compositionality over a sentiment treebank. In *Proceedings of the 2013 conference on empirical methods in natural language processing*, pages 1631–1642.

Emma Strubell, Ananya Ganesh, and Andrew McCallum. 2019. Energy and policy considerations for deep learning in NLP. In *Proceedings of the 57th Annual Meeting of the Association for Computational Linguistics*, pages 3645–3650, Florence, Italy. Association for Computational Linguistics.

Qizhe Xie, Zihang Dai, Eduard Hovy, Minh-Thang Luong, and Quoc V. Le. 2019. Unsupervised data augmentation for consistency training. *Computing Research Repository*, arXiv:1904.12848.

Xiang Zhang, Junbo Zhao, and Yann LeCun. 2015. Character-level convolutional networks for text classification. In C. Cortes, N. D. Lawrence, D. D. Lee, M. Sugiyama, and R. Garnett, editors, *Advances in Neural Information Processing Systems 28*, pages 649–657. Curran Associates, Inc.

## A Dataset Details

For each task except IMDb, we use one of the patterns and verbalizers introduced by Schick and Schütze (2021a). In the following, we describe in detail the patterns and verbalizers used.

**IMDb** For the IMDb Large Movie Review Dataset (Maas et al., 2011), the task is to estimate the binary sentiment of a movie review based on the review's text. We use the following pattern and verbalizer for an input review $a$:

$$P(a) = a. \text{ The movie is [MASK].}$$
$$v(0) = \text{bad} \quad v(1) = \text{good}$$

**Yelp** For the Yelp Reviews Full Star dataset (Zhang et al., 2015), the task is to estimate the rating that a customer gave to a restaurant on a 1-to 5-star scale based on their review's text. We use the following pattern for an input text $a$:

$$P(a) = a. \text{ In summary, the restaurant is [MASK].}$$

As a verbalizer $v$, we define:

$$\begin{array}{lll} v(1) = \text{terrible} & v(2) = \text{bad} & v(3) = \text{okay} \\ v(4) = \text{good} & v(5) = \text{great} & \end{array}$$

**AG's News** AG's News (Zhang et al., 2015) is a task to classify a news article as belonging to one of the categories *World* (1), *Sports* (2), *Business* (3) or *Science/Tech* (4). We define the following pattern for an input news text $a$:

$$P(a) = a. \text{ News Category: [MASK].}$$

Intuitively, we use a verbalizer that maps 1–4 to "World", "Sports", "Business" and "Science", respectively.

**Yahoo** Yahoo Questions (Zhang et al., 2015) is a text classification dataset. Given a question and an answer, the text has to be classified to one of ten possible categories. We make use of the following pattern for a input question $a$ and an answer $b$:

$$P(a, b) = a\ b. \text{ Question Category: [MASK].}$$

Our verbalizer maps labels 1–10 to the tokens "Society", "Science", "Health", "Education", "Computer", "Sports", "Business", "Entertainment", "Relationship" and "Politics".

# oBERTa: Improving Sparse Transfer Learning via improved initialization, distillation, and pruning regimes

Daniel Campos [1], Alexandre Marques[2], Mark Kurtz[2], and ChengXiang Zhai[1]

[1]Department of Computer Science, the University of Illinois Urbana-Champaign
[2]Neural Magic Inc.

## Abstract

In this paper, we introduce the range of oBERTa language models, an easy-to-use set of language models which allows Natural Language Processing (NLP) practitioners to obtain between 3.8 and 24.3 times faster models without expertise in model compression. Specifically, oBERTa extends existing work on pruning, knowledge distillation, and quantization and leverages frozen embeddings, improves distillation, and model initialization to deliver higher accuracy on a broad range of transfer tasks. In generating oBERTa, we explore how the highly optimized RoBERTa differs from the BERT for pruning during pre-training and fine-tuning. We find it less amenable to compression during fine-tuning. We explore the use of oBERTa on seven representative NLP tasks and find that the improved compression techniques allow a pruned oBERTa model to match the performance of $\text{BERT}_{\text{base}}$ and exceed the performance of Prune OFA Large on the SQUAD V1.1 Question Answering dataset, despite being 8x and 2x respectively faster in inference. We release our code, training regimes, and associated model for broad usage to encourage usage and experimentation. [1,2]

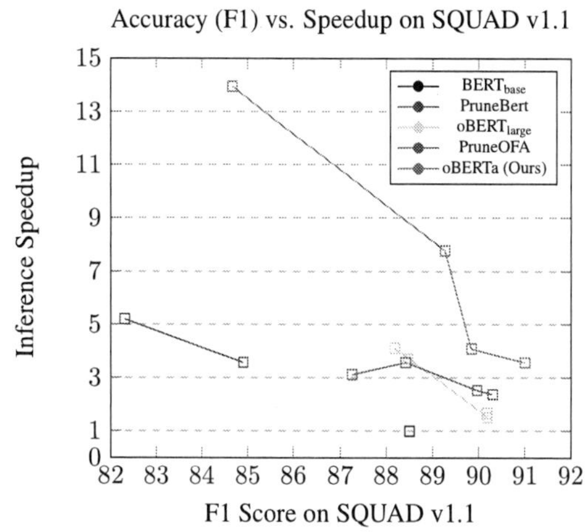


Figure 1: Performance of Sparse Language Models on the SQUAD V1.1 (Rajpurkar et al., 2016a) compared to an uncompressed $\text{BERT}_{\text{base}}$ (Devlin et al., 2019) with relation to realized inference improvements with regards to mean latency with a batch size of 1.

## 1 Introduction

The massive improvement in contextual word representations driven by the usage of the Transformer architecture (Vaswani et al., 2017) has led to the wide-scale deployment of language models. These models are customized for various use cases and tasks like question answering, sentiment analysis, information retrieval, and document classification and deployed into general domains and specialized domains such as financial, medical, and legal. While these models are effective, they commonly contain hundreds of millions of parameters, which can lead to slow inference times without using specialized hardware accelerations like graphics processing units (GPU) or Tensor Processing Units (TPU). Without hardware acceleration, the inference on CPUs can be slow and impractical for real-world deployments.

Approaches such as knowledge distillation (KD) (Hinton et al., 2015), quantization (Zafrir et al., 2019), and pruning (Kurtic et al., 2022) have been leveraged to improve model efficiency and, when paired with specialized inference engines[3], it is possible to accelerate inference times on CPUs and GPUs significantly. While there has been substantial effort to create effective methods for com-

[1]https://github.com/neuralmagic/sparseml/
[2]https://sparsezoo.neuralmagic.com/
[3]https://github.com/neuralmagic/deepsparse



*Proceedings of The Fourth Workshop on Simple and Efficient Natural Language Processing (SustaiNLP)*, pages 39–58
July 13, 2023 ©2023 Association for Computational Linguistics

pression (Jiao et al., 2020; Sun et al., 2020) and improved model performance (Liu et al., 2019), general users of language models have been slower to adopt these methods. Years after its release, the original $\text{BERT}_{\text{base}}$ uncased (Devlin et al., 2019) is still the most popular language model [4], followed by the slightly compressed DistilBERT (Sanh et al., 2019a) for latency-sensitive deployments. To enable broad adoption, regular users must be able to leverage more efficient language models without additional compression steps or tuning.

We present a case study on how to compress a language model for efficient CPU inference leveraging KD, structured pruning, unstructured sparsity, and quantization such that the compressed models can be applied to a broad range of natural language processing (NLP) tasks without expertise in compression of language models.

As part of this study, we release a set of efficient language models optimized to deliver the greatest improvement in inference while minimizing losses in accuracy. We then show how these models can be used for *sparse transfer learning* (Iofinova et al., 2021; Zafrir et al., 2021) such that most compression happens during the pre-training stage. The pre-trained sparse models can be transferred to various NLP tasks, preserving sparsity without extensive optimization. Using these sparse transfer models and the DeepSparse inference engine, we show these sparse models can be fine-tuned to produce task-specific sparse models with minimal accuracy loss and result in greatly improved inference speeds with minimal accuracy loss.

As shown in Figure 1, oBERTa provides state-of-the-art performance for sparse language models on the SQUAD v1.1 Question Answering dataset. oBERTa variants exceed the performance of $\text{BERT}_{\text{base}}$ despite being eight times faster, exceed the performance of Prune $\text{OFA}_{\text{large}}$ and $\text{oBERT}_{\text{large}}$ while being two to five times faster. In this paper, we focus on the following research questions:

- RQ1: Is RoBERTa more sensitive to unstructured pruning than BERT?
- RQ2: What is the impact of using a larger teacher for KD during the pruning of language models?
- RQ3: Can frozen embeddings improve the accuracy of pruned language models?

As part of our experimentation, we release the associated models and the training regimes to aid reproducibility and encourage efficient inference models.

In summary, our contributions are as follows:

- We provide a thorough case study on how to compress a less studied language model[5], RoBERTa (Liu et al., 2019), and evaluate performance on a set of seven NLP tasks finding that it is possible to effectively compress a language model without using its original pretraining dataset.
- We demonstrate the impact of varying the size of teachers in KD, freezing embeddings, and variations in learning rates when applied to sparse language models.
- We demonstrate that our compressed models can be leveraged to deliver accuracy of over 91% on the popular SQUAD v1.1 (Rajpurkar et al., 2016a) Question Answering Task with nearly three times faster inference than the previous state-of-the-art uses of unstructured sparsity.

## 2 Background and Related work

While many methods to improve model efficiency exist, the same goal generally underpins them: given an original model $\theta$ with an accuracy of $acc(\theta)$ and an inference cost of $c(\theta)$ minimize the inference cost. While the methods used for compression can be highly optimized and specialized, they can commonly be used together to deliver massive improvements in inference speeds with minimal losses in accuracy.

**Transformer Based Language Models** such as BERT (Devlin et al., 2019) and T5 (Raffel et al., 2020) provide contextual language representations built on the Transformer architecture (Vaswani et al., 2017) which can be specialized and adapted for specific tasks and domains (Lee et al., 2020).

[4] Based on monthly downloads on the huggingface model hub in march 2023

[5] While the RoBERTa model was downloaded over 10m times in May 2023 on the huggingface hub it has not a model of focus for compression research.

Using these models, it becomes relatively easy to excel at a broad range of natural language processing tasks such as Question Answering, Text Classification, and sentiment analysis.
**Unstructured Pruning** is a compression approach that removes individual weights or groups of weights in a model by applying a mask or setting the weight values to 0. This compression approach has been broadly studied in computer vision (Han et al., 2015), and many methods can remove 70% or more of model weights with little to no loss in accuracy. Models pruned can be 20x smaller in terms of pure model size and, when paired with a sparsity-aware inference engine such as DeepSparse (Magic, 2023), provide 3-5x speedups in inference throughput.
Focused on language models, recent work has shown that it is possible to prune models during fine-tuning (Sanh et al., 2020) (Kurtić et al., 2022) or during pre-training (Zafrir et al., 2021) and transfer to novel domains (Campos et al., 2022) and datasets.
**Structured Pruning** is a compression approach that removes fundamental structural components in a language model such as individual attention heads (Voita et al., 2019) or entire model layers such as transformer encoders (Sanh et al., 2019b). Structural pruning has become one of the most popular methods for inference optimization as it is easy to estimate the speedups and implement.
**Freezing Embeddings**, as introduced by Devlin et al. (Devlin et al., 2019), involves training the embedding layer of a language model and then toggling the ability to continue to optimize, or not, the values of in the embeddings as training continues.
**Knowledge Distillation** (Hinton et al., 2015) is a training method where a model is not explicitly a compression method but a training method where a model, called the *student* learns to emulate a *teacher* model which is commonly larger or better performing. The loss extracted from the original training data in KD is augmented or replaced by KL divergence between the student and teacher model.
KD leverages the hardness parameter $h$ to control the mixture of regular and distillation loss (with a higher distillation favoring the KL divergence loss) and a temperature parameter $t$ to control the softness of the distribution.
As applied to language models, the approach has been used to improve the performance of structurally pruned language models resulting in models like DistilBERT (Sanh et al., 2019b) and TinyBERT (Jiao et al., 2020).
**Quantization** reduces the precision for the model weights and activations to lower the computational requirements of model execution. While researchers have explored reducing representation to binary representations (Pouransari and Tuzel, 2020), current hardware limits inference speedups to 8 or 4-bit representations. Quantization can be applied after the model is trained in a one-shot fashion, but this can lead to large losses in accuracy because of rounding errors. To avoid this pitfall, quantization is applied as quantization-aware training (QAT), where the forward pass of the model is simulated with lower precision. In contrast, the backward pass happens in full precision. By using QAT models, learn to be robust to rounding errors and can result in quantization having little to no loss in accuracy. In language models, research has produced quantized language models such as Q8BERT (Zafrir et al., 2019) and is commonly used in conjunction with structured and unstructured pruning (Zafrir et al., 2021) as a way of introducing compounding compression.
Additional approaches such as early exiting (Xin et al., 2020) or token pruning (Kim et al., 2021) have also improved inference efficiency. Still, the inference improvements can be very dataset dependent and, as a result, out of our experimentation frame. For a broader survey on compression approaches, we recommend Treviso et al. recent work (Treviso et al., 2022)

## 3 Improving Sparse Transfer Learning

While quantization and pruning have been well studied as applied to language models, work has studied the compression $\text{BERT}_{\text{base}}$ or $\text{BERT}_{\text{large}}$. Despite existing research, we find that a clear case study that explores how best to create a family of compressed models is lacking, and this work seeks to remedy that. As part of our research, we compare the impact of varying pruning methods, pruning stage, teachers for KD, and freezing portions of the model as applied to the RoBERTa language model.

While performing task-specific compression allows NLP practitioners to broadly adopt improvements in inference efficiency, having access to pre-optimized models is key. We produce a family of 8 general purpose language models, collectively called oBERTa, which progressively get smaller and faster with minimal losses in accuracy.

The oBERTa models leverage a combination of structured and unstructured pruning to provide a set of compressed models which can meet a wide set of latency needs. This compression approach has not been extensively documented nor discussed. Our approach to producing the oBERTA models builds on prior explorations of the combination of compression methods (Kurtić et al., 2022) and addresses compression approaches in a staged manner as shown in Figure 2.

First, we create three structural variants starting with a RoBERTa$_{\text{base}}$ model. The base uses 12 transformer layers, the medium uses 6, and the small uses 3. Following prior work, we select interleaved layers for the 6-layer model and the first, middle, and last layers for the 3-layer model. Then, each of these 3 models is further pre-trained using masked language modeling on the Wikipedia-Bookcorpus text dataset, leveraging KD from a RoBERTa$_{\text{large}}$ teacher. After that, each model is pruned using gradual magnitude pruning (GMP) to a desired sparsity level (90% and 95%) during additional pre-training based on masked language modeling, similar to Zafir et al. (Zafrir et al., 2021). Further background on the RoBERTA model and why we did not prune using the WebText corpus can be found in the appendix.

After pre-training, the sparsity profile is fixed, and models are fine-tuned and quantized on their target task with a small set of variable hyperparameters. Experimentation on the impact of larger teachers, frozen embeddings, and variations in pruning algorithms are discussed in subsequent portions of this work.

### 3.1 Downstream Compression

We explore the impact of introducing unstructured sparsity during task-specific fine-tuning. We repeat each experiment with three different seeds and report the average F1 and Exact Match (EM) metrics in tables 2 and 3. Following a basic hyperparameter sweep, our baseline RoBERTa$_{\text{base}}$ model achieves a performance of 83.95 EM and 91.13 F1 in the broadly used question-answering benchmark SQUAD V1.1 (Rajpurkar et al., 2016a).

We also perform unstructured pruning varying the sparsity 50-95% and the pruning method: GMP and Optimal BERT Surgeon (OBS) (Kurtić et al., 2022). We prune each model for eight epochs, followed by an additional two epochs to allow the network to stabilize and re-converge. Knowledge distillation is used during training with the dense baseline model as a teacher, hardness set to 1.0 and temperature set to 5.0. Further hyperparameters are in the appendix A.7.

Table 1 shows the impact of sparsity on BERT$_{\text{base}}$, as reported by previous work. Comparing these results with tables 2 and 3, we conclude that RoBERTa is more sensitive to pruning than BERT, although RoBERTa$_{\text{base}}$ pruned with OBS remains substantially more accurate than BERT$_{\text{base}}$ for the same level of sparsity.

Table 2 shows that pruning RoBERTA$_{\text{base}}$ to 90% with OBS results in a relative drop in F1 of 1.59%, which is three times the relative drop reported for BERT$_{\text{base}}$ with the same pruning algorithm. Moreover, table 3 shows that RoBERTA$_{\text{base}}$ becomes very sensitive to pruning with GMP for sparsities above 85%, with the relative drop in F1 increasing almost threefold between 85% and 90% sparsity. We conjecture that RoBERTa is more sensitive to pruning than BERT because the latter is relatively under-trained (Liu et al., 2019), making the more optimized RoBERTa more sensitive to the loss in expressivity caused by pruning.

| Model | Sparsity | F1 | Impact |
|---|---|---|---|
| BERT$_{\text{base}}$ (Devlin et al., 2019) | 0 | 88.50 | N/A |
| BERT$_{\text{large}}$ (Devlin et al., 2019) | 0 | 90.9 | N/A |
| RoBERTa$_{\text{base}}$ (Liu et al., 2019) | 0 | 91.13 | N/A |
| RoBERTA$_{\text{large}}$ (Liu et al., 2019) | 0 | 94.60 | N/A |
| PruneBert$_{\text{base}}$ (Sanh et al., 2020) | 90 | 84.90 | -4.07 % |
| PruneOFA$_{\text{large}}$ (Zafrir et al., 2021) | 90 | 87.25 | -1.41 % |
| oBERT$_{\text{large}}$ (Kurtić et al., 2022) | 90 | 87.98 | -0.58% |
| $GMP_{\star\,\text{large}}$ (Kurtic and Alistarh, 2022) | 90 | 86.7 | -2.03% |

Table 1: Performance of existing dense and sparse language models on the SQUAD v1.1 Question Answering Dataset

### 3.2 Upstream Compression

Based on our fine-tuning experiments, achieving a high degree of sparsity on the RoBERTA model

| Sparsity (%) | EM | Impact | F1 | Impact |
|---|---|---|---|---|
| 50 | 84.80 | 1.01% | 91.49 | 0.40% |
| 60 | 84.64 | 0.82% | 91.33 | 0.22% |
| 70 | 84.42 | 0.56% | 91.13 | 0.00% |
| 80 | 84.64 | 0.82% | 91.33 | 0.22% |
| 85 | 82.89 | -1.26% | 90.12 | -1.11% |
| 90 | 82.48 | -1.75% | 89.68 | -1.59% |
| 95 | 79.01 | -5.89% | 87.05 | -4.47% |

Table 2: Impact of Sparsity introduced by OBS on the F1 and EM scores of pruned RoBERTa models on the SQUAD V1.1 Dataset

| Sparsity (%) | EM | Impact | F1 | Impact |
|---|---|---|---|---|
| 50 | 84.90 | 1.13% | 91.46 | 0.36% |
| 60 | 84.27 | 0.38% | 90.91 | -0.24% |
| 70 | 83.37 | -0.69% | 90.30 | -0.91% |
| 80 | 81.64 | -2.76% | 88.86 | -2.49% |
| 85 | 81.64 | -2.76% | 88.86 | -2.49% |
| 90 | 76.51 | -8.86% | 84.90 | -6.83% |
| 95 | 69.39 | -17.34% | 79.35 | -12.93% |

Table 3: Impact of Sparsity introduced by GMP on the F1 and EM scores of pruned RoBERTa models on the SQUAD V1.1 Dataset

leads to improvements in performance, but there are greater than expected losses in accuracy. Additionally, such compression is task-specific and non-amortizable, so we explore how best to generate general pruned RoBERTa models. While we eventually apply the winning set of training combinations to all of our variants of oBERTa, we first seek to answer the following questions: Does GMP or OBS perform better during pretraining pruning? Does Freezing the Embeddings during pretraining pruning further improve performance? Does the use of larger teachers further improve performance?

We prune various models while varying individual variables during pretraining to evaluate these questions. We experiment by pruning an oBERTa$_{base}$ (12 layers) model to 90% and 95% sparsity on all non-embedding layers. All pretraining pruning happens using the Wikipedia-BookCorpus dataset, where we train for five epochs using a learning rate of 5e-5 and a batch size of 256 using 4 A100 GPUS. To evaluate the impact of these models, we evaluate performance on the previously used SQUAD v1.1 question-answering dataset, where we train with a fixed training regime of 10 epochs with a learning rate of 1.5e-4 based on the work of Kurtic et al. We train without KD for each finetuning run with an unpruned RoBERTa$_{base}$ or an unpruned RoBERTa$_{large}$. Details for the hyperparameters used to train all teacher models can be found in the appendix A.5.

Comparing the use of OBS vs. GMP as shown

| | GMP | | | | OBS | | | |
|---|---|---|---|---|---|---|---|---|
| Model | F1 | Impact | EM | Impact | F1 | Impact | EM | Impact |
| RoBERTA$_{base}$ | 92.18 | 0.00% | 85.59 | 0.00% | 92.18 | 0.00% | 85.59 | 0.00% |
| oBERTa 90% No KD | 88.34 | -4.17% | 80.19 | -6.31% | 87.72 | -4.83% | 79.35 | -7.29% |
| oBERTa 90% RoBERTA$_{base}$ KD | 88.75 | -3.72% | 81.35 | -4.95% | 88.60 | -3.88% | 81.37 | -4.93% |
| oBERTa 90% RoBERTA$_{large}$ KD | 89.65 | -2.75% | 83.12 | -2.88% | 89.63 | -2.76% | 82.94 | -3.09% |
| oBERTa 95% No KD | 86.58 | -6.07% | 78.81 | -7.92% | 84.90 | -7.90% | 76.82 | -10.25% |
| oBERTa 95% RoBERTA$_{base}$ KD | 86.99 | -5.63% | 79.41 | -7.22% | 86.14 | -6.55% | 78.63 | -8.13% |
| oBERTa 95% RoBERTA$_{large}$ KD | 87.60 | -4.97% | 80.44 | -6.01% | 86.14 | -6.55% | 79.84 | -6.72% |

Table 4: Impact on F1 of SQUAD V1.1 of using OBS vs. GMP as the pruning method during pretraining. Impact measures the relative loss in performance vs. the unpruned RoBERTa$_{base}$ baseline.

in table 4, we can see that GMP consistently outperforms OBS. This is the opposite of what is seen when pruning downstream or, in prior work, pruning BERT. Without access to the original training corpus OBS is likely unable to leverage the loss aware saliency importance as well as it can when it has the original dataset.

Evaluating the impact of variations in the hardness

| | Hardness 0.5 | | | | Hardness 1.0 | | | |
|---|---|---|---|---|---|---|---|---|
| Model | F1 | Impact | EM | Impact | F1 | Impact | EM | Impact |
| RoBERTA$_{base}$ | 92.18 | 0.00% | 85.59 | 0.00% | 92.18 | 0.00% | 85.59 | 0.00% |
| oBERTa 90% No KD | 88.21 | -4.31% | 80.19 | -6.31% | 88.34 | -4.17% | 80.19 | -6.31% |
| oBERTa 90% Base KD | 89.19 | -3.25% | 81.74 | -4.50% | 88.75 | -3.72% | 81.35 | -4.95% |
| oBERTa 90% Large KD | 90.14 | -2.21% | 83.51 | -2.43% | 89.65 | -2.75% | 83.12 | -2.88% |
| oBERTa-95 No KD | 85.82 | -6.90% | 77.77 | -9.14% | 86.58 | -6.07% | 78.81 | -7.92% |
| oBERTa-95 Base KD | 86.98 | -5.64% | 79.23 | -7.43% | 86.99 | -5.63% | 79.41 | -7.22% |
| oBERTa-95 Large KD | 87.66 | -4.91% | 80.40 | -6.07% | 87.60 | -4.97% | 80.44 | -6.01% |

Table 5: Impact on F1 of SQUAD V1.1 by hardness in KD during pretraining pruning. Impact measures the relative loss in performance vs. the unpruned RoBERTa$_{base}$ baseline.

of KD as shown in table 5, there is a bit more of a muted set of conclusions. The 95% sparse models perform better with a hardness of 1.0, while the 90% models do better with a hardness of 0.5. Given that our goal is to preserve most of the RoBERTa model without actually using its large dataset, we set our hardness to 1.0 as it keeps the model from explicitly learning the new dataset.

When we evaluate the impact of freezing embeddings during pre-training, as shown in table 6, we find strong evidence that using frozen embeddings consistently leads to worse performance and, as a result, does not freeze embeddings during our model pruning. Looking at the impact of varying the size of the teacher for pretraining KD as shown in table 7, we unsurprisingly find clear evidence

| | Frozen Embeddings | | | | Trained Embeddings | | | |
|---|---|---|---|---|---|---|---|---|
| Model | F1 | Impact | EM | Impact | F1 | Impact | EM | Impact |
| $RoBERTa_{base}$ | 92.18 | 0.00% | 85.59 | 0.00% | 92.18 | 0.00% | 85.59 | 0.00% |
| $oBERTa_{base}$ 90% no KD | 87.71 | -4.85% | 79.62 | -6.98% | 88.21 | -4.31% | 80.19 | -6.31% |
| $oBERTa_{base}$ 90% $RoBERTa_{base}$ KD | 89.7 | -2.69% | 81.74 | -4.50% | 89.19 | -3.24% | 83.07 | -2.94% |
| $oBERTa_{base}$ 90% $RoBERTa_{large}$ KD | 89.59 | -2.81% | 82.98 | -3.05% | 90.14 | -2.21% | 83.51 | -2.43% |

Table 6: Impact on F1 of SQUAD V1.1 concerning the use of frozen embeddings or not during pretraining pruning. Impact measures the relative loss in performance vs. the unpruned $RoBERTa_{base}$ baseline.

that using a larger teacher during pretraining pruning leads to improvements in performance.

Using these experiments, we generate the recipe,

| | Base Upstream Teacher | | | | Large Upstream Teacher | | | |
|---|---|---|---|---|---|---|---|---|
| Model | F1 | Impact | EM | Impact | F1 | Impact | EM | Impact |
| $RoBERTA_{base}$ | 92.18 | 0.00% | 85.59 | 0.00% | 92.18 | 0.00% | 85.59 | 0.00% |
| oBERTa 90% no KD | 88.34 | -4.17% | 80.59 | -5.84% | 88.1 | -4.43% | 80.06 | -6.46% |
| oBERTa 90% Base KD | 88.75 | -3.72% | 81.35 | -4.95% | 89.22 | -3.21% | 82.02 | -4.17% |
| oBERTa 90% Large KD | 89.65 | -2.74% | 83.12 | -2.89% | 89.98 | -2.39% | 83.14 | -2.86% |

Table 7: Impact on F1 of SQUAD V1.1 with respect variation is the size of the teacher in KD during pretraining pruning. Impact measures the relative loss in performance vs. the unpruned $RoBERTa_{base}$ baseline.

which we then use to create the many variants of oBERTa. We evaluate their performance in Table 17 where it is important to note that these results are accuracy, loss, and perplexity relative to the RoBERTa-large teacher, not the true dataset. The compression recipe, as shown in Figure 2 is as follows:

1. Starting with a pre-trained language model, removing some portion of transformer layers in an interleaved fashion.
2. Using Knowledge Distillation from a large uncompressed model, pre-train the pruned model with a hardness of 1.0 and without freezing embeddings.
3. Using Knowledge Distillation from a large uncompressed model, prune during further pretraining using GMP where sparsity levels are enforced at the parameter level. The resulting model is the sparse-transfer-student.
4. Train an uncompressed large language model on the desired NLP task's dataset. This is the sparse-transfer teacher.
5. Using the sparse-transfer teacher fine-tune the sparse-transfer-student with knowledge distillation to convergence. Experiment with the use of frozen embeddings and various sizes of sparse-transfer teachers.
6. Using the fine-tuned sparse-transfer student and teacher, train with quantization-aware training. If embeddings were frozen during initial fine-tuning they should be unfrozen here.

## 4 Experimental Results

Based on the aforementioned experiments, we generate 8 variants of oBERTa, each with a different size and sparsity profile; details can be found in table 18. Within this table, we report the impact on the model size as measured by the raw and compressed size of the ONNX [6] model file. Embeddings are unpruned and each layer is pruned to the target sparsity profile independent of the rest of the model. As a result, the overall sparsity profile may vary as modules in the network may not be able to reach exactly 90% or 95% sparsity.

Using these *inference-optimized* models, we evaluate their *sparse transfer* performance by finetuning these models on their target task using a fixed training regime and minor hyperparameter exploration. For each task, we train them for 10 epochs or 20 (10 of which are Quantization Aware Training), with the longer schedule being reserved for models which are being quantized.

We evaluate performance on a benchmark of diverse NLP tasks ranging from question answering, sentiment analysis, document classification, token classification, and text classification. For question answering, we leverage the SQuAD v1.1 (Rajpurkar et al., 2016a) and SQuAD V2.0 (Rajpurkar et al., 2018) datasets. We leverage the SST-2 (Socher et al., 2013) dataset for sentiment analysis. For text classification, we use the Quora Duplicate Query Detection (QQP) (SambitSekhar, 2017) and the MNLI (Williams et al., 2018) datasets. We leverage the IMDB (Maas et al., 2011) dataset for document classification and CONLL2003 (Tjong Kim Sang and De Meulder, 2003) for token classification.

Looking at performance on question answering as shown in table 8 and 9. Moving to text classification on QQP and MNLI as shown in tables 11 and 10 Shifting focus to document classification

[6]https://onnx.ai/

| | Sparse Transfer | | | Sparse Transfer With Quantization | | |
|---|---|---|---|---|---|---|
| model | F1 | Recovery | EM | F1 | Recovery | EM |
| oBERTa$_{base}$ | 92.15 | 100.00% | 85.78 | 93.18 | 101.11% | 87.29 |
| oBERTa$_{base}$ 90% | 90.95 | 98.69% | 84.42 | 89.46 | 97.08% | 82.61 |
| oBERTa$_{base}$ 95% | 89.84 | 97.49% | 83.08 | 89.23 | 96.83% | 81.12 |
| oBERTa$_{MEDIUM}$ | 90.37 | 98.06% | 83.84 | 83.77 | 90.91% | 90.37 |
| oBERTa$_{MEDIUM}$ 90% | 89.26 | 96.86% | 82.18 | 88.65 | 96.20% | 81.88 |
| oBERTa$_{SMALL}$ | 84.87 | 92.09% | 76.55 | 84.82 | 92.05% | 76.77 |
| oBERTa$_{SMALL}$ 90% | 84.66 | 91.87% | 76.18 | 82.18 | 92.18% | 74.21 |

Table 8: Sparse Transfer performance of the oBERTA family on the SQUAD V1.1 dataset. The sparse transfer was performed over 10 epochs and sparse transfer with quantization over 20. Recovery is based on the relative performance of the unpruned oBERTa$_{base}$.

| | Sparse Transfer | | | Sparse Transfer With Quantization | | |
|---|---|---|---|---|---|---|
| model | F1 | Recovery | EM | F1 | Recovery | EM |
| oBERTa$_{base}$ | 82.77 | 100.00% | 79.56 | 85.298 | 103.06% | 82.347 |
| oBERTa$_{base}$ 90% | 81.33 | 98.26% | 78.27 | 81.43 | 98.38% | 78.92 |
| oBERTa$_{base}$ 95% | 77.98 | 94.22% | 74.67 | 78.09 | 94.35% | 74.82 |
| oBERTa$_{MEDIUM}$ | 77.51 | 93.65% | 74.25 | 78.137 | 94.41% | 75.179 |
| oBERTa$_{MEDIUM}$ 90% | 76.64 | 92.60% | 73.34 | 76.24 | 92.11% | 73.51 |
| oBERTa$_{SMALL}$ | 71.54 | 86.44% | 67.93 | 71.591 | 86.50% | 68.087 |
| oBERTa$_{SMALL}$ 90% | 70.79 | 85.53% | 67.31 | 69.35 | 87.79% | 65.21 |

Table 9: Sparse Transfer performance of the oBERTA family on the SQUAD V2.0 dataset. The sparse transfer was performed over 10 epochs, and sparse transfer with quantization over 20. Recovery is based on the relative performance of the unpruned oBERTa$_{base}$.

| | Sparse Transfer | | | Sparse Transfer With Quantization | | |
|---|---|---|---|---|---|---|
| model | Accuracy | Recovery | Accuracy(MM) | Accuracy | Recovery | Accuracy(MM) |
| oBERTa$_{base}$ | 87.88% | 100.00% | 87.57% | 88.06% | 100.20% | 88.01% |
| oBERTa$_{base}$ 90% | 85.17% | 96.91% | 84.73% | 85.09% | 96.83% | 84.76% |
| oBERTa$_{base}$ 95% | 84.32% | 95.95% | 84.08% | 83.73% | 95.28% | 83.83% |
| oBERTa$_{MEDIUM}$ | 85.29% | 97.05% | 85.17% | 83.62% | 95.15% | 83.74% |
| oBERTa$_{MEDIUM}$ 90% | 81.61% | 92.87% | 81.32% | 82.37% | 93.73% | 81.79% |
| oBERTa$_{SMALL}$ | 80.80% | 91.95% | 81.55% | 81.10% | 92.29% | 81.51% |
| oBERTa$_{SMALL}$ 90% | 79.23% | 90.15% | 79.24% | 79.14% | 90.06% | 79.42% |

Table 10: Sparse Transfer performance of the oBERTA family on the MNLI dataset. Sparse transfer was performed over 10 epochs and sparse transfer with quantization over 20. Recovery is based on the relative performance of the unpruned oBERTa$_{base}$.

| | Sparse Transfer | | | | Sparse Transfer With Quantization | | | |
|---|---|---|---|---|---|---|---|---|
| model | Accuracy | Recovery | F1 | Combined | Accuracy | Recovery | F1 | Combined |
| oBERTa$_{base}$ | 91.52% | 100.00% | 90.09% | 88.66% | 89.86% | 98.18% | 88.12% | 86.73% |
| oBERTa$_{base}$ 90% | 91.01% | 99.44% | 89.47% | 87.92% | 91.21% | 99.66% | 89.68% | 88.16% |
| oBERTa$_{base}$ 95% | 90.85% | 99.26% | 89.21% | 87.58% | 90.72% | 99.12% | 89.08% | 0.87% |
| oBERTa$_{MEDIUM}$ | 91.35% | 99.81% | 89.90% | 88.44% | 91.33% | 99.79% | 89.80% | 88.28% |
| oBERTa$_{MEDIUM}$ 90% | 90.48% | 98.86% | 88.85% | 87.21% | 90.60% | 99.00% | 89.01% | 87.42% |
| oBERTa$_{SMALL}$ | 90.72% | 99.13% | 89.21% | 87.71% | 89.74 | 98.06% | 87.99 | 86.25 |
| oBERTa$_{SMALL}$ 90% | 89.74% | 98.06% | 87.99% | 86.25% | 89.73 | 98.04% | 87.98 | 86.08 |

Table 11: Sparse Transfer performance of the oBERTA family on the QQP dataset. The sparse transfer was performed over ten epochs, and sparse transfer with quantization over 20. Recovery is based on the relative performance of the unpruned oBERTa$_{base}$.

as shown in table 12 and sentiment analysis in 13 Finally, looking at performance on token classification as shown in table 14

### 4.1 Inference Benchmark

To evaluate the performance of our inference-optimized models, we benchmark performance using the popular DeepSparse library version 1.3.2 [7] and an Intel Xeon Gold 6238R Processor. Performance is measured using models that have been *sparse-transferred* to the SQuAD v1.1 dataset and exported to a standard ONNX model format. Benchmarks are run on 4 and 24 cores and a sequence length of 384 with batch sizes of 1, 16, and 64. For each model, the benchmark is run for 60 seconds with a warm-up period of 10 seconds, and we report the throughput (items per second) and the mean, median, and standard deviation per item latency. We present a set of summary statistics of relative speedup across batch sizes and infer-

| | Sparse Transfer | | Sparse Transfer With Quantization | |
|---|---|---|---|---|
| model | Accuracy | Recovery | Accuracy | Recovery |
| oBERTa$_{base}$ | 95.24% | 100.00% | 95.44% | 100.21% |
| oBERTa$_{base}$ 90% | 93.64% | 98.32% | 93.28 | 97.94% |
| oBERTa$_{base}$ 95% | 93.48% | 98.15% | 92.80 | 97.23% |
| oBERTa$_{MEDIUM}$ | 93.36% | 98.03% | 94.08 | 98.78% |
| oBERTa$_{MEDIUM}$ 90% | 92.24% | 96.85% | 92.08 | 96.69% |
| oBERTa$_{SMALL}$ | 93.04% | 97.69% | 92.52 | 97.15% |
| oBERTa$_{SMALL}$ 90% | 91.60% | 96.18% | 91.28 | 95.84% |

Table 12: Sparse Transfer performance of the oBERTA family on the IMDB dataset. The sparse transfer was performed over ten epochs, and sparse transfer with quantization over 20. Recovery is based on the relative performance of the unpruned oBERTa$_{base}$.

| | Sparse Transfer | | Sparse Transfer With Quantization | |
|---|---|---|---|---|
| model | Accuracy | Recovery | Accuracy | Recovery |
| oBERTa$_{base}$ | 94.60 | 100.00% | 92.66 | 97.95% |
| oBERTa$_{base}$ 90% | 92.78 | 98.08% | 92.546 | 97.83% |
| oBERTa$_{base}$ 95% | 91.51 | 96.74% | 91.399 | 96.62% |
| oBERTa$_{MEDIUM}$ | 92.89 | 98.19% | 91.06 | 96.26% |
| oBERTa$_{MEDIUM}$ 90% | 88.76 | 93.83% | 89.91 | 95.04% |
| oBERTa$_{SMALL}$ | 90.48 | 95.64% | 91.28 | 96.49% |
| oBERTa$_{SMALL}$ 90% | 89.34 | 94.44% | 88.65 | 93.71% |

Table 13: Sparse Transfer performance of the oBERTA family on the SST-2 dataset. The sparse transfer was performed over ten epochs, and sparse transfer with quantization over 20. Recovery is based on the relative performance of the unpruned oBERTa$_{base}$.

| | Sparse Transfer | | | Sparse Transfer With Quantization | | |
|---|---|---|---|---|---|---|
| model | Accuracy | Recovery | F1 | Accuracy | Recovery | F1 |
| oBERTa$_{base}$ | 99.26% | 100.00% | 95.51% | 99.30% | 100.05% | 95.98% |
| oBERTa$_{base}$ 90% | 99.11% | 99.85% | 94.98% | 99.05% | 99.79% | 94.51% |
| oBERTa$_{base}$ 95% | 98.89% | 99.63% | 93.32% | 98.75% | 99.48% | 92.61% |
| oBERTa$_{MEDIUM}$ | 99.04% | 99.77% | 94.39% | 99.18% | 99.92% | 95.15% |
| oBERTa$_{MEDIUM}$ 90% | 98.79% | 99.53% | 93.31% | 98.73% | 99.46% | 92.70% |
| oBERTa$_{SMALL}$ | 99.01% | 99.75% | 94.00% | 98.98% | 99.72% | 94.13% |
| oBERTa$_{SMALL}$ 90% | 98.47% | 99.20% | 91.13% | 98.25% | 98.98% | 89.79% |

Table 14: Sparse Transfer performance of the oBERTA family on the CONLL-2003 dataset. The sparse transfer was performed over ten epochs, and sparse transfer with quantization over 20. Recovery is based on the relative performance of the unpruned oBERTa$_{base}$.

[7] pip install deepsparse==1.3.2

| | 24 Cores | | | 4 Cores | | |
|---|---|---|---|---|---|---|
| Model | BS 1 | BS 16 | BS 64 | BS 1 | BS 16 | BS 64 |
| $BERT_{base}$ | 1.00 | 1.00 | 1.00 | 1.00 | 1.00 | 1.00 |
| $oBERTa_{base}$ | 1.00 | 1.00 | 1.00 | 1.00 | 1.00 | 1.00 |
| $oBERTa_{base}$ Quantized | 3.10 | 4.29 | 4.46 | 4.09 | 4.31 | 4.32 |
| $oBERTa_{base}$ 90% | 3.29 | 3.80 | 3.80 | 3.60 | 3.34 | 3.40 |
| $oBERTa_{base}$ 90% Quantized | 4.12 | 7.05 | 7.37 | 7.67 | 7.59 | 7.40 |
| $oBERTa_{base}$ 95% | 8.72 | 4.56 | 4.65 | 4.12 | 3.85 | 4.37 |
| $oBERTa_{base}$ 95% Quantized | 4.73 | 8.22 | 8.56 | 9.41 | 9.06 | 8.68 |
| $oBERTa_{MEDIUM}$ | 1.96 | 1.99 | 1.99 | 1.96 | 1.99 | 2.02 |
| $oBERTa_{MEDIUM}$ Quantized | 6.20 | 8.04 | 8.44 | 8.43 | 8.33 | 8.45 |
| $oBERTa_{MEDIUM}$ 90% | 6.35 | 7.41 | 6.84 | 7.83 | 6.56 | 6.72 |
| $oBERTa_{MEDIUM}$ 90% Quantized | 8.94 | 12.86 | 13.65 | 14.99 | 14.81 | 14.95 |
| $oBERTa_{SMALL}$ | 3.89 | 3.96 | 3.99 | 3.95 | 3.97 | 4.03 |
| $oBERTa_{SMALL}$ Quantized | 12.47 | 14.12 | 14.08 | 15.50 | 15.48 | 15.70 |
| $oBERTa_{SMALL}$ 90% | 12.22 | 14.40 | 14.67 | 14.05 | 14.19 | 14.13 |
| $oBERTa_{SMALL}$ 90% Quantized | 16.21 | 21.35 | 23.96 | 29.77 | 27.14 | 27.58 |

Table 15: Latency reduction of the oBERTa family concerning the unpruned $oBERTa_{base}$ as measured on 24 and 4 cores. Speedup is measured relative to the latency reduction in MS/batch, and BS refers to batch size.

ence server configurations as shown in table 15. Full inference performance results can be found in the appendix. In analyzing performance, we can see that the introduction of quantization to a dense model delivers roughly a 4x speedup while quantization on sparse models is closer to 2x. With the introduction of sparsity, 90% leads to slightly under 4x speedup, while 95% leads to slightly over 4x. The impact of structural pruning is roughly equivalent to the size of the as a 6-layer model is two times faster than a 12-layer, and a 3-layer model is four times faster. Combing compression forms is only partially additive, as a small (3-layer) 90% quantized model performance is 24x vs the expected 32x (4x from structural pruning, 2x quantization, 4x unstructured pruning.

Looking at the variation in a speedup by batch size and the number of cores, we can see that allocating more cores leads to a smaller gap in inference speedup, especially with small batches. From this, we extract that compression is significant when performing streaming inference (batch size 1) on smaller CPUs.

Next, we go ahead and benchmark the oBERTa model performance against existing sparse-transfer models such as oBERT and PruneOFA using the models that have been published [8] in Neural Magic's Sparse-Zoo [9]. We run these models using four cores and a batch size of 1 and compare their speedup (or slowdown) relative to their performance on the SQUAD v1.1 question-answering benchmark. Results can be found in table 16 and full results in 45. Looking at the improvements in accuracy and inference throughput, we find the oBERTa models are 1.3 to 4 times better than models with approximately the same accuracy.

Looking at the competitive results, we find

| | | Vs. $BERT_{base}$ | | Vs. $BERT_{large}$ | |
|---|---|---|---|---|---|
| Model | F1 | Recovery | Speedup | Recovery | Speedup |
| $oBERTa_{base}$ 90% | 91.00 | 102.77% | 3.57 | 100.44% | 20.21 |
| $oBERT_{large}$ 95% Quantized | 90.21 | 101.87% | 3.41 | 99.57% | 19.31 |
| $prunedOFA_{large}$ 90% Quantized | 89.96 | 101.59% | 2.38 | 99.29% | 13.47 |
| $oBERTa_{base}$ 90% Quantized | 89.46 | 101.03% | 7.62 | 98.74% | 43.07 |
| $oBERTa_{MEDIUM}$ 90% | 89.26 | 98.99% | 7.78 | 96.75% | 43.99 |
| $obert_{base}$ 90% Quantized | 88.00 | 99.38% | 6.96 | 97.13% | 39.37 |
| $oBERTa_{SMALL}$ 90% | 84.66 | 90.97% | 13.95 | 88.91% | 78.91 |
| pruneBERT 90% | 84.90 | 95.88% | 3.57 | 93.71% | 73.82 |

Table 16: Speedups of the oBERTa-family compared to existing published sparse models compared to the performance of $BERT_{base}$ and BERT-large. Speedup measures the reduction in latency of MS/batch. $oBERTa_{base}$ 90% exceeds the accuracy of $oBERT_{large}$ 95% quantized despite being faster, $oBERTa_{base}$ 90% quantized performs at the level of $pruneOFA_{large}$ 90% Quantized despite being 3x faster, $oBERTa_{MEDIUM}$ 90% can outperform $oBERT_{base}$ 90% Quantized despite being 30% faster, and $oBERTa_{SMALL}$ 90% performs on par with pruneBERT 90% despite being nearly four times faster.

that the oBERTa-* models can deliver significant gains in performance (F1) relative to speedups. The $oBERTa_{base}$Pruned 90% Quantized model achieves an undertaking that nearly matches pruneOFA-large 90% Quantized while delivering nearly 13x faster inference. Similarly, the $oBERTA_{SMALL}$ 90% model provides similar accuracy to PruneBERT despite being over four times faster.

## 5 Discussion

**Sparse Models require higher learning rates** as shown in the tables in A.8 sparse language models can be used as general-purpose contextual language models but require the use of a much higher learning rate. When using structurally pruned models like the 6-layer $oBERTa_{MEDIUM}$ and the 3-layer $oBERTa_{SMALL}$, the optimal learning rate does not vary much within the same task despite the model size. With the introduction of sparsity, the learning rate needs to scale, usually by a factor of five or ten. We find this counterintuitive as the sparse models have fewer parameters to *tune*, so we would expect

[8] Since the PruneBERT model is not available in the zoo, we extrapolate numbers using the performance of our $oBERTa_{base}$ pruned 90% as both models feature 12 transformer encoders and 90% sparsity.

[9] https://sparsezoo.neuralmagic.com/

them to prefer a much lower learning rate. We attribute this to the loss of expressivity in the network driven by its sparsity. Since the network has fewer degrees of freedom to optimize the points which can be optimized move much more than those that cannot.

**Larger models compress better** as shown by the gap between the sparse and dense models and the gap between models and their quantized counterparts. While 12-layer models can receive 90 or 95 % sparsity and quantization with little to no loss in accuracy, the three and 6-layer models see a much bigger dip. This aligns with Li et al. 2020 (Li et al., 2020) in which they demonstrate that larger models are more robust to pruning and quantization. Empirically, this makes sense as the smaller models have *fewer degrees of freedom*, and other portions of the network cannot counteract the reduction in expressivity caused by pruning and quantization.

**Bigger Teachers are not always better** as shown in the table in A.9 the introduction of larger teachers does not always lead to improvements in accuracy. The impact is highly task and model dependent as some datasets like MNLI or QQP see little impact in using larger teachers, yet datasets like SQUAD or SQUAD v2.0 see large impacts, which are even more pronounced when the student model is smaller.

**Frozen embeddings can help**, but not always. As shown by A.10 the impact of freezing the embeddings is highly task-specific and inconsistent across tasks or models. In question answering, freezing leads to 1-2 point movement for unpruned models and 5-7 points for pruned models. In other tasks like QQP and MNLI, the impact of frozen embeddings tends to be minor or none.

## 6 Limitations

While our approach is effective at compressing models, it is not the most efficient. In order to discover the most optimal compression approaches and evaluate their performance performed hundreds of experiments. As a result, scaling our approach to every novel language understanding language model is not tractable. Another limitation of our work is we did not track the complete compute utilization of our entire experimentation process but we can provide some estimates. Experiments in pruning during fine-tuning leveraged a single V100 16 GB GPU and took approximately 14 hours per experiment. The pre-training of structurally pruned models with knowledge distillation required 4 A100 40GB GPUs for approximately 72 hours. Pruning during pre-training with Knowledge distillation required approximately 100 hours on the same setup. Task-specific fine-tuning happened on a single V100 16GB GPU and depending on the size of the task was anywhere from a few minutes to 20 hours. Based on all of our experiments we estimate 400 V100 hours of pruning during fine-tuning, roughly 16,000 A100 hours[10] for pretraining, and assuming an average of 10 V100 hours per sparse transfer run, a total of 4000 V100 hours for sparse-transfer and sparse-transfer with quantization.

## 7 Conclusion and Future Work

## References

Daniel Fernando Campos, Alexandre Marques, Tuan Anh D. Nguyen, Mark Kurtz, and ChengXiang Zhai. 2022. Sparse*bert: Sparse models are robust. *ArXiv*, abs/2205.12452.

Alexis Conneau, Kartikay Khandelwal, Naman Goyal, Vishrav Chaudhary, Guillaume Wenzek, Francisco Guzmán, Edouard Grave, Myle Ott, Luke Zettlemoyer, and Veselin Stoyanov. 2019. Unsupervised cross-lingual representation learning at scale.

J. Devlin, Ming-Wei Chang, Kenton Lee, and Kristina Toutanova. 2019. Bert: Pre-training of deep bidirectional transformers for language understanding. In *NAACL*.

Wikimedia Foundation. 2021. Wikimedia downloads.

Song Han, Huizi Mao, and William J. Dally. 2015. A deep neural network compression pipeline: Pruning, quantization, huffman encoding. *ArXiv*.

Geoffrey E. Hinton, Oriol Vinyals, and J. Dean. 2015. Distilling the knowledge in a neural network. *ArXiv*, abs/1503.02531.

Eugenia Iofinova, Alexandra Peste, Mark Kurtz, and Dan Alistarh. 2021. How well do sparse imagenet models transfer? *2022 IEEE/CVF Conference on Computer Vision and Pattern Recognition (CVPR)*, pages 12256–12266.

Xiaoqi Jiao, Yichun Yin, Lifeng Shang, Xin Jiang, Xiao Chen, Linlin Li, Fang Wang, and Qun Liu. 2020. Tinybert: Distilling bert for natural language understanding. *ArXiv*, abs/1909.10351.

[10]4000 hours and 4 A100 GPUS per hour

Sehoon Kim, Sheng Shen, David Thorsley, Amir Gholami, Joseph Hassoun, and Kurt Keutzer. 2021. Learned token pruning for transformers. *Proceedings of the 28th ACM SIGKDD Conference on Knowledge Discovery and Data Mining*.

Eldar Kurtic and Dan Alistarh. 2022. Gmp*: Well-tuned global magnitude pruning can outperform most bert-pruning methods. *ArXiv*, abs/2210.06384.

Eldar Kurtic, Daniel Fernando Campos, Tuan Nguyen, Elias Frantar, Mark Kurtz, Ben Fineran, Michael Goin, and Dan Alistarh. 2022. The optimal bert surgeon: Scalable and accurate second-order pruning for large language models. *ArXiv*, abs/2203.07259.

Eldar Kurtić, Daniel Fernando Campos, Tuan Nguyen, Elias Frantar, Mark Kurtz, Ben Fineran, Michael Goin, and Dan Alistarh. 2022. The optimal bert surgeon: Scalable and accurate second-order pruning for large language models. *ArXiv*, abs/2203.07259.

Zhen-Zhong Lan, Mingda Chen, Sebastian Goodman, Kevin Gimpel, Piyush Sharma, and Radu Soricut. 2019. Albert: A lite bert for self-supervised learning of language representations. *ArXiv*, abs/1909.11942.

Jinhyuk Lee, Wonjin Yoon, Sungdong Kim, Donghyeon Kim, Sunkyu Kim, Chan Ho So, and Jaewoo Kang. 2020. Biobert: a pre-trained biomedical language representation model for biomedical text mining. *Bioinformatics*, 36:1234 – 1240.

Zhuohan Li, Eric Wallace, Sheng Shen, Kevin Lin, K. Keutzer, D. Klein, and Joseph Gonzalez. 2020. Train large, then compress: Rethinking model size for efficient training and inference of transformers. *ArXiv*, abs/2002.11794.

Yinhan Liu, Myle Ott, Naman Goyal, Jingfei Du, Mandar Joshi, Danqi Chen, Omer Levy, Mike Lewis, Luke Zettlemoyer, and Veselin Stoyanov. 2019. Roberta: A robustly optimized bert pretraining approach. *ArXiv*, abs/1907.11692.

Andrew L. Maas, Raymond E. Daly, Peter T. Pham, Dan Huang, Andrew Y. Ng, and Christopher Potts. 2011. Learning word vectors for sentiment analysis. In *Proceedings of the 49th Annual Meeting of the Association for Computational Linguistics: Human Language Technologies*, pages 142–150, Portland, Oregon, USA. Association for Computational Linguistics.

Neural Magic. 2023. [link].

Hadi Pouransari and Oncel Tuzel. 2020. Least squares binary quantization of neural networks. *2020 IEEE/CVF Conference on Computer Vision and Pattern Recognition Workshops (CVPRW)*, pages 2986–2996.

Colin Raffel, Noam M. Shazeer, Adam Roberts, Katherine Lee, Sharan Narang, Michael Matena, Yanqi Zhou, Wei Li, and Peter J. Liu. 2020. Exploring the limits of transfer learning with a unified text-to-text transformer. *ArXiv*, abs/1910.10683.

Pranav Rajpurkar, Robin Jia, and Percy Liang. 2018. Know what you don't know: Unanswerable questions for squad. In *Annual Meeting of the Association for Computational Linguistics*.

Pranav Rajpurkar, Jian Zhang, Konstantin Lopyrev, and Percy Liang. 2016a. Squad: 100, 000+ questions for machine comprehension of text. In *EMNLP*.

Pranav Rajpurkar, Jian Zhang, Konstantin Lopyrev, and Percy Liang. 2016b. Squad: 100,000+ questions for machine comprehension of text. In *EMNLP*.

SambitSekhar. 2017. First quora dataset release: Question pairs.

Victor Sanh, Lysandre Debut, Julien Chaumond, and Thomas Wolf. 2019a. Distilbert, a distilled version of bert: smaller, faster, cheaper and lighter. *ArXiv*, abs/1910.01108.

Victor Sanh, Lysandre Debut, Julien Chaumond, and Thomas Wolf. 2019b. Distilbert, a distilled version of bert: smaller, faster, cheaper and lighter. *arXiv preprint arXiv:1910.01108*.

Victor Sanh, Thomas Wolf, and Alexander M. Rush. 2020. Movement pruning: Adaptive sparsity by fine-tuning. *ArXiv*, abs/2005.07683.

S. Shankar. 2017. Identifying quora question pairs having the same intent. In *QQP*.

Richard Socher, Alex Perelygin, Jean Wu, Jason Chuang, Christopher D. Manning, Andrew Ng, and Christopher Potts. 2013. Recursive deep models for semantic compositionality over a sentiment treebank. In *Proceedings of the 2013 Conference on Empirical Methods in Natural Language Processing*, pages 1631–1642, Seattle, Washington, USA. Association for Computational Linguistics.

Zhiqing Sun, Hongkun Yu, Xiaodan Song, Renjie Liu, Yiming Yang, and Denny Zhou. 2020. Mobilebert: a compact task-agnostic bert for resource-limited devices. In *ACL*.

Erik F. Tjong Kim Sang and Fien De Meulder. 2003. Introduction to the CoNLL-2003 shared task: Language-independent named entity recognition. In *Proceedings of the Seventh Conference on Natural Language Learning at HLT-NAACL 2003*, pages 142–147.

Marcos Vinícius Treviso, Tianchu Ji, Ji-Ung Lee, Betty van Aken, Qingqing Cao, Manuel R. Ciosici, Michael Hassid, Kenneth Heafield, Sara Hooker, Pedro Henrique Martins, André F. T. Martins, Peter Milder, Colin Raffel, Edwin Simpson, Noam Slonim, Niranjan Balasubramanian, Leon Derczynski, and Roy Schwartz. 2022. Efficient methods for natural language processing: A survey. *ArXiv*, abs/2209.00099.

Ashish Vaswani, Noam M. Shazeer, Niki Parmar, Jakob Uszkoreit, Llion Jones, Aidan N. Gomez, Lukasz Kaiser, and Illia Polosukhin. 2017. Attention is all you need. *ArXiv*, abs/1706.03762.

Elena Voita, David Talbot, F. Moiseev, Rico Sennrich, and Ivan Titov. 2019. Analyzing multi-head self-attention: Specialized heads do the heavy lifting, the rest can be pruned. In *ACL*.

Adina Williams, Nikita Nangia, and Samuel Bowman. 2018. A broad-coverage challenge corpus for sentence understanding through inference. In *Proceedings of the 2018 Conference of the North American Chapter of the Association for Computational Linguistics: Human Language Technologies, Volume 1 (Long Papers)*, pages 1112–1122. Association for Computational Linguistics.

Ji Xin, Raphael Tang, Jaejun Lee, Yaoliang Yu, and Jimmy J. Lin. 2020. Deebert: Dynamic early exiting for accelerating bert inference. In *ACL*.

Ofir Zafrir, Guy Boudoukh, Peter Izsak, and Moshe Wasserblat. 2019. Q8bert: Quantized 8bit bert. *2019 Fifth Workshop on Energy Efficient Machine Learning and Cognitive Computing - NeurIPS Edition (EMC2-NIPS)*, pages 36–39.

Ofir Zafrir, Ariel Larey, Guy Boudoukh, Haihao Shen, and Moshe Wasserblat. 2021. Prune once for all: Sparse pre-trained language models. *ArXiv*, abs/2111.05754.

Yukun Zhu, Ryan Kiros, Richard S. Zemel, Ruslan Salakhutdinov, Raquel Urtasun, Antonio Torralba, and Sanja Fidler. 2015. Aligning books and movies: Towards story-like visual explanations by watching movies and reading books. *2015 IEEE International Conference on Computer Vision (ICCV)*, pages 19–27.

# A Appendix

## A.1 Model Generation Approach

oBERTa models are generated in a multi-stage approach with details found in figure 2

## A.2 Roberta and Training Methodology

RoBERTa (Liu et al., 2019) is a language model that can best be considered more robust and optimized for the popular BERT model. While the models share architectures, their training differs as RoBERTA uses a 160 GB corpus for 10 epochs compared to the 4GB one used by BERT. As a result, the training time of RoBERTA is about 100 times higher than its predecessor.
Given this high cost of training and the regular need for longer training when pruning a model (Kurtić et al., 2022), we focus on compressing RoBERTa without following its expensive pre-training regime. Our research leverages the popular open-source compression library SparseML[11] to implement unstructured pruning, structured pruning, and quantization via quantization-aware training. In all our experiments, we prune each network component independently using either GMP or OBS (Kurtic et al.). One exception is the embeddings layer, which we do not prune.

Table 17: Pretraining performance using knowledge distillation from a RoBERTa large model.

| Model | ACC | Loss | Perplexity |
|---|---|---|---|
| oBERTa$_{\text{base}}$ | 0.580 | 3.775 | 43.593 |
| oBERTa$_{\text{base}}$ 90% | 0.506 | 4.448 | 85.420 |
| oBERTa$_{\text{base}}$ 95% | 0.439 | 4.734 | 113.702 |
| oBERTa$_{\text{medium}}$ | 0.533 | 4.296 | 73.391 |
| oBERTa$_{\text{medium}}$ 90% | 0.631 | 1.896 | 6.662 |
| oBERTa$_{\text{small}}$ | 0.465 | 4.561 | 95.670 |
| oBERTa$_{\text{small}}$ 90% | 0.404 | 4.669 | 106.614 |

## A.3 Model Details

Model details can be found in table 18

## A.4 Dataset Details

Dataset statistics are detailed in Table 19.

## A.5 Teacher models

Performance of the RoBERTa$_{\text{base}}$and RoBERTa$_{\text{large}}$ models on our sparse transfer datasets. We explore the optimal hyperparameters relative to performance in published results as shown in table 20 and 21

## A.6 Upstream Pruning

Following the findings that more extensive teachers distill better (Liu et al., 2019) and our experiments, we use both RoBERTa$_{\text{base}}$and RoBERTa$_{\text{large}}$ as teachers eventually find the large model works better. Using this teacher, we use the parameters shown in table 22 to prune the models for oBERTa. This same set of parameters is applied to the structurally pruned models, but there is no induced sparsity.

[11]https://github.com/neuralmagic/sparseml

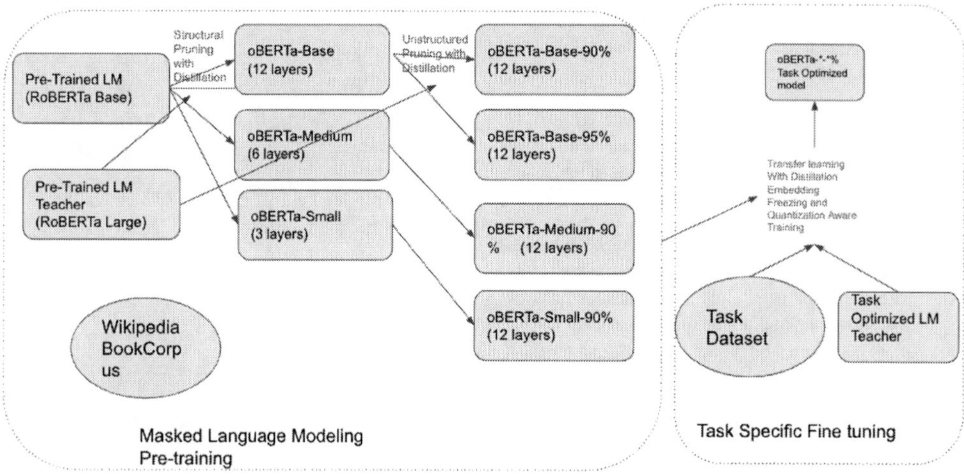


Figure 2: The set of oBERTa language models follows a compounding compression approach. First models are structurally pruned and further pre-trained using KD and a RoBERTa$_{large}$ teacher. Next, each model is pruned during additional pre-training to a target sparsity. After pruning, the sparsity pattern is locked, and models are fine-tuned with KD on specialized NLP tasks. During fine-tuning, models may be quantized for additional improvements in inference efficiency.

| Model | Parameters | Prunable | Sparse | Sparsity | size (MB) | Compression | GZIP size (MB) | Compression |
|---|---|---|---|---|---|---|---|---|
| oBERTa$_{base}$ | 124,647,170 | 85,526,016 | 1,539 | 0.0% | 474 | 1.00 | 435 | 1.00 |
| oBERTa$_{base}$ Quantized | 124,647,170 | 85,526,016 | 1,539 | 0.0% | 119 | 3.98 | 85 | 5.12 |
| oBERTa$_{base}$ 90% | 124,647,170 | 85,526,016 | 76,442,738 | 89.4% | 474 | 1.00 | 183 | 2.38 |
| oBERTa$_{base}$ 90% Quantized | 124,647,170 | 85,526,016 | 76,442,738 | 89.4% | 119 | 3.98 | 42 | 10.36 |
| oBERTa$_{base}$ 95% | 124,647,170 | 85,526,016 | 80,689,466 | 94.3% | 474 | 1.00 | 163 | 2.67 |
| oBERTa$_{base}$ 95% Quantized | 124,647,170 | 85,526,016 | 80,689,466 | 94.3% | 119 | 3.98 | 37 | 11.76 |
| oBERTa$_{MEDIUM}$ | 82,119,938 | 43,058,688 | 1,538 | 0.0% | 312 | 1.52 | 289 | 1.51 |
| oBERTa$_{MEDIUM}$ Quantized | 82,119,938 | 43,058,688 | 1,538 | 0.0% | 78 | 6.08 | 53 | 8.21 |
| oBERTa$_{MEDIUM}$ 90% | 82,119,938 | 43,058,688 | 38,222,138 | 88.8% | 312 | 1.52 | 161 | 2.70 |
| oBERTa$_{MEDIUM}$ 90% Quantized | 82,119,938 | 43,058,688 | 38,222,138 | 88.8% | 78 | 6.08 | 33 | 13.18 |
| oBERTa$_{SMALL}$ | 60,856,322 | 21,825,024 | 1,538 | 0.0% | 233 | 2.03 | 214 | 2.03 |
| oBERTa$_{SMALL}$ Quantized | 60,856,322 | 21,825,024 | 1,538 | 0.0% | 60 | 7.90 | 39 | 11.15 |
| oBERTa$_{SMALL}$ 90% | 60,856,322 | 21,825,024 | 19,111,068 | 87.6% | 233 | 2.03 | 149 | 2.92 |
| oBERTa$_{SMALL}$ 90% Quantized | 60,856,322 | 21,825,024 | 19,111,838 | 87.6% | 60 | 7.90 | 30 | 14.50 |

Table 18: Description of the oBERTa model family and their sparsity and size. Prunable parameters are the sum of all non-embedding parameters in the model. Since sparsity profiles are assigned at a module level, overall sparsity profiles do not perfectly match the target 90% or 95% which are targeted.

### A.7 Sparse Transfer Hyper-parameters

Our work aims not to produce the highest possible performance of a sparse language model. Instead, we aim to make light language models that perform well on various tasks with minimal hyperparameter optimization. As a result, in all of our experiments, we leverage the parameters shown in 23 and 24 and perform a grid search over them.

### A.8 Learning Rate

In our exploration of sparse transfer learning, we perform a wide study on the impact of the optimal learning rate for each task and each model in the oBERTa family. The results as shown in table 25

### A.9 Knowledge Distillation

In our exploration of sparse transfer learning, we perform a wide study on the impact of knowledge distillation. Across tasks, we look at the impact using no teacher, RoBERTa$_{base}$and RoBERTa$_{large}$

| Dataset | Train | Eval |
|---|---|---|
| SQuAD v1.1 (examples) | 87599 | 10570 |
| SQuAD v2.0 (examples) | 130319 | 11873 |
| MNLI (examples) | 392702 | 19628 |
| QQP (examples) | 363,846 | 40,430 |
| IMDB (examples) | 25000 | 25000 |
| CONLL2003 (examples) | 14041 | 3250 |
| SST2 (examples) | 67349 | 872 |
| Wikipedia (words) | 6078422 | - |
| TBC (words) | 74004228 | - |

Table 19: Statistics for training and evaluation datasets

as shown in tables 26,27,28,29,30,31

### A.10 Freezing Embeddings

In our exploration of sparse transfer learning, we perform a wide study on the impact of freezing the embeddings during finetuning. Across tasks, we look at the impact of frozen and unfrozen embeddings as shown in tables 32,33,34,35,36, and 37. Besides question answering, we do not find a strong trend with the impact of frozen embeddings. In some tasks, sparse and dense models perform better with frozen embeddings while not for others. Focusing on question answering, by using frozen embeddings dense models see large losses in F1 score and the opposite can be seen for pruned models.

### A.11 Inference Benchmarks

We provide full results for our experiments in benchmarking the impact of compression on inference efficiency as shown in tables 45,43,42,38,40,39,44,44

### A.12 Limitations

While much of our work has focused on showcasing the broad usability of compressed language models, they are not without fault. While our experiments focus on the compression of RoBERTa, the size of its training dataset makes complete exploration of the ability of pruning during pretraining somewhat limited. The work in the paper shows the ability to compress RoBERTa on a smaller pretraining dataset but does not contrast it with the impact of compression on the full dataset.

A second limitation of our work is the high computational demand required for creating public domain sparse language models. Despite amortizing the cost of compression to a few pretraining training regimes, the reduction of other language models like ALBERT (Lan et al., 2019) or XLM-R (Conneau et al., 2019) require completely new training, pruning, and transfer experiments.

### A.13 Responsible NLP Research - Reproducibility Checklist

#### A.13.1 Scientific Artifacts

**Datasets.** We experiment with well-established benchmarks with usage in many broad domains. We do not perform any modification or augmentation in any dataset. Since datasets are not modified, we did not look for any personal or sensitive content.
In our pre-training experiments, we leverage the Toronto Book Corpus (TBC) (Zhu et al., 2015)[12] and the Wikipedia (Foundation, 2021)[13]. For finetuning we make use of SQuAD v1.1 (Rajpurkar et al., 2016b) [14], SQuAD v2.0 (Rajpurkar et al., 2018) [15], Quora Duplicate Question Dataset (QQP) (Shankar, 2017)[16], and Multi-Genre Natural Language Inference (MNLI) (Williams et al., 2018) [17], Large Movie Review Dataset (IMDB) (Maas et al., 2011)[18], Stanford Sentiment Treebank (SST-2) (Socher et al., 2013)[19], and the shared task of CoNLL-2003 concerns language-independent named entity recognition (CONLL-2003) (Tjong Kim Sang and De Meulder, 2003)[20]datasets.

**Models.** The model used as a starting point for all of our experiments is RoBERta, publicly available via HuggingFace Hub [21]. All other models presented in this paper will be released in openly-available repositories along with their compression recipes, training metrics, and hyper-parameters.

[12]https://huggingface.co/datasets/bookcorpus
[13]https://huggingface.co/datasets/wikipedia
[14]https://huggingface.co/datasets/squad
[15]https://huggingface.co/datasets/squadv2
[16]https://huggingface.co/datasets/glue
[17]https://huggingface.co/datasets/glue
[18]https://huggingface.co/datasets/imdb
[19]https://huggingface.co/datasets/glue
[20]https://huggingface.co/datasets/conll2003
[21]https://huggingface.co/bert-base-uncased

| Model | Training Epochs | Batch Size | Learning Rate | Weight Decay | Warmup | Target Metric | Target Score | Actual | Recall |
|---|---|---|---|---|---|---|---|---|---|
| SQUAD V1.1 | 3 | 16 | 1.00E-05 | 0 | 0 | F1 | 90.40 | 92.15 | 101.94% |
| SQUAD V2.0 | 3 | 16 | 3.00E-05 | 0 | 0 | F1 | 82.91 | 83.53 | 100.74% |
| QQP | 5 | 16 | 2.00E-05 | 0 | 0 | ACC | 91.90 | 91.52 | 99.59% |
| MNLI | 3 | 16 | 1.00E-05 | 0 | 0 | ACC | 87.60 | 87.88 | 100.31% |
| SST-2 | 3 | 16 | 2.00E-05 | 0 | 0 | ACC | 94.80 | 94.61 | 99.80% |
| CONLL2003 | 3 | 16 | 3.00E-05 | 0 | 0 | ACC | 99.10 | 99.29 | 100.19% |
| IMDB | 3 | 16 | 1.00E-05 | 0 | 0 | ACC | 94.67 | 95.24 | 100.60% |

Table 20: Training parameters along with performance metrics and the recovery vs. the published performance of the same model for the RoBERTa base model

| Model | Training Epochs | Batch Size | Learning Rate | Weight Decay | Warmup | Target Metric | Target Score | Actual | Recall |
|---|---|---|---|---|---|---|---|---|---|
| SQUAD V1.1 | 3 | 16 | 1.00E-05 | 0 | 0 | F1 | 94.50 | 94.62 | 100.12% |
| SQUAD V2.0 | 3 | 16 | 1.00E-05 | 0 | 0 | F1 | 89.40 | 89.14 | 99.71% |
| QQP | 3 | 16 | 1.00E-05 | 0 | 0 | ACC | 92.20 | 91.76 | 99.52% |
| MNLI | 3 | 16 | 1.00E-05 | 0 | 0 | ACC | 90.20 | 90.61 | 100.45% |
| SST-2 | 3 | 16 | 1.00E-05 | 0 | 0 | ACC | 96.40 | 96.22 | 99.81% |
| CONLL2003 | 3 | 16 | 3.00E-05 | 0 | 0 | ACC | 99.10 | 99.39 | 100.29% |
| IMDB | 3 | 16 | 1.00E-05 | 0 | 0 | ACC | 94.67 | 96.12 | 101.53% |

Table 21: Training parameters along with performance metrics and the recovery vs. the published performance of the same model for the RoBERTa large model

#### A.13.2 Computational Experiments

**Upstream.** During upstream pruning due to the large size of language models and their associated teachers we leverage 4x A100 40GB NVIDIA GPUs. We train for 5 epochs and an entire training and pruning run takes approximately 72 hours. Since the cost of such a large compute instance is high, these experiments were only run with a single seed and without major hyper-parameter exploration.

**Sparse-Transfer** Our experimentation on finetuning our compressed models uses the workhorse 16GB V100. Our sparse-transfer datasets vary greatly in size and as a result, so do experiments. Finetuning for CONL2003 takes less than 10 minutes while larger datasets like QQP take about 24 hours. Due to the number of datasets which we evaluate and the number of models in the oBERTa family, we only perform experimentation with a single fixed seed.

**DeepSparse inference.** We pair our compressed models with DeepSparse (Magic, 2023) a publicly-available sparsity-aware CPU inference engine. All models are exported using the standard ONNX[22] format. For our competitive benchmarking against existing compressed language models, we leverage the model representations shared in the SparseZoo [23]. This approach means that some older models such as oBERT may have had less optimized ONNA exports. We believe this difference in exportation causes the nearly 4x improvement in the performance of oBERTa base vs bert-base.

#### A.13.3 Computational Packages

All of our experimentation is done using public libraries and datasets to ensure extensibility and reproducibility. Our experimentation is done using NeuralMagic's SparseML [24] which has specialized integration with HuggingFace's Transformers [25] and Datasets [26] libraries.

[22]https://onnx.ai/

[23]https://sparsezoo.neuralmagic.com/

[24]https://github.com/neuralmagic/sparseml

[25]https://github.com/huggingface/transformers

[26]https://github.com/huggingface/datasets

| | 5 Epochs |
|---|---|
| Datasets | BookCorpus & English Wikipedia |
| Batch size | 256 |
| Initial learning rate<br>Learning rate schedule<br>Learning rate rewinds | 5e-4<br>linear decay with rewinds<br>periodic every 0.5 epochs |
| Max sequence length<br>Weight decay | 512<br>0.01 |
| Knowledge Distillation<br>(hardness, temperature) | (1.0, 5.5) |
| Student model<br>Teacher model | dense oBERTa-* model<br>$\text{RoBERTa}_{\text{large}}$ |
| Pruning frequency | 100x per epoch |
| Initial Sparsity | 0.7 for 12 layer model, 0.5 for the 6-layer, and 0.3 for the 3-layer |

Table 22: Upstream pruning hyper-parameters.

| | 10 Epochs |
|---|---|
| Initial learning rate<br>Learning rate schedule | 2.1e-4,1.9e-4,1.7e-4,1.5e-4,1.3e-4,1.1e-4,9e-5,7e-5,5e-5,3e-5,2e-5,1e-5<br>linear decay to 0 |
| Batch size | 12 |
| Weight Decay | 0.0, 0.01, 0.05, 0.1 |
| Knowledge Distillation hardness | 1.0, 0.0 |
| Frozen Embeddings | 1.0, 0.0 |
| Knowledge Distillation temperature | 7.0 |
| Knowledge Distillation Teacher | $\text{RoBERTa}_{\text{base}}$, $\text{RoBERTa}_{\text{large}}$ |

Table 23: Sparse-transfer learning hyper-parameters used to fine-tune upstream-pruned models at downstream tasks. Each Experiment tunes this set of parameters to find a task-specific optimal combination.

| | 20 Epochs |
|---|---|
| Initial learning rate<br>Learning rate schedule | 2.1e-4,1.9e-4,1.7e-4,1.5e-4,1.3e-4,1.1e-4,9e-5,7e-5,5e-5,3e-5,2e-5,1e-5<br>linear decay to 0. Rewind to 5e-5 for QAT at epoch 10 |
| Freeze Batch Norm Epoch | 18 |
| Batch size | 12 |
| Weight Decay | 0.0, 0.01, 0.05, 0.1 |
| Knowledge Distillation hardness | 1.0, 0.0 |
| Frozen Embeddings | 1.0, 0.0 |
| Frozen Embeddings Schedule | Frozen until epoch 10, unfrozen for QAT |
| Knowledge Distillation temperature | 7.0 |
| Knowledge Distillation Teacher | $\text{RoBERTa}_{\text{base}}$, $\text{RoBERTa}_{\text{large}}$ |

Table 24: Sparse-transfer learning with Quantization hyper-parameters used to fine-tune upstream-pruned models at downstream tasks. Each Experiment tunes this set of parameters to find a task-specific optimal combination.

| | Optimal Learning Rate | | | | | | |
|---|---|---|---|---|---|---|---|
| model | SQUAD | SQUAD V2 | MNLI | QQP | IMDB | SST2 | CONLL2003 |
| RoBERTa$_{base}$ | 1.00E-05 | 3.00E-05 | 1.00E-05 | 2.00E-05 | 1.00E-05 | 2.00E-05 | 3.00E-05 |
| RoBERTa$_{large}$ | 1.00E-05 | 1.00E-05 | 1.00E-05 | 1.00E-05 | 1.00E-05 | 1.00E-05 | 3.00E-05 |
| oBERTa$_{base}$ | 1.00E-05 | 1.00E-05 | 1.00E-05 | 2.00E-05 | 1.00E-05 | 2.00E-05 | 3.00E-05 |
| oBERTa$_{base}$ 90% | 1.50E-04 | 1.50E-04 | 7.00E-05 | 1.70E-04 | 1.30E-04 | 9.00E-05 | 1.50E-04 |
| oBERTa$_{base}$ 95% | 1.50E-04 | 1.30E-04 | 9.00E-05 | 2.10E-04 | 1.30E-04 | 9.00E-05 | 5.00E-05 |
| oBERTa$_{MEDIUM}$ | 5.00E-05 | 5.00E-05 | 2.00E-05 | 3.00E-05 | 3.00E-05 | 2.00E-05 | 3.00E-05 |
| oBERTa$_{MEDIUM}$ 90% | 1.50E-04 | 1.30E-04 | 1.50E-04 | 1.50E-04 | 5.00E-05 | 1.50E-04 | 1.50E-04 |
| oBERTa$_{SMALL}$ | 1.50E-04 | 1.50E-04 | 3.00E-05 | 5.00E-05 | 3.00E-05 | 5.00E-05 | 3.00E-05 |
| oBERTa$_{SMALL}$ 90% | 1.50E-04 | 1.50E-04 | 2.10E-04 | 2.10E-04 | 1.50E-04 | 2.10E-04 | 1.90E-04 |

Table 25: Sparse-transfer learning with Quantization hyper-parameters used to fine-tune upstream-pruned models at downstream tasks. Each Experiment tunes this set of parameters to find a task-specific optimal combination.

| model | No KD | KD-Base | KD-Large |
|---|---|---|---|
| oBERTa$_{base}$(Target) | 91.52% | N/A | N/A |
| oBERTa$_{base}$ 90% | 91.97 | 92.78 | 92.55 |
| oBERTa$_{base}$ 95% | 91.40 | 91.17 | 91.514 |
| oBERTa$_{MEDIUM}$ | 90.94 | 91.86 | 91.78 |
| oBERTa$_{MEDIUM}$ 90% | 87.16 | 87.16 | 89.56 |
| oBERTa$_{SMALL}$ | 89.56 | 88.65 | 90.83 |
| oBERTa$_{SMALL}$ 90% | 85.58 | 89.22 | 89.45 |

Table 26: Impact of knowledge distillation on the accuracy (matched) MNLI Dataset across model sizes for the various sizes of oBERTa as compared to the regularly trained baseline

| model | No KD | KD-Base | KD-Large |
|---|---|---|---|
| oBERTa$_{base}$(Target) | 91.52 | N/A | N/A |
| oBERTa$_{base}$ 90% | 63.18 | 91.01 | 90.93 |
| oBERTa$_{base}$ 95% | 90.46 | 90.45 | 90.72 |
| oBERTa$_{MEDIUM}$ | 90.75 | 90.96 | 90.96 |
| oBERTa$_{MEDIUM}$ 90% | 89.93 | 90.41 | 89.82 |
| oBERTa$_{SMALL}$ | 86.63 | 87.34 | 87.65 |
| oBERTa$_{SMALL}$ 90% | 88.72 | 89.40 | 87.50 |

Table 27: Impact of knowledge distillation on the accuracy QQP Dataset across model sizes for the various sizes of oBERTa as compared to the regularly trained baseline

| model | No KD | KD-Base | KD-Large |
|---|---|---|---|
| oBERTa$_{base}$(Target) | 91.52 | N/A | N/A |
| oBERTa$_{base}$ 90% | 91.97 | 92.78 | 92.55 |
| oBERTa$_{base}$ 95% | 91.4 | 91.17 | 91.514 |
| oBERTa$_{MEDIUM}$ | 90.94 | 91.86 | 91.78 |
| oBERTa$_{MEDIUM}$ 90% | 87.16 | 87.16 | 89.56 |
| oBERTa$_{SMALL}$ | 89.56 | 88.65 | 90.83 |
| oBERTa$_{SMALL}$ 90% | 85.58 | 89.22 | 89.45 |

Table 28: Impact of knowledge distillation on the accuracy SST-2 Dataset across model sizes for the various sizes of oBERTa as compared to the regularly trained baseline

| model | No KD | KD-Base | KD-Large |
|---|---|---|---|
| oBERTa$_{base}$(Target) | 91.52% | N/A | N/A |
| oBERTa$_{base}$ 90% | 99.17 | 99.08 | 99.11 |
| oBERTa$_{base}$ 95% | 98.89 | 98.47 | 97.51 |
| oBERTa$_{MEDIUM}$ | 99.21 | 99.16 | 99.19 |
| oBERTa$_{MEDIUM}$ 90% | 99.01 | 98.8 | 98.79 |
| oBERTa$_{SMALL}$ | 99.05 | 98.95 | 98.94 |
| oBERTa$_{SMALL}$ 90% | 98.88 | 98.55 | 98.55 |

Table 29: Impact of knowledge distillation on the accuracy on the CONLL2003 Dataset across model sizes for the various sizes of oBERTa as compared to the regularly trained baseline

| model | No KD | KD-Base | KD-Large |
|---|---|---|---|
| oBERTa$_{base}$(Target) | 91.52% | N/A | N/A |
| oBERTa$_{base}$ 90% | 89.01 | 90.86 | 90.92 |
| oBERTa$_{base}$ 95% | 87.06 | 89.84 | 89.21 |
| oBERTa$_{MEDIUM}$ | 84.36 | 88.20 | 85.74 |
| oBERTa$_{MEDIUM}$ 90% | 84.71 | 89.26 | 88.61 |
| oBERTa$_{SMALL}$ | 82.00 | 80.77 | 77.08 |
| oBERTa$_{SMALL}$ 90% | 73.31 | 84.66 | 83.13 |

Table 30: Impact of knowledge distillation on the F1 SQUAD v1.1 Dataset across model sizes for the various sizes of oBERTa as compared to the regularly trained baseline

| model | No KD | KD-Base | KD-Large |
|---|---|---|---|
| oBERTa$_{base}$(Target) | 91.52% | N/A | N/A |
| oBERTa$_{base}$ 90% | 75.57852204 | 80.25256971 | 81.32561567 |
| oBERTa$_{base}$ 95% | 72.61 | 77.67 | 77.98 |
| oBERTa$_{MEDIUM}$ | 69.42634 | 70.97328 | 71.55996 |
| oBERTa$_{MEDIUM}$ 90% | 68.25281 | 76.02975 | 76.64135 |
| oBERTa$_{SMALL}$ | 66.8281 | 62.9573 | 63.1224 |
| oBERTa$_{SMALL}$ 90% | 55.3959 | 70.0796 | 70.7913 |

Table 31: Impact of knowledge distillation on the F1 SQUAD v2.0 Dataset across model sizes for the various sizes of oBERTa as compared to the regularly trained baseline

| model | Frozen | Unfrozen |
|---|---|---|
| oBERTa$_{base}$ (Target) | N/A | 87.88% |
| oBERTa$_{base}$ 90% | 84.50 | 83.81 |
| oBERTa$_{base}$ 95% | 83.91 | 83.41 |
| oBERTa$_{MEDIUM}$ | 84.37 | 83.32 |
| oBERTa$_{MEDIUM}$ 90% | 81.61 | 77.00 |
| oBERTa$_{SMALL}$ | 80.24 | 80.36 |
| oBERTa$_{SMALL}$ 90% | 78.46 | 74.25 |

Table 32: Impact of frozen vs trained embeddings on the accuracy (matched) MNLI Dataset across model sizes for the various sizes of oBERTa as compared to the uncompressed baseline

| model | Frozen | Unfrozen |
|---|---|---|
| oBERTa$_{base}$ (Target) | N/A | 91.52% |
| oBERTa$_{base}$ 90% | 90.93% | 90.99% |
| oBERTa$_{base}$ 95% | 90.72% | 90.85% |
| oBERTa$_{MEDIUM}$ | 90.96% | 91.35% |
| oBERTa$_{MEDIUM}$ 90% | 89.82% | 90.48% |
| oBERTa$_{SMALL}$ | 90.59% | 90.72% |
| oBERTa$_{SMALL}$ 90% | 89.40% | 89.74% |

Table 33: Impact of frozen vs trained embeddings on the accuracy on QQP across model sizes for the various sizes of oBERTa as compared to the uncompressed baseline

| model | Frozen | Unfrozen |
|---|---|---|
| oBERTa$_{base}$ (Target) | N/A | 91.52% |
| oBERTa$_{base}$ 90% | 92.55 | 91.74 |
| oBERTa$_{base}$ 95% | 91.514 | 91.4 |
| oBERTa$_{MEDIUM}$ | 91.78 | 92.89 |
| oBERTa$_{MEDIUM}$ 90% | 89.56 | 88.76 |
| oBERTa$_{SMALL}$ | 90.83 | 90.48 |
| oBERTa$_{SMALL}$ 90% | 89.45 | 89.34 |

Table 34: Impact of frozen vs trained embeddings on the accuracy SST2 Dataset across model sizes for the various sizes of oBERTa as compared to the uncompressed baseline

| model | Frozen | Unfrozen |
|---|---|---|
| oBERTa$_{base}$ (Target) | N/A | 91.52% |
| oBERTa$_{base}$ 90% | 97.51 | 98.55 |
| oBERTa$_{base}$ 95% | 99.11 | 99.13 |
| oBERTa$_{MEDIUM}$ | 99.19 | 99.18 |
| oBERTa$_{MEDIUM}$ 90% | 98.79 | 98.9 |
| oBERTa$_{SMALL}$ | 98.94 | 98.94 |
| oBERTa$_{SMALL}$ 90% | 98.55 | 98.69 |

Table 35: Impact of frozen vs trained embeddings on the accuracy on CONLL2003 Dataset across model sizes for the various sizes of oBERTa as compared to the uncompressed baseline

| model | Frozen | Unfrozen |
|---|---|---|
| oBERTa$_{base}$ (Target) | N/A | 91.52% |
| oBERTa$_{base}$ 90% | 90.92 | 83.99 |
| oBERTa$_{base}$ 95% | 89.21 | 87.08 |
| oBERTa$_{MEDIUM}$ | 85.74 | 89.95 |
| oBERTa$_{MEDIUM}$ 90% | 88.61 | 86.63 |
| oBERTa$_{SMALL}$ | 77.08 | 84.64 |
| oBERTa$_{SMALL}$ 90% | 83.13 | 77.43 |

Table 36: Impact of frozen vs trained embeddings on SQUAD v1.1 F1 across model sizes for the various sizes of oBERTa as compared to the uncompressed baseline

| model | Frozen | Unfrozen |
|---|---|---|
| oBERTa$_{base}$ (Target) | N/A | 91.52% |
| oBERTa$_{base}$ 90% | 71.56 | 78.05 |
| oBERTa$_{base}$ 95% | 81.33 | 78.45 |
| oBERTa$_{MEDIUM}$ | 77.98 | 76.86 |
| oBERTa$_{MEDIUM}$ 90% | 76.64 | 72.77 |
| oBERTa$_{SMALL}$ | 71.32 | 63.12 |
| oBERTa$_{SMALL}$ 90% | 70.79 | 59.38 |

Table 37: Impact of frozen vs trained embeddings on the SQUAD v2.0 Dataset across model sizes for the various sizes of oBERTa as compared to the uncompressed baseline

| model | Throughput (items/sec) | Speedup | Latency Mean (ms/batch) | Latency Median (ms/batch | Latency Std (ms/batch) |
|---|---|---|---|---|---|
| oBERTa$_{\text{base}}$ | 16.69 | 1.00 | 59.90 | 59.82 | 1.02 |
| oBERTa$_{\text{base}}$ Quantized | 51.68 | 3.10 | 19.34 | 19.28 | 0.58 |
| oBERTa$_{\text{base}}$ 90% | 54.87 | 3.29 | 18.21 | 18.15 | 0.31 |
| oBERTa$_{\text{base}}$ 90% Quantized | 68.70 | 4.12 | 14.55 | 14.50 | 0.20 |
| oBERTa$_{\text{base}}$ 95% | 145.57 | 8.72 | 6.86 | 6.86 | 0.11 |
| oBERTa$_{\text{base}}$ 95% Quantized | 78.90 | 4.73 | 12.66 | 12.68 | 0.31 |
| oBERTa$_{\text{MEDIUM}}$ | 32.78 | 1.96 | 30.49 | 30.44 | 1.19 |
| oBERTa$_{\text{MEDIUM}}$ Quantized | 103.47 | 6.20 | 9.65 | 9.60 | 0.57 |
| oBERTa$_{\text{MEDIUM}}$ 90% | 106.01 | 6.35 | 9.42 | 9.34 | 0.28 |
| oBERTa$_{\text{MEDIUM}}$ 90% Quantized | 149.25 | 8.94 | 6.69 | 6.65 | 0.42 |
| oBERTa$_{\text{SMALL}}$ | 64.93 | 3.89 | 15.39 | 15.31 | 0.66 |
| oBERTa$_{\text{SMALL}}$ Quantized | 208.09 | 12.47 | 4.80 | 4.78 | 0.28 |
| oBERTa$_{\text{SMALL}}$ 90% | 203.95 | 12.22 | 4.89 | 4.86 | 0.33 |
| oBERTa$_{\text{SMALL}}$ 90% Quantized | 270.63 | 16.21 | 3.69 | 3.68 | 0.25 |

Table 38: Inference performance of the oBERTa model family using a batch size of 1, 24 cores, and a sequence length of 384

| model | Throughput (items/sec) | Speedup | Latency Mean (ms/batch) | Latency Median (ms/batch | Latency Std (ms/batch) |
|---|---|---|---|---|---|
| oBERTa$_{\text{base}}$ | 19.55 | 1.00 | 818.23 | 811.93 | 15.52 |
| oBERTa$_{\text{base}}$ Quantized | 83.92 | 4.29 | 190.65 | 189.55 | 4.21 |
| oBERTa$_{\text{base}}$ 90% | 74.29 | 3.80 | 215.35 | 214.31 | 2.47 |
| oBERTa$_{\text{base}}$ 90% Quantized | 137.83 | 7.05 | 116.07 | 115.43 | 2.56 |
| oBERTa$_{\text{base}}$ 95% | 89.07 | 4.56 | 179.62 | 178.92 | 3.19 |
| oBERTa$_{\text{base}}$ 95% Quantized | 160.68 | 8.22 | 99.56 | 98.91 | 2.63 |
| oBERTa$_{\text{MEDIUM}}$ | 38.95 | 1.99 | 410.73 | 408.13 | 6.11 |
| oBERTa$_{\text{MEDIUM}}$ Quantized | 157.12 | 8.04 | 101.82 | 101.27 | 2.21 |
| oBERTa$_{\text{MEDIUM}}$ 90% | 144.95 | 7.41 | 110.37 | 109.62 | 1.56 |
| oBERTa$_{\text{MEDIUM}}$ 90% Quantized | 251.32 | 12.86 | 63.65 | 63.40 | 1.76 |
| oBERTa$_{\text{SMALL}}$ | 77.49 | 3.96 | 206.46 | 205.75 | 2.07 |
| oBERTa$_{\text{SMALL}}$ Quantized | 276.10 | 14.12 | 57.94 | 57.43 | 1.63 |
| oBERTa$_{\text{SMALL}}$ 90% | 281.57 | 14.40 | 56.81 | 56.73 | 0.64 |
| oBERTa$_{\text{SMALL}}$ 90% Quantized | 417.35 | 21.35 | 38.32 | 38.01 | 1.55 |

Table 39: Inference performance of the oBERTa model family using a batch size of 16, 24 cores, and a sequence length of 384

| model | Throughput (items/sec) | Speedup | Latency Mean (ms/batch) | Latency Median (ms/batch | Latency Std (ms/batch) |
|---|---|---|---|---|---|
| oBERTa$_{\text{base}}$ | 19.02 | 1.00 | 3365.11 | 3352.63 | 29.49 |
| oBERTa$_{\text{base}}$ Quantized | 84.80 | 4.46 | 754.73 | 749.38 | 18.69 |
| oBERTa$_{\text{base}}$ 90% | 72.22 | 3.80 | 886.13 | 881.75 | 10.65 |
| oBERTa$_{\text{base}}$ 90% Quantized | 140.14 | 7.37 | 456.67 | 453.59 | 11.03 |
| oBERTa$_{\text{base}}$ 95% | 88.35 | 4.64 | 724.41 | 720.43 | 10.85 |
| oBERTa$_{\text{base}}$ 95% Quantized | 162.76 | 8.56 | 393.21 | 390.45 | 12.15 |
| oBERTa$_{\text{MEDIUM}}$ | 37.94 | 1.99 | 1686.85 | 1685.03 | 8.09 |
| oBERTa$_{\text{MEDIUM}}$ Quantized | 160.48 | 8.44 | 398.80 | 396.47 | 9.27 |
| oBERTa$_{\text{MEDIUM}}$ 90% | 130.02 | 6.84 | 492.22 | 486.90 | 9.64 |
| oBERTa$_{\text{MEDIUM}}$ 90% Quantized | 259.51 | 13.64 | 246.61 | 244.54 | 7.13 |
| oBERTa$_{\text{SMALL}}$ | 75.81 | 3.99 | 844.15 | 841.30 | 8.72 |
| oBERTa$_{\text{SMALL}}$ Quantized | 267.70 | 14.07 | 239.06 | 237.86 | 7.02 |
| oBERTa$_{\text{SMALL}}$ 90% | 278.93 | 14.67 | 229.43 | 228.41 | 3.43 |
| oBERTa$_{\text{SMALL}}$ 90% Quantized | 455.71 | 23.96 | 140.43 | 139.81 | 5.40 |

Table 40: Inference performance of the oBERTa model family using a batch size of 64, 24 cores, and a sequence length of 384

| model | Throughput (items/sec) | Speedup | Latency Mean (ms/batch) | Latency Median (ms/batch | Latency Std (ms/batch) |
|---|---|---|---|---|---|
| oBERTa$_{\text{base}}$ | 4.89 | 1.00 | 204.65 | 204.93 | 1.82 |
| oBERTa$_{\text{base}}$ Quantized | 20.01 | 4.09 | 49.95 | 49.88 | 0.66 |
| oBERTa$_{\text{base}}$ 90% | 17.60 | 3.60 | 56.82 | 56.70 | 0.72 |
| oBERTa$_{\text{base}}$ 90% Quantized | 37.50 | 7.67 | 26.66 | 26.61 | 0.38 |
| oBERTa$_{\text{base}}$ 95% | 20.15 | 4.12 | 49.62 | 49.60 | 0.54 |
| oBERTa$_{\text{base}}$ 95% Quantized | 46.02 | 9.41 | 21.72 | 21.70 | 0.31 |
| oBERTa$_{\text{MEDIUM}}$ | 9.59 | 1.96 | 104.28 | 104.33 | 0.90 |
| oBERTa$_{\text{MEDIUM}}$ Quantized | 41.23 | 8.43 | 24.25 | 24.18 | 0.33 |
| oBERTa$_{\text{MEDIUM}}$ 90% | 38.30 | 7.83 | 26.10 | 26.05 | 0.41 |
| oBERTa$_{\text{MEDIUM}}$ 90% Quantized | 73.28 | 14.99 | 13.64 | 13.60 | 0.19 |
| oBERTa$_{\text{SMALL}}$ | 19.31 | 3.95 | 51.78 | 51.74 | 0.35 |
| oBERTa$_{\text{SMALL}}$ Quantized | 75.81 | 15.50 | 13.18 | 13.18 | 0.19 |
| oBERTa$_{\text{SMALL}}$ 90% | 68.70 | 14.05 | 14.55 | 14.50 | 0.20 |
| oBERTa$_{\text{SMALL}}$ 90% Quantized | 145.57 | 29.77 | 6.86 | 6.86 | 0.11 |

Table 41: Inference performance of the oBERTa model family using a batch size of 1, 4 cores, and a sequence length of 384

| model | Throughput (items/sec) | Speedup | Latency Mean (ms/batch) | Latency Median (ms/batch | Latency Std (ms/batch) |
|---|---|---|---|---|---|
| oBERTa$_{base}$ | 5.14 | 1.00 | 3113.07 | 3113.92 | 19.89 |
| oBERTa$_{base}$ Quantized | 22.14 | 4.31 | 722.72 | 719.24 | 11.40 |
| oBERTa$_{base}$ 90% | 17.15 | 3.34 | 932.97 | 931.21 | 5.76 |
| oBERTa$_{base}$ 90% Quantized | 39.03 | 7.59 | 409.90 | 408.71 | 4.64 |
| oBERTa$_{base}$ 95% | 19.80 | 3.85 | 808.16 | 806.80 | 4.15 |
| oBERTa$_{base}$ 95% Quantized | 46.54 | 9.06 | 343.75 | 342.75 | 4.12 |
| oBERTa$_{MEDIUM}$ | 10.24 | 1.99 | 1563.00 | 1557.90 | 16.53 |
| oBERTa$_{MEDIUM}$ Quantized | 42.82 | 8.33 | 373.61 | 372.88 | 4.05 |
| oBERTa$_{MEDIUM}$ 90% | 33.69 | 6.56 | 474.88 | 474.25 | 3.64 |
| oBERTa$_{MEDIUM}$ 90% Quantized | 76.10 | 14.81 | 210.24 | 209.41 | 2.45 |
| oBERTa$_{SMALL}$ | 20.41 | 3.97 | 783.81 | 782.99 | 6.59 |
| oBERTa$_{SMALL}$ Quantized | 79.57 | 15.48 | 201.07 | 200.60 | 2.12 |
| oBERTa$_{SMALL}$ 90% | 72.92 | 14.19 | 219.40 | 218.84 | 2.53 |
| oBERTa$_{SMALL}$ 90% Quantized | 139.50 | 27.14 | 114.68 | 114.45 | 1.53 |

Table 42: Inference performance of the oBERTa model family using a batch size of 16, 4 cores, and a sequence length of 384

| model | Throughput (items/sec) | Speedup | Latency Mean (ms/batch) | Latency Median (ms/batch | Latency Std (ms/batch) |
|---|---|---|---|---|---|
| oBERTa$_{base}$ | 5.06 | 1.00 | 12655.34 | 12680.81 | 57.78 |
| oBERTa$_{base}$ Quantized | 21.88 | 4.32 | 2924.89 | 2921.95 | 31.78 |
| oBERTa$_{base}$ 90% | 17.18 | 3.40 | 3724.72 | 3724.23 | 15.27 |
| oBERTa$_{base}$ 90% Quantized | 37.44 | 7.40 | 1709.44 | 1699.64 | 26.97 |
| oBERTa$_{base}$ 95% | 22.13 | 4.37 | 2892.15 | 2893.08 | 22.94 |
| oBERTa$_{base}$ 95% Quantized | 43.94 | 8.68 | 1456.53 | 1451.76 | 20.45 |
| oBERTa$_{MEDIUM}$ | 10.21 | 2.02 | 1567.70 | 1562.90 | 14.53 |
| oBERTa$_{MEDIUM}$ Quantized | 42.74 | 8.45 | 374.35 | 373.15 | 4.00 |
| oBERTa$_{MEDIUM}$ 90% | 33.99 | 6.72 | 470.67 | 469.99 | 3.58 |
| oBERTa$_{MEDIUM}$ 90% Quantized | 75.64 | 14.95 | 211.53 | 210.80 | 2.61 |
| oBERTa$_{SMALL}$ | 20.42 | 4.03 | 783.67 | 783.29 | 5.16 |
| oBERTa$_{SMALL}$ Quantized | 79.44 | 15.70 | 201.40 | 201.43 | 2.90 |
| oBERTa$_{SMALL}$ 90% | 71.50 | 14.13 | 223.77 | 223.41 | 1.78 |
| oBERTa$_{SMALL}$ 90% Quantized | 139.55 | 27.58 | 114.65 | 114.48 | 1.53 |

Table 43: Inference performance of the oBERTa model family using a batch size of 64, 4 cores, and a sequence length of 384

| Model | Throughput (items/sec) | Speedup vs BERT-Base | Speedup vs BERT-Large | Latency Mean (ms/batch) | Latency Median (ms/batch | Latency Std (ms/batch) |
|---|---|---|---|---|---|---|
| bert$_{base}$ | 4.923 | 1.00 | 5.65 | 203.1165 | 202.7077 | 1.3646 |
| bert-large | 0.8706 | 0.18 | 1.00 | 1148.6105 | 1145.145 | 9.5526 |
| oBERTa$_{base}$ | 4.89 | 0.99 | 5.61 | 204.65 | 204.93 | 1.82 |
| oBERTa$_{base}$ Quantized | 20.01 | 4.07 | 22.99 | 49.95 | 49.88 | 0.66 |
| oBERTa$_{base}$ 90% | 17.60 | 3.57 | 20.21 | 56.82 | 56.70 | 0.72 |
| oBERTa$_{base}$ 90% Quantized | 37.50 | 7.62 | 43.07 | 26.66 | 26.61 | 0.38 |
| oBERTa$_{base}$ 95% | 20.15 | 4.09 | 23.14 | 49.62 | 49.60 | 0.54 |
| oBERTa$_{base}$ 95% Quantized | 46.02 | 9.35 | 52.86 | 21.72 | 21.70 | 0.31 |
| oBERTa$_{MEDIUM}$ | 9.59 | 1.95 | 11.01 | 104.28 | 104.33 | 0.90 |
| oBERTa$_{MEDIUM}$ Quantized | 41.23 | 8.37 | 47.36 | 24.25 | 24.18 | 0.33 |
| oBERTa$_{MEDIUM}$ 90% | 38.30 | 7.78 | 43.99 | 26.10 | 26.05 | 0.41 |
| oBERTa$_{MEDIUM}$ 90% Quantized | 73.28 | 14.89 | 84.18 | 13.64 | 13.60 | 0.19 |
| oBERTa$_{SMALL}$ | 19.31 | 3.92 | 22.18 | 51.78 | 51.74 | 0.35 |
| oBERTa$_{SMALL}$ Quantized | 75.81 | 15.40 | 87.07 | 13.18 | 13.18 | 0.19 |
| oBERTa$_{SMALL}$ 90% | 68.70 | 13.95 | 78.91 | 14.55 | 14.50 | 0.20 |
| oBERTa$_{SMALL}$ 90% Quantized | 145.57 | 29.57 | 167.21 | 6.86 | 6.86 | 0.11 |
| pruneOFA-large 80% Quantized | 12.7315 | 2.59 | 14.62 | 78.5322 | 78.3961 | 0.4826 |
| prunedOFA-large 90% Quantized | 11.7265 | 2.38 | 13.47 | 85.2647 | 85.1616 | 0.4292 |
| obert-large | 0.876 | 0.18 | 1.01 | 1141.5707 | 1138.5756 | 9.0121 |
| obert-large 95% | 7.508 | 1.53 | 8.62 | 133.1785 | 132.9672 | 1.0091 |
| obert-large 95% Quantized | 16.8077 | 3.41 | 19.31 | 59.4828 | 59.322 | 0.6445 |
| pruneBERT | 17.60 | 3.57 | 20.21 | 56.82 | 56.70 | 0.72 |
| obert-large 97% | 8.0414 | 1.63 | 9.24 | 124.3431 | 124.1421 | 1.0249 |
| obert-large 97% Quantized | 15.8631 | 3.22 | 18.22 | 63.0278 | 62.9979 | 0.6018 |
| obert$_{base}$ 90% | 18.2881 | 3.71 | 21.01 | 54.6688 | 54.5896 | 0.5476 |
| obert$_{base}$ 90% Quantized | 34.2797 | 6.96 | 39.37 | 29.1616 | 29.0977 | 0.3156 |
| obert$_{base}$ 95% | 25.1818 | 5.12 | 28.92 | 39.6997 | 39.5986 | 0.5805 |
| obert$_{base}$ 95% Quantized | 40.6387 | 8.25 | 46.68 | 24.5986 | 24.5222 | 0.3231 |

Table 44: Inference performance of the other sparse models using a batch size of 1, 4 cores, and a sequence length of 384 comparing the oBERTa models to previous sparse language models such as pruneOFA (Zafrir et al., 2021) PruneBERT (Sanh et al., 2020) and oBERT (Kurtić et al., 2022)

| | | Vs. BERT-Base | | Vs. BERT-Large | |
|---|---|---|---|---|---|
| Model | F1 | Recovery | Speed up | Recovery | Speed up |
| $BERT_{base}$ | 88.55 | 100.00% | 1.00 | 97.74% | 5.65 |
| BERT-large | 90.60 | 102.32% | 0.18 | 100.00% | 1.00 |
| $oBERTa_{base}$ | 92.20 | 104.12% | 0.99 | 101.77% | 5.61 |
| $oBERTa_{base}$ Quantized | 93.18 | 105.23% | 4.07 | 102.85% | 22.99 |
| $oBERTa_{base}$ 90% | 91.00 | 102.77% | 3.57 | 100.44% | 20.21 |
| $oBERTa_{base}$ 90% Quantized | 89.46 | 101.03% | 7.62 | 98.74% | 43.07 |
| $oBERTa_{base}$ 95% | 89.84 | 101.46% | 4.09 | 99.16% | 23.14 |
| $oBERTa_{base}$ 95% Quantized | 88.40 | 99.83% | 9.35 | 97.57% | 52.86 |
| $oBERTa_{MEDIUM}$ | 90.36 | 102.04% | 1.95 | 99.74% | 11.01 |
| $oBERTa_{MEDIUM}$ Quantized | 90.37 | 102.06% | 8.37 | 99.75% | 47.36 |
| $oBERTa_{MEDIUM}$ 90% | 89.26 | 100.80% | 7.78 | 98.52% | 43.99 |
| $oBERTa_{MEDIUM}$ 90% Quantized | 86.93 | 98.17% | 14.89 | 95.95% | 84.18 |
| $oBERTa_{SMALL}$ | 84.87 | 95.84% | 3.92 | 93.68% | 22.18 |
| $oBERTa_{SMALL}$ Quantized | 84.82 | 95.79% | 15.40 | 93.62% | 87.07 |
| $oBERTa_{SMALL}$ 90% | 84.66 | 95.61% | 13.95 | 93.45% | 78.91 |
| $oBERTa_{SMALL}$ 90% Quantized | 78.71 | 88.89% | 29.57 | 86.88% | 167.21 |
| pruneOFA-large 80% Quantized | 90.30 | 101.98% | 2.59 | 99.67% | 14.62 |
| pruneOFA-large 90% Quantized | 89.96 | 101.59% | 2.38 | 99.29% | 13.47 |
| oBERT-large 95% | 90.19 | 101.85% | 1.53 | 99.55% | 1.01 |
| oBERT-large 95% Quantized | 90.21 | 101.87% | 3.41 | 99.57% | 8.62 |
| pruneBERT | 84.90 | 95.88% | 3.41 | 93.71% | 19.31 |
| oBERT-large 97% | 90.18 | 101.84% | 13.05 | 99.54% | 73.82 |
| oBERT-large 97% Quantized | 90.13 | 101.78% | 1.63 | 99.48% | 9.24 |
| $oBERT_{base}$ 90% | 88.47 | 99.91% | 3.22 | 97.65% | 18.22 |
| $oBERT_{base}$ 90% Quantized | 88.00 | 99.38% | 3.71 | 97.13% | 21.01 |
| $oBERT_{base}$ 95% | 88.19 | 99.59% | 6.96 | 97.34% | 39.37 |
| $oBERT_{base}$ 95% Quantized | 88.11 | 99.50% | 5.12 | 97.25% | 28.92 |

Table 45: Speedups of the oBERTa-family as compared to existing published sparse models as compared to the performance of $BERT_{base}$ and BERT-large. Speedup measures the reduction in latency of MS/batch.

# Quick Dense Retrievers Consume KALE: Post Training Kullback–Leibler Alignment of Embeddings for Asymmetrical dual encoders

Daniel Campos [*], Alessandro Magnani[2], and ChengXiang Zhai[1]

[1]Department of Computer Science, the University of Illinois Urbana-Champaign
[2]Walmart Labs

## Abstract

In this paper, we consider the problem of improving the inference latency of language model-based dense retrieval systems by introducing structural compression and model size asymmetry between the context and query encoders. First, we investigate the impact of pre and post-training compression on the MSMARCO, Natural Questions, TriviaQA, SQUAD, and SCIFACT, finding that asymmetry in the dual-encoders in dense retrieval can lead to improved inference efficiency. Knowing this, we introduce *Kullback–Leibler Alignment of Embeddings* (KALE), an efficient and accurate method for increasing the inference efficiency of dense retrieval methods by pruning and aligning the query encoder after training. Specifically, KALE extends traditional Knowledge Distillation after bi-encoder training, allowing for effective query encoder compression without full retraining or index generation. Using KALE and asymmetric training, we can generate models which exceed the performance of DistilBERT despite having 3x faster inference.

## 1 Introduction

A bi-encoder-based retrieval, often called dense retrieval, is a retrieval function that leverages the vector representation of queries and documents as a proxy for relevance. Using two encoders, one for the query and one for the document, the input data is mapped into a common latent space where closeness becomes a proxy for relevance.

Dense retrievers have become increasingly popular due to their ability to capture the semantic relationships between query and document terms. However, bi-encoder-based models can also be computationally expensive, particularly when dealing

* Corresponding author: dcampos3@illinois.edu

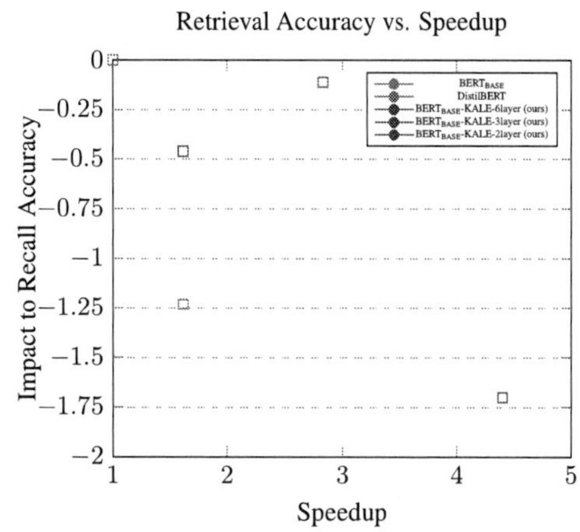


Figure 1: Using KALE and asymmetric training on the lead to when measuring QPS vs. Recall at 100 on the NQ dataset. Using Asymmetry and KALE, it is possible to 3x QPS with nearly no loss in accuracy and 4.5x with under 2% loss in accuracy. We calculate QPS as the mean number of queries per second with a batch size of 1 and a max sequence length of 32 on a T4 GPU. Impact on retrieval accuracy is measured by the relative drop in retrieval accuracy at 100

with large datasets. As a result, there has been a growing interest in methods for compressing these models to reduce their computational complexity without sacrificing performance.

While the use of smaller models (Wang et al., 2020) has provided a path to improving model performance, compression cannot be adjusted to suit varying latency needs. In other words, a model must match latency requirements before it can be experimented with. Additionally, since bi-encoders require a complete index generation to evaluate performance iteratively compressing models and



*Proceedings of The Fourth Workshop on Simple and Efficient Natural Language Processing (SustaiNLP)*, pages 59–77
July 13, 2023 

retraining them can be very expensive. Seeing the bottleneck caused by trying to train compressed models for retrieval we explore approaches to compress models after training. By doing so it becomes cheaper to evaluate the impact of compression of retrieval and generate variants of many sizes.

In this paper, we explore the role of asymmetry in the size of query and document encoders that leverage language models. Through experiments on several benchmarks, we demonstrate that our approach can significantly reduce the number of parameters in the bi-encoder model without sacrificing performance.

As shown in figure 1, the combination of asymmetric bi-encoders and post-training KALE allows for 3x more QPS than an uncompressed bi-encoder with less than 1% loss in accuracy and nearly 5x with less than 2%.

Building on the favorable implications of asymmetry for efficient inference, we introduce a compression mechanism called **K**ullback-Leibler **Al**lingment of **E**mbeddings (KALE). KALE uses an alignment of representations to compress models without requiring any form of retraining or index regeneration.

To ground our approaches, we evaluate the effectiveness of KALE and asymmetry on several benchmark datasets and compare the results to existing efficient inference approaches.

The following research questions drive our work:

- Is the performance of dense retrieval methods more driven by the query or document encoder size?
- Is it possible to compress query encoders without retraining and index regeneration?
- How can dense retrieval asymmetry and post-training alignment be leveraged to improve query encoder latency?

It is in answering these questions that we deliver the following contributions:

- We present the first robust studies on the role of document-query encoder symmetry, demonstrating that the size of the document encoder dominates performance.
- We introduce and demonstrate the effectiveness of KALE, a post-training compression and alignment approach demonstrating its effectiveness and
- We empirically demonstrate on various benchmarks how Asymmetric Compression can lead to 4.5 better QPS with 1% loss in recall accuracy at 100.

## 2 Related Work

**Transformer Based Language Models** such as BERT (Devlin et al., 2019) provide contextual language representations built on the Transformer architecture (Vaswani et al., 2017) which can be specialized and adapted for specific tasks and domains (Lee et al., 2020). Using contextual word representations, it becomes relatively easy to excel at a broad range of natural language processing tasks such as Question Answering, Text Classification, and sentiment analysis.

**Bi-Encoders**, commonly called dual-encoders or dense retrievers, decompose ranking by leveraging the inner product of query and document representations to produce a relevance score for query document pairs. While not as accurate at cross-encoders (Reimers and Gurevych, 2019), they are more efficient for inference and easier to deploy. Bi-encoder document representations are query invariant, allowing them to be pre-computed and loaded into an Approximate Nearest Neighbor (ANN) such as FAISS (Johnson et al., 2019).

At runtime, a query is an encoder into a latent space, and the $k$ documents are retrieved using a nearest neighbor algorithm such as HNSW (Malkov and Yashunin, 2016). Since the entire document index has already been created the retrieval latency is limited to a single call of the query encoder.

Bi-encoders commonly leverage LLM such as BERT (Devlin et al., 2019) to retrieve short passages of text leading to the task descriptor of Dense Passage Retrievers (DPR) (Karpukhin et al., 2020). Driven by their efficiency in deployment and relevance performance, DPR-based models have rapidly become the building blocks for systems doing product search (Magnani et al., 2022), open domain question answering (Karpukhin et al., 2020) and customer support (Mesquita et al., 2022).

**Efficient Inference** study methods and models which decrease the model execution cost while

minimizing the losses to model performance.
Knowledge Distillation (Hinton et al., 2015) is a training method where a model, called the *student*, learns to emulate a *teacher* model, which is commonly larger or better performing than the *student*.
Unstructured pruning removes individual weights or groups of weights in a model by applying a mask or setting the weight values to 0. When paired with a sparsity-aware inference engine, it is possible to gain 3-5x speedups in inference throughput with little to no loss in accuracy (Kurtić et al., 2022).
Structured pruning removes fundamental structural components in a language model, such as individual attention heads (Voita et al., 2019) or entire model layers (Sanh et al., 2019). Removing entire model layers is one of the most pervasive approaches, as latency gains are easy to realize, and pruning is straightforward.
While their training regimes may differ, models like DistilBERT (Sanh et al., 2019) and TinyBERT (Jiao et al., 2020), and MiniLM (Wang et al., 2020) leverage structural pruning as ways of generation 2-10x speedups.
Methods like quantization (Pouransari and Tuzel, 2020) (Zafrir et al., 2019), early exiting (Xin et al., 2020) or token pruning (Kim et al., 2021) have been effective in other NLP tasks. Still, our work primarily focuses on structured pruning and its relationship with asymmetry. We leave studying the impacts of asymmetry on these compression methods to future work.
**Asymmetrical deep learning** broadly refers to any non-uniformity in shape or attribute of models. Traditional modeling approaches favor uniformity as it is preferable for optimization algorithms (Mihaylova and Martins, 2019), and using models for inference should match training as closely as possible (Ranzato et al., 2015) as improvements in training loss during optimization result in improvements in model performance during inference. However, this does not account for cost or latency asymmetries during usage. Kasai et al. demonstrated how the sequence-to-sequence encoder depth dominates language model performance for machine translation (Kasai et al., 2020). Tay et al. 2021 extend this work by finding a *Deep-Narrow* which shows that for broad language modeling, it is possible to have 50% fewer parameters and a 40% faster inference with no loss in accuracy.
**Embedding Distillation** Concurrent to our work on bi-encoder compression, Kim et al. 2023 study how distillation in embeddings leads to general compression of bi-encoders and cross-encoders (Kim et al., 2023). Our work differs from theirs as we focus on the role of asymmetry between query and document encoders and how to leverage it for improved inference efficiency.

## 3 Method

The use of representation models for retrieval begins with a document space $d$ and a query space $q$ where each of which is generated by some model $m$. Models do not need to share the same initialization, shape, or size, but their representation vectors must share size without some projection. These two models learn a notion of relevance by training to minimize the distance of positive query-document pairs as shown in equation 1 where $\mathbf{x}$ is a query vector and $\mathbf{y}$ is a document vector, and $\cdot$ denotes the dot product of the vectors.

$$L = 1 - \frac{\mathbf{x} \cdot \mathbf{y}}{|\mathbf{x}||\mathbf{y}|} \quad (1)$$

The query and document encoder models are commonly initialized with a pre-trained language model such as BERT. Then, using pairs of labels for positive relevance scores for queries and documents, the models are trained to minimize the distance between queries and their relevant documents (Karpukhin et al., 2020)
While it is common practice to initialize the query encoder and document encoder with identical language models, this ignores the cost asymmetry of the usage patterns. The document encoder is usually only used once during a large-scale batch generation of the index. Index generation happens in a latency-insensitive environment and can easily leverage many GPUs and large batch sizes to improve efficiency.
The query encoder runs every time a user issues a query, which can be irregular and sporadically. The query encoder responds to each user query independently. Thus, query encoders often use a batch size of 1 and commonly leverage small inference-optimized hardware like the T4 GPU or small CPUs.

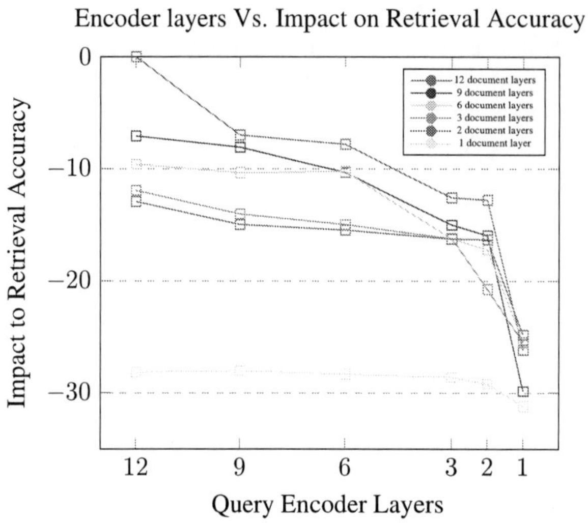


Figure 2: Measuring the impact on recall at 20 on the NQ retrieval dataset by varying the number of transformer layers for the query encoder and document encoder

Since the document encoder does not run very often, any improvement in latency produces a single fixed gain utterly dependent on the corpus size and index refresh cycle. The query encoder's user-facing nature means latency improvements occur whenever a user queries.

### 3.1 Role of model symmetry with Bi-encoders

Since the query encoder runs many times online and the document encoder runs once, offline, we question: Is there some form of asymmetry between the query encoder and the document encoder that can be exploited? Do the two encoders need to be compressed symmetrically?

To answer this question, we explore the impact on the performance of pruning the query and document encoders on the NQ passage retrieval dataset (Kwiatkowski et al., 2019). Using a BERT-base uncased model with 12 transformer encoder layers, we generate structurally pruned models with 9,6,3,2 and 1 layer. We also further pre-train the three and six-layer models using knowledge distillation, represented as $6_{KD}$ and $3_{KD}$, from a 12-layer model on the Wikipedia-book corpus similar to distilBERT (Sanh et al., 2019).

Then, using each of these seven models, we train dense retrieval models on the NQ passage retrieval dataset with variations of query and document models resulting in 72 variants. With each of these models, we generate a full index and evaluate retrieval performance on the development portion of the dataset. We do not tune any parameters to avoid overfitting and to explore asymmetry without overoptimizing. Each model's retrieval accuracy is evaluated with retrieval sets of depth 20, 100, and 200. We compare the impact of varying the encoders to the uncompressed baseline and a distilBERT model (denoted by $6_{db}$).

Looking at the impact of symmetric compression

Table 1: Impact of Structural pruning before fine-tuning on Retrieval Accuracy on NQ passage retrieval dataset

| Layers *enc* | Top 20 | Impact | Top 100 | Impact | Top 200 | Impact |
|---|---|---|---|---|---|---|
| 12 | 79.86% | 0.00% | 85.84% | 0.00% | 88.42% | 0.00% |
| $6_{db}$ | 73.88% | -7.49% | 84.74% | -1.29% | 87.26% | -1.31% |
| 9 | 73.41% | -8.08% | 83.68% | -2.51% | 86.51% | -2.16% |
| $6_{KD}$ | 75.04% | -6.04% | 85.15% | -0.80% | 87.45% | -1.10% |
| 6 | 71.69% | -10.23% | 83.30% | -2.96% | 86.04% | -2.69% |
| $3_{KD}$ | 73.32% | -8.19% | 83.43% | -2.80% | 86.20% | -2.51% |
| 3 | 66.93% | -16.20% | 80.61% | -6.09% | 84.49% | -4.45% |
| 2 | 66.87% | -16.27% | 80.42% | -6.32% | 83.85% | -5.17% |
| 1 | 54.96% | -31.18% | 71.88% | -16.26% | 76.73% | -13.22% |

as shown in table 1, we see that the impact of compression is more pronounced with a small recall set as retrieval accuracy impact at 20 is 3x that of at 200. As shown in table 1 we observe major accuracy gains by fine-tuning the pruned model with a 4% gap between 6 and $6_{KD}$ and a 8% gap between 3 and $3_{KD}$ with a 4% gap for recall at 20 on the NQ dataset.

Looking at the impact of asymmetry of the depth

of encoders as shown in table 2 and figure 2 we find there is the size of the query and document encoders cause similar impacts on retrieval accuracy. A retriever with 3 layers in the query encoder and 12 in the document encoder loses 11.9% of its retrieval accuracy and 12.55% when the sizes of the document encoder and query encoders are flipped. These asymmetric retrievers perform better than the symmetric 3-layer models, which lose 16.2% which highlights the ability to improve retrieval performance by having non-uniform compression. It is worth noting that having a larger document encoder is preferable to a larger query encoder which supports the notion that the document encoder is more important than the query encoder (Li and Lin, 2021).// Similar results can be seen with the introduction of fine-tuned three and 6-layer models as shown in table 6. Unsurprisingly, KD-optimized language models outperform non-distilled models, and any asymmetrical variant that leverages a distilled model outperforms the un-distilled variant. Without further optimization, a model with a distilled 3-layer query encoder and a 12-layer document encoder will outperform a model with symmetrical 6-layer models despite being 2x faster.

## 3.2 Inference Benchmarks

To evaluate the impact of structural pruning, we benchmark inference speeds of query encoding while varying the number of transformer layers. We perform benchmarking using an Intel Xeon Gold 6238R Processor and a T4 Nvidia GPU. For each model, we evaluate the performance on encoding 6500 queries with a batch size of one and a max context length of 32. For CPU inference, we evaluate the performance of models using the ONNX library [1], and for GPU inference, we evaluate native Pytorch inference. We repeat each run five times to ensure consistency and report the mean. Summary statistics can be found in table 3 and full results, including percentile, standard deviation, and confidence intervals, can be found in the appendix .5.

Table 2: Impact of Structural pruning before fine-tuning on Retrieval Accuracy on NQ passage retrieval dataset

| $layers_q$ | $layers_d$ | Top 20 | Impact | Top 100 | Impact | Top 200 | Impact |
|---|---|---|---|---|---|---|---|
| 12 | 12 | 79.86% | 0.00% | 85.84% | 0.00% | 88.42% | 0.00% |
| 9 | 12 | 74.27% | -7.00% | 84.40% | -1.67% | 86.95% | -1.66% |
| 6 | 12 | 73.63% | -7.80% | 84.27% | -1.83% | 86.79% | -1.85% |
| 3 | 12 | 69.83% | -12.55% | 82.58% | -3.80% | 85.35% | -3.48% |
| 2 | 12 | 69.67% | -12.76% | 82.19% | -4.25% | 84.68% | -4.23% |
| 1 | 12 | 59.00% | -26.12% | 75.37% | -12.19% | 81.00% | -8.39% |
| 12 | 9 | 74.21% | -7.07% | 84.40% | -1.67% | 87.06% | -1.53% |
| 9 | 9 | 73.41% | -8.08% | 83.68% | -2.51% | 86.51% | -2.16% |
| 6 | 9 | 71.63% | -10.30% | 83.05% | -3.25% | 85.98% | -2.76% |
| 3 | 9 | 67.89% | -14.98% | 80.94% | -5.71% | 84.79% | -4.10% |
| 2 | 9 | 67.15% | -15.92% | 80.53% | -6.19% | 83.66% | -5.39% |
| 1 | 9 | 56.04% | -29.83% | 73.35% | -14.55% | 78.12% | -11.65% |
| 12 | 6 | 72.22% | -9.57% | 83.41% | -2.83% | 85.84% | -2.91% |
| 9 | 6 | 71.61% | -10.33% | 83.30% | -2.96% | 85.93% | -2.82% |
| 6 | 6 | 71.69% | -10.23% | 83.30% | -2.96% | 86.04% | -2.69% |
| 3 | 6 | 66.93% | -16.20% | 80.28% | -6.48% | 83.96% | -5.04% |
| 2 | 6 | 66.12% | -17.20% | 80.33% | -6.42% | 83.49% | -5.58% |
| 1 | 6 | 59.53% | -25.46% | 75.37% | -12.19% | 79.83% | -9.71% |
| 12 | 3 | 70.36% | -11.90% | 81.72% | -4.80% | 84.60% | -4.32% |
| 9 | 3 | 68.67% | -14.01% | 80.47% | -6.25% | 84.46% | -4.48% |
| 6 | 3 | 67.92% | -14.95% | 80.06% | -6.74% | 83.85% | -5.17% |
| 3 | 3 | 66.93% | -16.20% | 80.61% | -6.09% | 84.49% | -4.45% |
| 2 | 3 | 63.30% | -20.74% | 78.37% | -8.71% | 83.02% | -6.11% |
| 1 | 3 | 59.53% | -25.46% | 75.68% | -11.84% | 80.08% | -9.43% |
| 12 | 2 | 69.56% | -12.90% | 81.33% | -5.25% | 84.49% | -4.45% |
| 9 | 2 | 67.92% | -14.95% | 80.75% | -5.93% | 84.32% | -4.64% |
| 6 | 2 | 67.53% | -15.43% | 80.33% | -6.42% | 83.82% | -5.20% |
| 3 | 2 | 66.90% | -16.23% | 80.36% | -6.38% | 84.24% | -4.73% |
| 2 | 2 | 66.87% | -16.27% | 80.42% | -6.32% | 83.85% | -5.17% |
| 1 | 2 | 60.06% | -24.80% | 75.29% | -12.29% | 79.75% | -9.80% |
| 12 | 1 | 57.40% | -28.13% | 73.24% | -14.68% | 78.56% | -11.15% |
| 9 | 1 | 57.51% | -27.99% | 73.24% | -14.68% | 77.87% | -11.94% |
| 6 | 1 | 57.26% | -28.30% | 73.52% | -14.35% | 78.34% | -11.40% |
| 3 | 1 | 57.04% | -28.58% | 73.93% | -13.87% | 78.39% | -11.34% |
| 2 | 1 | 56.57% | -29.17% | 73.71% | -14.13% | 77.98% | -11.81% |
| 1 | 1 | 54.96% | -31.18% | 71.88% | -16.26% | 76.73% | -13.22% |

| layers | size | compressed size | method | QPS | Speedup |
|---|---|---|---|---|---|
| 12 | 418 | 387 | GPU | 105.852 | 1.00 |
| 9 | 337 | 212 | GPU | 139.494 | 1.32 |
| 6 | 256 | 236 | GPU | 172.338 | 1.63 |
| 3 | 175 | 161 | GPU | 299.45 | 2.83 |
| 2 | 148 | 136 | GPU | 441.422 | 4.17 |
| 1 | 121 | 111 | GPU | 660.64 | 6.24 |
| 12 | 418 | 387 | CPU | 47.278 | 1.00 |
| 9 | 337 | 212 | CPU | 63.24 | 1.34 |
| 6 | 256 | 236 | CPU | 90.386 | 1.91 |
| 3 | 175 | 161 | CPU | 166.012 | 3.51 |
| 2 | 148 | 136 | CPU | 229.666 | 4.86 |
| 1 | 121 | 111 | CPU | 378.534 | 8.01 |

Table 3: Variation in model throughput according to the serving method and the number of transformer layers. Structural pruning can lead to a 6 and 8-layer performance increase on GPU and CPU and pruning a model to 3 layers allows a CPU to offer better inference performance than the GPU.

Table 4: Impact of structural pruning with and without KALE on Accuracy at 100 across various datasets.

| Layers | KALE | NQ | TriviaQA | MSMARCO | SCIFACT | SQUAD |
|---|---|---|---|---|---|---|
| 12 | N/A | 85.84% | 85.84% | 88.77% | 90.70% | 77.16% |
| 9 | N | 79.97% | 79.97% | 82.01% | 71.07% | 71.38% |
| 9 | Y | 84.90% | 84.90% | 86.16% | 84.87% | 73.54% |
| 6 | N | 68.20% | 68.20% | 72.68% | 22.98% | 59.97% |
| 6 | Y | 83.68% | 83.68% | 84.68% | 85.13% | 69.87% |
| 3 | N | 43.88% | 43.88% | 11.39% | 40.80% | 34.42% |
| 3 | Y | 81.14% | 81.14% | 82.11% | 82.57% | 64.37% |
| 2 | N | 46.90% | 46.90% | 31.46% | 42.66% | 37.01% |
| 2 | Y | 81.94% | 81.94% | 81.96% | 82.57% | 63.72% |
| 1 | N | 12.22% | 12.22% | 0.00% | 3.17% | 11.66% |
| 1 | Y | 71.33% | 71.33% | 54.36% | 66.83% | 51.39% |

## 4 KL Alignment of Embeddings

While training asymmetric models can improve latency, it requires novel training regimes and experimentation, and existing workloads need to regenerate their entire index to take advantage of any inference speedups. Generation of the passage index can take longer than model training (Karpukhin et al., 2020), which makes regenerating a new index and retraining a model to meet changing latency requirements an inefficient experimentation pathway.

Moreover, coupling asymmetry into training makes generating query encoder variants more difficult, as each encoder requires its own index and document encoder.

Motivated by this bottleneck, we introduce **K**ullback-Leibler **Al**lingment of **E**mbeddings (KALE), a simple method of improving bi-encoder latency by aligning the embeddings of compressed models. KALE is applied after model training and leverages large batch sizes to make compression **computationally inexpensive** and **independent of training**. A single V100 GPU KALE can produce a compressed query encoder in less than 5 minutes.

First, a bi-encoder model trains with separate query and document encoders. When training is complete, the document encoder, $e_{document}$, is frozen, and using the query encoder, $e_q$, a structurally pruned copy, $e_{q'}$, is made. Then, using a sample of queries, the $e_{q'}$ model is fine-tuned to minimize the KL divergence of their query representations as shown in equation 2. While the KL divergence is a measure of differences in probability distributions it has been applied successfully for representation alignment (Kim et al., 2023). To leverage it, we treat each of the representation vectors as a probability over a set of logits.

$$D_{\mathrm{KL}}(e_{q'} \parallel e_q) = \sum_{x \in \mathcal{X}} e_{q'}(x) \log \left( \frac{e_{q'}(x)}{e_q(x)} \right). \quad (2)$$

We explored the use of various distance functions such as cosine similarity, Manhattan distance, and the KL divergence but found little sensitivity in any metric besides KL divergence. We believe this is due to us freezing the document representations, and as a result, cosine distance allows the query embeddings to *drift* more than probability distribution matching methods. To explore this further, we experiment with tuning the temperature for the KL divergence and add a loss scaling factor but find a temperature of one and a scaling factor of ten to be most optimal.

Additionally, we explored using a contrastive loss with random negative and hard negatives mined from the trained encoder but found no positive impact for either method. We leave further exploration of training objective improvement for future work.

### 4.1 Experimental Results

We evaluate the effectiveness of KALE by taking uncompressed $\text{BERT}_{\text{BASE}}$ models and pruning them with and without KALE on a variety of well-established passage retrieval benchmarks. First, models are trained, and indexes are generated using un-optimized $\text{BERT}_{\text{BASE}}$ models. Next, the document encoders are frozen, and the query encoders are structurally pruned to have 9,6,3,2 or 1 transformer layer. Finally, query encoders are aligned using KALE, and we compare the performance of compressed models by comparing the impact on retrieval accuracy at 20,100, and 200.

To aid reproducibility, each model is trained using the Tevatron (Gao et al., 2022) [2] library, which makes use of hugginface's transformers to provide a simple interface for exploring neural ranking models. Our experiments focus on the plain $\text{BERT}_{\text{BASE}}$-uncased 12-layer transformer model. While never more capable models exist, the unaltered BERT model is widely used in production workloads, which our experiments seek to emulate. Our work aims not to produce the highest possible retrieval accuracy for a dense encoder. Instead, our goal is to find the role of asymmetry in bi-encoder models. As a result, we leverage the well-established parameters in all of our experiments without using an advanced methodology like contrastive or curriculum learning.

There are fewer parameters for using KALE, and we deliberately do not optimize on anything but the loss between $e_q$ and $e_{q'}$. In general, higher degrees of pruning require longer training with smaller batches.

[1] https://onnx.ai/

[2] https://github.com/texttron/tevatron

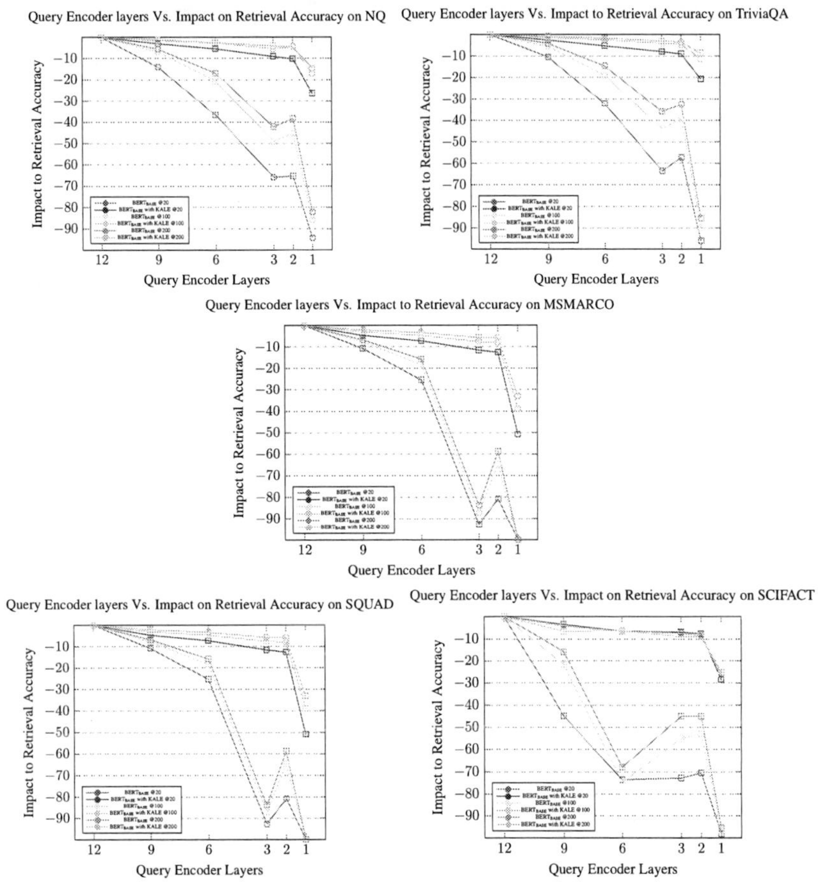


Figure 3: Impact of structural pruning with and without KALE on the NQ, MSMARCO, TriviaQA, SciFACT, and SQuAD Passage Retrieval dataset with the recall set sizes of 20,100, and 200. Across datasets, we see a consistent trend where KALE is effective but most effective when the network is heavily pruned and recall set sizes are small. When the model is pruned to 2 or 1 layer with a recall set size of 20, the difference between using KALE or not can be up to 10 times the loss in recall accuracy

**Datasets** We use a wide variety of standard dense retrieval benchmarks, including MSMARCO V1.1 [3] (Campos et al., 2016), NQ Passage Ranking [4] (Kwiatkowski et al., 2019), SciFact Passage Ranking [5] (Wadden et al., 2020), TriviaQA passage Ranking [6] (Joshi et al., 2017), and SQUAD Passage Ranking [7] (Rajpurkar et al., 2016).
For each dataset, we evaluate performance by measuring the recall accuracy with retrieval depths of 20,100, and 200. Additionally, for the MSMARCO dataset, we also report MRR@10; for Scifact, we also report NDCG @10 and RR@10.
**Computational Experiments** Our experimentation on fine-tuning our compressed models uses a 16 GB V100 GPU. Experiments in bi-encoder model training leverage 1 V100 for the MS-MARCO and 4 for each other experiment. Due to the vast number of models and datasets we train on, each experiment happens with the same fixed seed.

### 4.2 Evaluating KALE

We compare the performance of using KALE for post-training compression in figure 3 across the five datasets and see a fairly consistent trend. When the recall set is small and the query encoders are pruned to a high degree, the impact of KALE is most visible, often driving over 50 improvements in retrieval accuracy. Additionally, using KALE allows the models to have a steady and gradual drop in recall accuracy relative to speedup instead of the sharp drop shown by the regular usage of structural pruning. Without KALE, post-training compression causes a 20-50% loss in retrieval accuracy. With the use of KALE, these losses are cut to 1-10%. In practice, this allows using one or 2-layer encoder models running with CPU-based inference with minor impacts on accuracy.

We also notice a surprising performance improvement between 3 and 2-layer query encoders with and without KALE. We believe this shows the phenomena studied elsewhere: the first and last layers do most of the work (Oh et al., 2022).

| Model | Layers | KALE | MSMARCO | NQ | TriviaQA | SQUAD | SCIFACTS |
|---|---|---|---|---|---|---|---|
| $BERT_{BASE}$ | 12 | N | 88.77% | 85.84% | 85.03% | 77.16% | 90.70% |
| $BERT_{BASE}$ | 6 | Y | 84.68% | 83.68% | 83.01% | 69.87% | 85.13% |
| $6_{kd} - 6_{kd}$ | 6 | N | 88.19% | 85.15% | 84.96% | 71.94% | 91.23% |
| $6_{db} - 6_{db}$ | 6 | N | 88.35% | 84.74% | 84.83% | 71.69% | 89.37% |
| $6_{kd} - 3_{kd}$ | 6 | N | 86.50% | 85.37% | 84.04% | 70.89% | 89.20% |
| $BERT_{BASE}$ | 3 | Y | 82.11% | 81.14% | 81.67% | 64.37% | 82.57% |
| $3_{kd} - 3_{kd}$ | 3 | N | 86.13% | 83.66% | 84.11% | 71.98% | 89.40% |
| $3_{kd} - 6_{kd}$ | 3 | N | 84.79% | 85.76% | 83.91% | 67.85% | 88.63% |
| $6_{kd} - 3_{kd}$ | 3 | Y | 82.95% | 83.43% | 82.33% | 63.77% | 90.37% |
| $6_{kd} - 6_{kd}$ | 3 | Y | 86.75% | 80.78% | 83.48% | 64.14% | 91.70% |
| $BERT_{BASE}$ | 2 | Y | 81.96% | 81.94% | 81.23% | 67.00% | 82.57% |
| $3_{kd} - 3_{kd}$ | 2 | Y | 84.23% | 82.71% | 83.02% | 67.02% | 91.33% |
| $3_{kd} - 6_{kd}$ | 2 | Y | 85.57% | 84.27% | 82.90% | 62.75% | 88.37% |
| $6_{kd} - 3_{kd}$ | 2 | Y | 83.24% | 83.02% | 82.13% | 62.52% | 89.93% |
| $6_{kd} - 6_{kd}$ | 2 | Y | 85.77% | 80.39% | 83.32% | 52.74% | 91.93% |
| $BERT_{BASE}$ | 1 | Y | 48.05% | 71.33% | 75.40% | 51.39% | 66.83% |
| $3_{kd} - 3_{kd}$ | 1 | Y | 66.69% | 77.17% | 80.82% | 55.62% | 76.03% |
| $3_{kd} - 6_{kd}$ | 1 | Y | 72.13% | 79.81% | 80.23% | 52.26% | 78.67% |
| $6_{kd} - 3_{kd}$ | 1 | Y | 71.26% | 76.57% | 78.65% | 50.88% | 77.07% |
| $6_{kd} - 6_{kd}$ | 1 | Y | 70.70% | 74.71% | 80.31% | 52.74% | 77.89% |

Table 5: Impact of model asymmetry and use of KALE for structural pruning on the Retrieval at 100 accuracies across various datasets. Layers refer to the number of transformer encoder layers in the query encoder.

### 4.3 Aiding Asymmetry with KALE

Seeking to optimize compression further, we combine KALE with asymmetrical finetuning and evaluate the results similarly to our earlier experiments. Results on the impact of KALE and asymmetry on the five datasets on the recall accuracy at 100 can be found in table 5 where $3_{kd} - 6_{kd}$ denotes a three-layer query encoder and six-layer document encoder, $3_{kd} - 3_{kd}$ denotes dual three layer encoders. Full results and metrics for each task can be found in the appendix section .4.

First, it is immediately observable that post-training compression via KALE performs worse than models natively designed for that size. We believe this is due to the convergence of the KALE models to have *some distance* from the uncompressed model because of dropout. We experimented with not using dropout in KALE, but model performance quickly suffered.
Looking at the best retrieval accuracy vs. the model speedups shown in figure 4, we can see a substantial variation in the impact of compression across datasets. In tasks like SCIfacts, it is possible to get over 4x speedup while improving accuracy, while on tasks like SQuAD, even minor speedups lead to major losses in accuracy. We believe this variation is driven by the relative difficulty of each dataset, where easier tasks are more compressible than harder tasks.
We believe these variations in results highlight the utility of post-training compression methods like KALE. Given the task variability in the impact of

[3]https://huggingface.co/datasets/Tevatron/msmarco-passage

[4]https://huggingface.co/datasets/Tevatron/wikipedia-nq

[5]https://huggingface.co/datasets/Tevatron/scifact

[6]https://huggingface.co/datasets/Tevatron/wikipedia-trivia

[7]https://huggingface.co/datasets/Tevatron/wikipedia-squad

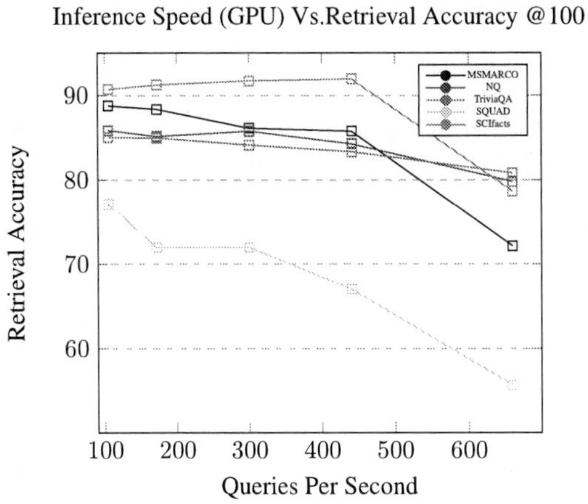


Figure 4: The impact on retrieval accuracy of the best combinations of asymmetrical training and KALE across the NQ, MSMARCO, TriviaQA, SQUAD, and SCIfacts retrieval datasets

compression, iteration speed and cost are essential to effectively tuning model inference speed and accuracy.

## 5 Limitations

While our work makes a broad study on how to improve model efficiency our scope is limited. Our work is limited to the usage of BERT-base and it is not clear how our compression approaches scale to more varied architectures like the sequence-to-sequence models used by DocT5 (Lee et al., 2022) or more optimized models like RoBERTa (Liu et al., 2019) or compressed models like MiniLM (Wang et al., 2020).

## 6 Conclusion and Future Work

In this work, we have demonstrated how the use of asymmetry between the query and document encoders in bi-encoder models can be leveraged for improved inference efficiencies across CPUs and GPUs. Using our post-training compression framework, KALE, we can compress models up to 6x with little loss in accuracy. Compressing models without regenerating the document index or the document encoder makes it practical to have many query encoders tailored to each use case's latency needs.

In the future, we wish to study how asymmetry in retrieval can be implemented with models which are widely different and may have different hidden sizes, such as using MiniLM for the query model and RoBERTA-Large for the document model.

## References

Daniel Fernando Campos, Tri Nguyen, Mir Rosenberg, Xia Song, Jianfeng Gao, Saurabh Tiwary, Rangan Majumder, Li Deng, and Bhaskar Mitra. 2016. Ms marco: A human generated machine reading comprehension dataset. *ArXiv*, abs/1611.09268.

J. Devlin, Ming-Wei Chang, Kenton Lee, and Kristina Toutanova. 2019. Bert: Pre-training of deep bidirectional transformers for language understanding. In *NAACL*.

Luyu Gao, Xueguang Ma, Jimmy J. Lin, and Jamie Callan. 2022. Tevatron: An efficient and flexible toolkit for dense retrieval. *ArXiv*, abs/2203.05765.

Geoffrey E. Hinton, Oriol Vinyals, and J. Dean. 2015. Distilling the knowledge in a neural network. *ArXiv*, abs/1503.02531.

Xiaoqi Jiao, Yichun Yin, Lifeng Shang, Xin Jiang, Xiao Chen, Linlin Li, Fang Wang, and Qun Liu. 2020. Tinybert: Distilling bert for natural language understanding. *ArXiv*, abs/1909.10351.

Jeff Johnson, Matthijs Douze, and Hervé Jégou. 2019. Billion-scale similarity search with GPUs. *IEEE Transactions on Big Data*, 7(3):535–547.

Mandar Joshi, Eunsol Choi, Daniel S. Weld, and Luke Zettlemoyer. 2017. Triviaqa: A large scale distantly supervised challenge dataset for reading comprehension. In *ACL*.

Vladimir Karpukhin, Barlas Oğuz, Sewon Min, Patrick Lewis, Ledell Yu Wu, Sergey Edunov, Danqi Chen, and Wen tau Yih. 2020. Dense passage retrieval for open-domain question answering. *ArXiv*, abs/2004.04906.

Jungo Kasai, Nikolaos Pappas, Hao Peng, James Cross, and Noah A. Smith. 2020. Deep encoder, shallow decoder: Reevaluating non-autoregressive machine translation. In *International Conference on Learning Representations*.

Sehoon Kim, Sheng Shen, David Thorsley, Amir Gholami, Joseph Hassoun, and Kurt Keutzer. 2021. Learned token pruning for transformers. *Proceedings of the 28th ACM SIGKDD Conference on Knowledge Discovery and Data Mining*.

Seungyeon Kim, Ankit Singh Rawat, Manzil Zaheer, Sadeep Jayasumana, Veeranjaneyulu Sadhanala, Wittawat Jitkrittum, Aditya Krishna Menon, Rob Fergus, and Surinder Kumar. 2023. Embeddistill: A geometric knowledge distillation for information retrieval. *ArXiv*, abs/2301.12005.

Eldar Kurtić, Daniel Fernando Campos, Tuan Nguyen, Elias Frantar, Mark Kurtz, Ben Fineran, Michael Goin, and Dan Alistarh. 2022. The optimal bert surgeon: Scalable and accurate second-order pruning for large language models. *ArXiv*, abs/2203.07259.

Tom Kwiatkowski, Jennimaria Palomaki, Olivia Redfield, Michael Collins, Ankur P. Parikh, Chris Alberti, Danielle Epstein, Illia Polosukhin, Jacob Devlin, Kenton Lee, Kristina Toutanova, Llion Jones, Matthew Kelcey, Ming-Wei Chang, Andrew M. Dai, Jakob Uszkoreit, Quoc V. Le, and Slav Petrov. 2019. Natural questions: A benchmark for question answering research. *Transactions of the Association for Computational Linguistics*, 7:453–466.

Chia-Hsuan Lee, Aditya Siddhant, Viresh Ratnakar, and Melvin Johnson. 2022. DOCmT5: Document-level pretraining of multilingual language models. In *Findings of the Association for Computational Linguistics: NAACL 2022*, pages 425–437, Seattle, United States. Association for Computational Linguistics.

Jinhyuk Lee, Wonjin Yoon, Sungdong Kim, Donghyeon Kim, Sunkyu Kim, Chan Ho So, and Jaewoo Kang. 2020. Biobert: a pre-trained biomedical language representation model for biomedical text mining. *Bioinformatics*, 36:1234–1240.

Minghan Li and Jimmy J. Lin. 2021. Encoder adaptation of dense passage retrieval for open-domain question answering. *ArXiv*, abs/2110.01599.

Yinhan Liu, Myle Ott, Naman Goyal, Jingfei Du, Mandar Joshi, Danqi Chen, Omer Levy, Mike Lewis, Luke Zettlemoyer, and Veselin Stoyanov. 2019. Roberta: A robustly optimized bert pretraining approach. *ArXiv*, abs/1907.11692.

Alessandro Magnani, Feng Liu, Suthee Chaidaroon, Sachin Yadav, Praveen Reddy Suram, Ajit Puthenputhussery, Sijie Chen, Min Xie, Anirudh Kashi, Tony Lee, and Ciya Liao. 2022. Semantic retrieval at walmart. *Proceedings of the 28th ACM SIGKDD Conference on Knowledge Discovery and Data Mining*.

Yu A. Malkov and Dmitry A. Yashunin. 2016. Efficient and robust approximate nearest neighbor search using hierarchical navigable small world graphs. *IEEE Transactions on Pattern Analysis and Machine Intelligence*, 42:824–836.

Tiago Mesquita, Bruno Martins, and Mariana Almeida. 2022. Dense template retrieval for customer support. In *COLING*.

Tsvetomila Mihaylova and André F. T. Martins. 2019. Scheduled sampling for transformers. *ArXiv*, abs/1906.07651.

Dongsuk Oh, Yejin Kim, Hodong Lee, Huimin Huang, and Heu-Jeoung Lim. 2022. Don't judge a language model by its last layer: Contrastive learning with layer-wise attention pooling. *ArXiv*, abs/2209.05972.

Hadi Pouransari and Oncel Tuzel. 2020. Least squares binary quantization of neural networks. *2020 IEEE/CVF Conference on Computer Vision and Pattern Recognition Workshops (CVPRW)*, pages 2986–2996.

Pranav Rajpurkar, Jian Zhang, Konstantin Lopyrev, and Percy Liang. 2016. Squad: 100, 000+ questions for machine comprehension of text. In *EMNLP*.

Marc'Aurelio Ranzato, Sumit Chopra, Michael Auli, and Wojciech Zaremba. 2015. Sequence level training with recurrent neural networks. *CoRR*, abs/1511.06732.

Nils Reimers and Iryna Gurevych. 2019. Sentence-bert: Sentence embeddings using siamese bert-networks. *ArXiv*, abs/1908.10084.

Victor Sanh, Lysandre Debut, Julien Chaumond, and Thomas Wolf. 2019. Distilbert, a distilled version of bert: smaller, faster, cheaper and lighter. *arXiv preprint arXiv:1910.01108*.

Victor Sanh, Thomas Wolf, and Alexander M. Rush. 2020. Movement pruning: Adaptive sparsity by fine-tuning. *ArXiv*, abs/2005.07683.

Ashish Vaswani, Noam M. Shazeer, Niki Parmar, Jakob Uszkoreit, Llion Jones, Aidan N. Gomez, Lukasz Kaiser, and Illia Polosukhin. 2017. Attention is all you need. *ArXiv*, abs/1706.03762.

Elena Voita, David Talbot, F. Moiseev, Rico Sennrich, and Ivan Titov. 2019. Analyzing multi-head self-attention: Specialized heads do the heavy lifting, the rest can be pruned. In *ACL*.

David Wadden, Shanchuan Lin, Kyle Lo, Lucy Lu Wang, Madeleine van Zuylen, Arman Cohan, and Hannaneh Hajishirzi. 2020. Fact or fiction: Verifying scientific claims. In *EMNLP*.

Wenhui Wang, Furu Wei, Li Dong, Hangbo Bao, Nan Yang, and Ming Zhou. 2020. Minilm: Deep self-attention distillation for task-agnostic compression of pre-trained transformers. *arXiv preprint arXiv:2002.10957*.

Ji Xin, Raphael Tang, Jaejun Lee, Yaoliang Yu, and Jimmy J. Lin. 2020. Deebert: Dynamic early exiting for accelerating bert inference. In *ACL*.

Ofir Zafrir, Guy Boudoukh, Peter Izsak, and Moshe Wasserblat. 2019. Q8bert: Quantized 8bit bert. *2019 Fifth Workshop on Energy Efficient Machine Learning and Cognitive Computing - NeurIPS Edition (EMC2-NIPS)*, pages 36–39.

## .1 Asymmetrical Dense Retrieval

the impact of structural pruning with asymmetrical dense retrieval can be found in table 6. Similar to other works studying the use of knowledge distillation found (Sanh et al., 2020), the use of distillation improves performance by a non-negligible level.

Table 6: Impact of Structural pruning with knowledge distilled variants before fine-tuning on Retrieval Accuracy on NQ passage retrieval dataset

| $layers_q$ | $layers_d$ | Top 20 | Impact | Top 100 | Impact | Top 200 | Impact |
|---|---|---|---|---|---|---|---|
| 12 | 12 | 79.86% | 0.00% | 85.84% | 0.00% | 88.42% | 0.00% |
| $6_{distilbert}$ | $6_{distilbert}$ | 73.88% | -7.49% | 84.74% | -1.29% | 87.26% | -1.31% |
| $6_{KD}$ | 12 | 73.99% | -7.35% | 84.32% | -1.77% | 86.65% | -2.00% |
| $6_{KD}$ | 9 | 71.63% | -10.30% | 83.16% | -3.12% | 85.82% | -2.94% |
| $6_{KD}$ | 6 | 71.00% | -11.10% | 82.35% | -4.06% | 85.48% | -3.32% |
| $6_{KD}$ | 3 | 68.42% | -14.32% | 80.94% | -5.71% | 84.24% | -4.73% |
| $6_{KD}$ | 2 | 68.39% | -14.36% | 80.58% | -6.13% | 84.02% | -4.98% |
| $6_{KD}$ | 1 | 56.62% | -29.10% | 72.24% | -15.84% | 77.81% | -12.00% |
| $3_{KD}$ | 12 | 71.72% | -10.20% | 83.21% | -3.06% | 85.90% | -2.85% |
| $3_{KD}$ | 9 | 68.95% | -13.66% | 81.75% | -4.77% | 84.79% | -4.10% |
| $3_{KD}$ | 6 | 68.09% | -14.74% | 81.52% | -5.03% | 84.76% | -4.13% |
| $3_{KD}$ | 3 | 65.84% | -17.55% | 79.58% | -7.29% | 83.41% | -5.67% |
| $3_{KD}$ | 2 | 66.81% | -16.34% | 79.50% | -7.38% | 82.71% | -6.45% |
| $3_{KD}$ | 1 | 54.46% | -31.81% | 71.44% | -16.77% | 76.59% | -13.38% |
| 12 | $6_{KD}$ | 78.78% | -1.35% | 85.84% | 0.01% | 87.45% | -1.10% |
| 9 | $6_{KD}$ | 77.26% | -3.26% | 85.18% | -0.77% | 87.34% | -1.22% |
| 6 | $6_{KD}$ | 76.45% | -4.26% | 84.96% | -1.03% | 87.06% | -1.53% |
| $6_{KD}$ | $6_{KD}$ | 75.04% | -6.03% | 85.15% | -0.80% | 87.45% | -1.10% |
| 3 | $6_{KD}$ | 74.49% | -6.73% | 84.24% | -1.87% | 86.54% | -2.13% |
| $3_{KD}$ | $6_{KD}$ | 77.01% | -3.57% | 85.76% | -0.09% | 87.42% | -1.13% |
| 2 | $6_{KD}$ | 74.43% | -6.80% | 83.68% | -2.51% | 86.32% | -2.38% |
| 1 | $6_{KD}$ | 68.09% | -14.74% | 79.22% | -7.71% | 83.19% | -5.92% |
| 12 | $3_{KD}$ | 76.45% | -4.26% | 84.49% | -1.58% | 86.70% | -1.94% |
| 9 | $3_{KD}$ | 76.12% | -4.68% | 84.29% | -1.80% | 86.26% | -2.44% |
| 6 | $3_{KD}$ | 75.15% | -5.89% | 83.43% | -2.80% | 86.45% | -2.22% |
| $6_{KD}$ | $3_{KD}$ | 77.40% | -3.09% | 85.37% | -0.54% | 87.48% | -1.06% |
| $3_{KD}$ | $3_{KD}$ | 73.32% | -8.18% | 83.43% | -2.80% | 86.20% | -2.51% |
| 3 | $3_{KD}$ | 71.88% | -9.99% | 83.66% | -2.54% | 86.37% | -2.32% |
| 2 | $3_{KD}$ | 72.22% | -9.56% | 81.93% | -4.55% | 85.08% | -3.77% |
| 1 | $3_{KD}$ | 67.31% | -15.71% | 79.25% | -7.67% | 82.77% | -6.39% |

## .2 Dense Retrieval and KALE Hyperparameters

Our experiments focus on minimal hyperparameter optimization. For training of the dense retrievers, we use the datasets described in 7 where the shorter training lengths and smaller batch sizes correspond to MSMARCO while the other datasets leverage the longer and larger training. For the use of KALE we perform task-specific grid search using the parameters described by 8.

## .3 KALE

As shown in table 9, we explore the impact of KALE for the NQ dataset, in table 10, we explore the impact on TriviaQA, in table 11, we evaluate

| Parameter | Possible Values |
|---|---|
| Training Length | 3,40 Epochs |
| Initial learning rate | 1e-5, 5e-5, 5e-6 |
| Learning rate schedule | Linear |
| Batch size | 8,128, |
| Negative Passages | 1,8 |

Table 7: Hyperparmaters used to train bi-encoder models for retrieval

| Parameter | Possible Values |
|---|---|
| Training Length | 1,10,100 Epochs |
| Initial learning rate | 5e-5, 5e-4, 5e-6 |
| Learning rate schedule | constant |
| Batch size | 4,64,256 |
| Loss Temperature | 1, 10 |

Table 8: Hyperparmaters used by KALE for aligning the embeddings of a pruned model with its uncompressed target.

the MSARCO passage retrieval, in table 12 we explore Scifacts, and in table 13 we explore SQUAD. The impact of pruning and KALE is fairly consistent across datasets, but there are larger losses on some smaller datasets, such as SCIfacts and SQUAD.

## .4 KALE and Asymmetric Training

Building on the impact of asymmetry and KALE, we explore comparing them across various datasets as shown in 14, 15,16, 17, 18.

## .5 Inference Benchmarks

Evaluation of inference on GPU can be found in 25,26,27,28 ,29,30 while CPU results can be found in 19, 20, 21, 22, 23, 24.

| Layers | KALE | Top 20 | Impact | Top 100 | Impact | Top 200 | Impact |
|---|---|---|---|---|---|---|---|
| 12 | N/A | 79.86% | 0.00% | 85.84% | 0.00% | 88.42% | 0.00% |
| 9 | N | 68.70% | -13.97% | 79.97% | -6.84% | 83.55% | -5.51% |
| 9 | Y | 77.40% | -3.08% | 84.90% | -1.10% | 87.04% | -1.56% |
| 6 | N | 50.69% | -36.53% | 68.20% | -20.55% | 73.52% | -16.85% |
| 6 | Y | 75.51% | -5.45% | 83.68% | -2.52% | 86.18% | -2.53% |
| 3 | N | 27.34% | -65.77% | 43.88% | -48.88% | 51.19% | -42.11% |
| 3 | Y | 72.69% | -8.98% | 81.14% | -5.48% | 84.76% | -4.14% |
| 2 | N | 27.81% | -65.18% | 46.90% | -45.36% | 54.54% | -38.32% |
| 2 | Y | 71.83% | -10.06% | 81.94% | -4.54% | 84.54% | -4.39% |
| 1 | N | 4.57% | -94.28% | 12.22% | -85.76% | 15.87% | -82.05% |
| 1 | Y | 58.86% | -26.30% | 71.33% | -16.90% | 75.65% | -14.44% |

Table 9: Impact of structural pruning with and without KALE on the NQ retrieval dataset

| Layers | KALE | Top 20 | Impact | Top 100 | Impact | Top 200 | Impact |
|---|---|---|---|---|---|---|---|
| 12 | N/A | 79.43% | 0.00% | 85.84% | 0.00% | 86.63% | 0.00% |
| 9 | N | 71.16% | -10.41% | 79.97% | -5.35% | 83.13% | -4.04% |
| 9 | Y | 77.46% | -2.48% | 84.90% | -1.28% | 85.95% | -0.78% |
| 6 | N | 53.98% | -32.04% | 68.20% | -18.91% | 74.05% | -14.52% |
| 6 | Y | 75.37% | -5.11% | 83.68% | -2.38% | 85.25% | -1.59% |
| 3 | N | 28.99% | -63.50% | 43.88% | -43.84% | 55.62% | -35.80% |
| 3 | Y | 73.17% | -7.88% | 81.14% | -3.95% | 84.04% | -2.99% |
| 2 | N | 33.98% | -57.22% | 46.90% | -39.29% | 58.52% | -32.45% |
| 2 | Y | 72.39% | -8.86% | 81.94% | -4.47% | 83.64% | -3.45% |
| 1 | N | 3.15% | -96.03% | 12.22% | -90.02% | 12.49% | -85.58% |
| 1 | Y | 63.04% | -20.63% | 71.33% | -11.33% | 79.23% | -8.54% |

Table 10: Impact of structural pruning with and without KALE on the TriviaQA retrieval dataset

| Layers | KALE | MRR@10 | Impact | Top 20 | Impact | Top 100 | Impact | Top 200 | Impact |
|---|---|---|---|---|---|---|---|---|---|
| 12 | N/A | 32.47% | 0.00% | 70.47% | 0.00% | 88.77% | 0.00% | 93.84% | 0.00% |
| 9 | N | 27.68% | -14.74% | 62.97% | -10.65% | 82.01% | -7.62% | 87.62% | -6.63% |
| 9 | Y | 30.38% | -6.43% | 67.21% | -4.64% | 86.16% | -2.94% | 91.85% | -2.12% |
| 6 | N | 20.86% | -35.75% | 52.66% | -25.27% | 72.68% | -18.12% | 79.20% | -15.60% |
| 6 | Y | 28.71% | -11.57% | 65.44% | -7.14% | 84.68% | -4.60% | 90.74% | -3.30% |
| 3 | N | 1.49% | -95.42% | 5.10% | -92.76% | 11.39% | -87.17% | 15.16% | -83.85% |
| 3 | Y | 26.56% | -18.19% | 62.36% | -11.51% | 82.11% | -7.50% | 88.51% | -5.68% |
| 2 | N | 3.48% | -89.28% | 13.55% | -80.77% | 31.46% | -64.56% | 38.71% | -58.75% |
| 2 | Y | 26.10% | -19.61% | 61.68% | -12.48% | 81.96% | -7.67% | 88.41% | -5.79% |
| 1 | N | 0.00% | -100.00% | 0.00% | -100.00% | 0.00% | -100.00% | 0.00% | -100.00% |
| 1 | Y | 13.16% | -59.47% | 34.64% | -50.84% | 54.36% | -38.77% | 62.82% | -33.05% |

Table 11: Impact of structural pruning with and without KALE on the MSMARCO retrieval dataset

| Layers | KALE | RR@10 | Impact | recall 10 | Impact | NDCG@10 | Impact | Top 20 | Impact | Top 100 | Impact | Top 200 | Impact |
|---|---|---|---|---|---|---|---|---|---|---|---|---|---|
| 12 | N/A | 59.11% | 0.00% | 78.71% | 0.00% | 62.55% | 0.00% | 82.38% | 0.00% | 90.70% | 0.00% | 93.77% | 0.00% |
| 9 | N | 25.30% | -57.20% | 39.66% | -49.61% | 27.46% | -56.10% | 45.43% | -44.85% | 71.07% | -21.64% | 79.03% | -15.72% |
| 9 | Y | 59.76% | 1.10% | 74.86% | -4.89% | 62.26% | -0.46% | 79.63% | -3.34% | 84.87% | -6.43% | 89.90% | -4.13% |
| 6 | N | 8.67% | -85.33% | 15.06% | -80.87% | 9.16% | -85.36% | 21.75% | -73.60% | 22.98% | -74.66% | 30.17$ | -67.83% |
| 6 | Y | 54.99% | -6.97% | 72.53% | -7.85% | 58.22% | -6.92% | 77.07% | -6.45% | 85.13% | -6.14% | 87.70% | -6.47% |
| 3 | N | 9.00% | -84.77% | 16.00% | -79.67% | 9.72% | -84.46% | 22.40% | -72.81% | 40.80% | -55.02% | 51.56% | -45.01% |
| 3 | Y | 55.18% | -6.65% | 77.22% | -1.89% | 58.30% | -6.79% | 76.73% | -6.86% | 82.57% | -8.96% | 86.90% | -7.33% |
| 2 | N | 9.65% | -83.67% | 16.93% | -78.49% | 10.39% | -83.39% | 24.26% | -70.55% | 42.66% | -52.97% | 51.49% | -45.09% |
| 2 | Y | 54.45% | -7.88% | 71.72% | -8.88% | 57.71% | -7.74% | 76.07% | -7.66% | 82.57% | -8.96% | 85.90% | -8.39% |
| 1 | N | 0.30% | -99.49% | 13.30% | -83.10% | 0.49% | -99.22% | 1.50% | -98.18% | 3.17% | -96.50% | 4.23% | -95.49% |
| 1 | Y | 40.52% | -31.45% | 55.25% | -29.81% | 43.23% | -30.89% | 59.00% | -28.38% | 66.83% | -26.32% | 70.22% | -25.11% |

Table 12: Impact of structural pruning with and without KALE on the SCIFACTS retrieval dataset

| Layers | KALE | Top 20 | Impact | Top 100 | Impact | Top 200 | Impact |
|---|---|---|---|---|---|---|---|
| 12 | N/A | 63.82% | 0.00% | 77.16% | 0.00% | 81.06% | 0.00% |
| 9 | N | 56.16% | -12.00% | 71.38% | -7.49% | 76.41% | -5.74% |
| 9 | Y | 58.74% | -7.96% | 73.54% | -4.69% | 78.51% | -3.15% |
| 6 | N | 42.79% | -32.95% | 59.97% | -22.28% | 66.63% | -17.80% |
| 6 | Y | 53.51% | -16.15% | 69.87% | -9.45% | 75.03% | -7.44% |
| 3 | N | 18.67% | -70.75% | 34.42% | -55.39% | 42.02% | -48.16% |
| 3 | Y | 47.62% | -25.38% | 64.37% | -16.58% | 69.89% | -13.78% |
| 2 | N | 20.82% | -67.38% | 37.01% | -52.03% | 45.01% | -44.47% |
| 2 | Y | 46.60% | -26.98% | 63.72% | -17.42% | 69.53% | -14.22% |
| 1 | N | 5.30% | -91.70% | 11.66% | -84.89% | 15.88% | -80.41% |
| 1 | Y | 34.72% | -45.60% | 51.39% | -33.40% | 58.01% | -28.44% |

Table 13: Impact of structural pruning with and without KALE on the SQUAD retrieval dataset

| Model | Layers | KALE | MRR@10 | Impact | Top 20 | Impact | Top 100 |
|---|---|---|---|---|---|---|---|
| BERT-base | 12 | N | 32.47% | 0.00% | 70.47% | 0.00% | 88.77% |
| BERT-base | 6 | Y | 28.71% | -11.57% | 65.44% | -7.14% | 84.68% |
| $6_{kd} - 6_{kd}$ | 6 | N | 32.21% | -0.78% | 69.94% | -0.75% | 88.19% |
| $6_{db} - 6_{db}$ | 6 | N | 32.13% | -1.02% | 70.37% | -0.14% | 88.35% |
| $6_{kd} - 3_{kd}$ | 6 | N | 30.44% | -6.24% | 67.82% | -3.76% | 86.50% |
| BERT-base | 3 | Y | 26.56% | -18.19% | 62.36% | -11.51% | 82.11% |
| $3_{kd} - 3_{kd}$ | 3 | N | 30.01% | -7.56% | 67.42% | -4.33% | 86.13% |
| $3_{kd} - 6_{kd}$ | 3 | N | 29.60% | -8.82% | 66.53% | -5.59% | 84.79% |
| $6_{kd} - 3_{kd}$ | 3 | Y | 28.19% | -13.16% | 64.00% | -9.19% | 82.95% |
| $6_{kd} - 6_{kd}$ | 3 | Y | 30.40% | -6.37% | 67.62% | -4.05% | 86.75% |
| BERT-base | 2 | Y | 26.10% | -19.61% | 61.68% | -12.48% | 81.96% |
| $3_{kd} - 3_{kd}$ | 2 | Y | 28.57% | -12.00% | 65.67% | -6.81% | 84.23% |
| $3_{kd} - 6_{kd}$ | 2 | Y | 29.52% | -9.09% | 66.16% | -6.12% | 85.57% |
| $6_{kd} - 3_{kd}$ | 2 | Y | 28.07% | -13.54% | 64.28% | -8.78% | 83.24% |
| $6_{kd} - 6_{kd}$ | 2 | Y | 30.00% | -7.58% | 66.91% | -5.06% | 85.77% |
| BERT-base | 1 | Y | 10.87% | -66.53% | 29.80% | -57.71% | 48.05% |
| $3_{kd} - 3_{kd}$ | 1 | Y | 19.09% | -41.21% | 47.56% | -32.51% | 66.69% |
| $3_{kd} - 6_{kd}$ | 1 | Y | 21.74% | -33.04% | 52.29% | -25.80% | 72.13% |
| $6_{kd} - 3_{kd}$ | 1 | Y | 20.82% | -35.88% | 50.92% | -27.75% | 71.26% |
| $6_{kd} - 6_{kd}$ | 1 | Y | 20.67% | -36.33% | 51.81% | -26.49% | 70.70% |

Table 14: Impact of model asymmetry and use of KALE for structural pruning on the MSMARCO retrieval dataset

| Model | Layers | KALE | recall 20 | Impact | recall 100 | Impact | recall 200 |
|---|---|---|---|---|---|---|---|
| BERT-base | 12 | N | 79.86% | 0.00% | 85.84% | 0.00% | 88.42% |
| BERT-base | 6 | Y | 75.51% | -5.45% | 83.68% | -2.52% | 86.18% |
| $6_{kd} - 6_{kd}$ | 6 | N | 75.04% | -6.03% | 85.15% | -0.80% | 87.45% |
| $6_{db} - 6_{db}$ | 6 | N | 73.88% | -7.49% | 84.74% | -1.29% | 87.26% |
| $6_{kd} - 3_{kd}$ | 6 | N | 77.40% | -3.09% | 85.37% | -0.54% | 87.48% |
| BERT-base | 3 | Y | 72.69% | -8.98% | 81.14% | -5.48% | 84.76% |
| $3_{kd} - 3_{kd}$ | 3 | N | 71.88% | -9.99% | 83.66% | -2.54% | 86.37% |
| $3_{kd} - 6_{kd}$ | 3 | N | 77.01% | -3.57% | 85.76% | -0.09% | 87.42% |
| $6_{kd} - 3_{kd}$ | 3 | Y | 74.16% | -7.14% | 83.43% | -2.81% | 85.62% |
| $6_{kd} - 6_{kd}$ | 3 | Y | 69.28% | -13.25% | 80.78% | -5.89% | 84.10% |
| BERT-base | 2 | Y | 71.83% | -10.06% | 81.94% | -4.54% | 84.54% |
| $3_{kd} - 3_{kd}$ | 2 | Y | 70.08% | -12.25% | 82.71% | -3.65% | 85.60% |
| $3_{kd} - 6_{kd}$ | 2 | Y | 75.40% | -5.58% | 84.27% | -1.83% | 86.81% |
| $6_{kd} - 3_{kd}$ | 2 | Y | 73.49% | -7.98% | 83.02% | -3.29% | 85.76% |
| $6_{kd} - 6_{kd}$ | 2 | Y | 68.42% | -14.33% | 80.39% | -6.35% | 83.57% |
| BERT-base | 1 | Y | 58.86% | -26.30% | 71.33% | -16.90% | 75.65% |
| $3_{kd} - 3_{kd}$ | 1 | Y | 62.69% | -21.50% | 77.17% | -10.10% | 81.33% |
| $3_{kd} - 6_{kd}$ | 1 | Y | 68.14% | -14.68% | 79.81% | -7.02% | 82.94% |
| $6_{kd} - 3_{kd}$ | 1 | Y | 63.82% | -20.09% | 76.57% | -10.80% | 80.33% |
| $6_{kd} - 6_{kd}$ | 1 | Y | 60.03% | -24.83% | 74.71% | -12.97% | 78.64% |

Table 15: Impact of model asymmetry and use of KALE for structural pruning on the NQ retrieval dataset

| Model | Layers | KALE | recall 20 | Impact | recall 100 | Impact | recall 200 |
|---|---|---|---|---|---|---|---|
| BERT-base | 12 | N | 79.43% | 0.00% | 85.03% | 0.00% | 86.63% |
| BERT-base | 6 | Y | 75.37% | -5.11% | 83.01% | -2.38% | 85.25% |
| $6_{kd} - 6_{kd}$ | 6 | N | 79.44% | 0.01% | 84.96% | -0.08% | 86.60% |
| $6_{db} - 6_{db}$ | 6 | N | 78.96% | -0.59% | 84.83% | -0.23% | 86.61% |
| $6_{kd} - 3_{kd}$ | 6 | N | 77.31% | -2.67% | 84.04% | -1.17% | 85.62% |
| BERT-base | 3 | Y | 73.17% | -7.88% | 81.67% | -3.95% | 84.04% |
| $3_{kd} - 3_{kd}$ | 3 | N | 77.80% | -2.05% | 84.11% | -1.09% | 85.96% |
| $3_{kd} - 6_{kd}$ | 3 | N | 77.52% | -2.40% | 83.91% | -1.31% | 85.72% |
| $6_{kd} - 3_{kd}$ | 3 | Y | 74.98% | -5.60% | 82.33% | -3.18% | 84.35% |
| $6_{kd} - 6_{kd}$ | 3 | Y | 76.76% | -3.36% | 83.48% | -1.82% | 85.40% |
| BERT-base | 2 | Y | 72.39% | -8.86% | 81.23% | -4.47% | 83.64% |
| $3_{kd} - 3_{kd}$ | 2 | Y | 76.48% | -3.71% | 83.02% | -2.36% | 85.16% |
| $3_{kd} - 6_{kd}$ | 2 | Y | 75.98% | -4.34% | 82.90% | -2.50% | 85.00% |
| $6_{kd} - 3_{kd}$ | 2 | Y | 74.60% | -6.08% | 82.13% | -3.41% | 84.44% |
| $6_{kd} - 6_{kd}$ | 2 | Y | 76.56% | -3.61% | 83.32% | -2.01% | 85.49% |
| BERT-base | 1 | Y | 63.04% | -20.63% | 75.40% | -11.33% | 79.23% |
| $3_{kd} - 3_{kd}$ | 1 | Y | 71.66% | -9.78% | 80.82% | -4.95% | 83.56% |
| $3_{kd} - 6_{kd}$ | 1 | Y | 71.13% | -10.45% | 80.23% | -5.65% | 82.86% |
| $6_{kd} - 3_{kd}$ | 1 | Y | 68.11% | -14.25% | 78.65% | -7.50% | 81.89% |
| $6_{kd} - 6_{kd}$ | 1 | Y | 70.91% | -10.73% | 80.31% | -5.55% | 83.05% |

Table 16: Impact of model asymmetry and use of KALE for structural pruning on the TriviaQA retrieval dataset

| Model | Layers | KALE | recall 20 | Impact | recall 100 | Impact | recall 200 |
|---|---|---|---|---|---|---|---|
| BERT-base | 12 | N | 63.82% | 0.00% | 77.16% | 0.00% | 81.06% |
| BERT-base | 6 | Y | 53.51% | -16.15% | 69.87% | -9.45% | 75.03% |
| $6_{kd} - 6_{kd}$ | 6 | N | 54.80% | -14.14% | 71.94% | -6.77% | 77.73% |
| $6_{db} - 6_{db}$ | 6 | N | 54.60% | -14.45% | 71.69% | -7.08% | 77.23% |
| $6_{kd} - 3_{kd}$ | 6 | N | 52.97% | -17.00% | 70.89% | -8.13% | 76.68% |
| BERT-base | 3 | Y | 47.62% | -25.38% | 64.37% | -16.58% | 69.89% |
| $3_{kd} - 3_{kd}$ | 3 | N | 55.05% | -13.74% | 71.98% | -6.72% | 77.76% |
| $3_{kd} - 6_{kd}$ | 3 | N | 48.86% | -23.43% | 67.85% | -12.06% | 74.04% |
| $6_{kd} - 3_{kd}$ | 3 | Y | 44.65% | -30.04% | 63.77% | -17.35% | 70.79% |
| $6_{kd} - 6_{kd}$ | 3 | Y | 45.36% | -28.93% | 64.14% | -16.87% | 71.07% |
| BERT-base | 2 | Y | 48.43% | -24.11% | 67.02% | -13.14% | 73.19% |
| $3_{kd} - 3_{kd}$ | 2 | Y | 48.43% | -24.11% | 67.02% | -13.14% | 73.19% |
| $3_{kd} - 6_{kd}$ | 2 | Y | 43.45% | -31.92% | 62.75% | -18.68% | 69.74% |
| $6_{kd} - 3_{kd}$ | 2 | Y | 42.90% | -32.78% | 62.52% | -18.97% | 69.47% |
| $6_{kd} - 6_{kd}$ | 2 | Y | 35.08% | -45.03% | 52.74% | -31.65% | 59.93% |
| BERT-base | 1 | Y | 34.72% | -45.60% | 51.39% | -33.40% | 58.01% |
| $3_{kd} - 3_{kd}$ | 1 | Y | 36.19% | -43.29% | 55.62% | -27.92% | 62.92% |
| $3_{kd} - 6_{kd}$ | 1 | Y | 34.75% | -45.55% | 52.26% | -32.27% | 59.35% |
| $6_{kd} - 3_{kd}$ | 1 | Y | 32.18% | -49.58% | 50.88% | -34.06% | 58.52% |
| $6_{kd} - 6_{kd}$ | 1 | Y | 35.08% | -45.03% | 52.74% | -31.65% | 59.93% |

Table 17: Impact of model asymmetry and use of KALE for structural pruning on the SQUAD retrieval dataset

| Model | Layers | KALE | recip_rank | Impact | NDC@10 | Impact | Recall 20 |
|---|---|---|---|---|---|---|---|
| BERT-base | 12 | N | 59.11% | 0.00% | 62.55% | 0.00% | 82.38% |
| BERT-base | 6 | Y | 54.99% | -6.97% | 58.22% | -6.92% | 77.07% |
| $6_{kd} - 6_{kd}$ | 6 | N | 65.52% | 10.84% | 67.87% | 8.51% | 83.92% |
| $6_{db} - 6_{db}$ | 6 | N | 66.25% | 12.08% | 67.81% | 8.41% | 82.16% |
| $6_{kd} - 3_{kd}$ | 6 | N | 61.90% | 4.72% | 65.30% | 4.40% | 82.48% |
| BERT-base | 3 | Y | 55.18% | -6.65% | 58.30% | -6.79% | 76.73% |
| $3_{kd} - 3_{kd}$ | 3 | N | 65.32% | 10.51% | 67.51% | 7.93% | 84.36% |
| $3_{kd} - 6_{kd}$ | 3 | N | 62.78% | 6.21% | 64.86% | 3.69% | 79.80% |
| $6_{kd} - 3_{kd}$ | 3 | Y | 62.07% | 5.01% | 64.73% | 3.49% | 82.57% |
| $6_{kd} - 6_{kd}$ | 3 | Y | 61.82% | 4.58% | 65.41% | 4.57% | 82.41% |
| BERT-base | 2 | Y | 54.45% | -7.88% | 57.71% | -7.74% | 76.07% |
| $3_{kd} - 3_{kd}$ | 2 | Y | 61.78% | 4.52% | 64.78% | 3.57% | 82.76% |
| $3_{kd} - 6_{kd}$ | 2 | Y | 61.41% | 3.89% | 63.61% | 1.69% | 82.46% |
| $6_{kd} - 3_{kd}$ | 2 | Y | 61.82% | 4.58% | 64.80% | 3.60% | 82.51% |
| $6_{kd} - 6_{kd}$ | 2 | Y | 62.09% | 5.04% | 65.27% | 4.35% | 81.51% |
| BERT-base | 1 | Y | 40.52% | -31.45% | 43.23% | -30.89% | 59.00% |
| $3_{kd} - 3_{kd}$ | 1 | Y | 42.93% | -27.37% | 44.19% | -29.35% | 61.06% |
| $3_{kd} - 6_{kd}$ | 1 | Y | 42.33% | -28.39% | 44.03% | -29.61% | 63.33% |
| $6_{kd} - 3_{kd}$ | 1 | Y | 42.72% | -27.73% | 45.68% | -26.97% | 65.81% |
| $6_{kd} - 6_{kd}$ | 1 | Y | 45.60% | -22.86% | 48.83% | -21.93% | 69.11% |

Table 18: Impact of model asymmetry and use of KALE for structural pruning on the SCIFACTS retrieval dataset

| | items/sec | Full Time | Mean Time | 95th | 50th | 5th | 99th |
|---|---|---|---|---|---|---|---|
| Run 1 | 44.890 | 80.414 | 2.17E-02 | 2.92E-02 | 2.09E-02 | 1.97E-02 | 3.07E-02 |
| Run 2 | 48.370 | 74.628 | 2.01E-02 | 2.11E-02 | 2.00E-02 | 1.96E-02 | 2.22E-02 |
| Run 3 | 47.290 | 76.334 | 2.06E-02 | 2.19E-02 | 2.04E-02 | 1.96E-02 | 2.28E-02 |
| Run 4 | 48.260 | 74.810 | 2.01E-02 | 2.13E-02 | 2.00E-02 | 1.95E-02 | 2.22E-02 |
| Run 5 | 47.580 | 75.872 | 2.04E-02 | 2.14E-02 | 2.03E-02 | 1.98E-02 | 2.28E-02 |
| average | 47.278 | 76.412 | 2.06E-02 | 2.30E-02 | 2.03E-02 | 1.96E-02 | 2.41E-02 |
| stdev | 1.410 | 2.348 | 6.46E-04 | 3.49E-03 | 3.65E-04 | 1.04E-04 | 3.68E-03 |
| CI | 1.236 | 2.058 | 5.66E-04 | 3.06E-03 | 3.20E-04 | 9.14E-05 | 3.23E-03 |
| Lower | 46.042 | 74.353 | 2.00E-02 | 1.99E-02 | 2.00E-02 | 1.96E-02 | 2.09E-02 |
| High | 48.514 | 78.470 | 2.12E-02 | 2.60E-02 | 2.06E-02 | 1.97E-02 | 2.74E-02 |

Table 19: Inference Benchmark for 12-layer Query encoder on a CPU using ONNX

| | items/sec | Full Time | Mean Time | 95th | 50th | 5th | 99th |
|---|---|---|---|---|---|---|---|
| Run 1 | 63.200 | 57.808 | 1.54E-02 | 1.65E-02 | 1.52E-02 | 1.49E-02 | 2.20E-02 |
| Run 2 | 63.570 | 56.787 | 1.52E-02 | 1.60E-02 | 1.50E-02 | 1.48E-02 | 1.70E-02 |
| Run 3 | 62.740 | 57.537 | 1.54E-02 | 1.64E-02 | 1.52E-02 | 1.48E-02 | 1.76E-02 |
| Run 4 | 63.440 | 56.908 | 1.52E-02 | 1.59E-02 | 1.51E-02 | 1.48E-02 | 1.70E-02 |
| Run 5 | 63.250 | 57.077 | 1.53E-02 | 1.60E-02 | 1.51E-02 | 1.48E-02 | 1.69E-02 |
| average | 63.240 | 57.223 | 1.53E-02 | 1.62E-02 | 1.51E-02 | 1.48E-02 | 1.81E-02 |
| stdev | 0.316 | 0.433 | 1.16E-04 | 2.49E-04 | 6.48E-05 | 6.69E-05 | 2.20E-03 |
| CI | 0.277 | 0.380 | 1.02E-04 | 2.18E-04 | 5.68E-05 | 5.86E-05 | 1.93E-03 |
| Lower | 62.963 | 56.844 | 1.52E-02 | 1.59E-02 | 1.51E-02 | 1.48E-02 | 1.62E-02 |
| High | 63.517 | 57.603 | 1.54E-02 | 1.64E-02 | 1.52E-02 | 1.49E-02 | 2.00E-02 |

Table 20: Inference Benchmark for 9-layer Query encoder on a CPU using ONNX

| | items/sec | Full Time | Mean Time | 95th | 50th | 5th | 99th |
|---|---|---|---|---|---|---|---|
| Run 1 | 91.090 | 39.631 | 1.04E-02 | 1.11E-02 | 1.03E-02 | 1.02E-02 | 1.19E-02 |
| Run 2 | 90.990 | 39.677 | 1.04E-02 | 1.11E-02 | 1.03E-02 | 1.01E-02 | 1.22E-02 |
| Run 3 | 91.290 | 39.547 | 1.04E-02 | 1.11E-02 | 1.03E-02 | 1.01E-02 | 1.22E-02 |
| Run 4 | 89.420 | 40.372 | 1.06E-02 | 1.24E-02 | 1.02E-02 | 1.01E-02 | 1.51E-02 |
| Run 5 | 89.140 | 40.499 | 1.07E-02 | 1.21E-02 | 1.03E-02 | 1.01E-02 | 1.49E-02 |
| average | 90.386 | 39.945 | 1.05E-02 | 1.16E-02 | 1.03E-02 | 1.01E-02 | 1.32E-02 |
| stdev | 1.020 | 0.452 | 1.23E-04 | 6.03E-04 | 3.95E-05 | 4.27E-05 | 1.61E-03 |
| CI | 0.894 | 0.396 | 1.08E-04 | 5.29E-04 | 3.47E-05 | 3.74E-05 | 1.41E-03 |
| Lower | 89.492 | 39.549 | 1.04E-02 | 1.10E-02 | 1.03E-02 | 1.01E-02 | 1.18E-02 |
| High | 91.280 | 40.342 | 1.06E-02 | 1.21E-02 | 1.03E-02 | 1.02E-02 | 1.47E-02 |

Table 21: Inference Benchmark for 6-layer Query encoder on a CPU using ONNX

| | items/sec | Full Time | Mean Time | 95th | 50th | 5th | 99th |
|---|---|---|---|---|---|---|---|
| Run 1 | 166.340 | 21.704 | 5.47E-03 | 5.84E-03 | 5.40E-03 | 5.35E-03 | 6.34E-03 |
| Run 2 | 164.830 | 21.902 | 5.53E-03 | 6.14E-03 | 5.40E-03 | 5.31E-03 | 7.35E-03 |
| Run 3 | 167.570 | 21.544 | 5.43E-03 | 5.87E-03 | 5.34E-03 | 5.30E-03 | 6.42E-03 |
| Run 4 | 165.370 | 21.830 | 5.51E-03 | 6.11E-03 | 5.39E-03 | 5.30E-03 | 6.96E-03 |
| Run 5 | 165.950 | 21.755 | 5.49E-03 | 5.92E-03 | 5.40E-03 | 5.32E-03 | 6.54E-03 |
| average | 166.012 | 21.747 | 5.49E-03 | 5.98E-03 | 5.39E-03 | 5.32E-03 | 6.72E-03 |
| stdev | 1.043 | 0.136 | 3.58E-05 | 1.41E-04 | 2.49E-05 | 2.20E-05 | 4.23E-04 |
| CI | 0.914 | 0.119 | 3.14E-05 | 1.23E-04 | 2.18E-05 | 1.93E-05 | 3.71E-04 |
| Lower | 165.098 | 21.628 | 5.45E-03 | 5.86E-03 | 5.37E-03 | 5.30E-03 | 6.35E-03 |
| High | 166.926 | 21.867 | 5.52E-03 | 6.10E-03 | 5.41E-03 | 5.33E-03 | 7.09E-03 |
| BERT-base | 2 | Y | 54.45% | -7.88% | 57.71% | -7.74% | 76.07% |

Table 22: Inference Benchmark for 3-layer Query encoder on a CPU using ONNX

| | items/sec | Full Time | Mean Time | 95th | 50th | 5th | 99th |
|---|---|---|---|---|---|---|---|
| Run 1 | 228.690 | 15.786 | 3.85E-03 | 4.53E-03 | 3.72E-03 | 3.67E-03 | 5.29E-03 |
| Run 2 | 230.420 | 15.668 | 3.81E-03 | 4.24E-03 | 3.74E-03 | 3.65E-03 | 4.72E-03 |
| Run 3 | 228.800 | 15.779 | 3.84E-03 | 4.23E-03 | 3.77E-03 | 3.73E-03 | 4.68E-03 |
| Run 4 | 230.530 | 15.661 | 3.81E-03 | 4.23E-03 | 3.74E-03 | 3.68E-03 | 4.63E-03 |
| Run 5 | 229.890 | 15.704 | 3.82E-03 | 4.25E-03 | 3.75E-03 | 3.70E-03 | 4.64E-03 |
| average | 229.666 | 15.720 | 3.83E-03 | 4.29E-03 | 3.74E-03 | 3.69E-03 | 4.79E-03 |
| stdev | 0.876 | 0.060 | 1.72E-05 | 1.32E-04 | 1.84E-05 | 3.00E-05 | 2.81E-04 |
| CI | 0.768 | 0.053 | 1.51E-05 | 1.16E-04 | 1.61E-05 | 2.63E-05 | 2.47E-04 |
| Lower | 228.898 | 15.667 | 3.81E-03 | 4.18E-03 | 3.73E-03 | 3.66E-03 | 4.55E-03 |
| High | 230.434 | 15.772 | 3.84E-03 | 4.41E-03 | 3.76E-03 | 3.71E-03 | 5.04E-03 |

Table 23: Inference Benchmark for 2 layer Query encoder on a CPU using ONNX

| | items/sec | Full Time | Mean Time | 95th | 50th | 5th | 99th |
|---|---|---|---|---|---|---|---|
| Run 1 | 378.680 | 9.534 | 2.14E-03 | 2.39E-03 | 2.10E-03 | 2.08E-03 | 2.88E-03 |
| Run 2 | 378.950 | 9.528 | 2.14E-03 | 2.31E-03 | 2.11E-03 | 2.08E-03 | 2.66E-03 |
| Run 3 | 377.750 | 9.558 | 2.13E-03 | 2.30E-03 | 2.12E-03 | 2.06E-03 | 2.67E-03 |
| Run 4 | 376.560 | 9.588 | 2.16E-03 | 2.35E-03 | 2.12E-03 | 2.06E-03 | 2.74E-03 |
| Run 5 | 380.730 | 9.483 | 2.14E-03 | 2.30E-03 | 2.11E-03 | 2.08E-03 | 2.66E-03 |
| average | 378.534 | 9.538 | 2.15E-03 | 2.33E-03 | 2.11E-03 | 2.07E-03 | 2.72E-03 |
| stdev | 1.543 | 0.039 | 7.46E-06 | 3.64E-05 | 8.72E-06 | 9.49E-06 | 9.64E-05 |
| CI | 1.353 | 0.034 | 6.54E-06 | 3.19E-05 | 7.65E-06 | 8.31E-06 | 8.45E-05 |
| Lower | 377.181 | 9.504 | 2.14E-03 | 2.30E-03 | 2.11E-03 | 2.06E-03 | 2.64E-03 |
| High | 379.887 | 9.572 | 2.15E-03 | 2.36E-03 | 2.12E-03 | 2.08E-03 | 2.81E-03 |

Table 24: Inference Benchmark for 1 layer Query encoder on a CPU using ONNX

| | items/sec | Full Time | Mean Time | 95th | 50th | 5th | 99th |
|---|---|---|---|---|---|---|---|
| Run 1 | 103.16 | 35.00 | 9.22E-03 | 9.33E-03 | 9.16E-03 | 9.08E-03 | 1.20E-02 |
| Run 2 | 111.51 | 32.36 | 8.50E-03 | 8.61E-03 | 8.47E-03 | 8.42E-03 | 8.73E-03 |
| Run 3 | 114.02 | 31.66 | 8.31E-03 | 8.41E-03 | 8.28E-03 | 8.22E-03 | 8.60E-03 |
| Run 4 | 90.39 | 39.94 | 1.06E-02 | 1.07E-02 | 1.05E-02 | 1.04E-02 | 1.25E-02 |
| Run 5 | 110.18 | 32.77 | 8.62E-03 | 8.74E-03 | 8.58E-03 | 8.51E-03 | 9.06E-03 |
| average | 105.85 | 34.35 | 9.04E-03 | 9.15E-03 | 9.00E-03 | 8.93E-03 | 1.02E-02 |
| stdev | 9.54 | 3.37 | 9.17E-04 | 9.19E-04 | 9.04E-04 | 9.02E-04 | 1.92E-03 |
| CI | 8.36 | 2.95 | 8.04E-04 | 8.06E-04 | 7.92E-04 | 7.91E-04 | 1.68E-03 |
| Lower | 97.49 | 31.40 | 8.24E-03 | 8.35E-03 | 8.21E-03 | 8.14E-03 | 8.50E-03 |
| High | 114.21 | 37.30 | 9.85E-03 | 9.96E-03 | 9.79E-03 | 9.73E-03 | 1.19E-02 |

Table 25: Inference Benchmark for 12-layer Query encoder on a T4 GPU

| | items/sec | Full Time | Mean Time | 95th | 50th | 5th | 99th |
|---|---|---|---|---|---|---|---|
| Run 1 | 140.35 | 25.72 | 6.69E-03 | 6.78E-03 | 6.66E-03 | 6.61E-03 | 6.94E-03 |
| Run 2 | 148.25 | 24.35 | 6.31E-03 | 6.52E-03 | 6.26E-03 | 6.22E-03 | 6.64E-03 |
| Run 3 | 147.04 | 24.55 | 6.37E-03 | 6.47E-03 | 6.32E-03 | 6.28E-03 | 7.19E-03 |
| Run 4 | 116.15 | 31.08 | 8.14E-03 | 8.25E-03 | 8.09E-03 | 8.01E-03 | 1.09E-02 |
| Run 5 | 145.68 | 24.78 | 6.44E-03 | 6.50E-03 | 6.39E-03 | 6.35E-03 | 8.83E-03 |
| average | 139.49 | 26.10 | 6.79E-03 | 6.91E-03 | 6.74E-03 | 6.69E-03 | 8.11E-03 |
| stdev | 13.39 | 2.84 | 7.70E-04 | 7.62E-04 | 7.66E-04 | 7.52E-04 | 1.79E-03 |
| CI | 11.74 | 2.49 | 6.75E-04 | 6.68E-04 | 6.72E-04 | 6.59E-04 | 1.57E-03 |
| Lower | 127.75 | 23.61 | 6.11E-03 | 6.24E-03 | 6.07E-03 | 6.04E-03 | 6.54E-03 |
| High | 151.23 | 28.58 | 7.46E-03 | 7.57E-03 | 7.42E-03 | 7.35E-03 | 9.67E-03 |

Table 26: Inference Benchmark for 9-layer Query encoder on a T4 GPU

| | items/sec | Full Time | Mean Time | 95th | 50th | 5th | 99th |
|---|---|---|---|---|---|---|---|
| Run 1 | 163.72 | 22.05 | 5.67E-03 | 5.75E-03 | 5.62E-03 | 5.56E-03 | 7.75E-03 |
| Run 2 | 161.90 | 22.30 | 5.74E-03 | 5.81E-03 | 5.70E-03 | 5.63E-03 | 6.17E-03 |
| Run 3 | 165.07 | 21.87 | 5.62E-03 | 5.70E-03 | 5.58E-03 | 5.51E-03 | 6.86E-03 |
| Run 4 | 189.71 | 19.03 | 4.84E-03 | 4.92E-03 | 4.82E-03 | 4.77E-03 | 5.07E-03 |
| Run 5 | 181.29 | 19.91 | 5.07E-03 | 5.92E-03 | 4.94E-03 | 4.88E-03 | 6.68E-03 |
| average | 172.34 | 21.03 | 5.39E-03 | 5.62E-03 | 5.33E-03 | 5.27E-03 | 6.51E-03 |
| stdev | 12.43 | 1.47 | 4.07E-04 | 3.99E-04 | 4.17E-04 | 4.11E-04 | 9.85E-04 |
| CI | 10.89 | 1.29 | 3.56E-04 | 3.50E-04 | 3.65E-04 | 3.61E-04 | 8.63E-04 |
| Lower | 161.44 | 19.75 | 5.03E-03 | 5.27E-03 | 4.97E-03 | 4.91E-03 | 5.64E-03 |
| High | 183.23 | 22.32 | 5.74E-03 | 5.97E-03 | 5.70E-03 | 5.63E-03 | 7.37E-03 |

Table 27: Inference Benchmark for 6-layer Query encoder on a T4 GPU

| | items/sec | Full Time | Mean Time | 95th | 50th | 5th | 99th |
|---|---|---|---|---|---|---|---|
| Run 1 | 269.73 | 13.39 | 3.28E-03 | 3.30E-03 | 3.26E-03 | 3.20E-03 | 3.87E-03 |
| Run 2 | 282.90 | 12.76 | 3.12E-03 | 3.38E-03 | 3.23E-03 | 2.65E-03 | 4.39E-03 |
| Run 3 | 268.47 | 13.45 | 3.30E-03 | 3.31E-03 | 3.28E-03 | 3.25E-03 | 3.76E-03 |
| Run 4 | 318.47 | 11.34 | 2.74E-03 | 2.79E-03 | 2.72E-03 | 2.69E-03 | 3.17E-03 |
| Run 5 | 357.68 | 10.09 | 2.43E-03 | 2.50E-03 | 2.41E-03 | 2.39E-03 | 2.69E-03 |
| average | 299.45 | 12.21 | 2.97E-03 | 3.05E-03 | 2.98E-03 | 2.84E-03 | 3.58E-03 |
| stdev | 38.31 | 1.45 | 3.78E-04 | 3.90E-04 | 3.93E-04 | 3.75E-04 | 6.58E-04 |
| CI | 33.58 | 1.27 | 3.31E-04 | 3.42E-04 | 3.45E-04 | 3.29E-04 | 5.77E-04 |
| Lower | 265.87 | 10.93 | 2.64E-03 | 2.71E-03 | 2.64E-03 | 2.51E-03 | 3.00E-03 |
| High | 333.03 | 13.48 | 3.30E-03 | 3.40E-03 | 3.33E-03 | 3.16E-03 | 4.16E-03 |

Table 28: Inference Benchmark for 3-layer Query encoder on a T4 GPU

| | items/sec | Full Time | Mean Time | 95th | 50th | 5th | 99th |
|---|---|---|---|---|---|---|---|
| Run 1 | 465.83 | 7.75 | 1.78E-03 | 1.83E-03 | 1.76E-03 | 1.74E-03 | 2.53E-03 |
| Run 2 | 435.46 | 8.29 | 1.92E-03 | 2.01E-03 | 1.91E-03 | 1.89E-03 | 2.04E-03 |
| Run 3 | 471.01 | 7.67 | 1.77E-03 | 1.84E-03 | 1.75E-03 | 1.74E-03 | 1.95E-03 |
| Run 4 | 413.49 | 8.73 | 2.02E-03 | 2.06E-03 | 2.00E-03 | 1.96E-03 | 2.61E-03 |
| Run 5 | 421.32 | 8.57 | 1.98E-03 | 2.05E-03 | 1.96E-03 | 1.94E-03 | 2.07E-03 |
| average | 441.42 | 8.20 | 1.89E-03 | 1.96E-03 | 1.88E-03 | 1.86E-03 | 2.24E-03 |
| stdev | 25.94 | 0.48 | 1.15E-04 | 1.12E-04 | 1.15E-04 | 1.07E-04 | 3.07E-04 |
| CI | 22.73 | 0.42 | 1.00E-04 | 9.83E-05 | 1.01E-04 | 9.34E-05 | 2.69E-04 |
| Lower | 418.69 | 7.78 | 1.79E-03 | 1.86E-03 | 1.78E-03 | 1.76E-03 | 1.97E-03 |
| High | 464.16 | 8.62 | 1.99E-03 | 2.05E-03 | 1.98E-03 | 1.95E-03 | 2.51E-03 |

Table 29: Inference Benchmark for 2-layer Query encoder on a T4 GPU

| | items/sec | Full Time | Mean Time | 95th | 50th | 5th | 99th |
|---|---|---|---|---|---|---|---|
| Run 1 | 627.64 | 5.75 | 1.22E-03 | 1.26E-03 | 1.21E-03 | 1.20E-03 | 1.28E-03 |
| Run 2 | 673.96 | 5.36 | 1.13E-03 | 1.18E-03 | 1.12E-03 | 1.11E-03 | 1.22E-03 |
| Run 3 | 651.45 | 5.54 | 1.18E-03 | 1.24E-03 | 1.17E-03 | 1.16E-03 | 1.28E-03 |
| Run 4 | 677.99 | 5.33 | 1.12E-03 | 1.19E-03 | 1.11E-03 | 1.10E-03 | 1.22E-03 |
| Run 5 | 672.16 | 5.37 | 1.13E-03 | 1.18E-03 | 1.12E-03 | 1.11E-03 | 1.22E-03 |
| average | 660.64 | 5.47 | 1.15E-03 | 1.21E-03 | 1.14E-03 | 1.14E-03 | 1.24E-03 |
| stdev | 21.12 | 0.18 | 4.28E-05 | 3.74E-05 | 4.44E-05 | 4.25E-05 | 3.30E-05 |
| CI | 18.51 | 0.16 | 3.75E-05 | 3.27E-05 | 3.89E-05 | 3.72E-05 | 2.89E-05 |
| Lower | 642.13 | 5.31 | 1.12E-03 | 1.18E-03 | 1.11E-03 | 1.10E-03 | 1.21E-03 |
| High | 679.15 | 5.63 | 1.19E-03 | 1.24E-03 | 1.18E-03 | 1.17E-03 | 1.27E-03 |

Table 30: Inference Benchmark for 1-layer Query encoder on a T4 GPU

# Lessons on Parameter Sharing across Layers in Transformers

**Sho Takase*** **Shun Kiyono**
LINE Corporation
{sho.takase, shun.kiyono}@linecorp.com

## Abstract

We propose a novel parameter sharing method for Transformers (Vaswani et al., 2017). The proposed approach relaxes a widely used technique, which shares the parameters of one layer with all layers such as Universal Transformers (Dehghani et al., 2019), to improve the efficiency. We propose three strategies: SEQUENCE, CYCLE, and CYCLE (REV) to assign parameters to each layer. Experimental results show that the proposed strategies are efficient in terms of the parameter size and computational time in the machine translation task. We also demonstrate that the proposed strategies are effective in the configuration where we use many training data such as the recent WMT competition. Moreover, we indicate that the proposed strategies are also more efficient than the previous approach (Dehghani et al., 2019) on automatic speech recognition and language modeling tasks.

## 1 Introduction

Transformer-based methods have achieved notable performance in various NLP tasks (Vaswani et al., 2017; Devlin et al., 2019; Brown et al., 2020). In particular, Brown et al. (2020) indicated that the larger parameter size we prepare, the better performance the model achieves. However, the model which is composed of many parameters occupies a large part of a GPU memory capacity. Thus, it is important to explore a parameter efficient way, which achieves better performance than a basic model with the same parameter size.

Parameter sharing is a widely used technique as a parameter efficient way (Dehghani et al., 2019; Dabre and Fujita, 2019; Lan et al., 2020). Dehghani et al. (2019) proposed Universal Transformer which consists of parameters for only one layer of a Transformer-based encoder-decoder, and uses these parameters $N$ times for an $N$-layered encoder-decoder. Dabre and Fujita (2019) and Lan et al. (2020) also used such parameter sharing across layers for their Transformers.

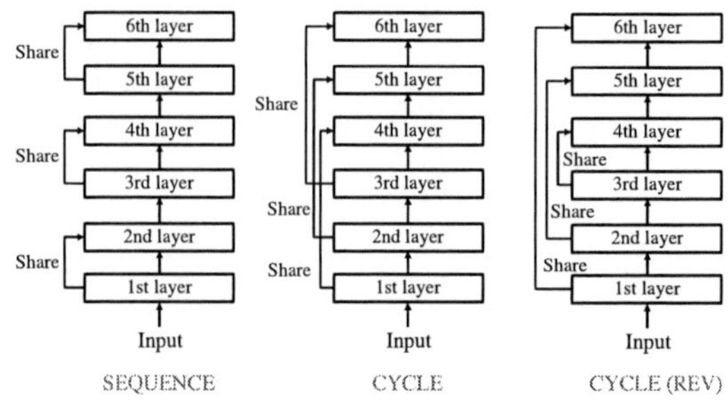


Figure 1: Examples of three parameter assignment strategies proposed in this study when we set $M = 3$ and $N = 6$.

Dehghani et al. (2019) reported that Universal Transformer achieved better performance than the vanilla Transformer in machine translation if the parameter sizes of both models are (almost) the same. However, when we prepare the same number of parameters for Universal Transformer and vanilla Transformer, the dimension sizes of each layer in Universal Transformer are much larger than ones in the vanilla Transformer. Thus, Universal Transformer requires much more computational time since its weight matrices are larger. For example, Universal Transformer requires twice as much training time as the vanilla Transformer in WMT English-to-German dataset, which is a widely used machine translation dataset (see Table 1).

In this paper, we propose a new parameter sharing method that is faster than using the same parameters for all layers such as Universal Transformers. Universal Transformers raise their expressiveness power by increasing the size of weight matrices for each layer. On the other hand, stacking (more) layers is another promising approach to raise expressiveness power of neural methods (He et al., 2016). Thus, the most straight-forward way to

* A part of this work was done when the author was at Tokyo Institute of Technology.



*Proceedings of The Fourth Workshop on Simple and Efficient Natural Language Processing (SustaiNLP)*, pages 78–90
July 13, 2023 

make Universal Transformers faster is stacking layers with smaller weight matrices for each layer. However, the approach using the same parameters for all layers limits the improvement of stacking layers (Dabre and Fujita, 2019). Therefore, instead of preparing parameters for only one layer, we prepare parameters for $M$ layers to construct an $N$-layered encoder-decoder, where $1 \leq M \leq N$. In other words, the proposed method relaxes the parameter sharing strategy in previous studies (Dehghani et al., 2019; Dabre and Fujita, 2019; Lan et al., 2020). Because this relaxation addresses the above limitation of improvement by stacking layers, the proposed method can be fast by stacking layers with using small weight matrices for each layer. For the actual parameter assignment strategies, we provide several simple examples (Figure 1) and investigate their performance empirically. The main focus of this study is to demonstrate that such simple strategies can be a better alternative to the existing parameter sharing strategy used in Universal Transformers.

We mainly conduct experiments on machine translation datasets. Experimental results show that the proposed method achieves slightly better scores to the previous method, that assigns parameters of one layer to all layers, with smaller computational time. In addition, we indicate that the proposed method outperforms the previous parameter sharing method when we spend almost the same training time. Moreover, we conduct experiments on automatic speech recognition and language modeling tasks (Section 4 and Appendix A). Experimental results on these tasks also indicate that the proposed method are also efficient in these situations.

## 2 Proposed Method

As described in Section 1, we use parameters for $M$ layers in the construction of an $N$-layered Transformer-based encoder-decoder. We provide three examples for the parameter assignment: SEQUENCE, CYCLE, and CYCLE (REV). This section describes these parameter assignment strategies.

Figure 1 shows examples of three parameter assignment strategies for an encoder side when we set $M = 3$ and $N = 6$. Let $\text{enc}_i$ be the $i$-th layer of an encoder. Figure 2 describes the algorithm to assign each parameter to each layer of the encoder. For the decoder side, we assign each parameter with the same manner.

**Algorithm** Encoder Construction

**Input:** the total number of layers $N$, number of independent layers $M$, sharing strategy TYPE $\in$ {SEQUENCE, CYCLE, CYCLE (REV)}
**Output:** $\text{enc}_1, ..., \text{enc}_N$

**for** $i$ in $[1, ..., N]$ **do**
  **if** $i == 1$ **then**
    $\text{enc}_i \leftarrow$ CreateNewLayer
  **else if** TYPE == SEQUENCE **then**
    **if** $(i-1) \bmod \lfloor N/M \rfloor == 0$ **then**
      $\text{enc}_i \leftarrow$ CreateNewLayer
    **else**
      $\text{enc}_i \leftarrow \text{enc}_{i-1}$
  **else if** TYPE == CYCLE **then**
    **if** $i \leq M$ **then**
      $\text{enc}_i \leftarrow$ CreateNewLayer
    **else**
      $\text{enc}_i \leftarrow \text{enc}_{((i-1) \bmod M)+1}$
  **else if** TYPE == CYCLE (REV) **then**
    **if** $i \leq M$ **then**
      $\text{enc}_i \leftarrow$ CreateNewLayer
    **else if** $i \leq (M \times (\lceil N/M \rceil - 1))$ **then**
      $\text{enc}_i \leftarrow \text{enc}_{((i-1) \bmod M)+1}$
    **else**
      $\text{enc}_i \leftarrow \text{enc}_{M-((i-1) \bmod M)}$

Figure 2: Proposed parameter assignment strategies for encoder construction. CreateNewLayer is a function that creates a new encoder layer.

### 2.1 SEQUENCE

The simplest strategy is to assign the same parameters to sequential $\lfloor N/M \rfloor$ layers. We name this strategy SEQUENCE. For example, when we set $M = 3$ and $N = 6$, two sequential layers share their parameters as illustrated in Figure 1.

### 2.2 CYCLE

In CYCLE, we stack $M$ layers whose parameters are independent from each other. Then, we repeat stacking the $M$ layers with the identical order to the first $M$ layers until the total number of layers reaches $N$. When we set $M = 3$ and $N = 6$, we stack 3 layers twice as illustrated in Figure 1.

### 2.3 CYCLE (REV)

Liu et al. (2020) and Takase et al. (2022) reported that higher decoder layers tends to obtain larger gradient norms[1]. Their report implies that higher layers require more degrees of freedom than lower layers for their expressiveness. In other words, lower layers probably have redundant parameters compared to higher layers. Thus, we propose the CYCLE (REV) strategy reusing parameters of lower layers in higher layers.

In this strategy, we repeat stacking $M$ layers in the same manner as CYCLE until $M * (\lceil N/M \rceil - 1)$ layers. For the remaining layers, we stack $M$ layers in the reverse order. When we set $M = 3$ and $N = 6$, we stack 3 layers and then stack the 3 layers in the reverse order as in Figure 1. Thus, the lowest layer and highest layer share parameters.

## 3 Experiments on Machine Translation

We investigate the efficiency of the proposed parameter sharing strategies. In detail, we indicate that our proposed strategies are faster than Universal Transformers while achieving comparable (or better) performance when we use the same parameter size. In this section, we conduct experiments on machine translation datasets. First, we focus on the English-to-German translation task because this task is widely used in the previous studies (Vaswani et al., 2017; Ott et al., 2018; Dehghani et al., 2019; Kiyono et al., 2020). We conduct comparisons based on following aspects: (i) comparison with Universal Transformers in terms of efficiency and (ii) comparison with models without parameter sharing across layers to investigate whether our proposed strategies can achieve comparable (or better) performance to the models with larger memory footprint.

In addition to the widely used training data, we conduct experiments on a large amount of training dataset in the English-to-German translation task. Then, we investigate if our findings are consistent in other language direction (i.e., German-to-English) and other language pair (i.e., English-to-French and French-to-English). We describe details in the following subsections.

### 3.1 Standard Setting

#### 3.1.1 Datasets

We used the WMT 2016 training dataset, which is widely used in previous studies (Vaswani et al., 2017; Ott et al., 2018; Takase and Kiyono, 2021). This dataset contains 4.5M English-German sentence pairs. Following previous studies, we constructed a vocabulary set with BPE (Sennrich et al., 2016b) in the same manner. We set the number of BPE merge operations at 32K and shared the vocabulary between the source and target languages. We measured case-sensitive detokenized BLEU with SacreBLEU (Post, 2018)[2].

#### 3.1.2 Methods

For the proposed parameter assignment strategies, we fixed $M = 6$ and set $N = 12, 18$ based on the Vanilla configuration below. We compare the proposed strategies with the following baselines.

**Vanilla**: This is the original Transformer (base) setting in (Vaswani et al., 2017). To stabilize the training, we applied Admin (Liu et al., 2020). See Section 5 for more details of Admin.

**Universal**: As the parameter sharing strategy in previous studies such as Universal Transformers (Dehghani et al., 2019), we set $M = 1$[3]. In this setting, we increased the dimensions of each layer for a fair comparison in terms of the number of parameters. This configuration corresponds to the Universal Transformer base setting in (Dehghani et al., 2019). Moreover, we prepared the model using twice as many layers to investigate the effect of stacking many layers in Universal Transformers. We call this setting **Universal (deep)**. In addition, we prepared **Universal (small)** whose dimension sizes are the identical to ones of Transformer (base).

Furthermore, we prepare two models that consist of a large number of parameters for reference.

**Vanilla (big)**: This is the original Transformer (big) setting in (Vaswani et al., 2017).

**Vanilla (deep)**: We stacked layers until $N = 18$ in the Vanilla configuration.

[1]In particular, this property is observed during warm-up when we use the post layer normalization (Post-LN) setting, which is originally used in Vaswani et al. (2017) and widely used in machine translation.

[2]The BLEU score computed by SacreBLEU is often lower than the score obtained by the procedure of Vaswani et al. (2017) as reported in Ott et al. (2018). In fact, when we used the same procedure as Vaswani et al. (2017), SEQUENCE of $M = 6, N = 12$ in Table 1 achieved 29.40 in the averaged BLEU score in newstest2014 and the best model in Table 2 achieved 35.14 in the averaged BLEU score in newstest2014. However, since Post (2018) encouraged using SacreBLEU for the compatibility of WMT results, we used SacreBLEU.

[3]The original Universal Transformers (Dehghani et al., 2019) use the sinusoidal positional encoding for each layer and adaptive computation time technique (Graves, 2017) but we omitted them in this study to focus on the difference among parameter sharing strategies.

| Method | $M$ | $N$ | #Params | Speed | 2010 | 2011 | 2012 | 2013 | 2014 | 2015 | 2016 | Avg. |
|---|---|---|---|---|---|---|---|---|---|---|---|---|
| Vanilla | 6 | 6 | 61M | ×2.02 | 24.14 | 21.93 | 22.25 | 26.14 | 27.05 | 29.59 | 34.23 | 26.48 |
| Universal | 1 | 6 | 63M | ×1.00 | 24.37 | 22.33 | 22.70 | 26.40 | 27.65 | 30.24 | 34.60 | 26.90 |
| Universal (deep) | 1 | 12 | 63M | ×0.52 | 24.42 | 22.30 | 22.61 | 26.52 | 27.76 | 29.75 | 34.01 | 26.77 |
| Universal (small) | 1 | 6 | 24M | ×2.52 | 22.89 | 21.11 | 21.29 | 24.75 | 24.71 | 28.16 | 32.81 | 25.10 |
| SEQUENCE | 6 | 12 | 61M | ×1.31 | 24.65 | 22.32 | 22.83 | **26.98** | 27.88 | 30.27 | **34.99** | **27.13** |
| CYCLE | 6 | 12 | 61M | ×1.31 | 24.51 | 22.43 | 22.69 | 26.61 | **27.91** | **30.37** | 34.77 | 27.04 |
| CYCLE (REV) | 6 | 12 | 61M | ×1.31 | **24.66** | **22.47** | **22.87** | 26.68 | 27.72 | **30.37** | 34.81 | 27.08 |
| SEQUENCE | 6 | 18 | 61M | ×0.98 | 24.53 | 22.44 | 22.73 | 26.59 | 27.73 | 30.30 | 34.80 | 27.02 |
| CYCLE | 6 | 18 | 61M | ×0.98 | 24.74 | 22.60 | 23.04 | **26.89** | **28.14** | 30.54 | 34.79 | 27.25 |
| CYCLE (REV) | 6 | 18 | 61M | ×0.98 | **24.93** | **22.77** | **23.09** | 26.88 | 28.09 | **30.60** | **34.84** | **27.31** |
| Methods consisting of a large number of parameters for reference | | | | | | | | | | | | |
| Vanilla (big) | 6 | 6 | 210M | ×0.81 | 24.31 | 22.21 | 22.75 | 26.39 | 28.28 | 30.35 | 33.40 | 26.81 |
| Vanilla (deep) | 18 | 18 | 149M | ×0.96 | 24.54 | 22.30 | 22.75 | 26.57 | 28.03 | 30.24 | 34.19 | 26.94 |

Table 1: The number of layers, number of parameters, computational speeds based on the Universal configuration, BLEU scores on newstest2010-2016, and averaged scores when we trained each method on widely used WMT 2016 English-to-German training dataset. Scores in bold denote the best results for each set. The results of our proposed strategies are statistically significant ($p < 0.05$) in comparison with Universal. The lowest part indicates results of methods consisting of a large number of parameters for reference.

#### 3.1.3 Results

Table 1 shows BLEU scores on newstest2010-2016 for each method. We trained three models with different random seeds, and reported the averaged scores. Table 1 also shows the total number of parameters and computational speeds[4]. The computational speed is based on the speed of Universal.

**(i) Comparison with Universal in terms of efficiency** In the comparison between Universal and Vanilla, Universal achieved better scores although their parameter sizes are almost the same. This result is consistent with the report in (Dehghani et al., 2019). However, the training time of Universal is more than twice as much as the one of Vanilla. In addition, Universal (deep) didn't improve the performance from Universal, and thus stacking many layers have small effect on BLEU scores when the model shares parameters of one layer with all layers.

In contrast, the proposed strategies (SEQUENCE, CYCLE, and CYCLE (REV)) were faster and achieved slightly better scores than Universal when we set $M = 6$ and $N = 12$. Thus, our proposed parameter sharing strategies are more efficient than Universal in terms of the parameter size and computational time.

In comparison among Universal (small) and the proposed strategies, Universal (small) was faster[5] but the configuration drastically sacrificed BLEU scores. These results imply that the strategy in Universal Transformer, which shares parameters of one layer with all layers, damages computational time or the quality of output sequences. In comparison with those Universal configurations, our proposed strategies improved both of the computational speed and BLEU scores.

Figure 3 illustrates the negative log-likelihood (NLL) values on newstest2013 for each training step. In this figure, we used $M = 6$ and $N = 12$ for our proposed strategies. This figure shows that Universal achieved better NLL values in the beginning of the training but the proposed strategies outperformed others when the training step is larger than 15,000. When we have finished training, the proposed strategies achieved better NLL values than Universal (and Vanilla). This result also indicates that the proposed strategies achieved better performance. We emphasize that the proposed strategies reached this better performance with small computational time in comparison with Universal because the proposed strategies are faster as in Table 1.

**(ii) Comparison with models without parameter sharing across layers** The lowest part of Table 1 indicates results when we prepared more parameters. We trained these models to investigate the performance of models without parameter sharing across layers. In other words, the purpose of these settings are comparison with models using larger memory footprint. As shown in Table 1, the proposed strategies achieved better performance than

[4]We regard processed tokens per second during the training as the computational speed.

[5]We used the same dimension sizes for Vanilla and Universal (small) but their training speeds are different from each other. Since Universal (small) consists of small parameters, the computational time for updating is smaller than Vanilla.

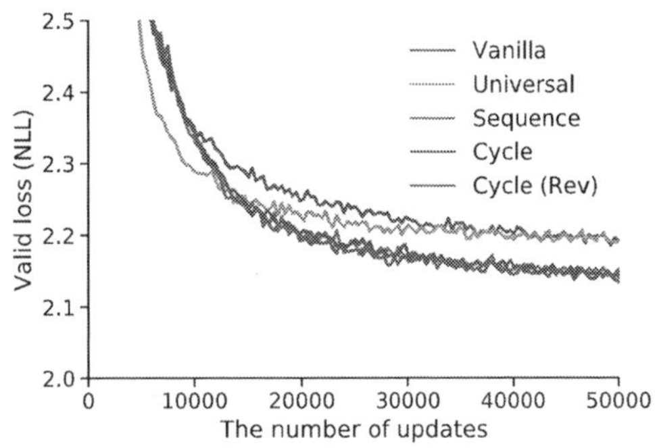


Figure 3: Negative log-likelihood (NLL) of each method on newstest2013. For our proposed parameter sharing strategies, we used $M = 6$ and $N = 12$.

models consisting of a large number of parameters in the averaged BLEU scores of newstest2010-2016. This result implies that the proposed parameter sharing strategies are not only efficient but also effective in constructing better encoder-decoder models.

## 3.2 High Resource Setting

### 3.2.1 Datasets

In the high resource setting, we constructed 44.2M translation sentence pairs as a training dataset with the procedures of (Kiyono et al., 2020) which achieved the best result in the WMT 2020 news translation task. In addition, we augmented the training data by using the back-translation technique (Sennrich et al., 2016a) in the same manner as (Kiyono et al., 2020). We obtained 284.3M pairs as synthetic training data. For evaluation, we add newstest2018 and 2019 to the set used in Section 3.1 to because (Kiyono et al., 2020) used these two test sets. In the same as Section 3.1, we measured case-sensitive detokenized BLEU with SacreBLEU.

### 3.2.2 Methods

We used the original Transformer (big) setting (Vaswani et al., 2017) as our baseline in using genuine training data. We call this setting **Vanilla** in this experiment. Moreover, we also prepared **Universal**, which shares the parameters with all layers, namely, $M = 1, N = 6$. We increased the dimensions of each layer in Universal to make their parameter size almost the same as others. For the proposed strategies, we used $M = 6$ and $N = 12$.

In using both of the genuine and synthetic (back-translated) datasets, we applied CYCLE (REV) to the BASE setting in (Kiyono et al., 2020) because CYCLE (REV) achieved the best BLEU scores on most test sets in Table 1. We also used $M = 6$ and $N = 12$ in this configuration. We compare the reported scores of the best model in (Kiyono et al., 2020). Their model is composed of 9 layers (i.e., $M = 9$ and $N = 9$); thus, it contains considerably more parameters than ours.

### 3.2.3 Results

Table 2 shows BLEU scores of each method on each test set. Similar to the experiments in Section 3.1, we reported the averaged scores of three models trained with different random seeds. Table 2 also shows the total number of parameters[6].

Table 2 shows that the proposed strategies achieved better BLEU scores than Vanilla and Universal when we prepared almost the same number of parameters. This result indicates that the proposed strategies are also parameter efficient in the high resource setting. In addition, since we used $M = 6$ and $N = 12$ for proposed strategies, they are also more efficient than Universal in terms of computational time (see Table 1).

When we used additional synthetic data for training in the same manner as (Kiyono et al., 2020), CYCLE (REV) achieved comparable BLEU scores to the best system of (Kiyono et al., 2020) except for newstest2019[7] even though the parameter size of CYCLE (REV) was smaller than theirs. This result indicates that CYCLE (REV) is also efficient in the construction of models for recent competitive tasks. In addition, this result implies that our proposed strategies can be used in the configuration where we train many parameters with a tremendous amount of data such as recent pre-trained language models, e.g., GPT series (Brown et al., 2020). We investigate the effect of the proposed strategies on language models in Appendix A.

## 3.3 Other Direction and Language Pair

### 3.3.1 Datasets

We conduct experiments on the other direction and language pair. For the German-to-English training dataset, we used the identical data in Section 3.1. For English-to-French and French-to-English, we

[6]The parameter sizes of Vanilla (big) in Table 1 and Vanilla in Table 2 are different from each other due to the difference of sharing embeddings. Following (Kiyono et al., 2020), we did not share embeddings in the high resource setting.

[7]For newstest2019, synthetic data might harm the quality of a model because models trained with only genuine data outperformed those trained with both data.

| Method | #Params | 2010 | 2011 | 2012 | 2013 | 2014 | 2015 | 2016 | 2018 | 2019 | Avg. |
|---|---|---|---|---|---|---|---|---|---|---|---|
| Genuine training data | | | | | | | | | | | |
| Vanilla | 242M | 26.53 | 24.09 | 24.51 | 28.51 | 31.40 | 33.52 | 39.08 | 47.11 | 42.80 | 33.06 |
| Universal | 249M | 27.00 | 24.20 | 24.96 | 28.94 | 31.73 | 33.53 | 39.38 | 47.54 | 43.11 | 33.38 |
| SEQUENCE | 242M | 27.31 | 24.24 | 24.86 | 29.15 | 31.90 | 33.84 | 39.93 | 48.15 | 43.12 | 33.61 |
| CYCLE | 242M | 27.23 | 24.45 | 25.13 | 29.12 | **32.10** | **34.04** | 39.82 | 48.11 | 43.19 | 33.69 |
| CYCLE (REV) | 242M | **27.37** | **24.46** | **25.14** | **29.16** | 32.06 | 33.98 | **40.28** | **48.34** | **43.43** | **33.80** |
| + Synthetic (back-translated) data | | | | | | | | | | | |
| Kiyono et al. (2020) | 514M | - | - | - | - | 33.1 | - | - | **49.6** | **42.7** | - |
| CYCLE (REV) | 343M | **28.29** | **24.99** | **25.98** | **30.01** | **33.54** | **34.93** | **41.37** | **49.55** | 42.18 | **34.54** |

Table 2: BLEU scores on newstest2010-2016, 2018, and 2019. We add newstest2018 and 2019 to the set in the standard setting to compare the top system on WMT 2020 (Kiyono et al., 2020).

| | | | German-to-English | | English-to-French | | French-to-English | |
|---|---|---|---|---|---|---|---|---|
| Method | $M$ | $N$ | 2013 | 2014 | 2013 | 2014 | 2013 | 2014 |
| Vanilla | 6 | 6 | 30.48 | 30.96 | 33.41 | 38.41 | 33.48 | 36.06 |
| Universal | 1 | 6 | 31.06 | 31.32 | 33.58 | 38.84 | 33.83 | 37.11 |
| SEQUENCE | 6 | 18 | 31.31 | 31.97 | 34.49 | **40.18** | **34.26** | 37.45 |
| CYCLE | 6 | 18 | **31.46** | **32.18** | 34.50 | 40.17 | 33.97 | **37.59** |
| CYCLE (REV) | 6 | 18 | 31.32 | 32.12 | **34.67** | 40.13 | 34.16 | 37.32 |

Table 3: The number of layers and BLEU scores on each dataset. Each method is composed of almost the same number of parameters.

used the WMT 2014 training dataset. We applied the same pre-processing as in (Ott et al., 2018), and used 35.8M English-French sentence pairs. Each configuration, we used newstest2013 and newstest2014 as valid and test sets, respectively. We also measured case-sensitive detokenized BLEU with SacreBLEU in these experiments.

#### 3.3.2 Methods

We compare our proposed strategies with baselines used in Section 3.1. We used the Transformer (base) setting with Admin as **Vanilla** and prepared **Universal** which is $M = 1, N = 6$ with large dimension sizes for each internal layer. For the proposed strategies, we used $M = 6$ and $N = 18$. In these configurations, the training time of proposed strategies are almost the same as one of Universal as described in Table 1.

#### 3.3.3 Results

Table 3 shows BLEU scores of each method on each dataset. This table indicates that Universal outperformed Vanilla in all datasets. The proposed parameter sharing strategies (SEQUENCE, CYCLE, and CYCLE (REV)) achieved better scores than Universal in all datasets. These results are consistent with results in Table 1. These results also indicate that the proposed strategies are more efficient than Universal, which shares parameters of one layer with all layers, because they achieved better performance with almost the same parameter size and computational time.

In the comparison among the proposed strategies, CYCLE and CYCLE (REV) outperformed SEQUENCE on German-to-English but it is difficult to conclude that CYCLE and CYCLE (REV) are superior to SEQUENCE on English-to-French and French-to-English. This result implies that the best strategy might depend on a language pair[8]. However, we emphasize that our proposed strategies outperformed Universal. For applying our proposed parameter sharing strategies to other datasets, we recommend using SEQUENCE as a first step because it is the easiest to implement.

## 4 Experiments on Automatic Speech Recognition

### 4.1 Datasets

To investigate the effect of our proposed strategies on other modality, we conduct comparisons on the automatic speech recognition (ASR) task. We used the de-facto standard English ASR benchmark dataset: LibriSpeech (Panayotov et al., 2015). The dataset contains 1,000 hours of English speech from audiobooks. We used the standard splits of LibriSpeech; used all available training data for training and two configurations (clean and other) of development and test sets for evaluation. We

[8]Section 4 and Appendix A imply that a sort of task and Transformer architectures also have an influence on the performance of proposed strategies.

| Method | Enc M | Enc N | Dec M | Dec N | #Params | Speed | Dev clean | Dev other | Test clean | Test other |
|---|---|---|---|---|---|---|---|---|---|---|
| Vanilla | 6 | 6 | 6 | 6 | 52M | ×2.94 | 3.98 | 9.06 | 4.18 | 9.18 |
| Universal | 1 | 6 | 1 | 6 | 54M | ×1.00 | 3.73 | 8.85 | 4.14 | 8.80 |
| SEQUENCE | 8 | 16 | 4 | 8 | 50M | ×1.41 | 3.16 | **7.84** | **3.32** | **7.71** |
| CYCLE | 8 | 16 | 4 | 8 | 50M | ×1.41 | 3.28 | 7.86 | 3.57 | 7.97 |
| CYCLE (REV) | 8 | 16 | 4 | 8 | 50M | ×1.41 | **3.11** | 8.10 | 3.60 | 8.11 |

Table 4: The parameter sizes, computational speeds based on the Universal configuration, and word error rates of each method. For word error rates, lower is better. Scores in bold denote the best results for each set.

applied the same pre-processing as in (Wang et al., 2020). We measured word error rate on each set.

### 4.2 Methods

We also compare our proposed strategies with baselines in Section 3. As the base architecture, we used Transformer based speech-to-text model (T-Md) described in (Wang et al., 2020). In contrast to the Post-LN architecture, which is the original Transformer architecture (Vaswani et al., 2017), the Transformer in T-Md consists of the Pre-LN configuration. We prepared 6 layers for the encoder and decoder in **Vanilla** and **Universal**. For proposed strategies, we stacked more layers for the encoder side in the same as in (Wang et al., 2020). We prepared $N = 16$ and $M = 8$ for the encoder side, and $N = 8$ and $M = 4$ for the decoder side.

### 4.3 Results

Table 4 shows word error rates of each method on each dataset. This table indicates that Universal outperformed Vanilla in all sets. The proposed parameter sharing strategies (SEQUENCE, CYCLE, and CYCLE (REV)) achieved better scores than Universal in all sets even though they are faster than Universal. These results are consistent with results in machine translation experiments in Section 3. Thus, the proposed strategies are also more efficient in the ASR task.

In contrast to machine translation experiments, SEQUENCE outperformed CYCLE and CYCLE (REV) in the ASR task. We consider that this result might be caused by the difference of tasks. In addition, the cause might be the difference of layer normalization positions in the Transformer architecture. We used Post-LN based method (Admin) (Liu et al., 2020) in machine translation experiments, but Pre-LN based method in this ASR task. Liu et al. (2020) and Takase et al. (2022) demonstrated that the position of the layer normalization has a strong effect on the property of Transformers. The experimental results in language modeling (Appendix A) also imply that SEQUENCE is more appropriate when we use the Pre-LN based Transformer. The main focus of this study is empirical comparisons to the widely used parameter sharing strategy, Universal (Dehghani et al., 2019), but we will address theoretical analyses on the training dynamics in the future to understand the relation between parameter sharing strategies and Transformer architectures.

## 5 Related Work

**Parameter Sharing** In the past decade, various studies reported that a large amount of training data improve the performance in NLP tasks (Suzuki and Isozaki, 2008; Brants et al., 2007; Mikolov et al., 2013; Sennrich et al., 2016a; Edunov et al., 2018). Moreover, recent studies indicated that the larger parameter size we prepare, the better performance the model achieves when we have a large amount of training data (Devlin et al., 2019; Brown et al., 2020). In fact, the best system on the WMT 2020 news translation task is composed of about 10 times as many parameters as the widely used Transformer (base) setting (Kiyono et al., 2020). However, due to the limitation on a GPU memory capacity, we have to explore a parameter efficient way, which achieves better performance while saving the parameter size.

Parameter sharing is a widely used technique as a parameter efficient way (Dehghani et al., 2019; Dabre and Fujita, 2019; Xia et al., 2019; Lan et al., 2020). Dehghani et al. (2019) proposed Universal Transformer. Their method requires parameters for only one layer (i.e., $M = 1$) of a Transformer-based encoder-decoder, and shares these parameters with $N$ layers. Dabre and Fujita (2019) investigated the effectiveness of Transformer sharing parameters of one layer across all layers on various translation datasets. Lan et al. (2020) used this parameter sharing strategy to construct a parameter efficient model. As reported in these studies, we can achieve better performance by the Transformer sharing parameters of one layer across all layers when we use the same parameter size as the original Transformer. However, this strategy requires much more computational time as described in Table 1 because weight matrices for each layer are much larger. To solve this problem, we propose a new parameter sharing strategies that prepare parameters for $M$ layers and assign them into $N$ layers, where $1 \leq M \leq N$. Experimental results show that our proposed strategies are more efficient than the method sharing parameters of one layer with across layers (Dehghani et al., 2019; Dabre and Fujita, 2019; Lan et al., 2020). In addition, experimental results imply that the proposed parameter sharing strategies are effective to improve the performance. In fact, in language modeling, previous studies demonstrated that the parameter sharing is useful to improve the performance (Melis et al., 2018; Merity et al., 2018; Takase et al., 2018),

Xia et al. (2019) proposed an encoder-decoder which shares parameters of the encoder part and decoder part. Xiao et al. (2019) proposed the method to share the attention weights to make the computation of Transformers fast. These techniques are orthogonal to our proposed method. Thus, we can combine them to improve the efficiency of parameters and computational time.

**Training Acceleration** In this study, we explore a parameter efficient method. On the other hand, recent studies proposed method to accelerate the training. Li et al. (2020) proposed a training strategy for a deep Transformer. Their strategy trains a shallow model and then stacks layers to construct a deep model. They repeat this procedure until the desired deep model. They indicated that their strategy was faster than the training of whole parameters of a deep Transformer. Takase and Kiyono (2021) compared regularization methods in terms of training time. Their experimental results show that the simple regularizations such as word dropout are more efficient than complex ones such as adversarial perturbations. We can use those findings to accelerate the training of our proposed strategies.

**Deep Transformers** To raise expressiveness power of Transformers, we stack many layers in the proposed method. The stability of training deep Transformers depends on their architectures (Nguyen and Salazar, 2019; Xiong et al., 2020; Liu et al., 2020). Transformer architectures can be categorized into two types based on the position of layer normalizations: Post-LN and Pre-LN. Most of recent studies used the Pre-LN setting when they stacked many layers (Wang et al., 2019; Brown et al., 2020) because Pre-LN makes the training process more stable than the Post-LN setting, which is used in the original Transformer (Nguyen and Salazar, 2019; Xiong et al., 2020). On the other hand, several studies proposed methods to stabilize the training of Post-LN based Transformers (Liu et al., 2020; Takase et al., 2022). In this study, we used Admin (Liu et al., 2020) in machine translation experiments because it stabilizes the training of Post-LN based Transformers while keeping the advantages of Post-LN in the machine translation task. For other experiments, we used the Pre-LN configuration based on the implementations of baselines. These experiments show that our proposed strategies are effective in major two architectures: Post-LN and Pre-LN.

## 6 Conclusion

We proposed three parameter sharing strategies: SEQUENCE, CYCLE, and CYCLE (REV), for the internal layers in Transformers. In contrast to the previous strategy, which prepares parameters for only one layer and shares them across layers such as Universal Transformers (Dehghani et al., 2019), the proposed strategies prepare parameters for $M$ layers to construct $N$ layers. The proposed strategies stack layers whose weight matrices are smaller than ones of Universal Transformers to raise expressiveness power while saving computational time.

Experimental results in the standard machine translation setting show that the proposed strategies achieved slightly better BLEU scores to those of Universal with a small computational time when we prepared almost the same parameters for each method ($M = 6$ and $N = 12$). In addition, the proposed strategies outperformed Universal under the same computational budgets ($M = 6$ and $N = 18$). Thus, the proposed strategies are efficient in terms of the parameter size and computational time. Through additional experiments, we indicated that the proposed strategies are also more efficient than Universal in the high resource setting, other language pairs, and another modality (speech-to-text).

## Limitations

As described in Section 1, the purpose of this study is to relax the existing parameter sharing strategy which shares the parameters of one layer with all layers (Dehghani et al., 2019; Dabre and Fujita, 2019; Lan et al., 2020). Experimental results indicate that the proposed simple parameter sharing strategies can be a better alternative to the existing method. As many studies on neural methods, this study also depend on empirical observations. In other words, this study lacks theoretical justifications for proposed parameter sharing strategies.

We conducted experiments on various situations. We mainly focused on sequence-to-sequence tasks and trained each model from scratch. Our conducted experiments indicated the efficiency of the proposed strategies but we did not conduct experiments on the pre-training and then fine-tuning configuration such as comparison with BERT (Devlin et al., 2019) due to the limitation of our computational budgets. Thus, it is difficult to claim that the proposed strategies are also more efficient in such configuration. In addition, we have to investigate the effectiveness in a more realistic situation. For example, we will investigate the performance of the combination of our proposed method, which is the parameter efficient way for internal layers, and a parameter efficient embedding such as Takase and Kobayashi (2020).

Through experiments in various configurations, it is difficult to conclude which strategy is the best. Experimental results imply that the best strategy depends on the task and Transformer architecture (Post-LN or Pre-LN). Such phenomena are reported in previous studies (Press et al., 2020; Gulati et al., 2020). In fact, the architecture explored by Press et al. (2020) is better in the language modeling task but ineffective in the machine translation task. Since it is intractable to investigate a tremendous amount of possible parameter assignment way due to the limitation of computational budgets, there might be a superior way to three simple strategies proposed in this paper. However, we emphasize that all our proposed strategies are more efficient than the Universal configuration. Because the purpose of our experiments is not to detect the best parameter sharing strategy but to indicate that our proposed parameter sharing strategies are more efficient than the Universal configuration, we consider that our conducted experiments are sufficient to verify our claims.

## Ethics Statement

As discussed in Strubell et al. (2019), recent neural models require substantial energy consumption. To address this issue, we explore a parameter efficient way for Transformers in this study. We believe that our proposed strategies are effective to reduce the energy consumption.

On the other hand, we spent a large amount of computational costs to investigate the usefulness of our proposed strategies in various situations. Appendix B indicates our used GPUs and the number of updates that correspond to the computational costs.

## Acknowledgements

We thank the anonymous reviewers for their insightful suggestions. A part of this work was supported by JSPS KAKENHI Grant Number JP21K17800 and JST ACT-X Grant Number JPMJAX200I.

## References

Alexei Baevski and Michael Auli. 2019. Adaptive input representations for neural language modeling. In *Proceedings of ICLR*.

Thorsten Brants, Ashok C. Popat, Peng Xu, Franz J. Och, and Jeffrey Dean. 2007. Large language models in machine translation. In *Proceedings of EMNLP-CoNLL*, pages 858–867.

Tom Brown, Benjamin Mann, Nick Ryder, Melanie Subbiah, Jared D Kaplan, Prafulla Dhariwal, Arvind Neelakantan, Pranav Shyam, Girish Sastry, Amanda Askell, Sandhini Agarwal, Ariel Herbert-Voss, Gretchen Krueger, Tom Henighan, Rewon Child, Aditya Ramesh, Daniel Ziegler, Jeffrey Wu, Clemens Winter, Chris Hesse, Mark Chen, Eric Sigler, Mateusz Litwin, Scott Gray, Benjamin Chess, Jack Clark, Christopher Berner, Sam McCandlish, Alec Radford, Ilya Sutskever, and Dario Amodei. 2020. Language models are few-shot learners. In *NeurIPS*, pages 1877–1901.

Raj Dabre and Atsushi Fujita. 2019. Recurrent stacking of layers for compact neural machine translation models. *Proceedings of AAAI*, 33:6292–6299.

Mostafa Dehghani, Stephan Gouws, Oriol Vinyals, Jakob Uszkoreit, and Łukasz Kaiser. 2019. Universal transformers. In *Proceedings of ICLR*.

Jacob Devlin, Ming-Wei Chang, Kenton Lee, and Kristina Toutanova. 2019. BERT: Pre-training of deep bidirectional transformers for language understanding. In *Proceedings of NAACL-HLT*, pages 4171–4186.

Sergey Edunov, Myle Ott, Michael Auli, and David Grangier. 2018. Understanding back-translation at scale. In *Proceedings of EMNLP*, pages 489–500.

Alex Graves. 2017. Adaptive computation time for recurrent neural networks.

Anmol Gulati, James Qin, Chung-Cheng Chiu, Niki Parmar, Yu Zhang, Jiahui Yu, Wei Han, Shibo Wang, Zhengdong Zhang, Yonghui Wu, and Ruoming Pang. 2020. Conformer: Convolution-augmented transformer for speech recognition. In *Proceedings of the 21st Annual Conference of the International Speech Communication Association (INTERSPEECH)*, pages 5036–5040.

Kaiming He, Xiangyu Zhang, Shaoqing Ren, and Jian Sun. 2016. Deep residual learning for image recognition. In *Proceedings of CVPR*, pages 770–778.

Shun Kiyono, Takumi Ito, Ryuto Konno, Makoto Morishita, and Jun Suzuki. 2020. Tohoku-AIP-NTT at WMT 2020 news translation task. In *Proceedings of WMT*, pages 145–155.

Zhenzhong Lan, Mingda Chen, Sebastian Goodman, Kevin Gimpel, Piyush Sharma, and Radu Soricut. 2020. ALBERT: A lite bert for self-supervised learning of language representations. In *Proceedings of ICLR*.

Bei Li, Ziyang Wang, Hui Liu, Yufan Jiang, Quan Du, Tong Xiao, Huizhen Wang, and Jingbo Zhu. 2020. Shallow-to-deep training for neural machine translation. In *Proceedings of EMNLP*, pages 995–1005.

Liyuan Liu, Xiaodong Liu, Jianfeng Gao, Weizhu Chen, and Jiawei Han. 2020. Understanding the difficulty of training transformers. In *Proceedings of EMNLP*, pages 5747–5763.

Gábor Melis, Chris Dyer, and Phil Blunsom. 2018. On the state of the art of evaluation in neural language models. *Proceedings of ICLR*.

Stephen Merity, Nitish Shirish Keskar, and Richard Socher. 2018. Regularizing and Optimizing LSTM Language Models. In *Proceedings of ICLR*.

Stephen Merity, Caiming Xiong, James Bradbury, and Richard Socher. 2017. Pointer sentinel mixture models. In *Proceedings of ICLR*.

Tomas Mikolov, Ilya Sutskever, Kai Chen, Greg S Corrado, and Jeff Dean. 2013. Distributed representations of words and phrases and their compositionality. In *NIPS*, volume 26.

Toan Q. Nguyen and Julian Salazar. 2019. Transformers without tears: Improving the normalization of self-attention. In *Proceedings of IWSLT*.

Myle Ott, Sergey Edunov, David Grangier, and Michael Auli. 2018. Scaling neural machine translation. In *Proceedings of WMT*, pages 1–9.

Vassil Panayotov, Guoguo Chen, Daniel Povey, and Sanjeev Khudanpur. 2015. Librispeech: An asr corpus based on public domain audio books. In *ICASSP*, pages 5206–5210.

Matt Post. 2018. A call for clarity in reporting BLEU scores. In *Proceedings of WMT*, pages 186–191.

Ofir Press, Noah A. Smith, and Omer Levy. 2020. Improving transformer models by reordering their sublayers. In *Proceedings of the 58th Annual Meeting of the Association for Computational Linguistics (ACL)*, pages 2996–3005.

Rico Sennrich, Barry Haddow, and Alexandra Birch. 2016a. Improving neural machine translation models with monolingual data. In *Proceedings of ACL*, pages 86–96.

Rico Sennrich, Barry Haddow, and Alexandra Birch. 2016b. Neural machine translation of rare words with subword units. In *Proceedings of ACL*, pages 1715–1725.

Emma Strubell, Ananya Ganesh, and Andrew McCallum. 2019. Energy and policy considerations for deep learning in NLP. In *Proceedings of the 57th Annual Meeting of the Association for Computational Linguistics (ACL)*, pages 3645–3650.

Jun Suzuki and Hideki Isozaki. 2008. Semi-supervised sequential labeling and segmentation using giga-word scale unlabeled data. In *Proceedings of ACL*, pages 665–673.

Sho Takase and Shun Kiyono. 2021. Rethinking perturbations in encoder-decoders for fast training. In *Proceedings of NAACL-HLT*, pages 5767–5780.

Sho Takase, Shun Kiyono, Sosuke Kobayashi, and Jun Suzuki. 2022. B2t connection: Serving stability and performance in deep transformers. *arXiv preprint arXiv:2206.00330*.

Sho Takase and Sosuke Kobayashi. 2020. All word embeddings from one embedding. In *Advances in Neural Information Processing Systems 33 (NeurIPS)*, pages 3775–3785.

Sho Takase, Jun Suzuki, and Masaaki Nagata. 2018. Direct output connection for a high-rank language model. In *Proceedings of EMNLP*, pages 4599–4609.

Ashish Vaswani, Noam Shazeer, Niki Parmar, Jakob Uszkoreit, Llion Jones, Aidan N Gomez, Ł ukasz Kaiser, and Illia Polosukhin. 2017. Attention is all you need. In *NIPS*, pages 5998–6008.

Changhan Wang, Yun Tang, Xutai Ma, Anne Wu, Dmytro Okhonko, and Juan Pino. 2020. Fairseq S2T: Fast speech-to-text modeling with fairseq. In *Proceedings of AACL-IJCNLP*, pages 33–39.

Qiang Wang, Bei Li, Tong Xiao, Jingbo Zhu, Changliang Li, Derek F. Wong, and Lidia S. Chao. 2019. Learning deep transformer models for machine translation. In *Proceedings of ACL*, pages 1810–1822.

Yingce Xia, Tianyu He, Xu Tan, Fei Tian, Di He, and Tao Qin. 2019. Tied transformers: Neural machine translation with shared encoder and decoder. *Proceedings of AAAI*, 33(01):5466–5473.

Tong Xiao, Yinqiao Li, Jingbo Zhu, Zhengtao Yu, and Tongran Liu. 2019. Sharing attention weights for fast transformer. In *Proceedings of IJCAI*, pages 5292–5298.

Ruibin Xiong, Yunchang Yang, Di He, Kai Zheng, Shuxin Zheng, Chen Xing, Huishuai Zhang, Yanyan Lan, Liwei Wang, and Tie-Yan Liu. 2020. On layer normalization in the transformer architecture. In *Proceedings of ICML*.

# A Experiments on Language Modeling

## A.1 Dataset

We focused Transformer-based encoder-decoders in the main experiments of this paper. However, recent studies often employed the decoder side only as a pre-trained model. Thus, we conduct experiments on the language modeling task to investigate the efficiency of our proposed strategies when we use the decoder side only. We used Wikitext-103 (Merity et al., 2017) which contains a large amount of training data. We measured perplexity of validation and test sets.

## A.2 Methods

We used the Transformer with adaptive inputs (Baevski and Auli, 2019) as the base architecture. In the same as in Baevski and Auli (2019), the Transformer in the language modeling consists of the Pre-LN configuration. We set $N = 6$ for **Vanilla** and **Universal**. For the proposed strategies, we set $N = 12$ and $M = 6$.

## A.3 Results

Table 5 shows perplexities of each method. This table indicates that Vanilla achieved better performance than Universal. Thus, the sharing parameters of one layer with all layers might not be suitable for a large-scaled language modeling task. In contrast, the proposed strategies outperformed Vanilla. This result indicates that our proposed strategies are also more efficient than Universal in the language modeling.

Through the comparison among proposed strategies, SEQUENCE achieved the best perplexity. As described in Section 4, SEQUENCE might be more appropriate to the Transformer with the Pre-LN configuration. To explore the reason, we believe that we have to conduct the theoretical analysis of the Transformer during its training. We address this issue in the future study.

The lower part of Table 5 shows the reported score of Baevski and Auli (2019), our reproduced score, and SEQUENCE with more parameters. This part indicates that SEQUENCE achieved better perplexities than others even though the parameter size of SEQUENCE is smaller. Therefore, SEQUENCE is also efficient when we prepare a large amount of parameters for a language model.

| Method | #Params | Valid | Test |
|---|---|---|---|
| Vanilla | 121M | 20.39 | 21.13 |
| Universal | 121M | 22.75 | 23.84 |
| SEQUENCE | 121M | **18.97** | **19.69** |
| CYCLE | 121M | 19.00 | **19.69** |
| CYCLE (REV) | 121M | 19.60 | 20.24 |
| Models with more parameters | | | |
| Baevski and Auli (2019)† | 247M | 18.53 | 19.24 |
| Baevski and Auli (2019) | 247M | - | 18.7 |
| SEQUENCE | 234M | **17.71** | **18.55** |

Table 5: The parameter sizes and perplexities of each method. The lower part indicates scores reported in Baevski and Auli (2019) and the score of SEQUENCE with more parameters. Scores in bold denote the best results for each set. † represents our re-run of Baevski and Auli (2019).

# B Details of Experimental Settings

We used NVIDIATesla V100 GPUs for all experiments. Table 6 shows the hyper-parameters for training in each task. The descriptions in our code also help to understand configurations in this study.

| Params | Machine Translation | ASR | Language Model |
|---|---|---|---|
| Leaning rate | 0.001 | 0.001 | 0.001 |
| Scheduler | inverse sqrt | inverse sqrt | inverse sqrt |
| Adam $\beta$ | (0.9, 0.98) | (0.9, 0.98) | (0.9, 0.98) |
| Warmup updates | 4k | 4k | 2k |
| Max updates | 50k | 150k | 50k |

Table 6: Hyper-parameters used in our experiments.

# To Asymmetry and Beyond: Structured Pruning of Sequence to Sequence Models for Improved Inference Efficiency *

Daniel Campos[1,2] and ChengXiang Zhai[1]

[1]Department of Computer Science, the University of Illinois Urbana-Champaign
[2]Neeva Inc.

## Abstract

Sequence-to-sequence language models can be used to produce abstractive summaries which are coherent, relevant, and concise. Still, model sizes can make deployment in latency-sensitive or web-scale implementations difficult. This paper studies the relationship between model size, structured pruning, inference efficiency, and summarization accuracy on widely used summarization datasets. We show that model accuracy is tied to the encoder size while inference efficiency is connected to the decoder. Using asymmetric pruning can lead to nearly 3x improvement in inference latency with 1 point loss in Rouge-2. Moreover, we find both the average degradation and the role of asymmetry to be consistent across model sizes and variations in datasets. We release our code[1], training regimes, and associated model [2] for broad usage to encourage usage and experimentation.

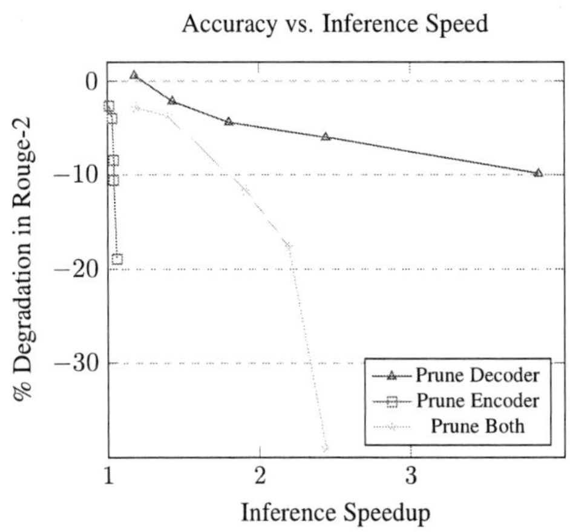


Figure 1: Impact of Asymmetrical Pruning on inference speedups and ROUGE-2 degradation on Query Independent Web Summarization. Inference Time is the mean inference time for a batch size of 1 on an A10 GPU over seven iterations.

## 1 Introduction

The application of sequence-to-sequence language models has become an important tool for natural language processing tasks such as machine translation (Sutskever et al., 2014), audio transcription (Radford et al., 2022), and abstractive summarization (Raffel et al., 2020). Sequence-to-sequence models effectively turn each of these aforementioned tasks into two-step problems: extraction and generation, and heavily condition the generation on the input.

Besides ensuring on-topic responses sequence to sequence models have the added benefit of being able to map inputs to targets with varying lengths and modalities in ways encoder or decoder-only systems cannot.

When used for abstractive summarization, sequence-to-sequence modeling has two steps, extraction using the encoder and generation using the decoder, which usually involves repeated execution until an end-of-sequence token is emitted. Since the encoder runs once on the input (Sutskever et al., 2014) its cost of execution is proportional to the batch size. The cost of decoder execution can be highly variable based on the generation length (Tay et al., 2021). Despite the broad study of sequence-to-sequence models (Raffel et al., 2020) and how they compress (Li et al., 2022), the role of model symmetry as applied to inference efficiency and model accuracy

* Corresponding author: dcampos3@illinois.edu

[1]https://github.com/spacemanidol/Efficient-Web-Scale-Absractive-Summarization

[2]https://huggingface.co/spacemanidol



*Proceedings of The Fourth Workshop on Simple and Efficient Natural Language Processing (SustaiNLP)*, pages 91–109
July 13, 2023 

is lacking.
Recent advances in scaling language models have led to a wide study on *scaling laws* as applied to language model performance (Kaplan et al., 2020), training data size (Hoffmann et al., 2022), machine translation (Henighan et al., 2020), and even reinforcement learning (Neumann and Gros, 2022).
We build on this work and study the impact of scaling on abstractive summarization and what role model asymmetry has in it. This asymmetry can manifest in various ways, such as the number of layers and hidden units in the encoder and decoder and the type of attention mechanisms used.
In this paper, we explore the role of asymmetry in the number of layers in encoder-decoder language modeling for summarization and its impact on the performance of these models. As shown in Figure 1, the symmetry of pruning drives the impact on accuracy and inference speedups for sequence-to-sequence models.
The following research questions drive our work:

- What scaling laws can be observed in abstractive summarization?
- What impact does encoder-decoder asymmetry have on abstractive summarization accuracy?
- What impact does encoder-decoder asymmetry have on abstractive summarization inference efficiency?
- What is asymmetries impact on accuracy and inference efficiency does scale have in encoder-decoder models for abstractive summarization?

It is in answering these questions that we deliver the following contributions:

- We present the first robust study on scaling laws applied to the compression of sequence-to-sequence modeling.
- We demonstrate that the asymmetric inference cost of sequence-to-sequence models leads to asymmetric pruning for optimal inference efficient compression.
- We empirically demonstrate on a wide variety of benchmarks how Asymmetric Compression can lead to a 2.7x inference speedup with no loss in accuracy on the XSUM dataset.

## 2 Related Work

**Transformer Based Language Models** such as BERT (Devlin et al., 2019) and T5 (Raffel et al., 2020) provide contextual language representations built on the Transformer architecture (Vaswani et al., 2017) which can be specialized and adapted for specific tasks and domains (Lee et al., 2020). Using these models, it becomes relatively easy to excel at a broad range of natural language processing tasks such as question answering, text classification, and sentiment analysis.
**Scaling Laws** has become an increasingly important area of study as models' size and training data grows. Performance of the transformer-based language model improves with the relation to model size (Radford, 2018) and that larger models outperform smaller models (Brown et al., 2020) on most NLP tasks. Increasing the training corpus size can lead to large improvements in performance, and model sizes can have a *optimal* training data size (Hoffmann et al., 2022). Li et al. (2020) (Li et al., 2020) explore the relationship between model size and training efficiency finding larger models train faster and are more robust to pruning and quantization (Na et al., 2022).
**Asymmetrical in sequence-to-sequence models** broadly refers to non-uniformity between encoder and decoder model shape or attributes. Training and inference procedures should match as closely as possible (Ranzato et al., 2015) (Mihaylova and Martins, 2019) as improvements in training loss during optimization result in improvements in model performance during Inference. While this may lead to the best model performance, it ignores the variable inference cost of sequence-to-sequence models.
During Inference, latency is dominated by the asymmetric execution of the language model. The auto-encoding encoder executes once over the entire input sequence, while the auto-regressive decoder executes iteratively until an end-of-sequence token is produced.
Kasai et al. demonstrated how the sequence-to-sequence language model performance for ma-

Table 1: Information about the architecture and attributes of the FLAN-T5 models

| Model | Size(MBs) | Parameters | Encoder Layers | Parameters Encoder | Decoder Layers | Parameters decoder | Ratio End:Dec | Hidden Size |
|---|---|---|---|---|---|---|---|---|
| Flan-t5-small [3] | 146 | 60511616 | 8 | 35332800 | 8 | 41628352 | 0.849 | 512 |
| Flan-t5-base [4] | 472 | 222903552 | 12 | 109628544 | 12 | 137949312 | 0.795 | 768 |
| Flan-t5-large [5] | 1500 | 750251008 | 24 | 341231104 | 24 | 441918976 | 0.772 | 1024 |

chine translation is dominated by the encoder depth (Kasai et al., 2020). Tay et al. 2021 extend this work by finding a *DeepNarrow* which shows that for broad language modeling, it is possible to have 50% fewer parameters and a 40% faster inference with no loss in accuracy (Tay et al., 2021).

**Efficient Inference** for language modeling is a growing area of study that broadly focuses on reducing the inference cost without losses in accuracy.

Unstructured Pruning has been broadly studied (Han et al., 2015) (Sanh et al., 2020) (Kurtić et al., 2022) (Zafrir et al., 2021) (Campos et al., 2022) but realizing speedups can be difficult.

Structured Pruning removes fundamental structural components in a language model such as individual attention heads (Voita et al., 2019) or entire model layers such as transformer encoders (Sanh et al., 2019). Rosenfeld et al. 2020 demonstrate that unstructured pruning impacts follow scaling laws (Rosenfeld et al., 2020) where larger models can be pruned with greater ease.

**Compressing Sequence-to-sequence** is a growing area of study where approaches from regular, efficient Inference has shown some transfer ability. Shleifer et al. show that it is possible to gain 1.93x speedup on a BART summarization model by applying structural pruning (Shleifer and Rush, 2020) but find compression approaches differ in their success depending on the dataset. Leveraging semi-structured pruning, Lagunas et al. can gain a 1.19 speedup (Lagunas et al., 2021) for minor losses in accuracy. While they find that the encoder is easier to prune than the decoder, they do not use this evidence of asymmetry to speed up performance further.

Li et al. investigate how to enable quantization, finding that without specialized distillation during quantization, performance collapses (Li et al., 2022). Leveraging that generation occurs iteratively, and some tokens are easier to generate than other CALM (Schuster et al., 2022) apply early exiting to improve inference speed by 1.4x. While existing work has found interest in asymmetry, it has not been studied directly, nor has relationships in model scale been explored.

While there are other approaches such as knowledge distillation (Hinton et al., 2015) (Sanh et al., 2019) (Jiao et al., 2020), quantization (Zafrir et al., 2019), early exiting (Xin et al., 2020) and token pruning (Kim et al., 2021) these are not the focus on our work as understanding the impact of many variables together limits the depth of our exploration. We leave further study of the interplay between summarization and quantization, unstructured pruning, structured pruning, and knowledge distillation for future work.

## 3 Scale and Abstractive Summarization

### 3.1 Background

**Sequence-to-sequence language models** such as BART (Lewis et al., 2021), T5 (Raffel et al., 2020), and PEGASUS (Zhang et al., 2020) combine transformer encoders and decoders to produce models which can adapt to novel tasks and reach top performance on tasks ranging from information retrieval (Nogueira et al., 2020) to summarization (Raffel et al., 2020).

We focus on the instruction-tuned FLAN-T5 models (Wei et al., 2021) as their performance is competitive and they feature wide variations in model size ranging from 60 million to 11 billion parameters and given the cost of training the larger variants, focus on the small, base, and large variants. Details on model size and architecture can be found in table 1.

**Abstractive summarization** is a method of sequence compression where a source document $D$ is transformed into a target document $d_{sum}$, which is shorter but faithful to the input.

**Datasets** of use are a combination of public and academic benchmarks and a proprietary web search dataset. The CNN/DailyMail (CNNDM) (See et al., 2017) and XSUM (Narayan et al., 2018) datasets are based on the summarization of English new language models. The Query Independent

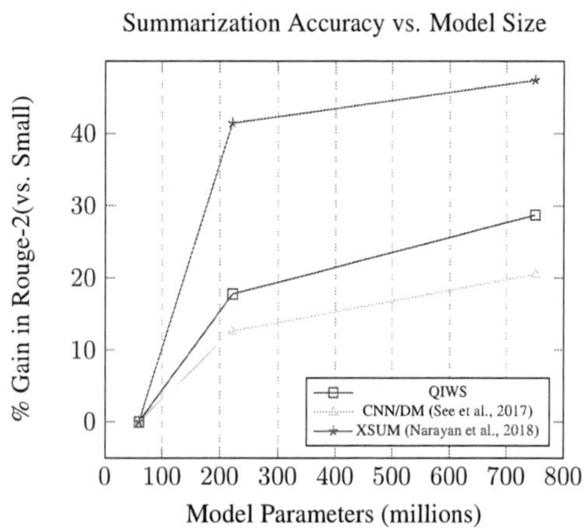


Figure 2: Model Size vs. Gain to summarization accuracy as measured by the relative Gain in rouge-2 vs. the small model.

Web Summary (QIWS) is a proprietary corpus of abstractive summaries of web pages that are used to create informative contextual snippets for search engine users. It is important to note the differences in compression factor in each dataset as each impact how decoder-driven inference latency is. Further information on the makeup of each dataset can be found in table 11.

**Metrics** For each dataset, we evaluate model performance by measuring the ROUGE-1 (R-1), ROUGE-2 (R-2), ROUGE-L (R-L), RougeSum-L (RSL) [6] (Lin, 2004), and Generation Length (GenL) on the test portion of the dataset. To aid the reproducibility and extension of our work, we experiment using HuggingFace's Transformers [7], release our training and pruning scripts [8] and model variants for datasets that are publicly available datasets [9].

### 3.2 Scaling Laws for Abstract Summarization

To study the role of scale in abstractive summarization, we train small, base, and large models of the three datasets mentioned above. We do not study the XL (3B) and XXL (11B) as they are expensive and slow to train.

For all of our experiments, we train on various hardware but fix the batch size to 64 using gradient accumulation and leverage the hyperparameters in 12. While further hyperparameter optimization and instruction tuning would likely lead to further gains in accuracy, our work is not focused on absolute Gains but on the relative relation of scale.

As shown in 2, 13, 14, and 15, there is a substantial role between scale and performance, but there is a substantial variation across datasets.

Datasets with short candidate summaries, such as XSUM, see nearly three times the impact compared to the long summaries of QIWS and CNNDM. During qualitative evaluations, the role of scale can easily be observed as smaller models generate more short keyword summaries while introducing scale makes responses more natural.

### 3.3 Inference Benchmark

To evaluate the impact of asymmetry on inference, we run experiments on the throughput of each model. Using an A10 GPU and the models from our QIWS datasets, we evaluate performance with a max sequence length of 1024, a max summary of 256, and batch sizes 1, 8, and 16 using native inference in PyTorch. We report the mean and standard deviation of timings on seven runs.

In comparing the impact of scale on R-2 vs. the effects on latency across batch sizes in 2, 4, 3 it becomes clear that larger models are more expensive to execute significantly as batch sizes increase. This is because of potential differences in output length within a batch as the batch completes when all sequences have produced an *EOS* token. To alleviate this issue bottleneck, improved streaming methods for improved batching have been proposed (Yang et al., 2020) but can be challenging to manage.

## 4 To Asymmetry and Beyond

While prior work has studied how to improve inference and tangentially explored the asymmetry between the encoder and decoder, we study that explicitly and across model scales. We focus our studies on **structural pruning** as inference gains are easy to realize, and this approach is highly

[6] Rouge-L is sentence level vs. RougeSum-L is summary level

[7] https://github.com/huggingface/transformers

[8] https://github.com/spacemanidol/Efficient-Web-Scale-Absractive-Summarization

[9] https://huggingface.co/spacemanidol

Table 2: Impact of scale on inference throughput for abstractive summarization models trained on the XSUM dataset. Latency is measured in MS/batch and the impact is the impact to latency vs. the small model

| Model | R-2 | Gain | BS 1 Latency | Impact | BS 8 Latency | Impact | BS 16 Latency | Impact |
|---|---|---|---|---|---|---|---|---|
| small | 17.55 | 0.00% | 138 | 1 | 230 | 1 | 330 | 1 |
| base | 19.77 | 12.63% | 199 | 1.44 | 550 | 2.39 | 931 | 2.82 |
| large | 21.15 | 20.51% | 445 | 3.22 | 1480 | 6.43 | 2700 | 8.18 |

Table 3: Impact of scale on inference throughput for abstractive summarization models trained on the QIWS dataset. Latency is measured in MS/batch and the impact is the impact to latency vs. the small model

| Model | R-2 | Gain | BS 1 Latency | Impact | BS 8 Latency | Impact | BS 16 Latency | Impact |
|---|---|---|---|---|---|---|---|---|
| small | 29.03 | 0 | 524 | 1 | 653 | 1 | 729 | 1 |
| base | 34.19 | 17.77% | 746 | 1.42 | 1060 | 1.62 | 1310 | 1.80 |
| large | 37.37 | 28.72% | 1,430 | 2.73 | 2240 | 3.43 | 3320 | 4.55 |

Table 4: Impact of scale on inference throughput for abstractive summarization models trained on the CNNDM dataset.Latency is measured in MS/batch and the impact is the impact to latency vs. the small model

| Model | R-2 | Gain | BS 1 Latency | Impact | BS 8 Latency | Impact | BS 16 Latency | Impact |
|---|---|---|---|---|---|---|---|---|
| small | 11.09 | 0 | 171 | 1.00 | 252 | 1.00 | 344 | 1.00 |
| base | 15.69 | 41.50% | 255 | 1.49 | 550 | 2.18 | 845 | 2.46 |
| large | 16.34 | 47.41% | 525 | 3.07 | 1370 | 5.44 | 2300 | 6.69 |

Table 5: Relation between scale and asymmetry on model performance on the QIWS dataset. As shown by the results in **bold** pruning only the decoder leads to less degradation than just the encoder or both, across all scales.

| | | Small | | Base | | Large | |
|---|---|---|---|---|---|---|---|
| $l_{enc}$ | $l_{dec}$ | R-2 | $R$ | R-2 | $R$ | R-2 | $R$ |
| 6 | 6 | 29.03 | 100.00% | 34.19 | 100.00% | 37.37 | 100.00% |
| 6 | 5 | 28.90 | 99.55% | 34.00 | 99.44% | 37.59 | 100.59% |
| 6 | 4 | 28.56 | 98.40% | 34.50 | 100.91% | 36.56 | 97.84% |
| 6 | 3 | 27.94 | **96.24%** | 33.70 | **98.58%** | 35.74 | **95.64%** |
| 6 | 2 | 24.85 | 85.61% | 31.93 | 93.38% | 35.13 | 94.01% |
| 6 | 1 | 15.41 | 53.08% | 28.05 | 82.03% | 33.69 | 90.15% |
| 5 | 6 | 27.92 | 96.17% | 33.57 | 98.18% | 36.39 | 97.38% |
| 4 | 6 | 27.75 | 95.60% | 33.06 | 96.69% | 35.90 | 96.07% |
| 3 | 6 | 25.20 | **86.82%** | 32.23 | **94.28%** | 34.22 | **91.58%** |
| 2 | 6 | 23.67 | 81.55% | 27.47 | 80.35% | 33.42 | 89.43% |
| 1 | 6 | 18.23 | 62.79% | 25.57 | 74.78% | 30.31 | 81.11% |
| 5 | 5 | 26.82 | 92.38% | 32.88 | 96.18% | 36.32 | 97.20% |
| 4 | 4 | 26.62 | 91.72% | 32.81 | 95.96% | 35.98 | 96.29% |
| 3 | 3 | 23.12 | **79.64%** | 28.70 | **83.95%** | 33.00 | **88.31%** |
| 2 | 2 | 19.14 | 65.92% | 26.53 | 77.60% | 30.78 | 82.38% |
| 1 | 1 | 6.09 | 20.99% | 19.64 | 57.43% | 22.77 | 60.94% |

compatible with other methods like quantization and unstructured pruning. We do not study how asymmetry is impacted by unstructured pruning or quantization as these methods are difficult to combine optimized libraries like FasterTransformers[10]. Following Shleifer et al., we adopt the "Shink and then fine" (STF) tune approach for compression. First, a model is trained until convergence on a fine-tuning summarization task. Then, entire layers are removed from the encoder, decoder, or both, and the model is further fine-tuned until it has re-converged. We do not study the use of knowledge distillation to avoid the additional training overhead without guaranteed improvements following Shleifer et al.'s results.

Each model we study has a uniform number of encoder and decoder layers, so we prune only the encoders, decoders, and a symmetric combination of the two combinations. We used our three scales of uncompressed models (small, base, large), and we pruned the model in multiples of 1 on the encoder, the decoder, and both. After pruning, models are fine-tuned again and evaluated. This means that for each dataset, we have 16 variants for each model size leading to 48 models per dataset and 144 models overall.

Given the wide number of models and the cost of multiple seeds or model-specific optimization, we train each model once and do not optimize the parameters for each model. While this leads to a worse-than-ideal performance, our goal is not to hyper-optimize models but explore where there is high sensitivity. To save space, we use the shorthand $l_{enc}$ and $l_{dec}$ to refer to the number portion of transformer encoder and decoder layers (out of 6), and $R$ refers to the percentage performance recall vs. uncompressed baseline. Detailed results have been moved to the A.3 to save space.

[10]https://github.com/NVIDIA/FasterTransformer

Table 6: Relation between scale and asymmetry on model performance on the CNNDM dataset. As shown by the results in **bold** as the model size grows the impact of pruning becomes more muted

| | | Small | | Base | | Large | |
|---|---|---|---|---|---|---|---|
| $l_{enc}$ | $l_{dec}$ | R-2 | $R$ | R-2 | $R$ | R-2 | $R$ |
| 6 | 6 | 17.55 | 100.00% | 19.77 | 100.00% | 21.15 | 100.00% |
| 6 | 5 | 17.68 | 100.74% | 19.92 | 100.76% | 21.30 | 100.69% |
| 6 | 4 | 17.27 | 98.36% | 19.85 | 100.42% | 21.32 | 100.81% |
| 6 | 3 | 16.40 | **93.43%** | 18.85 | **95.37%** | 21.08 | **99.66%** |
| 6 | 2 | 15.35 | 87.42% | 18.68 | 94.51% | 20.67 | 97.73% |
| 6 | 1 | 11.33 | 64.57% | 16.48 | 83.38% | 19.49 | 92.12% |
| 5 | 6 | 17.69 | 100.81% | 19.92 | 100.76% | 21.13 | 99.88% |
| 4 | 6 | 17.35 | 98.84% | 19.67 | 99.50% | 20.83 | 98.47% |
| 3 | 6 | 16.80 | **95.70%** | 18.85 | **95.37%** | 20.53 | **97.06%** |
| 2 | 6 | 15.54 | 88.51% | 18.22 | 92.14% | 19.74 | 93.33% |
| 1 | 6 | 13.31 | 75.83% | 17.06 | 86.27% | 18.68 | 88.31% |
| 5 | 5 | 17.07 | 97.23% | 19.72 | 99.74% | 21.23 | 100.34% |
| 4 | 4 | 16.20 | 92.28% | 19.17 | 96.99% | 20.90 | 98.81% |
| 3 | 3 | 14.91 | **84.95%** | 17.46 | **88.29%** | 20.13 | **95.16%** |
| 2 | 2 | 11.97 | 68.17% | 15.87 | 80.26% | 18.47 | 87.30% |
| 1 | 1 | 6.05 | 34.45% | 12.23 | 61.88% | 15.51 | 73.32% |

Table 7: Scale and Pruning on XSUM dataset

| | | Small | | Base | | Large | |
|---|---|---|---|---|---|---|---|
| $l_{enc}$ | $l_{dec}$ | R-2 | $R$ | R-2 | $R$ | R-2 | $R$ |
| 6 | 6 | 11.09 | 100.00% | 15.69 | 100.00% | 16.34 | 100.00% |
| 6 | 5 | 11.61 | 104.74% | 15.27 | 97.35% | 19.80 | 121.16% |
| 6 | 4 | 11.43 | 103.12% | 14.91 | 95.03% | 19.30 | 118.09% |
| 6 | 3 | 11.24 | 101.36% | 15.40 | 98.17% | 18.92 | 115.77% |
| 6 | 2 | 10.53 | 94.98% | 15.19 | 96.82% | 17.96 | 109.93% |
| 6 | 1 | 6.03 | 54.42% | 13.73 | 87.53% | 16.47 | 100.76% |
| 5 | 6 | 11.18 | 100.82% | 15.92 | 101.47% | 19.43 | 118.88% |
| 4 | 6 | 10.61 | 95.68% | 14.10 | 89.91% | 18.33 | 112.16% |
| 3 | 6 | 10.11 | 91.16% | 13.84 | 88.21% | 16.90 | 103.39% |
| 2 | 6 | 8.59 | 77.52% | 12.10 | 77.12% | 14.97 | 91.61% |
| 1 | 6 | 7.70 | 69.43% | 10.27 | 65.47% | 12.52 | 76.63% |
| 5 | 5 | 10.73 | 96.76% | 15.72 | 100.22% | 19.18 | 117.38% |
| 4 | 4 | 10.19 | 91.96% | 14.30 | 91.15% | 17.56 | 107.43% |
| 3 | 3 | 9.50 | 85.69% | 12.44 | 79.32% | 15.89 | 97.21% |
| 2 | 2 | 7.31 | 65.91% | 10.67 | 68.05% | 12.15 | 74.34% |
| 1 | 1 | 4.00 | 36.09% | 7.74 | 49.35% | 8.96 | 54.86% |

### 4.1 Scale and Pruning

Looking at abridged results in 5, 6, and 7, there is a clear scaling law as smaller models see much larger drops in performance when compressed to the same degree. For example, on the QIWS dataset, compression to $\frac{1}{6}$ of the layers on the encoder and decoder cause an 80% drop in R-2 on a small model but only 40% on the larger model. This scale comparison is 65% to 26% on CNNDM and 64% to 45% on XSUM datasets.

Similar scaling results hold with encoder or decoder pruning, where compressing large models lead to a 5x lower loss in performance than small models. As the model's size grows, the impact of decoder vs. encoder-only pruning becomes more muted. On the CNNDM dataset, the gap between the decoder only and encoder only pruned to $\frac{1}{6}$ is 10% with the FLAN-T5 small but only 4% with the large variant. When comparing asymmetric and symmetric, the gap is even further pronounced where the small gap is 30% while the large is 20%.

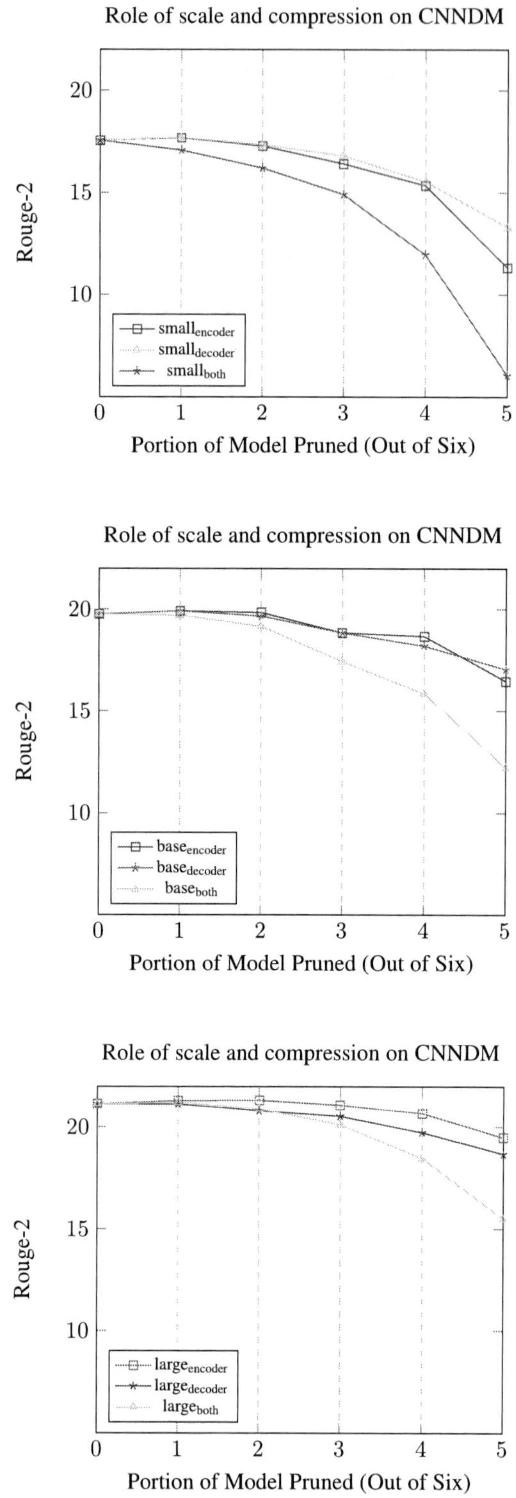


Figure 3: Relationship between model compression, model size, and summarization accuracy measured by rouge-2 vs. Number Layers. small$_{encoder}$ refers to a FLAN-T5 small which has only pruned the encoder, small$_{decoder}$ for only the decoder, and small$_{both}$ for the encoder and decoder

As shown in Figure 3, the impact of compression becomes more muted as the model size grows. In other words, larger models are more compressible and amenable to asymmetry in this compression. The impact of asymmetry is easiest to understand as it is not surprising that complete pruning of a model leads to higher losses than partial pruning across datasets and model sizes. While this finding is not immediately surprising, evaluating the inference costs becomes important.

## 4.2 Inference Benchmarks

We evaluate the impact of asymmetry in a similar method to our scale experiments. Using an A10 GPU, we evaluate performance for summarization on a portion of each model's respective evaluation datasets with a max sequence length of 1024, a max summary length of 256, and batch sizes 1, 8, and 16. We choose these batch sizes to represent streaming workloads (batch size 1), real-time results for the top results from a search query (batch size 8i), and max throughput given the A10's memory budget (batch size 16)

| | | QIWS | | CNN/DailyMail | | XSUM | |
|---|---|---|---|---|---|---|---|
| $l_{enc}$ | $l_{dec}$ | Impact | Speedup | Impact | Speedup | Impact | Speedup |
| 6 | 3 | -4.36% | 1.80 | -0.34% | 1.65 | 15.77% | 1.64 |
| 6 | 2 | -5.99% | 2.44 | -2.27% | 2.03 | 9.93% | 2.07 |
| 6 | 1 | -9.85% | 3.83 | -7.88% | 2.70 | **0.76%** | **2.71** |
| 3 | 6 | -8.42% | 1.04 | -2.94% | 1.14 | 3.39% | 1.16 |
| 2 | 6 | -10.57% | 1.04 | -6.67% | 1.19 | -8.39% | 1.21 |
| 1 | 6 | -18.89% | 1.06 | -11.69% | 1.27 | **-23.37%** | **1.30** |
| 3 | 3 | -11.69% | 1.91 | -4.84% | 1.94 | -2.79% | 2.06 |
| 2 | 2 | -17.62% | 2.20 | -12.70% | 2.78 | -25.66% | 2.83 |
| 1 | 1 | -39.06% | 2.44 | -26.68% | 4.96 | **-45.14%** | **4.84** |

Table 8: Relationship between accuracy and speedup of encoder only, the decoder only, encoder and decoder pruning on FLAN-T5 Large models on CNN/DM, XSUM, and QIWS. Speedup is measured by comparing the improvements in latency for batch size one vs. the uncompressed baseline. The impact is the relative loss of Rouge-2 of compressed models vs. the uncompressed baseline.

Looking at the focused set of results for large models across datasets in table 8 on the impact of R-2 vs. inference speedup, we can see a clear relationship between asymmetry and inference efficiency. While detailed inference results can be found in the appendix A.4 on this focused set of results, we can see that pruning only the encoder leads to no more than 30% improvement in inference efficiency at a sizable loss in accuracy. Pruning the model symmetrically leads to realizable inference improvements of up to 5x at the expense of summarization accuracy.

Alternatively, when only the decoder is pruned, it is possible to see most of the inference speedups seen during constant pruning with a substantially lower impact on accuracy. On the CNN/DM dataset, constant pruning leads to 8% better inference but losses nearly four times the performance of non-uniform compression.

| | | Small | | Base | | Large | |
|---|---|---|---|---|---|---|---|
| $l_{enc}$ | $l_{dec}$ | Impact | Speedup | Impact | Speedup | Impact | Speedup |
| 6 | 6 | -3.76% | 1.79 | -1.42% | 1.76 | -4.36% | 1.80 |
| 6 | 6 | -14.39% | 2.69 | -6.62% | 2.13 | -5.99% | 2.44 |
| 6 | 6 | -46.92% | 3.97 | -17.97% | 3.69 | **-9.85%** | **3.83** |
| 3 | 3 | -13.18% | 1.02 | -5.72% | 1.04 | -8.42% | 1.04 |
| 2 | 2 | -18.45% | 1.02 | -19.65% | 1.05 | -10.57% | 1.04 |
| 1 | 1 | -37.21% | 1.03 | -25.22% | 1.06 | **-18.89%** | **1.06** |
| 3 | 3 | -20.36% | 1.40 | -16.05% | 1.86 | -11.69% | 1.91 |
| 2 | 2 | -34.08% | 1.30 | -22.40% | 2.48 | -17.62% | 2.20 |
| 1 | 1 | -79.01% | 3.91 | -42.57% | 3.95 | **-39.06%** | **2.44** |

Table 9: Relationship between accuracy and speedup of encoder only, decoder only, encoder and decoder pruning on FLAN-T5 models on QIWS concerning model size. Speedup is measured by comparing the improvements in latency for batch size one vs. the uncompressed baseline. The impact is the relative loss of Rouge-2 of compressed models vs. the uncompressed baseline.

| $l_{enc}$ | $l_{dec}$ | Impact | Speedup (BS1) | Speedup (BS8) | Speedup (BS16) |
|---|---|---|---|---|---|
| 6 | 3 | -0.34% | 1.65 | 1.18 | 1.15 |
| 6 | 2 | -2.27% | 2.03 | 1.25 | 1.22 |
| 6 | 1 | -7.88% | **2.70** | **1.36** | **1.29** |
| 6 | 3 | -2.94% | 1.14 | 1.48 | 1.54 |
| 6 | 2 | -6.67% | 1.19 | 1.68 | 1.89 |
| 6 | 1 | -11.69% | **1.27** | **2.21** | **2.43** |
| 3 | 3 | -4.84% | 1.94 | 1.96 | 1.97 |
| 2 | 2 | -12.70% | 2.78 | 2.88 | 2.92 |
| 1 | 1 | -26.68% | **4.96** | **5.54** | **5.64** |

Table 10: Relationship between accuracy and speedup of encoder only, decoder only, encoder and decoder pruning on FLAN-T5 large models on CNN with variation in inference batch size. Speedup is measured by comparing the improvements in latency vs. the uncompressed baseline at various batch sizes. The impact is the relative loss of Rouge-2 of compressed models vs. the uncompressed baseline.

# 5 Discussion

## 5.1 Scale, Inference, and Pruning

As shown in table 9, the gains found by pruning are extremely consistent independently with scaling.

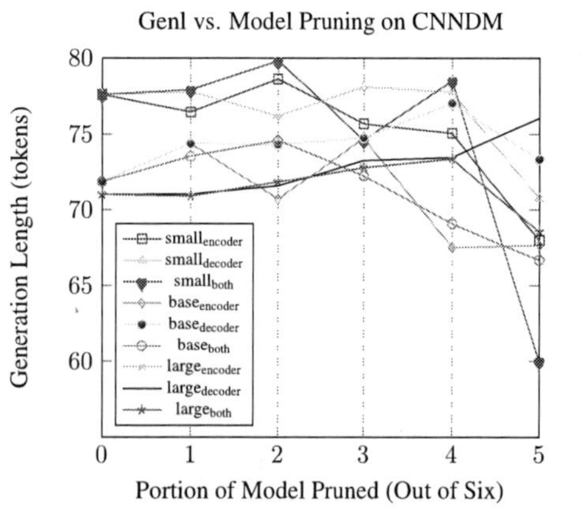


Figure 4: Role of scale and compression on generation length

Pruning only the encoder leads to a 4-6% improvement in latency, and pruning just the decoder leads to 400%, as does uniform compression. This is expected as structural pruning removes a constant portion of the network, which leads to consistent latency gains irrespective of model scale.

## 5.2 Scale, Pruning and Generated length

Despite expecting a significant trend in the role of scale and pruning in a generation, we do not see any noticeable trends. As shown in figures 6 and 4, there is no discernible trend of the Role of scale and pruning in generation length. There is a minor jump in generation length from FLAN-T5 small to FLAN-T5 base across all datasets but no such jump from FLAN-T5 base to FLAN-T5 large. We believe this is because the smaller models are less fluent and need more tokens to ensure accurate coverage. As models scale, this is no longer needed, and the models converge to a uniform summary length.

## 5.3 Asymmetry with large batches

Despite the allures of asymmetrical pruning, it is not without fault. As shown in table 10 and Figure 5, the improvements in inference efficiency are heavily influenced by the batch size. When the batch size is minimal, the difference in the type of non-uniformity has a significant impact

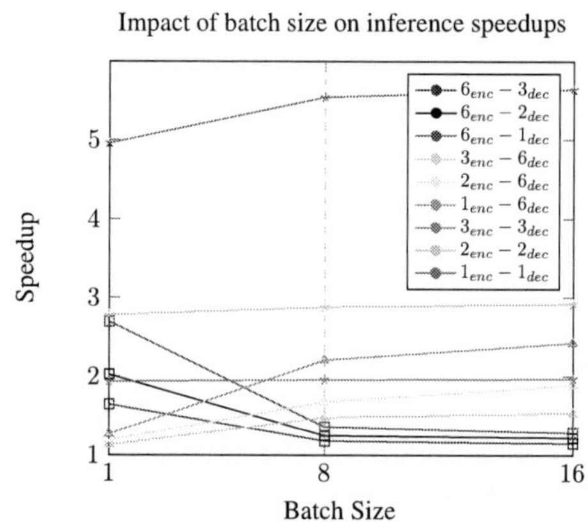


Figure 5: Relationship between inference batch size and realized inference speedup with uniform and no uniform pruning of FLAN-T5 large on CNNDM

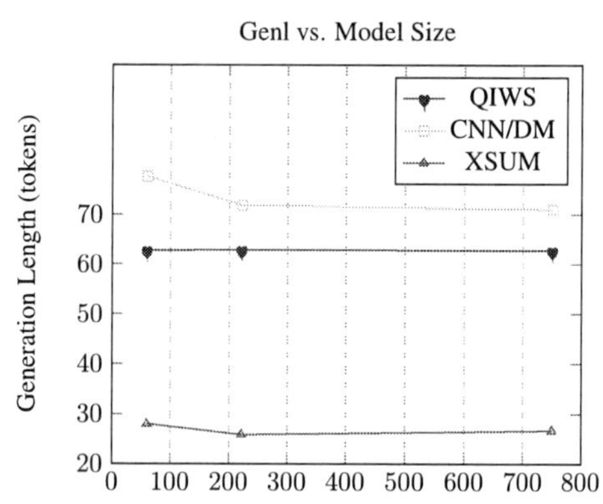


Figure 6: Role of scale on generation length

on inference efficiency. As batches scale, the speedup from encoder only or decoder only becomes much closer and becomes minor when compared to uniform methods. This indicates why further work on improving generative inference methods is highly relevant, as this problem impacts other efficiency-driven processes like CALM (Schuster et al., 2022).

## 6 Conclusion and Future Work

In this work, we explore the role of symmetry in the pruning of sequence-to-sequence models for abstractive summarization, finding that pruning asymmetrically can lead to inference speedups with low losses in accuracy. Our work also explores the relationship between model scale and the sensitivity to pruning, finding that larger models see lower losses when pruned. This compresses FLAN-T5 models to deliver 3x inference gains with a 1 Rouge-2 point loss.

In future work, we seek to study how pseudo labeling, early exiting, and quantization can be combined to improve further the inference efficiency of sequence-to-sequence models.

## References


Tom B. Brown, Benjamin Mann, Nick Ryder, Melanie Subbiah, Jared Kaplan, Prafulla Dhariwal, Arvind Neelakantan, Pranav Shyam, Girish Sastry, Amanda Askell, Sandhini Agarwal, Ariel Herbert-Voss, Gretchen Krueger, T. J. Henighan, Rewon Child, Aditya Ramesh, Daniel M. Ziegler, Jeff Wu, Clemens Winter, Christopher Hesse, Mark Chen, Eric Sigler, Mateusz Litwin, Scott Gray, Benjamin Chess, Jack Clark, Christopher Berner, Sam McCandlish, Alec Radford, Ilya Sutskever, and Dario Amodei. 2020. Language models are few-shot learners. *ArXiv*, abs/2005.14165.

Daniel Fernando Campos, Alexandre Marques, Tuan Anh D. Nguyen, Mark Kurtz, and ChengXiang Zhai. 2022. Sparse*bert: Sparse models are robust. *ArXiv*, abs/2205.12452.

J. Devlin, Ming-Wei Chang, Kenton Lee, and Kristina Toutanova. 2019. Bert: Pre-training of deep bidirectional transformers for language understanding. In *NAACL*.

Song Han, Huizi Mao, and William J. Dally. 2015. A deep neural network compression pipeline: Pruning, quantization, huffman encoding. *ArXiv*.

T. J. Henighan, Jared Kaplan, Mor Katz, Mark Chen, Christopher Hesse, Jacob Jackson, Heewoo Jun, Tom B. Brown, Prafulla Dhariwal, Scott Gray, Chris Hallacy, Benjamin Mann, Alec Radford, Aditya Ramesh, Nick Ryder, Daniel M. Ziegler, John Schulman, Dario Amodei, and Sam McCandlish. 2020. Scaling laws for autoregressive generative modeling. *ArXiv*, abs/2010.14701.

Geoffrey E. Hinton, Oriol Vinyals, and J. Dean. 2015. Distilling the knowledge in a neural network. *ArXiv*, abs/1503.02531.

Jordan Hoffmann, Sebastian Borgeaud, Arthur Mensch, Elena Buchatskaya, Trevor Cai, Eliza Rutherford, Diego de Las Casas, Lisa Anne Hendricks, Johannes Welbl, Aidan Clark, Tom Hennigan, Eric Noland, Katie Millican, George van den Driessche, Bogdan Damoc, Aurelia Guy, Simon Osindero, Karen Simonyan, Erich Elsen, Jack W. Rae, Oriol Vinyals, and L. Sifre. 2022. Training compute-optimal large language models. *ArXiv*, abs/2203.15556.

Xiaoqi Jiao, Yichun Yin, Lifeng Shang, Xin Jiang, Xiao Chen, Linlin Li, Fang Wang, and Qun Liu. 2020. Tinybert: Distilling bert for natural language understanding. *ArXiv*, abs/1909.10351.

Jared Kaplan, Sam McCandlish, T. J. Henighan, Tom B. Brown, Benjamin Chess, Rewon Child, Scott Gray, Alec Radford, Jeff Wu, and Dario Amodei. 2020. Scaling laws for neural language models. *ArXiv*, abs/2001.08361.

Jungo Kasai, Nikolaos Pappas, Hao Peng, James Cross, and Noah A. Smith. 2020. Deep encoder, shallow decoder: Reevaluating non-autoregressive machine translation. In *International Conference on Learning Representations*.

Sehoon Kim, Sheng Shen, David Thorsley, Amir Gholami, Joseph Hassoun, and Kurt Keutzer. 2021. Learned token pruning for transformers. *Proceedings of the 28th ACM SIGKDD Conference on Knowledge Discovery and Data Mining*.

Eldar Kurtić, Daniel Fernando Campos, Tuan Nguyen, Elias Frantar, Mark Kurtz, Ben Fineran, Michael Goin, and Dan Alistarh. 2022. The optimal bert surgeon: Scalable and accurate second-order pruning for large language models. *ArXiv*, abs/2203.07259.

François Lagunas, Ella Charlaix, Victor Sanh, and Alexander M. Rush. 2021. Block pruning for faster transformers. *ArXiv*, abs/2109.04838.

Jinhyuk Lee, Wonjin Yoon, Sungdong Kim, Donghyeon Kim, Sunkyu Kim, Chan Ho So, and Jaewoo Kang. 2020. Biobert: a pre-trained biomedical language representation model for biomedical text mining. *Bioinformatics*, 36:1234–1240.

Patrick Lewis, Yuxiang Wu, Linqing Liu, Pasquale Minervini, Heinrich Küttler, Aleksandra Piktus, Pontus Stenetorp, and Sebastian Riedel. 2021. PAQ: 65 million probably-asked questions and what you can do with them. *Transactions of the Association for Computational Linguistics*, 9:1098–1115.

Zheng Li, Zijian Wang, Ming Tan, Ramesh Nallapati, Parminder Bhatia, Andrew O. Arnold, Bing Xiang, and Dan Roth. 2022. Dq-bart: Efficient sequence-to-sequence model via joint distillation and quantization. In *Annual Meeting of the Association for Computational Linguistics*.

Zhuohan Li, Eric Wallace, Sheng Shen, Kevin Lin, K. Keutzer, D. Klein, and Joseph Gonzalez. 2020. Train large, then compress: Rethinking model size for efficient training and inference of transformers. *ArXiv*, abs/2002.11794.

Chin-Yew Lin. 2004. ROUGE: A package for automatic evaluation of summaries. In *Text Summarization Branches Out*, pages 74–81, Barcelona, Spain. Association for Computational Linguistics.

Tsvetomila Mihaylova and André F. T. Martins. 2019. Scheduled sampling for transformers. *ArXiv*, abs/1906.07651.

Clara Na, Sanket Vaibhav Mehta, and Emma Strubell. 2022. Train flat, then compress: Sharpness-aware minimization learns more compressible models. *ArXiv*, abs/2205.12694.

Shashi Narayan, Shay B. Cohen, and Mirella Lapata. 2018. Don't give me the details, just the summary! topic-aware convolutional neural networks for extreme summarization. *ArXiv*, abs/1808.08745.

Oren Neumann and Claudius Gros. 2022. Scaling laws for a multi-agent reinforcement learning model. *ArXiv*, abs/2210.00849.

Rodrigo Nogueira, Zhiying Jiang, Ronak Pradeep, and Jimmy J. Lin. 2020. Document ranking with a pretrained sequence-to-sequence model. In *Findings*.

Alec Radford. 2018. Improving language understanding by generative pre-training.

Alec Radford, Jong Wook Kim, Tao Xu, Greg Brockman, Christine McLeavey, and Ilya Sutskever. 2022. Robust speech recognition via large-scale weak supervision. *ArXiv*, abs/2212.04356.

Colin Raffel, Noam M. Shazeer, Adam Roberts, Katherine Lee, Sharan Narang, Michael Matena, Yanqi Zhou, Wei Li, and Peter J. Liu. 2020. Exploring the limits of transfer learning with a unified text-to-text transformer. *ArXiv*, abs/1910.10683.

Marc'Aurelio Ranzato, Sumit Chopra, Michael Auli, and Wojciech Zaremba. 2015. Sequence level training with recurrent neural networks. *CoRR*, abs/1511.06732.

Jonathan S. Rosenfeld, Jonathan Frankle, Michael Carbin, and Nir Shavit. 2020. On the predictability of pruning across scales. *ArXiv*, abs/2006.10621.

Victor Sanh, Lysandre Debut, Julien Chaumond, and Thomas Wolf. 2019. Distilbert, a distilled version of bert: smaller, faster, cheaper and lighter. *arXiv preprint arXiv:1910.01108*.

Victor Sanh, Thomas Wolf, and Alexander M. Rush. 2020. Movement pruning: Adaptive sparsity by fine-tuning. *ArXiv*, abs/2005.07683.

Tal Schuster, Adam Fisch, Jai Gupta, Mostafa Dehghani, Dara Bahri, Vinh Quang Tran, Yi Tay, and Donald Metzler. 2022. Confident adaptive language modeling. *ArXiv*, abs/2207.07061.

Abigail See, Peter J. Liu, and Christopher D. Manning. 2017. Get to the point: Summarization with pointer-generator networks. In *Proceedings of the 55th Annual Meeting of the Association for Computational Linguistics (Volume 1: Long Papers)*, pages 1073–1083, Vancouver, Canada. Association for Computational Linguistics.

Sam Shleifer and Alexander M. Rush. 2020. Pre-trained summarization distillation. *ArXiv*, abs/2010.13002.

Ilya Sutskever, Oriol Vinyals, and Quoc V. Le. 2014. Sequence to sequence learning with neural networks. In *NIPS*.

Yi Tay, Mostafa Dehghani, Jinfeng Rao, William Fedus, Samira Abnar, Hyung Won Chung, Sharan Narang, Dani Yogatama, Ashish Vaswani, and Donald Metzler. 2021. Scale efficiently: Insights from pre-training and fine-tuning transformers. *ArXiv*, abs/2109.10686.

Ashish Vaswani, Noam M. Shazeer, Niki Parmar, Jakob Uszkoreit, Llion Jones, Aidan N. Gomez, Lukasz Kaiser, and Illia Polosukhin. 2017. Attention is all you need. *ArXiv*, abs/1706.03762.

Elena Voita, David Talbot, F. Moiseev, Rico Sennrich, and Ivan Titov. 2019. Analyzing multi-head self-attention: Specialized heads do the heavy lifting, the rest can be pruned. In *ACL*.

Jason Wei, Maarten Bosma, Vincent Zhao, Kelvin Guu, Adams Wei Yu, Brian Lester, Nan Du, Andrew M. Dai, and Quoc V. Le. 2021. Finetuned language models are zero-shot learners. *ArXiv*, abs/2109.01652.

Ji Xin, Raphael Tang, Jaejun Lee, Yaoliang Yu, and Jimmy J. Lin. 2020. Deebert: Dynamic early exiting for accelerating bert inference. In *ACL*.

Kevin Yang, Violet Yao, John DeNero, and Dan Klein. 2020. A streaming approach for efficient batched beam search. In *Conference on Empirical Methods in Natural Language Processing*.

Ofir Zafrir, Guy Boudoukh, Peter Izsak, and Moshe Wasserblat. 2019. Q8bert: Quantized 8bit bert. *2019 Fifth Workshop on Energy Efficient Machine Learning and Cognitive Computing - NeurIPS Edition (EMC2-NIPS)*, pages 36–39.

Ofir Zafrir, Ariel Larey, Guy Boudoukh, Haihao Shen, and Moshe Wasserblat. 2021. Prune once for all: Sparse pre-trained language models. *ArXiv*, abs/2111.05754.

Jingqing Zhang, Yao Zhao, Mohammad Saleh, and Peter J. Liu. 2020. Pegasus: Pre-training with extracted gap-sentences for abstractive summarization. *ArXiv*, abs/1912.08777.

# A Appendix

## A.1 Training Details

In all of our experiments, we leverage the parameters shown in 12 on the datasets shown in 11

## A.2 Scale and Abstractive summarization

The role of model scale on performance on the QIWS, CNN/DM, and XSUM datasets can be found in tables 14,13, and 15

## A.3 Asymmetry in Summarization

The role of the model scale, structural pruning, and asymmetry on performance on the QIWS, CNN/DM, and XSUM datasets can be found in tables 22,23,24,16,17,18,19,20, and 21.

## A.4 Inference Benchmarks

Detailed variations in latency measurements across batch size, scale, structural pruning, and asymmetry on performance on the QIWS, CNN/DM, and XSUM datasets can be found in tables 25,26, 27, 28,29, 30, 33, 31, and 32.

## A.5 Responsible NLP Research - Reproducibility Checklist

### A.5.1 Scientific Artifacts

**Datasets.** We perform our experimentation on well-established benchmarks using many broad domains and a proprietary web summarization dataset. We do not perform any modification or augmentation on public benchmarks in any dataset.

**Models.** The model used as a starting point for all of our experiments is the family of flan-t5 models, publicly available via HuggingFace Hub [13]. All other models presented in this paper are openly-available in the hugging face hub.

### A.5.2 Computational Experiments

Our experimentation on finetuning our compressed models uses a single 40GB A100. Finetuning time varies across datasets ranging from 1 hour for T5-small to 24 hours for T5-Large.

### A.5.3 Computational Packages

All of our experimentation is done using public libraries and datasets to ensure extensibility and reproducibility. Our investigation is done using HuggingFace's Transformers [14] and Datasets [15].

[13] https://huggingface.co/bert-base-uncased

[14] https://github.com/huggingface/transformers

[15] https://github.com/huggingface/datasets

Table 11: Statistics for the abstractive summarization datasets which we study. Source and Summary refer to the number of words in each, and the compression factor is the ratio between the two on the train portion of the dataset.

| Dataset | Train | Validation | Test | Source | Summary | Compression |
|---|---|---|---|---|---|---|
| CNNDM [11] | 287,113 | 13,368 | 11,490 | 691.87 | 51.57 | 14.80 |
| XSUM [12] | 204,045 | 11,332 | 11,334 | 373.86 | 21.09 | 18.70 |
| QIWS | 10000 | 1000 | 1000 | 1410.12 | 73.78 | 19.11 |

| HyperParameter | Value |
|---|---|
| Training Length | 3,10 Epochs |
| Initial learning rate<br>Learning rate schedule | 1e-4<br>constant |
| Batch size | 64 |
| Weight Decay | 0.01, 0.05, 0.1 |

Table 12: Training Hyperparameters for summarization experiments

| Model | R-1 | Impact | R-2 | Impact | RSL | Impact | R-L | Impact | Genl | Impact |
|---|---|---|---|---|---|---|---|---|---|---|
| small | 50.22 | 0.00% | 29.03 | 0.00% | 45.87 | 0.00% | 40.19 | 0.00% | 62.79 | 0.00% |
| base | 54.84 | 9.20% | 34.19 | 17.77% | 50.38 | 9.83% | 44.68 | 11.18% | 62.91 | 0.19% |
| large | 57.81 | 15.11% | 37.37 | 28.72% | 53.14 | 15.84% | 48.16 | 19.84% | 62.85 | 0.10% |

Table 13: Impact of Scale on summarization performance on QIWS dataset

| Model | R-1 | Impact | R-2 | Impact | RSL | Impact | R-L | Impact | Genl | Impact |
|---|---|---|---|---|---|---|---|---|---|---|
| small | 39.31 | 0.00% | 17.55 | 0.00% | 36.50 | 0.00% | 27.97 | 0.00% | 77.62 | 0.00% |
| base | 42.14 | 7.20% | 19.77 | 12.63% | 39.32 | 7.75% | 30.15 | 7.80% | 71.86 | -7.42% |
| large | 43.99 | 11.90% | 21.15 | 20.51% | 41.12 | 12.68% | 31.64 | 13.11% | 71.01 | -8.51% |

Table 14: Impact of Scale on summarization performance on CNNDM dataset

| Model | R-1 | Impact | R-2 | Impact | RSL | Impact | R-L | Impact | Genl | Impact |
|---|---|---|---|---|---|---|---|---|---|---|
| small | 33.2675 | 0.00% | 11.09 | 0.00% | 26.17 | 0.00% | 26.17 | 0.00% | 28.01 | 0.00% |
| base | 38.7782 | 16.56% | 15.69 | 41.45% | 31.14 | 19.01% | 31.15 | 19.04% | 25.92 | -7.48% |
| large | 39.7125 | 19.36% | 16.34 | 47.36% | 31.72 | 21.21% | 31.72 | 21.23% | 26.74 | -4.54% |

Table 15: Impact of Scale on summarization performance on XSUM dataset

Table 16: The relation between pruning asymmetry and symmetry for a FLAN-T5 small model on the CNN/DailyMail Abstractive Summarization Dataset

| $l_{enc}$ | $l_{dec}$ | R-1 | Impact | R-2 | Impact | RSL | Impact | R-L | Impact | GenL | Impact |
|---|---|---|---|---|---|---|---|---|---|---|---|
| 8 | 8 | 39.31 | 0.00% | 17.55 | 0.00% | 36.50 | 0.00% | 27.97 | 0.00% | 77.62 | 0.00% |
| 8 | 6 | 39.33 | 0.04% | 17.68 | 0.74% | 36.54 | 0.13% | 28.21 | 0.87% | 76.46 | -1.49% |
| 8 | 5 | 38.75 | -1.42% | 17.27 | -1.64% | 36.01 | -1.32% | 27.91 | -0.23% | 78.63 | 1.31% |
| 8 | 4 | 37.18 | -5.42% | 16.40 | -6.57% | 34.46 | -5.58% | 27.22 | -2.70% | 75.69 | -2.48% |
| 8 | 2 | 35.47 | -9.76% | 15.35 | -12.58% | 32.78 | -10.17% | 26.28 | -6.06% | 75.08 | -3.27% |
| 8 | 1 | 29.27 | -25.55% | 11.33 | -35.43% | 26.97 | -26.09% | 22.33 | -20.18% | 67.99 | -12.40% |
| 6 | 8 | 39.59 | 0.71% | 17.69 | 0.81% | 36.80 | 0.83% | 28.08 | 0.39% | 77.81 | 0.25% |
| 5 | 8 | 39.12 | -0.47% | 17.35 | -1.16% | 36.38 | -0.31% | 27.73 | -0.88% | 76.22 | -1.80% |
| 4 | 8 | 38.57 | -1.87% | 16.80 | -4.30% | 35.79 | -1.92% | 27.15 | -2.92% | 78.13 | 0.67% |
| 2 | 8 | 36.82 | -6.32% | 15.54 | -11.49% | 34.00 | -6.84% | 25.79 | -7.78% | 77.77 | 0.20% |
| 1 | 8 | 33.58 | -14.58% | 13.31 | -24.17% | 30.96 | -15.16% | 23.72 | -15.19% | 70.79 | -8.79% |
| 6 | 6 | 38.59 | -1.82% | 17.07 | -2.77% | 35.80 | -1.91% | 27.55 | -1.52% | 77.93 | 0.41% |
| 5 | 5 | 37.31 | -5.08% | 16.20 | -7.72% | 34.60 | -5.19% | 26.83 | -4.07% | 79.83 | 2.85% |
| 4 | 4 | 35.28 | -10.25% | 14.91 | -15.05% | 32.54 | -10.85% | 25.74 | -7.98% | 74.61 | -3.88% |
| 2 | 2 | 30.79 | -21.66% | 11.97 | -31.83% | 28.03 | -23.19% | 22.88 | -18.19% | 78.53 | 1.18% |
| 1 | 1 | 21.30 | -45.80% | 6.05 | -65.55% | 19.57 | -46.39% | 16.62 | -40.56% | 60.03 | -22.66% |

Table 17: The relation between pruning asymmetry and symmetry for a FLAN-T5 base model on the CNN/DailyMail Abstractive Summarization Dataset

| $l_{enc}$ | $l_{dec}$ | R-1 | Impact | R-2 | Impact | RSL | Impact | R-L | Impact | GenL | Impact |
|---|---|---|---|---|---|---|---|---|---|---|---|
| 12 | 12 | 42.14 | 0.00% | 19.77 | 0.00% | 39.32 | 0.00% | 30.15 | 0.00% | 71.86 | 0.00% |
| 12 | 10 | 42.49 | 0.84% | 19.92 | 0.76% | 39.62 | 0.75% | 30.27 | 0.40% | 74.38 | 3.51% |
| 12 | 8 | 42.28 | 0.34% | 19.85 | 0.42% | 39.48 | 0.41% | 30.35 | 0.64% | 70.74 | -1.56% |
| 12 | 6 | 41.30 | -1.99% | 18.85 | -4.63% | 38.44 | -2.25% | 29.16 | -3.28% | 74.76 | 4.04% |
| 12 | 4 | 40.31 | -4.34% | 18.68 | -5.49% | 37.71 | -4.10% | 29.45 | -2.33% | 67.52 | -6.04% |
| 12 | 2 | 36.75 | -12.80% | 16.48 | -16.62% | 34.22 | -12.97% | 27.61 | -8.43% | 67.67 | -5.82% |
| 10 | 12 | 42.49 | 0.84% | 19.92 | 0.76% | 39.62 | 0.75% | 30.27 | 0.40% | 74.38 | 3.51% |
| 8 | 12 | 42.27 | 0.31% | 19.67 | -0.50% | 39.41 | 0.22% | 29.99 | -0.52% | 74.34 | 3.45% |
| 6 | 12 | 41.30 | -1.99% | 18.85 | -4.63% | 38.44 | -2.25% | 29.16 | -3.28% | 74.76 | 4.04% |
| 4 | 12 | 40.51 | -3.86% | 18.22 | -7.86% | 37.66 | -4.23% | 28.42 | -5.75% | 77.04 | 7.21% |
| 2 | 12 | 39.03 | -7.38% | 17.06 | -13.73% | 36.15 | -8.08% | 27.23 | -9.69% | 73.36 | 2.09% |
| 10 | 10 | 42.19 | 0.13% | 19.72 | -0.26% | 39.38 | 0.14% | 30.12 | -0.11% | 73.56 | 2.37% |
| 8 | 8 | 41.64 | -1.18% | 19.17 | -3.01% | 38.83 | -1.26% | 29.60 | -1.84% | 74.59 | 3.80% |
| 6 | 6 | 39.33 | -6.67% | 17.46 | -11.71% | 36.67 | -6.74% | 28.07 | -6.92% | 72.27 | 0.57% |
| 4 | 4 | 36.99 | -12.23% | 15.87 | -19.74% | 34.43 | -12.43% | 26.63 | -11.68% | 69.08 | -3.87% |
| 2 | 2 | 30.99 | -26.45% | 12.23 | -38.12% | 28.43 | -27.71% | 23.28 | -22.79% | 66.70 | -7.18% |

Table 18: The relation between pruning asymmetry and symmetry for a FLAN-T5 large model on the CNN/DailyMail Abstractive Summarization Dataset

| $l_{enc}$ | $l_{dec}$ | R-1 | Impact | R-2 | Impact | RSL | Impact | R-L | Impact | GenL | Impact |
|---|---|---|---|---|---|---|---|---|---|---|---|
| 24 | 24 | 43.99 | 0.00% | 21.15 | 0.00% | 41.12 | 0.00% | 31.64 | 0.00% | 71.01 | 0.00% |
| 24 | 20 | 44.15 | 0.37% | 21.30 | 0.69% | 41.31 | 0.46% | 31.73 | 0.31% | 71.20 | 0.26% |
| 24 | 16 | 44.10 | 0.27% | 21.32 | 0.81% | 41.29 | 0.39% | 31.83 | 0.60% | 70.19 | -1.16% |
| 24 | 12 | 43.74 | -0.57% | 21.08 | -0.34% | 40.97 | -0.38% | 31.60 | -0.13% | 69.99 | -1.44% |
| 24 | 8 | 43.35 | -1.45% | 20.67 | -2.27% | 40.58 | -1.32% | 31.29 | -1.11% | 72.88 | 2.63% |
| 24 | 4 | 41.42 | -5.84% | 19.49 | -7.88% | 38.78 | -5.69% | 30.35 | -4.06% | 70.39 | -0.89% |
| 20 | 24 | 44.10 | 0.26% | 21.13 | -0.12% | 41.28 | 0.38% | 31.58 | -0.17% | 71.04 | 0.04% |
| 16 | 24 | 43.76 | -0.52% | 20.83 | -1.53% | 40.92 | -0.49% | 31.22 | -1.31% | 71.59 | 0.80% |
| 12 | 24 | 43.33 | -1.50% | 20.53 | -2.94% | 40.43 | -1.68% | 30.82 | -2.58% | 73.28 | 3.20% |
| 8 | 24 | 42.46 | -3.48% | 19.74 | -6.67% | 39.64 | -3.60% | 29.98 | -5.23% | 73.47 | 3.46% |
| 4 | 24 | 41.25 | -6.23% | 18.68 | -11.69% | 38.30 | -6.86% | 28.78 | -9.04% | 76.05 | 7.08% |
| 20 | 20 | 44.10 | 0.25% | 21.23 | 0.34% | 41.25 | 0.32% | 31.65 | 0.05% | 70.90 | -0.16% |
| 16 | 16 | 43.69 | -0.67% | 20.90 | -1.19% | 40.86 | -0.64% | 31.30 | -1.06% | 71.85 | 1.18% |
| 12 | 12 | 42.81 | -2.67% | 20.13 | -4.84% | 39.97 | -2.80% | 30.58 | -3.33% | 72.81 | 2.53% |
| 8 | 8 | 40.57 | -7.78% | 18.47 | -12.70% | 37.82 | -8.04% | 28.96 | -8.46% | 73.39 | 3.34% |
| 4 | 4 | 36.11 | -17.91% | 15.51 | -26.68% | 33.48 | -18.59% | 26.30 | -16.88% | 68.58 | -3.43% |

Table 19: The relation between pruning asymmetry and symmetry for a FLAN-T5 small model on the Query Independent Web Snippets Abstractive Summarization Dataset

| $l_{enc}$ | $l_{dec}$ | R-1 | Impact | R-2 | Impact | RSL | Impact | R-L | Impact | GenL | Impact |
|---|---|---|---|---|---|---|---|---|---|---|---|
| 8 | 8 | 50.22 | 100.00% | 29.03 | 100.00% | 45.87 | 100.00% | 40.19 | 100.00% | 62.79 | 100.00% |
| 8 | 6 | 50.20 | 99.96% | 28.90 | 99.55% | 45.80 | 99.83% | 40.45 | 100.65% | 62.81 | 100.03% |
| 8 | 5 | 49.74 | 99.04% | 28.56 | 98.40% | 45.55 | 99.30% | 40.27 | 100.20% | 62.68 | 99.83% |
| 8 | 4 | 48.59 | 96.74% | 27.94 | 96.24% | 44.65 | 97.33% | 39.27 | 97.70% | 62.67 | 99.82% |
| 8 | 2 | 45.36 | 90.32% | 24.85 | 85.61% | 41.38 | 90.21% | 36.92 | 91.87% | 62.68 | 99.84% |
| 8 | 1 | 34.47 | 68.64% | 15.41 | 53.08% | 31.00 | 67.58% | 27.68 | 68.88% | 61.68 | 98.24% |
| 6 | 8 | 49.32 | 98.21% | 27.92 | 96.17% | 44.72 | 97.48% | 39.10 | 97.28% | 62.90 | 100.18% |
| 5 | 8 | 49.08 | 97.72% | 27.75 | 95.60% | 44.29 | 96.56% | 38.76 | 96.45% | 62.87 | 100.13% |
| 4 | 8 | 46.40 | 92.39% | 25.20 | 86.82% | 41.81 | 91.14% | 36.71 | 91.34% | 62.74 | 99.93% |
| 2 | 8 | 45.08 | 89.77% | 23.67 | 81.55% | 40.44 | 35.31% | 35.31 | 87.85% | 62.82 | 100.06% |
| 1 | 8 | 39.81 | 79.26% | 18.23 | 62.79% | 35.39 | 77.14% | 29.97 | 74.56% | 62.83 | 100.07% |
| 6 | 6 | 48.47 | 96.51% | 26.82 | 92.38% | 43.88 | 95.66% | 38.38 | 95.49% | 62.81 | 100.04% |
| 5 | 5 | 47.55 | 94.68% | 26.62 | 91.72% | 43.13 | 94.02% | 37.99 | 94.51% | 62.67 | 99.81% |
| 4 | 4 | 42.33 | 84.28% | 23.12 | 79.64% | 39.89 | 86.95% | 33.39 | 83.08% | 62.71 | 99.88% |
| 2 | 2 | 39.69 | 79.02% | 19.14 | 65.92% | 35.49 | 77.36% | 30.90 | 76.89% | 62.79 | 100.00% |
| 1 | 1 | 22.98 | 45.75% | 6.09 | 20.99% | 20.52 | 44.74% | 18.36 | 45.69% | 61.90 | 98.58% |

Table 20: The relation between pruning asymmetry and symmetry for a FLAN-T5 base model on the Query Independent Web Snippets Abstractive Summarization Dataset

| $l_{enc}$ | $l_{dec}$ | R-1 | Impact | R-2 | Impact | RSL | Impact | R-L | Impact | GenL | Impact |
|---|---|---|---|---|---|---|---|---|---|---|---|
| 12 | 12 | 54.84 | 0.00% | 34.19 | 0.00% | 50.38 | 0.00% | 44.68 | 0.00% | 62.91 | 0.00% |
| 12 | 10 | 55.02 | 0.33% | 34.00 | -0.56% | 50.20 | -0.35% | 44.67 | -0.02% | 62.79 | -0.19% |
| 12 | 8 | 55.97 | 2.05% | 34.50 | 0.91% | 51.12 | 1.48% | 44.90 | 0.48% | 62.75 | -0.24% |
| 12 | 6 | 54.54 | -0.55% | 33.70 | -1.42% | 49.94 | -0.87% | 44.19 | -1.11% | 62.81 | -0.16% |
| 12 | 4 | 52.64 | -4.01% | 31.93 | -6.62% | 47.28 | -6.16% | 42.98 | -3.81% | 62.85 | -0.09% |
| 12 | 2 | 49.02 | -10.61% | 28.05 | -17.97% | 44.98 | -10.71% | 40.36 | -9.68% | 62.89 | -0.02% |
| 10 | 12 | 54.23 | -1.11% | 33.57 | -1.82% | 49.93 | -0.89% | 44.00 | -1.52% | 62.87 | -0.05% |
| 8 | 12 | 54.02 | -1.50% | 33.06 | -3.31% | 49.49 | -1.76% | 43.80 | -1.96% | 62.85 | -0.09% |
| 6 | 12 | 48.74 | -11.13% | 32.23 | -5.72% | 48.74 | -3.26% | 42.92 | -3.95% | 62.82 | -0.14% |
| 4 | 12 | 47.93 | -12.61% | 27.47 | -19.65% | 46.21 | -8.28% | 39.77 | -11.00% | 62.79 | -0.19% |
| 2 | 12 | 47.45 | -13.48% | 25.57 | -25.22% | 43.20 | -14.26% | 37.69 | -15.66% | 62.77 | -0.22% |
| 10 | 10 | 54.25 | -1.08% | 32.88 | -3.82% | 49.51 | -1.72% | 43.24 | -3.23% | 62.82 | -0.13% |
| 8 | 8 | 53.89 | -1.73% | 32.81 | -4.04% | 49.32 | -2.10% | 43.77 | -2.04% | 62.82 | -0.14% |
| 6 | 6 | 50.26 | -8.34% | 28.70 | -16.05% | 45.62 | -9.45% | 40.05 | -10.37% | 62.82 | -0.13% |
| 4 | 4 | 47.77 | -12.89% | 26.53 | -22.40% | 43.34 | -13.97% | 37.85 | -15.29% | 62.84 | -0.10% |
| 2 | 2 | 39.59 | -27.80% | 19.64 | -42.57% | 35.80 | -28.95% | 31.38 | -29.78% | 62.85 | -0.09% |

Table 21: The relation between pruning asymmetry and symmetry for a FLAN-T5 large model on the Query Independent Web Snippets Abstractive Summarization Dataset

| $l_{enc}$ | $l_{dec}$ | R-1 | Impact | R-2 | Impact | RSL | Impact | R-L | Impact | GenL | Impact |
|---|---|---|---|---|---|---|---|---|---|---|---|
| 24 | 24 | 57.81 | 100.00% | 37.37 | 100.00% | 53.14 | 100.00% | 48.16 | 100.00% | 62.85 | 100.00% |
| 24 | 20 | 58.21 | 100.69% | 37.59 | 100.59% | 53.44 | 100.58% | 48.46 | 100.62% | 62.80 | 99.91% |
| 24 | 16 | 57.25 | 99.04% | 36.56 | 97.84% | 52.71 | 99.19% | 47.71 | 99.06% | 62.83 | 99.97% |
| 24 | 12 | 56.78 | 98.21% | 35.74 | 95.64% | 52.34 | 98.49% | 46.81 | 97.18% | 62.78 | 99.88% |
| 24 | 8 | 56.19 | 97.19% | 35.13 | 94.01% | 51.59 | 97.08% | 45.68 | 94.85% | 62.79 | 99.90% |
| 24 | 4 | 54.53 | 94.32% | 33.69 | 90.15% | 50.00 | 94.10% | 44.65 | 92.71% | 62.83 | 99.97% |
| 20 | 24 | 57.34 | 99.19% | 36.39 | 97.38% | 52.66 | 99.10% | 47.28 | 98.18% | 62.81 | 99.93% |
| 16 | 24 | 56.26 | 97.33% | 35.90 | 96.07% | 51.04 | 96.04% | 46.82 | 97.22% | 62.81 | 99.93% |
| 12 | 24 | 55.31 | 95.67% | 34.22 | 91.58% | 50.60 | 95.23% | 45.11 | 93.66% | 62.88 | 100.04% |
| 8 | 24 | 54.80 | 94.79% | 33.42 | 89.43% | 49.95 | 94.00% | 44.11 | 91.59% | 62.70 | 99.76% |
| 4 | 24 | 51.40 | 88.92% | 30.31 | 81.11% | 46.49 | 87.48% | 41.12 | 85.38% | 62.70 | 99.75% |
| 20 | 20 | 56.81 | 98.28% | 36.32 | 97.20% | 52.21 | 98.25% | 46.82 | 97.21% | 62.69 | 99.74% |
| 16 | 16 | 56.10 | 97.05% | 35.98 | 96.29% | 51.05 | 96.07% | 45.89 | 95.28% | 62.71 | 99.76% |
| 12 | 12 | 54.16 | 93.70% | 33.00 | 88.31% | 49.58 | 93.31% | 44.80 | 93.02% | 62.77 | 99.87% |
| 8 | 8 | 51.77 | 89.55% | 30.78 | 82.38% | 47.31 | 89.03% | 41.32 | 85.79% | 62.73 | 99.81% |
| 4 | 4 | 45.70 | 79.06% | 22.77 | 60.94% | 41.36 | 77.84% | 36.09 | 74.94% | 62.70 | 99.76% |

Table 22: The relation between pruning asymmetry and symmetry for a FLAN-T5 small model on the Extreme Summarization (XSUM) Abstractive Summarization Dataset

| $l_{enc}$ | $l_{dec}$ | R-1 | Impact | R-2 | Impact | RSL | Impact | R-L | Impact | GenL | Impact |
|---|---|---|---|---|---|---|---|---|---|---|---|
| 8 | 8 | 33.27 | 0.00% | 11.09 | 0.00% | 26.17 | 0.00% | 26.17 | 0.00% | 28.01 | 0.00% |
| 8 | 6 | 33.79 | 1.56% | 11.61 | 4.74% | 26.73 | 2.14% | 26.74 | 2.18% | 27.79 | -0.78% |
| 8 | 5 | 33.47 | 0.61% | 11.43 | 3.12% | 26.64 | 1.81% | 26.65 | 1.83% | 27.40 | -2.18% |
| 8 | 3 | 33.04 | -0.69% | 11.24 | 1.36% | 26.26 | 0.36% | 26.27 | 0.38% | 28.08 | 0.26% |
| 8 | 2 | 31.48 | -5.36% | 10.53 | -5.02% | 25.39 | -2.99% | 25.38 | -3.01% | 26.58 | -5.13% |
| 8 | 1 | 23.16 | -30.39% | 6.03 | -45.58% | 19.02 | -27.32% | 19.02 | -27.33% | 36.68 | 30.93% |
| 5 | 8 | 33.31 | 0.13% | 11.18 | 0.82% | 26.16 | -0.04% | 26.16 | -0.06% | 28.31 | 1.08% |
| 5 | 8 | 32.55 | -2.15% | 10.61 | -4.32% | 25.50 | -2.55% | 25.50 | -2.55% | 28.35 | 1.19% |
| 3 | 8 | 31.82 | -4.36% | 10.11 | -8.84% | 24.92 | -4.78% | 24.92 | -4.77% | 28.43 | 1.50% |
| 2 | 8 | 29.65 | -10.87% | 8.59 | -22.48% | 23.02 | -12.02% | 23.02 | -12.03% | 27.90 | -0.39% |
| 1 | 8 | 28.46 | -14.46% | 7.70 | -30.57% | 22.09 | -15.60% | 22.09 | -15.59% | 27.87 | -0.50% |
| 6 | 6 | 32.50 | -2.29% | 10.73 | -3.24% | 25.67 | -1.90% | 25.68 | -1.88% | 28.07 | 0.19% |
| 5 | 5 | 31.77 | -4.50% | 10.19 | -8.04% | 25.14 | -3.94% | 25.14 | -3.95% | 28.09 | 0.29% |
| 3 | 3 | 30.42 | -8.57% | 9.50 | -14.31% | 24.16 | -7.66% | 24.16 | -7.67% | 27.91 | -0.38% |
| 2 | 2 | 26.71 | -19.70% | 7.31 | -34.09% | 21.38 | -18.30% | 21.38 | -18.31% | 26.35 | -5.93% |
| 1 | 1 | 19.54 | -41.26% | 4.00 | -63.91% | 16.00 | -38.86% | 16.00 | -38.87% | 35.73 | 27.54% |

Table 23: The relation between pruning asymmetry and symmetry for a FLAN-T5 base model on the Extreme Summarization (XSUM) Abstractive Summarization Dataset

| $l_{enc}$ | $l_{dec}$ | R-1 | Impact | R-2 | Impact | RSL | Impact | R-L | Impact | GenL | Impact |
|---|---|---|---|---|---|---|---|---|---|---|---|
| 12 | 12 | 38.78 | 0.00% | 15.69 | 0.00% | 31.14 | 0.00% | 31.15 | 0.00% | 25.92 | 0.00% |
| 12 | 10 | 38.46 | -0.83% | 15.27 | -2.65% | 30.70 | -1.43% | 30.71 | -1.42% | 26.72 | 3.11% |
| 12 | 8 | 38.11 | -1.72% | 14.91 | -4.97% | 30.34 | -2.59% | 30.34 | -2.60% | 27.64 | 6.65% |
| 12 | 6 | 38.55 | -0.58% | 15.40 | -1.83% | 30.87 | -0.87% | 30.88 | -0.87% | 27.42 | 5.80% |
| 12 | 4 | 38.04 | -1.91% | 15.19 | -3.18% | 30.63 | -1.64% | 29.65 | -4.82% | 26.40 | 1.85% |
| 12 | 2 | 35.39 | -8.74% | 13.73 | -12.47% | 28.96 | -7.02% | 28.96 | -7.03% | 27.55 | 6.32% |
| 10 | 12 | 39.04 | 0.68% | 15.92 | 1.47% | 31.22 | 0.24% | 31.23 | 0.25% | 26.89 | 3.75% |
| 8 | 12 | 37.05 | -4.45% | 14.10 | -10.09% | 29.29 | -5.95% | 29.30 | -5.93% | 27.68 | 6.82% |
| 6 | 12 | 36.45 | -6.01% | 13.84 | -11.79% | 28.96 | -7.02% | 28.96 | -7.02% | 27.21 | 4.99% |
| 4 | 12 | 34.32 | -11.48% | 12.10 | -22.88% | 26.99 | -13.35% | 26.99 | -13.34% | 27.20 | 4.94% |
| 2 | 12 | 31.88 | -17.78% | 10.27 | -34.53% | 24.85 | -20.21% | 24.85 | -20.22% | 28.22 | 8.88% |
| 10 | 10 | 38.80 | 0.05% | 15.72 | 0.22% | 31.07 | -0.25% | 31.08 | -0.23% | 26.92 | 3.88% |
| 8 | 8 | 37.21 | -4.04% | 14.30 | -8.85% | 29.55 | -5.13% | 29.54 | -5.15% | 27.40 | 5.72% |
| 6 | 6 | 34.92 | -9.95% | 12.44 | -20.68% | 27.56 | -11.51% | 27.57 | -11.50% | 27.72 | 6.96% |
| 4 | 4 | 32.48 | -16.24% | 10.67 | -31.95% | 25.49 | -18.15% | 25.50 | -18.14% | 27.98 | 7.98% |
| 2 | 2 | 27.44 | -29.23% | 7.74 | -50.65% | 21.95 | -29.51% | 21.96 | -29.52% | 29.38 | 13.38% |

Table 24: The relation between pruning asymmetry and symmetry for a FLAN-T5 large model on the Extreme Summarization (XSUM) Abstractive Summarization Dataset

| $l_{enc}$ | $l_{dec}$ | R-1 | Impact | R-2 | Impact | RSL | Impact | R-L | Impact | GenL | Impact |
|---|---|---|---|---|---|---|---|---|---|---|---|
| 24 | 24 | 39.71 | 0.00% | 16.34 | 0.00% | 31.72 | 0.00% | 31.72 | 0.01% | 26.74 | 0.00% |
| 24 | 20 | 43.18 | 8.74% | 19.80 | 21.17% | 35.21 | 11.01% | 35.22 | 11.04% | 25.91 | -3.10% |
| 24 | 16 | 42.73 | 7.59% | 19.30 | 18.10% | 34.76 | 9.58% | 34.76 | 9.59% | 26.40 | -1.29% |
| 24 | 12 | 42.34 | 6.61% | 18.92 | 15.78% | 34.52 | 8.84% | 34.53 | 8.87% | 25.49 | -4.68% |
| 24 | 8 | 41.30 | 4.00% | 17.96 | 9.94% | 33.73 | 6.34% | 33.75 | 6.39% | 25.02 | -6.45% |
| 24 | 4 | 39.55 | -0.40% | 16.47 | 0.77% | 32.25 | 1.66% | 32.25 | 1.68% | 26.30 | -1.64% |
| 20 | 24 | 42.77 | 7.71% | 19.43 | 18.90% | 34.83 | 9.82% | 34.84 | 9.83% | 26.18 | -2.09% |
| 16 | 24 | 41.55 | 4.63% | 18.33 | 12.17% | 33.64 | 6.05% | 33.65 | 6.07% | 26.33 | -1.53% |
| 12 | 24 | 39.95 | 0.61% | 16.90 | 3.40% | 32.13 | 1.29% | 32.14 | 1.31% | 27.14 | -100.00% |
| 8 | 24 | 37.57 | -5.39% | 14.97 | -8.38% | 29.94 | -5.61% | 29.94 | -5.60% | 25.99 | -100.00% |
| 4 | 24 | 34.81 | -12.35% | 12.52 | -23.36% | 27.32 | -13.86% | 27.32 | -13.86% | 27.61 | -100.00% |
| 20 | 20 | 42.48 | 6.98% | 19.18 | 17.39% | 34.62 | 9.13% | 34.62 | 9.13% | 25.84 | -3.36% |
| 16 | 16 | 40.78 | 2.69% | 17.56 | 7.44% | 32.99 | 4.00% | 33.00 | 4.02% | 26.47 | -1.00% |
| 12 | 12 | 38.94 | 6.98% | 15.89 | -2.78% | 31.21 | -1.61% | 31.22 | -1.58% | 26.59 | -0.57% |
| 8 | 8 | 34.65 | -12.75% | 12.15 | -25.65% | 27.36 | -13.76% | 27.36 | -13.73% | 28.16 | 5.30% |
| 4 | 4 | 29.82 | -24.91% | 8.96 | -45.14% | 23.59 | -25.62% | 23.60 | -25.60% | 28.10 | 5.09% |

Table 25: Role of model symmetry in inference efficiency on FLAN-T5 small model on the QIWS dataset

| $l_{enc}$ | $l_{dec}$ | R-2 | Impact | BS 1 | STD | Speedup | BS 8 | STD | Speedup | BS 16 | STD | Speedup |
|---|---|---|---|---|---|---|---|---|---|---|---|---|
| 8 | 8 | 29.03 | 0.00% | 524 | 3.95 | 1.00 | 653 | 2.49 | 1.00 | 729 | 5.12 | 1.00 |
| 8 | 6 | 28.90 | -0.45% | 406 | 1.28 | 1.29 | 514 | 5.02 | 1.27 | 583 | 2.47 | 1.25 |
| 8 | 5 | 28.56 | -1.60% | 348 | 2.34 | 1.51 | 455 | 1.6 | 1.44 | 527 | 1.85 | 1.38 |
| 8 | 4 | 27.94 | -3.76% | 293 | 3.35 | 1.79 | 394 | 6.32 | 1.66 | 469 | 2.65 | 1.55 |
| 8 | 2 | 24.85 | -14.39% | 195 | 1.61 | 2.69 | 353 | 3.38 | 1.85 | 426 | 6.38 | 1.71 |
| 8 | 1 | 15.41 | -46.92% | 132 | 0.959 | 3.97 | 211 | 2.82 | 3.09 | 389 | 2.94 | 1.87 |
| 6 | 8 | 27.92 | -3.83% | 512 | 5.15 | 1.02 | 626 | 4.19 | 1.04 | 684 | 2.81 | 1.07 |
| 5 | 8 | 27.75 | -4.40% | 508 | 3.56 | 1.03 | 617 | 4.91 | 1.06 | 666 | 4.16 | 1.09 |
| 4 | 8 | 25.20 | -13.18% | 514 | 3.55 | 1.02 | 603 | 4.52 | 1.08 | 639 | 2.08 | 1.14 |
| 2 | 8 | 23.67 | -18.45% | 514 | 514 | 1.02 | 585 | 5.36 | 1.12 | 608 | 4.45 | 1.20 |
| 1 | 8 | 18.23 | -37.21% | 510 | 5.81 | 1.03 | 574 | 4.21 | 1.14 | 595 | 7.06 | 1.23 |
| 6 | 6 | 26.82 | -7.62% | 407 | 5.26 | 1.29 | 496 | 8.77 | 1.32 | 548 | 1.97 | 1.33 |
| 5 | 5 | 26.62 | -8.28% | 346 | 6.84 | 1.51 | 430 | 3.54 | 1.52 | 480 | 12.4 | 1.52 |
| 4 | 4 | 23.12 | -20.36% | 375 | 4.25 | 1.40 | 441 | 6.92 | 1.48 | 478 | 10.6 | 1.53 |
| 2 | 2 | 19.14 | -34.08% | 402 | 2.05 | 1.30 | 452 | 9.84 | 1.44 | 476 | 8.29 | 1.53 |
| 1 | 1 | 6.09 | -79.01% | 134 | 6.2 | 3.91 | 527 | 3.03 | 1.24 | 549 | 13.4 | 1.33 |

Table 26: Role of model symmetry in inference efficiency on FLAN-T5 base model on the QIWS dataset

| $l_{enc}$ | $l_{dec}$ | R-2 | Impact | BS 1 | STD | Speedup | BS 8 | STD | Speedup | BS 16 | STD | Speedup |
|---|---|---|---|---|---|---|---|---|---|---|---|---|
| 12 | 12 | 34.19 | 0.00% | 746 | 11 | 1.00 | 1060 | 2.84 | 1.00 | 1310 | 6.8 | 1.00 |
| 12 | 10 | 34.00 | -0.56% | 625 | 3.27 | 1.19 | 943 | 4.69 | 1.12 | 1200 | 4.8 | 1.09 |
| 12 | 8 | 34.50 | 0.91% | 523 | 2.19 | 1.43 | 814 | 4.23 | 1.30 | 1070 | 5.34 | 1.22 |
| 12 | 6 | 33.70 | -1.42% | 425 | 1.92 | 1.76 | 652 | 3.39 | 1.63 | 970 | 4.79 | 1.35 |
| 12 | 4 | 31.93 | -6.62% | 350 | 1.32 | 2.13 | 510 | 3.1 | 2.08 | 815 | 2 | 1.61 |
| 12 | 2 | 28.05 | -17.97% | 202 | 1.41 | 3.69 | 451 | 2.92 | 2.35 | 762 | 0.911 | 1.72 |
| 10 | 12 | 33.57 | -1.82% | 710 | 6.2 | 1.05 | 995 | 2.74 | 1.07 | 1290 | 4.2 | 1.02 |
| 8 | 12 | 33.06 | -3.31% | 690 | 5.72 | 1.08 | 953 | 5.72 | 1.11 | 1270 | 4.3 | 1.03 |
| 6 | 12 | 32.23 | -5.72% | 716 | 8 | 1.04 | 944 | 7.22 | 1.12 | 1080 | 5.29 | 1.21 |
| 4 | 12 | 27.47 | -19.65% | 710 | 1.75 | 1.05 | 911 | 10.1 | 1.16 | 1,000 | 8.84 | 1.31 |
| 2 | 12 | 25.57 | -25.22% | 706 | 5.4 | 1.06 | 862 | 7.11 | 1.23 | 921 | 7.04 | 1.42 |
| 10 | 10 | 32.88 | -3.82% | 633 | 11.6 | 1.18 | 915 | 11 | 1.16 | 1120 | 5.51 | 1.17 |
| 8 | 8 | 32.81 | -4.04% | 512 | 4.98 | 1.46 | 737 | 9.78 | 1.44 | 911 | 4.98 | 1.44 |
| 6 | 6 | 28.70 | -16.05% | 401 | 3.16 | 1.86 | 572 | 4.73 | 1.85 | 702 | 1.57 | 1.87 |
| 4 | 4 | 26.53 | -22.40% | 301 | 2.92 | 2.48 | 415 | 3.01 | 2.55 | 509 | 0.997 | 2.57 |
| 2 | 2 | 19.64 | -42.57% | 189 | 1.98 | 3.95 | 312 | 2.88 | 3.40 | 389 | 0.892 | 3.37 |

Table 27: Role of model symmetry in inference efficiency on FLAN-T5 large model on the QIWS dataset

| $l_{enc}$ | $l_{dec}$ | R-2 | Impact | BS 1 | STD | Speedup | BS 8 | STD | Speedup | BS 16 | STD | Speedup |
|---|---|---|---|---|---|---|---|---|---|---|---|---|
| 24 | 24 | 37.37 | 0.00% | 1430 | 6.08 | 1.00 | 2240 | 4.81 | 1.00 | 3320 | 1.02 | 1.00 |
| 24 | 20 | 37.59 | 0.59% | 1210 | 4.73 | 1.18 | 1990 | 6.89 | 1.13 | 3010 | 2.63 | 1.10 |
| 24 | 16 | 36.56 | -2.16% | 1000 | 2.70 | 1.43 | 1750 | 5.92 | 1.28 | 2710 | 1.57 | 1.23 |
| 24 | 12 | 35.74 | -4.36% | 795 | 6.61 | 1.80 | 1510 | 10.40 | 1.48 | 2400 | 1.59 | 1.38 |
| 24 | 8 | 35.13 | -5.99% | 585 | 4.99 | 2.44 | 1260 | 7.14 | 1.78 | 2090 | 7.17 | 1.59 |
| 24 | 4 | 33.69 | -9.85% | 373 | 1.16 | 3.83 | 1030 | 10.50 | 2.17 | 1790 | 1.72 | 1.85 |
| 20 | 24 | 36.39 | -2.62% | 1410 | 3.66 | 1.01 | 2130 | 10.90 | 1.05 | 3090 | 5.98 | 1.07 |
| 16 | 24 | 35.90 | -3.93% | 1395 | 3.52 | 1.03 | 2060 | 9.89 | 1.09 | 2880 | 3.32 | 1.15 |
| 12 | 24 | 34.22 | -8.42% | 1380 | 5.20 | 1.04 | 1900 | 9.65 | 1.18 | 2630 | 0.81 | 1.26 |
| 8 | 24 | 33.42 | -10.57% | 1370 | 5.49 | 1.04 | 1790 | 19.00 | 1.25 | 2400 | 1.34 | 1.38 |
| 4 | 24 | 30.31 | -18.89% | 1350 | 7.33 | 1.06 | 1670 | 5.30 | 1.34 | 2170 | 2.79 | 1.53 |
| 20 | 20 | 36.32 | -2.80% | 1200 | 5.37 | 1.19 | 1880 | 7.89 | 1.19 | 2780 | 1.15 | 1.19 |
| 16 | 16 | 35.98 | -3.71% | 1020 | 3.49 | 1.40 | 1530 | 5.62 | 1.46 | 2230 | 1.80 | 1.49 |
| 12 | 12 | 33.00 | -11.69% | 749 | 5.30 | 1.91 | 1160 | 2.94 | 1.93 | 1710 | 0.89 | 1.94 |
| 8 | 8 | 30.78 | -17.62% | 650 | 3.32 | 2.20 | 970 | 2.78 | 2.31 | 1550 | 0.79 | 2.14 |
| 4 | 4 | 22.77 | -39.06% | 585 | 2.23 | 2.44 | 890 | 3.21 | 2.52 | 1450 | 0.92 | 2.29 |

Table 28: Role of model symmetry in inference efficiency on FLAN-T5 small model on the CNNDM dataset

| $l_{enc}$ | $l_{dec}$ | R-2 | Impact | BS 1 | STD | Speedup | BS 8 | STD | Speedup | BS 16 | STD | Speedup |
|---|---|---|---|---|---|---|---|---|---|---|---|---|
| 8 | 8 | 17.55 | 0.00% | 138 | 5.05 | 1.00 | 230 | 7.61 | 1.00 | 330 | 3.71 | 1.00 |
| 8 | 6 | 17.68 | 0.74% | 133 | 0.292 | 1.04 | 211 | 0.425 | 1.09 | 300 | 0.954 | 1.10 |
| 8 | 5 | 17.27 | -1.64% | 116 | 0.196 | 1.19 | 193 | 0.448 | 1.19 | 279 | 0.537 | 1.18 |
| 8 | 4 | 16.40 | -6.57% | 98.1 | 0.242 | 1.41 | 174 | 0.153 | 1.32 | 259 | 0.424 | 1.27 |
| 8 | 2 | 15.35 | -12.58% | 63.2 | 0.207 | 2.18 | 137 | 0.1 | 1.68 | 218 | 0.303 | 1.51 |
| 8 | 1 | 11.33 | -35.43% | 45.7 | 0.106 | 3.02 | 118 | 0.0827 | 1.95 | 198 | 0.148 | 1.67 |
| 6 | 8 | 17.69 | 0.81% | 166 | 0.303 | 0.83 | 230 | 1.42 | 1.00 | 303 | 1.06 | 1.09 |
| 5 | 8 | 17.35 | -1.16% | 165 | 0.267 | 0.84 | 219 | 0.521 | 1.05 | 283 | 1.13 | 1.17 |
| 4 | 8 | 16.80 | -4.30% | 164 | 0.185 | 0.84 | 211 | 0.89 | 1.09 | 265 | 1.85 | 1.25 |
| 2 | 8 | 15.54 | -11.49% | 162 | 332 | 0.85 | 191 | 0.332 | 1.20 | 226 | 625 | 1.46 |
| 1 | 8 | 13.31 | -24.17% | 161 | 0.626 | 0.86 | 180 | 0.423 | 1.28 | 206 | 0.55 | 1.60 |
| 6 | 6 | 17.07 | -2.77% | 131 | 0.617 | 1.05 | 192 | 0.247 | 1.20 | 261 | 0.768 | 1.26 |
| 5 | 5 | 16.20 | -7.72% | 113 | 0.306 | 1.22 | 164 | 0.642 | 1.40 | 220 | 1.36 | 1.50 |
| 4 | 4 | 14.91 | -15.05% | 95.1 | 0.0955 | 1.45 | 135 | 0.21 | 1.70 | 182 | 0.268 | 1.81 |
| 2 | 2 | 11.97 | -31.83% | 57.8 | 0.27 | 2.39 | 78.9 | 0.078 | 2.92 | 103 | 0.238 | 3.20 |
| 1 | 1 | 6.05 | -65.55% | 39.1 | 0.136 | 3.53 | 50.2 | 0.132 | 4.58 | 63.4 | 0.0845 | 5.21 |

Table 29: Role of model symmetry in inference efficiency on FLAN-T5 base model on the CNNDM dataset

| $l_{enc}$ | $l_{dec}$ | R-2 | Impact | BS 1 | STD | Speedup | BS 8 | STD | Speedup | BS 16 | STD | Speedup |
|---|---|---|---|---|---|---|---|---|---|---|---|---|
| 12 | 12 | 19.77 | 0.00% | 199 | 3.74 | 1.00 | 550 | 3.81 | 1.00 | 931 | 2.09 | 1.00 |
| 12 | 10 | 19.92 | 0.76% | 179 | 3.31 | 1.11 | 524 | 16.2 | 1.05 | 889 | 4.41 | 1.05 |
| 12 | 8 | 19.85 | 0.42% | 155 | 4.50 | 1.28 | 493 | 14 | 1.12 | 884 | 3.61 | 1.05 |
| 12 | 6 | 18.85 | -4.63% | 126 | 1.95 | 1.58 | 449 | 5.88 | 1.22 | 800 | 4.59 | 1.16 |
| 12 | 4 | 18.68 | -5.49% | 99.2 | 1.02 | 2.01 | 405 | 1.41 | 1.36 | 737 | 5.06 | 1.26 |
| 12 | 2 | 16.48 | -16.62% | 75.3 | 0.85 | 2.64 | 372 | 1.98 | 1.48 | 697 | 4.55 | 1.34 |
| 10 | 12 | 19.92 | 0.76% | 198 | 4.75 | 1.01 | 495 | 14.5 | 1.11 | 811 | 1.18 | 1.15 |
| 8 | 12 | 19.67 | -0.50% | 196 | 3.72 | 1.02 | 441 | 7.82 | 1.25 | 715 | 4.39 | 1.30 |
| 6 | 12 | 18.85 | -4.63% | 187 | 4.81 | 1.06 | 396 | 13.3 | 1.39 | 613 | 9.45 | 1.52 |
| 4 | 12 | 18.22 | -7.86% | 183 | 3.54 | 1.09 | 330 | 5.04 | 1.67 | 509 | 2.1 | 1.83 |
| 2 | 12 | 17.06 | -13.73% | 176 | 3.52 | 1.13 | 272 | 1.79 | 2.02 | 400 | 3.25 | 2.33 |
| 10 | 10 | 19.72 | -0.26% | 171 | 3.21 | 1.16 | 462 | 11.9 | 1.19 | 776 | 4.62 | 1.20 |
| 8 | 8 | 19.17 | -3.01% | 141 | 2.97 | 1.41 | 37 | 12.1 | 14.86 | 628 | 6.48 | 1.48 |
| 6 | 6 | 17.46 | -11.71% | 109 | 1.71 | 1.83 | 281 | 2.61 | 1.96 | 478 | 3.55 | 1.95 |
| 4 | 4 | 15.87 | -19.74% | 82.5 | 1.24 | 2.41 | 198 | 1.71 | 2.78 | 329 | 0.74 | 2.83 |
| 2 | 2 | 12.23 | -38.12% | 50.7 | 1.30 | 3.93 | 112 | 2.59 | 4.91 | 178 | 0.557 | 5.23 |

Table 30: Role of model symmetry in inference efficiency on FLAN-T5 LARGE model on the CNNDM dataset

| $l_{enc}$ | $l_{dec}$ | R-2 | Impact | BS 1 | STD | Speedup | BS 8 | STD | Speedup | BS 16 | STD | Speedup |
|---|---|---|---|---|---|---|---|---|---|---|---|---|
| 24 | 24 | 21.15 | 0.00% | 445 | 2.35 | 1.00 | 1480 | 20.1 | 1.00 | 2700 | 7.22 | 1.00 |
| 24 | 20 | 21.30 | 0.69% | 390 | 33.7 | 1.14 | 1390 | 4.24 | 1.06 | 2590 | 7.7 | 1.04 |
| 24 | 16 | 21.32 | 0.81% | 335 | 13.9 | 1.33 | 1330 | 7.7 | 1.11 | 2470 | 7.42 | 1.09 |
| 24 | 12 | 21.08 | -0.34% | 270 | 3.28 | 1.65 | 1250 | 11 | 1.18 | 2340 | 6.68 | 1.15 |
| 24 | 8 | 20.67 | -2.27% | 219 | 8.67 | 2.03 | 1180 | 8.17 | 1.25 | 2220 | 4.25 | 1.22 |
| 24 | 4 | 19.49 | -7.88% | 165 | 1.81 | 2.70 | 1090 | 6.6 | 1.36 | 2090 | 9.15 | 1.29 |
| 20 | 24 | 21.13 | -0.12% | 418 | 13.8 | 1.06 | 1320 | 15.3 | 1.12 | 2400 | 7.26 | 1.13 |
| 16 | 24 | 20.83 | -1.53% | 421 | 16.8 | 1.06 | 1150 | 16 | 1.29 | 2080 | 6.07 | 1.30 |
| 12 | 24 | 20.53 | -2.94% | 391 | 12.5 | 1.14 | 1000 | 21.7 | 1.48 | 1750 | 8.18 | 1.54 |
| 8 | 24 | 19.74 | -6.67% | 373 | 13.1 | 1.19 | 882 | 6.92 | 1.68 | 1430 | 4.79 | 1.89 |
| 4 | 24 | 18.68 | -11.69% | 350 | 4.32 | 1.27 | 670 | 15 | 2.21 | 1110 | 3.21 | 2.43 |
| 20 | 20 | 21.23 | 0.34% | 359 | 4.3 | 1.24 | 1240 | 15.3 | 1.19 | 2260 | 6.73 | 1.19 |
| 16 | 16 | 20.90 | -1.19% | 1289 | 2.5 | 0.35 | 994 | 21.6 | 1.49 | 1820 | 4.27 | 1.48 |
| 12 | 12 | 20.13 | -4.84% | 229 | 12.1 | 1.94 | 756 | 12.6 | 1.96 | 1370 | 4.6 | 1.97 |
| 8 | 8 | 18.47 | -12.70% | 160 | 31.8 | 2.78 | 513 | 2.55 | 2.88 | 926 | 7.24 | 2.92 |
| 4 | 4 | 15.51 | -26.68% | 89.7 | 0.588 | 4.96 | 267 | 2.14 | 5.54 | 479 | 4.3 | 5.64 |

Table 31: Role of model symmetry in inference efficiency on FLAN-T5 small model on the XSUM dataset

| $l_{enc}$ | $l_{dec}$ | R-2 | Impact | BS 1 | STD | Speedup | BS 8 | STD | Speedup | BS 16 | STD | Speedup |
|---|---|---|---|---|---|---|---|---|---|---|---|---|
| 8 | 8 | 11.09 | 0.00% | 135 | 2.73 | 1.00 | 227 | 3.51 | 1.00 | 332 | 1.91 | 1.00 |
| 8 | 6 | 11.61 | 4.74% | 108 | 1.70 | 1.25 | 196 | 1.94 | 1.16 | 303 | 7.95 | 1.10 |
| 8 | 5 | 11.43 | 3.12% | 94.1 | 3.02 | 1.43 | 183 | 3.43 | 1.24 | 281 | 6.77 | 1.18 |
| 8 | 4 | 11.24 | 1.36% | 82.7 | 2.66 | 1.63 | 168 | 2.33 | 1.35 | 263 | 2.24 | 1.26 |
| 8 | 2 | 10.53 | -5.02% | 55.8 | 1.72 | 2.42 | 141 | 1.53 | 1.61 | 234 | 5.01 | 1.42 |
| 8 | 1 | 6.03 | -45.58% | 41.1 | 0.64 | 3.28 | 124 | 0.414 | 1.83 | 215 | 4.69 | 1.54 |
| 6 | 8 | 11.18 | 0.82% | 133 | 3.51 | 1.02 | 204 | 3.63 | 1.11 | 295 | 5.72 | 1.13 |
| 5 | 8 | 10.61 | -4.32% | 134 | 3.42 | 1.01 | 193 | 3.76 | 1.18 | 273 | 10.4 | 1.22 |
| 4 | 8 | 10.11 | -8.84% | 130 | 2.77 | 1.04 | 185 | 13.6 | 1.23 | 245 | 6.45 | 1.36 |
| 2 | 8 | 8.59 | -22.48% | 126 | 4.77 | 1.07 | 163 | 6 | 1.39 | 203 | 4.1 | 1.64 |
| 1 | 8 | 7.70 | -30.57% | 126 | 3.38 | 1.07 | 148 | 2.02 | 1.53 | 180 | 2.85 | 1.84 |
| 6 | 6 | 10.73 | -3.24% | 104 | 0.45 | 1.30 | 178 | 3.24 | 1.28 | 254 | 2.37 | 1.31 |
| 5 | 5 | 10.19 | -8.04% | 91.6 | 2.10 | 1.47 | 151 | 1.78 | 1.50 | 219 | 10.3 | 1.52 |
| 4 | 4 | 9.50 | -14.31% | 79 | 3.38 | 1.71 | 124 | 2.42 | 1.83 | 178 | 1.59 | 1.87 |
| 2 | 2 | 7.31 | -34.09% | 49.5 | 2.56 | 2.73 | 74.8 | 1.9 | 3.03 | 101 | 0.719 | 3.29 |
| 1 | 1 | 4.00 | -63.91% | 32 | 1.25 | 4.22 | 48.7 | 2.11 | 4.66 | 61.9 | 1.81 | 5.36 |

Table 32: Role of model symmetry in inference efficiency on FLAN-T5 base model on the XSUM dataset

| $l_{enc}$ | $l_{dec}$ | R-2 | Impact | BS 1 | STD | Speedup | BS 8 | STD | Speedup | BS 16 | STD | Speedup |
|---|---|---|---|---|---|---|---|---|---|---|---|---|
| 12 | 12 | 15.69 | 0.00% | 205 | 3.81 | 1.00 | 546 | 8.7 | 1.00 | 917 | 4.72 | 1.00 |
| 12 | 10 | 15.27 | -2.65% | 171 | 2.79 | 1.20 | 508 | 6.39 | 1.07 | 876 | 3.02 | 1.05 |
| 12 | 8 | 14.91 | -4.97% | 150 | 1.32 | 1.37 | 476 | 2.82 | 1.15 | 830 | 1.08 | 1.10 |
| 12 | 6 | 15.40 | -1.83% | 129 | 4.33 | 1.59 | 450 | 9.33 | 1.21 | 789 | 3.73 | 1.16 |
| 12 | 4 | 15.19 | -3.18% | 101 | 2.16 | 2.03 | 411 | 5.27 | 1.33 | 744 | 1.71 | 1.23 |
| 12 | 2 | 13.73 | -12.47% | 76 | 1.76 | 2.70 | 380 | 3.43 | 1.44 | 706 | 8.13 | 1.30 |
| 10 | 12 | 15.92 | 1.47% | 200 | 6.37 | 1.03 | 494 | 2.45 | 1.11 | 818 | 1.72 | 1.12 |
| 8 | 12 | 14.10 | -10.09% | 195 | 5.47 | 1.05 | 445 | 20.8 | 1.23 | 713 | 1.71 | 1.29 |
| 6 | 12 | 13.84 | -11.79% | 190 | 3.89 | 1.08 | 396 | 9.79 | 1.38 | 612 | 4.64 | 1.50 |
| 4 | 12 | 12.10 | -22.88% | 185 | 2.24 | 1.11 | 337 | 3.09 | 1.62 | 505 | 1.96 | 1.82 |
| 2 | 12 | 10.27 | -34.53% | 180 | 2.08 | 1.14 | 282 | 4.03 | 1.94 | 399 | 2.85 | 2.30 |
| 10 | 10 | 15.72 | 0.22% | 174 | 4.09 | 1.18 | 475 | 18.5 | 1.15 | 772 | 1.79 | 1.19 |
| 8 | 8 | 14.30 | -8.85% | 140 | 1.95 | 1.46 | 373 | 2.21 | 1.46 | 625 | 1.51 | 1.47 |
| 6 | 6 | 12.44 | -20.68% | 112 | 1.71 | 1.83 | 290 | 6.77 | 1.88 | 480 | 3.5 | 1.91 |
| 4 | 4 | 10.67 | -31.95% | 84.2 | 3.75 | 2.43 | 201 | 1.58 | 2.72 | 330 | 4.43 | 2.78 |
| 2 | 2 | 7.74 | -50.65% | 51.5 | 3.01 | 3.98 | 112 | 1.02 | 4.88 | 179 | 0.894 | 5.12 |

Table 33: Role of model symmetry in inference efficiency on FLAN-T5 large model on the XSUM dataset

| $l_{enc}$ | $l_{dec}$ | R-2 | Impact | BS 1 | STD | Speedup | BS 8 | STD | Speedup | BS 16 | STD | Speedup |
|---|---|---|---|---|---|---|---|---|---|---|---|---|
| 24 | 24 | 16.34 | 0.00% | 447 | 19.4 | 1.00 | 1480 | 23 | 1.00 | 2700 | 16.1 | 1.00 |
| 24 | 20 | 19.80 | 21.16% | 374 | 4.84 | 1.20 | 1410 | 17.5 | 1.05 | 2580 | 7.52 | 1.05 |
| 24 | 16 | 19.30 | 18.09% | 327 | 19.4 | 1.37 | 1320 | 8.18 | 1.12 | 2460 | 7.19 | 1.10 |
| 24 | 12 | 18.92 | 15.77% | 272 | 7.91 | 1.64 | 1240 | 7.06 | 1.19 | 2340 | 7.5 | 1.15 |
| 24 | 8 | 17.96 | 9.93% | 216 | 7.81 | 2.07 | 1170 | 11.4 | 1.26 | 2210 | 6.49 | 1.22 |
| 24 | 4 | 16.47 | 0.76% | 165 | 3.11 | 2.71 | 1090 | 3.66 | 1.36 | 2080 | 7.17 | 1.30 |
| 20 | 24 | 19.43 | 18.88% | 406 | 21.5 | 1.10 | 1310 | 11.5 | 1.13 | 2390 | 7.76 | 1.13 |
| 16 | 24 | 18.33 | 12.16% | 412 | 20.3 | 1.08 | 1140 | 6.88 | 1.30 | 2080 | 7.01 | 1.30 |
| 12 | 24 | 16.90 | 3.39% | 384 | 18.8 | 1.16 | 986 | 11 | 1.50 | 1750 | 686 | 1.54 |
| 8 | 24 | 14.97 | -8.39% | 369 | 8.87 | 1.21 | 822 | 15.5 | 1.80 | 1420 | 15.5 | 1.90 |
| 4 | 24 | 12.52 | -23.37% | 345 | 4.41 | 1.30 | 649 | 3.26 | 2.28 | 110 | 5.96 | 24.55 |
| 20 | 20 | 19.18 | 17.38% | 357 | 11.8 | 1.25 | 1230 | 13.2 | 1.20 | 2260 | 2.16 | 1.19 |
| 16 | 16 | 17.56 | 7.43% | 288 | 5.91 | 1.55 | 995 | 9.41 | 1.49 | 1820 | 5.33 | 1.48 |
| 12 | 12 | 15.89 | -2.79% | 217 | 3.09 | 2.06 | 748 | 3.25 | 1.98 | 1370 | 6.59 | 1.97 |
| 8 | 8 | 12.15 | -25.66% | 158 | 6.04 | 2.83 | 511 | 9.62 | 2.90 | 920 | 2.06 | 2.93 |
| 4 | 4 | 8.96 | -45.14% | 92.3 | 2.88 | 4.84 | 267 | 1.51 | 5.54 | 481 | 1.69 | 5.61 |

# Small is the New Big: Pre-finetuned Compact Models are Better for Asynchronous Active Learning

**Dantong Liu**
Amazon.com, Inc
Sunnyvale, United States
lidanton@amazon.com

**Kaushik Pavani**
Amazon.com, Inc
Seattle, United States
sripava@amazon.com

**Sunny Dasgupta**
Amazon.com, Inc
Seattle, United States
sunnyd@amazon.com

**Abstract**

We examine the effects of model size and pre-finetuning in an active learning setting where classifiers are trained from scratch on 14 binary and 3 multi-class text classification tasks. We make an important observation that, in realistic active learning settings, where the human annotator and the active learning system operate in asynchronous mode, a compact pre-finetuned 1-layer transformer model with 4.2 million parameters is 30% more label efficient when compared to the larger 24-layer 84 million parameter transformer model. Further, in line with previous studies, we note that pre-finetuning transformer models on related tasks improves label efficiency of downstream tasks by 12%-50%. The compact pre-finetuned model does not require GPUs, making it a viable solution for large-scale real-time inference with cheaper CPU options.

## 1 Introduction

Active learning is a popular approach used to reduce the manual labeling effort required to train a classifier. In active learning, we iteratively acquire labels from an annotator and use them to train a classifier.

Most existing academic literature (Huang and Zhou, 2013; Shao et al., 2019) on active learning assumes that manual labeling process can only happen after the model update is complete, making the active learning loop 'synchronous'. In practice, this implies that human annotators have to wait until an active learning iteration (training on labeled data and inference on all unlabeled data) process is complete before they can provide more labels. As pointed out by (Huang et al., 2021), in realistic production settings, 'synchronous' active learning will significantly decrease annotators' productivity. To this end, typical production systems such as Sagemaker GT (sag) employ 'asynchronous' active learning setup where the human annotators continuously provide annotations while the training and inference happen in the background.

*Pre-finetuning* proposed by Aghajanyan *et al* (2021) is a stage after pre-training to further refine representations before end-task finetuning. The purpose of the pre-finetuning step is to increase the similarity between data used for pre-training and downstream finetuning tasks (Phang et al., 2018; Pruksachatkun et al., 2020; Gururangan et al., 2020). Aghajanyan *et al* pose pre-finetuning as a Multi-task learning (MTL) problem on 47 tasks, and their experiments show that incorporating pre-finetuning to RoBERTa and BART models yields consistent improvements in downstream task finetuning, particularly in the low data regime.

In this work, we examine the effects of model size and pre-finetuning in a realistic asynchronous active learning setting on a diverse set of 14 binary and 3 multi-class text classification tasks. Our contributions are three-fold:

1. We present evidence that a small transformer model is ideal for use in large scale environments with asynchronous active learning setting. With a given training and inference infrastructure, large models, counter-intuitively, can increase the number of labeled data required to achieve precision/recall targets set by customers because of their slow training/inference speeds.
2. We conduct an extensive study surrounding the label efficiency of standard pre-trained representations and their respective pre-finetuned counterparts. We show empirical evidence that pre-finetuning helps to reduce the number of labeled data required to build transformer-based classifiers.
3. We present evidence that pre-finetuning can be formulated as a large-scale multi-label classification problem, which enables us to pre-finetune on a large corpus of 2664 classification tasks. This technique helps us learn



*Proceedings of The Fourth Workshop on Simple and Efficient Natural Language Processing (SustaiNLP)*, pages 110–120
July 13, 2023 ©2023 Association for Computational Linguistics

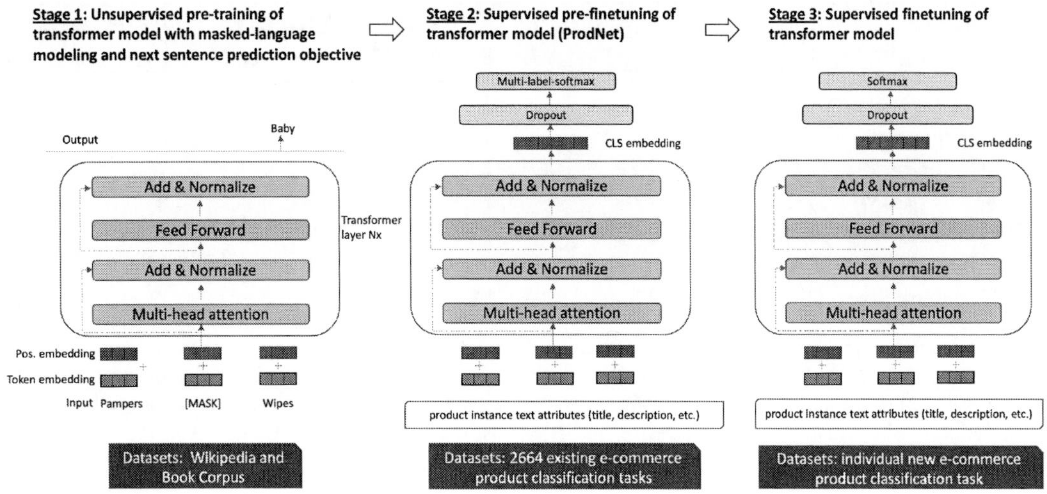


Figure 1: Besides standard pre-training (Stage 1) and then finetuning (Stage 3), our training procedure includes an intermediate pre-finetuning step (Stage 2) where we create ProdNet by training transformer model on data curated from thousands of existing classifiers.

from thousands of tasks simultaneously. To the best of our knowledge, this is the first work to realize the gain of pre-finetuning under a restricted latency budget in a large-scale asynchronous active learning setting.

## 2 Pre-Finetuning

### 2.1 Transformer Models

The details of various transformer architectures used in this study are shown in Table 2 in Appendix A.1. We perform pre-finetuning on BERT-variants models on e-commerce product classification tasks to create ProdNet variants (ProdNet-1L, ProdNet-2L, ProdNet-4L, ProdNet-6L, and ProdNet-24L-P). For example, we pre-finetune BERT-6L to create ProdNet-6L. The training process for creating ProdNet-based classifiers is illustrated in Fig. 1. We note the model parameters, training speed, and inference latency of various transformer models used in the study in Table 1. Note, the ProdNet variants have the same model architecture with the corresponding non-pre-finetuned counterparts (BERT variants). One major difference between BERT-24L-P model and the other BERT variants is that BERT-24L-P is unsupervised pre-trained using internal e-commerce product data while other BERT variants are pre-trained using public datasets. For the sake of readability, most of experiment results only include the results of 3 model pairs (underscored in Table 1), and we have verified that our conclusions hold for all 5 model pairs.

### 2.2 Pre-finetuning Datasets

To pre-finetune transformers, we selected 2664 proprietary binary classifiers created from Feb'20 to Sep'21 to classify the e-commerce products. We leverage human labeled training data from the selected binary classifiers, and aggregate all training samples from 2664 binary classifiers. Note that one instance may be a *member* of multiple binary classifiers. For e.g., a bundle instance with an 'eraser' and a 'ruler' may be a member of both 'eraser' and 'ruler' classifiers. Appendix A.2 shows the details of data used for pre-finetuning.

For each instance (product data), we use the *item_name* and *product_description* both for pre-finetuning and finetuning. We focused on the text attributes in this work, and the idea of creating ProdNet is readily generalized to image and multi-modal attributes.

### 2.3 Methodology

In the existing literature, a common approach for pre-finetuning is multi-task learning (MTL), and the number of tasks used has been fairly limited, e.g., 49 tasks were used in (Aghajanyan et al., 2021). Even at this scale, scientists have reported 'negative transfer', where the learning from upstream tasks can reduce accuracy of downstream tasks. Since we aim to learn from a large set of 2664 binary classification tasks, the traditional MTL approach does not scale. To this end, we formulate the pre-finetuning as a large multi-label classification problem using multi-label softmax loss

| Models → Parameters ↓ | BERT-1L ProdNet- 1L | BERT-2L ProdNet- 2L | BERT-4L ProdNet-4L | BERT-6L ProdNet-6L | BERT-24L-P ProdNet- 24L-P |
|---|---|---|---|---|---|
| # Trans. layers | 1 | 2 | 4 | 6 | 24 |
| Hidden layer size | 128 | 128 | 312 | 768 | 256 |
| # Attention head | 2 | 2 | 12 | 12 | 16 |
| Parameters (MM) | 4.2 | 4.4 | 14.5 | 66 | 84 |
| CPU infer. latency | 1.09 | 2.02 | 15.3 | 86 | 100 |
| GPU infer. latency | 0.16 | 0.18 | 0.4 | 8.6 | 10.6 |
| GPU training time | 28 | 32 | 54 | 197 | 233 |

Table 1: Inference latency (reported in milli-seconds) is the inference latency per instance computed on CPU (ml.c5.2xlarge) and GPU (ml.g4dn.xlarge) instances with batch size as 32 and max sequence length as 128. Training time is reported in seconds on a GPU (ml.g4dn.xlarge) instance with 2000 labeled data. We focus on three model pairs (underscored) for most of our experiments: BERT-1L vs. ProdNet-1L, BERT-2L vs. ProdNet-2L, and BERT-24L-P vs. ProdNet-24L-P.

function recommended by Mahajan *et al* (2018). While the solution is not generic to all multi-task problems with heterogeneous tasks, it is ideal for our use case since all our tasks of interest are binary classification tasks, which can be combined to create a multi-label dataset. The details about multi-label softmax loss and our experiments are shown in Appendix A.3.

## 3 Finetuning

We perform asynchronous active learning experiments on the selected finetuning tasks to examine the effects of model size and pre-finetuning in an active learning setting.

### 3.1 Active Learning

To measure the label efficiency of a classifier, we employ pool-based active learning setting (detailed in Appendix A.4) (Lewis and Gale, 1994; Settles, 2009; Gal et al., 2017). In each active learning iteration, we perform two operations: 1) judiciously select a subset of unlabeled instances for the data pool and send them to the annotator, and 2) train a classifier using new and the previously labeled instances. We continue active learning until convergence criteria are achieved. We use two convergence criteria for experiments which exactly mimics a production setup: 1) the estimated recall/precision for each class-of-interest should be no smaller than the business-specified targets, and 2) predictions on unlabeled data should have stabilized (Bloodgood and Vijay-Shanker, 2014).

For experiments, we use a bot (in lieu of a human annotator) to do the labeling job. To simulate realistic production scenario, we adopt asynchronous active-learning and labeling *i.e.,* the bot keeps providing labels regardless of the progress of training /inference/query acquisition process in the active learning loop. Throughout our experiments, the bot provides 3000 labels per day to mimic the labeling speed of a human annotator.

### 3.2 Finetuning Datasets

The finetuning datasets were sourced from proprietary binary and multi-class e-commerce product classification tasks created from Oct'21 to Mar'22. We deliberately selected classification tasks created after Oct'21 to 1) simulate real-world scenario where the pre-finetuned model will be used for new classification tasks, and 2) avoid any overlap with the datasets used for pre-finetuning. We selected 14 diverse binary classification tasks with the positive class prevalence ranging from 0.13 to 0.88. We also selected 3 multi-class classification datasets with class cardinalities 10, 8, and 3, respectively. The datasets have a long-tail distribution in terms of class sizes. Since we use a bot for the labeling job to avoid the human-in-the-loop, we need fully-labeled datasets of the finetuning tasks as the source of labels used by the bot, and we also need to compute metrics on data pool, which acts as the test data for active learning experiments. To curate fully-labeled datasets, we employed trained human annotators to manually label all instances in data pool. Note the data pool size of the 17 selected finetuning tasks are ranging from 8M to 17K.

### 3.3 Metrics

The key metric of interest is the number of labeled data required for the active learning process to converge, since our goal is to require as few human annotations as possible to build a classifier which satisfies precision/recall targets set by customers. For each active learning experiment, we track the progression of class-level *recall*, and *precision* computed on data pool. We summarize the class-level metrics by reporting *macro*-recall and *macro*-precision. We choose *macro* over *micro* averaging because performance of each class is equally important for our use-case.

## 4 Experiments Results

**Results on binary and multi-class classification tasks**: Fig. 2 (a), and (b) show the relative number of labeled data required for active learning experiments to converge averaged across 14 binary classification tasks and 3 multi-class classification tasks, respectively. The results of individual task (including the targeted/achieved precision/recall and number of required labels) are reported in Table 7 and 8 in Appendix A.7. We observed that

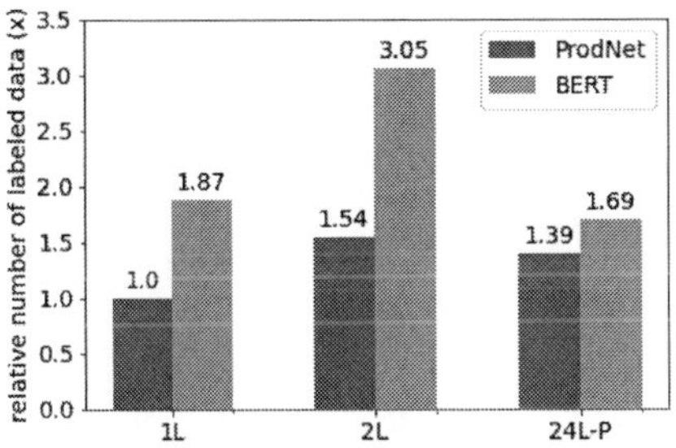


(a)

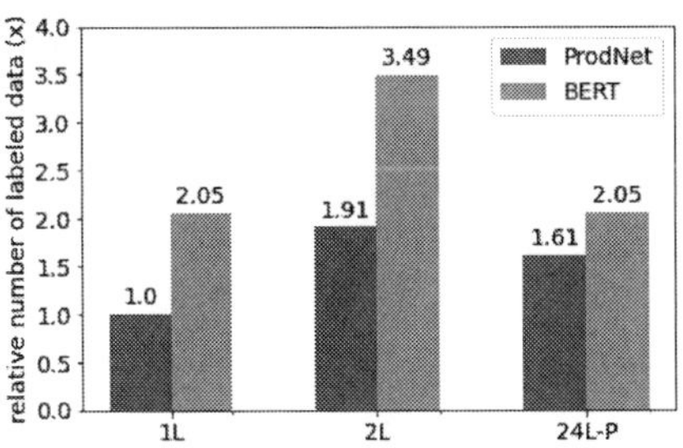


(b)

Figure 2: Average relative number of labeled data required for active learning experiments to converge (a) 14 binary classification tasks, and (b) 3 multi-class classification tasks.

- On average ProdNet-1L requires the least number of labeled data for model convergence among all the benchmarking models, increasing the label efficiency by 40% and 30% compared with ProdNet-2L and ProdNet-24L-P, respectively.
- The pre-finetuned models (ProdNet) consistently reduces the number of labeled data required for model convergence compared to the non-pre-finetuned counterparts. On average, ProdNet-1L requires 51% of labels required by BERT-1L classifier. Similarly, ProdNet-2L requires 50% of the labels that BERT-2L needs, and ProdNet-24L-P requires 88% of labels that BERT-24L-P model takes.
- The gain of pre-finetuning BERT-24L-P model is smaller when compared with the gain of pre-finetuning BERT-1L and BERT-2L. This is intuitive as BERT-24L-P model is unsupervised pre-trained using our internal product data, and it has already learnt internal product related information. In contrast, BERT-1L and BERT-2L are pre-trained using public corpora without the product specific information.
- Interestingly, even without the effect of pre-finetuning, BERT-1L is more label efficient than BERT-2L, which demonstrates the importance of smaller model size in the asynchronous active learning setting.

**Do bigger models mean fewer labels?** Fig. 3 illustrates the relative number of labeled data required for active learning experiments to converge versus number of parameters in the model on *FEE* dataset. The results show an interesting phenomenon that the number of labeled data required for active learning experiments to converge increases with the rising model parameter size. This is counter-intuitive, as larger models are usually better than smaller models for cases where the training and test datasets are fixed in academic settings. However, in an asynchronous active learning setting, larger models take longer to train and infer (*e.g.*, ProdNet-24L-P is $\sim$ 100 times slower than ProdNet-1L in CPU inference), thereby forcing human annotators to label 'stale' data. As such, larger models miss the opportunity to assist query acquisition module to select unlabeled instances effectively, and unnecessarily accumulate excessive labeled data from annotators. Smaller models, especially when pre-finetuned on 1000s of previously authored classifiers, provide a viable alternative with fast classifier authoring-time and low inference-cost. In addition, the compact pre-finetuned model does not require GPUs for inference, making it a viable solution for real-time

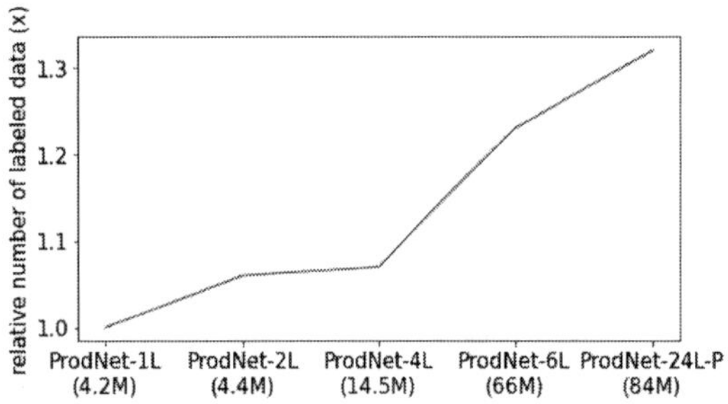


Figure 3: Relative number of labeled data required for active learning experiments to converge with model sizes on *FEE* dataset. *e.g.*, ProdNet-1L classifier requires $x$ labels to converge while ProdNet-2L needs $1.06x$ labels to converge.

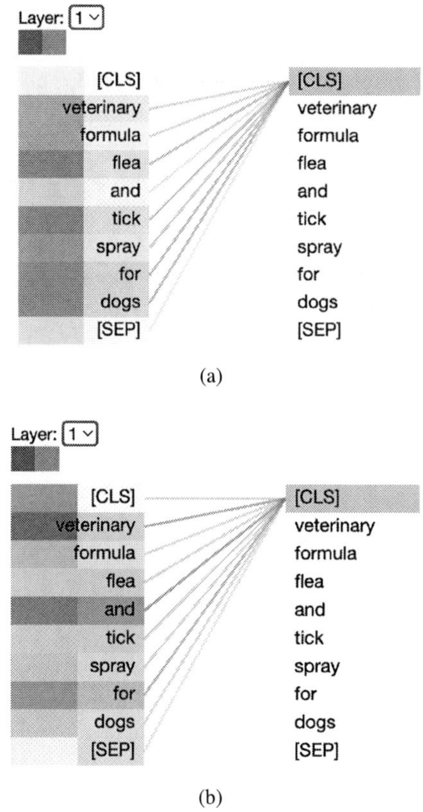


Figure 4: Attention visualization of (a) ProdNet-2L, and (b) BERT-2L

large-scale inference with cheaper CPU options.

**Why does ProdNet learn faster than the non-pre-finetuned counterpart?** Although researchers have cautioned against using attention as a reliable means of model interpretability (Serrano and Smith, 2019; Jain and Wallace, 2019), several recent works use attention weights to partially explain what words/tokens that are most influential to the model (Galassi et al., 2019; Letarte et al., 2018; Vashishth et al., 2019; Clark et al., 2019). To get an intuitive understanding if pre-finetuning helps, we illustrate attention weights[1] of the `[CLS]` token in the last layer for pre-finetuned (ProdNet-2L) and non-pre-finetuned (BERT-2L) models as shown in Fig.4. We choose to visualize `[CLS]` token since in downstream task finetuning, we pass the last layer `[CLS]` representation to a task-specific feed-forward layer and train the classifier end-to-end. It is worth mentioning that we visualize the attention of `[CLS]` token in the original ProdNet-2L (Stage 2 in Fig 1) and BERT-2L (Stage 1 in Fig 1) models without downstream tasks finetuning. Our rationale is that if a model is able to pay attention to the key information in downstream tasks before finetuning, then the model might learn faster when finetuned with the downstream task data (few-shot learning). The input text `Veterinary Formula Flea and Tick Spray for Dogs` is from the downstream task **PetCare** which aims to classify pet-care products designed to treat fleas, ticks, ringworm, or other parasites. The orange and blue color demonstrate the 2 attention heads of ProdNet-2L and BERT-2L. The darker color indicates more attention. In this example, we can observe that ProdNet-2L is able to pay more attention to `flea` and `tick` compared with BERT-2L. We hypothesize that pre-finetuning on relevant e-commerce product classification data helps the model understand potentially important words for the downstream task, thereby allowing the model to learn the downstream task faster.

Appendix A.8 shows additional results on the attention analysis.

## 5 Conclusion

In this paper, we present empirical evidence on 14 binary and 3 multi-class text classification tasks that compact transformer models consistently reduce number of labeled data required to build new classifiers in realistic asynchronous active learning settings when compared to larger models. Smaller models take less time for training and inference, and allow active learning query acquisition module to select next batch of informative instances more frequently, thereby allowing the classifier to learn fast. Further, we conclude that pre-finetuning helps compact models to learn even faster.

[1]We used BertViz for attention visualization https://github.com/jessevig/bertviz.

## References


Use amazon sagemaker ground truth to label data https://docs.aws.amazon.com/sagemaker/latest/dg/sms.html. In *Amazon Web Services*.

Armen Aghajanyan, Anchit Gupta, Akshat Shrivastava, Xilun Chen, Luke Zettlemoyer, and Sonal Gupta. 2021. Muppet: Massive multi-task representations with pre-finetuning. *CoRR*, abs/2101.11038.

Michael Bloodgood and K. Vijay-Shanker. 2014. A method for stopping active learning based on stabilizing predictions and the need for user-adjustable stopping. *CoRR*, abs/1409.5165.

Kevin Clark, Urvashi Khandelwal, Omer Levy, and Christopher D. Manning. 2019. What does BERT look at? an analysis of bert's attention. *CoRR*, abs/1906.04341.

Yarin Gal, Riashat Islam, and Zoubin Ghahramani. 2017. Deep bayesian active learning with image data. In *International Conference on Machine Learning*, pages 1183–1192. PMLR.

Andrea Galassi, Marco Lippi, and Paolo Torroni. 2019. Attention, please! A critical review of neural attention models in natural language processing. *CoRR*, abs/1902.02181.

Suchin Gururangan, Ana Marasović, Swabha Swayamdipta, Kyle Lo, Iz Beltagy, Doug Downey, and Noah A. Smith. 2020. Don't stop pretraining: Adapt language models to domains and tasks.

Sheng-Jun Huang and Zhi-Hua Zhou. 2013. Active query driven by uncertainty and diversity for incremental multi-label learning. In *2013 IEEE 13th International Conference on Data Mining*, pages 1079–1084.

Sheng-Jun Huang, Chen-Chen Zong, Kun-Peng Ning, and Hai-Bo Ye. 2021. Asynchronous active learning with distributed label querying. In *Proceedings of the Thirtieth International Joint Conference on Artificial Intelligence, IJCAI-21*, pages 2570–2576. International Joint Conferences on Artificial Intelligence Organization. Main Track.

Sarthak Jain and Byron C. Wallace. 2019. Attention is not explanation. *CoRR*, abs/1902.10186.

Xiaoqi Jiao, Yichun Yin, Lifeng Shang, Xin Jiang, Xiao Chen, Linlin Li, Fang Wang, and Qun Liu. 2019. Tinybert: Distilling BERT for natural language understanding. *CoRR*, abs/1909.10351.

Gaël Letarte, Frédérik Paradis, Philippe Giguère, and François Laviolette. 2018. Importance of self-attention for sentiment analysis. In *BlackboxNLP@EMNLP*.

David D Lewis and William A Gale. 1994. A sequential algorithm for training text classifiers. In *SIGIR'94*, pages 3–12. Springer.

Dhruv Mahajan, Ross Girshick, Vignesh Ramanathan, Kaiming He, Manohar Paluri, Yixuan Li, Ashwin Bharambe, and Laurens van der Maaten. 2018. Exploring the limits of weakly supervised pretraining. In *Proceedings of the European Conference on Computer Vision (ECCV)*.

Jason Phang, Thibault Févry, and Samuel R. Bowman. 2018. Sentence encoders on stilts: Supplementary training on intermediate labeled-data tasks. *CoRR*, abs/1811.01088.

Yada Pruksachatkun, Jason Phang, Haokun Liu, Phu Mon Htut, Xiaoyi Zhang, Richard Yuanzhe Pang, Clara Vania, Katharina Kann, and Samuel R. Bowman. 2020. Intermediate-task transfer learning with pretrained models for natural language understanding: When and why does it work?

Victor Sanh, Lysandre Debut, Julien Chaumond, and Thomas Wolf. 2019. Distilbert, a distilled version of BERT: smaller, faster, cheaper and lighter. *CoRR*, abs/1910.01108.

Sofia Serrano and Noah A. Smith. 2019. Is attention interpretable? *CoRR*, abs/1906.03731.

Burr Settles. 2009. Active learning literature survey.

Jingyu Shao, Qing Wang, and Fangbing Liu. 2019. Learning to sample: an active learning framework. *CoRR*, abs/1909.03585.

Iulia Turc, Ming-Wei Chang, Kenton Lee, and Kristina Toutanova. 2019. Well-read students learn better: The impact of student initialization on knowledge distillation. *CoRR*, abs/1908.08962.

Shikhar Vashishth, Shyam Upadhyay, Gaurav Singh Tomar, and Manaal Faruqui. 2019. Attention interpretability across NLP tasks. *CoRR*, abs/1909.11218.

# A Appendix

## A.1 Transformer models in study

Table 2 introduces the transformer models used in this study. We choose the BERT based models in our study as they are well-established models, and we focus on investigating the impact of different model sizes in the asynchronous active learning settings. The study can be easily extended to other transformer based models (e.g, RoBERTa)

## A.2 Pre-finetuning dataset

Table 3 illustrates the dataset that we used to pre-finetune transformers.

Table 4 shows dataset statistics for the supervised pre-finetuning.

## A.3 multi-label softmax

Due to the multi-label property of the pre-finetuning data, we formulate the pre-finetuning as a multi-label classification problem using multi-label softmax loss function recommended by Mahajan *et al* (Mahajan et al., 2018). multi-label softmax loss computes probabilities over all labels in the label space using a softmax activation and is trained to minimize the cross-entropy between the predicted softmax distribution and the target distribution of each instance. The target is a vector with $k$ non-zero entries, each set to $1/k$ corresponding to the $k \geq 1$ labels for the instance. We experimented both the conventional per-class sigmoid outputs with binary cross entropy loss and multi-label softmax. Results show using multi-label softmax loss function improves the top-1 accuracy by 20% compared with the model using per-class sigmoid outputs with binary cross entropy loss.

## A.4 Active learning strategy

To measure the label efficiency of a classifier $\mathcal{M}$, we employ pool-based active learning setting (Algorithm 1) (Lewis and Gale, 1994)(Settles, 2009)(Gal et al., 2017), consisting of a seed set of labeled instances $(x, y) \in \mathcal{D}_{\text{seed}}$ ($|\mathcal{D}_{\text{seed}}| = 100$) to initialize the classifier $\mathcal{M}$ in the first iteration, an unlabeled pool of data $\mathcal{D}_{\text{pool}}$, and a query acquisition function $\mathcal{A}(x, \mathcal{M})$ that ranks the next set of unlabeled instance $x \in \mathcal{D}_{\text{pool}}$ to be sent to the annotator. In each active learning iteration, we perform two operations: 1) judiciously select a subset of unlabeled instances and send them to the annotator, and 2) train a classifier using new and the previously labeled instances. To pick the next set of unlabeled instances for annotation, we take the trained classifier to perform inference on all instances in unlabeled data pool, rank them based on entropy score (calculated from the model prediction score) and select instances which have high entropy score (these are confusing instances that are most likely to increase the accuracy of the classifier in the next active learning iteration). We continue active learning until convergence criteria are achieved. We use two convergence criteria for experiments which exactly mimics a production setup: 1) the estimated recall/precision for each class-of-interest should be equal to or greater than the corresponding business-specified targets, and 2) predictions on unlabeled data should have stabilized (Bloodgood and Vijay-Shanker, 2014).

**Algorithm 1:** Active learning setup used in production and for experiments.

**Input**: Pool of unlabeled data $\mathcal{D}_{\text{pool}}$, Batch size $B$, Initial labeled dataset $\mathcal{S}$ (could be empty), Business targets on precision and recall
**Output**: Trained classifier $\mathcal{M}$ that meets business targets
**while** *convergence criteria are not met* **do**
    Rank instances from $\mathcal{D}_{\text{pool}}$ using query strategy $\mathcal{A}(x, \mathcal{M})$.
    Label top-ranked $B$ instances, add them to $\mathcal{S}$. (*Comment*: In production, human annotators provide labels, while in experiments a bot does the labeling job)
    Remove $\mathcal{S}$ from unlabeled data $\mathcal{D}_{\text{pool}} \leftarrow \mathcal{D}_{\text{pool}} \setminus \mathcal{S}$.
    (asynchronous process) Train the classifier $\mathcal{M}$ on $\mathcal{S}$.
    (asynchronous process) Predict $\mathcal{D}_{\text{pool}}$ using the classifier.
    (asynchronous process) Estimate current precision/recall using out-of-fold scores (k-fold cross validation)
**end**

## A.5 Data distribution in multi-class datasets

Table 5 presents the data distribution of the three multi-class datasets.

| Architecture | Description |
|---|---|
| BERT-24L-P | It is a internal BERT-based language model (84 million parameters). It is pre-trained on multilingual, multi-locale and multimodal (text + structured fields) e-commerce product data, and then pre-finetuned using the multi-task soft labels generated from the previously pre-trained teacher model with 500 million parameters. |
| BERT-6L | It is widely known as DistilBERT (Sanh et al., 2019), which is a 6-layer transformer model unsupervised pre-trained using English Wikipedia and Toronto Book Corpus. |
| BERT-4L | It is known as TinyBERT (Jiao et al., 2019). We used the 4 layer TinyBERT, which is distilled from the 12-layer BERT teacher model unsupervised pre-trained using English Wikipedia and Toronto Book Corpus. |
| BERT-2L | It is a 2-layer transformer model (Turc et al., 2019) unsupervised pre-trained with a masked language modeling objective on Book Corpus and English Wikipedia. |
| BERT-1L | In order to minimize the model size and investigate the impact of small transformer model, we extracted the first transformer layer from the BERT-2L and made it as a BERT-1L model. |

Table 2: Various transformer models under study (The model artifacts of BERT-6L, BERT-4L, BERT-2L used in this study are available in HuggingFace.).

| Classifier→ product instance↓ | C1 | C2 | C3 | ... | C2664 |
|---|---|---|---|---|---|
| A1 | 1 | 0 | 0 | ... | 0 |
| A2 | 0 | 1 | 1 | ... | 0 |
| ... | ... | ... | ... | ... | ... |
| An | 1 | 0 | 0 | ... | 0 |

Table 3: Illustration of dataset used to pre-finetune transformers. The rows of the table represent product instances, and the columns represent the 2664 binary classifiers used in our pre-finetuning. Each cell represents the membership of an product instance to a class. For example, if the class "C1" was created to identify "Face Masks", then product instance A1 was classified as a FaceMask and product instance A2 was not.

| $L$ | $n_{trn}$ | $n_{val}$ | $n_{tst}$ | $\bar{n}$ | $\bar{L}$ |
|---|---|---|---|---|---|
| 2664 | 4,607,904 | 918,894 | 820,839 | 2,383 | 2.62 |

Table 4: Statistics of the supervised pre-finetuning dataset. $L$ is number of classification tasks. $n_{trn}$, $n_{val}$, and $n_{tst}$ refer to number of instances in training, validation and test dataset, respectively. $\bar{n}$ is average number of instances per classification task and $\bar{L}$ is average number of labeled data per instance (product data)

Table 5: Multi-class datasets (*HS*, *FEE*, and *AB*) have long-tail distribution in terms of class sizes. $S$ denotes the relative size of each class. *E.g.*, the class HS-2 has 41.88% of 1.15M products in HS dataset.

| HS (1.15M) | | FEE (750K) | | AB (8.4M) | |
|---|---|---|---|---|---|
| Class | $S(\%)$ | Class | $S(\%)$ | Class | $S(\%)$ |
| HS-0 | 0.52 | T-0 | 50.56 | A-0 | 18.39 |
| HS-1 | 0.36 | T-1 | 6.36 | A-1 | 46.58 |
| HS-2 | 41.88 | T-2 | 30.84 | - | - |
| HS-3 | 25.81 | T-3 | 10.69 | - | - |
| HS-4 | 0.30 | T-4 | 0.53 | - | - |
| HS-5 | 0.44 | T-5 | 0.62 | - | - |
| HS-6 | 2.36 | T-6 | 0.28 | - | - |
| HS-7 | 11.10 | - | - | - | - |
| HS-8 | 14.65 | - | - | - | - |
| not-in-k | 2.59 | not-in-k | 0.12 | not-in-k | 35.03 |

| Hyperparameters | Pre-finetuning | Finetuning |
|---|---|---|
| Loss function | Multi-label softmax | Softmax |
| Train batch size | 32 | 32 |
| Val batch size | 32 | - |
| Dropout factor | 0.1 | 0.3 |
| Max seq length | 128 | 128 |
| Optimizer | AdamW | AdamW |
| Learning rate | $2e^{-5}$ | $2e^{-5}$ /$1e^{-4}$ |
| Weight decay | 0.01 | 0.01 |
| Early stopping | True | False |
| Max training epoch | 10 | 5 |

Table 6: Hyperparameters we used in the pre-finetuning and finetuning stages to train various transformer models. In downstream task finetuning, we use learning rate $2e^{-5}$ for BERT-6L and ProdNet-6L, and learning rate $1e^{-4}$ for rest of benchmarking transformer models. In order to fully utilize the labeled data for training, we do not use validation dataset in downstream task finetuning.

### A.6 Hyperparameters

Table 6 is the hyperparameters used in pre-finetuning and finetuning various transformer models.

### A.7 Per-task experiment results

Table 7 and Table 8 shows 1) the relative number of labeled data required for various active learning experiments to converge, and 2) the relative (macro) recall/(macro) precision of the models measured on data pool $\mathcal{D}_{\text{pool}}$, in the 14 binary classification tasks and 3 multi-class classification tasks, respectively.

### A.8 Why does ProdNet learn faster than the non-pre-finetuned counterpart?

To obtain a global understanding if pre-finetuning helps, we aggregate attention weights computed on 500 positive examples for four classification tasks (listed in Table 7). Specifically, we calculate the average attention for the key phrases a human expert deemed most critical to the classification task. For example, for PetCare products, the key phrases identified are *flea*, *tick*, *worm*, and *parasites*. The results are shown in Table 9. We observe that in general ProdNet-2L is able to pay more attention to the key tokens than BERT-2L. We hypothesize that pre-finetuning on relevant e-commerce product data helps the model understand potentially important words for the downstream task, thereby allowing the model to learn the downstream task faster.

| Models→ | ProdNet-1L | BERT-1L | ProdNet-2L | BERT-2L | ProdNet-24L-P | BERT-24L-P |
|---|---|---|---|---|---|---|
| Tasks ↓<br>(R/P target) | Top: relative number of labeled data<br>Bottom: relative recall(R)/precision(P) computed on data pool | | | | | |
| Speakers | *x* | 2.56*x* | 2.33*x* | 2.57*x* | 1.76*x* | 2.7*x* |
| (*r*/*p*) | 1.11*r*/*p* | 1.10*r*/1.02*p* | 1.11*r*/1.01*p* | 1.07*r*/*p* | 1.11*r*/1.02*p* | 1.11*r*/1.03*p* |
| Pillows | *x* | 1.43*x* | 1.09*x* | 2.05*x* | 1.08*x* | 1.74*x* |
| (*r*/*p*) | 1.09*r*/1.01*p* | 1.1*r*/1.01*p* | 1.07*r*/1.01*p* | 1.02*r*/1.02*p* | 1.11*r*/1.02*p* | 1.11*r*/1.03*p* |
| Plants | *x* | 1.80*x* | 2.12*x* | 5.87*x* | 1.32*x* | 1.47*x* |
| (*r*/*p*) | 1.01*r*/1.02*p* | *r*/1.03*p* | *r*/1.03*p* | *r*/1.04*p* | *r*/1.03*p* | 1.01*r*/1.03*p* |
| Bottle | *x* | 1.74*x* | 1.52*x* | 2.94*x* | 1.10*x* | 1.28*x* |
| (*r*/*p*) | 1.34*r*/1.01*p* | 1.38*r*/1.01*p* | 1.28*r*/*p* | 1.32*r*/1.01*p* | 1.32*r*/*p* | 1.3*r*/1.03*p* |
| Jackets | *x* | 1.32*x* | 1.79*x* | 2.40*x* | **0.99*x*** | 1.20*x* |
| (*r*/*p*) | 1.07*r*/1.02*p* | 1.06*r*/1.04*p* | 1.08*r*/1.02*p* | 1.08*r*/*p* | 1.1*r*/*p* | 1.13*r*/1.01*p* |
| Belt | *x* | 1.34*x* | 2.01*x* | 3.85*x* | 1.66*x* | 1.75*x* |
| (*r*/*p*) | 1.06*r*/1.01*p* | 1.05*r*/1.02*p* | 1.06*r*/1.02*p* | 1.05*r*/1.02*p* | 1.06*r*/1.04*p* | 1.06*r*/1.03*p* |
| Postcard | *x* | 1.37*x* | 2.10*x* | 3.10*x* | 1.47*x* | 1.55*x* |
| (*r*/*p*) | 1.16*r*/1.01*p* | 1.16*r*/1.01*p* | 1.17*r*/*p* | 1.15*r*/1.02*p* | 1.16*r*/1.02*p* | 1.16*r*/1.03*p* |
| PetCare | *x* | 1.57*x* | 1.25*x* | 2.12*x* | 1.74*x* | 2.17*x* |
| (*r*/*p*) | 1.12*r*/1.02*p* | 1.12*r*/1.03*p* | 1.12*r*/1.01*p* | 1.12*r*/1.02*p* | 1.12*r*/1.04*p* | 1.12*r*/1.04*p* |
| T39253 | *x* | 2.21*x* | 1.45*x* | 2.31*x* | 1.72*x* | 1.78*x* |
| (*r*/*p*) | 1.06*r*/*p* | 1.07*r*/1.01*p* | 1.04*r*/*p* | 1.05*r*/*p* | 1.08*r*/1.01*p* | 1.08*r*/1.02*p* |
| FireStarter | *x* | 2.98*x* | 1.22*x* | 2.01*x* | 1.89*x* | 2.32*x* |
| (*r*/*p*) | 1.08*r*/1.02*p* | 1.08*r*/1.03*p* | 1.08*r*/1.01*p* | 1.08*r*/1.02*p* | 1.08*r*/1.03*p* | 1.08*r*/1.04*p* |
| Batteries | *x* | 1.65*x* | 0.92*x* | 5.15*x* | **0.81*x*** | 1.52*x* |
| (*r*/*p*) | 1.25*r*/*p* | 1.24*r*/1.01*p* | 1.14*r*/1.01*p* | 1.24*r*/1.01*p* | 1.28*r*/1.01*p* | 1.28*r*/1.03*p* |
| Radio | *x* | 1.95*x* | 1.55*x* | 2.55*x* | 1.34*x* | 1.40*x* |
| (*r*/*p*) | 1.04*r*/1.04*p* | 1.01*r*/1.04*p* | 1.03*r*/1.04*p* | *r*/1.04*p* | 1.02*r*/1.04*p* | 1.03*r*/1.04*p* |
| GDevices | *x* | 2.02*x* | **0.96*x*** | 2.40*x* | 1.29*x* | 1.45*x* |
| (*r*/*p*) | 1.12*r*/1.01*p* | 1.13*r*/1.02*p* | 1.09*r*/1.01*p* | 1.13*r*/1.01*p* | 1.13*r*/1.02*p* | 1.13*r*/1.02*p* |
| Extg | *x* | 2.37*x* | 1.27*x* | 3.51*x* | 1.34*x* | 1.46*x* |
| (*r*/*p*) | 1.06*r*/1.01*p* | 1.07*r*/1.03*p* | 1.02*r*/1.01*p* | 1.05*r*/1.02*p* | 1.07*r*/1.03*p* | 1.07*r*/1.03*p* |

Table 7: For each classification task in the first column, we report the relative number of labeled data required to converge the active learning process by various classifiers. We also report the relative recall and precision measured on data pool $\mathcal{D}_{\text{pool}}$ as "recall/precision". For each classification task, we denoted the recall/precision targets set by customers as (*r*/*p*), and the number of labeled data required to converge with ProdNet-1L classifier as *x*. (Note: different classification tasks may have different recall/precision targets, and they require different number of labeled data to converge the experiments with ProdNet-1L classifier. Since we do not compare performance across different classification tasks, we use the same letters for the denotation of different tasks.) For example, on Speakers dataset the recall/precision targets are set as (*r*/*p*), the ProdNet-1L classifier achieved 1.11*r* recall at *p* precision when the active learning experiment converged at *x* labels, while the BERT-1L classifier achieved 1.10*r* recall at 1.02*p* precision when the active learning experiments converged at 2.56*x* labels. For each classification task, we highlight the least number of labeled data required for convergence in **bold**.

| Models→ | ProdNet-1L | BERT-1L | ProdNet-2L | BERT-2L | ProdNet-24L-P | BERT-24L-P |
|---|---|---|---|---|---|---|
| Tasks ↓ (R/P target) | Top: relative number of labeled data<br>Bottom: relative macro-recall/macro-precision computed on data pool | | | | | |
| HS<br>$(r/p)$ | $x$<br>$1.15r/1.13p$ | $2.71x$<br>$1.16r/1.17p$ | $2.30x$<br>$1.13r/1.12p$ | $3.48x$<br>$1.13r/1.11p$ | $1.08x$<br>$1.16r/1.17p$ | $1.09x$<br>$1.16r/1.17p$ |
| FEE<br>$(r/p)$ | $x$<br>$1.06r/1.07p$ | $1.84x$<br>$1.05r/1.08p$ | $1.06x$<br>$1.05r/1.07p$ | $3.12x$<br>$1.05r/1.06p$ | $1.32x$<br>$1.06r/1.07p$ | $1.35x$<br>$1.05r/1.08p$ |
| AB<br>$(r/p)$ | $x$<br>$1.08r/p$ | $1.60x$<br>$1.12r/p$ | $2.39x$<br>$1.04r/p$ | $3.89x$<br>$1.08r/p$ | $2.44x$<br>$1.08r/1.01p$ | $2.73x$<br>$1.05r/1.02p$ |

Table 8: For each multi-class classification task in the first column, we report the relative number of labeled data required to converge the active learning process by various classifiers. We also report relative macro-recall and macro-precision measured on data pool $\mathcal{D}_{\text{pool}}$. For example, on HS dataset the macro-recall/macro-precision targets are set as $(r/p)$, the ProdNet-1L classifier achieved $1.15r$ (macro-recall) at $1.13p$ (macro-precision) when the active learning experiment converged at $x$ labels, while the BERT-1L classifier achieved $1.16r$ (macro-recall) at $1.17p$ (macro-precision) when the active learning experiment converged at $2.71x$ labels. For each classification task, we highlight the least number of labeled data required for convergence in **bold**.

| Models→ | | ProdNet-2L | | BERT-2L | |
|---|---|---|---|---|---|
| Class rationale ↓ | Key token | Average attention | Token ranking | Average attention | Token ranking |
| **Task: PetCare** | | | | | |
| To classify pet-care products designed to prevent fleas, ticks, ringworm, or other parasites. | flea | **0.45** | **15%** | 0.36 | 50% |
| | worm | **0.44** | **16.7%** | 0.42 | 37.7% |
| | tick | **0.43** | **17.4%** | 0.39 | 44.3% |
| | parasites | **0.38** | **24.2%** | 0.33 | 56.2% |
| **Task: Speakers** | | | | | |
| To classify wireless battery operated portable speakers. | blue | **0.70** | **4.9%** | 0.39 | 52.6% |
| | portable | **0.60** | **11.2%** | 0.37 | 57.2% |
| | speaker | **0.40** | **35.3%** | 0.30 | 69.7% |
| | wireless | 0.29 | 52.1% | **0.48** | **34.7%** |
| **Task: Pillow** | | | | | |
| To classify pillows and cushions with feather fillings or inserts. | cushion | **0.42** | **23.1%** | 0.25 | 68.4% |
| | pillow | **0.60** | **24.0%** | 0.25 | 65.9% |
| | feather | 0.13 | 75.1% | **0.45** | **32.0%** |
| **Task: Seed** | | | | | |
| To classify seeds which are used for growing plants. | seed | **0.61** | **13.0%** | 0.31 | 50.4% |
| | plant | **0.60** | **13.6%** | 0.47 | 19.6% |
| | fruits | **0.42** | **36.0%** | 0.38 | 36.1% |
| | vegetable | **0.27** | **63.4%** | 0.24 | 64.8% |

Table 9: Global aggregation of attention values for key phrases of a classification task. We take 500 positive samples to the original ProdNet-2L and BERT-2L models without downstream task finetuning. We calculate the average attention of each token that the `[CLS]` token pays to in the last transformer layer. The average attention (higher the better) received by the identified key tokens is noted in the column *Avg. attention*. We also rank all the tokens in the 500 positive samples based on their average received attention, and calculate the rank of identified key tokens (smaller the better). Key tokens were identified by a trained expert who provided the labeled data required to train the classifiers.

# ADEPT: Adapter-based Efficient Prompt Tuning Approach for Language Models

**Aditya Shah, Surendrabikram Thapa, Aneesh Jain, Lifu Huang**
Department of Computer Science, Virginia Tech
{aditya31, surendrabikram, aneeshj, lifuh}@vt.edu

## Abstract

Fine-tuning large pre-trained models for downstream tasks can be really expensive. In the past, researchers have proposed various alternatives like adapter and prompt-based methods for tuning these large language models using minimal parameters. However, applying prompt-tuning for smaller language models has not been effective so far and not much work is done in pushing forward soft prompting for these smaller models. To improve the training efficiency of the language models and reduce the size of tuned parameters, we propose a novel Adapter-based Efficient Prompt Tuning approach (ADEPT). In this paper, we show that tuning the parameters of soft prompts with adapter modules while keeping the rest of the model frozen can be a promising method to optimize smaller language models for downstream tasks. Our method achieves up to *98% performance of full fine-tuning while using only 0.02% of total model parameters.*

## 1 Introduction

With the rapid advancement in computational facilities and the research in the field of Natural Language Processing (NLP), pre-trained language models (Peters et al., 2018; Conneau et al., 2018; Devlin et al., 2019; Yang et al., 2019; Raffel et al., 2020; Qiu et al., 2020; Xue et al., 2021; Doddapaneni et al., 2021) have been used widely in various tasks. These models use different statistical and probabilistic methods to decide the likelihood of a given sequence of words occurring in a sentence. To efficiently use the language models, researchers fine-tune these pre-trained language models on downstream tasks. With the conventional practices of fine-tuning the models, new parameters are generally introduced for every downstream task. However, this approach of fine-tuning language models becomes difficult especially when there are a lot of trainable parameters. With language models becoming larger and larger (Brown et al., 2020), we can often anticipate challenges related to maintaining multiple copies of model parameters for inference, training time, and lack of necessary computing power. The concept of prompt-tuning was introduced to improve parameter efficiency in the downstream tasks. In prompt tuning, there's no need for new parameters as we convert our problem into a language modeling task. This method can be promising, especially when there are very few training examples for e.g. few shot learning (Gao et al., 2021), where the standard fine-tuning would not be efficient.

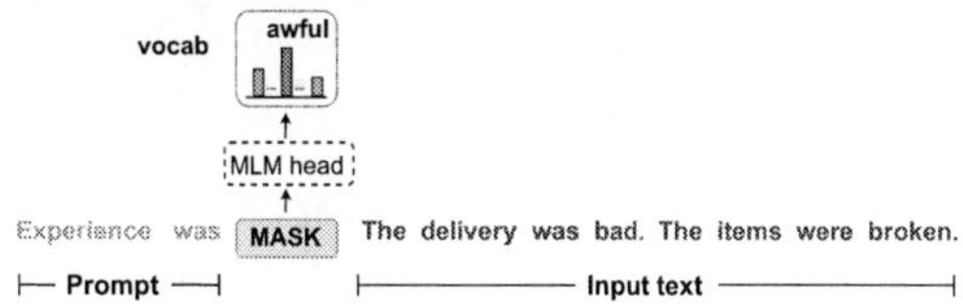


Figure 1: Prompt-based tuning using discrete prompt. The prompt "*Experience was*" with a [MASK] is prepended to the input text.

A *prompt* is usually a sequence of words or parameters that are appended or prepended to the input so that the given downstream task can be constructed as a language modeling problem (Liu et al., 2021a). An example is shown in Figure 1. In order to classify the sentiment of a given text, like an amazon product review "*The delivery was bad. The items were broken.*", we can prepend a prompt, such as "*Experience was*" or "*It was*", with a [MASK] to the sentence and anticipate the language model to predict a negative adjective such as "*awful*" for the [MASK] position.

As shown by Lester et al. (2021); Kim et al. (2021), soft prompt-tuning for smaller language models do not perform well when compared to traditional fine-tuning. This approach only works for significantly larger models ($\text{BERT}_{\text{large}}$, $\text{RoBERTa}_{\text{large}}$ , etc). In this paper, we propose a novel approach to leverage soft prompt tuning for smaller language models. We insert adapter modules in the language model, then jointly fine-tune the parameters of this adapter module along with soft prompts while keeping the rest of the model frozen. Through empirical results on 3 benchmark datasets from SuperGLUE (Wang et al., 2019) and 4 text classification datasets, we demonstrate the effectiveness of our proposed approach for these



*Proceedings of The Fourth Workshop on Simple and Efficient Natural Language Processing (SustaiNLP)*, pages 121–128
July 13, 2023 ©2023 Association for Computational Linguistics

smaller LM models (RoBERTa (Liu et al., 2019) and BERT (Devlin et al., 2019)). Our method optimizes only 0.02% of total model parameters during training and yet achieves better performance than other tuning strategies while being competitive to fine-tuning.

Our main contributions can be summarised as follows:

- a new Adapter-based Efficient Prompt Tuning (ADEPT) approach to leverage soft prompts for smaller language models - *"roberta-base"* and *"bert-base-cased"*.
- analyze the effectiveness of our approach with respect to other soft prompt-tuning and fine-tuning methods.
- an ablation study to investigate the importance of the number of prompt tokens and adapter hidden size.

## 2 Related Work

The effectiveness of prompt tuning was demonstrated by (Brown et al., 2020) where the authors showed that GPT-3 model could handle wide variety of tasks using only a few training examples. The use of prompts was first proposed by (Radford and Narasimhan, 2018). The authors showed that language models can perform well in few-shot and zero-shot settings through these natural language prompts. More recently, Jiang et al. (2020) proposed an approach to automatically discover better prompts in order to improve the factual knowledge retrieval from these language models. Moreover, Schick and Schütze (2021) introduced Pattern Exploiting Training (PET) which uses cloze-style phrases and achieves state-of-the-art performance on few supervised and semi-supervised tasks - classification on Yelp Reviews, AG's News, Yahoo Questions (Zhang et al., 2015) and MNLI (Williams et al., 2018). This work was further improved by (Tam et al., 2021) for few-shot natural language understanding without using any unlabeled data. In all of these approaches, prompts were manually designed in the form of discrete tokens. Thus, in such scenarios, it is important to design appropriate prompts based on different downstream tasks. The importance of prompt engineering and the complete paradigm of prompt tuning is summarized in Liu et al. (2021a).

In contrast to discrete prompts (Shin et al., 2020; Hambardzumyan et al., 2021; Gao et al., 2021; Reynolds and McDonell, 2021), soft prompts are randomly initialized vectors that are prepended or appended to the input text. The parameters of the entire language model are fixed and only the prompt parameters are fine-tuned. Liu et al. (2021b) showed that automatically searching better prompts in the continuous space gives competitive performance for natural language understanding. Soft prompts were initially proposed by Zhong et al. (2021) where OptiPrompt was proposed and outperformed discrete prompts on knowledge probing tasks. Li and Liang (2021) and Qin and Eisner (2021) used a similar idea for generation tasks where they prepended task-specific prompts in the input text and achieved comparable performance as the original model fine-tuning. Han et al. (2021) proposed prompt-tuning with rules (PTR) which significantly outperformed state-of-the-art baselines for relation classification tasks. The effectiveness of soft prompt-tuning was further leveraged by Lester et al. (2021) where they applied soft prompts on the T5 model and achieved a good performance on the SuperGLUE benchmark. Furthermore, Su et al. (2021); Vu et al. (2022) studied the transferability of prompt tuning across different tasks and models. They showed that soft prompts can be transferred to similar tasks without training and can be a good initialization for the underlying language model.

## 3 Approach

We propose a novel adapter-based prompt-tuning architecture for downstream classification tasks. Figure 2 shows an overview of the model. We use the pre-trained BERT (Devlin et al., 2019) and RoBERTa (Liu et al., 2019) from Hugging Face as the encoder. For soft prompt-tuning, we append soft prompt embedding in the input text using the same approach as Lester et al. (2021). Given an input text $X = [x_1, ..., x_n]$, where $x_i$ is the $i-$th token in the text and $n$ is the length of the sequence, we append prompt tokens $[p_1, p_2, ...\ p_m]$ where $m$ is the number of prompt tokens. We initialize these prompt tokens with embeddings obtained from random words in the vocabulary and update them during training, which shows better performance on downstream tasks than initializing them with random vectors. We found that initializing prompt tokens with random word embeddings instead of random vectors helps the model converge better on downstream tasks. The resulting input to the model becomes: $[p_1, ..., p_m, x_1, ..., x_n]$. We do not use any separator token between prompt vectors and tokens.

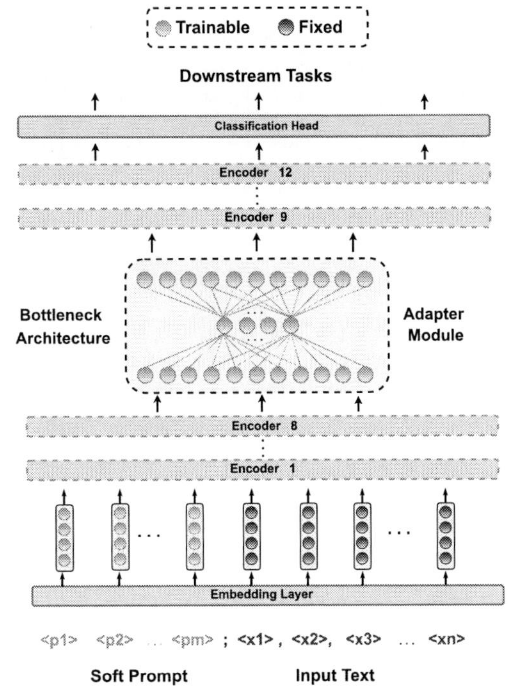


Figure 2: Overview of the ADEPT model. The adapter module is inserted between encoder layer 8 and layer 9. Parameters of prompt embeddings and this adapter module are tuned while the rest of the complete model and input text embeddings are frozen. ADEPT approach using RoBERTa/BERT tunes only $28K$ parameters (0.02% of $123M$ total parameters)

Inspired by the work of Bapna and Firat (2019); Houlsby et al. (2019); Pfeiffer et al. (2021); Rücklé et al. (2021); He et al. (2021), we insert adapter modules in the form of Multi-Layer Perceptron (MLP) between the encoder layers of the base transformer model. To reduce the number of parameters, we choose a bottleneck architecture for the adapter module. In a bottleneck architecture, the hidden layer also called as bottleneck size is much smaller than the input layer. If $d$ is the input size (number of neurons) of the MLP layer and $b$ is the bottleneck size (adapter hidden size), then the bottleneck architecture would require $2 \cdot d \cdot b + d + b$ parameters . When $b << d$, the total parameters are greatly reduced compared to a general MLP layer with $d \cdot d + d$ parameters. If the embedding dimension size is $e$ and the prompt length is $m$, then the trainable parameters for prompt embeddings is $m$ . $e$. So the total trainable parameters for the ADEPT model are just $[2 \cdot d \cdot b + (d + b)] + m \cdot e$. We use one adapter module with hidden size $b = 8$ and prompt length $m = 20$ in our implementation which is inserted between the $8^{th}$ and $9^{th}$ encoder layer [1]. For RoBERTa and BERT models, we have $d = e = 768$. So, total trainable parameters for the ADEPT model is only $28k$ while in standard fine-tuning, we update all the parameters ($123M$ parameters for *roberta-base* model.)

## 4 Experimental Setup

We conduct experiments on four classification datasets - *IMDB* (Maas et al., 2011), *AG's News* (Zhang et al., 2015) , *Yahoo Answers* (Zhang et al., 2015), Yelp - 5 (Zhang et al., 2015) and three datasets from SuperGLUE benchmark - Boolq (Clark et al., 2019), CommitmentBank (de Marneffe et al., 2019), and Recognizing Textual Entailment (RTE) . More details on data statistics and implementation details are described in Appendix A

To show the efficiency of our adapter-based prompt tuning approach, we compare it with several other training paradigms:

- **Prompt-tuning (PT):** fine-tune soft prompt embeddings while keeping the entire model frozen. The randomly initialized parameters of the classification head are also fixed.

- **Head-tuning (HT):** only fine-tune the classification head. The base transformer model is frozen.

- **Prompt + Head-tuning (PHT):** fine-tune soft prompt embeddings along with the parameters of the classification head. The base transformer model is frozen.

- **Fine-tuning (FT):** traditional fine-tuning where the entire model along with the classification head is trained.

[1]We experimented with different positions for the adapter module: between layer 4 and 5; between layer 6 and 7; between layer 8 and 9; between layer 10 and 11. We achieved the best results when the adapter module was inserted between layer 8 and layer 9. It stands out to the reason that the lower layers of BERT account for sentence and coarse linguistic structure while the higher layers are more domain-specific and help to learn task-specific parameters (Rogers et al., 2020). Attaching an adapter module between higher layers helps the adapter module parameters to converge better to downstream tasks

| Model | Method | IMDB | AG's News | Yahoo | Yelp-5 | BoolQ | CB | RTE |
|---|---|---|---|---|---|---|---|---|
| BERT | Prompt (PT) | 0.91 | 0.86 | 0.66 | 0.57 | 0.62 | 0.66 | 0.47 |
| | Head (HT) | 0.89 | 0.88 | 0.67 | 0.60 | 0.61 | 0.72 | 0.53 |
| | Prompt + Head (PHT) | 0.92 | 0.92 | 0.70 | 0.63 | 0.67 | 0.71 | 0.54 |
| | Fine-tune (FT) | 0.94 | 0.94 | 0.72 | 0.69 | 0.73 | 0.83 | 0.61 |
| | Adapter + Prompt (ADEPT) | 0.92 | 0.93 | 0.71 | 0.67 | 0.69 | 0.80 | 0.58 |
| RoBERTa | Prompt (PT) | 0.90 | 0.87 | 0.65 | 0.59 | 0.62 | 0.64 | 0.50 |
| | Head (HT) | 0.91 | 0.90 | 0.68 | 0.61 | 0.63 | 0.70 | 0.54 |
| | Prompt + Head (PHT) | 0.94 | 0.93 | 0.72 | 0.66 | 0.64 | 0.71 | 0.55 |
| | Fine-tune (FT) | 0.96 | 0.95 | 0.73 | 0.71 | 0.80 | 0.86 | 0.71 |
| | Adapter + Prompt (ADEPT) | 0.95 | 0.94 | 0.72 | 0.68 | 0.71 | 0.77 | 0.60 |

Table 1: Performance on all evaluation tasks. Each experiment is run for 3 trials and the average result is reported. For text classification tasks (IMDB, AG's News, Yahoo, Yelp-5), we report the test F-score; for Boolq, CommitmentBank (CB), and Recognizing Textual Entailment (RTE), we report the test accuracy. ADEPT approach results in better performance than Head-tuning (HT) and Prompt + Head-tuning (PHT) while using significantly lower parameters and is competitive to standard fine-tuning

- **Adapter + Prompt-tuning (ADEPT):** fine-tune soft prompt embeddings and adapter module parameters that are inserted in the encoder layer. The rest of the model and the randomly initialized parameters of the classification head are kept fixed.

## 5 Results

Table 1 shows the F-score and accuracy on all evaluation tasks under different training settings. Table 2 compares the model parameters and training metrics. We can see that ADEPT outperforms all the other methods which just tune the prompt or head layers using significantly lower parameters. By just tuning 0.02% parameters, ADEPT shows comparable performance as the method that fine-tunes all the parameters, demonstrating its significance in improving the training efficiency. It is interesting to see that although Head-tuning (HT) and Prompt + Head-tuning (PHT) methods have larger parameters to be optimized, the ADEPT method still achieves better results on the SuperGLUE dataset and requires lesser training time compared to the standard fine-tuning approach. We also observe that standard prompt-tuning requires about 2.5 times more steps to converge compared to fine-tuning approach and does not perform well for multi-class classification. A similar result was reported by Lester et al. (2021), where the authors claim that soft prompt based-tuning does not perform well for smaller language models.

Overall, attaching adapter modules between the encoder layers helps to retain the knowledge from pre-trained LMs and efficiently learn the required parameters to further improve the performance on downstream tasks. This helps the language model to better adapt to downstream tasks using minimal parameters. It achieves comparable performance as standard fine-tuning while being highly parameter efficient and requiring much lower training time. All these demonstrate the effectiveness of our proposed approach in improving the training and resource efficiency of language models.

| Method | # params | % params | time | Convergence |
|---|---|---|---|---|
| PT | *13K* | 0.01% | 0.9 $t$ | 2.5 $x$ steps |
| HT | *600K* | 0.48% | 0.5 $t$ | 2 $x$ steps |
| PHT | *620K* | 0.49% | 0.8 $t$ | 2 $x$ steps |
| FT | *123M* | 100% | $t$ | $x$ steps |
| ADEPT | *28K* | 0.02% | 0.7 $t$ | 1.5 $x$ steps |

Table 2: Model parameters and training metrics. $t$ and $x$ refer to training time and training steps respectively as required by standard fine-tuning. # params denotes the number of trainable parameters for every method. % params denotes % of parameters to be optimized compared to standard fine-tuning.

## 6 Conclusion

We proposed a novel adapter-based prompt-tuning approach for fine-tuning language models. Our results demonstrate the effectiveness of the approach on seven benchmark datasets. ADEPT achieves a significant performance boost over PT, HT, and PHT approaches and is comparable to the standard fine-tuning while using only 0.02% of the model parameters. Since adapter modules learn the required parameters for various NLU tasks, they help in retaining the knowledge of the pre-trained LM model when the encoder is frozen. Our work aims to facilitate the further research direction of using adapter-based prompt methods for tuning LMs.

## Limitations

Due to the limited resources, we could not experiment with this approach for larger language models such as *roberta-large* and *bert-large*. It would be interesting to investigate the performance of ADEPT with larger LMs.

In addition, we only evaluate the ADEPT approach on seven downstream tasks. It would also be interesting to test it on more broad natural language processing tasks, such as information extraction, natural language generation, question answering, and so on.

## Broader Impact

As discussed earlier, fine-tuning large pre-trained models for downstream tasks can be really expensive. The ADEPT approach can help AI practitioners to assess the abilities of LM without using a lot of resources. This approach of prompt tuning can also help smaller end users to take advantage of harnessing the power of LM with the minimal resources they have. It can be used by social scientists, Non-profit organizations, etc. to create a positive impact in society in spite of limited computing resources.

## Reproducibility

The code and resources for this work are available at our GitHub repository[2]. The code for training, testing, and producing plots are made available. The details on the model and hyperparameters are given in Appendix A.2. A brief introduction to the dataset used in this paper is given in Appendix A.1. Our implementation approach specific to all the dataset used are also explained.

## References

Ankur Bapna and Orhan Firat. 2019. Simple, scalable adaptation for neural machine translation. In *Proceedings of the 2019 Conference on Empirical Methods in Natural Language Processing and the 9th International Joint Conference on Natural Language Processing (EMNLP-IJCNLP)*, pages 1538–1548, Hong Kong, China. Association for Computational Linguistics.

Tom Brown, Benjamin Mann, Nick Ryder, Melanie Subbiah, Jared D Kaplan, Prafulla Dhariwal, Arvind Neelakantan, Pranav Shyam, Girish Sastry, Amanda Askell, Sandhini Agarwal, Ariel Herbert-Voss, Gretchen Krueger, Tom Henighan, Rewon Child, Aditya Ramesh, Daniel Ziegler, Jeffrey Wu, Clemens Winter, Chris Hesse, Mark Chen, Eric Sigler, Mateusz Litwin, Scott Gray, Benjamin Chess, Jack Clark, Christopher Berner, Sam McCandlish, Alec Radford, Ilya Sutskever, and Dario Amodei. 2020. Language models are few-shot learners. In *Advances in Neural Information Processing Systems*, volume 33, pages 1877–1901. Curran Associates, Inc.

Christopher Clark, Kenton Lee, Ming-Wei Chang, Tom Kwiatkowski, Michael Collins, and Kristina Toutanova. 2019. Boolq: Exploring the surprising difficulty of natural yes/no questions. In *NAACL*.

Alexis Conneau, Ruty Rinott, Guillaume Lample, Adina Williams, Samuel Bowman, Holger Schwenk, and Veselin Stoyanov. 2018. XNLI: Evaluating cross-lingual sentence representations. In *Proceedings of the 2018 Conference on Empirical Methods in Natural Language Processing*, pages 2475–2485, Brussels, Belgium. Association for Computational Linguistics.

Marie-Catherine de Marneffe, Mandy Simons, and Judith Tonhauser. 2019. The commitmentbank: Investigating projection in naturally occurring discourse.

Jacob Devlin, Ming-Wei Chang, Kenton Lee, and Kristina Toutanova. 2019. BERT: Pre-training of deep bidirectional transformers for language understanding. In *Proceedings of the 2019 Conference of the North American Chapter of the Association for Computational Linguistics: Human Language Technologies, Volume 1 (Long and Short Papers)*, pages 4171–4186, Minneapolis, Minnesota. Association for Computational Linguistics.

Sumanth Doddapaneni, Gowtham Ramesh, Mitesh M. Khapra, Anoop Kunchukuttan, and Pratyush Kumar. 2021. A primer on pretrained multilingual language models.

Tianyu Gao, Adam Fisch, and Danqi Chen. 2021. Making pre-trained language models better few-shot learners. In *Proceedings of the 59th Annual Meeting of the Association for Computational Linguistics and the 11th International Joint Conference on Natural Language Processing (Volume 1: Long Papers)*, pages 3816–3830, Online. Association for Computational Linguistics.

Karen Hambardzumyan, Hrant Khachatrian, and Jonathan May. 2021. WARP: Word-level Adversarial ReProgramming. In *Proceedings of the 59th Annual Meeting of the Association for Computational Linguistics and the 11th International Joint Conference on Natural Language Processing (Volume 1: Long Papers)*, pages 4921–4933, Online. Association for Computational Linguistics.

Xu Han, Weilin Zhao, Ning Ding, Zhiyuan Liu, and Maosong Sun. 2021. Ptr: Prompt tuning with rules for text classification.

[2]https://github.com/Aditya-shahh/ADEPT

Ruidan He, Linlin Liu, Hai Ye, Qingyu Tan, Bosheng Ding, Liying Cheng, Jia-Wei Low, Lidong Bing, and Luo Si. 2021. On the effectiveness of adapter-based tuning for pretrained language model adaptation.

Neil Houlsby, Andrei Giurgiu, Stanislaw Jastrzebski, Bruna Morrone, Quentin De Laroussilhe, Andrea Gesmundo, Mona Attariyan, and Sylvain Gelly. 2019. Parameter-efficient transfer learning for NLP. In *Proceedings of the 36th International Conference on Machine Learning*, volume 97 of *Proceedings of Machine Learning Research*, pages 2790–2799. PMLR.

Zhengbao Jiang, Frank F. Xu, Jun Araki, and Graham Neubig. 2020. How can we know what language models know?

Boseop Kim, HyoungSeok Kim, Sang-Woo Lee, Gichang Lee, Donghyun Kwak, Jeon Dong Hyeon, Sunghyun Park, Sungju Kim, Seonhoon Kim, Dongpil Seo, Heungsub Lee, Minyoung Jeong, Sungjae Lee, Minsub Kim, Suk Hyun Ko, Seokhun Kim, Taeyong Park, Jinuk Kim, Soyoung Kang, Na-Hyeon Ryu, Kang Min Yoo, Minsuk Chang, Soobin Suh, Sookyo In, Jinseong Park, Kyungduk Kim, Hiun Kim, Jisu Jeong, Yong Goo Yeo, Donghoon Ham, Dongju Park, Min Young Lee, Jaewook Kang, Inho Kang, Jung-Woo Ha, Woomyoung Park, and Nako Sung. 2021. What changes can large-scale language models bring? intensive study on HyperCLOVA: Billions-scale Korean generative pretrained transformers. In *Proceedings of the 2021 Conference on Empirical Methods in Natural Language Processing*, pages 3405–3424, Online and Punta Cana, Dominican Republic. Association for Computational Linguistics.

Brian Lester, Rami Al-Rfou, and Noah Constant. 2021. The power of scale for parameter-efficient prompt tuning. In *Proceedings of the 2021 Conference on Empirical Methods in Natural Language Processing*, pages 3045–3059, Online and Punta Cana, Dominican Republic. Association for Computational Linguistics.

Xiang Lisa Li and Percy Liang. 2021. Prefix-tuning: Optimizing continuous prompts for generation.

Pengfei Liu, Weizhe Yuan, Jinlan Fu, Zhengbao Jiang, Hiroaki Hayashi, and Graham Neubig. 2021a. Pretrain, prompt, and predict: A systematic survey of prompting methods in natural language processing.

Xiao Liu, Yanan Zheng, Zhengxiao Du, Ming Ding, Yujie Qian, Zhilin Yang, and Jie Tang. 2021b. GPT understands, too. *CoRR*, abs/2103.10385.

Yinhan Liu, Myle Ott, Naman Goyal, Jingfei Du, Mandar Joshi, Danqi Chen, Omer Levy, Mike Lewis, Luke Zettlemoyer, and Veselin Stoyanov. 2019. Roberta: A robustly optimized bert pretraining approach.

Andrew L. Maas, Raymond E. Daly, Peter T. Pham, Dan Huang, Andrew Y. Ng, and Christopher Potts. 2011. Learning word vectors for sentiment analysis. In *Proceedings of the 49th Annual Meeting of the Association for Computational Linguistics: Human Language Technologies*, pages 142–150, Portland, Oregon, USA. Association for Computational Linguistics.

Matthew E. Peters, Mark Neumann, Mohit Iyyer, Matt Gardner, Christopher Clark, Kenton Lee, and Luke Zettlemoyer. 2018. Deep contextualized word representations. In *Proceedings of the 2018 Conference of the North American Chapter of the Association for Computational Linguistics: Human Language Technologies, Volume 1 (Long Papers)*, pages 2227–2237, New Orleans, Louisiana. Association for Computational Linguistics.

Jonas Pfeiffer, Aishwarya Kamath, Andreas Rücklé, Kyunghyun Cho, and Iryna Gurevych. 2021. AdapterFusion: Non-destructive task composition for transfer learning. In *Proceedings of the 16th Conference of the European Chapter of the Association for Computational Linguistics: Main Volume*, pages 487–503, Online. Association for Computational Linguistics.

Guanghui Qin and Jason Eisner. 2021. Learning how to ask: Querying LMs with mixtures of soft prompts. In *Proceedings of the 2021 Conference of the North American Chapter of the Association for Computational Linguistics: Human Language Technologies*, pages 5203–5212, Online. Association for Computational Linguistics.

XiPeng Qiu, TianXiang Sun, YiGe Xu, YunFan Shao, Ning Dai, and XuanJing Huang. 2020. Pretrained models for natural language processing: A survey. *Science China Technological Sciences*, 63(10):1872–1897.

Alec Radford and Karthik Narasimhan. 2018. Improving language understanding by generative pretraining.

Colin Raffel, Noam Shazeer, Adam Roberts, Katherine Lee, Sharan Narang, Michael Matena, Yanqi Zhou, Wei Li, and Peter J. Liu. 2020. Exploring the limits of transfer learning with a unified text-to-text transformer. *J. Mach. Learn. Res.*, 21(1).

Laria Reynolds and Kyle McDonell. 2021. Prompt programming for large language models: Beyond the few-shot paradigm.

Anna Rogers, Olga Kovaleva, and Anna Rumshisky. 2020. A primer in bertology: What we know about how bert works.

Andreas Rücklé, Gregor Geigle, Max Glockner, Tilman Beck, Jonas Pfeiffer, Nils Reimers, and Iryna Gurevych. 2021. AdapterDrop: On the efficiency of adapters in transformers. In *Proceedings of the 2021 Conference on Empirical Methods in Natural*

*Language Processing*, pages 7930–7946, Online and Punta Cana, Dominican Republic. Association for Computational Linguistics.

Timo Schick and Hinrich Schütze. 2021. Exploiting cloze questions for few shot text classification and natural language inference.

Taylor Shin, Yasaman Razeghi, Robert L. Logan IV, Eric Wallace, and Sameer Singh. 2020. AutoPrompt: Eliciting Knowledge from Language Models with Automatically Generated Prompts. In *Proceedings of the 2020 Conference on Empirical Methods in Natural Language Processing (EMNLP)*, pages 4222–4235, Online. Association for Computational Linguistics.

Yusheng Su, Xiaozhi Wang, Yujia Qin, Chi-Min Chan, Yankai Lin, Zhiyuan Liu, Peng Li, Juanzi Li, Lei Hou, Maosong Sun, and Jie Zhou. 2021. On transferability of prompt tuning for natural language understanding.

Derek Tam, Rakesh R Menon, Mohit Bansal, Shashank Srivastava, and Colin Raffel. 2021. Improving and simplifying pattern exploiting training.

Tu Vu, Brian Lester, Noah Constant, Rami Al-Rfou', and Daniel Cer. 2022. SPoT: Better frozen model adaptation through soft prompt transfer. In *Proceedings of the 60th Annual Meeting of the Association for Computational Linguistics (Volume 1: Long Papers)*, pages 5039–5059, Dublin, Ireland. Association for Computational Linguistics.

Alex Wang, Yada Pruksachatkun, Nikita Nangia, Amanpreet Singh, Julian Michael, Felix Hill, Omer Levy, and Samuel Bowman. 2019. Superglue: A stickier benchmark for general-purpose language understanding systems. In *Advances in Neural Information Processing Systems*, volume 32. Curran Associates, Inc.

Adina Williams, Nikita Nangia, and Samuel Bowman. 2018. A broad-coverage challenge corpus for sentence understanding through inference. In *Proceedings of the 2018 Conference of the North American Chapter of the Association for Computational Linguistics: Human Language Technologies, Volume 1 (Long Papers)*, pages 1112–1122, New Orleans, Louisiana. Association for Computational Linguistics.

Linting Xue, Noah Constant, Adam Roberts, Mihir Kale, Rami Al-Rfou, Aditya Siddhant, Aditya Barua, and Colin Raffel. 2021. mT5: A massively multilingual pre-trained text-to-text transformer. In *Proceedings of the 2021 Conference of the North American Chapter of the Association for Computational Linguistics: Human Language Technologies*, pages 483–498, Online. Association for Computational Linguistics.

Zhilin Yang, Zihang Dai, Yiming Yang, Jaime Carbonell, Russ R Salakhutdinov, and Quoc V Le. 2019. Xlnet: Generalized autoregressive pretraining for language understanding. In *Advances in Neural Information Processing Systems*, volume 32. Curran Associates, Inc.

Xiang Zhang, Junbo Jake Zhao, and Yann LeCun. 2015. Character-level convolutional networks for text classification. *CoRR*, abs/1509.01626.

Zexuan Zhong, Dan Friedman, and Danqi Chen. 2021. Factual probing is [mask]: Learning vs. learning to recall.

# A Appendix

## A.1 Dataset

The data statistics along with number of examples and labels is shown in Table 3.

| Dataset | # train | # val | # test | # labels |
|---|---|---|---|---|
| IMDB | 40,000 | 5,000 | 5,000 | 2 |
| AG's News | 102,000 | 18,000 | 7,600 | 4 |
| Yahoo | 1,300,000 | 60,000 | 100,000 | 10 |
| Yelp-5 | 520,000 | 130,000 | 50,000 | 5 |
| Boolq | 9,427 | 3,270 | 3,245 | 3 |
| CB | 250 | 57 | 250 | 3 |
| RTE | 2,500 | 278 | 300 | 2 |

Table 3: Data statistics

**IMDB:** It is a binary sentiment analysis dataset that has a movie review and its respective label. The dataset consist of 2 labels - *"positive"* and *"negative"*.

**AG's News:** A news classification dataset where every example consists of a headline $h$, a text body $b$, and a label associated with it. The dataset consist of 4 labels - *"World"*, *"Sports"*, *"Business"*, and *"Science/Tech"*. For our implementation, we concatenate the headline and body - $[h : b]$ and use the concatenated text for the prediction.

**Yahoo Answers:** A topic classification dataset that consists of a question $q$, an answer $a$, and a label associated with it. The dataset consists of 10 labels - *"Society", "Science", "Health", "Education", "Computer", "Sports", "Business", "Entertainment", "Relationship", and "Politics"*. For our implementation, we concatenate the question and answer - $[q : a]$ and use the concatenated text for the prediction.

**Yelp-5** A review classification dataset where every example consists of a review and a label associated with it. The dataset consists of 5 labels in the form of numbers - (1 to 5).

**Boolq** Boolq is a question answering dataset for yes/no questions from the SuperGLUE benchmark. Each example is a triplet of (question, passage, and

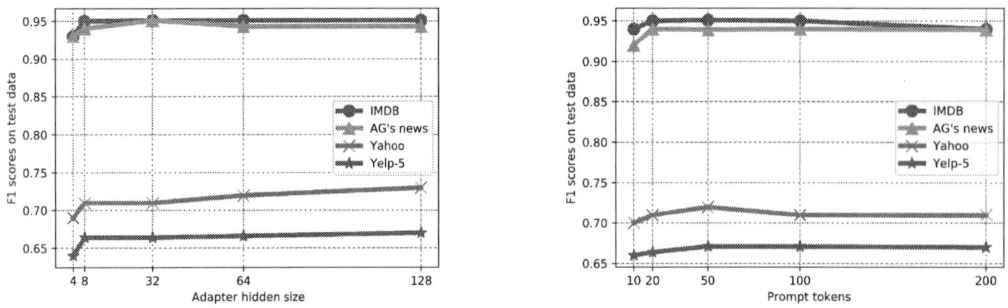


(a) Varying adapter size

(b) Varying # of prompt tokens

Figure 3: Test F-scores on the classification datasets using RoBERTa with ADEPT model In (a), number of prompt tokens is kept fixed $(m) = 20$ and adapter hidden size is varied. In (b), the adapter hidden size is kept fixed $(d) = 8$ and number of prompt tokens is varied.

answer). For our implementation, we concatenate the question and passage - *[q : p]* and use the concatenated text for the prediction. The dataset consist of 2 labels - *"yes"* and *"no"*

**CB** CommitmentBank (CB) is a three-class textual entailment dataset from the SuperGLUE benchmark. Each example is a triplet of (premise, hypothesis, and label). For our implementation, we concatenate the premise and hypothesis - *[p : h]* and use the concatenated text for the prediction. The dataset consist of 3 labels - *"contradiction"*, *"neutral"*, and *"entailment"*.

**RTE** Recognizing Textual Entailment (RTE) is a binary textual entailment dataset from the SuperGLUE benchmark. Each example is a triplet of (premise, hypothesis, and label). For our implementation, we concatenate the premise and hypothesis - *[p : h]* and use the concatenated text for the prediction. The dataset consist of 2 labels - *"entailment"* and *"not_entailment"*.

## A.2 Implementation details

We use *roberta-base* and *bert-base-cased* from Hugging Face[3]. For our experiment, the adapter module is inserted between the $8^{th}$ encoder layer and $9^{th}$ encoder layer of both models. We run each experiment for 3 trials and the average result is reported. The learning rate is $8e-4$ for ADEPT, prompt-tuning (PT), prompt-tuning + head (PHT), head-tuning (HT), and $2e-5$ for fine-tuning method. The batch size is 16 for all the methods. We train fine-tuning method for 10 epochs, the ADEPT model for 15 epochs, prompt-tuning + head and head-tuning for 20 epochs, and prompt-tuning for 25 epochs. We use AdamW optimizer and linear scheduler with 6% warmup steps for all the methods. For the ADEPT model, we use an adapter hidden size of 8 and the number of prompt tokens is 20 for ADEPT, PT, and PHT methods.

## A.3 Ablation Study

We analyze RoBERTa with the ADEPT model to show the impact of adapter hidden size and number of prompt tokens. We conduct two sets of experiments Figure 3a - for different adapter sizes and Figure 3b - for different prompt tokens.

**Adapter Hidden Size:** We train the ADEPT model for varying adapter sizes - (4, 8, 32, 64, 128), and the number of prompt tokens is kept as 20. As Figure 3a shows, the F-score is slightly improved as we increase the adapter size. Simpler data like IMDB do not benefit much from the increase in adapter size. Increasing adapter size beyond 32 brings 2 to 3% improvement for Yahoo and Yelp-5 dataset

**Number of Prompt Tokens:** We train the ADEPT model by varying the number of prompt tokens - (10, 20, 50, 100, 200) and keep the adapter hidden size fixed as 8. When the number of prompt tokens is beyond 50, the performance is decreased, indicating that adding trainable parameters in the input does not help much beyond a certain point.

[3]https://huggingface.co/

# NLU on Data Diets: Dynamic Data Subset Selection for NLP Classification Tasks

**Jean-Michel Attendu*** and **Jean-Philippe Corbeil***
Nuance Communications
{jattendu,jcorbeil}@microsoft.com

## Abstract

Finetuning large language models inflates the costs of NLU applications and remains the bottleneck of development cycles. Recent works in computer vision use data pruning to reduce training time. Pruned data selection with static methods is based on a score calculated for each training example prior to finetuning, which involves important computational overhead. Moreover, the score may not necessarily be representative of sample importance throughout the entire training duration. We propose to address these issues with a refined version of dynamic data pruning, a curriculum which periodically scores and discards unimportant examples during finetuning. Our method leverages an EL2N metric that we extend to the joint intent and slot classification task, and an initial finetuning phase on the full train set. Our results on the GLUE benchmark and four joint NLU datasets show a better time-accuracy trade-off compared to static methods. Our method preserves full accuracy while training on 50% of the data points and reduces computational times by up to 41%. If we tolerate instead a minor drop of accuracy of 1%, we can prune 80% of the training examples for a reduction in finetuning time reaching 66%.

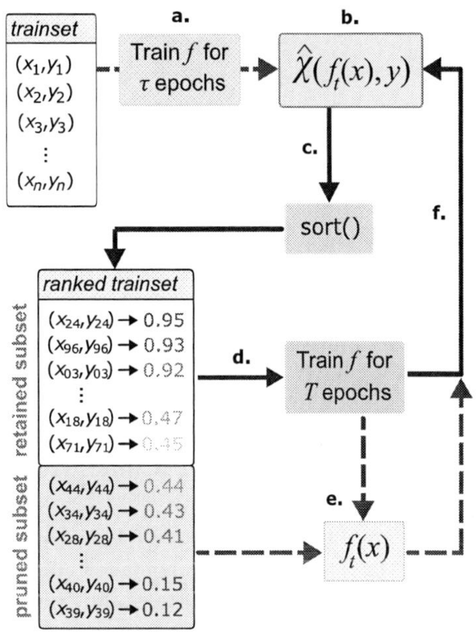


Figure 1: *a.* Model $f$ is trained for $\tau$ epochs with full train set. *b.* Importance function $\hat{\chi}$ assigns score to each training example $(x_i, y_i)$. *c.* Training examples are sorted according to their scores. *d.* Proportion of train set $(1-\rho)$ is retained to train model over a cycle of $T$ epochs. *e.* Resulting model is used to calculate a forward pass. *f.* Full training set is re-scored for the next cycle until completion.

## 1 Introduction

State-of-the-art natural language understanding (NLU) systems rely on finetuning large language models (LLMs) with considerable amounts of human-labelled examples. Such overparametrized models succeed at learning to classify nearly all training samples correctly. However, not all training examples are created equal: proper classification of out-of-distribution outliers requires more iterations for the model to converge. Moreover, many examples are correctly learned after only a few epochs of training and could be ignored further on without impacting test accuracy.

This raises a question about data efficiency: can we remove a proportion of training examples to reduce the number of calculations during finetuning while preserving accuracy at inference? Since finetuning LLMs is computationally intensive and represents a bottleneck in time and costs of development cycles of NLU applications, such an approach appears promising.

Previous works in computer vision suggest that an important fraction of training examples, up to 50% for some datasets, can be removed without significant loss in accuracy (Toneva et al., 2018; Paul

* Equal contributions.



*Proceedings of The Fourth Workshop on Simple and Efficient Natural Language Processing (SustaiNLP)*, pages 129–146
July 13, 2023 ©2023 Association for Computational Linguistics

et al., 2021; Raju et al., 2021). Assuming total train steps increase proportionally with the number of samples, this represents a considerable reduction of training costs while being completely compatible with other existing strategies to make finetuning more efficient (Gupta et al., 2015; Micikevicius et al., 2018; Zhang and He, 2020; Zaheer et al., 2020; Xiong et al., 2021). The core idea is to score each training example $(x_i, y_i)$ with an importance metric, and to remove a proportion of the samples based on ranked scores: the most important examples are kept, whereas others are discarded.

In this work, we expand the analysis of such a method to text classification across various datasets. In agreement with Raju et al. (2021), we observe that many examples have low importance when evaluated at early training but with high variability further on. Thus, a single evaluation often fails at predicting their impact on the loss at a later stage. To address this problem, we also adopt a curriculum in which pruning is performed periodically at a fixed number of epochs. The model is first trained with all examples for a few epochs before ranking is performed with respect to metric $\hat{\chi}$. Then, a proportion $\rho$ of the samples with the lowest scores is set aside, and the model is trained with the retained subset for a cycle of $T$ epochs. All examples are re-scored at every cycle's end to obtain an updated subset. New cycles are computed until training is complete. Since $\hat{\chi}$ is cheap to compute, the overhead of periodic calculations for a new pruned subset remains low. Figure 1 provides an overview of our proposed method.

Our contributions are as follows:

- We investigate the effectiveness of data pruning methods applied to text classification in reducing finetuning time while maintaining accuracy, including experimental results on six datasets from the GLUE benchmark and four joint NLU datasets.
- We improve the dynamic pruning method with a key initial training phase on the full train set and novel application of the EL2N score in a dynamic setting.
- We extend the EL2N importance score to multi-output text classifications supported by mathematical derivations, specifically for joint intent classification and slot filling.
- We release an open source version of our implementation[1] built around the *transformers* library (Wolf et al., 2020).

## 2 Related Work

Previous works have investigated data pruning methods based on metrics calculated from training characteristics. Toneva et al. (2018) propose to score examples based on their number of transitions from correct to incorrect classification over the course of training. They observed that training accuracy is not considerably affected by removing a significant proportion of the rarely forgotten training examples. Nevertheless, this method is not directly applicable to efficiency improvements since evaluating forgetting scores requires a full round of finetuning. Coleman et al. (2020) address this issue by conducting data selection using a small proxy model. However, this involves supporting an additional model, which makes the process more complex. Paul et al. (2021) derives GraNd and EL2N scores as approximations to sample importance (Alain et al., 2015; Katharopoulos and Fleuret, 2018). They observe that expectation over 10 initializations improves metric quality when evaluated early in training. Although this represents a considerable computational cost, they show that they can prune large proportions of low-importance samples without test accuracy reductions. Others have applied GraNd/EL2N scores to text datasets, notably in natural language inference (Fayyaz et al., 2022) and to reduce gender bias (Zayed et al., 2022). Sorscher et al. (2022) criticize previous work for experimenting only on two computer vision datasets: CIFAR-10 and CIFAR-100. Other metrics have been proposed (Sorscher et al., 2022; Mindermann et al., 2022; Yang et al., 2022), but they all involve further computations.

Raju et al. (2021) and Swayamdipta et al. (2020) observe that training dynamically separates examples in three categories: easy-to-learn, hard-to-learn and ambiguous. Ambiguous samples are characterized by higher variability across training, and an early evaluation of their importance metric can incorrectly predict late training behaviour. To address this, a curriculum is proposed to train on dynamically selected subsets, leading to better performance than EL2N-based static pruning and random subset selection at high pruning rates.

Other related topics also include coreset selection (Har-Peled and Kushal, 2005; Munteanu et al.,

[1] github.com/jpcorbeil-nuance/nlu_data_diets

2018; Campbell and Broderick, 2018), active learning (Ash et al., 2019; Kim, 2020; Park et al.), dataset size reduction (Mishra and Sachdeva, 2020) and curriculum learning (Bengio et al., 2009; Kumar et al., 2010; Platanios et al., 2019; Wan et al., 2020; Christopoulou et al., 2022).

## 3 Methods

### 3.1 Estimating Training Example Importance

Importance refers to the degree to which a particular training example affects the model's performance at learning to correctly classify other examples, as formally defined in Paul et al. (2021). A low-importance sample has little impact on training and can be removed without much effect.

We consider supervised classification, with training set $S$ composed of training examples $(x_i, y_i)$ with $i \in [1, N]$ and $N \in \mathbb{N}$, drawn i.i.d. from an unknown data distribution. Here, $x_i \in \mathbb{R}^d$ are the input vectors of dimension $d \in \mathbb{N}$ and $y_i \in \{0,1\}^K$ are one-hot labels with $K$ classes. Model $f$, composed of weights $w \in \mathcal{W} \subseteq \mathbb{R}^D$ with $D \in \mathbb{N}$, produces probability vector $p = f(x_i) \in [0,1]^K$, and is trained to estimate $y_i$ using the cross-entropy loss:

$$\mathcal{L}_i = -y_i^T \cdot log(f(x_i)). \tag{1}$$

Paul et al. (2021) showed that the norm of the gradient of $\mathcal{L}_i$ is an upper bound to the importance of sample $(x_i, y_i)$. They also introduced a computationally more efficient approximation known as the EL2N score:

$$\chi(x_i, y_i) = \mathbb{E}||f(x_i) - y_i||_2, \tag{2}$$

where the expectation is taken over the randomly initialized weights $w$ of model $f$.

#### 3.1.1 Extending EL2N to NLU

For the joint NLU task, each training example has sequence-level intent labels $y_i^{intent}$ and $M \in \mathbb{N}$ word-level slot labels $y_{i,m}^{slot}$ with $m \in \{1, M\}$. The loss for sample $i$ is expressed as:

$$\mathcal{L}_i^{nlu} = \mathcal{L}_i^{intent} + \sum_{m=1}^{M} \mathcal{L}_{i,m}^{slot}, \tag{3}$$

where intent and slot losses are calculated from eq. 1 with $y_i^{intent}$ and $y_{i,m}^{slot}$ respectively.

In order to estimate joint NLU sample importance, we extend the EL2N formulation to a such case in Appendix A. We provide a derivation for the EL2N score in three contexts: EL2N for sequence-level classification:

$$\hat{\chi}_{intent}(x_i, y_i) = ||f(x_i) - y_i^{intent}||_2, \tag{4}$$

EL2N for multiple-output classifications, which introduces a second $\ell_2$ norm over the sequence length:

$$\hat{\chi}_{slot}(x_i, y_i) = \sqrt{\sum_{m=1}^{M} ||f(x_i) - y_{i,m}^{slot}||_2^2}, \tag{5}$$

and for joint tasks, e.g. joint intent detection and slot filling:

$$\hat{\chi}_{nlu}(x_i, y_i) = \sqrt{\hat{\chi}_{intent}(x_i, y_i)^2 + \hat{\chi}_{slot}(x_i, y_i)^2}. \tag{6}$$

#### 3.1.2 Averaging $\hat{\chi}$ Over Time

Averaging EL2N over multiple initializations improves importance approximation, but increases compute costs. Instead, following Raju et al. (2021), we consider an exponential moving average (EMA) over time to evaluate $\hat{\chi}$:

$$\begin{aligned} \hat{\chi}_{ema}(x, y) \leftarrow & \alpha \cdot \hat{\chi}_{nlu}(x, y) \\ & + (1 - \alpha) \cdot \hat{\chi}_{ema}(x, y) \end{aligned} \tag{7}$$

This is possible since dynamic pruning is performed periodically over multiple cycles. Because importance estimation for some examples varies significantly across train steps, EMA provides an adequate trade-off between emphasizing the current estimate and leveraging previous evaluations.

### 3.2 Dynamic Pruning

With dynamic pruning, the model is trained for $\tau$ epochs, then, we train for cycles of $T$ epochs until training is complete. At the beginning of each cycle, we score all training examples with eq. 7, and the proportion with the highest scores is selected. In algorithm 1, we present pseudo-code for the proposed method, where $S'$ is the retained training subset and $E$ is the number of training epochs.

## 4 Experimental Details

### 4.1 Experimental Setup

In our experiments, we compare five methods:

- **Full Train Set**: baseline approach with standard training using the full train set.

**Algorithm 1:** Dynamic Pruning

**Inputs:** $S$, $f$, $\rho$, $T$, $\tau$, $E$
$S' \leftarrow \{\}$;
$\hat{\chi}_{ema} \leftarrow \{\}$;
$cycle \leftarrow 1$;
**for** *epoch in* $\tau$ **do**
  train $f$ with $S$;
**end**
**while** $cycle < \lfloor (E-\tau)/T \rfloor$ **do**
  $\hat{\chi}_{ema} \leftarrow \alpha\hat{\chi}_{nlu} + (1-\alpha)\hat{\chi}_{ema}$;
  *sort* $S$ with respect to $\hat{\chi}_{ema}$, $\downarrow$ order;
  $S' \leftarrow$ top $(1-\rho)$ elements from $S$;
  $cycle \leftarrow cycle + 1$;
  **for** *epoch in* $T$ **do**
    train $f$ with $S'$;
  **end**
**end**

- **Static Pruning**: method from Paul et al. (2021). The training subset is obtained from EL2N scores averaged over 10 randomly initialized models trained for 10 epochs, and finetuning is then performed on the fixed subset.

- **Single Pruning**: training is performed on the full trainset for $\tau$ epochs, followed by a single subset selection using EL2N. Finetuning is then performed on the fixed subset.

- **Dynamic Pruning**: proposed method which trains on the full trainset for $\tau$ epochs, followed by periodic data pruning using $\hat{\chi}_{ema}$ as described by algorithm 1.

- **Dynamic Random Pruning**: same as dynamic pruning, but the subset selection is random.

For the full train set method, we finetune the model for $E$ epochs. We assume that $E$ and $\tau$ correspond to constant numbers of training steps defined from the full training set size. For the other four methods, all experiments are performed over $E$ epochs, to which we remove a number of train steps equivalent to $\rho \cdot (E - \tau)$. We do not report results for the full train set method with reduced training steps as they are comparable to those of the dynamic random pruning method. The number of epochs $E$ is set to 10 for GLUE following Liu et al. (2019) and to 40 for the joint NLU tasks following Chen et al. (2019).

### 4.2 Datasets

We present two series of experiments to address text classification problems with either a single output or multiple outputs. For the single output case, we consider six datasets from the GLUE benchmark (Wang et al., 2019): COLA, MNLI, MRPC, QQP, RTE, and SST2. We exclude STS-B since it is a regression task, WNLI because it has a very small train set, and QNLI as it is an artificially built dataset.

For the multi-output case, we use four open-source joint NLU datasets: ATIS (Price, 1990; Tur et al., 2010), SNIPS (Coucke et al., 2018), SLURP (Bastianelli et al., 2020) and MTOP (Li et al., 2021) — English version only. All examples from these datasets are labelled with an intent (sequence-level class) and entity tags (token-level class). ATIS focuses on the airline travel domain, and the other three datasets represent voice assistants across various domains, such as music, weather, and calendar, among others. We use the original versions of these datasets without any modification.

Tables 2 and 3 in Appendix D provide the general characteristics of these datasets. Overall, they cover a large diversity of train set sizes and tasks. For the joint NLU tasks, we have a variety of domains, intents and entities.

### 4.3 Model Architecture

We use the pre-trained transformer model *RoBERTa base* (Liu et al., 2019). For the GLUE datasets, we use single sequences or concatenations of two sequences as model inputs for paraphrase detection and natural language inference (NLI) tasks. For the joint NLU tasks, we use the JointBERT approach (Chen et al., 2019). To handle entities, we apply a mask on special tokens as well as subsequent subwords if a word is decomposed into multiple subword tokens. Additionally, we reinitialize the last layer of the encoder (Kovaleva et al., 2019; Tamkin et al., 2020), which can improve the final performance.

### 4.4 Accuracy Evaluation

We evaluate the performance of our models on the GLUE datasets following the original instructions. Since the test sets are not publicly available, we report the averaged results on the development sets following previous approaches from (Devlin et al., 2019; Liu et al., 2019). Specifically, we report the accuracy metric for RTE and SST2, accuracy on the

Table 1: Median performances on 5 runs for the *dev* set of the GLUE benchmark for pruning rate of 50%. Static pruning is done with scores averaged on 10 runs of 10 epochs over 10 GPUs. All datasets are using $\tau = 1$ and $T = 2$, except for RTE set to $\tau = 3$ and $T = 1$ (marked by the asterisk *).

| | COLA | MNLI | MRPC | QQP | RTE | SST2 |
|---|---|---|---|---|---|---|
| **Full Train Set** | | | | | | |
| Score | 0.600 | 0.864 / 0.862 | 0.892 / 0.923 | 0.911 / 0.880 | 0.751 | 0.932 |
| Time (s) | 158.8 | 10053.0 | 89.0 | 8214.5 | 107.5 | 1314.8 |
| **Static Pruning** | | | | | | |
| Score | 0.587 | 0.852 / 0.850 | 0.857 / 0.892 | 0.895 / 0.864 | 0.517 | 0.933 |
| Relative Time | 152.6% | 151.2% | 150.7% | 146.5% | 150.8% | 150.7% |
| **Single Pruning** | | | | | | |
| Score | 0.586 | 0.778 / 0.775 | 0.854 / 0.887 | 0.909 / 0.879 | 0.746* | 0.937 |
| Relative Time | 58.0% | 56.5% | 56.6% | 53.1% | 68.2%* | 55.7% |
| **Dynamic Random Pruning** | | | | | | |
| Score | 0.578 | 0.853 / 0.855 | 0.863 / 0.902 | 0.899 / 0.867 | 0.753* | **0.938** |
| Relative Time | 56.0% | 54.5% | 55.1% | 54.3% | 65.8%* | 52.6% |
| **Dynamic Pruning (ours)** | | | | | | |
| Score | **0.590** | **0.863 / 0.863** | **0.882 / 0.915** | **0.912 / 0.881** | **0.773*** | 0.932 |
| Relative Time | 64.4% | 64.0% | 66.5% | 60.4% | 77.2%* | 62.0% |

matched and mismatched test set splits for MNLI, and both accuracy and F-1 metrics for MRPC and QQP. For COLA, we compute the Matthews correlation coefficient. For the joint NLU tasks, we focus on full-sequence accuracy, which requires matching both the intent and all the entities. We also provide the intent accuracy and entity micro F1 in Appendix F.

### 4.5 Runtime Evaluation

We report GPU finetuning time in minutes or seconds. To avoid the impact of CPU overhead, such as pre-processing and batching, we measure the time for each training step and forward pass for scoring EL2N separately, and then sum the results at the end of the fine-tuning process. We provide the mathematical expressions for the total GPU runtime and the minimum cycle $T_{min}$ to improve efficiency in Appendix B. Finally, we used 10 GPUs to parallelize the computation of EL2N scores with static pruning, as this method requires training 10 independent models.

## 5 Results

### 5.1 GLUE Benchmark

In Table 1, we present the results obtained on the GLUE benchmark with a 50% pruning rate. Overall, dynamic pruning achieves accuracy nearly on par with full training while reducing the finetuning time by approximately 30%. The largest accuracy decrease is observed on the COLA and MRPC datasets, at only 1% absolute. We also note that the smallest time reduction occurs on RTE and is due to the different pruning settings required by this dataset of smaller size. We observe a sharper drop in performance with single pruning and dynamic random pruning, despite being faster. Static pruning underperforms in terms of both accuracy and finetuning time. This is especially the case on the RTE dataset and is likely due to the combination of a high pruning rate and a smaller number of training examples. This suggests that dynamic pruning may be affected at lower data amounts, as reported for static pruning by Sorscher et al. (2022).

### 5.2 Joint Intent Classification and Slot Filling

In Figures 2 and 3, we present the full-sequence accuracy and GPU finetuning time obtained with the studied methods on the joint NLU tasks. In Appendix F, we also include the related intent accuracy and slot micro F1 score.

#### 5.2.1 Accuracy Analysis

Overall, our dynamic pruning method achieves accuracy comparable to full training, even when using aggressive pruning rates. It exhibits a flatter and smoother decrease compared to other techniques, which results in a better time-accuracy trade-off. For instance, at a pruning rate of 40%, our approach leads to similar scores as the full-training baseline while being about 25% faster. Other methods underperform by 0.5 to 2.5% in the same setting, excluding the ATIS dataset for which all methods perform above baseline. Single pruning outperforms static pruning in almost every setting, despite static pruning leveraging EL2N scores calculated from multiple models. This emphasizes the importance

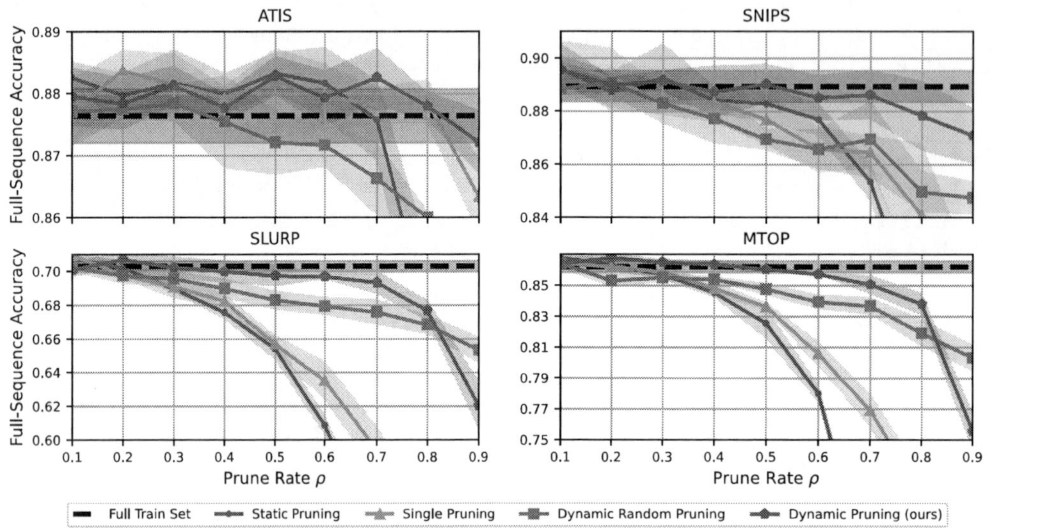


Figure 2: Full-sequence accuracy achieved on 40 epochs for different prune rates on joint NLU datasets applying: static pruning (EL2N from 10 runs of 10 epochs), single pruning, dynamic random pruning, and our dynamic pruning (EL2N with EMA). The dynamic methods are run with $\tau = 4$ and $T = 4$.

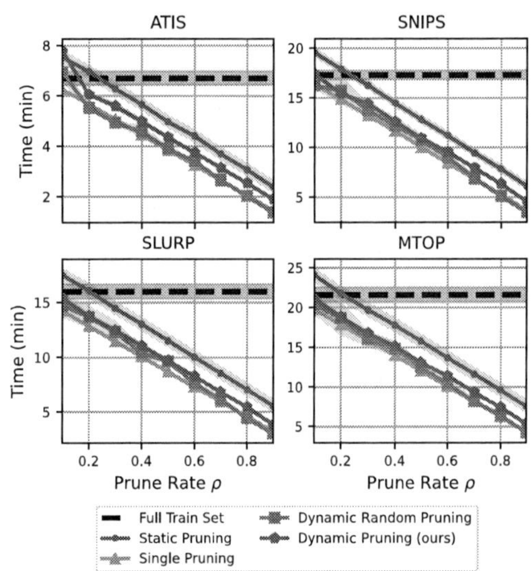


Figure 3: Finetuning time achieved on 40 epochs for different prune rates on joint NLU datasets applying: static pruning (EL2N from 10 runs of 10 epochs), single pruning, dynamic random pruning, and our dynamic pruning (EL2N with EMA). The dynamic methods are run with $\tau = 4$ and $T = 4$.

of the initial training phase on the full dataset. Surprisingly, dynamic random pruning performs better than static and single pruning methods. This is further discussed in section 6.

At an aggressive pruning rate of 80%, dynamic pruning only incurs a marginal drop of 1-2%, with a total finetuning time of nearly a third of the full training. In comparison, dynamic random pruning achieves a few absolute percentage points less than dynamic pruning, and static pruning decreases even faster. Single pruning shows a similar decrease, except on the ATIS dataset. At an extreme prune rate of 90%, dynamic random pruning performs better than dynamic pruning for two datasets: SLURP and MTOP. This is because these datasets have many mislabeled data points, usually associated with high-importance scores, as discussed in section 6. We also notice a significant decrease in accuracy from the static and single pruning methods for the same reason. Regarding domains, number of intents, and number of entities, SLURP and MTOP are the most complex.

Results on the ATIS dataset show a different trend, especially at a low prune rate. We observe an improvement over the full training set method for single, static and dynamic pruning, which perform equally well. ATIS is a smaller dataset with simple, repetitive samples on a single domain and consequently contains a larger proportion of easy-to-learn examples (see Section 6). Even at moderate prune rates, the composition of the pruned subset remains stable over time, explaining the adequate performance of the static method. At higher prune rates, the accuracy of static pruning drops abruptly.

Figures 7 and 8 of Appendix F show that our

dynamic pruning method preserves the full-trainset intent accuracy and slot micro F1 score with prune rates up to 80%.

### 5.2.2 Finetuning Time Analysis

Regarding finetuning time, we empirically observe the linearly decreasing relationship with $\rho$ as described by equation 31 in Appendix B. Dynamic random pruning is faster than dynamic pruning since it does not require the periodic forward passes needed for calculating $\hat{\chi}_{ema}$. However, we can observe from this difference that the overhead is relatively small compared to the whole training process. Single pruning, which only requires a single computation of the importance score, is faster than dynamic pruning. In contrast, static pruning is significantly slower due to the overhead from the initial 10 runs of 10 epochs, even if computations are parallelized across ten GPUs.

## 5.3 Balancing Accuracy and Efficiency

In this section, we present an analysis of the time-accuracy trade-off for our dynamic data pruning method in relation to $T$ and $\tau$ on the MTOP dataset, with a fixed prune rate of 70%. Similar trends are observed with the other datasets, as shown in Appendix F. The results are illustrated in Figures 4 and 5.

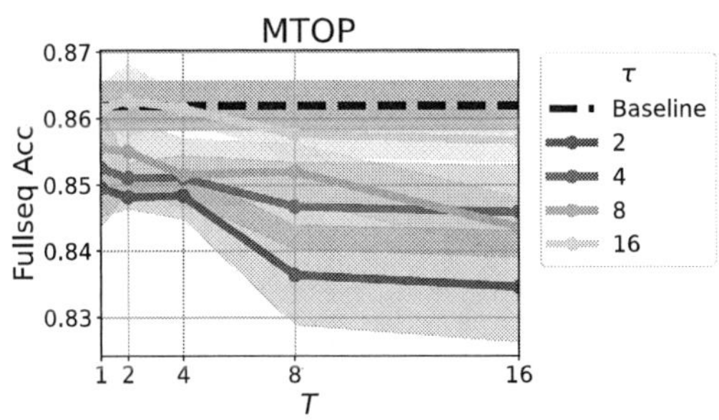


Figure 4: Full-sequence accuracy from a dynamic pruning of 70% for various $\tau$ and $T$ on the MTOP dataset.

We found that training on larger $\tau$ and considering shorter $T$ results in higher accuracy. We note that $\tau$ is key to our approach since it impacts accuracy the most. For instance, a $\tau$ of 2 is less effective than 16, while the difference between 4 and 8 is marginal. Despite pruning 70% of the data points, we achieved similar results to full training with $T = 2$ and $\tau = 16$. Considering that we are at a high prune rate, we can achieve a better time-accuracy trade-off at $T = 4$ and $\tau = 4$. This results in a marginal sacrifice of 1.2% for twice

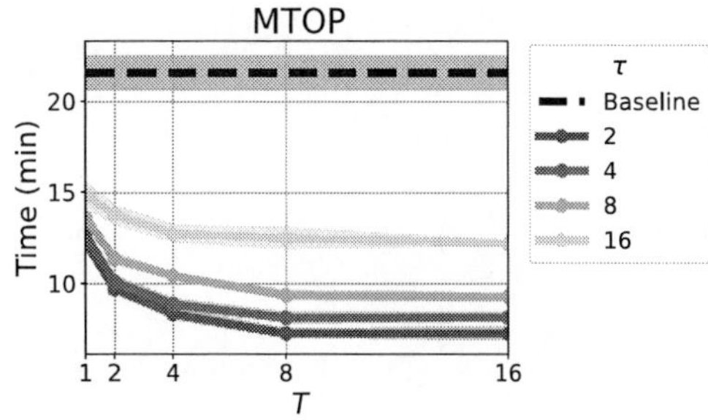


Figure 5: Finetuning time from a dynamic pruning of 70% for various $\tau$ and $T$ on the MTOP dataset.

the reduction in finetuning time. Specifically, the finetuning time is reduced from 826 s (−36%) to 533 s (−59%) compared to full training at 1295 s.

Furthermore, we observe the inverse relationship between the finetuning time and $T$ in Figure 5 as described by equation 31 in Appendix B. For small $T$, this inverse relationship significantly increases the computational time. For instance, the difference between $T = 1$ and $T = 2$ is nearly 2 minutes, while being negligible between 8 and 16.

Due to periodical re-evaluation of the pruned subset, we note that performance obtained with $\tau$, $\rho$, and $T$ is less sensible to dataset characteristics, and the time-accuracy trade-off it provides remains robust across various settings. We provide additional recommendations about selecting these parameters in Appendix E.

# 6 Data Selection Analysis

We analyze pruning dynamics for joint intent classification and slot filling. The analysis is presented for SLURP, but observations are similar to other datasets.

First, we present a data map in Figure 6*a*, that shows variance and mean of $\hat{\chi}_{nlu}$ over 10 cycles of $T = 4$ epochs for all training examples. The pruning proportion is set to 50%. We discern three regions delimited by dashed curves: the bottom-left corner (low variance, low mean) corresponds to easy-to-learn examples consistently pruned from the train set, the top (high mean) corresponds to hard-to-learn examples consistently retained, and examples in-between (mid/high variance, low/mid mean) are ambiguous.

Figure 6*b* shows the distribution for the number of times a given example is selected in the retained subset over ten pruning cycles. For SLURP, we observe that about a third of the examples are con-

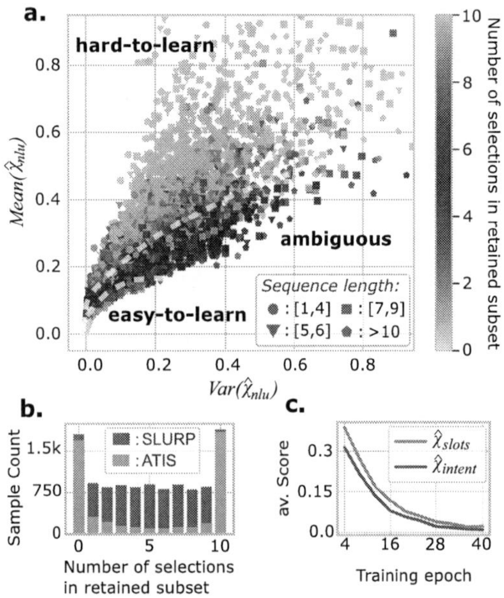


Figure 6: *a.* Data map for SLURP train set. Colours indicate the number of times an example is selected in the retained subset, and shapes show the sequence length. *b.* Distribution of the number of selections in retained subset over ten pruning cycles for SLURP and ATIS. *c.* Average intent and slots metrics with respect to epochs.

sistently either always selected or never selected, corresponding to hard-to-learn and easy-to-learn cases, respectively. Other examples are approximately evenly distributed across selection counts. In comparison, we also present the distribution for the ATIS dataset, for which most training examples are either never selected or always selected.

Figure 6*c* presents scoring metrics averaged over the full train set for intent and slot classifications with respect to the training epoch. On average, sequences have one intent classification term per 6.9 slot classification terms. Overall, contribution to $\hat{\chi}_{nlu}$ is comparable between intent and slots, meaning that individual score is typically smaller for slots. However, scores associated with the prevalent *no_entity* class are relatively low compared to other slot labels, which have a predominant contribution to $\hat{\chi}_{slots}$.

In Table 5 of Appendix F, we present 13 examples of easy-to-learn, hard-to-learn and ambiguous samples, with their score averaged over time and the number of selections with four different initializations. Examples with the highest score typically have mislabeled intent (1) or slot (2), or have an infrequent class label (3, 0.03% of all samples), or are unique (4). Examples with lowest $\hat{\chi}_{nlu}$ generally have short utterances with no entity label and with highly represented intent labels having many redundant tokens across class examples (see 5-7). Note that Spearman correlation between $\hat{\chi}_{nlu}$ and the number of words ($r = 0.096$), number of entities ($r = 0.205$) and intent class prevalence ($r = -0.109$) remains low when considering full train set.

Ambiguous examples, however, are more difficult to characterize qualitatively. We present several examples with an increasing scoring metric which are all under the same intent label for comparison purposes (see examples 8-13). There is no clear distinction between samples. In fact, when considering different initializations, the same ambiguous sample obtains different selection counts in the retained subset. This shows the necessity of using dynamic pruning: a static pruning algorithm will target easy-to-learn samples but will suffer from the variability of ambiguous samples. This high variability also explains the unexpectedly high performance of random pruning. Dynamic pruning can adjust the selection of ambiguous samples during training based on the model's performance, which leads to more efficient training.

When the proportion of ambiguous examples is low, as with the ATIS dataset, single and static pruning outperform random dynamic pruning, as shown in Figure 2, since the pruning subsets remain consistent across training.

## 7 Conclusion

In summary, this work presents a dynamic approach to data pruning to improve finetuning efficiency. It introduces an extension of the EL2N metric for multi-output classifications. We use this metric to periodically select a subset of the data during training in contrast to static pruning. We empirically show that our method provides a better trade-off between accuracy and efficiency, especially at high prune rates. We also show that this trade-off benefits from initial training with the full train set for a few epochs.

We apply our method to NLP classification datasets, particularly six tasks from the GLUE benchmark and four datasets for joint intent classification and slot filling. By pruning 50% of training examples, we preserve full accuracy on the test set while reducing the finetuning time by up to 41%. If we tolerate an accuracy reduction of 1% absolute, we can prune 80% of the training data, corresponding to time reductions of up to 66%. Finally, we provide insights into how performance is affected by the characteristics of the training set.

As future work, we envision further investigations including more natural language tasks, more challenging datasets (e.g. SuperGLUE) and improved importance approximations. Overall, dynamical evaluation of sample importance remains largely unexplored beyond improving efficiency, notably in data augmentation, active learning, mislabel detection or pre-training data selection.

## Limitations

This study is limited to classification tasks with an encoder architecture, short texts (e.g. utterances), datasets with at least several thousand examples, and a relatively low amount of mislabeled data. In theory, we could apply our method to longer texts, but our takeaways might not directly apply. For similar reasons, our conclusions could be different on very small datasets. Our approach is also sensible to mislabeled data points, but this weakness is mitigated by the fact that our method can contribute to improving the identification of such mislabels. We are also aware of further efficiency optimizations, such as calculating scores directly from mini-batches during training for the retained subset, which we leave to future work.

## Ethics Statement

We bring up two main ethical considerations. First, this empirical study uses a large language model requiring a considerable amount of computations (at most 1,500 GPU hours), which is not without environmental consequences. However, since this study aims at making training more efficient, it will help reduce energy consumption in the future. Moreover, this study focuses on accuracy as a measure of performance, which can hide pervasive effects on under-represented marginalized groups. However, since our method is about evaluating importance of training examples over train steps, it can lead to improving techniques to decrease bias in the training process, particularly when marginalized groups are under-represented in the data and therefore challenging to identify accurately.

## Acknowledgements

We would like to express our gratitude to François Beaulieu, Paul Vozila, Rupert Brook, and Alessandro Sordoni for their helpful comments. We also appreciate the valuable feedback provided by the anonymous reviewers, which contributed to the improvement of our paper.

## References

Guillaume Alain, Alex Lamb, Chinnadhurai Sankar, Aaron Courville, and Yoshua Bengio. 2015. Variance reduction in sgd by distributed importance sampling. *arXiv preprint arXiv:1511.06481*.

Jordan T Ash, Chicheng Zhang, Akshay Krishnamurthy, John Langford, and Alekh Agarwal. 2019. Deep batch active learning by diverse, uncertain gradient lower bounds. In *International Conference on Learning Representations*.

Emanuele Bastianelli, Andrea Vanzo, Pawel Swietojanski, and Verena Rieser. 2020. Slurp: A spoken language understanding resource package. In *Proceedings of the 2020 Conference on Empirical Methods in Natural Language Processing (EMNLP)*, pages 7252–7262.

Yoshua Bengio, Jérôme Louradour, Ronan Collobert, and Jason Weston. 2009. Curriculum learning. In *Proceedings of the 26th annual international conference on machine learning*, pages 41–48.

Trevor Campbell and Tamara Broderick. 2018. Bayesian coreset construction via greedy iterative geodesic ascent. In *International Conference on Machine Learning*, pages 698–706. PMLR.

Qian Chen, Zhu Zhuo, and Wen Wang. 2019. Bert for joint intent classification and slot filling. *arXiv preprint arXiv:1902.10909*.

Fenia Christopoulou, Gerasimos Lampouras, and Ignacio Iacobacci. 2022. Training dynamics for curriculum learning: A study on monolingual and cross-lingual NLU. In *Proceedings of the 2022 Conference on Empirical Methods in Natural Language Processing*, pages 2595–2611, Abu Dhabi, United Arab Emirates. Association for Computational Linguistics.

C Coleman, C Yeh, S Mussmann, B Mirzasoleiman, P Bailis, P Liang, J Leskovec, and M Zaharia. 2020. Selection via proxy: Efficient data selection for deep learning. In *International Conference on Learning Representations (ICLR)*.

Alice Coucke, Alaa Saade, Adrien Ball, Théodore Bluche, Alexandre Caulier, David Leroy, Clément Doumouro, Thibault Gisselbrecht, Francesco Caltagirone, Thibaut Lavril, et al. 2018. Snips voice platform: an embedded spoken language understanding system for private-by-design voice interfaces. *arXiv preprint arXiv:1805.10190*.

Jacob Devlin, Ming-Wei Chang, Kenton Lee, and Kristina Toutanova. 2019. Bert: Pre-training of deep bidirectional transformers for language understanding. In *Proceedings of NAACL-HLT*, pages 4171–4186.

Mohsen Fayyaz, Ehsan Aghazadeh, Ali Modarressi, Mohammad Taher Pilehvar, Yadollah Yaghoobzadeh, Samira Ebrahimi Kahou, and CIFAR Mila. 2022. Bert on a data diet: Finding important examples by gradient-based pruning.

Suyog Gupta, Ankur Agrawal, Kailash Gopalakrishnan, and Pritish Narayanan. 2015. Deep learning with limited numerical precision. In *International conference on machine learning*, pages 1737–1746. PMLR.

Sariel Har-Peled and Akash Kushal. 2005. Smaller coresets for k-median and k-means clustering. In *Proceedings of the twenty-first annual symposium on Computational geometry*, pages 126–134.

Angelos Katharopoulos and François Fleuret. 2018. Not all samples are created equal: Deep learning with importance sampling. In *International conference on machine learning*, pages 2525–2534. PMLR.

Yekyung Kim. 2020. Deep active learning for sequence labeling based on diversity and uncertainty in gradient. In *Proceedings of the 2nd Workshop on Life-long Learning for Spoken Language Systems*, pages 1–8.

Olga Kovaleva, Alexey Romanov, Anna Rogers, and Anna Rumshisky. 2019. Revealing the dark secrets of bert. In *Proceedings of the 2019 Conference on Empirical Methods in Natural Language Processing and the 9th International Joint Conference on Natural Language Processing (EMNLP-IJCNLP)*.

M Kumar, Benjamin Packer, and Daphne Koller. 2010. Self-paced learning for latent variable models. *Advances in neural information processing systems*, 23.

Quentin Lhoest, Albert Villanova del Moral, Yacine Jernite, Abhishek Thakur, Patrick von Platen, Suraj Patil, Julien Chaumond, Mariama Drame, Julien Plu, Lewis Tunstall, Joe Davison, Mario Šaško, Gunjan Chhablani, Bhavitvya Malik, Simon Brandeis, Teven Le Scao, Victor Sanh, Canwen Xu, Nicolas Patry, Angelina McMillan-Major, Philipp Schmid, Sylvain Gugger, Clément Delangue, Théo Matussière, Lysandre Debut, Stas Bekman, Pierric Cistac, Thibault Goehringer, Victor Mustar, François Lagunas, Alexander Rush, and Thomas Wolf. 2021. Datasets: A community library for natural language processing. In *Proceedings of the 2021 Conference on Empirical Methods in Natural Language Processing: System Demonstrations*, pages 175–184, Online and Punta Cana, Dominican Republic. Association for Computational Linguistics.

Haoran Li, Abhinav Arora, Shuohui Chen, Anchit Gupta, Sonal Gupta, and Yashar Mehdad. 2021. Mtop: A comprehensive multilingual task-oriented semantic parsing benchmark. In *Proceedings of the 16th Conference of the European Chapter of the Association for Computational Linguistics: Main Volume*, pages 2950–2962.

Yinhan Liu, Myle Ott, Naman Goyal, Jingfei Du, Mandar Joshi, Danqi Chen, Omer Levy, Mike Lewis, Luke Zettlemoyer, and Veselin Stoyanov. 2019. Roberta: A robustly optimized bert pretraining approach. *arXiv preprint arXiv:1907.11692*.

Paulius Micikevicius, Sharan Narang, Jonah Alben, Gregory Diamos, Erich Elsen, David Garcia, Boris Ginsburg, Michael Houston, Oleksii Kuchaiev, Ganesh Venkatesh, et al. 2018. Mixed precision training. In *International Conference on Learning Representations*.

Sören Mindermann, Jan M Brauner, Muhammed T Razzak, Mrinank Sharma, Andreas Kirsch, Winnie Xu, Benedikt Höltgen, Aidan N Gomez, Adrien Morisot, Sebastian Farquhar, et al. 2022. Prioritized training on points that are learnable, worth learning, and not yet learnt. In *International Conference on Machine Learning*, pages 15630–15649. PMLR.

Swaroop Mishra and Bhavdeep Singh Sachdeva. 2020. Do we need to create big datasets to learn a task? In *Proceedings of SustaiNLP: Workshop on Simple and Efficient Natural Language Processing*, pages 169–173.

Alexander Munteanu, Chris Schwiegelshohn, Christian Sohler, and David Woodruff. 2018. On coresets for logistic regression. *Advances in Neural Information Processing Systems*, 31.

Dongmin Park, Dimitris Papailiopoulos, and Kangwook Lee. Active learning is a strong baseline for data subset selection. In *Has it Trained Yet? NeurIPS 2022 Workshop*.

Adam Paszke, Sam Gross, Soumith Chintala, Gregory Chanan, Edward Yang, Zachary DeVito, Zeming Lin, Alban Desmaison, Luca Antiga, and Adam Lerer. 2017. Automatic differentiation in pytorch.

Adam Paszke, Sam Gross, Francisco Massa, Adam Lerer, James Bradbury, Gregory Chanan, Trevor Killeen, Zeming Lin, Natalia Gimelshein, Luca Antiga, Alban Desmaison, Andreas Kopf, Edward Yang, Zachary DeVito, Martin Raison, Alykhan Tejani, Sasank Chilamkurthy, Benoit Steiner, Lu Fang, Junjie Bai, and Soumith Chintala. 2019. Pytorch: An imperative style, high-performance deep learning library. In *Advances in Neural Information Processing Systems 32*, pages 8024–8035. Curran Associates, Inc.

Mansheej Paul, Surya Ganguli, and Gintare Karolina Dziugaite. 2021. Deep learning on a data diet: Finding important examples early in training. *Advances in Neural Information Processing Systems*, 34:20596–20607.

Emmanouil Antonios Platanios, Otilia Stretcu, Graham Neubig, Barnabás Poczós, and Tom Mitchell. 2019. Competence-based curriculum learning for neural machine translation. In *Proceedings of the 2019 Conference of the North American Chapter of the Association for Computational Linguistics: Human Language Technologies, Volume 1 (Long and Short Papers)*, pages 1162–1172.

Patti Price. 1990. Evaluation of spoken language systems: The atis domain. In *Speech and Natural Language: Proceedings of a Workshop Held at Hidden Valley, Pennsylvania, June 24-27, 1990.*

Ravi S Raju, Kyle Daruwalla, and Mikko Lipasti. 2021. Accelerating deep learning with dynamic data pruning. *arXiv preprint arXiv:2111.12621.*

Ben Sorscher, Robert Geirhos, Shashank Shekhar, Surya Ganguli, and Ari S Morcos. 2022. Beyond neural scaling laws: beating power law scaling via data pruning. In *Advances in Neural Information Processing Systems.*

Swabha Swayamdipta, Roy Schwartz, Nicholas Lourie, Yizhong Wang, Hannaneh Hajishirzi, Noah A Smith, and Yejin Choi. 2020. Dataset cartography: Mapping and diagnosing datasets with training dynamics. In *Proceedings of the 2020 Conference on Empirical Methods in Natural Language Processing (EMNLP)*, pages 9275–9293.

Alex Tamkin, Trisha Singh, Davide Giovanardi, and Noah Goodman. 2020. Investigating transferability in pretrained language models. In *Findings of the Association for Computational Linguistics: EMNLP 2020*, pages 1393–1401.

Mariya Toneva, Alessandro Sordoni, Remi Tachet des Combes, Adam Trischler, Yoshua Bengio, and Geoffrey J Gordon. 2018. An empirical study of example forgetting during deep neural network learning. In *International Conference on Learning Representations.*

Gokhan Tur, Dilek Hakkani-Tür, and Larry Heck. 2010. What is left to be understood in atis? In *2010 IEEE Spoken Language Technology Workshop*, pages 19–24. IEEE.

Yu Wan, Baosong Yang, Derek F Wong, Yikai Zhou, Lidia S Chao, Haibo Zhang, and Boxing Chen. 2020. Self-paced learning for neural machine translation. In *Proceedings of the 2020 Conference on Empirical Methods in Natural Language Processing (EMNLP)*, pages 1074–1080.

Alex Wang, Amanpreet Singh, Julian Michael, Felix Hill, Omer Levy, and Samuel R Bowman. 2019. Glue: A multi-task benchmark and analysis platform for natural language understanding. In *7th International Conference on Learning Representations, ICLR 2019.*

Thomas Wolf, Lysandre Debut, Victor Sanh, Julien Chaumond, Clement Delangue, Anthony Moi, Pierric Cistac, Tim Rault, Rémi Louf, Morgan Funtowicz, et al. 2020. Transformers: State-of-the-art natural language processing. In *Proceedings of the 2020 conference on empirical methods in natural language processing: system demonstrations*, pages 38–45.

Yunyang Xiong, Zhanpeng Zeng, Rudrasis Chakraborty, Mingxing Tan, Glenn Fung, Yin Li, and Vikas Singh. 2021. Nyströmformer: A nyström-based algorithm for approximating self-attention. In *Proceedings of the AAAI Conference on Artificial Intelligence*, volume 35, pages 14138–14148.

Shuo Yang, Zeke Xie, Hanyu Peng, Min Xu, Mingming Sun, and Ping Li. 2022. Dataset pruning: Reducing training data by examining generalization influence. *arXiv preprint arXiv:2205.09329.*

Manzil Zaheer, Guru Guruganesh, Kumar Avinava Dubey, Joshua Ainslie, Chris Alberti, Santiago Ontanon, Philip Pham, Anirudh Ravula, Qifan Wang, Li Yang, et al. 2020. Big bird: Transformers for longer sequences. *Advances in Neural Information Processing Systems*, 33:17283–17297.

Abdelrahman Zayed, Prasanna Parthasarathi, Goncalo Mordido, Hamid Palangi, Samira Shabanian, and Sarath Chandar. 2022. Deep learning on a healthy data diet: Finding important examples for fairness. *arXiv preprint arXiv:2211.11109.*

Minjia Zhang and Yuxiong He. 2020. Accelerating training of transformer-based language models with progressive layer dropping. *Advances in Neural Information Processing Systems*, 33:14011–14023.

## A Derivations of Pruning Metrics

### A.1 Unique Single-Label Classification on CLS token

We begin by defining the GraNd score, $\chi_t(x, y) \in \mathbb{R}_{\geq 0}$, at time $t > 0$ and for any sample data $(x, y)$ as a measure of sample importance (Paul et al., 2021):

$$\chi_t(x, y) = \mathrm{E}_{\mathbf{w}}\left[||g_t(x, y)||_2\right], \tag{8}$$

where $g_t$ is the gradient of the sample $(x, y)$ obtained with model $f$ at time $t$. For simplicity, we define $\chi'_t(x, y)$ as the same expression as in Equation (8) but without the expectation term. We compensate for the improvement of this expectation with dynamic pruning by leveraging the exponential moving average:

$$\chi'_t(x, y) = ||g_t(x, y)||_2. \tag{9}$$

Because processing per-sample gradients can be computationally burdensome, we look for an upper bound. First, we use the result from Katharopoulos and Fleuret (2018), which implies that the full gradient is upper bounded by a constant $\beta \in \mathbb{R}_{>0}$ multiplied by the gradient of the last classification layer. Let $G_t(x, y) \in \mathbb{R}^{K \times d}$ denote the gradient of the last classification layer, where $K, d \in \mathbb{N}$ (number of classes and hidden dimensions, respectively). We can write this result as

$$\chi'_t(x, y) \leq \beta ||G_t(x, y)||_2. \tag{10}$$

Since the last layer is a classification with the cross-entropy loss on a softmax activation, it naturally takes the form of a $K \times d$ matrix defined by the outer product of the error vector $\vec{p}(x) - \vec{y}$ and the transposed contextual word embedding $\vec{h}_{CLS}(x) \in \mathbb{R}^d$. For simplification purposes, we do not carry the notation marking the dependence on $x$ for $\vec{p}$ and $\vec{h}_{CLS}$:

$$G_t(x, y) = (\vec{p} - \vec{y})\, \vec{h}_{CLS}^T. \tag{11}$$

By replacing Equation (11) in Equation (10), we obtain

$$\chi'_t(x, y) \leq \beta ||\, (\vec{p} - \vec{y})\, \vec{h}_{CLS}^T ||_2. \tag{12}$$

Using the property of outer products, we can separate the matrix norm into the product of the vector norms:

$$\chi'_t(x, y) \leq \beta ||\vec{h}_{CLS}||_2 ||\vec{p} - \vec{y}||_2. \tag{13}$$

Given that we want to rank samples $\{(x, y)\}_{1..N}$ and that norm of the contextual word embeddings of $\vec{h}_{CLS}$ can roughly be assumed constant across samples due to layer normalization, we obtain:

$$\chi'_t(x, y) \propto ||\vec{p} - \vec{y}||_2 \tag{14}$$

This metric corresponds to the EL2N score proposed by Paul et al. (2021), and provides scoring function for intent classification:

$$\hat{\chi}_{intent}(x, y) = ||\vec{p}(x) - \vec{y}||_2 \tag{15}$$

## A.2 Sequence of Single-Label Classifications

The derivation for multi-output classification is similar to that of single-label classification shown above, with some modifications. In this case, we consider a summation over the sequence length $m \in [1, M]$, where $M \in \mathbb{N}$, to update the entity classifier with the sum of the gradients from all tokens. We assume that all sequences are padded up to length $M$.

To begin, we introduce the sequence-wise error vectors $\vec{\delta}_m = \vec{p}_m - \vec{y_m}$, and rewrite the gradient $G_t(x, y)$ of equation (11) as follows:

$$G_t(x, y) = \sum_{m=1}^{M} \vec{\delta}_m \vec{h}_m^T, \tag{16}$$

where $\vec{h}_m$ is the contextual embedding for the $m$-th token. By substitution in equation (10), we obtain the following upper bound:

$$\chi'_t(x, y) \leq \beta || \sum_{m=1}^{M} \vec{\delta}_m \vec{h}_m^T ||_2. \tag{17}$$

We then use the triangle inequality to derive a new bound as follows:

$$\chi'_t(x, y) \leq \beta \sum_{m=1}^{M} ||\vec{\delta}_m \vec{h}_m^T||_2. \tag{18}$$

Since the sum over $m \in [1, M]$ can be interpreted as a $\ell_1$ norm over the sequence, we replace it with a $\ell_2$ norm leveraging the equivalence of topology of $p$-norms. This norm is less sensitive to the sequence length and puts more emphasis on the highest norms. This results in a new upper bound:

$$\chi'_t(x, y) \leq \beta \sqrt{M \sum_{m=1}^{M} ||\vec{\delta}_m \vec{h}_m^T||_2^2}. \tag{19}$$

This substitution is better suited for our metric for two reasons. First, the square applied to each individual norm of element $m$ reduces the impact of small norms compared to larger ones, resulting in a metric that scales less with the length of the sequence $M$. Second, it matches the $\ell_2$ norm used in the previous section, which combines more naturally in the mathematical development of the next section for joint tasks.

We can apply the inner $\ell_2$ norm separately on the outer product of vectors. Since the amplitude of all contextual word embeddings $\vec{h}_m$ are similar, we can assume $||\vec{h}_m|| \approx ||\vec{h}_{m'}|| \approx ||\vec{h}||$ with $m' \in [1, M]$ across tokens. Thus, we obtain the following simplified bound:

$$\chi'_t(x, y) \leq \beta \sqrt{M} ||\vec{h}||_2 \sqrt{\sum_{m=1}^{M} ||\vec{\delta}_m||_2^2}. \tag{20}$$

Since we are interested in ranking samples $\{(x, y)\}_{1..N}$ by scores as before, we can simplify this bound for multi-output classification tasks such as slot filling. We also replace $\vec{\delta}_m$ by its definition.

$$\hat{\chi}_{slot}(x, y) = \sqrt{\sum_{m=1}^{M} ||\vec{p}_m(x) - \vec{y}_m||_2^2} \quad (21)$$

### A.3 Joint Single-Label Classification and Sequence of Single-Label Classification

We aim to combine the gradient matrices of two independent classification heads into one gradient matrix using an $\ell_2$ norm. We can use the direct sum to express this combination for a joint task, such as joint intent classification (indicated by the *int* superscript) and slot filling (indicated by the *slot* superscript). The direct sum of matrices generates a block diagonal matrix that combines two vector spaces. Under a norm, this matrix representation is equivalent to the flattened one.

Let us denote the gradient matrices as $G^{(int,t)}(x, y_{int})$ and $G^{(slot,t)}(x, y_{slot})$, where $t$ denotes the training step, $x$ is the input data, and $y_{int}$ and $y_{slot}$ is the corresponding labels. For simplification, we are leaving the dependence on $x$, $y_{int}$ and $y_{slot}$ on the right side of our equations. The combined gradient matrix is obtained by taking the direct sum of these matrices as follows:

$$G_t(x, y) = G^{(int,t)} \oplus G^{(slot,t)}. \quad (22)$$

Substituting this equation in (10), we get:

$$\chi'_t(x, y) \leq \beta ||G^{(int,t)} \oplus G^{(slot,t)}||_2. \quad (23)$$

We consider the squared Frobenius norm and apply the sum of square terms block-wise, where the off-diagonal zero terms are ignored. This gives us the sum of the square norms of each gradient matrix as follows:

$$\chi'_t(x, y)^2 \leq \beta^2 \left( ||G^{(int,t)}||_2^2 + ||G^{(slot,t)}||_2^2 \right). \quad (24)$$

Using the definitions of the gradient norms obtained from the previous derivations, we get the following:

$$\chi'_t(x, y)^2 \leq \beta^2 ||\vec{h}_{CLS}||_2^2 ||\vec{p}_{int} - \vec{y}_{int}||_2^2 + \beta^2 ||\vec{h}||_2^2 \sum_{m=1}^{M} ||\vec{p}_m - \vec{y}_m||_2^2. \quad (25)$$

As $||\vec{h}_{CLS}|| \approx ||\vec{h}||$ and by identification with the two previous derivations, we obtain the final form for the joint task, such as joint intent classification and slot filling, as follows:

$$\hat{\chi}_{nlu}(x, y) = \sqrt{\hat{\chi}_{intent}^2 + \hat{\chi}_{slot}^2}. \quad (26)$$

## B Derivations of GPU Runtime Equations

### B.1 GPU Runtime Dependency to Pruning Factor and Epoch Cycle

The total GPU time $\mathcal{T}$ contains three terms as follow

$$\mathcal{T} = \mathcal{T}_{init} + \mathcal{T}_{prune} + \mathcal{T}_{score}, \quad (27)$$

where $\mathcal{T}_{init}$ is the initial amount of epochs finetuned with the full training set, $\mathcal{T}_{prune}$ is the remaining amount of epochs to finetune with the pruned dataset, and $\mathcal{T}_{score}$ is the time to compute the importance score.

We define $\tau \leq E \in \mathbb{N}$, the epoch at which we start the data pruning and the total amount of epochs, respectively. We have $B \in \mathbb{N}$, the number of steps in one epoch (i.e. the ceiling of training set length divided by the batch size). We define an epoch cycle to prune the train data set as well $T \in \mathbb{N}$, with $T \leq E - \tau$. The proportion of pruned samples is defined by $\rho \in (0, 1)$. Finally, we have $\Delta t_{step} \in \mathbb{R}_{\geq 0}$, the average time to process one mini-batch, and $\Delta t_{forward} \in \mathbb{R}_{\geq 0}$, the time to compute a complete forward pass on the training dataset.

Then, we can explicitly formulate

$$\mathcal{T}_{init} = \tau B \Delta t_{step} \quad (28)$$

$$\mathcal{T}_{prune} = (E - \tau)(1 - \rho) B \Delta t_{step} \quad (29)$$

$$\mathcal{T}_{score} = \left\lfloor \frac{E - \tau}{T} \right\rfloor \Delta t_{forward}, \quad (30)$$

where $\lfloor \cdot \rfloor$ is the floor operator. Therefore, the complete GPU runtime equation based on eq. 27 takes the form

$$\mathcal{T} = EB\Delta t_{step} - (E - \tau) B \Delta t_{step}\rho + \left\lfloor \frac{E - \tau}{T} \right\rfloor \Delta t_{forward} \quad (31)$$

### B.2 Lower-Bound Epoch Cycle

We can find $T_{min}$, which is a lower bound to $T$, to achieve an effective pruning in terms of computational time. We need to satisfy:

$$\mathcal{T} < \mathcal{T}_{baseline} \tag{32}$$

Given the previous definitions, we can find

$$\mathcal{T}_{baseline} = EB\Delta t_{step} \tag{33}$$

Considering eq. 33 and 31 for $\mathcal{T}$, we deduce

$$T_{min} > \frac{\Delta t_{forward}}{\Delta t_{step} B \rho} \tag{34}$$

## C Training Setup

We use the following HuggingFace libraries distributed under the Apache License 2.0: transformers v4.21.3 (Wolf et al., 2020) and datasets v2.5.1 (Lhoest et al., 2021). We set our back-end to Pytorch v1.10.1 (Paszke et al., 2017, 2019). We used the Adam optimizer ($\beta_1 = 0.9$, $\beta_2 = 0.999$ and $\epsilon = 1 \times 10^{-8}$) with no warm up and no scheduler. We run fine-tunings and evaluations on an on-premise cluster of NVIDIA V100 32 Gb GPUs. All the results are the average of 5 runs with different random seeds unless it is stated otherwise.

We run our fine-tuning on the GLUE datasets with the following hyper-parameters: number of epochs of 10, a learning rate of $2 \times 10^{-5}$, a batch size of 32 and a maximum sequence length of 128 (except for the RTE dataset at 256). For the joint intent and slot filling datasets, we set: number of epochs of 40, a learning rate of $2 \times 10^{-5}$, a batch size of 32, a maximum sequence length of 50 and $\lambda = 0.5$. For $\hat{\chi}_{ema}$ calculations, we use $\alpha = 0.8$.

## D Dataset Statistics

In Tables 2 and 3, we provide the statistics about the GLUE datasets and the joint NLU datasets. We verify that all samples in the datasets do not contain offensive language and personal information.

Table 2: Statistics of GLUE datasets.

| Name | \|Train\| | \|Test\| | Task | Domain |
|---|---|---|---|---|
| COLA | 8.5k | 1k | Acceptability | Misc. |
| MNLI | 393k | 20k | NLI | Misc. |
| MRPC | 3.7k | 1.7k | Paraphrase | News |
| QQP | 364k | 391k | Paraphrase | QA questions |
| RTE | 2.5k | 3k | NLI | News, Wikipedia |
| SST2 | 67k | 1.8k | Sentiment | Movie reviews |

Table 3: Statistics of joint NLU Datasets.

| Name | \|Train\| | \|Test\| | Domains | Intents | Slots |
|---|---|---|---|---|---|
| ATIS | 5.0k | 893 | 1 | 26 | 129 |
| SNIPS | 13.0k | 700 | - | 7 | 53 |
| SLURP | 16.5k | 3.0k | 18 | 60 | 55 |
| MTOP | 15.7k | 4.4k | 11 | 117 | 78 |

## E Parameter Selection

Values for $\tau$, $\rho$, and $T$ must be selected to achieve the desired time-accuracy trade-off. A valid first step is to set $\tau$ at about 10% of $E$ for datasets with more than a few thousand samples or 20-40% for smaller datasets to achieve higher accuracy. Larger $\tau$ significantly hinders efficiency at the expense of accuracy. Then, we calculate $T_{min}$ as a lower bound to obtain an efficiency gain with a given prune rate $\rho$ using equation 34. We recommend $\rho \in [0.4, 0.7]$ depending if accuracy or efficiency is more important, respectively. Finally, we want to set $T$ such that it is above $T_{min}$ to be efficient but small enough to provide many pruning updates for higher accuracy — about ten cycles calculated with $\lfloor \frac{E-\tau}{T} \rfloor$ being a valid target. In Table 4 of Appendix F, we present values of $T_{min}$ for $\rho \in \{0.1, 0.5\}$ for all our datasets, along with the forward pass time $\Delta t_f$, train step time $\Delta t_{step}$ and the number of steps per epoch $B$.

## F Further Results

In Table 4, we show $T_{min}$ (i.e. the minimum cycle to achieve an efficiency improvement over the baseline) for $\rho \in \{0.1, 0.5\}$ for all datasets along their $\Delta t_{forward}$ and $\Delta t_{step}$.

Table 4: Minimum epoch per prune cycle $T(\rho) = T_{min}(\rho)$ for prune rates of 10% (0.1) and 50% (0.5). $\Delta t_f$ is equivalent to $\Delta t_{forward}$. We measure $\Delta t_f$ and $\Delta t_{step}$ based on the median of previous experiments. $B$ is calculated from the train set length and the batch size.

| | | $\Delta t_f$ | $\Delta t_{step}$ | $B$ | $T(0.1)$ | $T(0.5)$ |
|---|---|---|---|---|---|---|
| GLUE | COLA | 1.8 | 0.061 | 268 | 1.1 | 0.2 |
| | MNLI | 145.4 | 0.082 | 12272 | 1.4 | 0.3 |
| | MRPC | 1.8 | 0.076 | 115 | 2.0 | 0.4 |
| | QQP | 112.4 | 0.068 | 11371 | 1.4 | 0.3 |
| | RTE | 1.5 | 0.102 | 78 | 1.8 | 0.4 |
| | SST2 | 14.5 | 0.062 | 2105 | 1.1 | 0.2 |
| Joint NLU | ATIS | 3.7 | 0.065 | 156 | 3.6 | 0.7 |
| | MTOP | 8.3 | 0.065 | 490 | 2.6 | 0.5 |
| | SLURP | 5.9 | 0.066 | 360 | 2.5 | 0.5 |
| | SNIPS | 7.6 | 0.064 | 409 | 2.9 | 0.6 |

In Figures 7 and 8, we provide the intent accuracy and the slot micro F1 score for the joint intent classification and slot filling tasks as complementary results to sub-section 5.2.

In Figures 9 and 10, we present the extensive results on all joint NLU datasets for the experiments on the prune epoch cycle $T$ and prune epoch $\tau$.

In table 5, we present representative examples of hard-to-learn, easy-to-learn and ambiguous samples from fine-tunings on the SLURP dataset, as discussed in section 6.

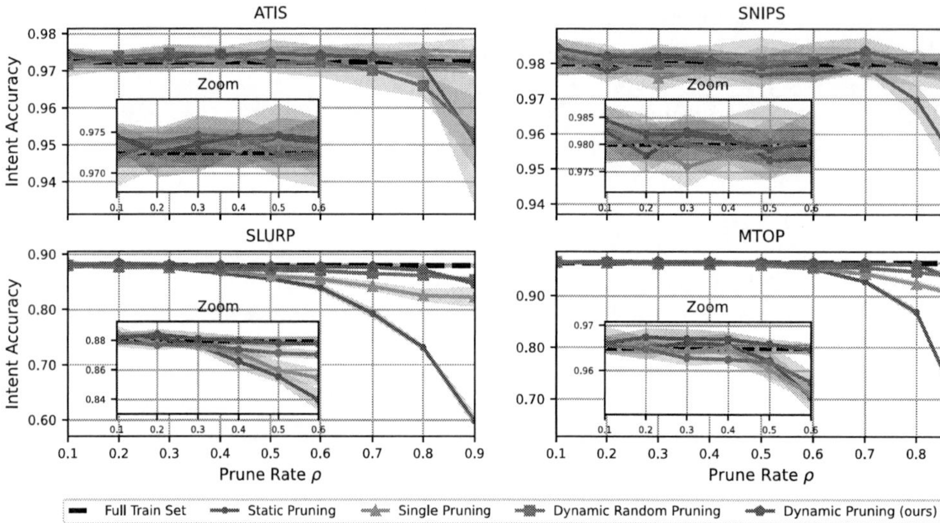


Figure 7: Intent accuracy achieved on 40 epochs for different prune rates applying: static pruning (EL2N from 10 runs of 10 epochs), single pruning, dynamic random pruning, and our dynamic pruning (EL2N with EMA). The dynamic methods are run with $\tau = 4$ and $T = 4$.

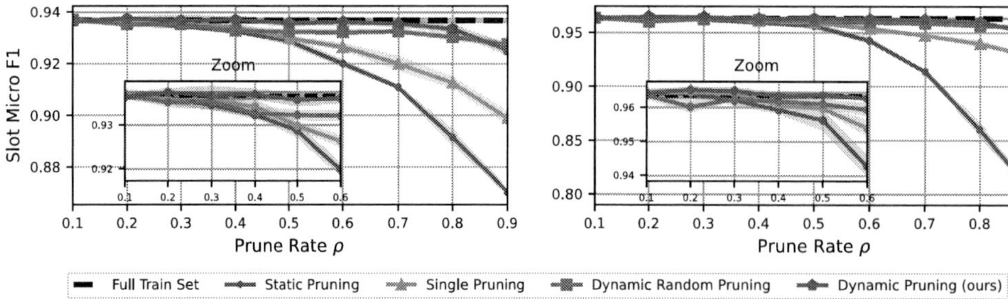


Figure 8: Slot Micro F1 score achieved on 40 epochs for different prune rates applying: static pruning (EL2N from 10 runs of 10 epochs), single pruning, dynamic random pruning, and our dynamic pruning (EL2N with EMA). The dynamic methods are run with $\tau = 4$ and $T = 4$.

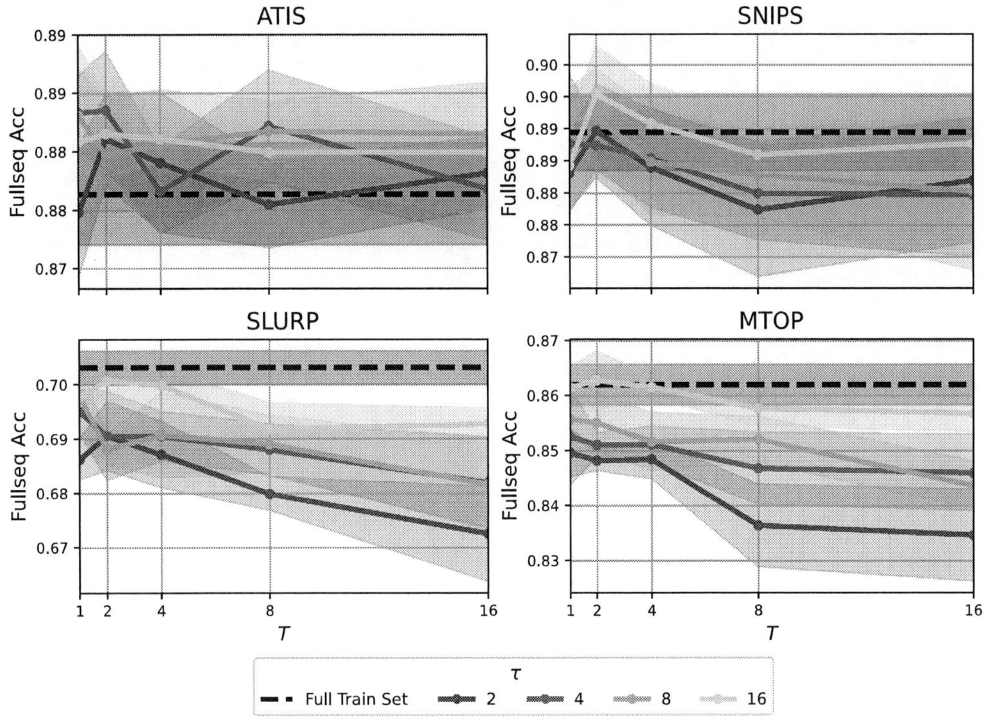


Figure 9: Full-sequence accuracy achieved on 40 epochs using our dynamic pruning (EL2N with EMA) across $T$ and $\tau$. We fixed the pruning rate to 70%.

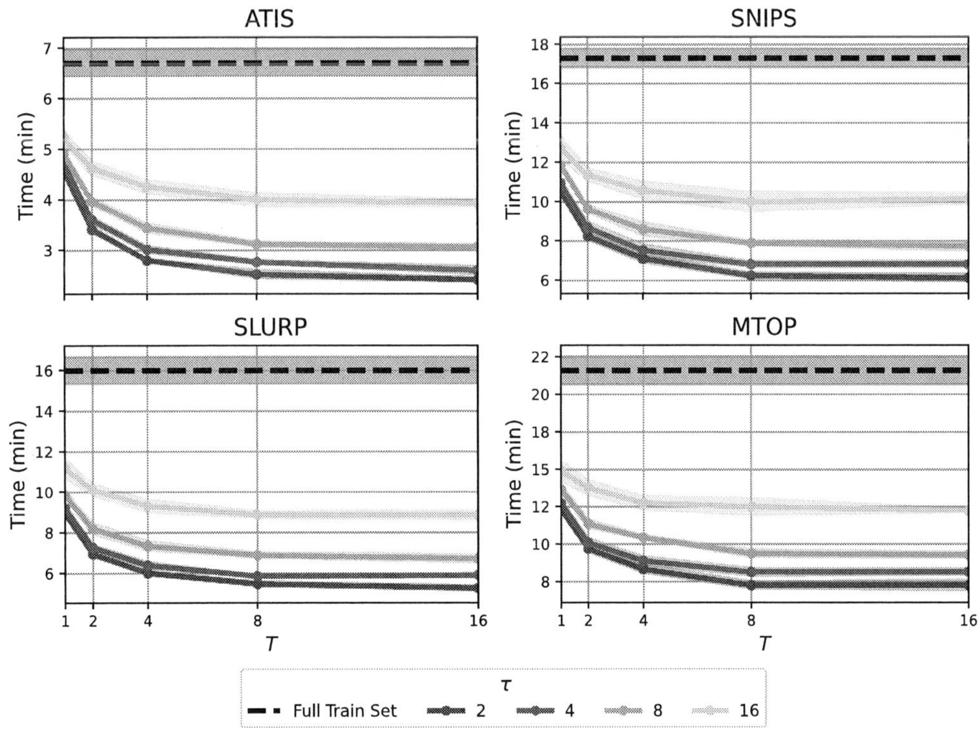


Figure 10: Finetuning time achieved on 40 epochs using our dynamic pruning (EL2N with EMA) across $T$ and $\tau$. We fixed the pruning rate to 70%.

Table 5: Examples for hard-to-learn, easy-to-learn and ambiguous samples for the SLURP dataset. # selection column shows the number of times a sample is selected in retained subset over ten pruning cycles for four different initializations.

| | Id | Intent label | Annotated utterance | # selections | *Av.* $\hat{X}_{nlu}$ |
|---|---|---|---|---|---|
| Hard-to-Learn | 1 | *calendar_set* | olly play [*song_name* : be warned] by [*artist_name* : tech nine] | 10, 10, 10, 10 | 1.291 |
| | 2 | *play_radio* | play my favorite [*device_type* : radio station] | 10, 10, 10, 10 | 1.018 |
| | 3 | *cooking_query* | what's the easiest and quickest way to cook a turkey | 10, 10, 10, 10 | 1.255 |
| | 4 | *general_joke* | tell me a joke [*joke_type* : about chickens] | 10, 10, 10, 10 | 0.984 |
| Easy-to-Learn | 5 | *calendar_set* | please add this event to my calendar | 0, 0, 0, 0 | 0.008 |
| | 6 | *calendar_set* | add an event | 0, 0, 0, 0 | 0.012 |
| | 7 | *calendar_set* | i need you to add this event to my calendar | 0, 0, 0, 0 | 0.08 |
| Ambiguous | 8 | *calendar_set* | mark [*relation* : dad's] [*event_name* : retirement dinner] for [*date* : april fourth] | 3, 5, 4, 5 | 0.116 |
| | 9 | *calendar_set* | add [*person* : mary's] [*event_name* : birthday] on the [*date* : twenty second] to my calendar please | 4, 2, 1, 4 | 0.152 |
| | 10 | *calendar_set* | can you add my [*relation* : brother's] [*event_name* : birthday dinner] at [*place_name* : rusk] for [*date* : march twenty third] | 5, 3, 6, 6 | 0.224 |
| | 11 | *calendar_set* | remind me about my [*date* : monday] [*event_name* : meeting] with [*person* : peter francis] [*time* : fifteen minutes] before the meeting | 6, 9, 5, 8 | 0.299 |
| | 12 | *calendar_set* | add [*event_name* : lee's birthday] to the calendar on [*date* : twenty two june] | 7, 4, 8, 7 | 0.369 |
| | 13 | *calendar_set* | please give me a two hour warning before [*date* : next saturdays] [*event_name* : meeting] | 8, 8, 9, 8 | 0.530 |

# On the Interactions of Structural Constraints and Data Resources for Structured Prediction

**Zhisong Zhang, Emma Strubell, Eduard Hovy**
Language Technologies Institute, Carnegie Mellon University
zhisongz@cs.cmu.edu, strubell@cmu.edu, hovy@cmu.edu

## Abstract

In this work, we provide an analysis on the interactions of the effectiveness of decoding with structural constraints and the amount of available training data for structured prediction tasks in NLP. Our exploration adopts a simple protocol that enforces constraints upon constraint-agnostic local models at testing time. With evaluations on three typical structured prediction tasks (named entity recognition, dependency parsing, and event argument extraction), we find that models trained with less data predict outputs with more structural violations in greedy decoding mode. Incorporating constraints provides consistent performance improvements and such benefits are larger in lower resource scenarios. Moreover, there are similar patterns with regard to the model sizes and more efficient models tend to enjoy more benefits. Finally, we also investigate settings with genre transfer and discover patterns that are related to domain discrepancies.

## 1 Introduction

Recently, neural models, especially those based on pre-trained contextualized representations, have brought impressive improvements for a variety of structured prediction tasks in NLP (Devlin et al., 2019; Kulmizev et al., 2019; Shi and Lin, 2019; Li et al., 2020a). More interestingly, the incorporation of powerful neural models seems to decrease the potential benefits brought by more complex structured output modeling. For example, for sequence labeling, it has been shown that reasonably good performance could be obtained even without any explicit modeling of the interactions of the output tags (Tan et al., 2018; Devlin et al., 2019). For dependency parsing, models that ignore tree constraints and cast the problem as head selection in training can still obtain impressive results (Dozat and Manning, 2017). Most of these previous results are obtained in fully supervised settings. While they show that with abundant training signals, better input modeling and representation learning could shadow the benefits brought by more complex structured modeling, it remains unclear for the cases where data resources are limited.

One of the most salient and important properties of structured prediction is that the output objects should follow specific structural constraints. For example, the output of a syntactic parser should be a well-formed tree and the output labels of an information extraction system need to follow certain type restrictions. In this work, we focus on the facet of structural constraints and explore its influence on structured prediction problems under scenarios with different amounts of training data. On the one hand, since we know the target outputs should conform to certain constraints, *explicitly* enforcing these constraints will likely bring benefits and sometimes even be a requirement. On the other hand, as neural models are developed to better represent input contexts, they might already be able to *implicitly* capture the output constraints by learning from the data. In particular, it would be unsurprising that the model could directly produce outputs that conform to constraints without explicit enforcement, given enough training data, since the training instances are presented as such.

Regarding the interactions between explicit incorporation of constraints and the amount of training data, we ask the following three research questions (RQs), which we aim to explore in this work:

**RQ1: What is the influence of constraints with different amounts of training data?**
With powerful neural networks and abundant training data, the model can be trained to implicitly capture structural constraints even without explicit enforcement. Nevertheless, it still remains unclear for the cases with limited data. We aim to explore how the incorporation of constraints influences the outputs and how such influences change with dif-



*Proceedings of The Fourth Workshop on Simple and Efficient Natural Language Processing (SustaiNLP)*, pages 147–157
July 13, 2023 ©2023 Association for Computational Linguistics

ferent amounts of training data.

**RQ2: What is the influence of constraints when using more efficient models?**
Although neural models can obtain impressive results, one shortcoming is that they are usually computationally expensive. Recently, there have been many works on improving model efficiency. Knowledge distillation is one of the most widely-utilized methods, learning a smaller student model from a larger teacher model (Kim and Rush, 2016; Sanh et al., 2019; Jiao et al., 2020). An interesting question to explore is how these more efficient models interact with the explicit incorporation of structural constraints.

**RQ3: What is the influence of constraints for out-of-domain generalization?**
We usually expect the model to be able to generalize to scenarios that can be different from those represented by the training data, for example, to different domains or text genres. It will be interesting to explore how the constraints influence predictions for these cases and especially whether there are specific patterns with regard to the discrepancies between the source and the target.

To answer these questions, we conduct extensive experiments on three typical structured prediction tasks, including named entity recognition (NER), dependency parsing (DPAR) and an information extraction task of event argument extraction (EAE). We find that models trained with less training data tend to produce outputs that contain more structural violations when using constraint-agnostic greedy decoding. Further applying constrained decoding brings consistent performance improvements and the benefits are more prominent in lower data scenarios (§3.2). A similar trend can be found with regard to model size: Smaller models tend to output more violations with greedy decoding and benefit more from constrained decoding (§3.3). Finally, in cross-genre settings, we find a weak pattern with regard to genre discrepancies: More structural violations tend to be made with greedy decoding when transferring to more distant genres (§3.4).

## 2 Tasks and Models

### 2.1 Named Entity Recognition

Our first task is named entity recognition (NER), which aims to extract entity mentions from raw texts and can be typically cast as a sequence labeling problem. We adopt a simple NER model

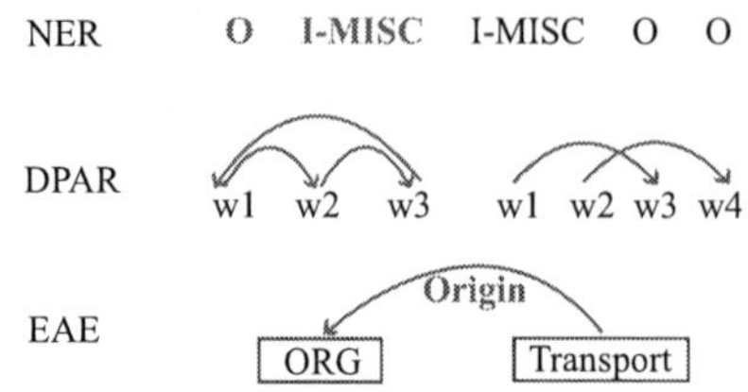


Figure 1: Examples of structural violations (marked in red). For NER, the tag transition from 'O' to 'I-MISC' is illegal. For DPAR, the left subtree contains a loop while the right one has crossing edges. For EAE, the ORIGIN role cannot be assigned to an ORG entity.

that utilizes a pre-trained BERT model as the encoder and a softmax layer to predict the output tags. We adopt the typical BIO tagging scheme (Ramshaw and Marcus, 1995), specifying tags for the **B**eginning, the **I**nside and the **O**utside of an entity span.

More specifically, for an input sequence of words $[w_1, w_2, \cdots, w_n]$, our model aims to assign a sequence of BIO tags $[t_1, t_2, \cdots, t_n]$ for them. The probability of each output tag is locally normalized for each word:

$$p(t_i|w_i) = \frac{\exp \text{score}(t_i|w_i)}{\sum_{t' \in \mathcal{T}} \exp \text{score}(t'|w_i)}$$

Here, the score$(\cdot)$ function is realized as a linear layer stacked upon the word representations[1] and $\mathcal{T}$ denotes the output tag space.

With the BIO tagging scheme, there are hard constraints between tags of consecutive tokens: The **I** tag must follow a **B** or **I** tag of the same entity type. For example, the tagged sequence "O I-MISC I-MISC O O" is erroneous because the transition "O $\rightarrow$ I-MISC" is illegal. One solution to mitigate this problem is to forbid such illegal transitions in decoding. This can be achieved by incorporating a transition matrix $M \in \mathcal{R}^{|\mathcal{T}| \times |\mathcal{T}|}$, where the entries corresponding to illegal tag transitions are filled with $-\infty$ and the legal ones are filled with 0. For the decoding process, we define the score of a tag sequence as:

$$s(t_1, t_2, \cdots, t_n) = \sum_i \log p(t_i|w_i) + \sum_i M_{t_i, t_{i+1}}$$

In this way, the highest scoring tag sequence will not contain transition violations. This decoding

[1] If a word is split into multiple tokens, we simply take its first sub-token.

problem can be solved efficiently by the Viterbi algorithm (Viterbi, 1967). If not enforcing these constraints, the second term of the sequence score can be dropped and the decoding will be greedily finding the maximally-scored tag for each token individually.

Notice that this treatment resembles conditional random field (CRF) based models (Lafferty et al., 2001), wherein the main difference is that we utilize a locally normalized model and the transition matrix is manually specified to exclude illegal transitions. In our preliminary experiments, we also tried CRF models but did not find obvious benefits compared to local models when adopting the same underlying pre-trained model.

### 2.2 Dependency Parsing

We further consider dependency parsing (DPAR) (Kübler et al., 2009), which aims to parse the input sentence into well-formed tree structures. We adopt the widely utilized first-order graph-based parser (McDonald et al., 2005). Similar to NER, we adopt the pre-trained BERT encoder to provide the contextualized representations for the input tokens and stack a biaffine scorer (Dozat and Manning, 2017) to assign scores for the dependency edges. For training, we adopt a local model that views the problem as a head-finding classification task for each input token (Dozat and Manning, 2017; Zhang et al., 2017). At testing time, we further consider tree constraints with specific decoding algorithms. Since we are mainly interested in structural tree constraints, we only perform unlabeled parsing.

More specifically, for an input sequence of words $[w_1, w_2, \cdots, w_n]$, we aim to find the dependency head words $[h_1, h_2, \cdots, h_n]$ for the input word sequence. With local normalization, this can be viewed as a head classification problem:

$$p(h_i|w_i) = \frac{\exp \text{score}(h_i|w_i)}{\sum_{h' \in \{R, w_1, w_2, \cdots, w_n\}} \exp \text{score}(h'|w_i)}$$

Here we add an artificial target $R$ to the output space to cover the case of root nodes. The score$(\cdot)$ function is realized with a biaffine module that produces head-modifier scores for the input pair of words.

We consider two constraints for the output structures. First, there should not be any cycles in the output graphs, otherwise, they will not be trees. Moreover, we consider the projectivity constraint,[2] which specifies that there are no edges that cross each other. We adopt Eisner's algorithm (Eisner, 1996) for the constrained decoding, which is a dynamic programming algorithm that searches the highest scored trees in the constrained output space. If not considering any of these constraints, we greedily predict the head word for each token based on the head classification probabilities.

### 2.3 Event Argument Extraction

Finally, we consider event argument extraction (EAE), an information extraction task that aims to extract arguments for the event mentions from the texts (Ahn, 2006). For a pair of event trigger and entity mention, this task aims to link them with an argument role indicating that the entity can play such a role in the event frame. If no such role is possible, then no links are added. We again adopt a pre-trained BERT encoder for encoding and further stack a task-specific predictor, which is a biaffine scorer, similar to dependency parsing. The main difference is that here we perform local normalization for each event-entity pair since there are no constraints on how many other mentions that one mention can be linked to for event argument extraction. To better explore real application scenarios, we train an extra sequence labeler to extract event and entity mentions rather than using gold mentions. This mention detection model is the same as the one described in our NER experiments.

More specifically, our model takes a pair of event trigger and entity mention ($m_t$ and $m_e$) and assigns the probabilities of argument roles to them:

$$p(r|m_t, m_e) = \frac{\exp \text{score}(r|m_t, m_e)}{\sum_{r' \in \mathcal{R} \cup \{\epsilon\}} \exp \text{score}(r'|m_t, m_e)}$$

Here, $\mathcal{R}$ denotes the role labeling space and we further include an option of $\epsilon$ to denote there are no argument relations between the event trigger and entity mention. The score function is realized with a biaffine module that produces argument scores for the input mention pair. Since a mention may contain multiple words, we concatenate the word representations of the starting and ending words to form the mention's input vector.

In event extraction, there are constraints on the mention (event and entity) types and argument role

[2]We only perform experiments on English, which is a highly projective language. Extensions to non-projective languages are left to future work.

| Data | Split | #Sent. | #Token | #Event | #Entity | #Argument | #Relation |
|---|---|---|---|---|---|---|---|
| CoNLL03 | train | 14.0K | 203.6K | - | 23.5K | - | - |
| | dev | 3.3K | 51.4K | - | 5.9K | - | - |
| | test | 3.5K | 46.4K | - | 5.6K | - | - |
| UD-EWT | train | 12.5K | 204.6K | - | - | - | - |
| | dev | 2.0K | 25.1K | - | - | - | - |
| | test | 2.1K | 25.1K | - | - | - | - |
| ACE05 | train | 14.4K | 215.2K | 3.7K | 38.0K | 5.7K | 6.2K |
| | dev | 2.5K | 34.5K | 0.5K | 6.0K | 0.7K | 0.8K |
| | test | 4.0K | 61.5K | 1.1K | 10.8K | 1.7K | 1.7K |

Table 1: Data statistics of the datasets utilized in our main experiments.

labels. For example, the PERSON role of a MARRY event should have the entity type of PER, while the DESTINATION or ORIGIN roles of a TRANSPORT should have entity types denoting places (GPE, LOC or FAC). We adopt a simple method to incorporate such constraints in decoding by ignoring (masking out) the roles that are not possible according to the event and entity types. The role constraints are manually collected according to the event annotation guideline (LDC, 2005). If not considering these role constraints, we simply adopt greedy prediction for each event-entity pair.

## 3 Experiments

### 3.1 Settings

**Data.** Our experiments are conducted on widely utilized English datasets. In our main experiments, we adopt the CoNLL-2003 English dataset[3] (Tjong Kim Sang and De Meulder, 2003) for NER and the English Web Treebank (EWT) from Universal Dependencies[4] v2.10 (Nivre et al., 2020) for DPAR. In the genre transfer experiments for NER and DPAR, we utilize OntoNotes 5.0 dataset[5] (Weischedel et al., 2013) and split the data according to text genres. For the event task, we adopt the ACE05 dataset[6] (Walker et al., 2006), using the scripts from Lin et al. (2020) for the pre-processing.[7] Table 1 shows the data statistics.

**Model and training.** Unless otherwise specified, we adopt the pre-trained $\text{BERT}_{\text{base}}$ as the contextualized encoder for our models. The encoder is fined-tuned with the task-specific decoders in all the experiments. The number of model parameters is around 110M. We follow common practices for the settings of other hyper-parameters. Adam (Kingma and Ba, 2014) is utilized as the optimizer. The learning rate is initially set to 1e-5 for NER and 2e-5 for DPAR and EAE. It is further linearly decayed to 10% of the initial value throughout the training process. The models are trained for 20K steps with a batch size of around 512 tokens. We pick final models by the performance on the development set of each task. The original development sets are also down-sampled accordingly as the training sets to simulate scenarios with different data amounts. All the reported results are averaged over five runs with different random seeds.

| Task | Model | 5K | 20K | 100K |
|---|---|---|---|---|
| NER | Local | $84.27_{0.8}$ | $88.91_{0.6}$ | $91.24_{0.3}$ |
| | Global | $84.73_{0.1}$ | $88.92_{0.4}$ | $91.38_{0.2}$ |
| DPAR | Local | $84.57_{0.1}$ | $89.46_{0.2}$ | $91.95_{0.1}$ |
| | Global | $82.65_{0.3}$ | $88.92_{0.3}$ | $91.65_{0.2}$ |

Table 2: Comparisons between local and global models for NER (F1%) and DPAR (UAS%). Numbers in the subscripts denote standard deviation.

**Local normalization.** In our main experiments, we choose locally normalized models instead of more complex global models. Table 2 provides comparisons between the local and global models for NER and DPAR. For the global models, we use a standard linear-chain CRF (Lafferty et al., 2001) for NER and tree-CRF (Paskin, 2001) for DPAR. For these results, constrained decoding is applied since it is found to be helpful for both local and global models. The results show that there are no clear benefits of using global models over the simpler local models, probably due to the strong input context modeling capabilities of the underlying pre-trained encoders. Therefore, we simply adopt local models in our main experiments.

[3] https://www.clips.uantwerpen.be/conll2003/ner/
[4] https://universaldependencies.org/
[5] https://catalog.ldc.upenn.edu/LDC2013T19
[6] https://catalog.ldc.upenn.edu/LDC2006T06
[7] http://blender.cs.illinois.edu/software/oneie/

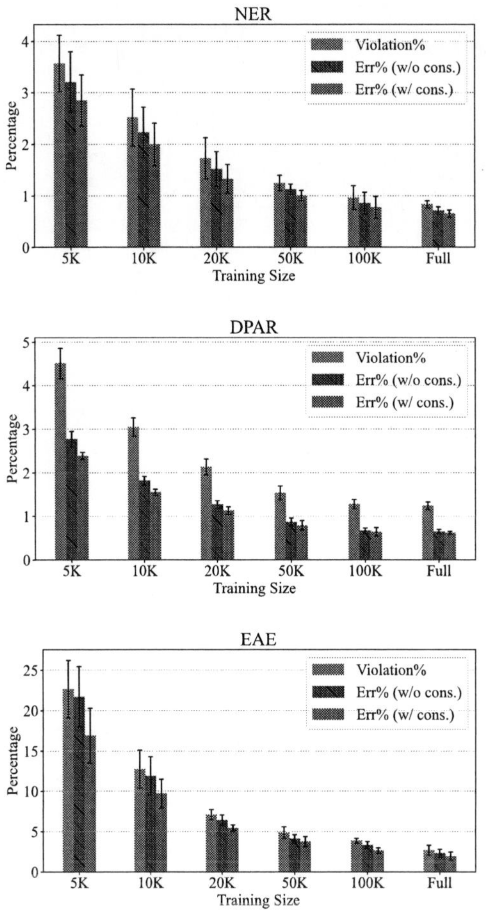


Figure 2: Illustrations of constraint violations and related error rates. Here, "Violation%" denotes the percentages of predicted items that violates structural constraints in the greedy decoding mode, and "Err%" denotes the percentages of the predicted items that violate the constraints and are incorrect at the same time.

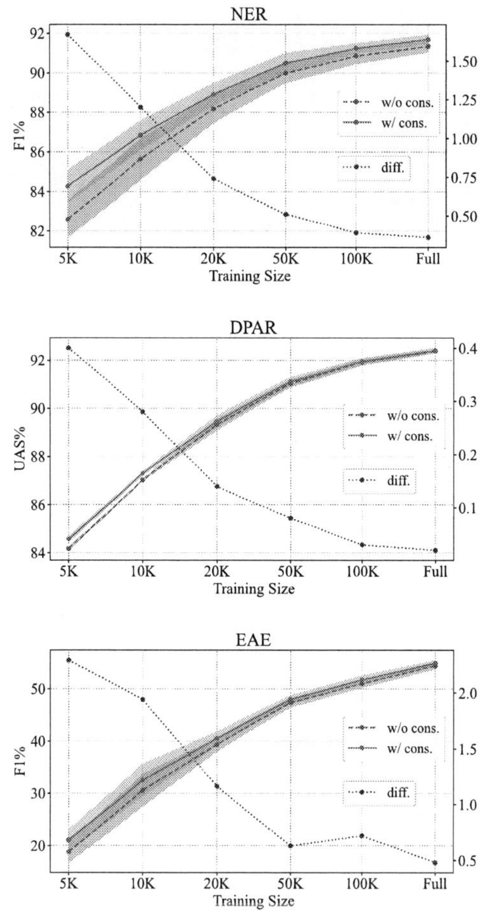


Figure 3: Test results with or without applying constraints against different training sizes. Here, $x$-axis denotes the training size (measured by the number of tokens). The left $y$-axis denotes the performance (F1% for NER, UAS% for DPAR and F1% for EAE). The right $y$-axis denotes the performance differences between the methods with or without constraints.

**Evaluation.** We adopt standard evaluation metrics for the tasks: Labeled F1 score for NER, unlabeled attachment score (UAS) for DPAR, labeled argument F1 score for EAE (Lin et al., 2020).

### 3.2 RQ1: On Training Data

We first investigate the effectiveness of incorporating constraints in decoding, plotting the rates of structural violations and related errors in Figure 2. For all the predicted items (all non-'O' tags for NER, all dependency edges for DPAR and all predicted argument links for EAE), we calculate the percentage of items that violate the structural constraints when using greedy decoding ("Violation%"). For NER, we analyze at the tag level and count the illegal tag transitions. For DPAR, we include the edges that are inside a loop (violating the acyclic constraint) or go across another edge (violating the projective constraint). For EAE, we count the argument links whose role does not comply with the types of the event and the entity that it connects. We further calculate "Err%", which denotes the percentage of the items that contain violations in greedy decoding and are wrongly predicted at the same time. Such error rates are calculated for both greedy (w/o cons.) and constrained (w/ cons.) modes, and the comparisons between these two can illustrate the amount of error reduction that constrained decoding can bring.

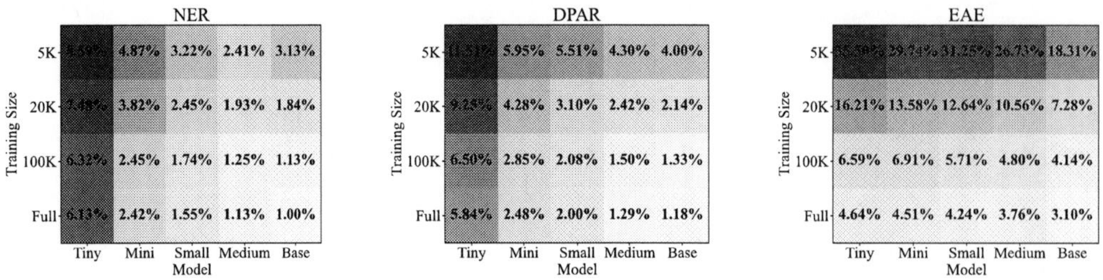


Figure 4: "Violation%" (percentages of predicted items that violates constraints with greedy decoding) with different models and amounts of training data. Here, $x$-axis denotes the underlying model while $y$-axis denotes training sizes.

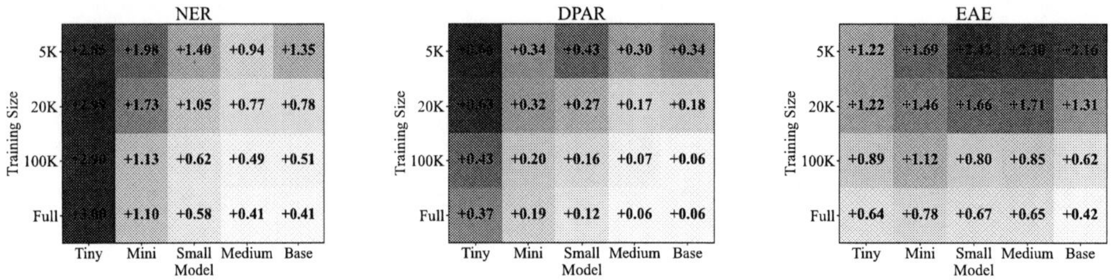


Figure 5: Performance improvements brought by constrained decoding with different models and amounts of training data. Here, $x$-axis denotes the underlying model while $y$-axis denotes training sizes.

The overall trends are consistent on all the tasks. As we have more training data, there are fewer structural violations without explicitly enforcing constraints, which indicates that the model can implicitly learn the constraints if given enough training data. Moreover, although constrained decoding can eliminate such violations, they do not always lead to the correct predictions; only a small portion of incorrect items can be corrected with constrained decoding, and such improvements are more prominent with less training data.

We further show the main test results in Figure 3. The general trends are again similar for all three tasks: Constraints provide consistent benefits for the model performance, and such benefits are larger as we have less training data. This corresponds well to the violation analysis in Figure 2: with enough training data, the model implicitly learns the structural constraints from the data and further enhancement of constrained decoding will make little difference; however, with less training data, explicitly enforcing constraints can help.

**RQ1 Takeaways:** Without incorporating constraints, there are more constraint violations from the predictions of the models trained with less data. By enforcing constraints in decoding, there can be consistent benefits for model performance and such improvements are greater with models learned with less training data.

### 3.3 RQ2: On Efficient Models

We further explore the influence of using more efficient models. We take the distilled versions of the BERT models from Turc et al. (2019) and repeat our previous experiments. Specifically, we consider five models (L=Layer Number, H=Dimension Size): Tiny (L=2, H=128), Mini (L=4, H=256), Small (L=4, H=512), Medium (L=8, H=512), and Base (L=12, H=768). We plot "Violation%" and performance differences in Figure 4 and Figure 5, respectively.

First, if looking at the axis of the training data size, the overall trends are similar to previous findings: There are more violations with less training data, and enforcing constraints helps more in lower-resource scenarios. This trend is generally consistent across all the underlying models. Moreover, comparing across the model axis brings more interesting findings. Overall, the smaller models tend to output predictions with more violations if adopting greedy decoding and incorporating constraints generally bring more performance improvements for smaller models. The reason for this trend might be that smaller models contain fewer parameters

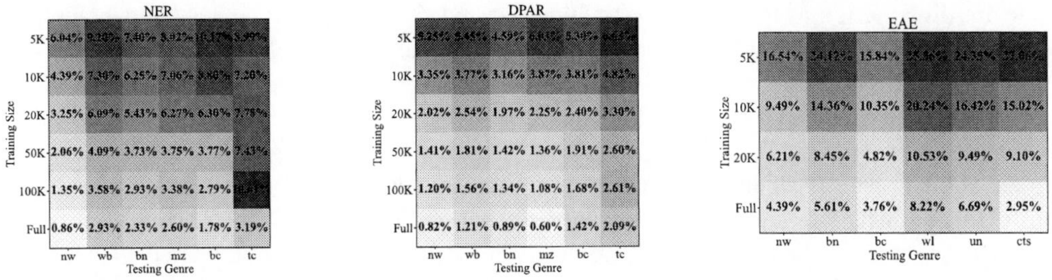


Figure 6: "Violation%" (percentages of predicted items that violates structural constraints) on different testing genres with different amounts of source training data ("nw" as the training source). Here, $x$-axis denotes the testing genres (which are sorted with the similarities to the source genre) while $y$-axis denotes training sizes.

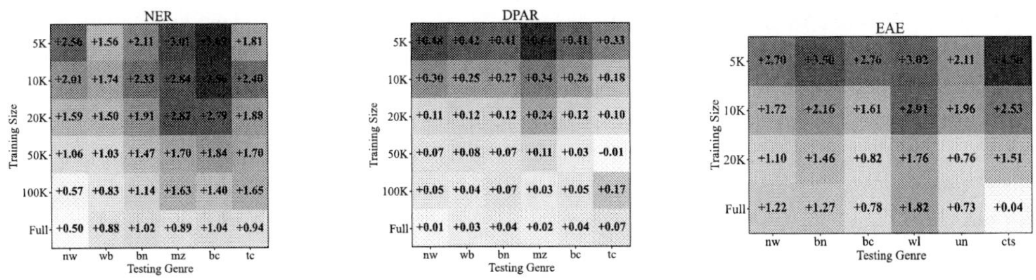


Figure 7: Performance improvements brought by constrained decoding on different testing genres with different amounts of source training data ("nw" as the training source). Here, $x$-axis denotes the testing genres (which are sorted with the similarities to the source genre) while $y$-axis denotes training sizes.

| | Tiny | Mini | Small | Medium | Base |
|---|---|---|---|---|---|
| $\text{NER}_{w/o}$ | 0.29 | 0.32 | 0.36 | 0.53 | 1.19 |
| $\text{NER}_{w/}$ | 0.56 | 0.59 | 0.64 | 0.80 | 1.45 |
| $\text{DPAR}_{w/o}$ | 0.23 | 0.26 | 0.33 | 0.47 | 1.07 |
| $\text{DPAR}_{w/}$ | 0.28 | 0.31 | 0.36 | 0.50 | 1.10 |

Table 3: Decoding speed (ms per sentence) without ($_{w/o}$) or with ($_{w/}$) constraints.

to learn all the patterns in the training data and such under-parameterization may bring difficulties in implicitly capturing the constraints.

Another interesting question is how decoding speed is influenced by the underlying model and the decoding algorithm. Table 3 presents the time required to decode one sentence for NER and DPAR. Here, we do not analyze the EAE task, since there are no complex algorithms involved for our constrained decoding for EAE and we did not find obvious speed differences between decoding methods with or without constraints. Generally, constrained decoding requires more computational cost compared with the constraint-agnostic greedy methods. This is not surprising since the constraint-agnostic decoding method simply predicts the locally maximally scored items while constrained decoding needs to invoke algorithms with higher complexity. With smaller models, constrained decoding brings relatively more cost because there are less intense computational requirements for the underlying encoder. This trend is especially obvious for the NER task, where constrained decoding costs nearly twice the time as greedy decoding when using the Tiny model. When adopting larger models, the encoder starts to require more computations and thus the relative extra cost brought by constrained decoding takes a smaller proportion.

**RQ2 Takeaways:** Smaller and more efficient models such as distilled versions of BERT tend to output predictions with more structural violations with greedy decoding, and constrained decoding generally brings more benefits.

### 3.4 RQ3: On Genre Transfer

Finally, we explore a transfer-learning scenario where there are discrepancies between the training and testing data distributions. Specifically, we consider transferring across different text genres. For these experiments, we utilize OntoNotes for NER and DPAR, and ACE05 for EAE. We take the newswire (nw) portion as the source for training and directly test the source-trained model on the test sets of other genres (in a zero-shot manner).

The results are shown in Figure 6 and 7, where the notations are similar to those in §3.3. In these results, similar patterns along the data size axis can be found: Incorporating constraints is more helpful in the cases with less training data and such trends generally hold for out-of-distribution testing scenarios (target genres that are not "nw") as well.

Another interesting dimension is the pattern along the axis of genres. In the figures, we sort the testing genres according to their similarities to the source (nw). To calculate the similarities between genres, we use the overlapping rate of vocabularies since lexical overlaps can be one important factor for the effectiveness of transfer. Overall, there is a weak trend that when transferring to more distant genres, greedy decoding tends to produce outputs with more structural violations. However, such a pattern is not consistent across all cases, and one potential reason might be the instability of model transfer. Moreover, there can be more appropriate measurements than our simple lexicon-based similarity that may better reflect how the predictions are influenced by constrained decoding across genres. We leave more explorations to future work.

**RQ3 Takeaways:** The previous patterns still generally hold for testing on out-of-domain instances with genre discrepancies: Models trained with less data tend to make more violations with greedy decoding and benefit more from constrained decoding. There is also a weak pattern when transferring to more distant genres, wherein greedy decoding tends to produce more violations.

## 4 Related Work

For structured prediction tasks, one important property is that the prediction outputs are complex objects with multiple interdependent variables. How to model such inter-dependencies is an important question for traditional NLP research. Classical algorithms for decoding and learning have been developed for various structured prediction tasks, including the Viterbi algorithm (Viterbi, 1967) and forward-backward algorithm (Baum et al., 1970) for sequence labeling, maximum spanning tree algorithm (Chu and Liu, 1965; Edmonds, 1967), Inside-Outside algorithm (Paskin, 2001) and Matrix-Tree Theorem (Koo et al., 2007; Smith and Smith, 2007; McDonald and Satta, 2007) for dependency parsing, as well as more complex algorithms for tasks involving more complicated graph structures (Rush and Collins, 2012; Burkett and Klein, 2013; Martins et al., 2015; Gormley and Eisner, 2015). Though recent developments in neural models and pre-trained language models have boosted the performance of simple local models, better modeling of the structured outputs have still been shown effective for various structured prediction tasks (Wang et al., 2019; Fonseca and Martins, 2020; Zhang et al., 2020; Wei et al., 2021).

For the output modeling of structured prediction tasks, the hard structural constraint is a key factor for the development of decoding and learning algorithms. To enhance general explicitly stated constraints, Roth and Yih (2004) tackle the decoding problem with Integer Linear Programming (ILP) and such paradigm has been applied to a range of structured NLP tasks (Denis and Baldridge, 2007; Roth and Yih, 2007; Clarke and Lapata, 2008; Punyakanok et al., 2008). In addition to enforcing well-formed output structures for decoding, constraints can be also incorporated to enhance model learning (Chang et al., 2008; Li et al., 2020b; Pan et al., 2020; Wang et al., 2020, 2021). While we mainly focus on simply applying constrained decoding with local models trained with different amounts of data, it would be interesting to explore the influences when further incorporating constraints at model training time.

## 5 Conclusion

In this work, we explore the interactions of constraint-based decoding algorithms and the amounts of training data for typical structured prediction tasks in NLP. Specifically, we train local models with different amounts of training data and analyze the influence of whether to adopt constrained decoding or not. The results show that when the model is trained with less data, the predictions contain more structural violations with greedy decoding and there are more benefits on model performance by further applying constrained decoding. Such patterns also generally hold with more efficient models and when transferring across text genres, where there are further interesting patterns with regard to model sizes and genre distances.

## Limitations

This work has several limitations. First, we only experiment on English datasets. It would be interesting to explore whether the general patterns hold for non-English languages with different structural properties. Moreover, we only explore incorporating hard constraints for decoding with local models at testing time. Exploring more applications of structural constraints, such as learning with constraints, or incorporating other types of constraints, such as soft ones, would be promising future directions. Finally, we only explore three simple sentence-level structured prediction tasks, while extentions can be made to more complex tasks with larger output space, such as text generation or document-level information extraction, where constraints may play more interesting roles.

## References


David Ahn. 2006. The stages of event extraction. In *Proceedings of the Workshop on Annotating and Reasoning about Time and Events*, pages 1–8, Sydney, Australia. Association for Computational Linguistics.

Leonard E Baum, Ted Petrie, George Soules, and Norman Weiss. 1970. A maximization technique occurring in the statistical analysis of probabilistic functions of markov chains. *The annals of mathematical statistics*, 41(1):164–171.

David Burkett and Dan Klein. 2013. Variational inference for structured NLP models. In *Proceedings of the 51st Annual Meeting of the Association for Computational Linguistics (Tutorials)*, pages 9–10, Sofia, Bulgaria. Association for Computational Linguistics.

Ming-Wei Chang, Lev-Arie Ratinov, Nicholas Rizzolo, and Dan Roth. 2008. Learning and inference with constraints. In *AAAI*, pages 1513–1518.

Y.J. Chu and T.H. Liu. 1965. On the shortest arborescence of a directed graph. *Scientia Sinica*, 14:1396–1400.

James Clarke and Mirella Lapata. 2008. Global inference for sentence compression: An integer linear programming approach. *Journal of Artificial Intelligence Research*, 31:399–429.

Pascal Denis and Jason Baldridge. 2007. Joint determination of anaphoricity and coreference resolution using integer programming. In *Human Language Technologies 2007: The Conference of the North American Chapter of the Association for Computational Linguistics; Proceedings of the Main Conference*, pages 236–243, Rochester, New York. Association for Computational Linguistics.

Jacob Devlin, Ming-Wei Chang, Kenton Lee, and Kristina Toutanova. 2019. BERT: Pre-training of deep bidirectional transformers for language understanding. In *Proceedings of the 2019 Conference of the North American Chapter of the Association for Computational Linguistics: Human Language Technologies, Volume 1 (Long and Short Papers)*, pages 4171–4186, Minneapolis, Minnesota. Association for Computational Linguistics.

Timothy Dozat and Christopher D. Manning. 2017. Deep biaffine attention for neural dependency parsing. In *ICLR*.

Jack Edmonds. 1967. Optimum branchings. *Journal of Research of the National Bureau of Standards, B*, 71:233–240.

Jason M. Eisner. 1996. Three new probabilistic models for dependency parsing: An exploration. In *COLING 1996 Volume 1: The 16th International Conference on Computational Linguistics*.

Erick Fonseca and André F. T. Martins. 2020. Revisiting higher-order dependency parsers. In *Proceedings of the 58th Annual Meeting of the Association for Computational Linguistics*, pages 8795–8800, Online. Association for Computational Linguistics.

Matthew R. Gormley and Jason Eisner. 2015. Structured belief propagation for NLP. In *Proceedings of the 53rd Annual Meeting of the Association for Computational Linguistics and the 7th International Joint Conference on Natural Language Processing: Tutorial Abstracts*, pages 5–6, Beijing, China. Association for Computational Linguistics.

Xiaoqi Jiao, Yichun Yin, Lifeng Shang, Xin Jiang, Xiao Chen, Linlin Li, Fang Wang, and Qun Liu. 2020. TinyBERT: Distilling BERT for natural language understanding. In *Findings of the Association for Computational Linguistics: EMNLP 2020*, pages 4163–4174, Online. Association for Computational Linguistics.

Yoon Kim and Alexander M. Rush. 2016. Sequence-level knowledge distillation. In *Proceedings of the 2016 Conference on Empirical Methods in Natural Language Processing*, pages 1317–1327, Austin, Texas. Association for Computational Linguistics.

Diederik P Kingma and Jimmy Ba. 2014. Adam: A method for stochastic optimization. *arXiv preprint arXiv:1412.6980*.

Terry Koo, Amir Globerson, Xavier Carreras, and Michael Collins. 2007. Structured prediction models via the matrix-tree theorem. In *Proceedings of the 2007 Joint Conference on Empirical Methods in Natural Language Processing and Computational Natural Language Learning (EMNLP-CoNLL)*, pages 141–150, Prague, Czech Republic. Association for Computational Linguistics.

Sandra Kübler, Ryan McDonald, and Joakim Nivre. 2009. Dependency parsing. *Synthesis lectures on human language technologies*, 1(1):1–127.

Artur Kulmizev, Miryam de Lhoneux, Johannes Gontrum, Elena Fano, and Joakim Nivre. 2019. Deep contextualized word embeddings in transition-based and graph-based dependency parsing - a tale of two parsers revisited. In *Proceedings of the 2019 Conference on Empirical Methods in Natural Language Processing and the 9th International Joint Conference on Natural Language Processing (EMNLP-IJCNLP)*, pages 2755–2768, Hong Kong, China. Association for Computational Linguistics.

John D Lafferty, Andrew McCallum, and Fernando CN Pereira. 2001. Conditional random fields: Probabilistic models for segmenting and labeling sequence data. In *Proceedings of the Eighteenth International Conference on Machine Learning*, pages 282–289.

LDC. 2005. ACE (automatic content extraction) english annotation guidelines for events version 5.4.3. *Linguistic Data Consortium.*

Jing Li, Aixin Sun, Jianglei Han, and Chenliang Li. 2020a. A survey on deep learning for named entity recognition. *IEEE Transactions on Knowledge and Data Engineering*, 34(1):50–70.

Tao Li, Parth Anand Jawale, Martha Palmer, and Vivek Srikumar. 2020b. Structured tuning for semantic role labeling. In *Proceedings of the 58th Annual Meeting of the Association for Computational Linguistics*, pages 8402–8412, Online. Association for Computational Linguistics.

Ying Lin, Heng Ji, Fei Huang, and Lingfei Wu. 2020. A joint neural model for information extraction with global features. In *Proceedings of the 58th Annual Meeting of the Association for Computational Linguistics*, pages 7999–8009, Online. Association for Computational Linguistics.

André FT Martins, Mário AT Figueiredo, Pedro MQ Aguiar, Noah A Smith, and Eric P Xing. 2015. Ad3: Alternating directions dual decomposition for map inference in graphical models. *The Journal of Machine Learning Research*, 16(1):495–545.

Ryan McDonald, Koby Crammer, and Fernando Pereira. 2005. Online large-margin training of dependency parsers. In *Proceedings of the 43rd Annual Meeting of the Association for Computational Linguistics (ACL'05)*, pages 91–98, Ann Arbor, Michigan. Association for Computational Linguistics.

Ryan McDonald and Giorgio Satta. 2007. On the complexity of non-projective data-driven dependency parsing. In *Proceedings of the Tenth International Conference on Parsing Technologies*, pages 121–132, Prague, Czech Republic. Association for Computational Linguistics.

Joakim Nivre, Marie-Catherine de Marneffe, Filip Ginter, Jan Hajič, Christopher D. Manning, Sampo Pyysalo, Sebastian Schuster, Francis Tyers, and Daniel Zeman. 2020. Universal Dependencies v2: An evergrowing multilingual treebank collection. In *Proceedings of the Twelfth Language Resources and Evaluation Conference*, pages 4034–4043, Marseille, France. European Language Resources Association.

Xingyuan Pan, Maitrey Mehta, and Vivek Srikumar. 2020. Learning constraints for structured prediction using rectifier networks. In *Proceedings of the 58th Annual Meeting of the Association for Computational Linguistics*, pages 4843–4858, Online. Association for Computational Linguistics.

Mark A Paskin. 2001. Cubic-time parsing and learning algorithms for grammatical bigram models.

Vasin Punyakanok, Dan Roth, and Wen-tau Yih. 2008. The importance of syntactic parsing and inference in semantic role labeling. *Computational Linguistics*, 34(2):257–287.

Lance Ramshaw and Mitch Marcus. 1995. Text chunking using transformation-based learning. In *Third Workshop on Very Large Corpora.*

Dan Roth and Wen-tau Yih. 2004. A linear programming formulation for global inference in natural language tasks. In *Proceedings of the Eighth Conference on Computational Natural Language Learning (CoNLL-2004) at HLT-NAACL 2004*, pages 1–8, Boston, Massachusetts, USA. Association for Computational Linguistics.

Dan Roth and Wen-tau Yih. 2007. Global inference for entity and relation identification via a linear programming formulation. *Introduction to statistical relational learning*, pages 553–580.

Alexander M Rush and MJ Collins. 2012. A tutorial on dual decomposition and lagrangian relaxation for inference in natural language processing. *Journal of Artificial Intelligence Research*, 45:305–362.

Victor Sanh, Lysandre Debut, Julien Chaumond, and Thomas Wolf. 2019. Distilbert, a distilled version of bert: smaller, faster, cheaper and lighter. *arXiv preprint arXiv:1910.01108.*

Peng Shi and Jimmy Lin. 2019. Simple bert models for relation extraction and semantic role labeling. *arXiv preprint arXiv:1904.05255.*

David A. Smith and Noah A. Smith. 2007. Probabilistic models of nonprojective dependency trees. In *Proceedings of the 2007 Joint Conference on Empirical Methods in Natural Language Processing and Computational Natural Language Learning (EMNLP-CoNLL)*, pages 132–140, Prague, Czech Republic. Association for Computational Linguistics.

Zhixing Tan, Mingxuan Wang, Jun Xie, Yidong Chen, and Xiaodong Shi. 2018. Deep semantic role labeling with self-attention. In *Proceedings of the AAAI Conference on Artificial Intelligence.*

Erik F. Tjong Kim Sang and Fien De Meulder. 2003. Introduction to the CoNLL-2003 shared task: Language-independent named entity recognition. In

*Proceedings of the Seventh Conference on Natural Language Learning at HLT-NAACL 2003*, pages 142–147.

Iulia Turc, Ming-Wei Chang, Kenton Lee, and Kristina Toutanova. 2019. Well-read students learn better: On the importance of pre-training compact models. *arXiv preprint arXiv:1908.08962*.

Andrew Viterbi. 1967. Error bounds for convolutional codes and an asymptotically optimum decoding algorithm. *IEEE transactions on Information Theory*, 13(2):260–269.

Christopher Walker, Stephanie Strassel, Julie Medero, and Kazuaki Maeda. 2006. ACE 2005 multilingual training corpus. *Linguistic Data Consortium*, 57.

Haoyu Wang, Muhao Chen, Hongming Zhang, and Dan Roth. 2020. Joint constrained learning for event-event relation extraction. In *Proceedings of the 2020 Conference on Empirical Methods in Natural Language Processing (EMNLP)*, pages 696–706, Online. Association for Computational Linguistics.

Haoyu Wang, Hongming Zhang, Muhao Chen, and Dan Roth. 2021. Learning constraints and descriptive segmentation for subevent detection. In *Proceedings of the 2021 Conference on Empirical Methods in Natural Language Processing*, pages 5216–5226, Online and Punta Cana, Dominican Republic. Association for Computational Linguistics.

Xinyu Wang, Jingxian Huang, and Kewei Tu. 2019. Second-order semantic dependency parsing with end-to-end neural networks. In *Proceedings of the 57th Annual Meeting of the Association for Computational Linguistics*, pages 4609–4618, Florence, Italy. Association for Computational Linguistics.

Tianwen Wei, Jianwei Qi, Shenghuan He, and Songtao Sun. 2021. Masked conditional random fields for sequence labeling. In *Proceedings of the 2021 Conference of the North American Chapter of the Association for Computational Linguistics: Human Language Technologies*, pages 2024–2035, Online. Association for Computational Linguistics.

Ralph Weischedel, Martha Palmer, Mitchell Marcus, Eduard Hovy, Sameer Pradhan, Lance Ramshaw, Nianwen Xue, Ann Taylor, Jeff Kaufman, Michelle Franchini, et al. 2013. Ontonotes release 5.0. *Linguistic Data Consortium, Philadelphia, PA*, 23.

Xingxing Zhang, Jianpeng Cheng, and Mirella Lapata. 2017. Dependency parsing as head selection. In *Proceedings of the 15th Conference of the European Chapter of the Association for Computational Linguistics: Volume 1, Long Papers*, pages 665–676, Valencia, Spain. Association for Computational Linguistics.

Yu Zhang, Zhenghua Li, and Min Zhang. 2020. Efficient second-order TreeCRF for neural dependency parsing. In *Proceedings of the 58th Annual Meeting of the Association for Computational Linguistics*, pages 3295–3305, Online. Association for Computational Linguistics.

# Can we Pretrain a SotA Legal Language Model on a Budget From Scratch?

**Joel Niklaus** and **Daniele Giofré**
Thomson Reuters Labs, Zug, Switzerland
firstname.lastname@thomsonreuters.com

## Abstract

Even though many efficient transformers have been proposed, only few such models are available for specialized domains. Additionally, since the pretraining process is extremely costly in general – but even more so as the sequence length increases – it is often only in reach of large research labs. One way of making pretraining cheaper is the Replaced Token Detection (RTD) task, by providing more signal during training compared to MLM, since the loss can be computed over all tokens. In this work, we train Longformer models with the efficient RTD task on long-context legal data to showcase that pretraining efficient LMs is possible using less than 12 GPU days. We evaluate the trained models on challenging summarization tasks requiring the model to summarize complex long texts. We find that both the small and base models outperform their baselines on the in-domain BillSum and out-of-domain PubMed tasks in their respective parameter range. We publish our models as a resource for researchers and practitioners.

## 1 Introduction

Pretrained transformer models have achieved excellent performance across various Natural Language Processing (NLP) tasks such as Text Classification (TC), Named Entity Recognition (NER), Question Answering (QA) and summarization (Devlin et al., 2019; Yang et al., 2020; He et al., 2021; Zhang et al., 2020a).

Transfer learning is to a large extent responsible for this success (Howard and Ruder, 2018). Usually, transformer models are pretrained in a self-supervised way on large unlabeled corpora (Devlin et al., 2019; Radford et al., 2018). Pretraining is very resource intensive (especially for large models), thus making it costly and only available for large organizations (Sharir et al., 2020). The Masked Language Modeling (MLM) task has been

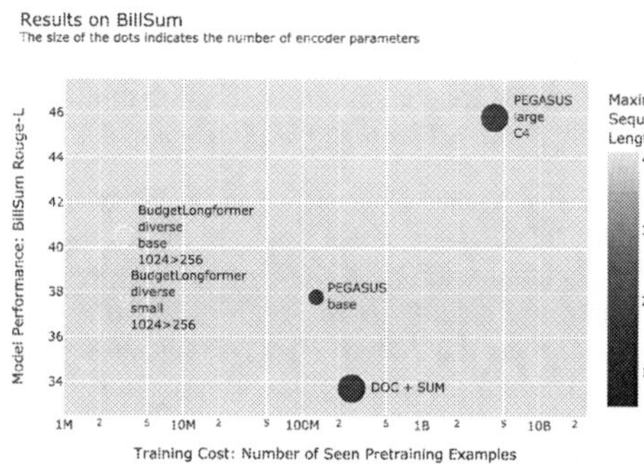


Figure 1: Results on BillSum (log-scaled x-axis)

very successful, with many models adopting the task in pretraining (Devlin et al., 2019; Liu et al., 2019; Beltagy et al., 2020; Zaheer et al., 2021). Since typically only 15% of the tokens are masked, the loss can be computed for those tokens only.

Clark et al. (2020) introduced the Replaced Token Detection (RTD) task, enabling loss computation on all tokens for efficient training. On the GLUE benchmark (Wang et al., 2018), ELECTRA matches RoBERTa (Liu et al., 2019) and XLNet (Yang et al., 2020) using 1/4 their compute. Although ELECTRA's training strategy seems very promising, to the best of our knowledge, only few works have adopted the RTD task so far (He et al., 2021; Kanakarajan et al., 2021).

On another note, domain-specific pretraining has been shown to improve downstream performance in many domains such as law (Chalkidis et al., 2020; Xiao et al., 2021), biology (Lee et al., 2019), scientific articles (Beltagy et al., 2019), clinical documents (Li et al., 2022), or even code (Chen et al., 2021a). Despite the vast amount of legal text and the importance of training legal models for downstream tasks, there has yet to be domain-specific pertaining coupled with the RTD task for law.

Pretraining on legal documents is especially challenging, given that legal documents tend to span multiple pages (ranging from 10s to 100s of pages, which translates to tens of thousands tokens). This



*Proceedings of The Fourth Workshop on Simple and Efficient Natural Language Processing (SustaiNLP)*, pages 158–182
July 13, 2023 ©2023 Association for Computational Linguistics

is incompatible with current transformer architectures (Vaswani et al., 2017) as they often prohibit efficient processing of sequences longer than 512 tokens on current hardware due to the quadratic time and memory requirement of the attention mechanism. To solve this problem, a rich body of research investigates how transformers can be adapted to efficiently process longer input (Tay et al., 2020b; Child et al., 2019; Beltagy et al., 2020; Zaheer et al., 2021; Roy et al., 2021; Kitaev et al., 2020; Tay et al., 2021; Lee-Thorp et al., 2021).

Longformer (Beltagy et al., 2020) is one of these efficient transformer architectures for long sequences, leveraging windowed and global attention. So far, to the best of our knowledge, there does not yet exist a public Longformer model pretrained on English legal data[1], although Xiao et al. (2021) have proven the effectiveness of the Longformer in dealing with long legal text in many Chinese-related tasks. This work aims to fill this gap.

To test the ability to grasp long-distance dependencies in the text, we mainly evaluated our models on the task of automatic (abstractive) summarization. It consists of capturing the most important concepts/ideas from the (long) document and then rewriting it in a shorter passage in a grammatical and logically coherent way (Chen et al., 2019).

In particular, we used the BillSum dataset (Kornilova and Eidelman, 2019), as a domain-specific summarization task, and the PubMed dataset (Cohan et al., 2018), to evaluate the model's ability outside the legal context (i.e., in the biomedical context). On BillSum, we achieve a new state-of-the-art (SOTA) (see Figure 1) in our parameter range. On Pubmed, we obtain comparable metrics even though the Language Model (LM) has only been pretrained on legal data and the tokenizer is also optimized for legal data (see Figure 2).

We emphasize that this performance was achieved with minimal pretraining due to the combination of the RTD task and the Longformer infrastructure making our LM very attractive from the perspective of building costs. For example, our model saw 3.2M examples during pretraining, while RoBERTa (Liu et al., 2019) or PEGASUS-large (Zhang et al., 2020a) saw 4.1B examples (nearly 1300x more). For reference, RoBERTa was trained for 1024 GPU days (>42x more than our base model), while our small and base models only used 12 and 24 GPU days respectively (16GB NVIDIA V100 GPUs for all models).[2]

[1]On the web there is a model based on Longformer in the legal domain, but it offers no model card (https://huggingface.co/saibo/legal-longformer-base-4096). Also, concurrent to our work, Mamakas et al. (2022) trained legal Longformer models, but they are private. Additionally, concurrently, Hua et al. (2022) trained Reformer (Kitaev et al., 2020) models with the RTD task on legal data.

#### Contributions

The contributions of this paper are three-fold:

- We train and release a new model pretrained on recently published curated English legal text (Henderson et al., 2022), capable of handling input spans longer than 512 tokens out of the box.
- Using Longformer and RTD, dubbed BudgetLongformer, we achieve a new SOTA on BillSum and PubMed compared to models of the same size. Our small model even outperforms a transformer base model (Vaswani et al., 2017) containing almost 4 times more encoder parameters (110M vs. 29M). On BillSum it performs on par with a PEGASUS base model (Zhang et al., 2020a) whose encoder is also almost 4 times larger and has been pretrained specifically for the abstractive summarization task in mind.
- We verified that pretraining with the RTD task is suitable for down-stream summarization tasks by evaluating our model on an out-of-domain benchmark (PubMed), obtaining comparable results with summarization-specific architectures.

#### Main Research Questions

In this work, we pose and examine three main research questions:

**RQ1**: *Is it possible to train a LM with domain (e.g. legal) expertise efficiently from scratch, reducing costs?*

**RQ2**: *How does our model compare with other models on the challenging legal domain-specific BillSum summarization benchmark?*

**RQ3**: *How well does our model compare with other models on the biomedical out-of-domain PubMed summarization benchmark?*

## 2 Related Work

### Domain-Specific Language Models

Previous work showed that domain-specific pretraining achieves promising results on datasets of specialized domains such as law (Chalkidis et al., 2020; Xiao et al., 2021), biology (Lee et al., 2019), scientific articles (Beltagy et al., 2019), clinical

[2]Although Zhang et al. (2020a) do not report the compute used, we expect it to be similar to RoBERTa.

documents (Li et al., 2022), or even code (Chen et al., 2021a).

Gururangan et al. (2020) show that continued pretraining on a RoBERTa checkpoint on biomedical data, scientific articles in computer science, and reviews, clearly improves downstream performance in the respective domain-specific datasets. The effect was less pronounced on news domain datasets, presumably because RoBERTa has seen many news articles during pretraining already.

**Long Document Processing**

In the past few years, a vast amount of research has been devoted to addressing the problem of quadratic time and memory complexity associated with the dense attention mechanism (Vaswani et al., 2017), practically limiting the maximum sequence length severely (often to 512 tokens) (Tay et al., 2020b; Child et al., 2019; Beltagy et al., 2020; Zaheer et al., 2021; Roy et al., 2021; Kitaev et al., 2020; Tay et al., 2021; Lee-Thorp et al., 2021). These research works have given rise to a new class of transformers, referred to as sparse transformers or efficient transformers (Tay et al., 2020b). Reducing the cost associated with the computation of the dense attention matrix while maintaining the same performance is the core idea behind efficient transformers. This is often achieved by introducing sparsity in the attention matrix in a variety of ways that may be fixed pattern such as local (windowed) attention (Child et al., 2019; Beltagy et al., 2020), global attention (Zaheer et al., 2021) or learnable patterns such as routing attention (Roy et al., 2021) and LSH attention (Kitaev et al., 2020) or a random pattern (Zaheer et al., 2021; Tay et al., 2021). Recently, Lee-Thorp et al. (2021) proposed to use Fourier transforms instead of the attention layer. Tay et al. (2020b) provide a comprehensive list of efficient transformers and the detailed description of their attention mechanism. (Tay et al., 2020a) proposed a series of tasks designed for testing the capabilities of these different models suitable for longer inputs. However, this so-called "Long Range Arena" considers mostly artificial tasks, with the goal of evaluating the models independent of any pretraining.

**Efficient Pretraining**

ELECTRA-style pretraining (Clark et al., 2020) has been shown to reduce training cost substantially, while matching the performance of SOTA LMs. ELECTRA leverages a smaller generator model (discarded after pretraining), that changes some tokens. The larger discriminator model (used for down-stream tasks) must predict for each token if it was changed by the generator or not, similar to how Generative Adversarial Networks (GANs) are trained (Goodfellow et al., 2014). This enables the loss to be relevant for every token, leading to much faster and thus more efficient training.

## 3 Datasets

### 3.1 Pile of Law

Henderson et al. (2022) recently released a large-scale English corpus suitable for pretraining LMs. It contains 256 GB of diverse legal text in English from various jurisdictions and judicial bodies including for example bills, court decisions and contracts from the US, Canada, and Europe even though the focus clearly lies on US data. While there are 28 US datasets available (253.25 GB or 99%), there is only 1 Canadian dataset[3] (243 MB or 0.09%), 3 European datasets[4] (2.3 GB or 0.9%), and 2 international datasets[5] (212 MB or 0.08%). The non-US datasets only cover the categories "Legal Case Opinions and Filings", "Laws" and "Conversations", but do not cover categories "Legal Analyses", "Contracts / Business Documents" and "Study Materials", whereas the US data is much more diverse and covers all categories.

### 3.2 BillSum

Kornilova and Eidelman (2019) introduced a legislative summarization dataset covering 21K US bills from 1993 to 2018. It is challenging due to the technical nature and complex structure of the bills. Additionally, the bills are rather long, ranging from 5K to 20K characters ($\sim$ 1K to 4K tokens[6]) with their summaries being up to 5K characters ($\sim$ 1K tokens) long (see Appendix C for more details).

### 3.3 PubMed

Cohan et al. (2018) introduced another challenging summarization dataset in a specialized domain (scientific articles from the biomedical domain). It includes 133K scientific papers together with their abstracts in English. The papers are 3K words long on average and the summaries (abstracts) 200

[3]Canadian Court Opinions (ON, BC)

[4]European Court of Human Rights Opinions, EUR-LEX and European Parliament Proceedings Parallel Corpus

[5]World Constitutions and U.N. General Debate Corpus

[6]Our experiments show that using our tokenizer, one token corresponds to 5.33 characters on average.

words. Thus, similar to the BillSum dataset, this dataset is well suited as a test bed for methods capable of long document summarization. Note, that in this dataset, the domain is vastly different from the legal domain (see Appendix C for more details).

## 4 BudgetLongformer

In the legal domain, it is especially important that models can handle long input. So far, there does not exist an English legal model capable of handling more than 512 tokens. Since many tasks in legal NLP are formulated as TC problems, a hierarchical architecture has been used frequently to process long documents (Chalkidis et al., 2019; Niklaus et al., 2021, 2022, 2023). This simple hierarchical architecture, however, cannot be easily adapted to solve the more complex sequence-to-sequence tasks like token classification or summarization because it compresses the long input sequence into a single token. For this reason, in this work, we pretrain a more versatile Longformer model. To make pretraining more affordable, we trained the well-proven Longformer model (Beltagy et al., 2020) with the RTD task proposed by Clark et al. (2020).

### 4.1 Longformer

We opted for the Longformer method over other efficient transformer architectures because it seems to work robustly[7] and is heavily used in the literature (Xiao et al., 2021; Dai et al., 2022; Maroudas et al., 2022). Longformer (Beltagy et al., 2020) proposed three sparse attention mechanisms: Sliding Window Attention, Dilated Sliding Window Attention and Global + Sliding Window. We follow their recommendations and use the Global + Sliding Window attention mechanism because we pretrain an encoder-only model.

### 4.2 Replaced Token Detection

Inspired by GAN training (Goodfellow et al., 2014), the RTD task adapts this training framework to NLP. The drawback of training with MLM is that the loss can only be computed for the masked tokens (usually 15%). With RTD training, a smaller generator model (usually 1/3 the size of the discriminator) solves the MLM task. The discriminator receives the predictions of the generator and determines for each token, whether it is original or changed by the generator. This leads to the loss being computed for each token for the discriminator, thus transporting more information per forward-pass and leading to more efficient training.

[7]164 models on huggingface hub as of January 3rd 2023

| PileOfLaw Subset | Dataset Size | # Words | # Documents |
|---|---|---|---|
| caselaw | | | |
| **CL Opinions** | **59.29GB** | **7.65B** | **3.39M** |
| diverse | | | |
| **Total** | **73.04GB** | **8.91B** | **2.1M** |
| CL Opinions | 8.74GB | 1.13B | 500K |
| CL Docket Entries | 17.49GB | 1.80B | 500K |
| U.S. State Codes | 6.77GB | 829.62M | 157 |
| U.S. Code | 0.27GB | 30.54M | 43 |
| EUR-Lex | 1.31GB | 191.65M | 106K |
| Edgar Contracts | 7.26GB | 0.97B | 500K |
| Atticus Contracts | 31.2GB | 3.96B | 488K |

Table 1: The datasets used for pretraining our models. CL is short for Court Listener

## 5 Experimental Setup

In this section, we describe how we set up the experiments. For all experiments, we used the huggingface transformers library (Wolf et al., 2020) available under an Apache 2.0 license and AMP mixed precision training and evaluation to reduce costs and GPU memory.

### 5.1 Tokenizer

We trained a byte-level BPE tokenizer (Wang et al., 2019) akin to Beltagy et al. (2020) with a large 64K token vocabulary to encode complex legal language well. We trained the tokenizer using the huggingface tokenizers library[8] on the entire PileOfLaw training split ($\sim$ 192GB, $\sim$ 22.5B tokens, $\sim$ 7.5M documents), covering a wide array of English (mostly US) legal texts without preprocessing/cleaning due to the high-quality data.

### 5.2 Pretraining

Henderson et al. (2022) have experienced difficulties when the language model was trained on the entire PileOfLaw. We believe that the highly imbalanced dataset concerning text types (contracts, court decisions, legislation, etc.) could have been a reason for the training instability.[9] This led us to do a sanity check by training only on caselaw first and then to subselect only the most important and largest subsets of the PileOfLaw for training the diverse model, leading to stable pretraining (see Section 6). On the contrary, on the summarization tasks, the diverse model – which includes more

[8]https://github.com/huggingface/tokenizers

[9]However, the large model size could also explain the training instability.

lexical and layout diversity of documents – turns out to perform better and train more robustly.

We trained the *caselaw* models on the training subset of "Court Listener Opinions" from the PileOfLaw (59.3 GB, 7.65B words, 3.39M documents). The *diverse* models were trained on caselaw ("Court Listener Opinions" & "Court Listener Docket Entries"), legislation ("US Code", "State Codes" & "EURLEX") and contracts ("Atticus Contracts" & "EDGAR Contracts"). To balance the training data, we limited the number of documents to 500K (this affects Court Listener Opinions, Court Listener Docket Entries and EDGAR Contracts (see Table 1 for more details). Our validation set consisted of 1000 randomly selected examples from the respective training set.[10] To maximally use the available data, we concatenated all the examples and cut them off in slices of the model's maximum sequence length (4096) – in batches of 1000 examples with multiprocessing to speed up data preparation. We dropped the last slice, since it will not contain 4096 tokens.

We trained both a small (29M parameters) and a base (159M parameters) model for each configuration (caselaw and diverse data). To reach 100K steps it took 68 hours (a bit less than 3 days) for the small model and 135 hours (a bit more than 5 days) for the base model on 4 16GB NVIDIA V100 GPUs. The achieved training and evaluation losses are shown in Table 7 in Appendix A. Interestingly, we find that the diverse models achieve lower training and evaluation losses. Please find more training details in Appendix A. Due to budget constraints, we trained for a maximum of 200K steps. Surprisingly, lower pretraining loss from 200K-step models did not transfer to downstream tasks. We hypothesize that a larger batch size might lead to improvements when training longer.

### 5.3 Downstream Benchmarks

For downstream finetuning, we paired our pretrained encoder model with a randomly initialized BART-base decoder model (Lewis et al., 2020).[11] For BillSum, we set the maximum input length to 1024 and the maximum target length to 256 to save compute. However, many summaries get cut off at 256 tokens. This is why we took our best model and trained it with maximum input length 4096 and maximum target length 1024 (see results in Table 5 and examples in Table 12). For PubMed, we set the maximum input length to 4096 and the maximum generation length to 512. Due to high training costs, we only trained our models with one random seed (42). Our models contain 29M (small) and 159M (base) parameters in the encoder and 96M parameters in the decoder, resulting in a total of 125M (small) and 255M (base) parameters.

### 5.4 Ablation Studies

We run two ablation studies on the BillSum dataset, testing the influence of the pretraining corpus and the number of pretraining steps. To reduce computational costs, we set the maximum input and generation lengths to 1024 and 128 respectively.

| # Steps | Size | Rouge-1 ↑ | Rouge-2 ↑ | Rouge-L ↑ |
|---|---|---|---|---|
| 100K | small | 51.62 | 30.84 | 40.22 |
| 200K | small | 49.02 | 27.02 | 36.98 |
| 100K | base | 56.10 | 36.50 | 45.17 |
| 200K | base | 55.30 | 35.47 | 44.30 |

Table 2: Models pretrained on caselaw only.

| Corpus | Size | Rouge-1 ↑ | Rouge-2 ↑ | Rouge-L ↑ |
|---|---|---|---|---|
| caselaw | small | 51.62 | 30.84 | 40.22 |
| diverse | small | 53.61 | 33.54 | 42.50 |
| caselaw | base | 56.10 | 36.50 | 45.17 |
| diverse | base | 54.87 | 35.63 | 44.21 |

Table 3: Models pretrained for 100K steps.

#### Pretraining Steps

Though train and evaluation losses decrease steadily with more pretraining steps (see Table 7), surprisingly, models trained longer underperform on the BillSum benchmark (see Table 2). We hypothesize the low pretraining batch size caused fast convergence to a local optimum, inhibiting further progress. Consequently, we use the 100K steps model checkpoints.

#### Pretraining Corpus

In total, we trained 4 models (small and base each on the caselaw and diverse corpora). In Table 3 we perform an ablation on the pretraining corpus. The results are inconclusive, with the diverse corpus outperforming for the small models and the caselaw corpus outperforming for the base models. The caselaw models were unstable during finetuning and even failed completely for some learning

[10] We used such a small validation set to save compute.

[11] Interestingly, the randomly initialized decoder yielded better results than when we used the weights from the pretrained huggingface checkpoint at https://huggingface.co/facebook/bart-base.

rates. Together with the fact that the diverse models reached lower pretraining losses (see Table 7), we focus on the diverse models for our experiments.

We acknowledge the necessity of more ablations. Because of limited compute, we opted for the safest and cheapest choices instead of ablating them (e.g. windowed and global attention, RTD pretraining task). Additionally, we put a focus on providing our models as a resource for further research in this area and for practitioners in the field of legal NLP. We thus leave further ablations for future work (w.r.t. pretraining task, more general domain corpora, efficient transformer method, etc.).

## 6 Results

In this section, we present results for the BillSum and PubMed datasets, conducting error analysis on generated summaries. Table 4 compares models in detail. All further experiments utilize models trained on the diverse dataset.

### 6.1 BillSum

We achieve a new SOTA on BillSum in the small and base parameter range and outperform models with almost 12 times more encoder parameters and others having seen more than 1200 times more pretraining examples. The results on BillSum are presented in Figure 1 and Table 5.

We observe that even our small diverse model clearly exceeds the baseline of the original article (DOC + SUM), even though their model is based on BERT-large, containing almost 12 times more encoder parameters and pretrained for 10x more steps. Even more surprisingly, our small diverse model is on par with the PEGASUS-base model (Zhang et al., 2020a) (37.58 vs. 37.78 Rouge-L), pretrained using the Gap-Sentences task specifically designed for abstractive summarization. PEGASUS-base contains almost 4 times more encoder parameters and has seen 40 times more training examples during pretraining (128M vs. 3.2M; see Table 4). Most surprisingly, it even outperforms an LED large model[12] (37.58 vs. 34.23 Rouge-L) using a much longer input length (16384 vs. 1024), containing more than 8 times as many encoder parameters (257M vs. 29M) and having seen more than 1200 times more examples during pretraining.

By scaling up our model to the base size and increasing the maximum input and generation length

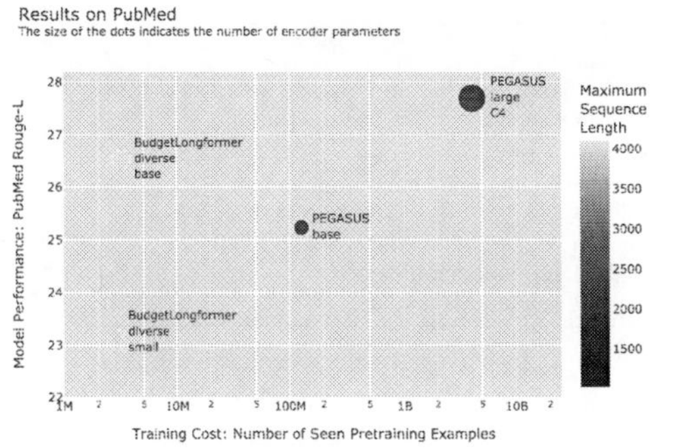


Figure 2: Results on PubMed (log-scaled x-axis)

to 4096 and 1024 tokens respectively, we even approach the performance of PEGASUS-large (43.23 vs. 45.8 Rouge-L). PEGASUS-large has seen three orders of magnitude more training examples during its pretraining in comparison to our model (4.1B vs. 3.2M) and contains almost twice as many encoder parameters (301M vs. 159M).

To conclude, it appears that pretraining with the RTD on (high-quality) in-domain data can be an effective and computationally cheap alternative to a summarization-specific model trained on web text (i.e. PEGASUS). Whether the gain is due to in-domain pretraining or the RTD task is inconclusive, and we leave these experiments for future work.

### 6.2 PubMed

We achieve a new SOTA on PubMed in the small and base parameter range and almost reach the performance of a PEGASUS large model pretrained with a summarization-specific task. The results on PubMed are presented in Figure 2 and Table 6.

Similar to the results on BillSum, our small model clearly outperforms the transformer-base model (23.24 vs. 19.02 Rouge-L) and approaches the PEGASUS-base model (23.24 vs. 25.2 Rouge-L) despite not being specifically pretrained for summarization and having seen significantly fewer examples during pretraining (3.2M vs. 128M). Similar again, our base model outperforms PEGASUS-base (26.53 vs. 25.23 Rouge-L) and almost reaches the performance of PEGASUS-large (26.53 vs. 27.69 Rouge-L) while having seen 1280 times fewer examples during pretraining (3.2M vs. 4.1B).

Our model is pretrained on the narrower domain of legal text, rather than broader C4 data used by PEGASUS. Furthermore, our model and tokenizer had no exposure to medical data in pretraining. This, combined with the high quality of legal data used in pretraining, may explain our model's good out-of-domain performance, similar to the findings

[12]https://huggingface.co/Artifact-AI/led_large_16384_billsum_summarization

| Model Name | Source | P. Steps | P. BS | # P. Examples | # Enc. Par | # Dec. Par | MaxSeqLen | Vocab |
|---|---|---|---|---|---|---|---|---|
| DOC + SUM | (Kornilova and Eidelman, 2019) | 1000K | 256 | 256M | 340M | – | 512 | 30K |
| Transformer base | (Zhang et al., 2020a) | – | – | – | 159M | 187M | 1024 | 96K |
| PEGASUS base | (Zhang et al., 2020a) | 500K | 256 | 128M | 159M | 187M | 1024 | 96K |
| PEGASUS large (C4) | (Zhang et al., 2020a) | 500K | 8192 | 4096M | 301M | 368M | 1024 | 96K |
| LED large | (Beltagy et al., 2020) | 500K | 8192 | 4096M | 257M | 254M | 16384 | 50K |
| LongT5 xl | (Guo et al., 2022) | 1000K | 2048 | 2048M | 1224M | 1626M | 16384 | 32K |
| BudgetLongformer small | ours | 100K | 32 | 3.2M | 29M | 96M | 4096 | 64K |
| BudgetLongformer base | ours | 100K | 32 | 3.2M | 159M | 96M | 4096 | 64K |

Table 4: Comparison of the evaluated models. For more information on the baselines, refer to the cited papers. (Abbreviations: P.: Pretraining, BS: Batch Size, Enc.: Encoder, Dec.: Decoder, Par: Parameters.)

| Model | Size | MaxInLen | MaxGenLen | Rouge-1 ↑ | Rouge-2 ↑ | Rouge-L ↑ |
|---|---|---|---|---|---|---|
| BudgetLongformer | small | 1024 | 256 | **49.85** | **29.63** | **37.58** |
| Transformer | base | 512 | 256 | 44.05 | 21.30 | 30.98 |
| PEGASUS | base | 512 | 256 | 51.42 | 29.68 | 37.78 |
| BudgetLongformer | base | 1024 | 256 | 52.70 | 32.97 | 40.50 |
| BudgetLongformer | base | 4096 | 1024 | **55.45** | **36.68** | **43.23** |
| DOC + SUM | large | 512 | 512 | 40.80 | 23.83 | 33.73 |
| PEGASUS (C4) | large | 1024 | 256 | **57.20** | **39.56** | **45.80** |
| LED | large | 16384 | 1024 | 47.84 | 26.34 | 34.23 |

Table 5: Results on BillSum. Best results per model size are in bold.

of Taylor et al. (2022). Even though our pretraining data is out-of-domain PubMed – whereas C4, likely contains medical data – compared to PEGASUS, our models perform similarly on PubMed as on BillSum. This makes us believe the gains stem mainly from the RTD pretraining task.

Krishna et al. (2022) find that pretraining on the downstream corpus can achieve similar results as pretraining on a large upstream corpus, significantly cutting costs. Finetuning a small model on BillSum cost us approx. half-day of a 16GB V100 GPU. Pretraining the small model for 100K steps cost approx. 12 GPU days[13]. Pretraining and finetuning a smaller model with the RTD task on a task specific corpus might be a suitable alternative to finetuning a larger general model, yielding similar performance with shorter inference time and costs.

### 6.3 Error Analysis

We conducted an error analysis by manually inspecting 25 random summaries. Example summaries are shown in Appendix D.

**Coherence** The inspected summaries were well-structured and emulated the specific style of the reference summaries in the respective domains[14].

[13]For the base model the numbers are approx. double

[14]In future work, we will corroborate these findings by performing human evaluations with domain experts.

**Consistency** We find the summaries mostly factually aligned with the source.[15] However, sometimes it copies formulas from the source text, but then mixes up numbers.[16]

**Fluency** Generally, we find the summaries to be fluent[17] and grammatically correct.

**Relevance** In general, the model summaries contain important content from the source document. However, we find repetitions to be a repeating issue in both BillSum and PubMed summarization. In the BillSum task, the model occasionally uses the same start of the sentence multiple times instead of providing a longer list [18]. It correctly imitates the lists often given in BillSum summaries, but then seems to struggle with continuing lists to more entries. Other times it manages well to formally continue the lists, but repeats list items. In the PubMed task, in one particular summary, a phrase

[15]e.g. "imaging guidance improved the accuracy of intra - articular injections of the knee ( 96.7% versus 81.0%, p < 0.001 ) and shoulder ( 97.3% versus 65.4%, p < 0.001 )"

[16]e.g. "[ a1c ( % ) = [ 0.021 mbg ( mg / dl ] + 4.3, r = 0.92 ) + 4.3, r = 0.58 ]"

[17]Repetitions are discussed in "Relevance"

[18]e.g. "**amends the agricultural marketing act of 1946 to** terminate the authority of the secretary of agriculture (usda) to: (1) livestock processing plant processing plant slaughter, and (2) slaughtering plant slaughter. **amends the agricultural marketing act of 1946 to**: (1) revise minimum reporting requirements; and (2) revise reporting requirements"

| Model | Size | MaxInLen | MaxGenLen | Rouge-1 ↑ | Rouge-2 ↑ | Rouge-L ↑ |
|---|---|---|---|---|---|---|
| BudgetLongformer | small | 4096 | 512 | **34.98** | **13.56** | **23.24** |
| Transformer | base | 512 | 256 | 33.94 | 7.43 | 19.02 |
| PEGASUS | base | 512 | 256 | 39.98 | 15.15 | 25.23 |
| BudgetLongformer | base | 4096 | 512 | **41.16** | **18.15** | **26.53** |
| PEGASUS (C4) | large | 1024 | 256 | **45.49** | **19.90** | **27.69** |
| LongT5 | xl | 16384 | 512 | **50.23** | **24.76** | **46.67** |

Table 6: Results on PubMed. Best results per model size are in bold.

gets repeated 10 times. Even in a high scoring example (Rougel: 62.2, RougeL: 48.5, 464 tokens summary length), a sentence is repeated three times. Here, in contrast to BillSum, the repetitions are also occurring on a lower level.[19]

Generally, the problems are similar in the BillSum and the PubMed tasks; however, they are less pronounced in the in-domain BillSum dataset.

## 7 Conclusions and Future Work

### 7.1 Answers to Main Research Questions

**RQ1**: *Is it possible to train a LM with domain (e.g. legal) expertise efficiently from scratch, reducing costs?* Yes, this work demonstrates the feasibility of pretraining a domain-expertise LM from scratch with minimal compute, matching performance of methods exposed to three orders of magnitude more pretraining examples. Particularly when a high-performing large teacher model is unavailable, our method is advisable.

**RQ2**: *How does our model compare with other models on the challenging legal domain-specific BillSum summarization benchmark?* Our LMs compare favorably to baselines on the challenging domain-specific summarization benchmark BillSum, necessitating long input processing. Our small model outperforms the larger PEGASUS-base, and our base model almost reaches the performance of the larger PEGASUS-large. Both baselines have been pretrained with much more compute and data, and additionally with a pretraining task crafted specifically for summarization.

**RQ3**: *How well does our model compare with other models on the biomedical out-of-domain PubMed summarization benchmark?* Our results on the out-of-domain PubMed summarization benchmark show that our models compare favorably to baselines. Again, our small model outperforms PEGASUS-base and our base model approaches PEGASUS large.

### 7.2 Conclusion

In this work, we show that we can successfully pretrain Longformer models with the RTD task on a Budget. Using very little pretraining, we can achieve SOTA performance on the challenging legal summarization task BillSum, outperforming PEGASUS, that has been pretrained specifically for summarization. Our model even outperforms PEGASUS on the out-of-domain PubMed dataset involving biomedical research articles. To sum up, we present a simple and extremely cheap way of pretraining a long-context LM in cases without the availability of a large teacher model.

### 7.3 Future Work

Future work could test our models on further legal downstream benchmarks such as LexGLUE (Chalkidis et al., 2021), ClassActionPrediction (Semo et al., 2022), CUAD (Hendrycks et al., 2021) or MultiLexSum (Shen et al., 2022). Additionally, one can test whether the out-of-domain results hold on other out-of-domain summarization datasets, such as BigPatent (Sharma et al., 2019) or ArXiv (Cohan et al., 2018). Future work could further scale up the models in terms of batch size, pretraining steps, parameter count and data size to test what further gains can be achieved. Additionally, to further save compute and enhance models, one could explore warm-starting ELECTRA pretraining from existing checkpoints.. The difficulty, of course, lies in getting a suitable generator and discriminator, trained with the same tokenizer. One possible setup might be Longformer-base as the generator and Longformer-large as the discriminator. Finally, one can investigate the use of other efficient transformers with the RTD task.

[19] e.g. "hemoglobin glycated hemoglobin ( hba1c )"

## Limitations

ELECTRA-style training has the disadvantage of the setup being slightly more complicated, requiring a generator and a discriminator. Additionally, the generator should be smaller than the discriminator to ensure stable training. This makes it difficult to warm start from available checkpoints, since two models of different sizes are required. Often, small models are not released, which makes it difficult to warm-start base models using the RTD task. We leave the direction of warm starting a large discriminator with a base generator to future work.

Except for EUR-LEX (1.31 GB or 1.8% of our diverse dataset), our models have only seen US data during the pretraining phase. So, while these models are expected to work well on US data or datasets with similar content such as heavily influenced by the US or mainly common-law based, legal data from Europe for example is expected to look very different (mainly civil-law based except for the UK) and often translated from the original European languages. Thus, our models are not expected to transfer well to such kind of data.

Because of insufficient compute, we were not able to scale up our models in terms of parameter size, batch size and number of pretraining steps. So while we can show that our approach scales well from the small to the base model, it is unknown if this continues to even larger model sizes. Although it is expected to produce better results, we do not know if using a higher batch size and more pretraining steps boosts performance significantly. Additionally, the lacking compute budget made evaluating on more and especially large datasets like BigPatent impossible. Therefore, we cannot give any conclusions at this point to whether our results are robust across a wide range of datasets.

So far, we did not evaluate our summarization models using newer reference-based metrics such as BERTScore (Zhang et al., 2020b) or BARTScore (Yuan et al., 2021), or reference-free metrics such as SUPERT (Gao et al., 2020) or Semantic Distribution Correlation (SDC) (Chen et al., 2021b). However, our baselines used ROUGE only, requiring us to rerun experiments for comparison using newer scores, straining our low compute budget.

So far, we did not have the resources to conduct a thorough human expert evaluation of the quality of our summarization outputs. Such an evaluation would be needed for production systems and for better comparison of models. However, it also requires highly educated medical experts (for PubMed) or lawyers with specific expertise in US bills (for BillSum) respectively, and thus a prohibitively high amount of resources.

For comparing the efficiency of pretraining, number of FLOPs would probably be best. We compared the models' efficiency based on the number of seen examples during pretraining, due to ready availability (most papers report batch size and number of steps, but few papers report FLOPs).

## Ethics Statement

Pretraining language models is a very compute-heavy process and thus leaves a large carbon footprint (Strubell et al., 2019; Patterson et al., 2021). Our method makes significantly reduces the compute requirements and thus the carbon footprint.

As with any large LM there is the risk of it producing biased or unfair output. Researchers using the model should put into place respective safeguards to identify biased and/or toxic language.

## References


Iz Beltagy, Kyle Lo, and Arman Cohan. 2019. SciBERT: A Pretrained Language Model for Scientific Text. *arXiv:1903.10676 [cs]*. ArXiv: 1903.10676.

Iz Beltagy, Matthew E. Peters, and Arman Cohan. 2020. Longformer: The Long-Document Transformer. *arXiv:2004.05150 [cs]*. ArXiv: 2004.05150.

Ilias Chalkidis, Ion Androutsopoulos, and Nikolaos Aletras. 2019. Neural Legal Judgment Prediction in English. In *Proceedings of the 57th Annual Meeting of the Association for Computational Linguistics*, pages 4317–4323, Florence, Italy. Association for Computational Linguistics.

Ilias Chalkidis, Manos Fergadiotis, Prodromos Malakasiotis, Nikolaos Aletras, and Ion Androutsopoulos. 2020. LEGAL-BERT: The Muppets straight out of Law School. *arXiv:2010.02559 [cs]*. ArXiv: 2010.02559.

Ilias Chalkidis, Abhik Jana, Dirk Hartung, Michael James Bommarito, Ion Androutsopoulos, Daniel Martin Katz, and Nikolaos Aletras. 2021. LexGLUE: A Benchmark Dataset for Legal Language Understanding in English. SSRN Scholarly Paper ID 3936759, Social Science Research Network, Rochester, NY.

Mark Chen, Jerry Tworek, Heewoo Jun, Qiming Yuan, Henrique Ponde de Oliveira Pinto, Jared Kaplan, Harri Edwards, Yuri Burda, Nicholas Joseph, Greg Brockman, Alex Ray, Raul Puri, Gretchen Krueger, Michael Petrov, Heidy Khlaaf, Girish Sastry, Pamela Mishkin, Brooke Chan, Scott Gray,

Nick Ryder, Mikhail Pavlov, Alethea Power, Lukasz Kaiser, Mohammad Bavarian, Clemens Winter, Philippe Tillet, Felipe Petroski Such, Dave Cummings, Matthias Plappert, Fotios Chantzis, Elizabeth Barnes, Ariel Herbert-Voss, William Hebgen Guss, Alex Nichol, Alex Paino, Nikolas Tezak, Jie Tang, Igor Babuschkin, Suchir Balaji, Shantanu Jain, William Saunders, Christopher Hesse, Andrew N. Carr, Jan Leike, Josh Achiam, Vedant Misra, Evan Morikawa, Alec Radford, Matthew Knight, Miles Brundage, Mira Murati, Katie Mayer, Peter Welinder, Bob McGrew, Dario Amodei, Sam McCandlish, Ilya Sutskever, and Wojciech Zaremba. 2021a. Evaluating Large Language Models Trained on Code. *arXiv:2107.03374 [cs]*. ArXiv: 2107.03374.

Wang Chen, Piji Li, and Irwin King. 2021b. A Training-free and Reference-free Summarization Evaluation Metric via Centrality-weighted Relevance and Self-referenced Redundancy. In *Proceedings of the 59th Annual Meeting of the Association for Computational Linguistics and the 11th International Joint Conference on Natural Language Processing (Volume 1: Long Papers)*, pages 404–414, Online. Association for Computational Linguistics.

Yangbin Chen, Yun Ma, Xudong Mao, and Qing Li. 2019. Multi-Task Learning for Abstractive and Extractive Summarization. *Data Science and Engineering*, 4(1):14–23.

Rewon Child, Scott Gray, Alec Radford, and Ilya Sutskever. 2019. Generating Long Sequences with Sparse Transformers. *arXiv:1904.10509 [cs, stat]*. ArXiv: 1904.10509.

Kevin Clark, Minh-Thang Luong, Quoc V. Le, and Christopher D. Manning. 2020. ELECTRA: Pre-training Text Encoders as Discriminators Rather Than Generators. *arXiv:2003.10555 [cs]*. ArXiv: 2003.10555.

Arman Cohan, Franck Dernoncourt, Doo Soon Kim, Trung Bui, Seokhwan Kim, Walter Chang, and Nazli Goharian. 2018. A Discourse-Aware Attention Model for Abstractive Summarization of Long Documents. In *Proceedings of the 2018 Conference of the North American Chapter of the Association for Computational Linguistics: Human Language Technologies, Volume 2 (Short Papers)*, pages 615–621, New Orleans, Louisiana. Association for Computational Linguistics.

Xiang Dai, Ilias Chalkidis, Sune Darkner, and Desmond Elliott. 2022. Revisiting Transformer-based Models for Long Document Classification. *arXiv:2204.06683 [cs]*. ArXiv: 2204.06683.

Jacob Devlin, Ming-Wei Chang, Kenton Lee, and Kristina Toutanova. 2019. BERT: Pre-training of Deep Bidirectional Transformers for Language Understanding. *arXiv:1810.04805 [cs]*. ArXiv: 1810.04805.

Yang Gao, Wei Zhao, and Steffen Eger. 2020. SUPERT: Towards New Frontiers in Unsupervised Evaluation Metrics for Multi-Document Summarization. In *Proceedings of the 58th Annual Meeting of the Association for Computational Linguistics*, pages 1347–1354, Online. Association for Computational Linguistics.

Ian J. Goodfellow, Jean Pouget-Abadie, Mehdi Mirza, Bing Xu, David Warde-Farley, Sherjil Ozair, Aaron Courville, and Yoshua Bengio. 2014. Generative Adversarial Networks. ArXiv:1406.2661 [cs, stat].

Mandy Guo, Joshua Ainslie, David Uthus, Santiago Ontanon, Jianmo Ni, Yun-Hsuan Sung, and Yinfei Yang. 2022. LongT5: Efficient text-to-text transformer for long sequences. In *Findings of the Association for Computational Linguistics: NAACL 2022*, pages 724–736, Seattle, United States. Association for Computational Linguistics.

Suchin Gururangan, Ana Marasović, Swabha Swayamdipta, Kyle Lo, Iz Beltagy, Doug Downey, and Noah A. Smith. 2020. Don't Stop Pretraining: Adapt Language Models to Domains and Tasks. *arXiv:2004.10964 [cs]*. ArXiv: 2004.10964.

Pengcheng He, Jianfeng Gao, and Weizhu Chen. 2021. DeBERTaV3: Improving DeBERTa using ELECTRA-Style Pre-Training with Gradient-Disentangled Embedding Sharing. *arXiv:2111.09543 [cs]*. ArXiv: 2111.09543.

Peter Henderson, Mark S. Krass, Lucia Zheng, Neel Guha, Christopher D. Manning, Dan Jurafsky, and Daniel E. Ho. 2022. Pile of Law: Learning Responsible Data Filtering from the Law and a 256GB Open-Source Legal Dataset. ArXiv:2207.00220 [cs].

Dan Hendrycks, Collin Burns, Anya Chen, and Spencer Ball. 2021. CUAD: An Expert-Annotated NLP Dataset for Legal Contract Review. ArXiv:2103.06268 [cs].

Jeremy Howard and Sebastian Ruder. 2018. Universal Language Model Fine-tuning for Text Classification. In *Proceedings of the 56th Annual Meeting of the Association for Computational Linguistics (Volume 1: Long Papers)*, pages 328–339, Melbourne, Australia. Association for Computational Linguistics.

Wenyue Hua, Yuchen Zhang, Zhe Chen, Josie Li, and Melanie Weber. 2022. LegalRelectra: Mixed-domain Language Modeling for Long-range Legal Text Comprehension. ArXiv:2212.08204 [cs].

Kamal raj Kanakarajan, Bhuvana Kundumani, and Malaikannan Sankarasubbu. 2021. BioELECTRA:Pretrained Biomedical text Encoder using Discriminators. In *Proceedings of the 20th Workshop on Biomedical Language Processing*, pages 143–154, Online. Association for Computational Linguistics.

Nikita Kitaev, Łukasz Kaiser, and Anselm Levskaya. 2020. Reformer: The Efficient Transformer. *arXiv:2001.04451 [cs, stat]*. ArXiv: 2001.04451.

Anastassia Kornilova and Vladimir Eidelman. 2019. BillSum: A Corpus for Automatic Summarization of US Legislation. In *Proceedings of the 2nd Workshop on New Frontiers in Summarization*, pages 48–56, Hong Kong, China. Association for Computational Linguistics.

Kundan Krishna, Saurabh Garg, Jeffrey P. Bigham, and Zachary C. Lipton. 2022. Downstream Datasets Make Surprisingly Good Pretraining Corpora. ArXiv:2209.14389 [cs].

Jinhyuk Lee, Wonjin Yoon, Sungdong Kim, Donghyeon Kim, Sunkyu Kim, Chan Ho So, and Jaewoo Kang. 2019. BioBERT: a pre-trained biomedical language representation model for biomedical text mining. *Bioinformatics*, page btz682. ArXiv: 1901.08746.

James Lee-Thorp, Joshua Ainslie, Ilya Eckstein, and Santiago Ontanon. 2021. FNet: Mixing Tokens with Fourier Transforms. *arXiv:2105.03824 [cs]*. ArXiv: 2105.03824.

Mike Lewis, Yinhan Liu, Naman Goyal, Marjan Ghazvininejad, Abdelrahman Mohamed, Omer Levy, Veselin Stoyanov, and Luke Zettlemoyer. 2020. BART: Denoising Sequence-to-Sequence Pretraining for Natural Language Generation, Translation, and Comprehension. In *Proceedings of the 58th Annual Meeting of the Association for Computational Linguistics*, pages 7871–7880, Online. Association for Computational Linguistics.

Yikuan Li, Ramsey M. Wehbe, Faraz S. Ahmad, Hanyin Wang, and Yuan Luo. 2022. Clinical-Longformer and Clinical-BigBird: Transformers for long clinical sequences. *arXiv:2201.11838 [cs]*. ArXiv: 2201.11838.

Yinhan Liu, Myle Ott, Naman Goyal, Jingfei Du, Mandar Joshi, Danqi Chen, Omer Levy, Mike Lewis, Luke Zettlemoyer, and Veselin Stoyanov. 2019. RoBERTa: A Robustly Optimized BERT Pretraining Approach. *arXiv:1907.11692 [cs]*. ArXiv: 1907.11692.

Dimitris Mamakas, Petros Tsotsi, Ion Androutsopoulos, and Ilias Chalkidis. 2022. Processing Long Legal Documents with Pre-trained Transformers: Modding LegalBERT and Longformer. ArXiv:2211.00974 [cs].

Stelios Maroudas, Sotiris Legkas, Prodromos Malakasiotis, and Ilias Chalkidis. 2022. Legal-Tech Open Diaries: Lesson learned on how to develop and deploy light-weight models in the era of humongous Language Models. ArXiv:2210.13086 [cs].

Joel Niklaus, Ilias Chalkidis, and Matthias Stürmer. 2021. Swiss-Judgment-Prediction: A Multilingual Legal Judgment Prediction Benchmark. In *Proceedings of the Natural Legal Language Processing Workshop 2021*, pages 19–35, Punta Cana, Dominican Republic. Association for Computational Linguistics.

Joel Niklaus, Veton Matoshi, Pooja Rani, Andrea Galassi, Matthias Stürmer, and Ilias Chalkidis. 2023. LEXTREME: A Multi-Lingual and Multi-Task Benchmark for the Legal Domain. ArXiv:2301.13126 [cs].

Joel Niklaus, Matthias Stürmer, and Ilias Chalkidis. 2022. An Empirical Study on Cross-X Transfer for Legal Judgment Prediction. In *Proceedings of the 2nd Conference of the Asia-Pacific Chapter of the Association for Computational Linguistics and the 12th International Joint Conference on Natural Language Processing (Volume 1: Long Papers)*, pages 32–46, Online only. Association for Computational Linguistics.

David Patterson, Joseph Gonzalez, Quoc Le, Chen Liang, Lluis-Miquel Munguia, Daniel Rothchild, David So, Maud Texier, and Jeff Dean. 2021. Carbon Emissions and Large Neural Network Training. *arXiv:2104.10350 [cs]*. ArXiv: 2104.10350.

Alec Radford, Karthik Narasimhan, Tim Salimans, and Ilya Sutskever. 2018. Improving Language Understanding by Generative Pre-Training. page 12.

Aurko Roy, Mohammad Saffar, Ashish Vaswani, and David Grangier. 2021. Efficient Content-Based Sparse Attention with Routing Transformers. *Transactions of the Association for Computational Linguistics*, 9:53–68. Place: Cambridge, MA Publisher: MIT Press.

Gil Semo, Dor Bernsohn, Ben Hagag, Gila Hayat, and Joel Niklaus. 2022. ClassActionPrediction: A Challenging Benchmark for Legal Judgment Prediction of Class Action Cases in the US. In *Proceedings of the Natural Legal Language Processing Workshop 2022*, pages 31–46, Abu Dhabi, United Arab Emirates (Hybrid). Association for Computational Linguistics.

Or Sharir, Barak Peleg, and Yoav Shoham. 2020. The Cost of Training NLP Models: A Concise Overview. ArXiv:2004.08900 [cs].

Eva Sharma, Chen Li, and Lu Wang. 2019. BIGPATENT: A Large-Scale Dataset for Abstractive and Coherent Summarization. In *Proceedings of the 57th Annual Meeting of the Association for Computational Linguistics*, pages 2204–2213, Florence, Italy. Association for Computational Linguistics.

Zejiang Shen, Kyle Lo, Lauren Yu, Nathan Dahlberg, Margo Schlanger, and Doug Downey. 2022. Multi-LexSum: Real-World Summaries of Civil Rights Lawsuits at Multiple Granularities. ArXiv:2206.10883 [cs].

Emma Strubell, Ananya Ganesh, and Andrew McCallum. 2019. Energy and Policy Considerations for Deep Learning in NLP. ArXiv:1906.02243 [cs].

Yi Tay, Dara Bahri, Donald Metzler, Da-Cheng Juan, Zhe Zhao, and Che Zheng. 2021. Synthesizer: Rethinking Self-Attention in Transformer Models. *arXiv:2005.00743 [cs]*. ArXiv: 2005.00743.

Yi Tay, Mostafa Dehghani, Samira Abnar, Yikang Shen, Dara Bahri, Philip Pham, Jinfeng Rao, Liu Yang, Sebastian Ruder, and Donald Metzler. 2020a. Long Range Arena: A Benchmark for Efficient Transformers. *arXiv:2011.04006 [cs]*. ArXiv: 2011.04006.

Yi Tay, Mostafa Dehghani, Dara Bahri, and Donald Metzler. 2020b. Efficient Transformers: A Survey. *arXiv:2009.06732 [cs]*. ArXiv: 2009.06732.

Ross Taylor, Marcin Kardas, Guillem Cucurull, Thomas Scialom, Anthony Hartshorn, Elvis Saravia, Andrew Poulton, Viktor Kerkez, and Robert Stojnic. 2022. Galactica: A Large Language Model for Science. ArXiv:2211.09085 [cs, stat].

Ashish Vaswani, Noam Shazeer, Niki Parmar, Jakob Uszkoreit, Llion Jones, Aidan N. Gomez, Lukasz Kaiser, and Illia Polosukhin. 2017. Attention Is All You Need. *arXiv:1706.03762 [cs]*. ArXiv: 1706.03762.

Alex Wang, Amanpreet Singh, Julian Michael, Felix Hill, Omer Levy, and Samuel Bowman. 2018. GLUE: A Multi-Task Benchmark and Analysis Platform for Natural Language Understanding. In *Proceedings of the 2018 EMNLP Workshop BlackboxNLP: Analyzing and Interpreting Neural Networks for NLP*, pages 353–355, Brussels, Belgium. Association for Computational Linguistics.

Changhan Wang, Kyunghyun Cho, and Jiatao Gu. 2019. Neural Machine Translation with Byte-Level Subwords. ArXiv:1909.03341 [cs].

Thomas Wolf, Lysandre Debut, Victor Sanh, Julien Chaumond, Clement Delangue, Anthony Moi, Pierric Cistac, Tim Rault, Remi Louf, Morgan Funtowicz, Joe Davison, Sam Shleifer, Patrick von Platen, Clara Ma, Yacine Jernite, Julien Plu, Canwen Xu, Teven Le Scao, Sylvain Gugger, Mariama Drame, Quentin Lhoest, and Alexander Rush. 2020. Transformers: State-of-the-Art Natural Language Processing. In *Proceedings of the 2020 Conference on Empirical Methods in Natural Language Processing: System Demonstrations*, pages 38–45, Online. Association for Computational Linguistics.

Chaojun Xiao, Xueyu Hu, Zhiyuan Liu, Cunchao Tu, and Maosong Sun. 2021. Lawformer: A pre-trained language model for Chinese legal long documents. *AI Open*, 2:79–84.

Zhilin Yang, Zihang Dai, Yiming Yang, Jaime Carbonell, Ruslan Salakhutdinov, and Quoc V. Le. 2020. XLNet: Generalized Autoregressive Pretraining for Language Understanding. *arXiv:1906.08237 [cs]*. ArXiv: 1906.08237.

Weizhe Yuan, Graham Neubig, and Pengfei Liu. 2021. BARTScore: Evaluating Generated Text as Text Generation. *arXiv:2106.11520 [cs]*. ArXiv: 2106.11520.

Manzil Zaheer, Guru Guruganesh, Avinava Dubey, Joshua Ainslie, Chris Alberti, Santiago Ontanon, Philip Pham, Anirudh Ravula, Qifan Wang, Li Yang, and Amr Ahmed. 2021. Big Bird: Transformers for Longer Sequences. *arXiv:2007.14062 [cs, stat]*. ArXiv: 2007.14062.

Jingqing Zhang, Yao Zhao, Mohammad Saleh, and Peter J. Liu. 2020a. PEGASUS: Pre-training with Extracted Gap-sentences for Abstractive Summarization. *arXiv:1912.08777 [cs]*. ArXiv: 1912.08777.

Tianyi Zhang, Varsha Kishore, Felix Wu, Kilian Q. Weinberger, and Yoav Artzi. 2020b. BERTScore: Evaluating Text Generation with BERT. *arXiv:1904.09675 [cs]*. ArXiv: 1904.09675.

## A Hyperparameters and Training Details

| Model | Data | # Steps | Train Loss | Eval Loss |
|---|---|---|---|---|
| small | caselaw | 50K | 14.61 | 15.78 |
| small | caselaw | 100K | 13.93 | 15.07 |
| small | caselaw | 150K | 13.63 | 14.77 |
| small | caselaw | 200K | 13.38 | 14.49 |
| small | diverse | 50K | 13.75 | 12.70 |
| small | diverse | 100K | 12.78 | 11.66 |
| small | diverse | 150K | 12.28 | 11.29 |
| small | diverse | 200K | 12.05 | 11.03 |
| base | caselaw | 50K | 12.40 | 13.76 |
| base | caselaw | 100K | 11.67 | 12.99 |
| base | caselaw | 150K | 11.31 | 12.58 |
| base | caselaw | 200K | 11.02 | 12.27 |
| base | diverse | 50K | 10.70 | 10.01 |
| base | diverse | 100K | 9.86 | 9.22 |
| base | diverse | 150K | 9.42 | 8.79 |
| base | diverse | 200K | 9.20 | 8.56 |

Table 7: Training and Evaluation losses for the different trained models. Note that these losses are the addition of the loss of the generator and the loss of the discriminator. Since the loss of the discriminator is much smaller, it is scaled by a factor of 50 to stabilize training.

In this section, we present additional details regarding training and the chosen hyperparameters.

### A.1 Pretraining

We pretrained our models with batch size 128 and learning rate 5e-4 and 3e-4 for the small and base models respectively. We used a Longformer attention window of 256. As described in by Clark et al. (2020), we used 10000 warm up steps and a 4 and 3 times smaller generator than the discriminator in the small and base version respectively. In contrast to Clark et al. (2020), we reduced the generator's depth (number of hidden layers) instead of its width (embedding size, hidden size and intermediate size). We used a MLM probability of 25% for the generators. The pretraining losses are shown in Table 7.

### A.2 Downstream Benchmarks

We finetuned on the summarization datasets using early stopping on the validation set with patience of 3 epochs. We used a batch size of 32 and learning rate of 7e-5 after tuning in {5e-4, 9e-5, 7e-5, 5e-5, 3e-5, 1e-5}. We used the bart-base default config for num_beams (4) and no_repeat_ngram_size (3).

Overall, we found the diverse models to be more robust in finetuning with less failed runs and typically higher performance.

### A.3 Compute Costs

For running the pretraining, we used an AWS p3.8xlarge instance with 4 16GB NVIDIA V100 GPUs. Training the four models to 200K steps each, took approx. 36 days or 144 GPU days in total (almost. 6 days and almost 12 days for the small and base models respectively). Previous debug runs additionally consumed approx. 12 GPU days. For running the finetuning experiments, we used an AWS p3.16xlarge instance with 8 16GB NVIDIA V100 GPUs. Running the BillSum, and PubMed experiments including debugging and hyperparameter tuning took approximately 25 and 7 GPU days in total respectively. Putting it all together, we trained our models for 176 16GB NVIDIA V100 GPU days.

## B Library Versions

We used the following versions to the libraries in a pip requirements.txt format:

```
datasets==2.4.0
huggingface-hub==0.9.0
nltk==3.7
pandas==1.3.5
rouge-score==0.1.2
scikit-learn==1.0.2
scipy==1.7.3
tokenizers==0.12.1
torch==1.12.1
tqdm==4.64.0
transformers==4.21.1
```

## C Data Details

We used our own tokenizer to calculate the number of tokens. In Tables 3, and 4 we show the data length distributions for the BillSum train and test splits. In Tables 5, 6, and 7 we show the data length distributions for the PubMed train, validation and test splits.

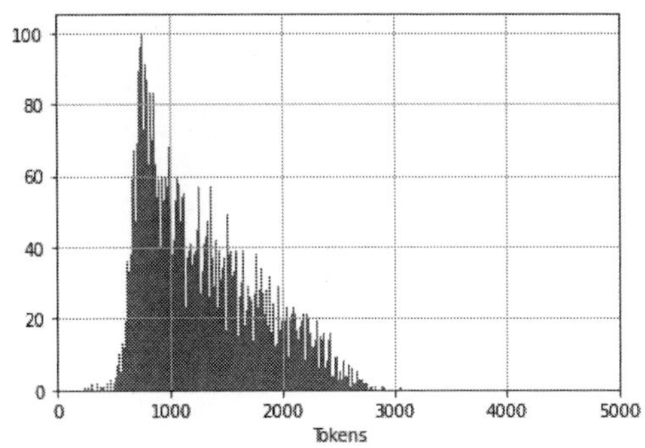


(a) **Input Text**
Mean: 1289, Median: 1166
75-Quant: 1644, 95-Quant: 2290, Max: 3055

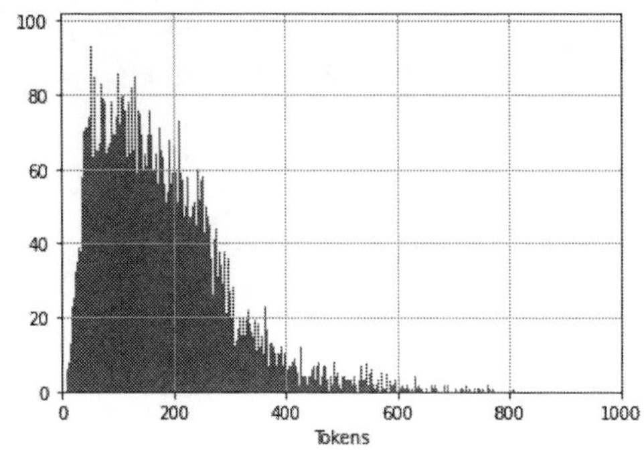


(b) **Summary**
Mean: 179, Median: 157
75-Quant: 240, 95-Quant: 398, Max: 808

Figure 3: Histograms for the BillSum training set (18949 samples).

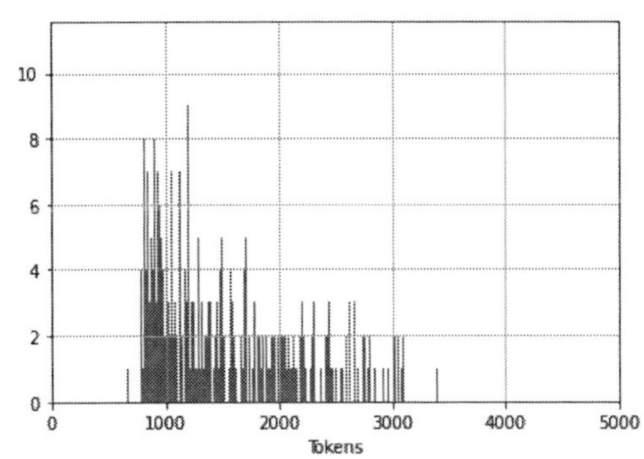


(a) **Input Text**
Mean: 1284, Median: 1164
75-Quant: 1629, 95-Quant: 2288, Max: 2957

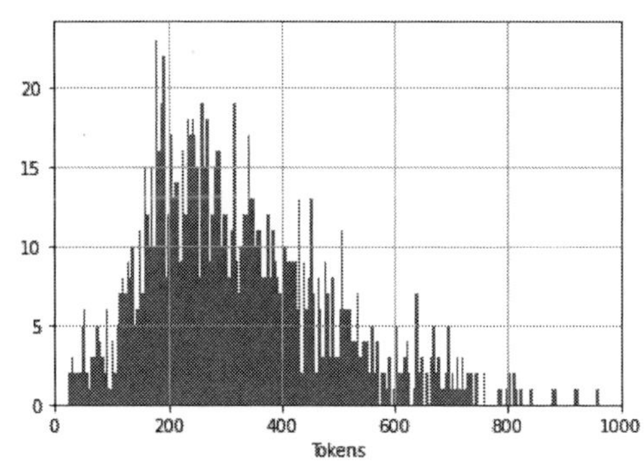


(b) **Summary**
Mean: 179, Median: 156
75-Quant: 239, 95-Quant: 394, Max: 787

Figure 4: Histograms for the BillSum test set (3269 samples).

## D Examples

Example summaries are displayed in Tables 8, 9, 10, 11, 12, 13, 13, 15, and 16. Since the documents are very long sometimes, we truncated them to the first 2500 characters. We sorted the examples by RougeL scores and show the bottom 5%, bottom 25%, top 75% and top 95% percentile.

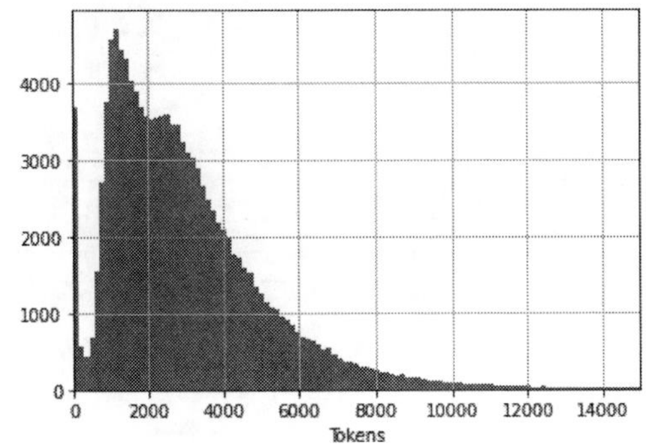


(a) **Input Text**
Mean: 3044, Median: 2572
75-Quant: 3996, 95-Quant: 7057, Max: 109759

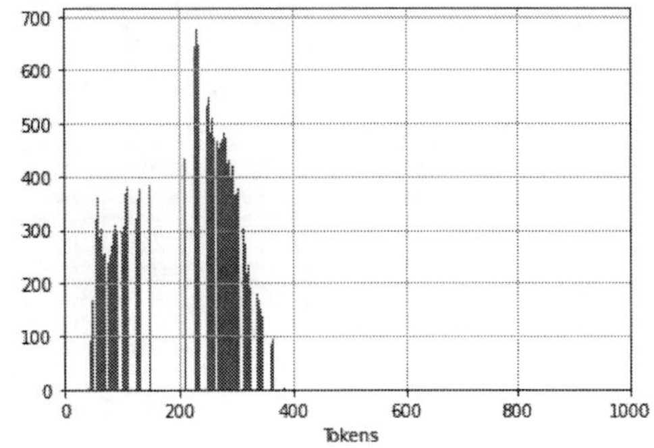


(b) **Summary**
Mean: 202, Median: 208
75-Quant: 262, 95-Quant: 326, Max: 391

Figure 5: Histograms for the PubMed train set (119924 samples).

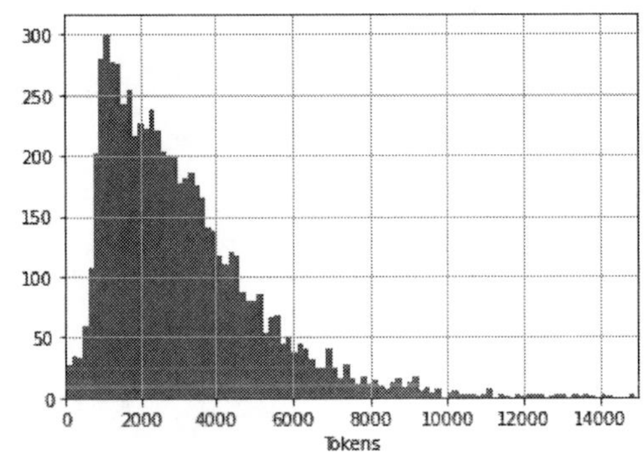


(a) **Input Text**
Mean: 3112, Median: 2609
75-Quant: 4011, 95-Quant: 6968, Max: 119269

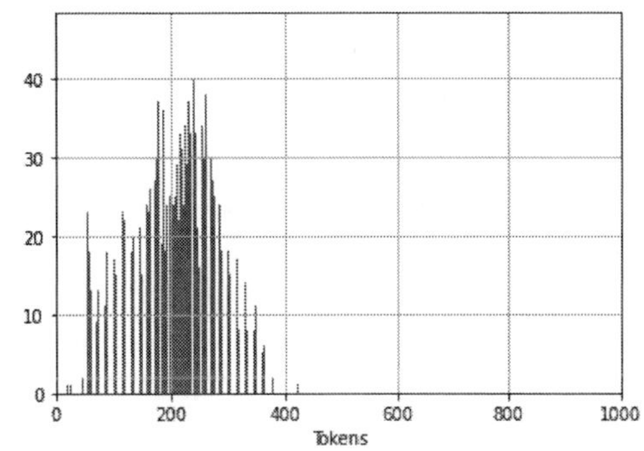


(b) **Summary**
Mean: 203, Median: 209
75-Quant: 263, 95-Quant: 330, Max: 518

Figure 6: Histograms for the PubMed validation set (6633 samples).

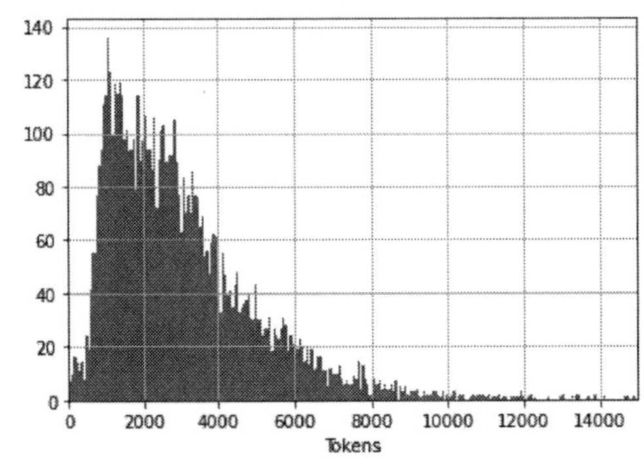


(a) **Input Text**
Mean: 3093, Median: 2596
75-Quant: 3964, 95-Quant: 6985, Max: 48750

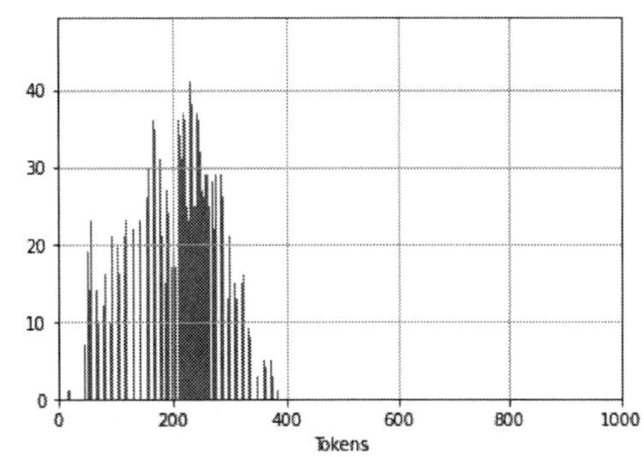


(b) **Summary**
Mean: 205, Median: 213
75-Quant: 265, 95-Quant: 329, Max: 506

Figure 7: Histograms for the PubMed test set (6658 samples).

| Bottom 5% example (Sorted by rougeL) | |
|---|---|
| Document | SECTION 1. SHORT TITLE.<br>This Act may be cited as the "Child Citizenship Act of 2000".<br>TITLE I–CITIZENSHIP FOR CERTAIN CHILDREN BORN OUTSIDE THE UNITED STATES<br>SEC. 101. AUTOMATIC ACQUISITION OF CITIZENSHIP FOR CERTAIN CHILDREN BORN OUTSIDE THE UNITED STATES.<br>(a) In General.–Section 320 of the Immigration and Nationality Act (8 U.S.C. 1431) is amended to read as follows:<br>"children born outside the united states and residing permanently in the united states; conditions under which citizenship automatically acquired<br>"Sec. 320. (a) A child born outside of the United States automatically becomes a citizen of the United States when all of the following conditions have been fulfilled: "(1) At least one parent of the child is a citizen of the United States, whether by birth or naturalization. "(2) The child is under the age of eighteen years. "(3) The child is residing in the United States in the legal and physical custody of the citizen parent pursuant to a lawful admission for permanent residence. "(b) Subsection (a) shall apply to a child adopted by a United States citizen parent if the child satisfies the requirements applicable to adopted children under section 101(b)(1).". (b) Clerical Amendment.–The table of sections of such Act is amended by striking the item relating to section 320 and inserting the following: "Sec. 320. Children born outside the United States and residing permanently in the United States; conditions under which citizenship automatically acquired.".<br>SEC. 102. ACQUISITION OF CERTIFICATE OF CITIZENSHIP FOR CERTAIN CHILDREN BORN OUTSIDE THE UNITED STATES.<br>(a) In General.–Section 322 of the Immigration and Nationality Act (8 U.S.C. 1433) is amended to read as follows:<br>"children born and residing outside the united states; conditions for acquiring certificate of citizenship<br>"Sec. 322. (a) A parent who is a citizen of the United States may apply for naturalization on behalf of a child born outside of the United States who has not acquired citizenship automatically under section 320. The Attorney General shall issue a certificate of citizenship to such parent upon proof, to the satisfaction of the Attorney General, that the following conditions have been fulfilled: "(1) At least one parent ... |
| Gold | Provides for issuance of a certificate of naturalization for a child born outside of the United States when the following conditions are met: (1) at least one parent is a U.S. citizen who has been present in the United States for not less than five years, at least two of which were after having attained the age of 14, or who has a citizen parent meeting such requirements; (2) the child is under 18 years old; and (3) the child is residing outside the United States in the legal and physical custody of the citizen parent, is temporarily and lawfully present in the United States, and is maintaining such lawful status. Applies such provision to an adopted child meeting certain definitional requirements who is adopted by a U.S. citizen parent. Title II: Protections for Certain Aliens Voting Based on Reasonable Belief of Citizenship - Amends the Immigration and Nationality Act respecting unlawful voting or false U.S. citizenship claims by permanent resident aliens under 16 years old having natural or adoptive U.S. citizen parents, to provide exceptions from certain provisions regarding deportability, moral character, inadmissability or related criminal penalties. |
| Model | table of contents: title i: citizenship for certain title ii: immigration and naturalization provisions title i: citizenship for certain children born outside the united states - amends the immigration and nationality act (ina) to revise naturalization requirements with respect to child born outside the united states. (sec. 102) amends the immigration and nationality act to revise requirements with respect to: (1) naturalization as a citizen of the united states; (2) naturalization of a u.s. citizen; (3) citizenship; (4) citizenship; (5) naturalization service; and (6) |
| Metrics | Rouge1: 35.9, Rouge2: 15.54, RougeL: 22.56, RougeLsum: 20.51, Summary length (tokens): 129 |
| **Bottom 25% example (Sorted by rougeL)** | |
| Document | SECTION 1. SHORT TITLE.<br>This Act may be cited as the "Effective Terrorists Prosecution Act of 2006".<br>SEC. 2. DEFINITION OF UNLAWFUL ENEMY COMBATANT.<br>Paragraph (1) of section 948a of title 10, United States Code (as enacted by the Military Commissions Act of 2006 (Public Law 109-366)), is amended to read as follows: "(1) Unlawful enemy combatant.–The term 'unlawful enemy combatant' means an individual who directly participates in hostilities as part of an armed conflict against the United States who is not a lawful enemy combatant. The term is used solely to designate individuals triable by military commission under this chapter.".<br>SEC. 3. DETERMINATION OF UNLAWFUL ENEMY COMBATANT STATUS BY COMBATANT STATUS REVIEW TRIBUNAL NOT DISPOSITIVE FOR PURPOSES OF JURISDICTION OF MILITARY COMMISSIONS.<br>Section 948d of title 10, United States Code (as enacted by the Military Commissions Act of 2006 (Public Law 109-366)), is amended– (1) by striking subsection (c); and (2) by redesignating subsection (d) as subsection (c).<br>SEC. 4. EXCLUSION FROM TRIAL BY MILITARY COMMISSION OF STATEMENTS OBTAINED BY COERCION.<br>Section 948r of title 10, United States Code (as enacted by the Military Commissions Act of 2006 (Public Law 109-366)), is amended by striking subsections (c) and (d) and inserting the following new subsection (c): "(c) Exclusion of Statements Obtained by Coercion.–A statement obtained by use of coercion shall not be admissible in a military commission under this chapter, except against a person accused of coercion as evidence that the statement was made.".<br>SEC. 5. DISCRETION OF MILITARY JUDGE TO EXCLUDE HEARSAY EVIDENCE DETERMINED TO BE UNRELIABLE OR LACKING IN PROBATIVE VALUE.<br>Section 949a(b)(2)(E)(ii) of title 10, United States Code (as enacted by the Military Commissions Act of 2006 (Public Law 109-366)), is amended by striking "if the party opposing the admission of the evidence demonstrates that the evidence is unreliable or lacking in probative value" and inserting "if the military judge determines, upon motion by counsel, that the evidence is unreliable or lacking in probative value".<br>SEC. 6. DISCRETION OF MILITARY JUDGE TO TAKE CERTAIN ACTIONS IN EVENT THAT A SUBSTITUTE FOR CLASSIFIED EXCULPATORY EVIDENCE IS INS... |
| Gold | Effective Terrorists Prosecution Act of 2006 - Amends federal armed forces provisions enacted by the Military Commissions Act of 2006 to, among other things: (1) exclude from military commission (commission) trials statements obtained by coercion; (2) allow a commission military judge to exclude hearsay evidence determined to be unreliable or lacking in probative value; (3) provide for review of commission decisions by the U.S. Court of Appeals for the Armed Forces rather than the Court of Military Commission Review; (4) revise generally provisions concerning the implementation of treaty obligations with respect to the U.S. prosecution of enemy combatants; (5) restore habeas corpus rights for individuals detained by the United States; and (6) provide for expedited judicial review of provisions of the Military Commissions Act of 2006. |
| Model | effective terrorists prosecution act of 2006 - amends federal armed forces law to revise the definition of " unlawful enemy combatant" to include an individual who directly participated in hostilities as part of an armed conflict against the united states who is not a lawful enemy combatant.<br>amends the military pay reform and reform act of 2006 to provide that a complaint obtained by mail or the military court of appeals for the u.s. military court of appeals for the armed forces who is not a lawful enemy combatant.<br>directs the u.s. military department of defense to review the record in each case, except against a person aggrieved by prosecution or |
| Metrics | Rouge1: 51.64, Rouge2: 24.64, RougeL: 33.8, RougeLsum: 37.56, Summary length (tokens): 129 |
| **Top 75% example (Sorted by rougeL)** | |
| Document | SECTION 1. SHORT TITLE.<br>This Act may be cited as the "Census Address List Improvement Act of 1994". SEC. 2. ADDRESS INFORMATION REVIEWED BY LOCAL GOVERNMENTS. (a) In General.–Chapter 1 of title 13, United States Code, is amended by adding after section 15 the following new section: "Sec. 16. Address information reviewed by States and local governments "(a) The Secretary, to assist efforts to ensure the accuracy of censuses and surveys under this title, shall– "(1) publish standards defining the content and structure of address information which States and local units of general purpose government may submit to the Secretary to be used in developing a national address list; "(2)(A) develop and publish a timetable for the Bureau to receive, review, and respond to submissions of information under paragraph (1) before the decennial census date; and "(B) provide for a response by the Bureau with respect to such submissions in which the Bureau specifies its determinations regarding such information and the reasons for such determinations; and "(3) be subject to the review process developed under section 3 of the Census Address List Improvement Act of 1994 relating to responses pursuant to paragraph (2). "(b)(1) The Secretary– "(A) shall provide officials who are designated as census liaisons by a local unit of general purpose government with access to census address information for the purpose of verifying the accuracy of the address information of the Bureau for census and survey purposes; and "(B) together with such access, should provide an explanation of duties and obligations under this title. "(2) Access under paragraph (1) shall be limited to address information concerning addresses within the local unit of general purpose government represented by the census liaison or an adjacent local unit of general purpose government. "(3) The Bureau should respond to each recommendation made by a census liaison concerning the accuracy of address information, including the determination (and reasons therefor) of the Bureau regarding each such recommendation. "(4) For the purposes of paragraph (1), in a case in which a local unit of general purpose government is within another local unit of general purpose government and is not independent of the enclosing unit, the census liaison shall be ... |
| Gold | Census Address List Improvement Act of 1994 - Directs the Secretary of Commerce to: (1) publish standards defining the content and structure of address information which States and local governments may submit to the Secretary to be used in developing a national address list; (2) develop and publish a timetable for the Bureau of the Census to receive, review, and respond to the submitted information before the decennial census date; (3) provide for a response by the Bureau that specifies its determinations regarding such information and the reasons for such determinations; and (4) be subject to the review process developed under this Act relating to such responses. Directs the Secretary to provide officials who are designated as census liaisons by local governments with access to census address information for the purpose of verifying the accuracy of the Bureau's address information for census and survey purposes and together with such access, provide an explanation of duties and obligations under this Act. Limits such access to the addresses within the local government represented by the census liaison or an adjacent local government. Requires the Bureau to respond to each recommendation made by a census liaison concerning the accuracy of address information, including the determination (and reasons therefor) of the Bureau regarding each such recommendation. Prohibits a census liaison from using information made available under this Act for purposes other than the purposes specified in this Act. Makes provisions that require, with exceptions, that such information be treated as confidential applicable to local government census liaisons. Imposes a fine and up to five years' imprisonment on whoever being or having been a census liaison wrongfully discloses such information. Requires: (1) the Administrator of the Office of Information and Regulatory Affairs, acting through the Chief Statistician, to develop an appeals process for those States and local governments which desire to appeal determinations of the Bureau; and (2) the Postal Service to provide to the Secretary for use by the Bureau such address, address- related, and point of postal delivery information, including postal delivery codes, determined by the Secretary to be appropriate for any census or survey being conducted by the Bureau. |
| Model | census address list improvement act of 1994 - directs the secretary of transportation to: (1) publish standards amending the content and structure of address information which states and local governments may submit to the secretary to the secretary to the secretary for such a national address list; (2) provide for a response by a census liaison with respect to such reports; and (3) provide for a response by a census liaison with respect to such reports. requires the secretary to: (1) provide officials who are designated as census liaison with access to census information; and (2) report annually to the congressional committees on the accuracy of |
| Metrics | Rouge1: 62.26, Rouge2: 41.9, RougeL: 50.0, RougeLsum: 52.83, Summary length (tokens): 129 |
| **Top 95% example (Sorted by rougeL)** | |
| Document | SECTION 1. SHORT TITLE.<br>This Act may be cited as the "National Geologic Mapping Reauthorization Act of 1996".<br>SEC. 2. FINDINGS.<br>Congress finds that– (1) in enacting the National Geologic Mapping Act of 1992 (43 U.S.C. 31a et seq.), Congress found, among other things, that– (A) during the 2 decades preceding enactment of that Act, the production of geologic maps had been drastically curtailed; (B) geologic maps are the primary data base for virtually all applied and basic earth-science investigations; (C) Federal agencies, State and local governments, private industry, and the general public depend on the information provided by geologic maps to determine the extent of potential environmental damage before embarking on projects that could lead to preventable, costly environmental problems or litigation; (D) the lack of proper geologic maps has led to the poor design of such structures as dams and waste- disposal facilities; (E) geologic maps have proven indispensable in the search for needed fossil fuel and mineral resources; and (F) a comprehensive nationwide program of geologic mapping is required in order to systematically build the Nation's geologic-map data base at a pace that responds to increasing demand; (2) the geologic mapping program called for by that Act has not been fully implemented; and (3) it is time for this important program to be fully implemented.<br>SEC. 3. REAUTHORIZATION AND AMENDMENT.<br>(a) Definitions.–Section 3 of the National Geologic Mapping Act of 1992 (43 U.S.C. 31b) is amended– (1) by striking "As used in this Act:" and inserting "In this Act:"; (2) by redesignating paragraphs (2), (3), (4), and (5) as paragraphs (3), (4), (5), and (6), respectively; (3) by inserting after paragraph (1) the following: "(2) Association.–The term 'Association' means the Association of American State Geologists."; and (4) in each paragraph that does not have a heading, by ... |
| Gold | National Geologic Mapping Reauthorization Act of 1996 - Amends the National Geologic Mapping Act of 1992 to establish a national cooperative geologic mapping program between the U.S. Geological Survey and State geological surveys. Establishes a geologic mapping advisory committee to advise the Director of the U.S. Geological Survey on planning and implementation of the geological mapping program. Authorizes appropriations. |
| Model | national geologic mapping reauthorization act of 1996 - amends the national geologic mapping act of 1992 to establish a national cooperative geologic mapping program within the united states geological survey (usgs) to be administered and administered through the association. establishes a national cooperative geologic mapping program between the united states geological survey and the association. authorizes appropriations. |
| Metrics | Rouge1: 74.14, Rouge2: 56.14, RougeL: 65.52, RougeLsum: 67.24, Summary length (tokens): 69 |

Table 8: Examples of the BillSum dataset using the model billsum-1024-128 small diverse

| Bottom 5% example (Sorted by rougeL) | |
|---|---|
| Document | SECTION 1. NATIONAL GUARD SUPPORT FOR BORDER CONTROL ACTIVITIES.<br>(a) Operation Jump Start.– (1) In general.–Not fewer than 6,000 National Guard personnel shall continue to be deployed along the international border between the United States and Mexico under Operation Jump Start until the date on which the Federal Government has achieved operational control of such border (as defined in section 2(b) of the Secure Fence Act of 2006 (Public Law 109- 367)). (2) Exemption.–National Guard personnel deployed pursuant to paragraph (1) shall not be included in the calculation to determine compliance with– (A) limits on end strength; or (B) limits on the number of National Guard personal that may be placed on active duty for operational support. (b) Support Authorized.–Chapter 1 of title 32, United States Code, is amended by inserting after section 112 the following: "Sec. 112a. Border control activities "(a) Funding Assistance.–The Secretary of Defense may provide funds to the Governor of a State who submits to the Secretary a State border control activities plan satisfying the requirements of subsection (c). Such funds shall be used for the following: "(1) The pay, allowances, clothing, subsistence, gratuities, travel, and related expenses, as authorized by State law, of personnel of the National Guard of that State used, while not in Federal service, for the purpose of border control activities. "(2) The operation and maintenance of the equipment and facilities of the National Guard of that State used for the purpose of border control activities. "(3) The procurement of services and equipment, and the leasing of equipment, for the National Guard of that State used for the purpose of border control activities. However, the use of such funds for the procurement of equipment may not exceed $5,000 per item, unless approval for procurement of equipment in excess of that amount is granted in advance by the Secretary of Defense. "(b) Use of Personnel Performing Full-Time National Guard Duty.– (1) Under regulations prescribed by the Secretary of Defense, personnel of the National Guard of a State may, in accordance with the State... |
| Gold | Provides for continued National Guard support for border control activities along the U.S.- Mexico border under Operation Jump Start until operational control of such border has been achieved.<br>Authorizes the Secretary of Defense to provide funding to a state that submits to the Secretary of State a state border control activities plan that meets certain requirements. Limits the number of National Guard that may be so deployed. |
| Model | (this measure has not been amended since it was passed by the senate on december 21, 2011. the summary of that version is repeated here.)<br>states that not fewer than six,000, national guard personnel shall continue to be deployed along the international border between the united states and mexico under operation jump start up to six,000 shall not be included in the annual calculation to determine compliance with: (1) limits on end strength or limits on the number of national guard personal that may be placed on active duty for operational support; and (2) the pay, allowances, and benefits of the national guard of a state shall |
| Metrics | Rouge1: 46.33, Rouge2: 14.86, RougeL: 22.6, RougeLsum: 32.77, Summary length (tokens): 129 |
| **Bottom 25% example (Sorted by rougeL)** | |
| Document | SECTION 1. SHORT TITLE.<br>This Act may be cited as the "International Commerce Enhancement Act".<br>SEC. 2. REFERENCES.<br>Except as otherwise specifically provided in this Act, whenever in this Act an amendment or repeal is expressed as the amendment or repeal of a section or other provision, the reference shall be considered to be made to a section or other provision of the Arms Export Control Act (22 U.S.C. 2751 et seq.).<br>SEC. 3. FOREIGN AND NATIONAL SECURITY POLICY OBJECTIVES AND RESTRAINTS.<br>(a) Value of Defense Articles and Services.–Section 3(d) (22 U.S.C. 2753(d)) is amended in paragraphs (1) and (3)(A)– (1) by striking "$14,000,000" each place it appears and inserting "$25,000,000"; and (2) by striking "$50,000,000" each place it appears and inserting "$85,000,000". (b) Transfers With Respect to NATO and Major Non-NATO Countries.– Section 3(d) (22 U.S.C. 2753(d)) is amended– (1) in paragraph (2)– (A) in subparagraph (A), by striking "Except as provided in subparagraph (B), unless" and inserting "Unless"; and (ii) in subparagraph (B) to read as follows: "(B) Subparagraph (A) shall not apply in the case of a proposed transfer to the North Atlantic Treaty Organization, or any member country of such Organization, Japan, Australia, or New Zealand."; and (iii) in subparagraph (C), by striking "or (B)"; and (2) in paragraph (3)– (A) in the second sentence of subparagraph (A), by striking "shall be submitted" and all that follows through "unless the President" and inserting "shall be submitted at least 30 calendar days before such consent is given in the case of a transfer to a country other than a country which is a member of the North Atlantic Treaty Organization, Japan, Australia, or New Zealand, unless the President"; (B) in the third sentence of subparagraph (A), by striking "(thus waiving the requirements of clause (i) or (ii), as the case may be, and of subparagraph (B))"; and (C) in subparagraph (B)– (i) by striking ... |
| Gold | International Commerce Enhancement Act - Amends the Arms Export Control Act to increase threshold values of major defense equipment or defense articles or related training or other defense services whose transfer or lease to foreign countries would require a presidential certification to Congress. Exempts from specified congressional oversight requirements any such transfers to North Atlantic Treaty Organization (NATO) countries, Japan, Australia, or New Zealand. |
| Model | international commerce enhancement act - amends the arms export control act to: (1) increase the amount of defense articles and services from $10 million to $10 million to $10 million the value of defense articles and services (currently, $10 million); (2) prohibit the transfer of defense articles or services to the north atlantic treaty organization (nato); and (3) prohibit the transfer of defense articles or services from the north atlantic treaty organization (nato) defense articles or services.<br>repeals the requirement that the transfer of defense articles or services from defense articles or services from the north atlantic treaty (nato) |
| Metrics | Rouge1: 44.72, Rouge2: 21.38, RougeL: 34.78, RougeLsum: 38.51, Summary length (tokens): 129 |
| **Top 75% example (Sorted by rougeL)** | |
| Document | SECTION 1. SHORT TITLE.<br>This Act may be cited as the "Family Education Reimbursement Act of 2005".<br>SEC. 2. FAMILY EDUCATION REIMBURSEMENT ACCOUNTS.<br>(a) Establishment.–The Secretary of Education, in consultation with the Secretary of Health and Human Services, shall– (1) establish a Family Education Reimbursement Account Program under which, at the direction of the parent of each displaced student who signs up under subsection (d), the Secretary provides reimbursement to enable the student or preschool-age child to attend the school or preschool program of his or her parent's choice during the 2005-2006 school year; (2) of the amount available to carry out this section for fiscal year 2006, use not more than one third of one percent of such amount for administrative expenses, including outreach, support services, and dissemination of information; and (3) contract with a nongovernmental entity to administer and operate the program. (b) Reimbursement.– (1) In general.–In carrying out this section, the Secretary– (A) shall allow the parent of the participating displaced student to select the school or preschool program to be attended by the student during the 2005- 2006 school year; (B) at the direction of the parent, shall provide reimbursement to that school or preschool program on a quarterly basis; and (C) in the case of a public school, may provide such reimbursement to the appropriate local fiscal agent for the school. (2) Amount.–In providing reimbursement under paragraph (1), the Secretary shall– (A) determine the amount of reimbursement to a school or preschool program based on the number of weeks during which the participating displaced student attended the school or preschool program during the preceding quarter; (B) subject to subparagraph (C), provide the same amount of reimbursement to each school and preschool program for each week of attendance by one participating displaced student; (C) not provide reimbursement... |
| Gold | Family Education Reimbursement Act of 2005 - Directs the Secretary of Education to establish a Family Education Reimbursement Account Program for families of students displaced by Hurricane Katrina or Hurricane Rita.<br>Provides for reimbursing parents for costs of such students or preschool-age children attending schools or preschool programs, chosen by the parents, during the 20052006 school year.<br>Requires the Secretary to make a contract with a nongovernmental entity to administer and operate the program. |
| Model | family education reimbursement act of 2005 - directs the secretary of education to establish a family education reimbursement account program under which, at the direction of the parent of each displaced student who signs up under the 2005- 2006 school year, the secretary of education shall: (1) provide reimbursement to the student or preschool child to attend the school or breakfast program of his or her parent's choice during the 2005- 2006- 2006 school year; (2) contract with a nongovernmental entity to administer and operate the program; and (3) contract with a nongovernmental entity to administer the program.<br>requires the secretary to develop and implement a web- |
| Metrics | Rouge1: 63.74, Rouge2: 44.44, RougeL: 52.75, RougeLsum: 61.54, Summary length (tokens): 129 |
| **Top 95% example (Sorted by rougeL)** | |
| Document | SECTION 1. SHORT TITLE.<br>This Act may be cited as the "Pharmaceutical Products Price Equity Act".<br>SEC. 2. FINDINGS.<br>The Congress finds the following: (1) Modern life enhancing and life sustaining drugs are the products of decades of scientific research and practice. (2) The refining and production of products by American pharmaceutical enterprises must be appropriately compensated. (3) The pricing of American pharmaceutical products varies greatly from country to country with the corporate owners of such products voluntarily assuming no losses by always selling their products above the cost of production. (4) Considering the vital life and death nature of pharmaceutical products, it is appropriate that the United States Government, in harmony with other nations belonging to the World Trade Organization, should engage in the reasonable regulation of the prices of pharmaceutical products.<br>SEC. 3. REASONABLE LIMITS ON PROFITS OF PHARMACEUTICAL PRODUCTS.<br>(a) Presidential Authority.–The President shall issue such orders and regulations, and establish such procedures and reporting requirements, as the President determines to be appropriate to ensure that no pharmaceutical product (as defined by the President in such regulation or order) is sold to any consumer in the United States at a price that is more than 6 percent above the average retail price at which such pharmaceutical product is sold in the 5 most industrialized, free-market countries, other than the United States, as determined by the President. (b) Delegation.–The President may delegate the performance of any function under this section to any officer of any Federal department or agency who has been appointed by the President, by and with the consent of the Senate. (c) Confidentiality of Information.–All information reported to or otherwise obtained by any person exercising any authority under this section which contains or relates to a trade secret or other matter referred to in section 1905 of title 18, United States Code, shall be considered confidential for purposes of that section, except that such information may be disclosed to any other officer or employee of the United States involved in carrying out this section solely for the purpose of carrying out, and enforcing compliance with, this section. (d) Subpoena Powe... |
| Gold | Pharmaceutical Products Price Equity Act - Directs the President to issue orders and regulations, and establish procedures and reporting requirements, to ensure that no pharmaceutical product is sold to any consumer in the United States at a price that is more than six percent above the average retail price at which such pharmaceutical product is sold in the five most industrialized, free-market countries, other than the United States. Sets forth enforcement and civil liability provisions. |
| Model | pharmaceutical products price equity act - directs the president to issue orders and regulations to ensure that no pharmaceutical product is sold to any consumer in the united states at a price more than six percent above the average retail price at which such product is sold in the five most industrialized, free-market countries, other than the united states. authorizes the president to delegate the performance of any such function to any federal department or agency who has been appointed by the president, by and with the consent of the senate, by and with the consent of the senate. |
| Metrics | Rouge1: 70.11, Rouge2: 63.95, RougeL: 68.97, RougeLsum: 68.97, Summary length (tokens): 113 |

Table 9: Examples of the BillSum dataset using the model billsum-1024-128 base diverse

| Bottom 5% example (Sorted by rougeL) | |
|---|---|
| Document | .–(1) For purposes of subsection (a)(2) and this subsection, the term 'joint resolution' means only a joint resolution introduced by a qualifying Member specified in paragraph (2) after the date on which the report of the President under subsection (a)(1) is received by the Congress– "(A) the matter after the resolving clause of which is as follows: 'That the Congress hereby concurs in the certification of the President relating to deployment of a National Missile Defense system as submitted to Congress pursuant to section 4(b) of the National Missile Defense Act of 1999.'; "(B) which does not have a preamble; and "(C) the title of which is as follows: 'Joint resolution relating to deployment of a National Missile Defense system.'. "(2) For purposes of this subsection, a qualifying Member described in this paragraph is– "(A) in the case of the House of Representatives, the majority leader or minority leader of the House of Representatives or a Member of the House of Representatives designated by the majority leader or minority leader; and "(B) in the case of the Senate, the majority leader or minority leader of the Senate or a Member of the Senate designated by the majority leader or minority leader. "(3) The provisions of paragraphs (3) through (8) of section 4(c) of the National Missile Defense Deployment Criteria Act of 2001 shall apply to a joint resolution under this subsection in the same manner as to a joint resolution under such section.".<br>SEC. 4. LIMITATION ON OBLIGATION OF FUNDS FOR PROCUREMENT FOR NATIONAL MISSILE DEFENSE SYSTEM.<br>(a) Limitation.–No funds appropriated to the Department of Defense for procurement may be obligated for the National Missile Defense system unless– (1) the President submits to Congress a report concerning testing of the National Missile Defense system against countermeasures that includes a certification described in subsection (b); and (2) a joint resolution concurring in the President's certification in such report is enacted as provided for in this section. (b) Presidential Certification.–A certification described in this subsection is a certification by the President that– (1) an adequate testing program for the National Missile ... |
| Gold | National Missile Defense Deployment Criteria Act of 2001 - Amends the National Missile Defense Act of 1999 to allow deployment of a national missile defense system (system) only if: (1) the system is technologically feasible; (2) system cost in relation to other Department of Defense (DOD) priorities will not lead to an overall reduction in national security by reducing resources available for other defense priorities; (3) the system will not diminish overall U.S. national security; (4) the system will not threaten to disrupt relations with U.S. nuclear allies, U.S. European allies, Russia, the People's Republic of China, and other nations; and (5) the threat of a long-range ballistic missile attack from a nation of concern is clearly demonstrated.Prohibits the President from directing DOD to deploy a system unless and until: (1) the President certifies to Congress that the above deployment conditions have been met; and (2) a joint resolution is enacted concurring in the President's certification.Prohibits DOD procurement funds from being obligated for a system unless: (1) the President certifies to Congress that adequate system tests have been undertaken to meet identified threats against countermeasures; and (2) a joint resolution is enacted concurring in the President's certification.Requires the Secretary of Defense to direct the Ballistic Missile Defense Organization to: (1) include specified system countermeasures in system ground and flight testing conducted before the system becomes operational; and (2) determine the extent to which the exoatmospheric kill vehicle and the system can reliably discriminate between warheads and such countermeasures. |
| Model | prohibits funds appropriated to the department of defense (dod) for procurement from being obligated for the national missile defense system unless the president certifies to congress that: (1) an adequate testing program for the system is in place to meet the threats identified in the report; and (2) an adequate ground and flight testing of the system has been conducted against the system that are likely to be used against the system and that other countries have or are likely to acquire. |
| Metrics | Rouge1: 40.69, Rouge2: 16.67, RougeL: 20.0, RougeLsum: 20.0, Summary length (tokens): 94 |
| **Bottom 25% example (Sorted by rougeL)** | |
| Document | TITLE I–FEDERAL AIRPORTS SECURITY ENHANCEMENT ACT<br>SEC. 101. SHORT TITLE.<br>This title may be cited as the "Federal Airports Security Enhancement Act".<br>SEC. 102. ESTABLISHMENT OF AIRPORT SECURITY COMMITTEES.<br>The Act of July 5, 1994 (49 U.S.C. 44935), is amended– (1) by striking section 44901 subparagraph (b) and inserting the following:<br>"SEC. 103. EMPLOYMENT STANDARDS AND TRAINING.".<br>(2) by striking section 44935 subparagraph (b) and inserting the following: "(a) Review and Recommendations.–The Administrator of the Federal Aviation Administration shall establish Security Committees at each airport location to be composed of representatives of the air carriers, airport operators, other interested parties and at least one representative from the Federal Protective Service, the Federal Bureau of Investigation, The Federal Aviation Administration and one member from each local jurisdiction that the airport may be located in or that may have jurisdictional authority for the airport facility. Each Airport Security Committee shall meet at least quarterly and shall make recommendations for minimum security countermeasures to the Administrator. The Federal Protective Service shall have primary responsibility for conducting on an ongoing basis security surveys and formulating recommendations to the Security Committee. The Administrator shall prescribe appropriate changes in existing procedures to improve that performance.".<br>SEC. 103. SCREENING PASSENGERS AND PROPERTY.<br>The Act of July 5, 1994 (49 U.S.C. 44935), is amended by striking section 44901, subparagraph (a), and inserting the following: "(a) General Requirements.–The Administrator of the Federal Aviation Administration shall prescribe regulations requiring screening of all passengers and property that will be carried in a cabin of an aircraft in air transportation or intrastate air transportation. The screening must take place before boarding and be carried out by a weapon detecting facility or procedure used or operated by an employee or agent of the Federal Protective Service. The Administrator– "(1) shall require that sufficient Federal Police Officers are posted at airport facilities to provide patrol duties during all hours of operations as well as supervise screening personnel; "(2) shall maintain sufficient numbers of Special Agents to provid... |
| Gold | Federal Airports Security Enhancement Act - Amends Federal aviation law to direct the Administrator of the Federal Aviation Administration (FAA) to establish at each airport a Security Committee which shall make recommendations for minimum security counter-measures. Requires the Administrator, on the basis of such recommendations, to prescribe appropriate changes to improve the performance of existing airport security procedures.Requires the screening of passengers and property that will be carried in a cabin of an aircraft to be carried out by Federal Protective Service employees or agents. (Currently, screening is carried out by employees or agents of an air carrier, interstate air carrier, or foreign air carrier).Authorizes the Administrator of the General Services Administration (GSA) to appoint police officers and special agents (currently, special policemen and nonuniformed special policemen) for the policing of all Federal buildings (including buildings under the control of the GSA). Sets forth certain additional powers of such officers and agents, including the authority to carry firearms and to police areas adjacent to Federal property.Establishes the Federal Protective Service as a separate operating service of the GSA. Calls for at least 1,000 full-time equivalent Service police officers to be assigned to areas outside of airport operations. Requires the Commissioner of the Service to prescribe minimum employment and training standards to be applied in the contracting of security personnel for the policing of buildings and areas controlled by the United States and GSA. Authorizes GSA to recover airport security costs from the FAA. |
| Model | table of contents: title i: federal airports security enhancement act title ii: miscellaneous provisions general federal airports security enhancement act - title i: federal airports security enhancement - amends the federal aviation act of 1992 to direct the administrator of the federal aviation administration (faa) to prescribe regulations requiring screening of all passengers and property that will be carried in a port of aircraft in air transportation or intrastate air transportation. (sec. 102) directs the administrator to prescribe regulations requiring screening of all passengers and property that will be carried out by the federal protective service, the federal bureau of investigation (fbi), the federal bureau of investigation (fbi), and one member from each local jurisdiction that the aircraft may be located in or that may have jurisdictional authority for the airport of an aircraft in air transportation or intrastate air transportation. (sec. 103) directs the administrator to prescribe regulations requiring screening of all passengers and property that will be carried out by a weapon detection facility or procedure used or operated by an employee or agent of the federal protective service. (sec. 103) authorizes the administrator to enter into agreements with state and local law enforcement authorities to obtain authority for, jointly with state and local law enforcement authorities. ( |
| Metrics | Rouge1: 52.44, Rouge2: 22.84, RougeL: 29.7, RougeLsum: 47.8, Summary length (tokens): 256 |
| **Top 75% example (Sorted by rougeL)** | |
| Document | SECTION 1. SHORT TITLE.<br>This Act may be cited as the "Patent and Trademark Office Authorization Act of 2002".<br>SEC. 2. AUTHORIZATION OF AMOUNTS AVAILABLE TO THE PATENT AND TRADEMARK OFFICE.<br>(a) In General.–There are authorized to be appropriated to the United States Patent and Trademark Office for salaries and necessary expenses for each of the fiscal years 2003 through 2008 an amount equal to the fees estimated by the Secretary of Commerce to be collected in each such fiscal year, respectively, under– (1) title 35, United States Code; and (2) the Act entitled "An Act to provide for the registration and protection of trademarks used in commerce, to carry out the provisions of certain international conventions, and for other purposes", approved July 5, 1946 (15 U.S.C. 1051 et seq.) (commonly referred to as the Trademark Act of 1946). (b) Estimates.–Not later than February 15, of each fiscal year, the Undersecretary of Commerce for Intellectual Property and the Director of the Patent and Trademark Office (in this Act referred to as the Director) shall submit an estimate of all fees referred to under subsection (a) to be collected in the next fiscal year to the chairman and ranking member of– (1) the Committees on Appropriations and Judiciary of the Senate; and (2) the Committees on Appropriations and Judiciary of the House of Representatives.<br>SEC. 3. ELECTRONIC FILING AND PROCESSING OF PATENT AND TRADEMARK APPLICATIONS.<br>(a) Electronic Filing and Processing.–Not later than December 1, 2004, the Director shall complete the development of an electronic system for the filing and processing of patent and trademark applications, that– (1) is user friendly; and (2) includes the necessary infrastructure to– (A) allow examiners and applicants to send all communications electronically; and (B) allow the Office to process, maintain, and search electronically the contents and history of each application. (b) Authorization of Appropriations.–Of amounts authorized under section 2, there are authorized to be appropriated to carry out subsection (a) of this section not more than $50,000,000 for each of fiscal years 2003 and 2004. Amounts made available under this subsection shall... |
| Gold | Patent and Trademark Office Authorization Act of 2002 - Authorizes appropriations to the U.S. Patent and Trademark Office for salaries and expenses for FY 2003 through 2008 in an amount equal to all patent and trademark fees estimated by the Secretary of Commerce (Secretary) to be collected in each such fiscal year.(Sec. 2) Requires the Under Secretary of Commerce for Intellectual Property and the Director of the Office (Director), by February 15 of each fiscal year, to report an estimate of all fees to be collected in the next fiscal year to the chairman and ranking member of specified congressional committees.(Sec. 3) Requires the Director, by December 1, 2004, to complete the development of an electronic system for the filing and processing of patent and trademark applications that: (1) is user friendly; and (2) includes the necessary infrastructure to allow examiners and applicants to send all communications electronically, and the Office to process, maintain, and search electronically the contents and history of each application. Authorizes appropriations for FY 2003 and 2004 for development of such system.(Sec. 4) Requires the Secretary, in each of the five calendar years following the enactment of this Act, to report to specified congressional committees on the progress made in implementing the 21st Century Strategic Plan issued on June 3, 2002, and on any amendments made to it.(Sec. 5) Amends Federal patent law to provide that previous citation by or to, or consideration by the Office of, a patent or printed publication does not preclude the existence of a substantial new question of patentability in patent reexamination proceedings.(Sec. 6) Revises requirements for appeals in inter partes reexamination proceedings to allow a third-party requester to appeal to the U.S. Court of Appeals for the Federal Circuit, or be a party to any appeal taken by the patent owner, with respect to any final decision favorable to the patentability of any original or proposed amended or new claim of the patent.Allows a third-party requester to appeal a decision of the Board of Patent Appeals and Interferences.Provides that a third-party requester in an inter partes reexamination proceeding dissatisfied with the final decision in an appeal to the Board may appeal the decision only to the U.S. Court of Appeals for the Federal Circuit. |
| Model | patent and trademark office authorization act of 2002 - authorizes appropriations to the u.s. patent and trademark office for fy 2003 through 2008. requires the director of the patent and trademark office to: (1) complete the development of an electronic system for the filing and processing of patent and trademark applications; and (2) submit an annual report to the congressional committees on progress made in implementing the 21st century strategic plan issued under the federal patent and trademark programs. |
| Metrics | Rouge1: 48.99, Rouge2: 39.86, RougeL: 44.3, RougeLsum: 48.32, Summary length (tokens): 94 |
| **Top 95% example (Sorted by rougeL)** | |
| Document | SECTION 1. SHORT TITLE.<br>This Act may be cited as the "Guidance, Understanding, and Information for Dual Eligibles (GUIDE) Act".<br>SEC. 2. FINDINGS; PURPOSE.<br>(a) Findings.–The Congress finds the following: (1) Nearly 8,800,000 Americans were eligible for benefits under the Medicare program and for medical assistance under Medicaid (dual eligible beneficiaries) in fiscal year 2005. Of these "dual eligible beneficiaries", almost 40 percent have cognitive impairments, including Alzheimer's disease, dementia, serious mental illnesses, and intellectual disabilities. Until December 31, 2005, dual eligible beneficiaries received outpatient prescription drug benefits through medical assistance under Medicaid. On January 1, 2006, drug coverage for dual eligibles switched from Medicaid to Medicare. (2) In 2008, 53 percent of dual eligible beneficiaries had medication access problems and of those, 27 percent experienced significant adverse clinical events. (3) Individuals with medication access issues experience significantly more adverse clinical events. Among dual eligible beneficiaries with mental illness who had medication access problems, 27 percent experienced significant adverse clinical events, which included emergency room visits and hospitalizations. (4) In total, over 1,000,000 dual eligible beneficiaries and low-income subsidy beneficiaries were automatically auto- enrolled to new benchmark prescription drug plans under part D of the Medicare program between 2006 and 2007. (5) Community providers are at the front line of helping the most vulnerable dual eligible beneficiaries obtain prescription drug coverage under the Medicare program and navigate complex enrollment and low-income subsidy eligibility requirements under such program. (b) Purpose.–It is the purpose of this bill to help low-income persons with cognitive impairments to enroll in and navigate the prescription drug benefit under the Medicare program by providing front line community providers who serve the population daily with financial assistance to conduct vigorous education and outreach and direct case management.<br>SEC. 3. MEDICARE PRESCRIPTION DRUG OUTREACH DEMONSTRATION PROGRAM FOR DUAL E... |
| Gold | Guidance, Understanding, and Information for Dual Eligibles (GUIDE) Act - Directs the Secretary of Health and Human Services to establish a three-year demonstration program under which the Secretary awards grants and contracts to appropriate, qualified community programs and clinics for individuals with intellectual or developmental disabilities, or certain programs under the Public Health Services Act, to employ qualified social workers and case managers to provide one-on-one counseling about benefits under part D (Voluntary Prescription Drug Benefit Program) of title XVIII (Medicare) of the Social Security Act (SSA) to a full-benefit dual eligible individual (eligible for benefits under both Medicare and SSA title XIX [Medicaid]) who has one or more mental disabilities. |
| Model | guidance, understanding, and information for dual eligible beneficiaries with intellectual or developmental disabilities act - directs the secretary of health and human services (hhs) to establish a three-year demonstration program under which the secretary awards grants and contracts to qualified community programs and clinics for individuals with intellectual or developmental disabilities or such programs to provide medicare prescription drug assistance to individuals with intellectual or developmental disabilities or such programs. |
| Metrics | Rouge1: 60.87, Rouge2: 47.25, RougeL: 58.7, RougeLsum: 58.7, Summary length (tokens): 80 |

Table 10: Examples of the BillSum dataset using the model billsum-1024-256 small diverse

| Bottom 5% example (Sorted by rougeL) | |
|---|---|
| Document | SECTION 1. SHORT TITLE.<br>This Act may be cited as the "Health Coverage Tax Credit Extension Act of 2015".<br>SEC. 2. EXTENSION AND MODIFICATION OF HEALTH COVERAGE TAX CREDIT.<br>(a) Extension.–Subparagraph (B) of section 35(b)(1) of the Internal Revenue Code of 1986 is amended by striking "before January 1, 2014" and inserting "before January 1, 2020". (b) Coordination With Credit for Coverage Under a Qualified Health Plan.–Subsection (g) of section 35 of the Internal Revenue Code of 1986 is amended– (1) by redesignating paragraph (11) as paragraph (13), and (2) by inserting after paragraph (10) the following new paragraphs: "(11) Election.– "(A) In general.–A taxpayer may elect to have this section apply for any eligible coverage month. "(B) Timing and applicability of election.–Except as the Secretary may provide– "(i) an election to have this section apply for any eligible coverage month in a taxable year shall be made not later than the due date (including extensions) for the return of tax for the taxable year, and "(ii) any election for this section to apply for an eligible coverage month shall apply for all subsequent eligible coverage months in the taxable year and, once made, shall be irrevocable with respect to such months. "(12) Coordination with premium tax credit.– "(A) In general.–An eligible coverage month to which the election under paragraph (11) applies shall not be treated as a coverage month (as defined in section 36B(c)(2)) for purposes of section 36B with respect to the taxpayer. "(B) Coordination with advance payments of premium tax credit.–In the case of a taxpayer who makes the election under paragraph (11) with respect to any eligible coverage month in a taxable year or on behalf of whom any advance payment is made under section 7527 with respect to any month in such taxable year– ... |
| Gold | Health Coverage Tax Credit Extension Act of 2015 This bill extends the tax credit for health insurance costs of a taxpayer and qualifying family members through 2019. The tax credit for health insurance costs is a refundable tax credit equal to 72.5% of the cost of qualified health coverage paid by an eligible individual [defined as an individual who is receiving a trade adjustment allowance, is eligible for the alternative trade adjustment assistance program, or is over age 55 and receives pension benefits from the Pension Benefit Guaranty Corporation (PBGC)]. The bill requires a taxpayer to make an election to have the tax credit apply for any eligible coverage month during a taxable year. An eligible coverage month is a month in which an eligible individual is covered by qualified health insurance, does not have other specified coverage, and is not imprisoned. The bill also directs the Departments of the Treasury, Health and Human Services, and Labor and the PBGC to conduct a public outreach, including on the Internet, to inform individuals eligible for the tax credit for health insurance costs on the extension of such credit and the availability of the election to claim such credit retroactively for coverage months beginning after December 31, 2013. |
| Model | health coverage tax credit extension act of 2015 this bill amends the internal revenue code, with respect to health care coverage, to: (1) extend through 2020 the tax credit for advance payments to individuals, (2) allow advance payments of advance payments of advance payments of advance payments, and (3) extend through 2018 the tax credit for advance payments of advance payments of advance payments to individuals. |
| Metrics | Rouge1: 26.37, Rouge2: 11.07, RougeL: 21.25, RougeLsum: 25.64, Summary length (tokens): 82 |
| **Bottom 25% example (Sorted by rougeL)** | |
| Document | SECTION 1. EXTENSION. (a) In General.–Chapter 5 of subtitle B of the Agricultural Marketing Act of 1946 (7 U.S.C. 1636 et seq.) is amended by adding at the end the following new section: "SEC. 260. TERMINATION OF AUTHORITY. "The authority provided by this subtitle terminates on September 30, 2010.". (b) Conforming Amendment and Extension.–Section 942 of the Livestock Mandatory Reporting Act of 1999 (7 U.S.C. 1635 note; Public Law 106-78) is amended by striking "terminate on September 30, 2005" and inserting "(other than section 911 of subtitle A and the amendments made by that section) terminate on September 30, 2010". SEC. 2. DEFINITIONS. (a) Base Market Hogs.–Section 231(4) of the Agricultural Marketing Act of 1946 (7 U.S.C. 1635i(4)) is amended to read as follows: "(4) Base market hog.–The term 'base market hog' means a barrow or gilt for which no discounts are subtracted from and no premiums are added to the base price.". (b) Boars.–Section 231(5) of such Act (7 U.S.C. 1635i(5)) is amended to read as follows: "(5) Boar.–The term 'boar' means a sexually-intact male swine.". (c) Packer of Sows and Boars.–Section 231(12) of such Act (7 U.S.C. 1635i(12)) is amended by– (1) striking subparagraph (B) and inserting the following new subparagraph: "(B) for any calendar year, the term includes only– "(i) a swine processing plant that slaughtered an average of at least 100,000 swine per year during the immediately preceding five calendar years; and "(ii) a person that slaughtered an average of at least 200,000 sows, boars, or any combination thereof, per year during the immediately preceding five calendar years; and"; and (2) in subparagraph (C)– (A) by inserting "or person" after "swine processing plant"; (B) by inserting "or person" after "plant capacity of the processing plant"; and (C) by inserting "or person" after "determining whether the processing plant". SEC. 3. REPORTING; BARROWS AND GILTS. Section 232(c) of the Agricultural Marketing Act of 1946 (7 U.S.C. 1635j(c)) is amended to read as follows: "(c) Daily Reporting; Barrows and Gilts.– "(1) Prior day report.– "(A) In general.–The corporate officers or officially d... |
| Gold | Amends the Agricultural Marketing Act of 1946 to extend the provisions of the Livestock Mandatory Price Reporting Act of 1999 through September 30, 2010.<br>Amends swine price reporting provisions. |
| Model | amends the agricultural marketing act of 1946 to terminate the authority of the secretary of agriculture (usda) to: (1) livestock processing plant processing plant slaughter, and (2) slaughtering plant slaughter.<br>amends the agricultural marketing act of 1946 to: (1) revise minimum reporting requirements; and (2) revise reporting requirements.<br>amends the agricultural marketing act of 1946 and the agricultural marketing act of 1946 to: (1) revise reporting requirements; and (2) revise reporting requirements. |
| Metrics | Rouge1: 33.66, Rouge2: 18.18, RougeL: 31.68, RougeLsum: 29.7, Summary length (tokens): 105 |
| **Top 75% example (Sorted by rougeL)** | |
| Document | SECTION 1. SHORT TITLE.<br>This Act may be cited as the "Maritime Administration Authorization Act for Fiscal Year 2001".<br>SEC. 2. AUTHORIZATION OF APPROPRIATIONS FOR FISCAL YEAR 2001.<br>Funds are hereby authorized to be appropriated, as Appropriations Acts may provide, for the use of the Department of Transportation for the Maritime Administration as follows: (1) For expenses necessary for operations and training activities, not to exceed $80,240,000 for the fiscal year ending September 30, 2001. (2) For the costs, as defined in section 502 of the Federal Credit Reform Act of 1990, of guaranteed loans authorized by title XI of the Merchant Marine Act, 1936 (46 U.S.C. App. 1271 et seq.), $50,000,000, to be available until expended. In addition, for administrative expenses related to loan guarantee commitments under title XI of that Act, $4,179,000.<br>SEC. 3. AMENDMENTS TO TITLE IX OF THE MERCHANT MARINE ACT, 1936.<br>(a) Title IX of the Merchant Marine Act, 1936 (46 U.S.C. App. 101 et seq.) is amended by adding at the end thereof the following:<br>"SEC. 910. DOCUMENTATION OF CERTAIN DRY CARGO VESSELS.<br>"(a) In General.–The restrictions of section 901(b)(1) of this Act concerning a vessel built in a foreign country shall not apply to a newly constructed drybulk or breakbulk vessel over 7,500 deadweight tons that has been delivered from a foreign shipyard or contracted for construction in a foreign shipyard before the earlier of– "(1) the date that is 1 year after the date of enactment of the Maritime Administration Authorization Act for Fiscal Year 2001; or "(2) the effective date of the OECD Shipbuilding Trade Agreement Act. "(b) Compliance With Certain U.S.-Build Requirements.–A vessel timely contracted for or delivered pursuant to this section and documented under the laws of the United States shall be deemed to have been United-States built for purposes of sections 901(b) and 901b of this Act if– "(1) following delivery by a foreign shipyard, the vessel has any additional shipyard work necessary to receive its initial Coast Guard certificate of inspection performed in a United States shipyard; "(2) the vessel is not documented in another country before being documented under the laws of the United States; "(3)... |
| Gold | (Sec. 3) Amends the Merchant Marine Act, 1936 to declare that certain restrictions concerning a vessel built in a foreign country shall not apply to a newly constructed drybulk or breakbulk vessel over 7,500 deadweight tons that has been delivered from a foreign shipyard or contracted for construction in a foreign shipyard before the earlier of two specified dates. Deems U.S.-built any vessel timely contracted for or delivered and documented under U.S. law, if certain conditions are met. (Sec. 4) Directs the Secretary of State, in coordination with the Secretary of Transportation, to initiate discussions in all appropriate international forums to establish an international standard for the scrapping of vessels in a safe and environmentally sound manner. Directs the Secretary of Transportation to develop, and report to specified congressional committees on, a program for the scrapping of obsolete National Defense Reserve Fleet Vessels. Amends the National Maritime Heritage Act of 1994 to extend, through September 30, 2006, the authority of the Secretary to dispose of certain vessels in the National Defense Reserve Fleet. Requires that such vessels be disposed of in the most cost effective manner to the United States, taking into account the need for disposal, the environment, and safety concerns. Amends Federal law to authorize the expenditure of funds from the National Defense Sealift Fund for costs related to the scrapping of National Defense Reserve Fleet vessels. Names vessels in the National Defense Reserve Fleet that may be scrapped in the United States or a foreign country. (Sec. 5) Requires the Maritime Administration (in its annual report to Congress and its estimated annual budget) to state separately the amount, source, intended use, and nature of any funds (other than funds appropriated to the Administration or to the Secretary for use by the Administration) administered, or subject to oversight, by the Administration. (Sec. 6) Amends Federal maritime law to authorize the Secretary of Transportation to make a grant to a National Maritime Enhancement Institute for maritime and maritime intermodal research as if the Institute were a university transportation center. (Sec. 7) Directs the Secretary to study maritime research and technology development, and report the results, including any recommendations, to Congress. Authorizes appropriations. (Sec. 8) Authorizes the Secretary to convey all right, title, and U.S. interest in the U.S.S. GLACIER (formerly of the National Defense Reserve Fleet) to the Glacier Society, Inc., Bridgeport, Connecticut. |
| Model | maritime administration authorization act for fiscal year 2001 - authorizes appropriations for the department of transportation (dot) for fy 2001 for: (1) operations and training activities; (2) training activities; and (3) administrative expenses.amends the merchant marine act, 1936 to make appropriations for fy 2001 through 2001 for the maritime administration.amends the merchant marine act, 1936 to apply certain restrictions concerning a vessel located in a foreign country to a newly constructed dry or breakable vessel over seven,500 feet that has been delivered from a foreign shipyard or contracted for construction in a foreign shipyard before the earlier of: (1) one year after enactment of this act, or (2) the effective date of the international maritime administration act. directs the secretary of state in coordination with the secretary of transportation to initiate discussions in all appropriate international forums in order to establish an international standard for the scrapping of vessels in a safe and environmentally sound manner. directs the secretary of state to initiate discussions in all appropriate international forums to establish an international standard for the scrapping of vessels in a safe and environmentally sound manner. |
| Metrics | Rouge1: 61.19, Rouge2: 41.5, RougeL: 47.76, RougeLsum: 57.21, Summary length (tokens): 222 |
| **Top 95% example (Sorted by rougeL)** | |
| Document | SECTION 1. SMALL BUSINESS EXPENSING PROVISIONS MADE PERMANENT.<br>(a) Increase in Small Business Expensing Made Permanent.– (1) In general.–Subsection (b) of section 179 of the Internal Revenue Code of 1986 (relating to limitations) is amended– (A) by striking "$25,000 ($125,000 in the case of taxable years beginning after 2006 and before 2011)" in paragraph (1) and inserting "$500,000", and (B) by striking "$200,000 ($500,000 in the case of taxable years beginning after 2006 and before 2011)" in paragraph (2) and inserting "$1,000,000". (2) Conforming amendment.–Section 179(b) of such Code is amended by striking paragraph (7). (b) Expensing for Computer Software Made Permanent.–Clause (ii) of section 179(d)(1)(A) of such Code is amended by striking "and which is placed in service in a taxable year beginning after 2002 and before 2011,". (c) Inflation Adjustment.– (1) So much of subparagraph (A) of section 179(b)(5) of such Code as precedes clause (i) thereof is amended to read as follows: "(A) In general.–In the case of any taxable year beginning in a calendar year after 2009, the $500,000 and $1,00,000 amounts in paragraphs (1) and (2) shall each be increased by an amount equal to–". (2) Section 179(b)(5)(A)(ii) of such Code is amended by striking "2006" and inserting "2008". (d) Effective Date.–The amendments made by this section shall apply to taxable years ending after the date of the enactment of this Act.<br>SEC. 2. DEDUCTION FOR PURCHASE OF DOMESTICALLY MANUFACTURED AUTOMOBILES.<br>(a) In General.–Part VII of subchapter B of chapter 1 of the Internal Revenue Code of 1986 (relating to additional itemized deductions for individuals) is amended by redesignating section 224 as section 225 and by inserting after section 223 the following new section:<br>"SEC. 224. DEDUCTION FOR PURCHASE OF DOMESTICALLY MANUFACTURED AUTOMOBILES.<br>"(a) Allowance of Deduction.–In the case of an individual, there shall be allowed as a deduction an amount equal to the cost of any qualified automobile placed in service by the taxpayer during the taxable year. "(b) Limitation Per Vehicle.–The amount of the ded... |
| Gold | Amends the Internal Revenue Code to: (1) increase and make permanent the expensing allowance for depreciable business assets; and (2) allow a tax deduction, up to $10,000, for the purchase of a motor vehicle manufactured in the United States. Terminates such tax deduction after 2010. |
| Model | amends the internal revenue code to make permanent: (1) the increased expensing allowance for depreciable business assets; and (2) the tax deduction for the purchase of manufactured manufactured automobiles. |
| Metrics | Rouge1: 72.0, Rouge2: 46.58, RougeL: 64.0, RougeLsum: 64.0, Summary length (tokens): 40 |

Table 11: Examples of the BillSum dataset using the model billsum-1024-256 base diverse

| Bottom 5% example (Sorted by rougeL) | |
|---|---|
| Document | SECTION 1. SHORT TITLE.<br>This Act may be cited as the "Public Health Equity Act".<br>SEC. 2. FINDINGS.<br>Congress finds that– (1) all communities and individuals are entitled to protection from occupational and other exposure to substances that are hazardous to the public health; (2) hazardous substances have had a disproportionate impact on the public health of poor and ethnic minority communities and individuals, resulting in exclusion from participation in, denial of benefits under, and discrimination under, programs and activities receiving Federal financial assistance; and (3) each Federal agency has an obligation to ensure that all federally assisted programs and activities that affect human health do not directly or through contractual arrangements use criteria, methods, or practices that cause discrimination on the ground of race, color, or national origin.<br>SEC. 3. PUBLIC HEALTH EQUITY.<br>The Public Health Service Act (42 U.S.C. 201 et seq.) is amended by adding at the end thereof the following new title:<br>"TITLE XXVII–PUBLIC HEALTH EQUITY<br>"SEC. 2701. DEFINITIONS.<br>"As used in this title: "(1) Activity; program.–The term 'program or activity' means any operation of– "(A)(i) a department, agency, special purpose district, or other instrumentality of a State or of a local government; or "(ii) the entity of such State or local government that distributes such assistance and each such department or agency (and each other State or local government entity) to which the assistance is extended, in the case of assistance to a State or local government; "(B)(i) a college, university, or other postsecondary institution, or a public system of higher education; or "(ii) a local educational agency (as defined in section 198(a)(10) of the Elementary and Secondary Education Act of 1965), system of vocational education, or other school system; "(C)(i) an entire corporation, partnership, or other private organization, or an entire sole ... |
| Gold | Public Health Equity Act - Amends the Public Health Service Act to add a new title, title XXVII: Public Health Equity. Prohibits, under such title, acts with discriminatory effect as well as intentionally discriminatory acts that result in disproportionate exposure to a covered substance on the basis of race, color, or national origin. Defines a covered substance to include certain hazardous materials, substances, contaminants, or chemicals listed, identified, or defined in specified laws. |
| Model | public health equity act - amends the public health service act to require the president to ensure that no person shall be excluded from participation in, be denied the benefits of, or being subject to discrimination under, any program or activity on the ground of race, color, or national origin.<br>requires the president to ensure that no person shall be excluded from participation in, be denied the benefits of, or being subject to discrimination under, any program or activity on the ground of race, color, or national origin.<br>requires the secretaries of labor, health and human services, the administrator of the health and human services, the administrator, and any other head of a federal agency with responsibility for providing federal financial assistance to a program or activity to issue regulations implementing such nondiscrimination requirements.<br>requires such regulations to: (1) declare that no person shall be excluded from participation in, be denied the benefits of, or be subject to discrimination under, any program or activity on the ground of race, color, or national origin; and (2) address actions of programs or activities that result in disproportionate exposure to a covered substance on the basis of race, color, or national origin. |
| Metrics | Rouge1: 28.89, Rouge2: 20.15, RougeL: 22.96, RougeLsum: 26.67, Summary length (tokens): 239 |
| **Bottom 25% example (Sorted by rougeL)** | |
| Document | SECTION 1. SHORT TITLE; REFERENCES TO TITLE 38, UNITED STATES CODE.<br>(a) Short Title.–This Act may be cited as the "Veterans Programs Improvement Act of 2003". (b) References.–Except as otherwise expressly provided, wherever in this Act an amendment is expressed in terms of an amendment to a section or other provision, the reference shall be considered to be made to a section or other provision of title 38, United States Code.<br>SEC. 2. INCREASE IN RATES OF DISABILITY COMPENSATION AND DEPENDENCY AND INDEMNITY COMPENSATION.<br>(a) Rate Adjustment.–The Secretary of Veterans Affairs shall, effective on December 1, 2003, increase the dollar amounts in effect for the payment of disability compensation and dependency and indemnity compensation by the Secretary, as specified in subsection (b). (b) Amounts To Be Increased.–The dollar amounts to be increased pursuant to subsection (a) are the following: (1) Compensation.–Each of the dollar amounts in effect under section 1114. (2) Additional compensation for dependents.–Each of the dollar amounts in effect under section 1115(1). (3) Clothing allowance.–The dollar amount in effect under section 1162. (4) New dic rates.–Each of the dollar amounts in effect under paragraphs (1) and (2) of section 1311(a). (5) Old dic rates.–Each of the dollar amounts in effect under section 1311(a)(3). (6) Additional dic for surviving spouses with minor children.–The dollar amount in effect under section 1311(b); (7) Additional dic for disability.–Each of the dollar amounts in effect under subsections (c) and (d) of section 1311. (8) DIC for dependent children.–Each of the dollar amounts in effect under sections 1313(a) and 1314. (c) Determination of Increase.– (1) The increase under subsection (a) shall be made in the dollar amounts specified in subsection (b) as in effect on November 30, 2003. (2) Except as provided in paragraph (3), each such amount shall be increased by the same percentage as the percentage by which benefit amounts payable under title II of the Social Security Act (42 U.S.C. 401 et seq.) are increased effective December 1, 2003, as a result of a determination under section 215(i) of such Act (42 U.S.C... |
| Gold | Veterans Programs Improvement Act of 2003 - Directs the Secretary of Veterans Affairs to increase, as of December 1, 2003, the rates of veterans' disability compensation, additional compensation for dependents, the clothing allowance for certain disabled adult children, and dependency and indemnity compensation for surviving spouses and children.<br>Makes the effective date for the award of death pension the same as that for the award of death compensation or dependency and indemnity compensation.<br>Excludes lump-sum insurance proceeds from income for purposes of eligibility for veterans' pensions.<br>Prohibits the payment of veterans' disability compensation for an alcohol- or drug-abuse related disability even if the the alcohol or drug abuse is secondary to a service-connected disability.<br>Provides alternative beneficiaries for National Service Life Insurance and United States Government Life Insurance proceeds when the first beneficiary does not make a claim.<br>Provides burial benefit eligibility for a veteran's surviving spouse who remarries following the veteran's death.<br>Makes permanent the authority for the State cemetery grants program.<br>Repeals the Department of Veterans Affairs Education Loan program.<br>Includes self-employment training under the Montgomery GI Bill. |
| Model | veterans programs improvement act of 2003 - directs the secretary of veterans affairs, effective on december 1, 2003, to increase the rates of disability and dependency and indemnity compensation (dic) through the department of veterans affairs (va), to: (1) increase the rates of disability compensation and dependency and indemnity compensation; (2) provide for additional compensation for dependents; (3) provide for additional compensation for dependents; (4) exclude lump-sum sales of any life insurance policy or policies on a veteran for purposes of pension benefits; (5) exclude lump-sum sales of any life insurance policy or policies on a veteran for purposes of pension benefits; (6) exclude lump-sum life insurance proceeds from the determinations of annual income for pension purposes; (7) provide for alternative beneficiaries for certain veterans' life insurance policies or policies on a veteran's service-connected disability; and (8) authorize the secretary to approve a program of self-employment on-employment in the department of veterans affairs education loan program.amends the veterans' advisory committee on education to: (1) repeal the requirement that a claimant and the claimant's representative is necessary to complete an application is not received by the secretary within one year from the date of such notification; (2) make permanent the same authority for state cemetery grants program; and (3) authorize the secretary to approve a program of self-employment on-employment in the department of america known as the department of veterans affairs. |
| Metrics | Rouge1: 60.71, Rouge2: 29.79, RougeL: 33.88, RougeLsum: 50.82, Summary length (tokens): 297 |
| **Top 75% example (Sorted by rougeL)** | |
| Document | SECTION 1. SHORT TITLE.<br>This Act may be cited as the "Cameron Gulbransen Kids and Cars Safety Act of 2003".<br>SEC. 2. EVALUATION OF DEVICES AND TECHNOLOGY TO REDUCE CHILD INJURY AND DEATH FROM PARKED OR UNATTENDED MOTOR VEHICLES.<br>(a) In General.–The Secretary of Transportation shall evaluate– (1) devices and technologies intended to reduce the incidence of child injury and child death occurring outside of parked motor vehicles in nontraffic, noncrash events, including backing-over incidents, that are caused by such vehicles, and determining which of those methods is the most effective; and (2) currently available technology to prevent injury and death of children left unattended inside of parked motor vehicles, including injury or death due to hyperthermia, power windows, or power sunroofs. (b) Report.–The Secretary of Transportation shall submit a report on the findings and determinations of the evaluation under this section to the Congress by not later than one year after the date of the enactment of this Act. (c) Completion of Rulemaking Regarding Power Windows.–The Secretary of Transportation shall by not later than 6 months after the submission of the report under subsection (b) complete any rulemaking begun before the date of the enactment of this Act regarding power windows and power window switches.<br>SEC. 3. DATABASE FOR TRACKING THE NUMBER AND TYPES OF INJURIES AND DEATHS IN NONTRAFFIC, NONCRASH EVENTS.<br>(a) Establishment.–The Secretary of Transportation shall establish a database of (or modify an existing database to include), and collect data regarding, the numbers and types of injuries and deaths in nontraffic, noncrash events involving motor vehicles. (b) Included Information.–The Secretary of Transportation shall collect and include in such database the following information: (1) The types, makes, models, and model years of motor vehicles involved in nontraffic, noncrash events. (2) Whether there was an operator of each motor vehicle in such events. (3) The age of each operator of such motor vehicles. (4) The age of each individual who suffered injury or death in such events. (5) Whether each motor vehicle had technology installed to detect individuals and objects behind it. (6... |
| Gold | Cameron Gulbransen Kids and Cars Safety Act of 2003 - Directs the Secretary of Transportation to: (1) evaluate devices and technologies to reduce child injuries and deaths occurring outside of parked motor vehicles in non-traffic, non-crash events or inside of parked vehicles when children are left unattended; (2) establish a database of, and collect data on, the number and types of injuries and deaths in such events; (3) evaluate technologies for detecting and preventing collisions with individuals and objects behind motor vehicles; (4) prescribe safety standards to require devices for detecting individuals and objects behind motor vehicles; and (5) prescribe safety standards for power windows and power sunroofs, including requirements for child-safe switches and auto reverse technology. |
| Model | tamarisk kids and cars safety act of 2003 - directs the secretary of transportation (dot) to evaluate: (1) devices and technologies intended to reduce the incidence of child injury and death occurring inside distant motor vehicles in nontraffic, noncrash events, and determine which are the most effective; and (2) currently available technology to prevent injury and death of children left behind the motor vehicles.<br>directs the secretary to: (1) establish a database of, and collect data regarding, the number and types of injuries and deaths in nontraffic, noncrash events involving motor vehicles; and (2) prescribe motor vehicle safety standards. |
| Metrics | Rouge1: 63.59, Rouge2: 37.21, RougeL: 50.69, RougeLsum: 49.77, Summary length (tokens): 132 |
| **Top 95% example (Sorted by rougeL)** | |
| Document | SECTION 1. FINDINGS.<br>The Congress finds the following: (1) As a Member of Congress from the Tenth Congressional District of Texas, as Majority Leader of the U.S. Senate, Vice- President and President of the United States, Lyndon Baines Johnson's accomplishments in the fields of civil rights, education, and economic opportunity rank among the greatest achievements of the past half century. (2) As President, Lyndon Johnson proposed, championed, led to passage, and signed into law on August 6, 1965, the Voting Rights Act of 1965, which swept away barriers impeding millions of Americans from meaningful participation in American political life. (3) On July 30, 1965, President Johnson signed into law the Social Security Amendments Act of 1965, popularly known as Medicare, which has transformed the delivery of health care in the United States and which, along with Social Security, reduced the rate of poverty among the elderly from 28.5 percent in 1966 to 9.1 percent in 2012. (4) On July 2, 1964, President Johnson secured passage and signed into law the most sweeping civil rights legislation since Reconstruction, the Civil Rights Act of 1964, which prohibits discrimination in employment, education, and public accommodations based on race, color, religion, or national origin. (5) On November 8, 1965, President Johnson signed into law the Higher Education Act, which provided need-based financial aid to students in the form of scholarships, work-study grants, and loans, and thus made higher education more accessible to populations of persons who were previously unable to attend college because of economic circumstances. (6) On October 3, 1965, President Johnson signed into law the Immigration and Naturalization Act of 1965, which transformed the Nation's immigration system by abolishing the racially based quota system that had defined American immigration policy for four decades and replaced it with a policy whose central purpose was family reunification, with a preference for immigrants with specific skill sets. (7) According to Robert A. Caro, the preeminent biographer of Lyndon Baines Johnson, with the s... |
| Gold | This bill directs the Speaker of the House and the President pro tempore of the Senate to arrange for the posthumous award of a Congressional Gold Medal to Lyndon Baines Johnson in recognition of his contributions to the nation, including passage of the Voting Rights Act of 1965, the Social Security Amendments Act (Medicare) of 1965, the Civil Rights Act of 1964, the Higher Education Act of 1965, and the Immigration and Naturalization Act of 1965. Requires such medal to be given to the Lyndon Baines Johnson Library and Museum following its award, where it will be available for display and research. |
| Model | this bill directs the speaker of the house of representatives and the president pro tempore of the senate to arrange for the posthumous award, on behalf of congress, of a gold medal to lyrics to lyrics in recognition of his contributions to the nation, including recognition of his contributions to the nation, including recognition of the landmark voting rights act of 1965, the civil rights act of 1964, the higher education act of 1965, and the immigration and naturalization act of 1965. |
| Metrics | Rouge1: 72.83, Rouge2: 62.64, RougeL: 68.48, RougeLsum: 68.48, Summary length (tokens): 97 |

Table 12: Examples of the BillSum dataset using the model billsum-4096-1024 base diverse

| | |
|---|---|
| Bottom 5% example (Sorted by rougeL) | |
| Document | in the last decade the amount of data regarding micrornas ( mirs ) and their target genes described in the literature has expanded tremendously . the volume of information on this new group of regulators ( i.e. , mirs ) has complicated attempts to integrate this data within existing metabolic and signalling networks . as regulators of gene expression in addition , a single mir can potentially regulate multiple different genes at the same time , leading to complex functional outcomes . however , from another perspective , the identification of groups of genes targeted by the same mir and the clustering of these genes within individual signalling pathways represents a means to understand the cross talk between multiple signalling networks and their role in a common biological process . the focus of this review is to summarize the validated groups of mirs functionally linked to the cross talk between tgf- , notch , and wnt signalling during the common biological process of epithelial - to - mesenchymal transition ( emt ) . in particular , this review will address whether the documented cross talk between these three important emt - associated pathways could be further reinforced by the identification of a signature of mirs , already depicted in the literature but not yet sharpened or clearly defined in this role . in the past years , many studies have elegantly described the role of tgf- , notch , and wnt pathways in promoting emt and emt - associated disorders including fibrosis and metastatic dissemination in cancer [ 16 ] . here we identify published and validated interactions between mirs and genes involved in tgf- , notch , and wnt signalling . this led to the discovery of a signature of 30 mirs each regulating all three pathways . we then searched for additional validated genes targeted by these 30 mirs and then further clustered these into the tgf- , notch , and wnt signalling pathways . interestingly , in our attempt to identify mirs that were common to all three of these signalling pathways , we found that the 30-mir signature strongly reinforced existing evidence supporting cross talk between these three pathways during emt . in this review we used tarbase v6.0 , the largest currently available manually curated mir target gene database , which includes targets derived from specific and high throughput experiments . using tarbase v6.0 we searched the collection of manually curated , experimentally validated mir - gene intera... |
| Gold | epithelial - to - mesenchymal transition ( emt ) is a reversible process by which cancer cells can switch from a sessile epithelial phenotype to an invasive mesenchymal state . emt enables tumor cells to become invasive , intravasate , survive in the circulation , extravasate , and colonize distant sites . paracrine heterotypic stroma - derived signals as well as paracrine homotypic or autocrine signals can mediate oncogenic emt and contribute to the acquisition of stem / progenitor cell properties , expansion of cancer stem cells , development of therapy resistance , and often lethal metastatic disease . emt is regulated by a variety of stimuli that trigger specific intracellular signalling pathways . altered microrna ( mir ) expression and perturbed signalling pathways have been associated with epithelial plasticity , including oncogenic emt . in this review we analyse and describe the interaction between experimentally validated mirs and their target genes in tgf- , notch , and wnt signalling pathways . interestingly , in this process , we identified a signature of 30 experimentally validated mirs and a cluster of validated target genes that seem to mediate the cross talk between tgf- , notch , and wnt signalling networks during emt and reinforce their connection to the regulation of epithelial plasticity in health and disease . |
| Model | micrornas ( mirs ) are a class of small noncoding rnas that regulate multiple gene expression at the same time, leading to complex functional outcomes. recent studies have shown that mirs regulate multiple different pathways at the same time, leading to complex functional outcomes. however, from another perspective, the identification of genes targeted by the same mir and the clustering of these genes within individual signalling pathways represents a means to understand the cross talk between multiple signalling pathways and their role in a common biological process. in this review , we summarize the published studies of mir-, notch, and wnt signalling in |
| Metrics | Rouge1: 20.22, Rouge2: 0.0, RougeL: 11.24, RougeLsum: 14.61, Summary length (tokens): 129 |
| Bottom 25% example (Sorted by rougeL) | |
| Document | mhc class ii molecules are heterodimeric cell surface glycoproteins that bind exogenously derived antigenic peptides and present them to cd4 t cells 12 . class ii and chains are translocated into the endoplasmic reticulum ( er ) , where they form nonamers with invariant ( ii ) chain 3 . ii chain prevents the binding of immunogenic peptides due to the presence of a 14amino acid domain ( clip ) that occupies the peptide - binding groove of / dimers 3 . after ii degradation in the endocytic pathway , the mhc - encoded molecules hla - dm ( or h2-m in the mouse ) and hla - do ( h2-o ) facilitate the removal of clip from / dimers , allowing peptide binding 456 . ii chain has been implicated in functions such as er export , endosome targeting , and even b cell maturation 37 . two alternatively spliced ii isoforms exist ( p31 and p41 ) , distinguished by a 64-residue domain in the lumenal portion of p41 8 . the isoforms are expressed differently in various apcs and regulate the presentation of certain antigen epitopes in b cells 9 . this difference may reflect protease inhibition by the amino acid insertion in p41 , as it has been shown to inhibit the lysosomal cysteine protease cathepsin l both in vitro and in vivo 910 . therefore , ii chain may contribute to the modulation of the proteolysis in the endocytic pathway and thus modulate antigen processing indirectly 1112 . we demonstrate here that ii chain deletion leads to the lysosomal degradation of h2-mb in apcs , suggesting that ii chain is required to prevent the proteolysis of h2-m and perhaps of other proteins . this feature may help explain how ii chain expression affects t cell selection and b cell maturation independently from its effect on mhc class ii traffic 131415 . c57bl/6 ( control ) and ii , ii p31 1416 , class ii , and class ii / ii mice ( the gift of p. marrack , university of colorado health sciences center , denver , co ) were kept in a pathogen - free environment for 78 wk before killing . splenocytes were obtained as described 7 . bone marrow derived dendritic cells ( dcs ) were cultured as described 17 . after purification , immature dcs were characterized by immunofluorescence and processed in parallel with the lps - treated dcs . the primers used here to detect i - a , h2-m , and h2-m are identical to the primers described previously 19 . 3 10 late dcs were pulse labeled with 7.5 mci / ml of [ s]methionine translabel ( icn ) and chased as described 17 . ... |
| Gold | the association of invariant ( ii ) chain with major histocompatibility complex ( mhc ) class ii dimers is required for proper antigen presentation to t cells by antigen - presenting cells . mice lacking ii chain have severe abnormalities in class ii transport , t cell selection , and b cell maturation . we demonstrate here that h2-m , which is required for efficient class ii antigenic peptide loading , is unexpectedly downregulated in splenocytes and mature dendritic cells ( dcs ) from ii/ mice . downregulation reflects an increased rate of degradation in ii/ cells . degradation apparently occurs within lysosomes , as it is prevented by cysteine protease inhibitors such as e64 , but not by the proteasome inhibitor lactacystin . thus , ii chain may act as a lysosomal protease inhibitor in b cells and dcs , with its deletion contributing indirectly to the loss of h2-m . |
| Model | mhc class ii molecules are heterodimeric cell surface glycoproteins that bind exogenously derived antigenic peptides and present them to cd4 t cells 12. type ii chains are translocated into the endoplasmic reticulum ( er ), where they form nonamers with invariant ( ii ) chain 3. type ii chains are translocated into the endoplasmic reticulum ( er ), where they form nonamers with invariant ( ii ) chain 3. type ii chains are translocated into the endoplasmic reticulum ( er ), where |
| Metrics | Rouge1: 27.67, Rouge2: 8.92, RougeL: 17.61, RougeLsum: 25.16, Summary length (tokens): 129 |
| Top 75% example (Sorted by rougeL) | |
| Document | stroke , after myocardial infarction ( mi ) , is the second leading reason for mortality in iran as with many countries worldwide . the epidemiology of stroke has already been investigated in the american , european , african , and asian countries . no comprehensive study has yet investigated the epidemiology of stroke , particularly in mi patients , in iran , one of the largest countries in southwest asia . stroke and mi share many risk factors , most prevalent of which are smoking , dyslipidemia , type 2 diabetes , and hypertension . the risk factors for stroke and mi , especially smoking , hypertension , and dyslipidemia are highly prevalent in iran , as well . according to projections urbanism , increased life expectancy , reduction in childbirth , aging and elderly population , epidemiological changes , socioeconomic status , geographical conditions , and lifestyles such as poor diet , stress , and low mobility are the main causes of the burden of noncommunicable diseases , particularly stroke . because the determinants of stroke in different communities are various , we require knowledge about the risk factors and determinants of mortality in a community for effective planning and selection of appropriate strategies for the prevention and management of stroke and heart attack as the most important causes of death . since no comprehensive study has yet been investigated the status and mortality determinants of stroke in mi patients in iran , this study is conducted to determine and compare the determinants of mortality due to stroke in mi patients . in this retrospective cohort study , the data obtained from the mi registry of iran 's cardiovascular diseases surveillance system were analyzed . around 20,750 hospitalized patients with mi with a new presentation ( hospitalized in 540 hospitals ) between april , 2012 and march , 2013 were enrolled . the study was approved by the management center of noncommunicable diseases and the department of cardiovascular diseases prevention of iran 's ministry of health and medical education ( approval no . the research followed the principles of the declaration of helsinki ; the researchers did not conduct any interventions on the patients , and an institutional review board approved this research . the study protocol was approved by an independent scientific review committee ( at shahid beheshti university medical of sciences ) ( no . inclusion criteria were determined according to the world... |
| Gold | background : the data and determinants of mortality due to stroke in myocardial infarction ( mi ) patients are unknown . this study was conducted to evaluate the differences in risk factors for hospital mortality among mi patients with and without stroke history.materials and methods : this study was a retrospective , cohort study ; 20,750 new patients with mi from april , 2012 to march , 2013 were followed up and their data were analyzed according to having or not having the stroke history . stroke and mi were defined based on the world health organization 's definition . the data were analyzed by logistic regression in stata software.results:of the 20,750 studied patients , 4293 had stroke history . the prevalence of stroke in the studied population was derived 20.96% ( confidence interval [ ci ] 95% : 20.1321.24 ) . of the patients , 2537 ( 59.1% ) had st - elevation mi ( stemi ) . mortality ratio in patients with and without stroke was obtained 18.8% and 10.3% , respectively . the prevalence of risk factors in mi patients with and without a stroke is various . the adjusted odds ratio of mortality in patients with stroke history was derived 7.02 ( 95% ci : 5.429 ) for chest pain resistant to treatment , 2.39 ( 95% ci : 1.972.9 ) for stemi , 3.02 ( 95% ci : 2.53.64 ) for lack of thrombolytic therapy , 2.2 ( 95% ci : 1.662.91 ) for heart failure , and 2.17 ( 95% ci : 1.62.9 ) for ventricular tachycardia.conclusion:with regards to the factors associated with mortality in this study , it is particularly necessary to control the mortality in mi patients with stroke history . more emphasis should be placed on the mi patients with the previous stroke over those without in the interventions developed for prevention and treatment , and for the prevention of avoidable mortalities . |
| Model | background : stroke and myocardial infarction ( mi ) share many risk factors, most prevalent of which are smoking, dyslipidemia, type 2 diabetes, and hypertension. the aim of this study was to determine and compare the determinants of stroke in mi patients.methods:in this retrospective cohort study, the data obtained from the mi registry of iran's cardiovascular diseases surveillance system were analyzed. patients with mi were defined by the date at mi diagnosis, hospital stay, and follow - up till discharge or death ( outcome ). odds ratio ( or ) of mortality for clinical and demographic risk factors were calculated by logistic regression.results |
| Metrics | Rouge1: 55.88, Rouge2: 20.79, RougeL: 31.37, RougeLsum: 51.96, Summary length (tokens): 129 |
| Top 95% example (Sorted by rougeL) | |
| Document | stroke commonly causes loss of motor function due to weakening of upper / lower extremity muscles1 . according to ryerson2 , use the affected upper extremity decreases because of the patient s dependency on the unaffected upper extremity for normal functions , which results in problems such as learned disuse , asymmetric postural patterns , contractures , and aggravated functional restrictions involving the affected upper extremity . therefore , to improve functions of the affected upper extremity in stroke patients , measures that maximize opportunities to use the affectedupper extremity are necessary . bilateral activities have been discussed as measures to improve the body symmetry and to reduce abnormal muscle tone3 , thereby promoting voluntary movement of the affected upper extremity4 . thus far , bilateral upper extremity coordination movements have been applied in the form of bilateral single exercises utilizing tasks such as figure imitation5 , robot arm upper extremity mechanisms6 and functional stretching7 , and bilateral complex exercises combined with the principle of motor learning , such as rhythmic acoustic8 , unaffected extremity weight addition9 , and active neuromuscular electrical stimulation in stroke patients10 . most previous studies have reported the positive effects of these exercises on motor function recovery in stroke patients . whitall et al.8 reported that when chronic hemiplegia patients underwent bilateral training to push and pull upper extremity apparatuses , including acoustic signals , their upper extremity functions were improved . in a study conducted by summer et al.7 with 12 chronic stroke patients , the movement time of the patients affected side upper extremity decreased and upper extremity functions showed more improvement when they performed tasks to hold objects by stretching both hands simultaneously then when they performed tasks to hold objects by stretching only one hand . however , lee su - jin11 advised that the tasks in those studies involved mostly gross motor exercises of the upper extremity and simple repetitive training tasks , and that they were not sufficient to improve patients grasping ability to hold objects with various sizes , shapes , and weights using the shoulder , elbow , wrist , and fingers . although studies that applied diverse functional training tasks including activities of daily living to symmetric bilateral upper ... |
| Gold | [ purpose ] the purpose of this study was to investigate the effects of task - oriented bilateral arm training and repetitive bilateral arm training on upper limb function and activities of daily living in stroke patients . [ subjects ] forty patients with hemiplegia resulting from stroke were divided into a task orientied bilateral arm training group ( n=20 ) and a repetitive bilateral arm training group ( n=20 ) . [ methods ] the task - oriented group underwent bilateral arm training with 5 functional tasks , and the repetitive group underwent bilateral arm training with rhythmin auditory cueing for 30 minutes / day , 5 times / week , for 12 weeks . [ results ] the upper limb function and the ability to perform activities of daily living improved significantly in both groups . although there were significant differences between the groups , the task - oriented group showed greater improvement in upper limb function and activities of daily living . [ conclusion ] we recommend bilateral arm training as well as adding functional task training as a clinical intervention to improve upper limb function activities of daily living in patients with hemiplegia . |
| Model | [ purpose ] the purpose of this study was to compare the effects of symmetric bilateral upper extremity exercises using diverse functional training tasks with the effects of repetitive bilateral upper extremity exercises including acoustic signals on the recovery of upper extremity function and daily living activities in stroke paitents. [ subjects and methods ] forty patients with hemiplegia resulting from stroke were randomly and equally assigned to a task - oriented bilateral arm training group ( tbg : 11 males, 9 females ) and a repetitive bilateral arm training group ( rbg : 13 males, 7 females ). both groups performed their exercises for |
| Metrics | Rouge1: 62.03, Rouge2: 34.59, RougeL: 50.27, RougeLsum: 60.96, Summary length (tokens): 129 |

Table 13: Examples of the PubMed dataset using the model pubmed-1024-128 small diverse

| Bottom 5% example (Sorted by rougeL) | |
|---|---|
| Document | cdnas containing the sequence of human wt - ftl and human mutant ftl498499instc were introduced into the pet-28a(+ ) expression vector ( novagen , emd chemicals inc . ) . the cdnas were cloned between the bamhi and xhoi sites , downstream from and in - frame with the sequence encoding an n - terminal his6 tag . to eliminate the his6 tag ( included in the expression vector ) , the sequence of the vector was modified by introducing the recognition sequence for cleavage by factor xa before the coding sequence of the ferritin genes . pcr amplification of the ferritin cdnas was performed using the upstream primer f1 5-tgg atc cat cga agg tcg tat gag ctc cca gat t-3 and the downstream primer r1 5-tta tgc ctc gag ccc tat tac ttt gca agg-3. f1 contains the factor xa sequence ( underlined ) . pet-28a(+ ) carrying wt - ftl and mt - ftl cdnas was transformed into bl21 ( de3 ) escherichia coli ( invitrogen ) . transformed cells were grown in luria broth medium ( lb ) containing 30 g / ml kanamycin ( invitrogen ) at 37 c up to an absorbance of 0.91.0 at 600 nm . bacteria were induced to overexpress recombinant proteins by adding 1 mm isopropyl thio–d - galactopyranoside ( icn biotechnologies ) for 12 h at 25 c . purification of recombinant wt- and mt - ftl homopolymers cells were harvested by centrifugation and frozen at -80 c . the cell pellets were suspended in 50 mm sodium phosphate , 500 mm nacl ( ph 7.4 ) , 1 mg / ml lysozyme , and a protease inhibitor mixture ( complete , roche applied science ) for 30 min . bacteria were disrupted by sonication , and the insoluble material was removed by centrifugation at 21,000 g for 30 min . the soluble fraction was purified by nickel iminodiacetic acid affinity chromatography using an akta purifier system ( ge healthcare ) . purified protein was eluted with 250 mm imidazole in 50 mm sodium phosphate ( ph 7.4 ) , 0.5 m nacl . recombinant proteins were diluted with 50 mm tris and 10% glycerol ( v / v ) down to an absorbance of 0.5 at 280 nm , and ferritins were cleaved from the his tag by digestion with factor xa protease ( ge healthcare ) ( 5 units / mg of protein ) . after being dialyzed against 50 mm tris , ph 8.0 , for 18 h , proteins were further purified by anion exchange chromatography ( mono q ) using a linear nacl elution gradient in 50 mm tris ( ph 8) . peak fractions were 95% pure based on s... |
| Gold | nucleotide insertions in the ferritin light chain ( ftl ) polypeptide gene cause hereditary ferritinopathy , a neurodegenerative disease characterized by abnormal accumulation of ferritin and iron in the central nervous system . here we describe for the first time the protein structure and iron storage function of the ftl mutant p.phe167serfsx26 ( mt - ftl ) , which has a c terminus altered in sequence and extended in length . mt - ftl polypeptides assembled spontaneously into soluble , spherical 24-mers that were ultrastructurally indistinguishable from those of the wild type . far - uv cd showed a decrease in -helical content , and 8-anilino-1-naphthalenesulfonate fluorescence revealed the appearance of hydrophobic binding sites . near - uv cd and proteolysis studies suggested little or no structural alteration outside of the c - terminal region . in contrast to wild type , mt - ftl homopolymers precipitated at much lower iron loading , had a diminished capacity to incorporate iron , and were less thermostable . however , precipitation was significantly reversed by addition of iron chelators both in vitro and in vivo . our results reveal substantial protein conformational changes localized at the 4-fold pore of mt - ftl homopolymers and imply that the c terminus of the mt - ftl polypeptide plays an important role in ferritin solubility , stability , and iron management . we propose that the protrusion of some portion of the c terminus above the spherical shell allows it to cross - link with other mutant polypeptides through iron bridging , leading to enhanced mutant precipitation by iron . our data suggest that hereditary ferritinopathy pathogenesis is likely to result from a combination of reduction in iron storage function and enhanced toxicity associated with iron - induced ferritin aggregates . |
| Model | apoferrin is a member of the nuclear receptor superfamily family of membrane proteins. apoferrin is a member of the family of apoferrin family. apoferrin is a member of the family of apoferrin family. apoferrin is a member of the family of apoferrin family. apoferrin is a member of the family of apoferrin family. apoferrin is a member of the family of apoferrin family. apoferrin is a member of the family of |
| Metrics | Rouge1: 13.33, Rouge2: 1.35, RougeL: 12.0, RougeLsum: 12.0, Summary length (tokens): 129 |
| Bottom 25% example (Sorted by rougeL) | |
| Document | intracellular signaling pathways transmit signals of various extracellular stimuli to their cytosolic and nuclear targets in order to induce biological responses , such as proliferation , differentiation , cell death and migration . when needed , the signals are transmitted from the cytoplasm to the nucleus via translocation of one or more components of each of the signaling pathways involved . thus , after stimulation , a large number of signaling proteins are rapidly translocated to the nucleus to induce and regulate many nuclear processes . however , despite the importance of stimulated nuclear signaling , the mechanisms by which these components reach the nucleus upon stimulation have been elucidated only for a few signaling pathways . classic nuclear shuttling is mediated by an importin- complex that binds to cargoes containing a nuclear localization signal ( nls ) , consisting of mono- or bi - partite clusters of basic amino acids [ 1 - 3 ] . this importin- complex often acts as a housekeeping mechanism that shuttles most nuclear proteins immediately to the nucleus after their translation . the relocalization of cargoes is followed by the dissociation of the proteins from the importins upon binding to rangtp , which exports the importins back to the cytoplasm , while the cargo remains in the nucleus . however , only a limited number of signaling proteins , such as nfb and erk5 ( extracellular signal - regulated kinase 5 ) [ 8 - 10 ] , use this machinery for their stimulated nuclear shuttle . aside from this canonical mechanism , importin- or similar karyopherins , termed -like importins , operate by binding to non - canonical nlss to mediate translocation without the assistance of importin-. the mechanism by which these components operate is much less understood and is currently under investigation . recently , several -like importins have been implicated in the stimulated nuclear translocation of signaling proteins . here , we propose that this group of importins might be responsible for the swift nuclear shuttling of many proteins following various stimuli . the rapid and robust activation of erk1/2 allows the phosphorylation and modulation of the activity of more than 300 proteins , which are localized either in the cytoplasm or the nucleus [ 13 - 15 ] . these substrates are important for the induction and regulation of cellular processes , including proliferation , differentiation , and migration amongst others [ 16 - ... |
| Gold | classic nuclear shuttling is mediated by an importin- heterodimer that binds to cargoes containing a nuclear localization signal , and shuttles most nuclear proteins immediately after their translation . aside from this canonical mechanism , kariopheryn-s or -like importins operate by binding to non - canonical nuclear localization signals to mediate translocation without the assistance of importin-. the mechanism by which these components operate is much less understood and is currently under investigation . recently , several -like importins have been implicated in the stimulated nuclear translocation of signaling proteins . here , we propose that this group of importins might be responsible for the swift nuclear shuttling of many proteins following various stimuli . |
| Model | the nuclear translocation signal ( nl ) is a key regulator of many cellular processes, including proliferation, differentiation, cell death, migration, and migration. recent studies have shown that the nuclear translocation signal ( nl ) is required for the induction and regulation of many nuclear processes, including proliferation, differentiation, migration, and migration. here , we discuss the role of nl in the regulation of the nuclear translocation signal ( nl ), as well as the mechanisms that regulate it. |
| Metrics | Rouge1: 33.33, Rouge2: 5.0, RougeL: 18.52, RougeLsum: 32.1, Summary length (tokens): 100 |
| Top 75% example (Sorted by rougeL) | |
| Document | helicobacter pylori is a stomach bacterium that colonizes ~50% of people globally.1 h. pylori is the primary risk factor for gastric cancer the third highest cause of global cancer morbidity.2 h. pylori infection rates are highly dependent on socioeconomic status ; ~80% of those living in low socioeconomic areas of latin america , asia , and eastern europe are infected , compared with < 20% of asymptomatic caucasians in the usa.3 h. pylori infection is treatable with different regimens of antibiotics,4 and eradication of h. pylori is a recognized way to lower incidence of gastric cancer.5 however , recurrence of infection is variable.6,7 and the emergence of antibiotic resistance compromises treatment efficacy . thus , determining the best course of treatment is important to improve treatment efficacy and to reduce recurrence of h. pylori infection . unfortunately , there is no broad consensus about an optimal antibiotic therapy for the treatment of h. pylori . for example , meta - analyses of european and asian clinical data compared the standard triple therapy ( amoxicillin , clarithromycin , and a proton - pump inhibitor for 714 days ) with 5- or 10-day quadruple therapy regimens ( adding metronidazole or tinidazole to the triple therapy ) and found that quadruple therapies are both significantly more effective and cheaper than the triple therapy.810 however , we previously published a study comparing eradication therapies in seven sites of six latin american countries that showed that the 14-day triple therapy was superior to the 5-day concomitant quadruple therapy , and no different than the 10-day sequential quadruple therapy.11,12 these inconsistencies reflect localized differences in antibiotic use practices , such as the use of clarithromycin for upper respiratory infections.13 the differences in efficacy of antibiotic therapy are supported by primary antibiotic resistance data . for example , h. pylori resistance to amoxicillin varied widely between africa ( 65.6% ) , europe ( 0.5% ) , asia ( 11.6% ) , and the americas ( 2.2%).12 even in the same region , patterns of resistance differ : within central and latin america , reported average metronidazole resistance varies from 30% in argentina to 83% in columbia , and tetracycline resistance varies from 2% in brazil to 33% in columbia.14 as such , characterizing local resistance patterns is important for selecting therapies with the highest likelihood of success . our research focus... |
| Gold | objectivesgastric carcinoma is the most common cancer and cause of cancer mortality in peru . helicobacter pylori , a bacterium that colonizes the human stomach , is a group 1 carcinogen due to its causal relationship to gastric carcinoma . while eradication of h. pylori can help prevent gastric cancer , characterizing regional antibiotic resistance patterns is necessary to determine targeted treatment for each region . thus , we examined primary antibiotic resistance in clinical isolates of h. pylori in lima , peru.materials and methodsh . pylori strains were isolated from gastric biopsies of patients with histologically proven h. pylori infection . primary antibiotic resistance among isolates was examined using e - test strips . isolates were examined for the presence of the caga pathogenicity island and the vaca m1/m2 alleles via polymerase chain reaction.resultsseventy-six isolates were recovered from gastric biopsies . clinical isolates showed evidence of antibiotic resistance to 1 ( 27.6% , n=21/76 ) , 2 ( 28.9% , n=22/76 ) , or 3 antibiotics ( 40.8% ) . of 76 isolates , eight ( 10.5% ) were resistant to amoxicillin and clarithromycin , which are part of the standard triple therapy for h. pylori infection . no trends were seen between the presence of caga , vaca m1 , or vaca m2 and antibiotic resistance.conclusionthe rate of antibiotic resistance among h. pylori isolates in lima , peru , is higher than expected and presents cause for concern . to develop more targeted eradication therapies for h. pylori in peru , more research is needed to better characterize antibiotic resistance among a larger number of clinical isolates prospectively . |
| Model | helicobacter pylori infection is the third most common cause of global cancer morbidity. eradication of helicobacter pylori is a recognized way to lower incidence of gastric cancer. however, there is no broad consensus about an optimal antibiotic therapy for the treatment of helicobacter pylori. we assessed primary antibiotic resistance to helicobacter pylori among 76 isolates from a cohort of patients recruited in lima, peru. primary antibiotic resistance to metronidazole, amoxicillin, tetracycline, clarithromycin, levofloxacin, and rifamp |
| Metrics | Rouge1: 50.0, Rouge2: 17.28, RougeL: 32.93, RougeLsum: 47.56, Summary length (tokens): 129 |
| Top 95% example (Sorted by rougeL) | |
| Document | in general , brain injury can occur due to sudden and severe head strike to a hard object , which can be mild , moderate or severe ( 1 ) . the main causes of head injury include traffic accidents , falling from heights , physical violence , accidents at work , inside home accidents and during exercise incidents . however , the most important cause of head trauma in iranian population is traffic accident ( 2 ) . among the warning signs of head trauma are nausea , vomiting , dizziness , headache , blurred vision , and loss of balance , difficulty in sleeping , memory problems , tinnitus and fatigue ( 3 ) . nausea and vomiting are the most common complications after minor head trauma that in addition to severe harassment of patients increases the risk of aspiration and intracranial pressure rising . ondansetron is a serotonin 5-ht3 receptor antagonist , which connects to the peripheral and central receptors of serotonin ( 1 ) . this drug is mostly used in nausea and vomiting after chemotherapy and surgery ( 2 ) . it does not have any effect on dopamine receptors thus ; it does not have extra pyramidal effect ( 3 ) . this drug has a half - life of 2 - 7 hours and is metabolized in the liver where it changes into glucuronide and sulfate which is inactive . its most common side effects include headaches , fatigue , diarrhea , constipation , dizziness and anxiety . the recommended dose for the treatment of nausea and vomiting is 4 - 8 milligrams ( 4 , 5 ) . metoclopramide as an old antiemetic is mostly used in high doses , before chemotherapy and for nausea and vomiting caused by various reasons ( 6 - 8 ) . this drug blocks the dopamine receptors on the peripheral and central dopamine receptors and increases the movement of the upper gastrointestinal tract without increasing secretion ( 9 , 10 ) . its intravenous absorption takes about 3 minutes and the peak of its effect is about 15 minute . this drug is metabolized in the liver and its half - life is approximately 4 - 5 hours ( 11 ) . its most common side effects include dystonia < 10% , fatigue , drowsiness , and flushing . based on the above - mentioned reasons , the present study was aimed to compare the antiemetic effects of metoclopramide and ondansetron in the treatment of post head trauma nausea and vomiting . study design and setting the study was a controlled , randomized , double blind clinical trial , which was conducted in the first 6 months of 2014 in al - zahra a... |
| Gold | introduction : nausea and vomiting are the most common complications after minor head trauma that increases the risk of intracranial pressure rising . therefore , the present study was aimed to compare the antiemetic effects of metoclopramide and ondansetron in the treatment of post - traumatic nausea and vomiting . methods : the study was a controlled , randomized , double blind clinical trial , which was conducted in the first 6 months of 2014 in emergency department al - zahra and kashani hospitals in isfahan , iran . the patients with minor head trauma associated with nausea and vomiting were randomly divided into 2 groups : treatment with metoclopramide ( 10mg/2ml , slow injection ) and treatment with ondansetron ( 4mg/2ml , slow injection ) . the comparison between the 2 groups was done regarding antiemetic efficacy and side effects using spss 21 statistical software . results:120 patients with minor head trauma were distributed and studied into two groups of 60 patients ( mean age 35.614.1 years ; 50.0% male ) . administration of both ondansetron and metoclopramide significantly reduced the severity of nausea ( p<0.001 ) . changes in the severity of nausea in both groups before and after the treatment revealed that nausea had been decreased significantly in both groups ( p < 0.001 ) . the incidence of fatigue ( p=0.44 ) , headache ( p=0.58 ) and dystonia ( p=0.06 ) had no significant difference in the two groups but the incidence of drowsiness and anxiety in the metoclopramide group was significantly higher ( p < 0.001 ) . conclusion : the present study indicated that the treatment effectiveness of ondansetron and metoclopramide are similar . however , incidence of drowsiness and anxiety in the metoclopramide was considerably higher . since these complications can have adverse effects on the treatment of patients with brain injury , it is suggested that it may be better to use ondansetron in these patients . |
| Model | background : head injury can occur due to sudden and severe head strike to a hard object, which can be mild, moderate or severe. metoclopramide as an old antiemetic is mostly used in high doses, before chemotherapy and for nausea and vomiting caused by various reasons. the present study was aimed to compare the antiemetic effects of metoclopramide and ondansetron in the treatment of post head trauma nausea and vomiting. methods : this randomized, double blind clinical trial was conducted in the first 6 months of 2014 in isfahan, iran. the patients were randomly divided into |
| Metrics | Rouge1: 59.69, Rouge2: 46.56, RougeL: 51.31, RougeLsum: 58.64, Summary length (tokens): 129 |

Table 14: Examples of the PubMed dataset using the model pubmed-1024-128 base diverse

| Bottom 5% example (Sorted by rougeL) | |
|---|---|
| Document | this study is an extension of a report on patients with type 1 diabetes at children 's hospital of new orleans ( 14 ) and was approved by the institutional review board at louisiana state university health sciences center , new orleans , louisiana . glucose data were downloaded from patient meters at each clinic visit . meter model and sampling protocols varied by patient preference and insurance provider . an average of three glucose measurements per day were recorded in a study using a similar self - monitoring protocol ( 7 ) . a1c was measured by national glycohemoglobin standardization program ( ngsp)-approved immunoassays ( 15 ) at the children 's hospital ( 184 patients ) or by commercial laboratories that presumably also used ngsp - approved methods ( 18 patients , including 4 low- , 7 moderate- , and 7 high - hgi subjects ) . a population regression equation { a1c ( % ) = [ 0.021 mbg ( mg / dl ) ] + 4.3 , r = 0.57 } was derived using mean mbg and mean a1c from 202 patients collected at 1,612 clinic visits as described elsewhere ( 14 ) . the same data were used to calculate hemoglobin glycation index ( hgi ) and to divide patients into low- , moderate- , and high - hgi groups . predicted a1c values were calculated at each clinic visit by inserting mbg into the regression equation . hgi values were calculated by subtracting predicted a1c from observed a1c measured at the same clinic visit . patients were divided into low- , moderate- , and high - hgi groups based on mean hgi tertile ( 33% ) rank ( low hgi , < 0.41 , n = 67 ; moderate hgi , 0.41 to 0.26 , n = 68 ; high hgi , > 0.26 , n = 67 ) . eag was calculated by inserting observed a1c into the adag linear regression equation ( eag [ mg / dl ] = [ 28.7 a1c ( % ) ] 46.7 , r = 0.92 ) ( 1 ) . a mean blood glucose index ( mbgi ) that quantifies the difference between mbg and eag was calculated by subtracting observed mbg from eag . descriptive statistics and linear regression analyses were generated using graphpad prism v. 4.03 ( graphpad software , san diego , ca ) . glucose data were downloaded from patient meters at each clinic visit . meter model and sampling protocols varied by patient preference and insurance provider . an average of three glucose measurements per day were recorded in a study using a similar self - monitoring protocol ( 7 ) . a1c was measured by national glycohemoglobin standardization program ( ngsp)-approved immunoassays ( 15 ) at the children 's ho... |
| Gold | objectivethe a1c - derived average glucose study recommended reporting a1c in estimated average glucose ( eag ) equivalents . we compared eag with self - monitored mean blood glucose ( mbg ) to determine whether eag is systematically biased due to biological variation in the relationship between mbg and a1c.research design and methodsmbg and a1c were recorded from charts of 202 pediatric type 1 diabetic patients at 1,612 clinic visits . patients were divided into groups with low , moderate , or high a1c bias based on a hemoglobin glycation index ( hgi).resultsthe mean sd values for mbg versus eag were as follows : total population , 194 34 vs. 196 36 mg / dl ; low - hgi group , 186 31 vs. 163 20 mg / dl ; moderate - hgi group , 195 28 vs. 193 19 mg / dl ; and high - hgi group , 199 42 vs. 230 31 mg / dl.conclusionseag underestimated mbg in low hgi patients and overestimated mbg in high hgi patients . disagreement between eag and mbg downloaded from patient glucose meters will cause confusion if eag is implemented for clinical use . |
| Model | objectiveto investigate the relationship between hemoglobin glycated hemoglobin ( hba1c ), hemoglobin glycated hemoglobin ( hba1c ), and hemoglobin glycated hemoglobin ( hba1c ) in children with type 1 diabetes.research design and methodsa1c was measured by national glycohemoglobin standardization program ( ngsp)-approved immunoassays at the children's hospital of new orleans. hba1c was measured by national glycohemoglobin standardization program ( ngsp)-approved immunoassays at the children's hospital of new orleans. hba1c was measured by national glycohemoglobin standardization program ( ngsp)-approved immunoassays at the children's hospital of new orleans. a population regression equation [ a1c ( % ) = [ 0.021 mbg ( mg / dl ] + 4.3, r = 0.92 ) + 4.3, r = 0.58 ] was derived using mean hba1c ( % ). a population regression equation [ a1c ( % ) = [ 0.021 mbg ( mg / dl ] + 4.3, r = 0.92 ) + 4.3, r = 0.92 ] was |
| Metrics | Rouge1: 19.4, Rouge2: 6.06, RougeL: 10.03, RougeLsum: 13.38, Summary length (tokens): 256 |
| **Bottom 25% example (Sorted by rougeL)** | |
| Document | the principal aim of this laboratory is the synthesis of conjugated unsaturated ketones as candidate antineoplastic agents . these compounds interact with thiols but in general , they have little or no affinity for amino and hydroxyl groups which are found in nucleic acids ( 1 - 3 ) . hence thiol alkylators may not have the genotoxic properties associated with a number of contemporary anticancer drugs ( 4 ) . however after an initial chemical insult , certain neoplasms are more vulnerable to a subsequent cytotoxic effect than various non - malignant cells ( 5 , 6 ) . hence by mounting the 1,5-diaryl-3-oxo-1,4-pentadienyl pharmacophore [ ar - c = c - c(o)-c = c - ar ] on heterocyclic and cycloaliphatic scaffolds , two sequential interactions with cellular thiols can take place which may be more detrimental to tumours than normal tissues . such considerations led to the development of 3,5-bis(benzylidene)-4-piperidones 1a - d which demonstrated potent cytotoxic properties with the ic50 values in the low micromolar range against human molt 4/c8 and cem t - lymphocytes as well as murine l1210 lymphocytic leukemia cells ( 7 , 8 ) . the hypothesis of sequential cytotoxicity was advanced that the 1,5-diaryl-3-oxo-1,4-pentadienyl group interacts at a primary binding site and a side chain on the piperidine nitrogen may align at an auxiliary binding site which could enhance cytotoxic potencies . in order to evaluate this hypothesis , a novel series of n - aroyl-3,5-bis(benzylidene)-4-piperidone derivatives 2 - 7 were synthesized ( 8 ) . in these compounds , the side chain contains atoms and groups capable of forming hydrogen and van der waals bonds and also an ionic bond in series 3 - 6 which could bind at an auxiliary binding site . when the potencies of the compounds in series 3 - 6 were compared with that of the analogs 1a - d which have the same aryl substituent , the ic50 values of the amides 3 - 6 were lower in 48% of the comparisons made while equipotency was noted in 35% of the cases ( 8) . the proposed primary and auxiliary binding sites of cytotoxic n - aroyl-3,5-bis(benzylidene)-4-piperidone analogs the objectives of the present investigation are two folds . first , to gain some insight into the physicochemical properties of the 3,5-bis(benzylidene)-4-piperidone derivatives 1 - 7 that influence cytotoxic potencies , and second , to derive predictive 2d - qsar models that will be helpful to design new analogs with improved bioactivity . t... |
| Gold | 1-[4-(2-alkylaminoethoxy ) phenylcarbonyl]-3,5-bis(arylidene)-4-piperidones are a novel class of potent cytotoxic agents . these compounds demonstrate low micromolar to submicromolar ic50 values against human molt 4/c8 and cem t - lymphocytes and murine leukemia l1210 cells . in this study , a comparative qsar investigation was performed on a series of 3,5-bis ( arylidene)-4-piperidones using different chemometric tools to develop the best predictive models for further development of analogs with improved cytotoxicity . all the qsar models were validated by internal validation tests . the qsar models obtained by ga - pls method were considered the best as compared to mlr method . the best qsar model obtained by ga - pls analysis on l1210 , cem and molt4/c8 demonstrated good predictively with r2pred values ranging from 0.94 - 0.80 . molecular density , topological ( x2a ) and geometrical indices of the molecules were found to be the most important factors for determining cytotoxic properties . |
| Model | in order to evaluate the physicochemical properties of the 3,5-bis(benzylidene)-4-piperidone derivatives 1 - 7 and 2 - 7 were synthesized. the compounds 1 - 7 showed potent cytotoxic property with ic50 values of 3 - 6. the compounds 1 - 7 showed potent cytotoxic property with ic50 values of 3 - 6. the compounds 1 - 7 showed potent cytotoxic property with ic50 values of 3 - 6. the compounds 1 - 7 showed potent cytotoxic property with ic50 values of 3 - 6. the compounds 1 - 7 showed potent cytotoxic property with ic50 values of 3 - 6. the compounds 1 - 7 showed potent cytotoxic property with ic50 values of 3 - 6. the compounds 1 - 7 showed potent cytotoxic property with ic50 values of 3 - 6. the compounds 1 - 7 showed potent cytotoxic property with ic50 values of 3 - 6. the compounds 1 - 7 showed potent cytotoxic property with ic50 values of 3 - 6. |
| Metrics | Rouge1: 21.38, Rouge2: 5.06, RougeL: 16.35, RougeLsum: 16.35, Summary length (tokens): 253 |
| **Top 75% example (Sorted by rougeL)** | |
| Document | educational evaluation ( ee ) is a formal process performed to evaluate the quality of effectiveness and/or value of a program , process , goal or curriculum.12 it deals with data collection and assessment of the progress of academic programs.34 by considering some principles related to educational measurements and data collection , ee may result in a better understanding of such programs.57 during the past thirty years , theorists have presented numerous methods of evaluation . worthen and sanders2 mentioned that more than 50 different evaluation approaches has been developed in recent decades . among these , methods based on internal criteria are known as the ones that can interpret the scientific , educational , and therapeutic authenticity of different educational groups.48 this is greatly welcomed by the academic community and is widely spread to all universities in the world . that is because this method provided a scientific , appropriate , precise , timely , and valid basis regarding the interpretation of decision making system quality and programming for its promotion and development.3 such a method was successfully carried out in four medical education groups at supervisory and expansion of medical education council secretariat of ministry of health , treatment and medical education of iran in 1995.8 ee has its most effect , value , and results when it can provide needed information to individuals which are directly related , as well as those who may be benefited from its results.346 educating dental professionals consists of theoretical and practical ( clinical , paraclinical , and laboratory ) courses , differing in duration , and educational curriculum among different countries . it might vary from 4 years ( e.g. , in india , turkey , and russia ) to 6 years or more ( e.g. , in iran consisting of 2 years of only basic medical sciences and 4 + years of dentistry courses ) . due to numerous practical educational units in dentistry education and with regard to expensive but very critical protocols for infection control , a great deal of resources is consumed in governmental universities of iran over training every general practitioner with a degree of doctorate of dental surgery . on the other hand , the quality of dental services plays an important role in public health . considering these issues , dentistry education needs to be cost - effective in terms of optimizing its quality . to date , the pace of advancements in dentistry... |
| Gold | background : educational evaluation is a process which deals with data collection and assessment of academic activities progress . in this research , educational evaluation of dentistry school of tehran university of medical sciences , which trains students in undergraduate and residency courses , was studied.methods:this descriptive study was done with a model of educational evaluation in ten steps and 13 fields including purposes and mission objectives , management and organization , academic board members , students , human resources and support , educational , research , health and treatment spaces , educational , diagnostic , research and laboratory tools , educational , research , health and treatment programs and courses , process of teaching and learning , evaluation and assessment , alumni , and patients satisfaction . data were collected using observation , interviews , questionnaires , and checklists.results:results of the study were mainly qualitative and in some cases quantitative , based on defined optimal situation . the total mean of qualitative results of educational evaluation of dentistry school in all 13 fields was 55.98% which is relatively desirable . in the case of quantitative ones , results of some fields such as treatment quality of patients and education and learning of the students were relatively desirable ( 61.32% and 60.16% respectively).conclusion : according to the results , educational goals and missions , educational and research facilities and spaces which were identified as the weakest areas need to be considered and paid more serious attention . |
| Model | background : educational evaluation ( ee ) is a formal process performed to evaluate the quality of effectiveness and/or value of a program, process, goal or curriculum. it deals with data collection and assessment of the progress of academic programs. the objective of this descriptive cross - sectional study was to assess the quality of education provided at dental school of tehran university of medical sciences.materials and methods : in this descriptive cross - sectional study, the efficacy of provided educational programs provided at dental school of tehran university of medical sciences educational groups in 2010 through this descriptive cross - sectional study was assessed in 13 fields. the data were analyzed using spss version 20.results:the overall quality of education provided in 13 fields. the most important quality of education was the quality of education. the most important quality of education was the quality of education. the most important quality of education was the quality of education. the most important quality of education was the quality of education. the most important quality of education was the quality of education. the most important quality of education was the quality of education. the most important quality of education was the quality of education. the most important quality of education was the quality of education. |
| Metrics | Rouge1: 39.32, Rouge2: 12.68, RougeL: 27.67, RougeLsum: 34.47, Summary length (tokens): 256 |
| **Top 95% example (Sorted by rougeL)** | |
| Document | the study population included patients over 18 years old who had an initial cabg or combined cabg and open chest aortic valve replacement ( avr ) , from april 1 , 1998 to october 31 , 2011 in ontario . the date of first cardiac surgery was the index date , and eligible patients were followed for 1 year with respect to major outcomes , and 5 years for mortality . preoperative data were included for 1 year prior to surgery , and outcomes for 1 year postoperatively . patients for whom sex , age , height , weight were missing , and patients living outside of ontario or of unknown residence were excluded . cardiac care network of ontario ( ccn ) data were used to identify baseline characteristics such as cardiac ejection fraction , number of grafts bypassed , prior myocardial infarction ( mi ) , emergency or elective surgery , and other co - morbidities . ccn data and the following datasets were combined from ices using deterministic linkage by unique ices key number identifiers : ontario health insurance plan , canadian institute of health information ( cihi ) discharge abstract database , national ambulatory care reporting system , same day surgery , and the registered persons database . patients who had undergone either isolated cabg or combined cabg / avr were selected from the cihi discharge abstract database . data for which other cardiac procedures had been performed during the same admission were excluded ( eg , percutaneous coronary intervention or other valve procedures ) . bmi was calculated as weight ( kg)/height ( m ) , and patients were divided into groups : underweight ( bmi < 20 kg / m ) , normal weight ( bmi 20.0 to 24.9 kg / m ) , overweight ( bmi 25.0 to 29.9 kg / m ) , obese ( bmi 30.0 to 34.9 kg / m ) , and morbidly obese ( bmi > 34.9 kg / m ) , closely based on world health organization ( who ) and health canada guidelines.1214 the following comorbidities were assessed for presence within 1 year prior to index date : diabetes , smoking history ( current or ever smoked ) , peripheral vascular disease ( pvd ) , chronic obstructive pulmonary disease ( copd ) , dialysis within 1 year prior to surgery , cerebrovascular disease ( cvd ) , congestive heart failure ( chf , from cihi ) , hypertension , elective or emergent surgery , creatinine . within 30 days prior to surgery , the following cardiac characteristics were captured : ejection fraction , prior mi , left main coronary disease , and previous cabg at date o... |
| Gold | backgroundthe obesity paradox reflects an observed relationship between obesity and decreased morbidity and mortality , suggesting improved health outcomes for obese individuals . studies examining the relationship between high body mass index ( bmi ) and adverse outcomes after cardiac surgery have reported conflicting results.methods and resultsthe study population ( n=78 762 ) was comprised of adult patients who had undergone first - time coronary artery bypass ( cabg ) or combined cabg / aortic valve replacement ( avr ) surgery from april 1 , 1998 to october 31 , 2011 in ontario ( data from the institute for clinical evaluative sciences ) . perioperative outcomes and 5-year mortality among pre - defined bmi ( kg / m2 ) categories ( underweight < 20 , normal weight 20 to 24.9 , overweight 25 to 29.9 , obese 30 to 34.9 , morbidly obese > 34.9 ) were compared using bivariate analyses and cox multivariate regression analysis to investigate multiple confounders on the relationship between bmi and adverse outcomes . a reverse j - shaped curve was found between bmi and mortality with their respective hazard ratios . independent of confounding variables , 30-day , 1-year , and 5-year survival rates were highest for the obese group of patients ( 99.1% [ 95% confidence interval ( ci ) , 98.9 to 99.2 ] , 97.6% [ 95% ci , 97.3 to 97.8 ] , and 90.0% [ 95% ci , 89.5 to 90.5 ] , respectively ) , and perioperative complications lowest . underweight and morbidly obese patients had higher mortality and incidence of adverse outcomes.conclusionsoverweight and obese patients had lower mortality and adverse perioperative outcomes after cardiac surgery compared with normal weight , underweight , and morbidly obese patients . the obesity paradox was confirmed for overweight and moderately obese patients . this may impact health resource planning , shifting the focus to morbidly obese and underweight patients prior to , during , and after cardiac surgery . |
| Model | backgroundthe aim of this study was to investigate the relationship between body mass index ( bmi ) and mortality in patients undergoing coronary artery bypass grafting ( cabg ) or open chest aortic valve replacement ( avr).methods and resultswe identified 1 year patients undergoing primary cabg or combined cabg and open chest aortic valve replacement ( avr ) from april 1, 1998 to october 31, 2011. patients were divided into groups : underweight ( bmi < 20 kg / m2 ), normal weight ( bmi 25.0 to 29.9 kg / m2 ), overweight ( bmi 25.0 to 29.9 kg / m2 ), obese ( bmi 30.0 to 29.9 kg / m2 ), and morbidly obese ( bmi > 34.9 kg / m2 ). patients were followed for 1 year with respect to major outcomes, and 5 years for mortality. cox proportional hazards regression analysis was used to investigate multiple confounders on the relationship between bmi and mortality, providing hazard ratios and 95% confidence intervals ( ci ). patients with bmi < 20 kg / m2 were more likely to die during the 5 years of follow - up ( hazard ratio [ hr ] |
| Metrics | Rouge1: 56.82, Rouge2: 26.29, RougeL: 40.91, RougeLsum: 50.0, Summary length (tokens): 256 |

Table 15: Examples of the PubMed dataset using the model pubmed-4096-512 small diverse

| | |
|---|---|
| Bottom 5% example (Sorted by rougeL) | |
| Document | in august , 4 months before presentation , a 35-year - old white woman of scots and english descent developed reddish urine for several days followed by eruption of vesicles and blisters on the dorsal surfaces of her hands and fingers , the sides of her nose , and her upper anterior chest , knees , and legs . she worked as a landscaping contractor and noticed that lesions occurred on areas exposed to sunlight , but application of sunscreen neither diminished the rate at which new lesions appeared , nor promoted healing of older lesions . her skin was fragile in areas of the lesions and the lesions healed slowly , often with scarring . she also developed dark brown pigmentation and the growth of fine black hair over her cheeks . she consumed three glasses of wine each week and had smoked electronic cigarettes for approximately 6 months , having changed from tobacco cigarettes . she had donated three units of blood for transfusion , but none in several years . she had no menses in the 12 months before presentation due to the effects of a contraceptive vaginal ring ( nuvaring ; etonogestrel / ethinyl estradiol ) . a dermatologist performed a punch biopsy of two skin lesions on her left forefinger and referred her for hematology evaluation and treatment . physical examination confirmed the presence of new vesicles and bullae with erythematous bases , some as large as 1 cm in diameter , and older lesions in various stages of erosion , resolution , and scarring in the anatomical distribution described above . lesions were most prominent on the dorsal surfaces of the hands and fingers ( fig . milia were scattered over areas affected with bullous lesions and were especially prominent on skin overlying finger joints . ( a ) before therapy , there were vesicles , bullae with erythematous bases , older lesions in various stages of erosion , resolution , scarring , and punctate milia , all typical of pct . ( b ) after iron depletion with phlebotomy , there were no active skin lesions , although hyperpigmentation , scarring , and milia ( especially over dorsal aspects of second and third interphalangeal joints ) persisted . punch biopsy specimens of skin were deposited in immunofluorescence transport medium , flash frozen , and cut for manual immunofluorescence staining . the sections were probed with fluorescein - labeled anti - human antibodies specific for igg , iga , igm , c3 , c5b-9 , and fibrinogen . complete blood count ( including ... |
| Gold | porphyria cutanea tarda ( pct ) is characterized by decreased uroporphyrinogen decarboxylase activity in hepatocytes , uroporphyrin i and heptacarboxyl porphyrin iii accumulation , photosensitivity dermatitis , and increased storage iron . in women , estrogen therapy , including oral contraceptives , postmenopausal hormone replacement , and tamoxifen for breast cancer treatment , is a risk factor for pct . we report the case of a woman who presented with pct , hfe c282y homozygosity , and hepatic iron overload and was using a contraceptive vaginal ring containing ethinyl estradiol , an estrogen . we discuss this case in the context of characteristics of other persons with pct , including common hfe mutations , iron overload , and estrogen exposure . |
| Model | a 35-year - old white woman of scots and english descent developed reddish urine for several days followed by eruption of vesicles and blisters on the dorsal surfaces of her hands and fingers, the sides of her nose, and her upper anterior chest, knees, and legs. skin biopsy specimens revealed linear glassy iga and igg deposition along the epidermal basement membrane zone and superficial dermal blood vessels, forming a doughnut pattern. the patient was treated with a levonorgestrel - releasing intrauterine contraceptive system ( skyla ). eight months after presentation, she underwent implantation of a levonorgestrel - releasing intrauterine contraceptive system ( skyla ). eight months after presentation, she underwent implantation of a levonorgestrel - releasing intrauterine contraceptive system ( skyla ). |
| Metrics | Rouge1: 20.56, Rouge2: 0.94, RougeL: 11.22, RougeLsum: 17.76, Summary length (tokens): 176 |
| Bottom 25% example (Sorted by rougeL) | |
| Document | this was a multicenter , community - based , retrospective observational study of patients with pns , ranging from 8 to 20 mm in diameter , presenting to 18 geographically representative outpatient pulmonary clinics across the united states . the study was approved at 15 sites by a central institutional review board and at three sites by local institutional review board approval . four hundred forty sites were identified based on investigator databases and claims data from a large insurance carrier whose coverage population was representative of the overall us population . of these , 77 sites expressed interest in participating , and 48 sites went on to sign confidentiality agreements . of these , 17 did not request additional information , leaving 31 sites undergoing qualification review . eighteen outpatient pulmonary clinics were chosen to participate based on the following criteria : ( 1 ) management of patients with pns , ( 2 ) availability of medical records , and ( 3 ) ability to perform data abstraction . in addition , investigators targeted enrollment of geographically diverse patients to limit the potential bias associated with differences in practice patterns and to account for variation in disease prevalence ( eg , endemic mycoses ) that could alter management decisions . patients were identified by querying databases ( eg , billing and scheduling systems ) using five international classification of diseases , ninth revision , clinical modification codes for pn ( 793.1 , 786.6 , 518.89 , 519.8 , 519.9 ) to ensure homogeneity in patient identification and inclusion . manual chart abstraction was then used to identify those who met the criteria . to minimize selection bias , the sites were not permitted to use additional codes during database query to identify patients . to ensure a systematic sample , inclusion criteria included age 40 years and 89 years at the time of nodule finding , presentation to a pulmonologist , nodule size 8 to 20 mm , and definitive diagnosis ascertained by tissue diagnosis or radiographic follow - up for 2 years . exclusion criteria included chest ct scan performed > 60 days prior to the initial visit , prior diagnosis of any cancer within 2 years of nodule detection , or incomplete chart data . patients were categorized into three groups by the most invasive procedure performed during management , as follows : surveillance ( serial imaging ) , biopsy ( ct scan - guided transthoracic needle aspi... |
| Gold | background : pulmonary nodules ( pns ) are a common reason for referral to pulmonologists . the majority of data for the evaluation and management of pns is derived from studies performed in academic medical centers . little is known about the prevalence and diagnosis of pns , the use of diagnostic testing , or the management of pns by community pulmonologists.methods:this multicenter observational record review evaluated 377 patients aged 40 to 89 years referred to 18 geographically diverse community pulmonary practices for intermediate pns ( 8 - 20 mm ) . study measures included the prevalence of malignancy , procedure / test use , and nodule pretest probability of malignancy as calculated by two previously validated models . the relationship between calculated pretest probability and management decisions was evaluated.results:the prevalence of malignancy was 25% ( n = 94 ) . nearly one - half of the patients ( 46% , n = 175 ) had surveillance alone . biopsy was performed on 125 patients ( 33.2% ) . a total of 77 patients ( 20.4% ) underwent surgery , of whom 35% ( n = 27 ) had benign disease . pet scan was used in 141 patients ( 37% ) . the false - positive rate for pet scan was 39% ( 95% ci , 27.1%-52.1% ) . pretest probability of malignancy calculations showed that 9.5% ( n = 36 ) were at a low risk , 79.6% ( n = 300 ) were at a moderate risk , and 10.8% ( n = 41 ) were at a high risk of malignancy . the rate of surgical resection was similar among the three groups ( 17% , 21% , 17% , respectively ; p = .69).conclusions : a substantial fraction of intermediate - sized nodules referred to pulmonologists ultimately prove to be lung cancer . despite advances in imaging and nonsurgical biopsy techniques , invasive sampling of low - risk nodules and surgical resection of benign nodules remain common , suggesting a lack of adherence to guidelines for the management of pns . |
| Model | objectivethe aim of this study was to document the prevalence of cancer ( 25% ) in patients with intermediate - sized pulmonary nodules referred to community pulmonologists.materials and methodsthis was a multicenter, community - based, observational study of patients with intermediate - sized pulmonary nodule who were referred to pulmonologists. patients were categorized into three groups by the most invasive procedure performed during management, as follows : surveillance ( serial imaging ), biopsy ( ct - guided transthoracic needle aspiration [ ttna ] or bronchoscopy ), or surgery ( including mediastinoscopy, video - assisted thorascopic surgery, and/or thoracotomy ). patients were categorized into three groups by the most invasive procedure performed during management, as follows : surveillance ( serial imaging ), biopsy ( ct - guided transthoracic needle aspiration [ ttna ] or bronchoscopy ), or surgery ( including mediastinoscopy, video - assisted thorascopic surgery, and/or thoracotomy ). patients were categorized into three groups by the most invasive procedure performed during management, as follows : surveillance ( serial imaging ), biopsy ( ct - guided transthoracic needle aspiration [ ttna ] or bronchoscopy ), or surgery ( including mediastinoscopy, video - assisted thorascopic surgery, and/or thoracotomy ). multivariate logistic regression was performed to identify factors associated with the use of an invasive diagnostic procedure.resultsof the 377 patients included, 283 ( 75% ) had a nodule that was benign, and 94 ( 25% ) had a malignant nodule. the overall accuracy of pet scanning was 74%, with a false - positive ( fp ) rate of 39% and a false - negative ( fn ) rate of 9%. the overall accuracy of pet scanning was 74%, with a false - positive ( fp ) rate of 39% and a false - negative ( fn ) rate of 9%. nodules measuring > 11 to 15 mm ( n = 48 ) had fn and fp rates of 9% and 36%, respectively.conclusionsthe prevalence of cancer in patients with intermediate - sized nodules was 25%. the rate of surgical resection for benign disease varied from 9% to 23% in screening trials and surgical series. |
| Metrics | Rouge1: 45.58, Rouge2: 9.56, RougeL: 18.37, RougeLsum: 38.1, Summary length (tokens): 470 |
| Top 75% example (Sorted by rougeL) | |
| Document | a total of 1,217 dead birds were shipped at 4c to the tropical medicine institute " pedro kouri " and identified by ornithology experts . brain , heart , and kidneys were removed and tested for wnv by using reverse transcription polymerase chain reaction ( rt - pcr ) ( 12 ) . briefly , rna was extracted by using the qiamp viral rna kit ( qiagen , inc . , valencia , ca , usa ) . primers wn212 ( 5-ttgtgttggctctcttggcgttctt-3 ) and wn619c ( 5-cagccgacagcactggacattcata-3 ) were used to detect viral rna . a second rt - pcr with primers wn9483 ( 5-cacctacgccctaaacactttcacc-3 ) and wn9794 ( 5-ggaacctgctgccaatcataccatc-3 ) was performed on the same rna preparation . serum specimens from horses in havana and havana province were tested for antibodies to wnv by using a competitive enzyme - linked immunosorbent assay ( elisa ) with monoclonal antibodies 3.1112 g and 6b6c-1 as described by blitvich et al . we tested 210 serum specimens from horses collected as part of an infectious anemia study . the immunoglobulin m ( igm ) test was not performed because horses were never suspected of having wnv and did not have any history of suspected viral encephalitis or other illness or symptoms . an inhibition value > 30% was used as the diagnostic criterion to identify flavivirus antibody ( table 1 ) . * wnv , west nile virus ; elisa , enzyme - linked immunosorbent assay ; prnt , plaque reduction neutralization test ; slev , saint louis encephalitis virus . the cuban health ministry and medical services division conducted surveillance for encephalitis of unknown origin in patients > 30 years of age . serum and cerebrospinal fluid specimens were shipped at 4c to the tropical medicine institute " pedro kouri . " human sera were screened for wnv igm and igg by using commercial igm and igg elisa kits ( focus technologies , cypress , ca , usa ) according to manufacturer 's instructions . hemagglutination - inhibition ( hi ) tests were also undertaken with wnv and saint louis encephalitis virus ( slev ) antigen ( 14 ) . reactive serum samples were further tested by a plaque reduction neutralization test ( prnt ) with wnv ( ny99 , ontario , canada , 2001 isolate ) , slev ( parton strain , american type culture collection catalog no . vr-1265 ) , and dengue virus ( dengue 2 , ng - c strain ) . prnt was performed to confirm wnv - specific antibody and was carried out as described previously ( 15 ) by using a neutral red double - overlay procedure . ho... |
| Gold | a surveillance system to detect west nile virus ( wnv ) was established in cuba in 2002 . wnv infection was confirmed by serologic assays in 4 asymptomatic horses and 3 humans with encephalitis in 2003 and 2004 . these results are the first reported evidence of wnv activity in cuba . |
| Model | we report the first evidence of antibodies to west nile virus ( wnv ) in horses and humans in cuba. antibodies were detected by plaque reduction neutralization test in 10 of 1,217 dead birds tested. these findings provide evidence that wnv and slev may co - circulate in cuba. |
| Metrics | Rouge1: 51.06, Rouge2: 17.39, RougeL: 31.91, RougeLsum: 46.81, Summary length (tokens): 64 |
| Top 95% example (Sorted by rougeL) | |
| Document | intra - articular injections of corticosteroids have been used for several decades in the management of inflammatory and degenerative joint conditions when first - line conservative therapies such as rest , ice , and anti - inflammatory medications fail to provide adequate symptom relief . based in part on this long history of successful utilization coupled with the findings of several randomized controlled trials , consensus statements and meta - analyses have concluded that intra - articular corticosteroid injections provide short - term patient benefit and clinical efficacy for chronic knee pain.13 more recently , various injectable hyaluronic acid agents have become commercially available and have enjoyed widespread clinical acceptance as an effective treatment for knee osteoarthritis . these agents are indicated for the treatment of the pain associated with osteoarthritis of the knee in patients who have failed to respond adequately to conservative nonpharmacologic therapy and simple analgesics , eg , acetaminophen . traditionally , intra - articular injections have been performed using anatomical landmarks to identify the correct trajectory for needle placement . however , different anatomical - guided injection techniques have yielded inconsistent intra - articular needle positioning due , in large part , to the fact that the physician can not directly visualize the area of interest , and variations in anatomy are common . incorrect needle placement has been partially attributed to variable clinical outcomes.410 furthermore , inaccurate corticosteroid injections in the knee , for example , may result in post - injection pain , crystal synovitis , hemarthrosis , joint sepsis , and steroid articular cartilage atrophy , as well as systemic effects , such as fluid retention or exacerbation of hypertension or diabetes mellitus.1 therefore , identification of methods and proper training to aid in correct needle placement during these procedures is warranted . various imaging modalities can be used to improve the accuracy of intra - articular injections , including fluoroscopy , computed tomography , and magnetic resonance imaging . however , musculoskeletal ultrasound is one of the most practical because it is rapid , safe , relatively inexpensive , emits no ionizing radiation , and can be performed in the outpatient clinical setting.11,12 ultrasound utilizes high - frequency sound waves to visualize soft tissues and bony structures and is a f... |
| Gold | intra - articular corticosteroid and hyaluronic acid injections provide short - term symptom amelioration for arthritic conditions involving structural damage or degenerative changes in the knee . conventional palpation - guided anatomical injections frequently result in inaccurate needle placement into extra - articular tissue and adjacent structures . the purpose of this review was to determine the effect of ultrasound guidance on the accuracy of needle placement , clinical outcomes , and cost - effectiveness in comparison with anatomical landmark - guided intra - articular large joint injections , with particular emphasis on the knee . a total of 13 relevant studies were identified ; five studied the knee , seven studied the shoulder , one used both the knee and shoulder , and none studied the hip . ultrasound was used in seven studies ; the remaining studies utilized air arthrography , fluoroscopy , magnetic resonance arthrography , or magnetic resonance imaging . across all studies ( using all imaging modalities and all joints ) , needle placement accuracy ranged from 63% to 100% with ultrasound and from 39% to 100% with conventional anatomical guidance . imaging guidance improved the accuracy of intra - articular injections of the knee ( 96.7% versus 81.0% , p < 0.001 ) and shoulder ( 97.3% versus 65.4% , p < 0.001 ) . in particular , ultrasound guidance of knee injections resulted in better accuracy than anatomical guidance ( 95.8% versus 77.8% , p < 0.001 ) , yielding an odds ratio of 6.4 ( 95% confidence interval 2.914 ) . ultrasound guidance notably improves injection accuracy in the target intra - articular joint space of large joints including the knee . the enhanced injection accuracy achieved with ultrasound needle guidance directly improves patient - reported clinical outcomes and cost - effectiveness . |
| Model | objectivethe purpose of this review was to determine the effect of ultrasound guidance on the accuracy of needle placement, clinical outcomes, and cost - effectiveness in comparison with anatomical landmark - guided intra - articular large joint injections, with particular emphasis on the knee.methodsthe peer - reviewed literature was searched using medline and relevant bibliographies published in english language journals through december 31, 2011 that compared the accuracy of intra - articular injections with anatomical landmark - guided intra - articular large joint injections, with particular emphasis on the knee.resultsa total of 13 studies met the entry criteria. needle placement accuracy ranged from 63% to 100% with ultrasound and from 39% to 100% with conventional anatomical guidance. imaging guidance improved the accuracy of intra - articular injections of the knee ( 96.7% versus 81.0%, p < 0.001 ) and shoulder ( 97.3% versus 65.4%, p < 0.001 ). imaging guidance improved the accuracy of intra - articular injections of the knee ( 96.7% versus 81.0%, p < 0.001 ) and shoulder ( 97.3% versus 65.4%, p < 0.001 ). imaging guidance improved the accuracy of intra - articular injections of the knee ( 96.7% versus 81.0%, p < 0.001 ) and shoulder ( 97.3% versus 65.4%, p < 0.001 ). in particular, ultrasound guidance of knee injections resulted in better accuracy than did anatomical guidance ( 95.8% versus 77.8%, p < 0.001 ). in particular, ultrasound guidance of knee injections resulted in better accuracy than did anatomical guidance ( 95.8% versus 77.8%, p < 0.001 ). in particular, ultrasound guidance of knee injections resulted in better accuracy than did anatomical guidance ( 95.8% versus 77.8%, p < 0.001).conclusionthe use of imaging guidance, in particular ultrasound, improves the accuracy of intra - articular injections in large joints, including the knee. furthermore, accurate ultrasound - guided intra - articular knee injections improve clinical outcomes and lower health care costs. |
| Metrics | Rouge1: 62.21, Rouge2: 43.74, RougeL: 48.51, RougeLsum: 58.7, Summary length (tokens): 464 |

Table 16: Examples of the PubMed dataset using the model pubmed-4096-512 base diverse

# Is a Video worth $n \times n$ Images? A Highly Efficient Approach to Transformer-based Video Question Answering

**Chenyang Lyu**[†] **Tianbo Ji**[‡*] **Yvette Graham**[¶] **Jennifer Foster**[†]
[†] School of Computing, Dublin City University, Dublin, Ireland
[‡] Nantong University, China
[¶] School of Computer Science and Statistics, Trinity College Dublin, Dublin, Ireland
chenyang.lyu2@mail.dcu.ie, ygraham@tcd.ie, jennifer.foster@dcu.ie
jitianbo@ntu.edu.cn

## Abstract

Conventional Transformer-based Video Question Answering (VideoQA) approaches generally encode frames independently through one or more image encoders followed by interaction between frames and question. However, such schema incur significant memory use and inevitably slow down the training and inference speed. In this work, we present a highly efficient approach for VideoQA based on existing vision-language pre-trained models where we concatenate video frames to a $n \times n$ matrix and then convert it to one *image*. By doing so, we reduce the use of the image encoder from $n^2$ to 1 while maintaining the temporal structure of the original video. Experimental results on MSRVTT and TrafficQA show that our proposed approach achieves state-of-the-art performance with nearly 4× faster speed and only 30% memory use. We show that by integrating our approach into VideoQA systems we can achieve comparable, even superior, performance with a significant speed up for training and inference. We believe the proposed approach can facilitate VideoQA-related research by reducing the computational requirements for those who have limited access to budgets and resources. Our code is publicly available at `https://github.com/lyuchenyang/Efficient-VideoQA` for research use.

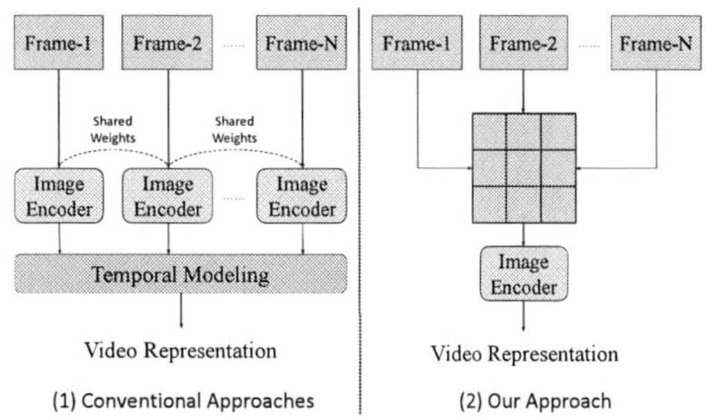


Figure 1: Conventional approach to encoding video frames for VideoQA and our proposed method.

## 1 Introduction

Transformer-based Video Question Answering (VideoQA) (Xu et al., 2016; Yu et al., 2018; Xu et al., 2021b; Bain et al., 2021; Lei et al., 2022) approaches relying on large scale vision transformers (Dosovitskiy et al., 2020) have achieved strong performance in recent years. However, such approaches typically encode multiple video frames separately through one or more *Image Encoders* (Lei et al., 2021; Luo et al., 2021; Xu et al., 2021a; Arnab et al., 2021; Zhong et al., 2022) followed by interaction with question representations. This requires significant memory use and inevitably slows down training and inference speed. In order to reduce the computational cost required for modeling video representations from frames, we propose to arrange the frames sampled from one video as a single image. Specifically, we sample $n^2$ frames from one video and concatenate them as a single image with $n \times n$ grids.

Figure 1 shows the difference between our method (right) and conventional methods (left). In general, conventional approaches either independently encode video frames (Luo et al., 2021; Xu et al., 2021a; Lei et al., 2021; Bain et al., 2022) which require $N$ forward passes, or encode the sequence of all patches in video frames (Bain et al., 2021; Arnab et al., 2021) which quadratically increases the computational cost in the attention modelling. Both types of aforementioned encoding approaches can be expected to negatively impact training and inference speed, whereas our proposed method reduces this need substantially, now requiring only a single forward pass.

Our method diverges from previous approaches in two ways: 1) it fully relies on existing available pre-trained vision-language models such as CLIP (Radford et al., 2021) without need for extra

*corresponding author



*Proceedings of The Fourth Workshop on Simple and Efficient Natural Language Processing (SustaiNLP)*, pages 183–189
July 13, 2023 ©2023 Association for Computational Linguistics

pre-training (Bain et al., 2021; Lei et al., 2022); 2) it considers a multi-frame video as a single image, dispensing with the need for positional embedding at the frame level (Bain et al., 2021), so only minor modifications to pre-trained models are necessary.

More importantly, our approach has three advantages: 1) higher computational efficiency[1]; 2) less memory use - our approach only uses an *Image Encoder* a single time; 3) our approach can be easily scaled up for large numbers of frames for long videos. Our approach also models a multiple-frame video as a single image while still (partially) maintaining the temporal structure of the original video.

To validate the effectiveness of our approach, we conduct experiments on two benchmark VideoQA datasets: MSRVTT-MC (Xu et al., 2016; Yu et al., 2018) and TrafficQA (Xu et al., 2021b). Results show that our approach achieves comparable or even superior performance compared to existing models with nearly 4× faster training and inference speed and vast reduction in memory use (30%). Our contribution can be summarised as follows:

- We propose a novel approach combining video frames as a single image to accelerate VideoQA systems ;
- Experimental results on MSRVTT-MC and TrafficQA show that our proposed approach achieves competitive performance with faster training-inference speed and lower memory use;
- We include additional experiments investigating options for arrangement of video frames for VideoQA;

## 2 Model Architecture

In this section, we introduce details of our approach, of which an overview is shown in Figure 2.

### 2.1 Vision Transformer

Generally Vision Transformer (ViT) (Dosovitskiy et al., 2020) flattens a single image to $m$ non-overlapping patches $v = \{p_0, p_1, ......, p_{m-1}\}$. All patches are fed into a linear projection and then regarded as discrete tokens in (Vaswani et al., 2017; Radford et al., 2018; Devlin et al., 2019) followed

[1]For example, the computational cost of Bain et al. (2021); Arnab et al. (2021) scales up quadratically w.r.t. the number of image patches whereas ours is invariant w.r.t. the number of image patches.

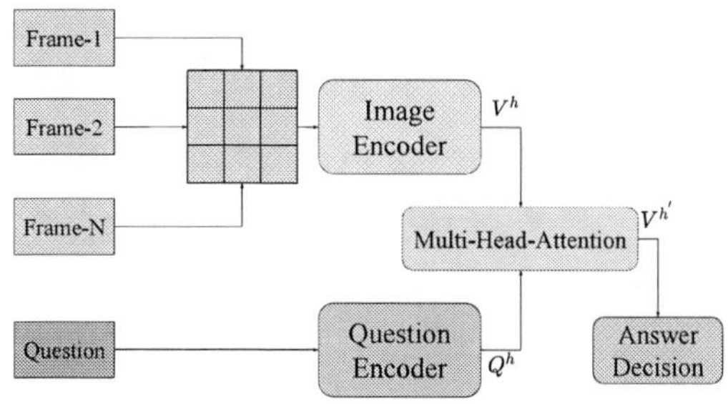


Figure 2: An overview of our proposed approach.

by transformer-based modeling (Vaswani et al., 2017; Dosovitskiy et al., 2020). The output feature is $v^h = \{h_0, h_1, ......, h_{m-1}\}$, where $E^h \in \mathbf{R}^{m \times d}$, $d$ is the dimension of the output feature for each patch.

For encoding a multiple-frame video, suppose that we have an input video $V = \{v_0, v_1, ......, v_{n-1}\}$ with $n$ frames, so for each frame $v_i$ ViT flattens it to $m$ non-overlapping patches $v_i = \{p_{i,0}, p_{i,1}, ......, p_{i,m-1}\}$. The patches for each frame are concatenated to form a sequence of patches:

$$V = \{p_{0,0}, ......, p_{0,m-1}, ......, p_{i,0}, \\ p_{i,1}, ......, p_{i,m-1}, ......\} \quad (1)$$

which are fed into (a) linear projection(s) followed by transformer-based modeling (Vaswani et al., 2017; Dosovitskiy et al., 2020)[2]. We thus obtain frame-level representations:

$$V^h = \{v_0, v_1, ......, v_{n-1}\} \quad (2)$$

where $V^h \in \mathbf{R}^{n \times d}$. [3]

### 2.2 Interaction with Question Representations

For a natural language question $Q = \{w_0, w_1, ......, w_{k-1}\}$ consisting of $k$ words, we use a textual transformer to encode $Q$ to obtain a sentence-level representation $Q^h \in \mathbf{R}^{1 \times d}$. Since in this work, we mainly focus on reducing the computational cost of encoding videos, we perform simple interactions between video representations $V^h$ and question representations $Q^h$:

[2]Frames can be encoded separately through one or more *Image Encoder* (Luo et al., 2021; Xu et al., 2021a; Bain et al., 2022) or all patches can also be concatenated and passed into one *Image Encoder* (Bain et al., 2021; Arnab et al., 2021)

[3]Patch-level representations $V^h = \{h_{0,0}, ......, h_{0,m-1}, ......, h_{i,0}, h_{i,1}, ......, h_{i,m-1}, ......\}$ are used in (Lei et al., 2021; Bain et al., 2021)

$$V^{h'} = \text{MULTI-HEAD-ATTENTION}(Q^h, V^h, V^h) \quad (3)$$

where $V^{h'} \in \mathbf{R}^{1\times d}$ is the question weighted representations and MULTI-HEAD-ATTENTION (Vaswani et al., 2017) performs attention between $V^h$ (key and value) and $Q^h$ (query).

### 2.3 Frames Transformation

When encoding multiple frames, the encoding schema in 2.1 incurs significant memory use and additionally impedes training and inference speed (Lei et al., 2021; Luo et al., 2021; Xu et al., 2021a; Lei et al., 2022). Therefore, we propose a novel strategy to reduce the computational cost associated with encoding videos by combining all frames into a single image arranged by $n \times n$ grids. Practically, we arrange all frames to a matrix, $M$, in which each entry corresponds to a frame. For a video with $n \times n$ frames, we put each frame into $M_{i,j}$ in a specific order. For example, frames can be arranged in $M$ via ascending or descending order (either vertically or horizontally) based on its index in the video.[4] Next, we convert $M$ to a single image. Therefore, regardless of how many frames we use, the number of tokenized patches (image tokens) is always a constant number, resulting in a computationally more efficient VideoQA system.

## 3 Experiments

### 3.1 Datasets

We conduct experiments on two benchmark datasets for VideoQA: MSRVTT-MC (Xu et al., 2016; Yu et al., 2018) and TrafficQA (Xu et al., 2021b), which are multi-choice VideoQA datasets – each video in MSRVTT-MC is associated with 5 candidate options whereas TrafficQA provides 4 options for each question. We follow the standard data split for MSRVTT-MC (Xu et al., 2016; Yu et al., 2018), where evaluation data have 2,990 videos. TrafficQA contains 62,535 QA pairs and 10,080 videos. We follow the standard split of TrafficQA: 56,460 QA pairs for training and 6,075 QA pairs for evaluation.

[4]The effect of various arrangement orders is shown in Sec 3.5.

| Models | Accuracy |
|---|---|
| JSFusion (Yu et al., 2018) | 83.4 |
| ActBERT (Zhu and Yang, 2020) | 85.7 |
| ClipBERT (Lei et al., 2021) | 88.2 |
| MERLOT (Zellers et al., 2021) | 90.9 |
| VIOLET (Fu et al., 2021) | 90.9 |
| VideoCLIP (Xu et al., 2021a) | 92.1 |
| All-in-One (Wang et al., 2022) | 92.0 |
| Singularity (Lei et al., 2022) | 92.1 |
| Ours + MULTI-FRAME | 92.1 (1.0×) |
| Ours + SINGLE-FRAME | 92.2 (3.9×) |

Table 1: Evaluation results on MSRVTT-MC (Xu et al., 2016; Yu et al., 2018) dataset. Number in bracket indicates the average of training and inference speed (↑), which is evaluated on Nvidia GTX 3090.

### 3.2 Experimental Setup

We use CLIP ViT-B/16 (Radford et al., 2021) [5] to initialize our IMAGE-ENCODER and TEXT-ENCODER. We evenly sample 9 frames from the videos in MSRVTT-MC and TrafficQA for the main experiment. We train our model for 20 epochs with a learning rate of 1e-6. The training batch size is 16. We use a maximum gradient norm of 1. The optimizer we used is AdamW (Loshchilov and Hutter, 2019), for which the $\epsilon$ is set to $1 \times 10^{-8}$.

### 3.3 Evaluation Results

We show the evaluation results on MSRVTT-MC (Xu et al., 2016; Yu et al., 2018) in Table 1. Furthermore, we conduct experiments on TrafficQA (Xu et al., 2021b) and the results are shown in Table 2. We present the results of separately encoding video frames (MULTI-FRAME) as in Figure 1 (left) and our approach that combines multiple video frames into a single image (SINGLE-FRAME). For SINGLE-FRAME, the frames are arranged in a matrix via horizontally descending order. The evaluation results show that our approach SINGLE-FRAME achieves comparable and even improved performance relative to strong baselines including VideoCLIP (Xu et al., 2021a), All-in-One (Wang et al., 2022), Singularity (Lei et al., 2022) and CMCIR (Liu et al., 2022). SINGLE-FRAME obtains a significant speed up (approaching ×4) compared to MULTI-FRAME approach while maintaining competitive performance. The memory use of SINGLE-FRAME is only 30% of MULTI-

[5]https://openai.com/blog/clip/

| Models | Accuracy |
|---|---|
| Q-type (random) (Xu et al., 2021b) | 25.0 |
| QE-LSTM (Xu et al., 2021b) | 25.2 |
| QA-LSTM (Xu et al., 2021b) | 26.7 |
| Avgpooling (Xu et al., 2021b) | 30.5 |
| CNN+LSTM (Xu et al., 2021b) | 30.8 |
| I3D+LSTM (Xu et al., 2021b) | 33.2 |
| VIS+LSTM (Ren et al., 2015) | 29.9 |
| BERT-VQA (Yang et al., 2020) | 33.7 |
| TVQA (Lei et al., 2018) | 35.2 |
| HCRN (Le et al., 2020) | 36.5 |
| Eclipse (Xu et al., 2021b) | 37.0 |
| ERM (Zhang et al., 2022) | 37.1 |
| TMBC (Luo et al., 2022) | 37.2 |
| CMCIR (Liu et al., 2022) | 38.6 |
| Ours + MULTI-FRAME | 39.7 (1.0×) |
| Ours + SINGLE-FRAME | 39.7 (3.8×) |

Table 2: Evaluation results on SUTD-TrafficQA (Xu et al., 2021b) dataset. Number in bracket indicates the average of training and inference speed (↑).

FRAME, which are compared on Nvidia GTX 3090. The results on two benchmark datasets have shown the effectiveness of our approach for improving the computational efficiency while maintaining accuracy of VideoQA systems.

### 3.4 Effect of Number of Frames

We investigate the effect of the number of video frames used by our approach during the training and inference process. The results are shown in Figure 3. We compare the performance of MULTI-FRAME and SINGLE-FRAME for number of frames ranging from 1 to 25[6] in Figure 3. Results show that: 1) Both MULTI-FRAME and SINGLE-FRAME systems can benefit from more video frames; 2) SINGLE-FRAME is capable of achieving comparable and even better performance against MULTI-FRAME; 3) MULTI-FRAME costs much more computational time than SINGLE-FRAME especially when using a large number of video frames. Therefore, our proposed SINGLE-FRAME approach is able to achieve higher efficiency as well as competitive accuracy.

### 3.5 Effect of Frame Order

We investigate the effect of the arrangement of video frames used to form a single frame. The

[6]For SINGLE-FRAME with a number of frames that is not a square number we up-sample it to the closest square number. For example, a SINGLE-FRAME that deals with 2 frames with index of $\{0, 1\}$, we upsample it to $\{0, 0, 1, 1\}$ as $2 \times 2$ images.

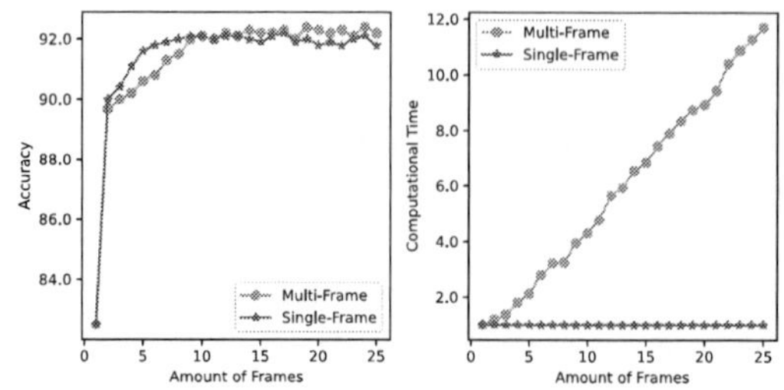


Figure 3: Evaluation results including accuracy (↑) and computational time (↓) on the effect of amount of video frames on MSRVTT-MC.

| Arrangement of Frames | 9 frames | 16 frames |
|---|---|---|
| Vertical-Ascent | 89.8 | 89.9 |
| Vertical-Descent | 89.1 | 89.5 |
| Horizontal-Ascent | 88.7 | 88.8 |
| Horizontal-Descent | 87.5 | 88.6 |
| Matrix (Vertical-Ascent) | 91.4 | 91.1 |
| Matrix (Vertical-Descent) | 91.9 | 91.8 |
| Matrix (Horizontal-Ascent) | 91.6 | 91.2 |
| Matrix (Horizontal-Descent) | 92.2 | 92.1 |
| Matrix (Random) | 90.5 | 90.7 |

Table 3: Evaluation results on the effect of the arrangement of video frames on MSRVTT-MC.

results of both the 9 frame and 16 frame configurations are shown in Table 3. We report the results of VERTICAL, HORIZONTAL and MATRIX via either ASCENDING or DESCENDING order.[7] The results in Table 3 reveal that both VERTICAL and HORIZONTAL perform worst, and this is likely due to configurations distorting the visual information since they essentially squeeze the video frames either vertically or horizontally. The MATRIX arrangement performs substantially better especially MATRIX (HORIZONTAL-DESCENT) and HORIZONTAL generally yielding better performance compared to VERTICAL under the MATRIX arrangement.

## 4 Conclusion and Future Work

In this paper, we propose a highly efficient method for VideoQA where we combine multiple video frames into one single image. By adapting our approach, the computational cost of VideoQA systems can be significantly reduced. To validate the effectiveness of our approach, we conduct experiments on two benchmark datasets, MSRVTT-MC and TrafficQA. Results show that our approach

[7]Examples are shown in Appendix A.1.

achieves competitive performance and faster training and inference speed (nearly 4× faster) and less memory consumption (30%). Our approach provides a way of significantly accelerating training and inference. In the future, we aim to explore how to adapt our approach to VideoQA with longer videos and additional video-related NLP tasks.


## Acknowledgements

This work was funded by Science Foundation Ireland through the SFI Centre for Research Training in Machine Learning (18/CRT/6183). We thank the reviewers for helpful feedback.


## Limitations

The two VideoQA datasets used in experiments are associated with relatively short videos. Therefore it would be better if more experiments could be conducted on VideoQA datasets with long videos to verify the effectiveness of our approach on a wider range of VideoQA tasks. Although the proposed approach in this paper can also be used in other video-language tasks, our experiments focuses on a specific video-language task - VideoQA. Experiments on more video-language tasks are needed to show that our approach are also effective in other video-language tasks.

## References


Anurag Arnab, Mostafa Dehghani, Georg Heigold, Chen Sun, Mario Lučić, and Cordelia Schmid. 2021. Vivit: A video vision transformer. In *Proceedings of the IEEE/CVF International Conference on Computer Vision*, pages 6836–6846.

Max Bain, Arsha Nagrani, Gül Varol, and Andrew Zisserman. 2021. Frozen in time: A joint video and image encoder for end-to-end retrieval. In *Proceedings of the IEEE/CVF International Conference on Computer Vision*, pages 1728–1738.

Max Bain, Arsha Nagrani, Gül Varol, and Andrew Zisserman. 2022. A clip-hitchhiker's guide to long video retrieval. *arXiv preprint arXiv:2205.08508*.

Jacob Devlin, Ming-Wei Chang, Kenton Lee, and Kristina Toutanova. 2019. BERT: Pre-training of deep bidirectional transformers for language understanding. In *Proceedings of the 2019 Conference of the North American Chapter of the Association for Computational Linguistics: Human Language Technologies, Volume 1 (Long and Short Papers)*, pages 4171–4186, Minneapolis, Minnesota. Association for Computational Linguistics.

Alexey Dosovitskiy, Lucas Beyer, Alexander Kolesnikov, Dirk Weissenborn, Xiaohua Zhai, Thomas Unterthiner, Mostafa Dehghani, Matthias Minderer, Georg Heigold, Sylvain Gelly, et al. 2020. An image is worth 16x16 words: Transformers for image recognition at scale. In *International Conference on Learning Representations*.

Tsu-Jui Fu, Linjie Li, Zhe Gan, Kevin Lin, William Yang Wang, Lijuan Wang, and Zicheng Liu. 2021. Violet: End-to-end video-language transformers with masked visual-token modeling. *arXiv preprint arXiv:2111.12681*.

Thao Minh Le, Vuong Le, Svetha Venkatesh, and Truyen Tran. 2020. Hierarchical conditional relation networks for video question answering. In *Proceedings of the IEEE/CVF conference on computer vision and pattern recognition*, pages 9972–9981.

Jie Lei, Tamara L Berg, and Mohit Bansal. 2022. Revealing single frame bias for video-and-language learning. *arXiv preprint arXiv:2206.03428*.

Jie Lei, Linjie Li, Luowei Zhou, Zhe Gan, Tamara L Berg, Mohit Bansal, and Jingjing Liu. 2021. Less is more: Clipbert for video-and-language learning via sparse sampling. In *Proceedings of the IEEE/CVF Conference on Computer Vision and Pattern Recognition*, pages 7331–7341.

Jie Lei, Licheng Yu, Mohit Bansal, and Tamara Berg. 2018. Tvqa: Localized, compositional video question answering. In *Proceedings of the 2018 Conference on Empirical Methods in Natural Language Processing*, pages 1369–1379.

Yang Liu, Guanbin Li, and Liang Lin. 2022. Cross-modal causal relational reasoning for event-level visual question answering. *arXiv preprint arXiv:2207.12647*.

Ilya Loshchilov and Frank Hutter. 2019. Decoupled weight decay regularization. In *International Conference on Learning Representations*.

Huaishao Luo, Lei Ji, Ming Zhong, Yang Chen, Wen Lei, Nan Duan, and Tianrui Li. 2021. Clip4clip: An empirical study of clip for end to end video clip retrieval. *arXiv preprint arXiv:2104.08860*.

Yuanmao Luo, Ruomei Wang, Fuwei Zhang, Fan Zhou, and Shujin Lin. 2022. Temporal-aware mechanism with bidirectional complementarity for video q&a. In *2022 IEEE International Conference on Systems, Man, and Cybernetics (SMC)*, pages 3273–3278. IEEE.

Alec Radford, Jong Wook Kim, Chris Hallacy, Aditya Ramesh, Gabriel Goh, Sandhini Agarwal, Girish Sastry, Amanda Askell, Pamela Mishkin, Jack Clark, et al. 2021. Learning transferable visual models from natural language supervision. In *International Conference on Machine Learning*, pages 8748–8763. PMLR.

Alec Radford, Karthik Narasimhan, Tim Salimans, and Ilya Sutskever. 2018. Improving language understanding by generative pre-training.

Mengye Ren, Ryan Kiros, and Richard Zemel. 2015. Exploring models and data for image question answering. *Advances in neural information processing systems*, 28.

Ashish Vaswani, Noam Shazeer, Niki Parmar, Jakob Uszkoreit, Llion Jones, Aidan N Gomez, Łukasz Kaiser, and Illia Polosukhin. 2017. Attention is all you need. *Advances in neural information processing systems*, 30.

Alex Jinpeng Wang, Yixiao Ge, Rui Yan, Yuying Ge, Xudong Lin, Guanyu Cai, Jianping Wu, Ying Shan, Xiaohu Qie, and Mike Zheng Shou. 2022. All in one: Exploring unified video-language pre-training.

Hu Xu, Gargi Ghosh, Po-Yao Huang, Dmytro Okhonko, Armen Aghajanyan, Florian Metze, Luke Zettlemoyer, and Christoph Feichtenhofer. 2021a. VideoCLIP: Contrastive pre-training for zero-shot video-text understanding. In *Proceedings of the 2021 Conference on Empirical Methods in Natural Language Processing*, pages 6787–6800, Online and Punta Cana, Dominican Republic. Association for Computational Linguistics.

Jun Xu, Tao Mei, Ting Yao, and Yong Rui. 2016. Msr-vtt: A large video description dataset for bridging video and language. In *Proceedings of the IEEE conference on computer vision and pattern recognition*, pages 5288–5296.

Li Xu, He Huang, and Jun Liu. 2021b. Sutd-trafficqa: A question answering benchmark and an efficient network for video reasoning over traffic events. In *Proceedings of the IEEE/CVF Conference on Computer Vision and Pattern Recognition*, pages 9878–9888.

Zekun Yang, Noa Garcia, Chenhui Chu, Mayu Otani, Yuta Nakashima, and Haruo Takemura. 2020. Bert representations for video question answering. In *Proceedings of the IEEE/CVF Winter Conference on Applications of Computer Vision*, pages 1556–1565.

Youngjae Yu, Jongseok Kim, and Gunhee Kim. 2018. A joint sequence fusion model for video question answering and retrieval. In *Proceedings of the European Conference on Computer Vision (ECCV)*, pages 471–487.

Rowan Zellers, Ximing Lu, Jack Hessel, Youngjae Yu, Jae Sung Park, Jize Cao, Ali Farhadi, and Yejin Choi. 2021. MERLOT: Multimodal neural script knowledge models. In *Advances in Neural Information Processing Systems*.

Fuwei Zhang, Ruomei Wang, Fan Zhou, and Yuanmao Luo. 2022. Erm: Energy-based refined-attention mechanism for video question answering. *IEEE Transactions on Circuits and Systems for Video Technology*.

Yaoyao Zhong, Wei Ji, Junbin Xiao, Yicong Li, Weihong Deng, and Tat-Seng Chua. 2022. Video question answering: Datasets, algorithms and challenges. *arXiv preprint arXiv:2203.01225*.

Linchao Zhu and Yi Yang. 2020. Actbert: Learning global-local video-text representations. In *Proceedings of the IEEE/CVF conference on computer vision and pattern recognition*, pages 8746–8755.

# A Appendix

## A.1 Examples of frames with different arrangement order

We present some examples of frames with different arrangement order in Figure 4, where we use 9 frames as examples. The arrangement orders are: (1) HORIZONTAL. (2) VERTICAL. (3) MATRIX (HORIZONTAL-ASCENT). (4) MATRIX (HORIZONTAL-DESCENT). (5) MATRIX (VERTICAL-ASCENT). (6) MATRIX (VERTICAL-DESCENT). The corresponding video frame indices are shown in Figure 5.

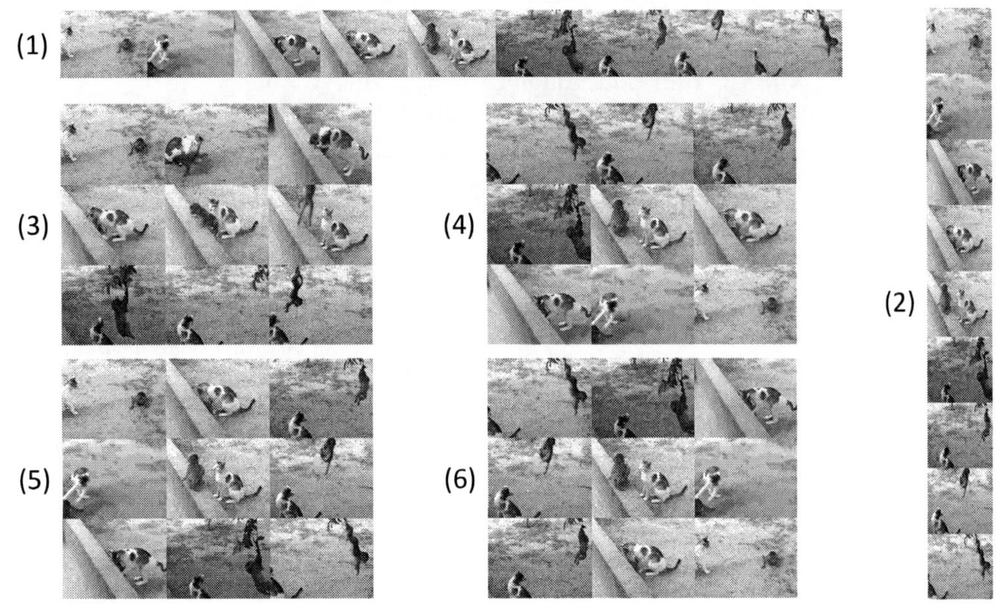


Figure 4: Frames arranged via different order.

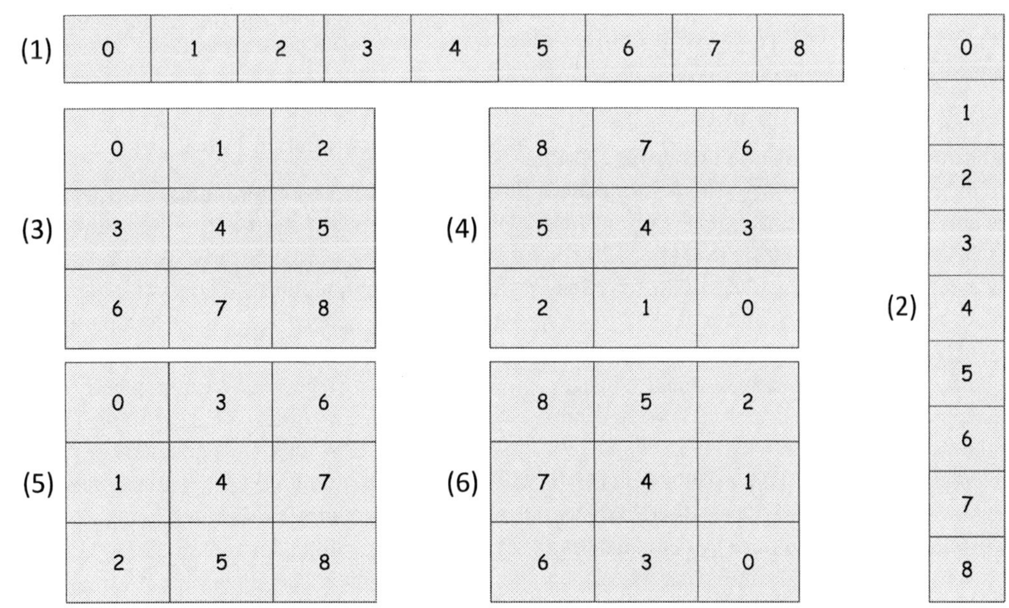


Figure 5: Corresponding frame index for different arrangement order.

# How to Unleash the Power of Large Language Models for Few-shot Relation Extraction?

**Xin Xu, Yuqi Zhu, Xiaohan Wang, Ningyu Zhang***
Zhejiang University & AZFT Joint Lab for Knowledge Engine
{xxucs, wangxh07, zhangningyu}@zju.edu.cn

## Abstract

Scaling language models have revolutionized widespread NLP tasks, yet little comprehensively explored few-shot relation extraction with large language models. In this paper, we investigate principal methodologies, in-context learning and data generation, for few-shot relation extraction via GPT-3.5 through exhaustive experiments. To enhance few-shot performance, we further propose task-related instructions and schema-constrained data generation. We observe that in-context learning can achieve performance on par with previous prompt learning approaches, and data generation with the large language model can boost previous solutions to obtain new state-of-the-art few-shot results on four widely-studied relation extraction datasets. We hope our work can inspire future research for the capabilities of large language models in few-shot relation extraction[1].

## 1 Introduction

Few-shot Relation Extraction (RE) appeals to many researchers in Natural Language Processing (NLP) due to the capability to extract textual information where only a few support examples are given (Han et al., 2018; Yang et al., 2021; Han et al., 2021a; Brody et al., 2021; Ma et al., 2023). Most previous works focus on fine-tuning (Soares et al., 2019; Ye et al., 2022) or prompt-tuning (Chen et al., 2022; Han et al., 2021b) with relatively small language models, e.g., RoBERTa (Liu et al., 2019). Recently, with the scaling of model size and corpus size, large language models (LLMs) such as ChatGPT (OpenAI, 2022) and GPT-4 (OpenAI, 2023a) have demonstrated powerful abilities by demonstrating only a few instances, a.k.a In-Context Learning (Dong et al., 2023). Although LLMs have achieved remarkable results in many NLP tasks, their potential in few-shot relation extraction has not been fully explored yet.

In this paper, we take GPT-3.5 (OpenAI, 2023b) as an exemplary LLM to investigate how to maximize the utilization of LLMs for the few-shot relation extraction task with in-context learning and data generation. Different from text classification, the relation extraction task contains rich predefined schemas (e.g., entity and relation type constraints) and a relatively large and complex classification space with noisy data. We further design two simple-yet-effective strategies to unleash the power of large language models better: **task-related instructions** and **schema-constrained data generation**. We conduct exhaustive experiments on four well-known relation extraction datasets. Empirical results indicate that LLMs can potentially be advantageous to few-shot relation extraction and boost previous prompt learning performance.

## 2 Background

### 2.1 Few-shot Relation Extraction

The relation extraction task aims to extract the relationship between head and tail entities within a plain context. Specifically, one instance for the relation extraction task consists of a context $\boldsymbol{x} = \{x_1, x_2, ..., h, ..., t, ..., x_{|\boldsymbol{x}|}\}$, head and tail entity mentions $\boldsymbol{h}$ and $\boldsymbol{t}$, entity types $\boldsymbol{t}_h$ and $\boldsymbol{t}_t$, and the relation $\boldsymbol{y} \in \mathcal{Y}$ between $\boldsymbol{h}$ and $\boldsymbol{t}$, where $\mathcal{Y}$ is the set of candidate relations. RE systems will predict $\boldsymbol{y}$ given $\boldsymbol{x}, \boldsymbol{h}, \boldsymbol{t}, \boldsymbol{t}_h$ and $\boldsymbol{t}_t$. For few-shot relation extraction, fine-tuning pre-trained language models (PLMs) is a direct solution (Han et al., 2019; Yamada et al., 2020; Joshi et al., 2020; Lyu and Chen, 2021; Zhou and Chen, 2022). To alleviate the gap between pre-training objectives and downstream applications, prompt tuning has recently been applied to relation extraction, especially for low-resource scenarios (Chen et al., 2022; Han et al., 2021b, 2022). Most of those approaches

* Corresponding author.

[1]Code is available in https://github.com/zjunlp/DeepKE/tree/main/example/llm.



*Proceedings of The Fourth Workshop on Simple and Efficient Natural Language Processing (SustaiNLP)*, pages 190–200
July 13, 2023 

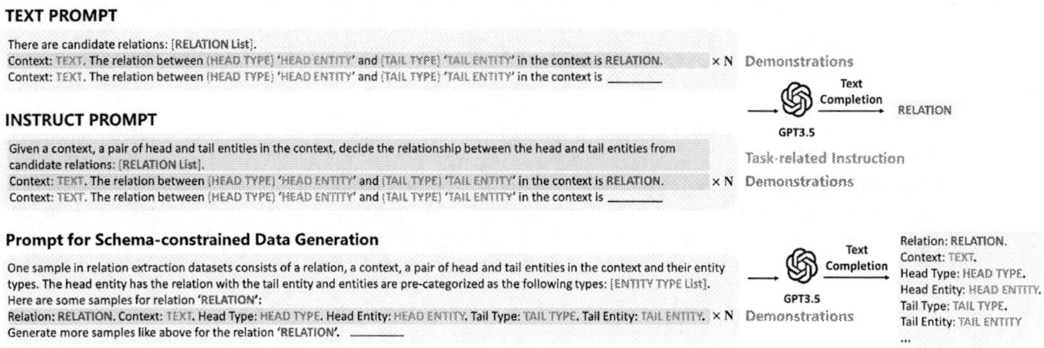


Figure 1: Strategies to unleash the power of LLMs for few-shot relation. HEAD TYPE and TAIL TYPE are schemas. HEAD ENTITY and TAIL ENTITY are entity mentions. RELATION refers the verbalized relation label words.

utilize relatively small language models (RoBERTa (Liu et al., 2019), GPT2 (Radford et al., 2019)), demonstrating empirical success regarding few-shot relation extraction performance. To date, large language models have demonstrated powerful abilities by prompting a few instances without tuning (Ding et al., 2022); however, the power of LLMs for few-shot relation extraction is little known.

### 2.2 Large Language Models

Large language models, trained with exceedingly large corpora and often with a great number of parameters ($\geq$10B), have achieved excellent performance in numerous downstream NLP tasks (Taylor et al., 2022; Zhang et al., 2022; Zeng et al., 2022; Chowdhery et al., 2022; Ouyang et al., 2022). Compared to relatively small language models (SLMs), LLMs are usually not open-source and can not be fine-tuned, which is challenging for downstream task adaptation. Therefore, in-context learning (Brown et al., 2020) is proposed to utilize prompts with a few demonstrations for few-shot learning. Previous studies (Yoo et al., 2021; Wang et al., 2021) have investigated using LLMs for text classification and generation. In this work, we take the first step to study few-shot RE with large language models, which brings new challenges and insights.

## 3 LLMs for Few-shot Relation Extraction

In this section, we introduce two strategies to utilize LLMs for relation extraction: 1) in-context learning (§3.1); 2) data generation (§3.2) with LLMs, as shown in Figure 1.

### 3.1 In-Context Learning with LLMs

The first strategy applies in-context learning (ICL) by providing LLMs with demonstrations in the prompt to elicit comprehension of the relation extraction task from LLMs. To this end, specific and compelling prompts for RE with demonstrations are manually constructed and designed to instruct LLMs to understand the relation extraction task and how to execute relation extraction. Considering aspects and characteristics of the relation extraction task, including task definition, candidate relation (label) words, entity types (schemas) and so on, we design prompts of different articulation and complexity to investigate how prompts help LLMs release the power of few-shot RE. First, **TEXT PROMPT** only contains essential elements for RE, including relation categories, contexts, and corresponding head and tail entities. Inspired by the fantastic performance of InstructGPT (Ouyang et al., 2022) and ChatGPT (OpenAI, 2022), we design the **task-related instruction** describing the relation extraction task and add it to the prompt, which is named **INSTRUCT PROMPT**. Meanwhile, according to previous few-shot RE works (Zhou and Chen, 2022), entity types (schemas) are helpful; therefore, we also explore the effectiveness of schemas in prompts.

### 3.2 Data Generation with LLMs

To complement the scarcity of labeled data, we introduce another strategy: data generation via LLMs. Specifically, we utilize specific prompts with descriptions of data forms to guide LLMs to generate more in-domain labeled data autonomously, which is subsequently employed to fine-tune a relatively small language model with existing few-shot labeled training data. We design the prompt to tell the essential components ($x, h, t, t_h, t_t$ and $y$) of one RE training instance and show few-shot instances as demonstrations to teach LLMs to comprehend

| | Method | TACRED | | TACREV | | RE-TACRED | | SciERC | |
|---|---|---|---|---|---|---|---|---|---|
| | | K=8 | K=16 | K=8 | K=16 | K=8 | K=16 | K=8 | K=16 |
| Baselines | SpanBERT (Joshi et al., 2020) | 8.4 | 17.5 | 5.2 | 5.7 | 14.2 | 29.3 | 29.0 | 38.7 |
| | LUKE (Yamada et al., 2020) | 9.5 | 21.5 | 9.8 | 22.0 | 14.1 | 37.5 | 33.2 | 48.9 |
| | GDPNet (Xue et al., 2021) | 11.8 | 22.5 | 8.3 | 20.8 | 18.8 | 48.0 | 33.5 | 42.3 |
| | TANL (Paolini et al., 2021) | 18.1 | 27.6 | 18.6 | 28.8 | 26.7 | 50.4 | 32.4 | 38.7 |
| | TYP Marker (Zhou and Chen, 2022) | 26.5 | 29.9 | 26.7 | 29.5 | 44.8 | 54.1 | 50.4 | 59.0 |
| | KnowPrompt (Chen et al., 2022) | 29.4 | 32.1 | 29.8 | 34.1 | 56.1 | 61.4 | 50.2 | 57.1 |
| GPT3 | In-context Learning† | 31.9 | | 32.4 | | 49.9 | | 46.6 | |
| | In-context Learning†(w/ Instruction) | 31.0 | | 31.9 | | 51.8 | | 48.8 | |
| | Data Generation (TYP Marker) | 35.8 | 36.6 | 36.7 | 36.5 | 58.4 | 60.6 | 63.2 | 64.3 |
| | Data Generation (KnowPrompt) | 37.9 | 37.4 | 42.6 | 41.0 | 62.7 | 66.2 | 58.6 | 67.8 |

Table 1: Micro F1 (%) of few-shot performance. † refers to the performance with one-shot demonstrations.

| Prompts | TACRED | TACREV | RE-TACRED | SciERC |
|---|---|---|---|---|
| TEXT | 31.9 | 32.4 | 49.9 | 46.6 |
| TEXT + Schema | 36.9 | 37.7 | 54.3 | 45.9 |
| INSTRUCT | 31.0 | 31.9 | 51.8 | 48.8 |
| INSTRUCT + Schema | 38.3 | 36.7 | 58.5 | 50.2 |

Table 2: Micro F1 (%) of performance on different prompt: TEXT PROMPT and INSTRUCT PROMPT.

features of labeled RE data. Note that schemas, such as types of relations and entities, are significant structural information in RE data. Therefore, we propose **schema-constrained data generation** by adding entity types as schema guidance to the prompt (in Figure 1) to boost performance. Then, the prompt is utilized to guide LLMs to create augmented relation extraction data that are converted into the expected format for future usage.

## 4 Experimental Setups

### 4.1 Methods and Datasets

**GPT-3.5** is utilized via OpenAI API[2] as the large language model in our experiments. We implement experiments on four relation extraction datasets, including TACRED (Zhang et al., 2017), TACREV (Alt et al., 2020), RE-TACRED (Stoica et al., 2021) and SciERC (Luan et al., 2018). Compared with the LLM, six baselines methods are conducted via relatively small models (details in Appendix A).

### 4.2 Few-shot Settings

**$K$ instances per relation ($K$-shot) are sampled for training and validation.** For all baselines, we use randomly sampled 8-shot and 16-shot datasets for training and validation. As for in-context learning, because GPT-3.5 has the limitation of maximum request tokens (4097 tokens) and the series of TACRED datasets have more than 40 relations, **one-shot demonstrations** can only be used, and the one-shot performance is reported in Table 1. For the same reason, to generate more labeled data for each relation independently, only three demonstrations for the relation are added to the prompts.

In-context learning is implemented on the four whole test sets. Different demonstrations are randomly sampled from the shuffled training set every time to avoid effects from permutations of demonstrations (Lu et al., 2021). As for data generation, generated data from GPT-3.5 and original few-shot training data are combined to fine-tune two baselines, TYP Marker (Zhou and Chen, 2022) and KnowPrompt (Chen et al., 2022). Using different shots of generated data will lead to different results. Therefore, we increasingly add generated $k$-shot ($k \in \{8, 16, 32, 48\}$) data to the original 8-shot and 16-shot training data respectively and report the best performance over $k$ in Tabel 1. More details are shown in Appendix A.3.

## 5 Results and Discussion

### 5.1 Main Findings for Relation Extraction

**In-context learning on LLMs can achieve comparable performance for RE with tuning relatively small PLMs.** From Table 1, we notice that ICL with only one-shot demonstrations can obtain competitive performance with full parameter tuning-based prompt learning baselines. Using LLMs via ICL does not necessitate any parameter updates, which contains the potential value of mak-

[2] https://platform.openai.com/docs/models/gpt-3-5

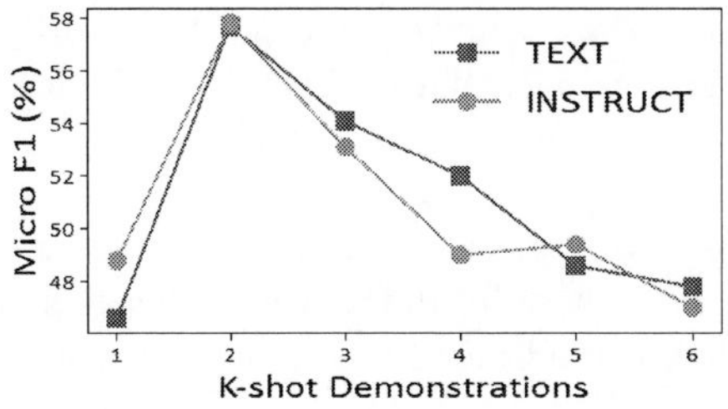


Figure 2: Micro F1 (%) of $k$ in-context demonstrations in SciERC.

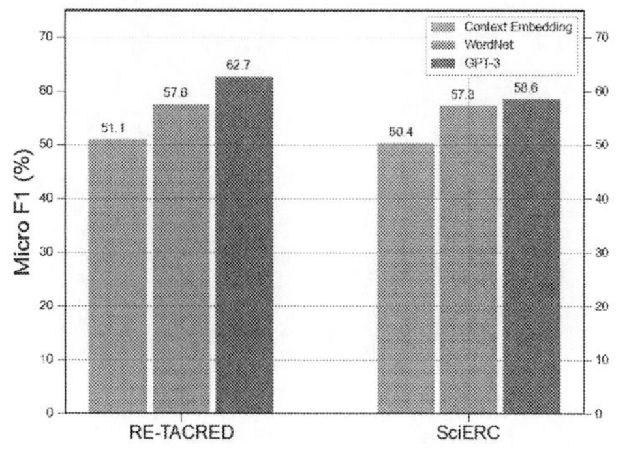


Figure 3: Performance of data generation with LLMs and different data augmentation methods. *Roberta* and *SciBERT* are used on RE-TACRED and SciERC, respectively, in the context embedding-based DA method.

ing models scenario-adaptable, unlike supervised learning requiring parameter optimization.

**Data generation with LLMs can boost previous solutions to obtain new state-of-the-art few-shot RE results.** We find that previous baselines can significantly improve with **10.7%** for 16-shot in SciERC and **6.6%** for 16-shot in RE-TACRED by simply using generated data from GPT-3.5 in Table 1. To be noted, data generation is a simple yet effective approach to elicit the power from the LLM to previous methods, and we demonstrate that using schema-constrained generation with LLMs can benefit all previous approaches with SLMs.

### 5.2 Prompts in In-context Learning with LLMs

**Instructions and schemas play an essential role in in-context learning for RE with LLMs.** From Table 2, we notice that the model with INSTRUCT PROMPT obtains better performance than TEXT PROMPT in most cases, indicating task-related information indeed helps to unlock more ability of LLMs for RE. Aberrant results are shown in TACRED and TACREV because incorrectly labeled demonstrations from the two datasets will violate the correct instruction fed into LLMs, which confuses LLMs and results on worse performance than ICL without the instruction. Moreover, adding schema information obtains much better performance, exhibiting the importance of pre-defined structural information for relation extraction.

**More demonstrations, counter-intuitively, may not lead to performance improvement for RE with LLMs.** We find performance will not improve even drop and the gap between INSTRUCT PROMPT and TEXT PROMPT becomes relatively smaller as the number of in-context demonstrations increases from Figure 2. We argue that there may be two reasons: 1) it is challenging to select representative demonstrations; 2) it is non-trivial for LLMs to understand structure prediction tasks with more large output (relation) space. More case studies for GPT-3.5 can be found in Appendix B.1.

### 5.3 Utility of Generated Data from LLMs

**Combining data generated from LLMs with original training data can yield better RE performance than from traditional data augmentation approaches.** We compare data generation through the LLM with previous widely used data generation approaches, such as substituting words in training sets with WordNet's synonyms and contextual word embedding in Figure 3 (details in Appendix A.3). Data generation with LLMs can obtain better performance than all others, indicating guiding LLMs to generate data is an effective method to compensate for the lack of labeled data.

**Using more and more generated data from LLMs can only boost RE performance to a certain extent, not continuously better.** From Figure 4, we observe that with more generated data, the result climbs up first and then declines, and is always higher than without generated data. We think low-quality generated data introduces much noise in the training course, according to the analysis on generated data in Appendix B.2, and LMs may have an anti-noise capacity (Song et al., 2020).

## 6 Discussion and Conclusion

In this paper, we take the first step to investigate how to utilize the large language model for few-shot relation extraction. We observe that task-related information, including instructions or

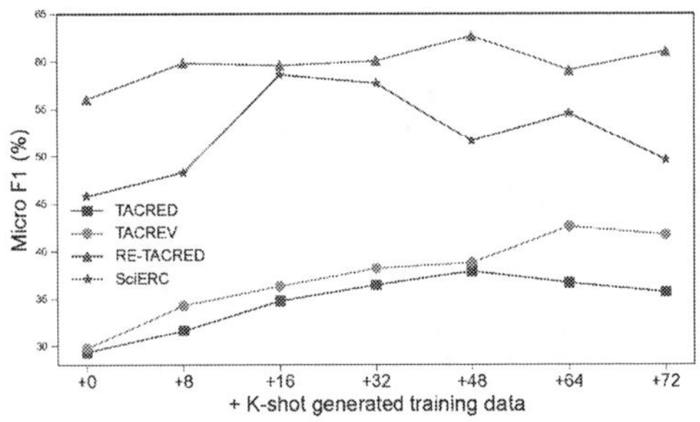


Figure 4: Micro F1 (%) of KnowPrompt with generated training data and original 8-shot data.

schemas, helps to elicit the capability of LLMs and boost few-shot relation extraction performance. At this stage, using LLMs to generate data may be a simple yet effective solution to enhance the power of foundation models (relatively small PLMs) for practical applications. We hope this work can deliver the benefits of using LLMs for the NLP community. Note that LLMs can make predictions only based on contexts combined with a few training examples as demonstrations. We argue that it has the potential to design sophisticated human-readable prompts for scenario-adaptable (e.g., low-shot and any domains) relation extraction.

## Acknowledgment

We would like to express gratitude to the anonymous reviewers for their kind comments. This work was supported by the National Natural Science Foundation of China (No.62206246), Zhejiang Provincial Natural Science Foundation of China (No. LGG22F030011), Ningbo Natural Science Foundation (2021J190), and Yongjiang Talent Introduction Programme (2021A-156-G), CAAI-Huawei MindSpore Open Fund.

## Limitations

Despite our best efforts, there may still be some limitations remaining in this paper.

**LLMs:** Due to the limited budgets, we can not afford all kinds of LLMs, so we only evaluate GPT-3.5 (*text-davinci-003*). We will try to investigate relation extraction with more LLMs, such as OPT (Zhang et al., 2022), GLM-130B (Zeng et al., 2022), or code language models (Bi et al., 2023) like Codex.

**Other Methods to utilize LLMs:** There are several other techniques to leverage LLMs, such as black-box optimization (Sun et al., 2022) and feature-based learning (Lang et al., 2022); however, we find that most of those approaches cannot directly be applied to relation extraction due to the large label space and complex schema structures. We leave these for future work to leverage other methods with LLMs for relation extraction.

**Datasets:** We only evaluate four relation extraction datasets and will try to investigate relation extraction performance with LLMs on more diverse datasets across different domains and languages.

## References

Christoph Alt, Aleksandra Gabryszak, and Leonhard Hennig. 2020. Tacred revisited: A thorough evaluation of the tacred relation extraction task. In *Proceedings of ACL*.

Iz Beltagy, Kyle Lo, and Arman Cohan. 2019. SciBERT: A pretrained language model for scientific text. In *Proceedings of the 2019 Conference on Empirical Methods in Natural Language Processing and the 9th International Joint Conference on Natural Language Processing (EMNLP-IJCNLP)*, pages 3615–3620, Hong Kong, China. Association for Computational Linguistics.

Zhen Bi, Jing Chen, Yinuo Jiang, Feiyu Xiong, Wei Guo, Huajun Chen, and Ningyu Zhang. 2023. Codekgc: Code language model for generative knowledge graph construction. *CoRR*, abs/2304.09048.

Sam Brody, Sichao Wu, and Adrian Benton. 2021. Towards realistic few-shot relation extraction. In *Proceedings of the 2021 Conference on Empirical Methods in Natural Language Processing*, pages 5338–5345, Online and Punta Cana, Dominican Republic. Association for Computational Linguistics.

Tom Brown, Benjamin Mann, Nick Ryder, Melanie Subbiah, Jared D Kaplan, Prafulla Dhariwal, Arvind Neelakantan, Pranav Shyam, Girish Sastry, Amanda Askell, Sandhini Agarwal, Ariel Herbert-Voss, Gretchen Krueger, Tom Henighan, Rewon Child, Aditya Ramesh, Daniel Ziegler, Jeffrey Wu, Clemens Winter, Chris Hesse, Mark Chen, Eric Sigler, Mateusz Litwin, Scott Gray, Benjamin Chess, Jack Clark, Christopher Berner, Sam McCandlish, Alec Radford, Ilya Sutskever, and Dario Amodei. 2020. Language models are few-shot learners. In *Advances in Neural Information Processing Systems*, volume 33, pages 1877–1901. Curran Associates, Inc.

Xiang Chen, Ningyu Zhang, Xin Xie, Shumin Deng, Yunzhi Yao, Chuanqi Tan, Fei Huang, Luo Si, and Huajun Chen. 2022. Knowprompt: Knowledge-aware prompt-tuning with synergistic optimization for relation extraction. In *WWW '22: The ACM Web*

*Conference 2022, Virtual Event, Lyon, France, April 25 - 29, 2022*, pages 2778–2788. ACM.

Aakanksha Chowdhery, Sharan Narang, Jacob Devlin, Maarten Bosma, Gaurav Mishra, Adam Roberts, Paul Barham, Hyung Won Chung, Charles Sutton, Sebastian Gehrmann, Parker Schuh, Kensen Shi, Sasha Tsvyashchenko, Joshua Maynez, Abhishek Rao, Parker Barnes, Yi Tay, Noam Shazeer, Vinodkumar Prabhakaran, Emily Reif, Nan Du, Ben Hutchinson, Reiner Pope, James Bradbury, Jacob Austin, Michael Isard, Guy Gur-Ari, Pengcheng Yin, Toju Duke, Anselm Levskaya, Sanjay Ghemawat, Sunipa Dev, Henryk Michalewski, Xavier Garcia, Vedant Misra, Kevin Robinson, Liam Fedus, Denny Zhou, Daphne Ippolito, David Luan, Hyeontaek Lim, Barret Zoph, Alexander Spiridonov, Ryan Sepassi, David Dohan, Shivani Agrawal, Mark Omernick, Andrew M. Dai, Thanumalayan Sankaranarayana Pillai, Marie Pellat, Aitor Lewkowycz, Erica Moreira, Rewon Child, Oleksandr Polozov, Katherine Lee, Zongwei Zhou, Xuezhi Wang, Brennan Saeta, Mark Diaz, Orhan Firat, Michele Catasta, Jason Wei, Kathy Meier-Hellstern, Douglas Eck, Jeff Dean, Slav Petrov, and Noah Fiedel. 2022. Palm: Scaling language modeling with pathways. *arXiv preprint*, abs/2204.02311.

Bosheng Ding, Chengwei Qin, Linlin Liu, Lidong Bing, Shafiq R. Joty, and Boyang Li. 2022. Is GPT-3 a good data annotator? *arXiv preprint*, abs/2212.10450.

Qingxiu Dong, Lei Li, Damai Dai, Ce Zheng, Zhiyong Wu, Baobao Chang, Xu Sun, Jingjing Xu, Lei Li, and Zhifang Sui. 2023. A survey for in-context learning. *arXiv preprint*, abs/2301.00234.

Jiale Han, Bo Cheng, and Wei Lu. 2021a. Exploring task difficulty for few-shot relation extraction. In *Proceedings of the 2021 Conference on Empirical Methods in Natural Language Processing, EMNLP 2021, Virtual Event / Punta Cana, Dominican Republic, 7-11 November, 2021*, pages 2605–2616. Association for Computational Linguistics.

Jiale Han, Shuai Zhao, Bo Cheng, Shengkun Ma, and Wei Lu. 2022. Generative prompt tuning for relation classification. In *Findings of the Association for Computational Linguistics: EMNLP 2022*, pages 3170–3185, Abu Dhabi, United Arab Emirates. Association for Computational Linguistics.

Xu Han, Tianyu Gao, Yuan Yao, Deming Ye, Zhiyuan Liu, and Maosong Sun. 2019. Opennre: An open and extensible toolkit for neural relation extraction. In *Proceedings of the 2019 Conference on Empirical Methods in Natural Language Processing and the 9th International Joint Conference on Natural Language Processing, EMNLP-IJCNLP 2019, Hong Kong, China, November 3-7, 2019 - System Demonstrations*, pages 169–174. Association for Computational Linguistics.

Xu Han, Weilin Zhao, Ning Ding, Zhiyuan Liu, and Maosong Sun. 2021b. PTR: prompt tuning with rules for text classification. *arXiv preprint*, abs/2105.11259.

Xu Han, Hao Zhu, Pengfei Yu, Ziyun Wang, Yuan Yao, Zhiyuan Liu, and Maosong Sun. 2018. FewRel: A large-scale supervised few-shot relation classification dataset with state-of-the-art evaluation. In *Proceedings of the 2018 Conference on Empirical Methods in Natural Language Processing*, pages 4803–4809, Brussels, Belgium. Association for Computational Linguistics.

Mandar Joshi, Danqi Chen, Yinhan Liu, Daniel S. Weld, Luke Zettlemoyer, and Omer Levy. 2020. Spanbert: Improving pre-training by representing and predicting spans. *Trans. Assoc. Comput. Linguistics*, 8:64–77.

Hunter Lang, Monica N. Agrawal, Yoon Kim, and David A. Sontag. 2022. Co-training improves prompt-based learning for large language models. In *International Conference on Machine Learning, ICML 2022, 17-23 July 2022, Baltimore, Maryland, USA*, volume 162 of *Proceedings of Machine Learning Research*, pages 11985–12003. PMLR.

Yinhan Liu, Myle Ott, Naman Goyal, Jingfei Du, Mandar Joshi, Danqi Chen, Omer Levy, Mike Lewis, Luke Zettlemoyer, and Veselin Stoyanov. 2019. Roberta: A robustly optimized BERT pretraining approach. *arXiv:1907.11692*, abs/1907.11692.

Yao Lu, Max Bartolo, Alastair Moore, Sebastian Riedel, and Pontus Stenetorp. 2021. Fantastically ordered prompts and where to find them: Overcoming few-shot prompt order sensitivity. *arXiv preprint*, abs/2104.08786.

Yi Luan, Luheng He, Mari Ostendorf, and Hannaneh Hajishirzi. 2018. Multi-task identification of entities, relations, and coreferencefor scientific knowledge graph construction. In *Proc. Conf. Empirical Methods Natural Language Process. (EMNLP)*.

Shengfei Lyu and Huanhuan Chen. 2021. Relation classification with entity type restriction. In *Findings of the Association for Computational Linguistics: ACL/IJCNLP 2021, Online Event, August 1-6, 2021*, volume ACL/IJCNLP 2021 of *Findings of ACL*, pages 390–395. Association for Computational Linguistics.

Yubo Ma, Yixin Cao, YongChing Hong, and Aixin Sun. 2023. Large language model is not a good few-shot information extractor, but a good reranker for hard samples! *CoRR*, abs/2303.08559.

OpenAI. 2022. Chatgpt: Optimizing language models for dialogue. `https://openai.com/blog/chatgpt/`.

OpenAI. 2023a. Gpt-4 technical report. *arXiv preprint*, abs/2303.08774.

OpenAI. 2023b. Text-davinci-003. `https://platform.openai.com/docs/models/text-davinci-003`.

Long Ouyang, Jeff Wu, Xu Jiang, Diogo Almeida, Carroll L. Wainwright, Pamela Mishkin, Chong Zhang, Sandhini Agarwal, Katarina Slama, Alex Ray, John Schulman, Jacob Hilton, Fraser Kelton, Luke Miller, Maddie Simens, Amanda Askell, Peter Welinder, Paul F. Christiano, Jan Leike, and Ryan Lowe. 2022. Training language models to follow instructions with human feedback. *arXiv preprint*, abs/2203.02155.

Giovanni Paolini, Ben Athiwaratkun, Jason Krone, Jie Ma, Alessandro Achille, Rishita Anubhai, Cícero Nogueira dos Santos, Bing Xiang, and Stefano Soatto. 2021. Structured prediction as translation between augmented natural languages. In *9th International Conference on Learning Representations, ICLR 2021, Virtual Event, Austria, May 3-7, 2021*. OpenReview.net.

Alec Radford, Jeffrey Wu, Rewon Child, David Luan, Dario Amodei, Ilya Sutskever, et al. 2019. Language models are unsupervised multitask learners. *OpenAI blog*, 1(8):9.

Livio Baldini Soares, Nicholas FitzGerald, Jeffrey Ling, and Tom Kwiatkowski. 2019. Matching the blanks: Distributional similarity for relation learning. In *Proceedings of the 57th Conference of the Association for Computational Linguistics, ACL 2019, Florence, Italy, July 28- August 2, 2019, Volume 1: Long Papers*, pages 2895–2905. Association for Computational Linguistics.

Hwanjun Song, Minseok Kim, Dongmin Park, and Jae-Gil Lee. 2020. Learning from noisy labels with deep neural networks: A survey. *arXiv preprint*, abs/2007.08199.

George Stoica, Emmanouil Antonios Platanios, and Barnabás Póczos. 2021. Re-tacred: Addressing shortcomings of the TACRED dataset. In *Thirty-Fifth AAAI Conference on Artificial Intelligence, AAAI 2021, Thirty-Third Conference on Innovative Applications of Artificial Intelligence, IAAI 2021, The Eleventh Symposium on Educational Advances in Artificial Intelligence, EAAI 2021, Virtual Event, February 2-9, 2021*, pages 13843–13850. AAAI Press.

Tianxiang Sun, Yunfan Shao, Hong Qian, Xuanjing Huang, and Xipeng Qiu. 2022. Black-box tuning for language-model-as-a-service. In *International Conference on Machine Learning, ICML 2022, 17-23 July 2022, Baltimore, Maryland, USA*, volume 162 of *Proceedings of Machine Learning Research*, pages 20841–20855. PMLR.

Ross Taylor, Marcin Kardas, Guillem Cucurull, Thomas Scialom, Anthony Hartshorn, Elvis Saravia, Andrew Poulton, Viktor Kerkez, and Robert Stojnic. 2022. Galactica: A large language model for science. *arXiv preprint*, abs/2211.09085.

Shuohang Wang, Yang Liu, Yichong Xu, Chenguang Zhu, and Michael Zeng. 2021. Want to reduce labeling cost? GPT-3 can help. In *Findings of the Association for Computational Linguistics: EMNLP 2021, Virtual Event / Punta Cana, Dominican Republic, 16-20 November, 2021*, pages 4195–4205. Association for Computational Linguistics.

Fuzhao Xue, Aixin Sun, Hao Zhang, and Eng Siong Chng. 2021. Gdpnet: Refining latent multi-view graph for relation extraction. In *Thirty-Fifth AAAI Conference on Artificial Intelligence, AAAI 2021, Thirty-Third Conference on Innovative Applications of Artificial Intelligence, IAAI 2021, The Eleventh Symposium on Educational Advances in Artificial Intelligence, EAAI 2021, Virtual Event, February 2-9, 2021*, pages 14194–14202. AAAI Press.

Ikuya Yamada, Akari Asai, Hiroyuki Shindo, Hideaki Takeda, and Yuji Matsumoto. 2020. LUKE: deep contextualized entity representations with entity-aware self-attention. In *Proceedings of the 2020 Conference on Empirical Methods in Natural Language Processing, EMNLP 2020, Online, November 16-20, 2020*, pages 6442–6454. Association for Computational Linguistics.

Shan Yang, Yongfei Zhang, Guanglin Niu, Qinghua Zhao, and Shiliang Pu. 2021. Entity concept-enhanced few-shot relation extraction. In *Proceedings of the 59th Annual Meeting of the Association for Computational Linguistics and the 11th International Joint Conference on Natural Language Processing, ACL/IJCNLP 2021, (Volume 2: Short Papers), Virtual Event, August 1-6, 2021*, pages 987–991. Association for Computational Linguistics.

Hongbin Ye, Ningyu Zhang, Hui Chen, and Huajun Chen. 2022. Generative knowledge graph construction: A review. In *Proceedings of the 2022 Conference on Empirical Methods in Natural Language Processing*, pages 1–17, Abu Dhabi, United Arab Emirates. Association for Computational Linguistics.

Kang Min Yoo, Dongju Park, Jaewook Kang, Sang-Woo Lee, and Woo-Myoung Park. 2021. Gpt3mix: Leveraging large-scale language models for text augmentation. In *Findings of the Association for Computational Linguistics: EMNLP 2021, Virtual Event / Punta Cana, Dominican Republic, 16-20 November, 2021*, pages 2225–2239. Association for Computational Linguistics.

Aohan Zeng, Xiao Liu, Zhengxiao Du, Zihan Wang, Hanyu Lai, Ming Ding, Zhuoyi Yang, Yifan Xu, Wendi Zheng, Xiao Xia, Weng Lam Tam, Zixuan Ma, Yufei Xue, Jidong Zhai, Wenguang Chen, Peng Zhang, Yuxiao Dong, and Jie Tang. 2022. GLM-130B: an open bilingual pre-trained model. *CoRR*, abs/2210.02414.

Susan Zhang, Stephen Roller, Naman Goyal, Mikel Artetxe, Moya Chen, Shuohui Chen, Christopher Dewan, Mona T. Diab, Xian Li, Xi Victoria Lin, Todor Mihaylov, Myle Ott, Sam Shleifer, Kurt Shuster, Daniel Simig, Punit Singh Koura, Anjali Sridhar, Tianlu Wang, and Luke Zettlemoyer. 2022. OPT: open pre-trained transformer language models. *CoRR*, abs/2205.01068.

Yuhao Zhang, Victor Zhong, Danqi Chen, Gabor Angeli, and Christopher D. Manning. 2017. Position-aware attention and supervised data improve slot filling. In *Proceedings of the 2017 Conference on Empirical Methods in Natural Language Processing (EMNLP 2017)*, pages 35–45.

Wenxuan Zhou and Muhao Chen. 2022. An improved baseline for sentence-level relation extraction. In *Proceedings of the 2nd Conference of the Asia-Pacific Chapter of the Association for Computational Linguistics and the 12th International Joint Conference on Natural Language Processing, AACL/IJCNLP 2022 - Volume 2: Short Papers, Online only, November 20-23, 2022*, pages 161–168. Association for Computational Linguistics.

# A Experimental Details

## A.1 Datasets

TACRED[3] is a widely used RE dataset. It has 42 relation labels, including *no_relation*, meaning no relation is found. TACREV[4] includes the same training set and relabeled development and test sets from TACRED. RE-TACRED[5] is a re-annotated version of TACRED with 40 relations. SciERC[6] has seven relation categories and is constructed in the scientific domain. All datasets are derived from their official webs without modification, including contents and train/test/dev splits.

## A.2 Baselines

We compare LLMs with recent baseline methods using relatively small models. 1) Normal fine-tuning methods: **SpanBERT** (Joshi et al., 2020), a span-based PLM; **LUKE** (Yamada et al., 2020), pre-trained contextualized representations of words and entities based on the bidirectional transformer; **GDPNet**, a gaussian dynamic time warping pooling net able to select important words for relation prediction; **TYP Marker** (Zhou and Chen, 2022), fine-tuning with entity typed markers. 2) Generative method: **TANL** (Paolini et al., 2021), framing a structured prediction language task as a translation task between augmented natural languages. 3) Prompt-tuning methods: **KnowPrompt**, knowledge-aware continuous prompt-based tuning with synergistic optimization.

## A.3 Implementation Details

Generated data with existing training data is then evaluated on KnowPrompt. Data augmentation methods with Word-Net's synonyms and contextual word embedding are achieved by *nlpaug*[7]. The parameter *temperature* in OpenAI API is set to 0 for precision in ICL and 1 for generating diverse RE data. One NVIDIA GeForce RTX 3090 GPU with 24GB memory is employed to run all experiments. We rerun the official code of baselines with their original settings except on the SciERC dataset. Due to the vertical domain of SciERC, *SciBERT* (Beltagy et al., 2019) is used in TYP Marker and KnowPrompt for fairness. And for another three datasets, *RoBERTa-large* is utilized in *TYP Marker* and *KnowPrompt*.

[3]https://nlp.stanford.edu/projects/tacred/

[4]https://github.com/DFKI-NLP/tacrev

[5]https://github.com/gstoica27/Re-TACRED

[6]http://nlp.cs.washington.edu/sciIE/

# B Case Analysis

## B.1 Wrong Cases from ICL

From Table 4, we notice that some RE instances are challenging for LLMs, and there are several limitations with LLMs: 1) LLMs are not good at clearly distinguishing the order between head and tail entities. 2) The same mention of head and tail entities will confuse LLMs. 4) If the distance between head and tail entities in the context is long, it is difficult for LLMs to decide the relation correctly. 5) Semantically-similar relation label words and entity mentions will puzzle LLMs because their embeddings are similar. 6) LLMs cannot afford very long instances since there is a large label space for relation extraction. 7) LLMs may mostly fail to extract those ambitious or wrongly labeled relations; those are also challenging for humans. More high-quality demonstrations may help mitigate these issues. And we think it is necessary to develop step-by-step (Chat-style) approaches with LLMs to extract limited relations in one stage.

## B.2 Generated Data from LLMs

There are some cases for generated data from GPT-3.5 in Table 5. Through human checks on 100 generated samples per dataset, about 78% generated data are corrected labeled and of a high quality (85% for TACRED, 82.5% for TACREV, 72% for RE-TACRED, 75% for SciERC). Meanwhile, we add generated data and original gold training data respectively to 8-shot datasets and fine-tune *KnowPrompt*, we evaluate the quality of generated data as shown in Table 3. We observe that labeled data generated by GPT-3.5 are mostly correct. As for TACRED and TACREV, generated data achieve more improvements than gold labeled data. Since

[7]https://github.com/makcedward/nlpaug

| 8-shot Dataset | TACRED | | TACREV | | RE-TACRED | | SciERC | |
|---|---|---|---|---|---|---|---|---|
| | generated | gold | generated | gold | generated | gold | generated | gold |
| add 0-shot | 29.35 | 29.35 | 29.77 | 29.77 | 56.05 | 56.05 | 45.80 | 45.80 |
| add 8-shot | 31.63 | 30.73 | 34.30 | 33.16 | 59.85 | 60.92 | 48.30 | 57.08 |
| add 16-shot | 34.78 | 31.88 | 36.33 | 33.49 | 59.59 | 61.30 | **58.62** | 65.15 |
| add 32-shot | 36.45 | 33.35 | 38.19 | 33.98 | 60.06 | 64.65 | 57.70 | 72.11 |
| add 48-shot | **37.89** | 33.97 | 38.80 | 35.06 | **62.67** | 65.56 | 51.64 | 74.29 |
| add 64-shot | 36.67 | 34.36 | **42.61** | 35.57 | 61.07 | 67.28 | 54.52 | 75.36 |
| add 72-shot | 35.69 | **34.58** | 41.72 | **35.96** | 59.09 | **67.43** | 49.59 | **75.87** |

Table 3: Micro F1 (%) of *KnowPrompt* after adding labeled data generated by GPT-3.5 or gold labeled data to 8-shot datasets.

there are many incorrect labeled data in TACRED and TACREV (Zhang et al., 2017; Alt et al., 2020), we think better performance results from GPT-3.5's help. However, we also find that Some generated data from GPT-3.5 are of less quality than gold data. As for RE-TACRED and SciERC, using more gold data perform better than generated data. Through human checks, some generated samples are too short and concatenated by some semantically irrelevant sentences. Meanwhile, big performance's difference on SciERC shows GPT-3.5 is not good at vertical domains such as science.

| Dataset | Case | Gold Relation | In-context Learning |
|---|---|---|---|
| TACRED | Context: And strangely enough , Cain's short , three-year tenure at the NRA is evidently the only period in his decades-long career during which he 's alleged to have been a sexual predator.<br>Head Type: ORGANIZATION. Head Entity: NRA.<br>Tail Type: PERSON. Tail Type: Cain | org:top_members/employees | per:employee_of |
| | Context: "I learn from students and I challenge them," says Heloise, 58, who took over the family hints business when her mother, also named Heloise, died in 1977.<br>Head Type: PERSON. Head Entity: Heloise.<br>Tail Type: PERSON. Tail Entity: Heloise. | per:parents | per:alternate_names |
| TACREV | Context: Anna Mae Pictou Aquash, a Mi ' kmaq Indian from Canada, was brutally murdered in 1975.<br>Head Type: PERSON. Head Entity: Anna Mae Pictou Aquash.<br>Tail Type: COUNTRY. Tail Entity: Canada. | per:country_of_birth | per:countries_of_residence |
| | Context: Messina Denaro has been trying to impose his power in Palermo, the Sicilian capital, and become the new head of the Sicilian Mafia, weakened by the arrest of Provenzano in April 2006.<br>Head Type: PERSON. Head Entity: his.<br>Tail Type: CITY. Tail Entity: Palermo. | no_relation | per:cities_of_residence |
| RE-TACRED | Context: They say Vladimir Ladyzhenskiy died late Saturday during the contest in southern Finland, while his Finnish rival Timo Kaukonen was rushed to a hospital.<br>Head Type: PERSON. Head Entity: Vladimir Ladyzhenskiy.<br>Tail Type: PERSON. Tail Entity: his. | per:identity | per:date_of_death |
| | President of the Central American Parliament (Parlacen) Jacinto Suarez said on Monday that the presidents of the Central American countries did not support Panama 's request of withdrawal from the Parlacen.<br>Head Type: ORGANIZATION. Head Entity: Central American Parliament.<br>Tail Type: PERSON. Tail Entity: Jacinto Suarez. | org:top_members/employees | per:title |
| SciERC | Context: We evaluate across two corpora (conversational telephone speech and broadcast news speech) on both human transcriptions and speech recognition output.<br>Head Type: OtherScientificTerm. Head Entity: transcriptions.<br>Tail Type: OtherScientific Term. Tail Entity: output. | CONJUNCTION | COMPARE |
| | Context: We validate this new method on nine standard person re-identification datasets including two large scale Market-1501 and CUHK03 datasets and show that we improve upon the current state-of-the-art methods on all of them.<br>Head Type: Material. Head Entity: CUHK03 datasets.<br>Tail Type: Material. Tail Entity: datasets. | HYPONYM-OF | PART-OF |

Table 4: Wrong cases predicted by GPT-3.5. The gold relation categories are listed in the third column and the results predicted by in-context learning are in the fourth column.

| Dataset | Case | Corrective Data |
|---|---|---|
| TACRED | Context: The American Cancer Society is headquartered in Atlanta and was founded in 1913 by 15 trained laywomen.<br>Head Type: ORGANIZATION. Head Entity: American Cancer Society.<br>**Tail Type: ORGANIZATION**. Tail Entity: 15 trained laywomen.<br>Relation: org:founded_by. | Tail Type: PERSON |
| | Context: Mary Brown, CEO of Brown Corp and renowned businesswoman, is a regular speaker at industry conferences and events.<br>Head Type: PERSON. Head Entity: Mary Brown.<br>**Tail Type: PERSON**. Tail Entity: CEO.<br>Relation: per:title. | Tail Type: TITLE |
| TACREV | Context: Gustav Mahler was born in Kalischt, Bohemia on July 7th, 1860.<br>Head Type: PERSON. Head Entity: Gustav Mahler.<br>**Tail Type: PERSON**. Tail Entity: 1860.<br>**Relation: per:country_of_birth**. | Tail Type: DATE<br>Relation: per:date_of_birth |
| | Context: MTN Nigeria, a subsidiary of South African-based MTN Group, has begun to list its shares on the Nigerian Stock Exchange.<br>Head Type: ORGANIZATION. Head Entity: MTN Group.<br>Tail Type: ORGANIZATION. Tail Entity: MTN Nigeria.<br>Relation: org:subsidiaries. | - |
| RE-TACRED | Context: Pope John Paul II was a hugely popular Catholic leader who was based in the Vatican City for most of his papacy.<br>Head Type: PERSON. Head Entity: Pope John Paul II.<br>**Tail Type: PERSON**. Tail Entity: Vatican City.<br>**Relation: per:countries_of_residence**. | Tail Type: CITY<br>Reltaion: per:cities_of_residence |
| | Context: French drug manufacturer Sanofi-Aventis dissolved its Chinese subsidiary Guangzhou Pharma following a bribery scandal.<br>Head Type: ORGANIZATION. Head Entity: Sanofi-Aventis.<br>Tail Type: ORGANIZATION. Tail Entity: Guangzhou Pharma.<br>Relation: org:dissolved. | - |
| SciERC | Context: The comparison between the two approaches indicates that the neural method produces far better results than the rule-based system.<br>Head Type: Method. Head Entity: neural method.<br>Tail Type: Method. Tail Entity: rule-based system.<br>Relation: COMPARE. | - |
| | Context: The combination of chromatography and mass spectrometry has enabled scientists to achieve unparalleled levels of proteome analysis.<br>Head Type: Method. Head Entity: mass spectrometry.<br>Tail Type: Method. Tail Entity: chromatography.<br>**Relation: FEATURE-OF**. | Relation: CONJUNCTION |

Table 5: Generated data from LLMs. Errors are bold in the second column and corrected in the third column.

# Prompting language models improves performance in imbalanced setting

**Jay Mohta**
Amazon
jaymoht@amazon.com

## Abstract

Prompting is a widely adopted technique for fine-tuning large language models. Recent research by Scao and Rush (2021) has demonstrated its effectiveness in improving few-shot learning performance compared to vanilla fine-tuning and also showed that prompting and vanilla fine tuning achieves similar performance in high data regime ($\sim>$ 2000 samples). This paper investigates the impact of imbalanced data distribution on prompting. Through rigorous experimentation on diverse datasets and models, our findings reveals that even in scenarios with high data regimes, prompting consistently outperforms vanilla fine-tuning by exhibiting average performance improvement of $2-5\%$.

## 1 Introduction

Fine tuning language models is a common strategy in Natural Language Processing (NLP), where a classifier head is added on top of the base language model to obtain the desired classification output. This approach has been applied to various NLP models, including RoBERTa (Liu et al., 2019), ALBERT (Lan et al., 2019), and DeBERTa (He et al., 2020), and has demonstrated exceptional performance on benchmark datasets such as GLUE (Wang et al., 2018) and SuperGLUE (Wang et al., 2019).

An alternate approach to adapting language models to downstream tasks involves the use of autoregressive text generation or prompt based fine tuning. This technique is commonly used in sequence-to-sequence models such as T5 (Raffel et al., 2019) leading to state-of-the-art performance on SuperGLUE benchmark. This type of fine tuning strategy has an added advantage of multi-task training (McCann et al., 2018). This technique has also shown to improve models zero shot capability (Puri and Catanzaro, 2019) where we can provide only task description and model is able to classify the input correctly.

Work by Scao and Rush (2021); Schick and Schütze (2020); Webson and Pavlick (2021) has shown that prompting language models really helps in few shot learning setting over vanilla fine tuned models. In high data regime setting prompting and vanilla fine tuned language models achieve the similar performance. However, these studies used balanced datasets where the number of examples from each class are equal.

The issue of class imbalance in machine learning is a well-known challenge, and occurs when the distribution of samples across classes is skewed. These types of problems are encountered in various real world settings like malware detection (Demirkiran et al., 2021), spam detection (Rao et al., 2023), medical domain (Altaf et al., 2023) and many more. Previous work by Buda et al. (2017); Leevy et al. (2018) has shown that if we use general supervised loss then it leads to poor generalization on the minority classes. In this work we ask the question: How does prompting impact performance in imbalanced setting? To the best of our knowledge this is the first work which explores impact of prompting in imbalanced setting.

In this work therefore we conduct an experimental study by varying imbalance ratio and compare performance of vanilla fine tuned model with that of prompting based models. Our study includes experiments with varying models like RoBERTa (Liu et al., 2019), ALBERT (Lan et al., 2019) and DeBERTa (He et al., 2020), and different datasets like RTE (Dagan et al., 2007), QQP (Chen et al., 2017) and MRPC (Lan et al., 2017). To study how different imbalance ratios affect performance we vary imbalance ratio from 0.1%-30%. We also compare the impact of model size on the performance of models in imbalanced settings i.e. for ALBERT we run experiments on large and its base counterpart. To make our finding more robust we experiment across different prompts as work by Webson and Pavlick (2021) points out that different



*Proceedings of The Fourth Workshop on Simple and Efficient Natural Language Processing (SustaiNLP)*, pages 201–211
July 13, 2023 ©2023 Association for Computational Linguistics

prompts could impact performance of the models. To isolate the impact of prompting we don't use any special technique like PET (Schick and Schütze, 2021), AdaPET (Tam et al., 2021) for performing fine tuning. We suspect that using those techniques may further improve performance of prompt based models.

Our results show that prompting helps in imbalanced setting over vanilla fine tuning in mild imbalanced setting even in high data regime by $2-5\%$ increase in performance on average. In high and no imbalanced setting the prompting and vanilla fine tuning gives a very similar performance. This insight will help practitioners decide what fine tuning strategy works the best for their use case.

The rest of the paper is organized as follows section 2 will provide some background on vanilla fine tuning and prompting. section 3 describes our experimental setup and results. We conclude in section 4 with a summary of our findings and suggestions for future work.

## 2 Background

The aim of this work is to evaluate the impact of prompting on language model performance compared to traditional fine tuning. To achieve this, we conduct experiments with different imbalance ratios from severe to mild to low/no imbalance. The following sections provides background on vanilla fine tuning, prompting based fine tuning and imbalanced classification problems before delving into our empirical study.

### 2.1 Vanilla fine tuning

This is very simple and widely adopted fine tuning stratgey where we add classifier head on the top of language models. In the case of RoBERTa, ALBERT and DeBERTa the classification head is added on top of $[CLS]$ token and the embedding generated for that token are fed into this classification head to generate the classification output.

### 2.2 Prompt based fine tuning

Prompting is a fine tuning technique that utilizes masked language modeling to obtain the classification output, converting each classification task into sequence-to-sequence problem. Similar to PET (Schick and Schütze, 2021), the prompt is decomposed into two parts: the *pattern* and the *verbalizer*. The pattern transforms the input into clozed task, i.e., a sequence with a $mask$ token that needs to be filled by the model, serving as the classification output. The verbalizer then converts the output space into a token or sequence of tokens in the vocabulary. The goal of prompting is to guide the model by providing a pattern that contains the $mask$ token, and for the model to predict the correct output based on the defined verbalizer pattern.

To illustrate the technique of prompting, consider an example from the RTE dataset (Dagan et al., 2007). The task is to predict whether the premise *No Weapons of Mass Destruction Found in Iraq Yet.* entails the hypothesis, *Weapons of Mass Destruction Found in Iraq*. The prompt is generated using the verbalizer pattern that maps entailment to *yes* and non-entailment to *no*. The prompt pattern is defined as follows

> ***Given*** No Weapons of Mass Destruction Found in Iraq Yet. ***Should we assume that*** Weapons of Mass Destruction Found in Iraq ***mask***

The bolded text represents the prompt pattern, while the non-bolded text is the sample from RTE dataset. The model predict $yes$ or $no$ at the $mask$ token based on the verbalizer pattern we defined. Different pattern-verbalizer pattern can be used for single task and prior work (Webson and Pavlick, 2021; Brown et al., 2020) has shown that different choices of prompt pattern and verbalizer pairs can impact the performance of the model. To ensure robust results, we experiment with various prompt pattern-verbalizer pairs.

### 2.3 Class imbalance

In this work we define something called imbalance ratio which represents how imbalanced is your train set. It is defined as follows

$$\text{Imbalance Ratio} = \frac{\text{Number of negative samples}}{\text{Total number of samples}} \tag{1}$$

In order to effectively study prompting based technique in class imbalance we start from an imbalance ratio of $0.1\%$, we incrementally increase the imbalance ratio up to 30%, allowing us to study the effect of various levels of class imbalance.

## 3 Experimental setting and results

We now present our main experimental results to show that prompting improves performance of the

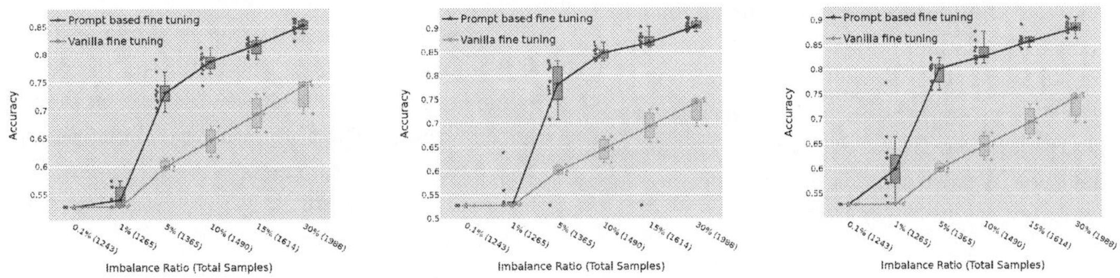


(a) RoBERTa (b) DeBERTa (c) ALBERT

Figure 1: These figures are similar to figures plotted in Webson and Pavlick (2021). Here each dot represents one prompt under one random seed (random seed controls different negative examples selected to create an imbalance). The plot compares fine tuning and prompt based tuning performance with varying imbalance ratios on RTE dataset (reported accuracies are on validation set). The boxes span from first quartile to third quartile while the lines inside the box mark the median.

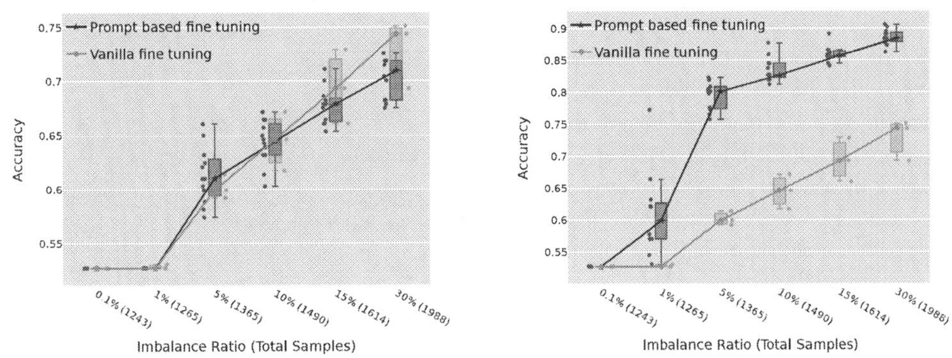


(a) ALBERT-Base (b) ALBERT-Large

Figure 2: Comparing performance of ALBERT-Base with ALBERT-Large on RTE dataset.

model than vanilla fine tuned model in imbalanced setting (even in high data regime). To improve the robustness of our results we experiment with different models, datasets and different training splits. In the following subsection we describe the setup and main takeways from the experiments.

### 3.1 Setup

We experimented with RoBERTa (Liu et al., 2019), ALBERT (Lan et al., 2019) and DeBERTa (He et al., 2020) pre-trained models. These are all encoder-only models trained using masked language modelling objective during pretraining phase. We experimented with different prompts from the open-source library *prompt-source* (Bach et al., 2022) to understand the impact of different prompts on performance. We provide experimental results on three different datasets Recognizing Textual Entailment (RTE) (Dagan et al., 2007), Quora Question Pairs (QQP) (Chen et al., 2017) and Microsoft Research Paraphrase Corpus (MPRC) (Lan et al., 2017). Except QQP which has $>$ 100k samples all other datasets have about 2400 samples. In order to check how prompting affect performance in imbalanced setting we experiment with different imbalance ratios defined in eq. (1). We start from as low as $0.1\%$ imbalance ratio and incrementally increase it up to $30\%$. To ensure the reliability of our results, we conduct multiple experiments by varying the random seed three times which is used for selecting a new subset of samples from the training set. On each downstream task we fine tune RoBERTa, ALBERT and DeBERTa using prompting based fine tuning and vanilla fine tuning with varying prompts and varying seeds. For all of our prompt based fine tuning experiments we use a learning rate of $1e-5$ and we train the model for 5 epochs. For all of our vanilla fine tuning experiments we use learning rate of $2e-5$ and train the model for 5 epochs as well. In the main text of the paper we provide results on RTE dataset. We ask the readers to refer to Appendix for results on all datasets. We also provide different prompts used for different datasets in appendix A.

### 3.2 Prompting improves performance in imabalanced setting

The results of our experiments are depicted in fig. 1. Our findings demonstrate that in high data regime and imbalanced settings, prompt-based fine tuning consistently outperforms vanilla fine tuning. In scenarios where the imbalance ratio is between $0.1\%$ and $1\%$, both prompt-based and vanilla models perform similarly, almost equivalent to predicting the more labels class. However, when the imbalance ratio is between $5\%$ and $15\%$, we observe significant improvement in the performance of prompt-based models compared to vanilla fine tuning. Especially, for RTE dataset we observe $10-15\%$ improvement in performance across different models. The difference in performance between the two methods becomes smaller at $30\%$ imbalance ratio. As stated by previous studies (Brown et al., 2020; Webson and Pavlick, 2021), in balanced high data regimes, the performance of prompt-based models becomes similar to vanilla fine tuning. For more comprehensive results obtained from various datasets and models, please refer to appendix B. Overall, our findings indicates that when dealing with an imbalance ratio ranging from $5\%$ to $15\%$ there is an average improvement in performance of approximately $2-5\%$.

As shown in fig. 2, the comparison of the performance between the prompted model and ALBERT-Base and Large reveals that using the base models of these models does not significantly improve performance. Both the vanilla fine-tuned model and the prompt-based fine-tuned model yield similar results. This finding aligns with previous studies such as (Schick and Schütze, 2021; Tam et al., 2021), which also noted that prompted base models (or smaller models) do not enhance performance in the few-shot learning setting. The same holds true for imbalanced settings, as indicated by our results. For further analysis of different model sizes, please refer to appendix C in the paper.

## 4 Conclusion

This paper investigated the impact of prompt-based fine-tuning and vanilla fine-tuning on the performance of models in high data regimes and imbalanced settings. The findings revealed that prompt-based fine-tuning outperforms vanilla fine-tuning by about $2-5\%$, particularly in scenarios where the imbalance ratio is between $5\%$ to $15\%$. The results in balanced high data regimes were in accordance with previous studies, showing that prompt-based models perform similarly to vanilla fine-tuning. A comparison between the prompted base models and large models found that the former did not provide significant improvement in performance. To explain these phenomenons we aim to further study the pretraining dataset on the performance the models, as the output distribution of masked language modelling may play a role in the enhanced performance of prompt-based models compared to vanilla fine-tuned models.

## References

Fouzia Altaf, Syed M. S. Islam, Naeem Khalid Janjua, and Naveed Akhtar. 2023. Pre-text representation transfer for deep learning with limited imbalanced data : Application to ct-based covid-19 detection. *ArXiv*, abs/2301.08888.

Stephen H. Bach, Victor Sanh, Zheng-Xin Yong, Albert Webson, Colin Raffel, Nihal V. Nayak, Abheesht Sharma, Taewoon Kim, M Saiful Bari, Thibault Fevry, Zaid Alyafeai, Manan Dey, Andrea Santilli, Zhiqing Sun, Srulik Ben-David, Canwen Xu, Gunjan Chhablani, Han Wang, Jason Alan Fries, Maged S. Al-shaibani, Shanya Sharma, Urmish Thakker, Khalid Almubarak, Xiangru Tang, Xiangru Tang, Mike Tian-Jian Jiang, and Alexander M. Rush. 2022. Promptsource: An integrated development environment and repository for natural language prompts.

Tom B. Brown, Benjamin Mann, Nick Ryder, Melanie Subbiah, Jared Kaplan, Prafulla Dhariwal, Arvind Neelakantan, Pranav Shyam, Girish Sastry, Amanda Askell, Sandhini Agarwal, Ariel Herbert-Voss, Gretchen Krueger, T. J. Henighan, Rewon Child, Aditya Ramesh, Daniel M. Ziegler, Jeff Wu, Clemens Winter, Christopher Hesse, Mark Chen, Eric Sigler, Mateusz Litwin, Scott Gray, Benjamin Chess, Jack Clark, Christopher Berner, Sam McCandlish, Alec Radford, Ilya Sutskever, and Dario Amodei. 2020. Language models are few-shot learners. *ArXiv*, abs/2005.14165.

Mateusz Buda, Atsuto Maki, and Maciej A. Mazurowski. 2017. A systematic study of the class imbalance problem in convolutional neural networks. *Neural networks : the official journal of the International Neural Network Society*, 106:249–259.

Zihang Chen, Hongbo Zhang, Xiaoji Zhang, and Leqi Zhao. 2017. Quora question pairs.

Ido Dagan, Oren Glickman, and Bernardo Magnini. 2007. The pascal recognising textual entailment challenge. In *Machine Learning Challenges Workshop*.

Ferhat Demirkiran, Aykut Çayir, Uğur Ünal, and Hasan Dag. 2021. An ensemble of pre-trained transformer models for imbalanced multiclass malware classification. *Comput. Secur.*, 121:102846.

Pengcheng He, Xiaodong Liu, Jianfeng Gao, and Weizhu Chen. 2020. Deberta: Decoding-enhanced bert with disentangled attention. *ArXiv*, abs/2006.03654.

Wuwei Lan, Siyu Qiu, Hua He, and Wei Xu. 2017. A continuously growing dataset of sentential paraphrases. *arXiv preprint arXiv:1708.00391*.

Zhenzhong Lan, Mingda Chen, Sebastian Goodman, Kevin Gimpel, Piyush Sharma, and Radu Soricut. 2019. Albert: A lite bert for self-supervised learning of language representations. *ArXiv*, abs/1909.11942.

Joffrey L. Leevy, Taghi M. Khoshgoftaar, Richard A. Bauder, and Naeem Seliya. 2018. A survey on addressing high-class imbalance in big data. *Journal of Big Data*, 5:1–30.

Yinhan Liu, Myle Ott, Naman Goyal, Jingfei Du, Mandar Joshi, Danqi Chen, Omer Levy, Mike Lewis, Luke Zettlemoyer, and Veselin Stoyanov. 2019. Roberta: A robustly optimized bert pretraining approach. *ArXiv*, abs/1907.11692.

Bryan McCann, Nitish Shirish Keskar, Caiming Xiong, and Richard Socher. 2018. The natural language decathlon: Multitask learning as question answering. *arXiv preprint arXiv:1806.08730*.

Raul Puri and Bryan Catanzaro. 2019. Zero-shot text classification with generative language models. *arXiv preprint arXiv:1912.10165*.

Colin Raffel, Noam M. Shazeer, Adam Roberts, Katherine Lee, Sharan Narang, Michael Matena, Yanqi Zhou, Wei Li, and Peter J. Liu. 2019. Exploring the limits of transfer learning with a unified text-to-text transformer. *ArXiv*, abs/1910.10683.

Sanjeev Rao, Anil Kumar Verma, and Tarunpreet Bhatia. 2023. Hybrid ensemble framework with self-attention mechanism for social spam detection on imbalanced data. *Expert Systems with Applications*.

Teven Le Scao and Alexander M. Rush. 2021. How many data points is a prompt worth? In *North American Chapter of the Association for Computational Linguistics*.

Timo Schick and Hinrich Schütze. 2020. It's not just size that matters: Small language models are also few-shot learners. *arXiv preprint arXiv:2009.07118*.

Timo Schick and Hinrich Schütze. 2021. True few-shot learning with prompts—a real-world perspective. *Transactions of the Association for Computational Linguistics*, 10:716–731.

Derek Tam, Rakesh R Menon, Mohit Bansal, Shashank Srivastava, and Colin Raffel. 2021. Improving and simplifying pattern exploiting training. In *Conference on Empirical Methods in Natural Language Processing*.

Alex Wang, Yada Pruksachatkun, Nikita Nangia, Amanpreet Singh, Julian Michael, Felix Hill, Omer Levy, and Samuel R. Bowman. 2019. Superglue: A stickier benchmark for general-purpose language understanding systems. *ArXiv*, abs/1905.00537.

Alex Wang, Amanpreet Singh, Julian Michael, Felix Hill, Omer Levy, and Samuel R. Bowman. 2018. Glue: A multi-task benchmark and analysis platform for natural language understanding. In *BlackboxNLP@EMNLP*.

Albert Webson and Ellie Pavlick. 2021. Do prompt-based models really understand the meaning of their prompts? *ArXiv*, abs/2109.01247.

# A Different prompts used for different datasets

This section describes the different prompts and verbalizer patterns used for the experiments.

| Dataset | Patterns | Verbalizer |
|---|---|---|
| RTE | Given {premise} Should we assume that {hypothesis} is true? | yes-no |
| | {premise} Based on the previous passage, is it true that {hypothesis}? | yes-no |
| | Given {premise} Is it guaranteed true that {hypothesis}? | yes-no |
| | Suppose {premise} Can we infer that {hypothesis}? | yes-no |
| QQP | Can an answer to {question1} also be used to answer {question2}? | yes-no |
| | I received the questions {question1} and {question2}. Are they duplicates? | yes-no |
| | Are the questions {question1} and {question2} asking the same thing? | yes-no |
| | I am an administrator on the website Quora. There are two posts, one that asks {question1} and another that asks {question2}. I can merge questions if they are asking the same thing. Can I merge these two questions? | yes-no |
| MRPC | Are the following two sentences equivalent? {sentence1}. {sentence2} | yes-no |
| | I want to know whether the following two sentences mean the same thing. {sentence1}. {sentence2} | yes-no |
| | Do the following two sentences mean the same thing? {sentence1}. {sentence2} | yes-no |
| | Can I replace the sentence {sentence1} with the sentence {sentence2} and have it mean the same thing? | yes-no |

Table 1: Table showing different Datasets, Patterns, and Verbalizers.

## B Prompt based fine tuning vs vanilla fine tuning on different datasets and models

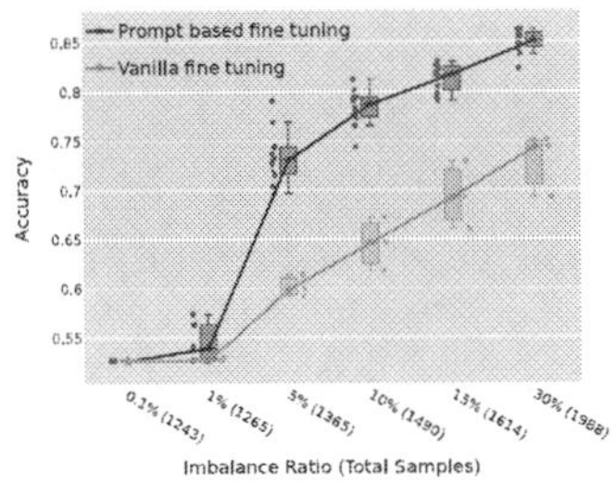


(a) RoBERTa

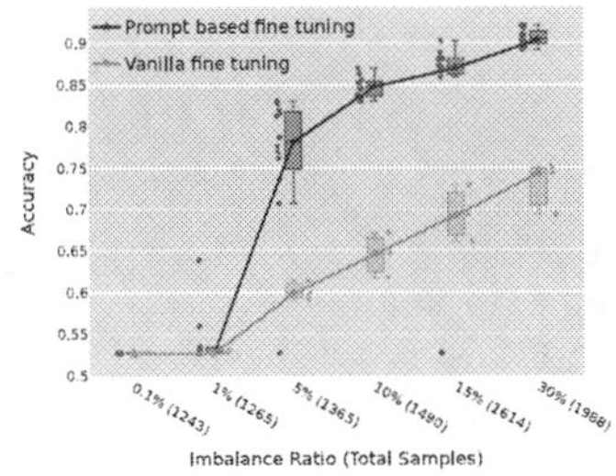


(b) DeBERTa

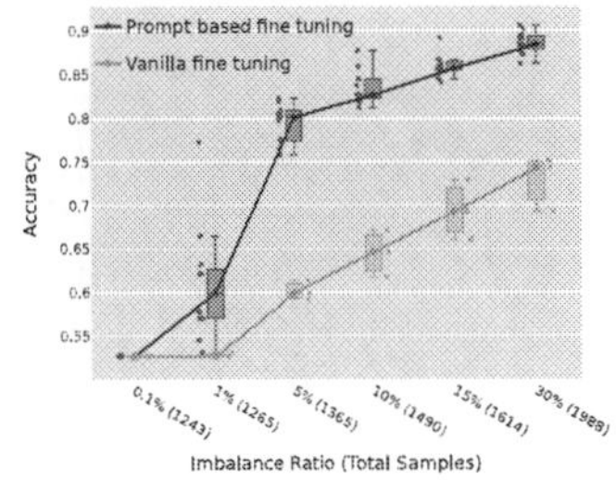


(c) ALBERT

Figure 3: RTE dataset performance on different models

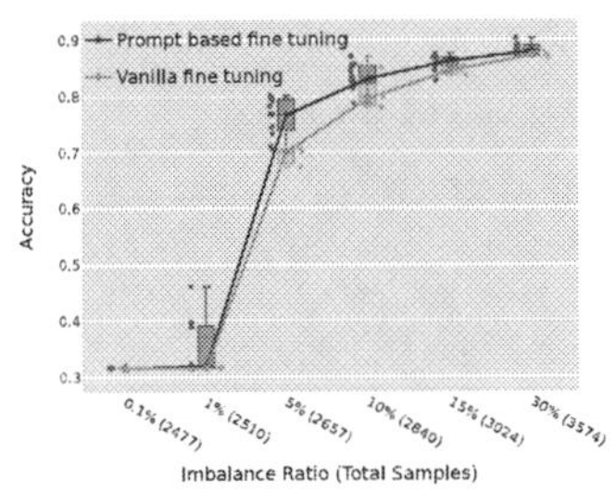


(a) RoBERTa

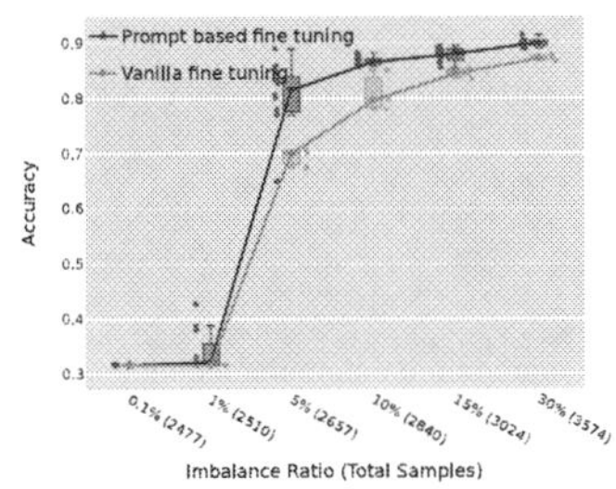


(b) DeBERTa

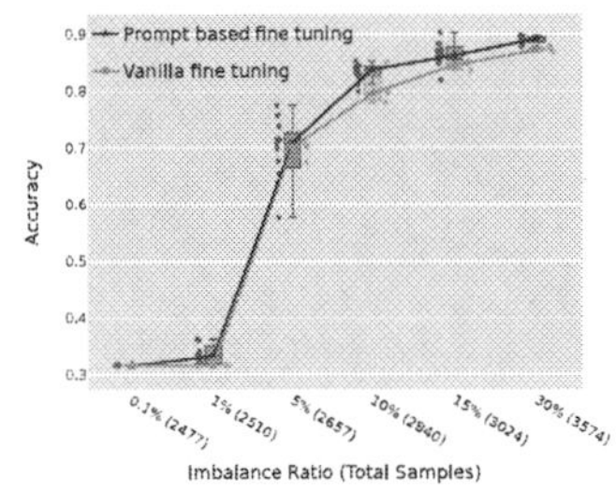


(c) ALBERT

Figure 4: MRPC dataset performance on different models

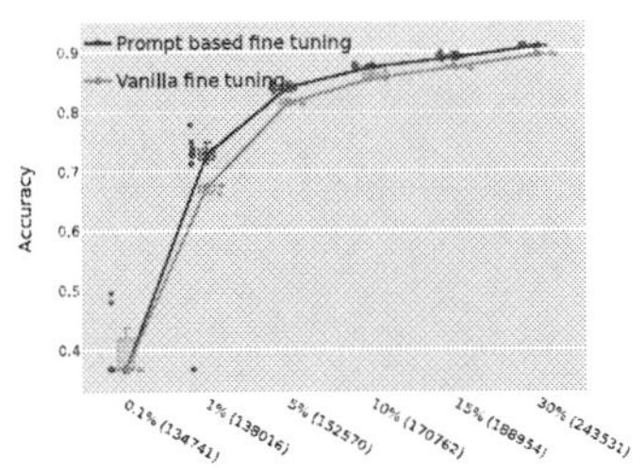


(a) RoBERTa

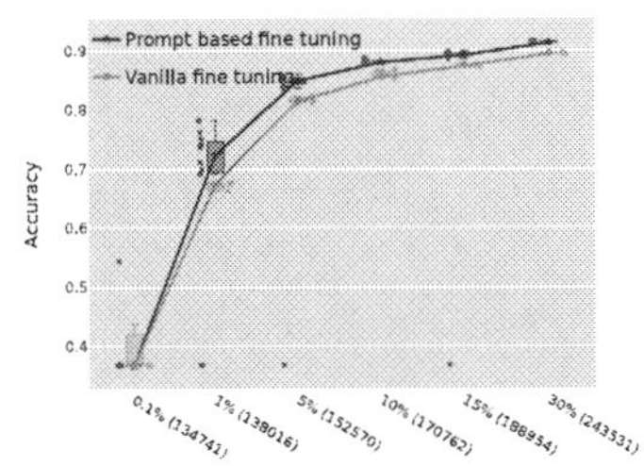


(b) DeBERTa

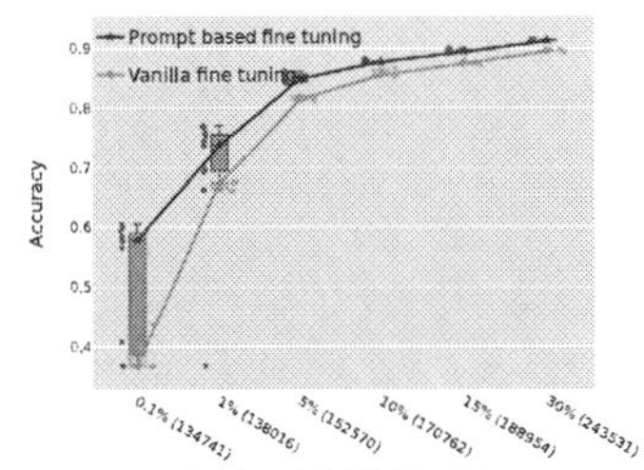


(c) ALBERT

Figure 5: QQP dataset performance on different models

## C Large vs base model comparison on different datasets

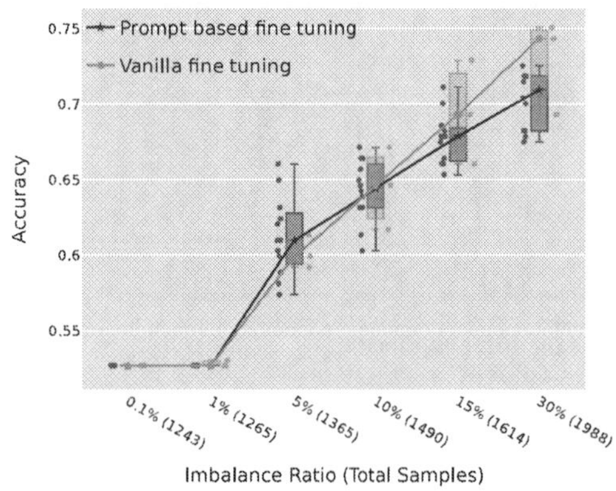


(a) ALBERT-Base

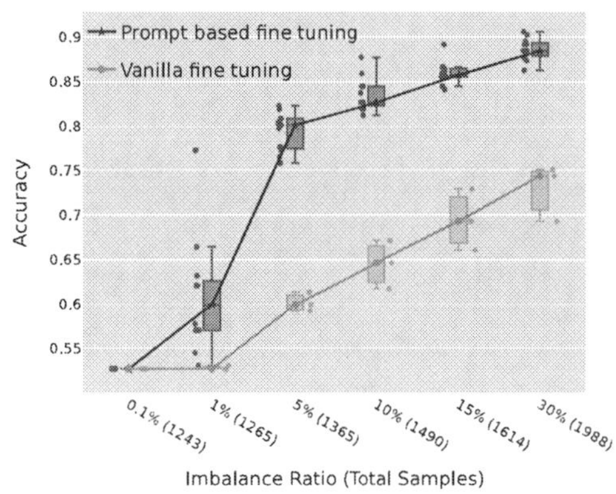


(b) ALBERT-Large

Figure 6: Comparing performance of ALBERT-Base with ALBERT-Large on RTE dataset

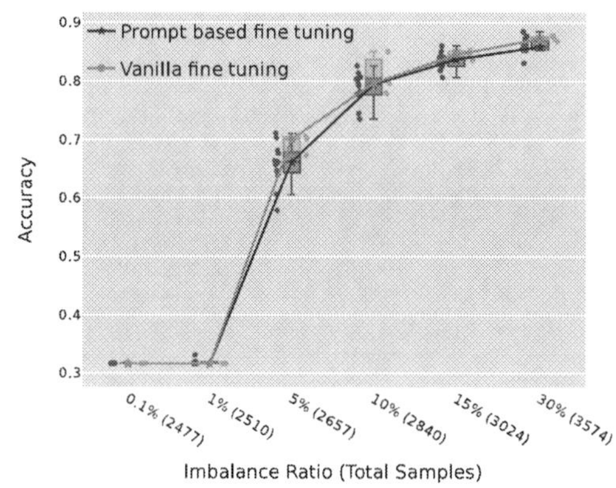


(a) ALBERT-Base

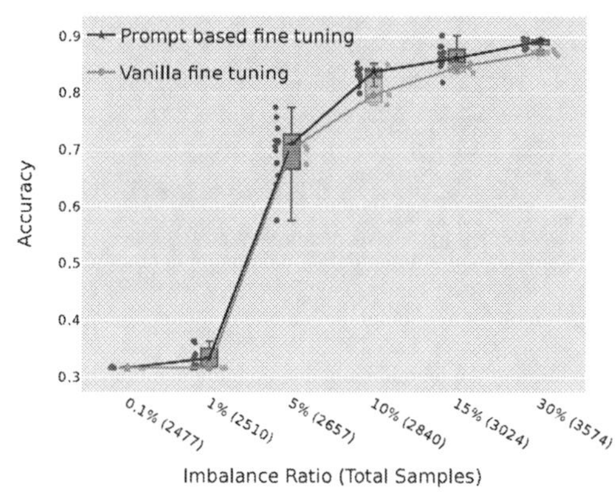


(b) ALBERT-Large

Figure 7: Comparing performance of ALBERT-Base with ALBERT-Large on MRPC dataset

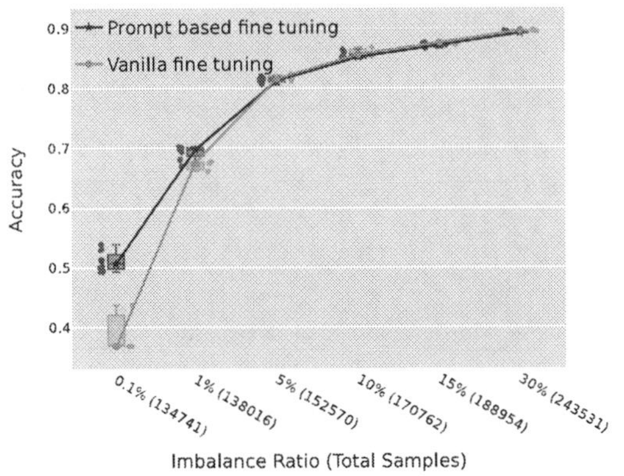


(a) ALBERT-Base

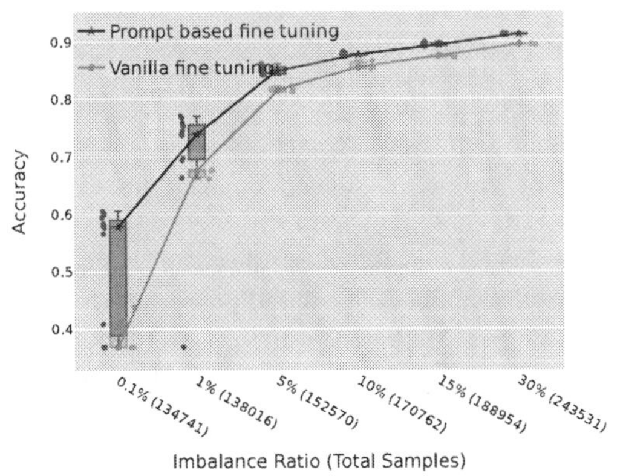


(b) ALBERT-Large

Figure 8: Comparing performance of ALBERT-Base with ALBERT-Large on QQP dataset

# KGQA Without Retraining

**Nick McKenna**
University of Edinburgh
nick.mckenna@ed.ac.uk

**Priyanka Sen**
Amazon Alexa AI
sepriyan@amazon.co.uk

## Abstract

Popular models for Knowledge Graph Question Answering (KGQA), including semantic parsing and End-to-End (E2E) models, decode into a constrained space of KG relations. Although E2E models accommodate novel entities at test-time, this constraint means they cannot access novel relations, requiring expensive and time-consuming retraining whenever a new relation is added to the KG. We propose KG-Flex, a new architecture for E2E KGQA that instead decodes into a continuous embedding space of relations, which enables use of novel relations at test-time. KG-Flex is the first to support KG updates with entirely novel triples, free of retraining, while still supporting end-to-end training with simple, weak supervision of (Q, A) pairs. Our architecture saves on time, energy, and data resources for retraining, yet we retain performance on standard benchmarks. We further demonstrate zero-shot use of novel relations, achieving up to 82% of baseline hit@1 on three QA datasets. KG-Flex can also fine-tune, requiring significantly shorter time than full retraining; fine-tuning on target data for 10% of full training increases hit@1 to 89-100% of baseline.

## 1 Introduction

Knowledge Graph Question Answering (KGQA) is the task of answering questions using facts in a Knowledge Graph (KG). Common approaches to KGQA include semantic parsing (Rongali et al., 2020) and End-to-End (E2E) Question Answering techniques (Cohen et al., 2020). E2E approaches are promising due to being composed of entirely differentiable operations, including program prediction and execution using a Differentiable KG (DKG), and the ease of training with simple (question, answer) pairs. However, these methods decode into a constrained space of KG relations which are then used to traverse the KG. While this works well for benchmark datasets where the KGs are static, it fails to scale to real use cases where KGs are frequently updated.

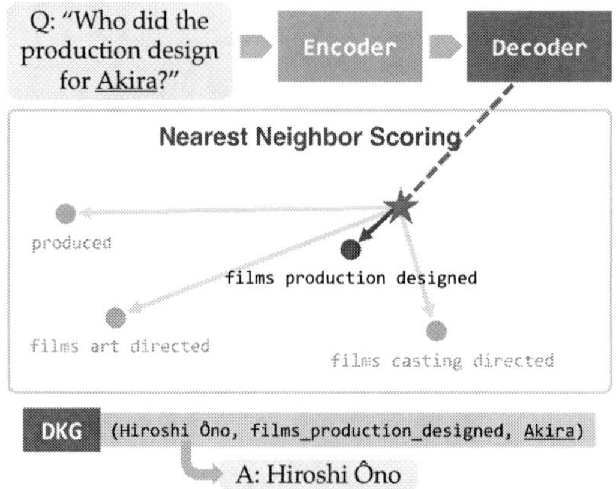


Figure 1: KG-Flex enables KG updates with new entities or relations at test-time without retraining. Given a question, an embedding is predicted in the space of (pre-computed) KG relation embeddings. Available relations are scored relatively by distance to prediction.

For example, Wikidata (Vrandečić and Krötzsch, 2014) is a commonly used Knowledge Graph that is actively updated. Between March 2022 and March 2023, the number of reported properties (relations in Wikidata) increased from 9.7K to 10.9K. At the time of writing, there are almost 200 new properties proposed for addition, including relations about new platforms or services (e.g., *Patreon user ID*, *Peacock ID*), and relations improving existing ontologies (e.g., *Pokemon category*, *alternate universe counterpart*).

In order to handle new relations, most KGQA methods require full retraining to learn a new output space of possible relations. These methods also require additional training data with examples using the new relations. We argue that incrementally updating the KG should not require full model retraining, a mostly redundant process which is energy- and time-intensive.

We present KG-Flex, an E2E model architecture that overcomes this problem by instead decoding



*Proceedings of The Fourth Workshop on Simple and Efficient Natural Language Processing (SustaiNLP)*, pages 212–218
July 13, 2023 ©2023 Association for Computational Linguistics

into an open embedding space in which relations are expressed in natural language. Given an input question, the model predicts the answer relation *embedding*, and available triples in the KG are scored against the prediction via their relations (example in Figure 1). KG-Flex is the first End-to-End KGQA model that allows updates to both KG entities and relations at test-time, without retraining.

We show that KG-Flex retains performance on standard benchmarks compared to a similar model, while demonstrating additional capabilities. In a zero-shot setting in three QA datasets, KG-Flex scores between 40-82% of baseline hit@1 on questions using relations that were held out during training time, a task which is impossible for previous models using a fixed decoder. Further, by fine-tuning for 10% of full training, scores are increased to 89-100% of baseline.

## 2 Related Work

Traditional approaches to KGQA involve semantic parsing of natural language into logical forms. Semantic parsing models use a constrained decoder over the output space of symbols. Since models such as Rongali et al. (2020) treat relations as whole symbols, adding new relations requires increasing the decoder output size and retraining the model. Further, collecting new training data of natural language to logical forms (e.g., SPARQL) is expensive (Finegan-Dollak et al., 2018).

Other techniques transform queries and KG triples to an embedding space (Saxena et al., 2020; Sun et al., 2020). These methods do not require annotated KG queries, however, adding new relations requires retraining to update the model.

Recent End-to-End methods for KGQA (Cohen et al., 2020; Sen et al., 2021) are weakly supervised with (question, answer) pairs which, conditioned on a question, predict a probability distribution over KG relations. Execution on the KG involves following relations and returning probabilistically weighted answer entities. While E2E methods also do not require supervision of KG pathways, they still constrain relation decoding, which means that adding new relations requires retraining.

Previous work in expanding the flexibility of KGQA models at test-time include Ravishankar et al. (2021), using a two-step process of first predicting an intermediate query template, then adding KG-specific relations. However, this method still relies on expensive SPARQL query annotation for training data. Oguz et al. (2022) propose a method to unify structured and unstructured data sources by converting them all into text, however this sacrifices the useful structure of Knowledge Graphs.

## 3 KG-Flex

We introduce KG-Flex, a novel KGQA architecture that is designed for unconstrained relation decoding, and can be trained end-to-end using only weak supervision of questions and answers. KG-Flex is an encoder-decoder model using a Differentiable Knowledge Graph, in the family of End-to-End KGQA models such as ReifKB (Cohen et al., 2020) and Rigel-based models (Sen et al., 2021; Saffari et al., 2021). We make key changes in the decoder to enable the use of new relations at test-time. KG-Flex has 4 key stages.

### 3.1 Precompute KG Relation Embeddings

Ahead of train- or test-time, we pre-compute vector embeddings for all relations available in KG triples (in training and test, these are frozen). To do so, every KG relation $r_i \in \mathcal{R}$ is lightly preprocessed into natural language and encoded as a vector $\mathbf{r}_i \in \mathbb{R}^h$, $h = 768$, using the RoBERTa-base v2 Sentence Transformer (Reimers and Gurevych, 2019).

- **Freebase** (Bollacker et al., 2008) property IDs are preprocessed into the template "(type) property", e.g., *film.film_festival.location* ⇒ "(film festival) location"
- **Wikidata** property label text is already in natural language, e.g., "place of birth"
- **MetaQA** relations have underscores replaced with spaces, e.g., *directed_by* ⇒ "directed by"

### 3.2 Encode Question Text

At train- and test-time, a natural language question is encoded with RoBERTa-base v2 Sentence Transformer, into a vector representation $\mathbf{q} \in \mathbb{R}^h$. This is similar to earlier E2E models like Rigel (Sen et al., 2021), which uses a RoBERTa encoder.

### 3.3 Decode Relation Embedding

The decoder is the key improvement in KG-Flex, which predicts from amongst the relations available in the KG, unconstrained from a fixed schema. Conditioned on the question encoding $\mathbf{q}$, the KG-Flex decoder predicts an *embedding* for a relation which answers the question. All available relations are scored based on their Euclidean distance to

| | WebQ | SimpleQ | MetaQA 1-hop | MetaQA 2-hop | MetaQA 3-hop |
|---|---|---|---|---|---|
| MemNN (Bordes et al., 2015) | 22.7 | 61.6 | – | – | – |
| KVMemNet (Miller et al., 2016) | 46.7 | – | 95.8 | 25.1 | 10.1 |
| GraftNet (Sun et al., 2018) | 66.4 | – | 97.0 | 94.8 | 77.7 |
| PullNet (Sun et al., 2019) | 68.1 | – | 97.0 | 99.9 | 91.4 |
| KBQA Adapter (Wu et al., 2019) | – | 72.0 | – | – | – |
| EmbedKGQA (Saxena et al., 2020) | 66.6 | – | 97.5 | 98.8 | 94.8 |
| TransferNet (Shi et al., 2021) | **71.4** | – | 97.5 | **100.0** | **100.0** |
| ReifKB (Cohen et al., 2020) | 52.7 | – | 96.2 | 81.1 | 72.3 |
| Rigel (Sen et al., 2021) | 69.2 | **79.9** | 97.5 | 87.1 | 89.6 |
| KG-Flex (ours) | 68.9 | 79.2 | **97.6** | 90.1 | 87.2 |

Table 1: KG-Flex compared to baselines on three standard QA tasks: WebQuestions (WebQ), SimpleQuestions (SimpleQ), and MetaQA. Compared to the similar model Rigel, KG-Flex scores within 3 percentage points.

the prediction, and these scores are converted to a probability distribution via a softmax.

As in Sen et al. (2021) and Saffari et al. (2021), the decoding step is performed for $T$ "hops" in the KG, where the hyperparameter $T$ is fixed before training[1]. An attention mechanism is jointly learned as part of the model which predicts how many hops (up to $T$) is required for a given question, conditioned on $\mathbf{q}$. This is used to weight final entity predictions. For example, answering "What's the mascot of Obama's alma mater?" requires two hops from the entity *Obama*: first the ALMA-MATER relation, then MASCOT, so entities fetched in hop 2 will be weighted most heavily.

For each hop $t \in [1, T]$, we apply a decoder transformation $D_t \in \mathbb{R}^{(th)\times h}$ (with bias $\mathbf{b}_t \in \mathbb{R}^h$). $D_t$ predicts a relation embedding $\mathbf{z}_t \in \mathbb{R}^h$, given the encoded question vector $\mathbf{q} \in \mathbb{R}^h$ and any predictions of earlier hops $\mathbf{z}_{<t}$.

$$\begin{aligned}\mathbf{z}_1 &= tanh(\mathbf{q}D_1 + \mathbf{b}_1)\\ \mathbf{z}_2 &= tanh([\mathbf{q};\mathbf{z}_1]D_2 + \mathbf{b}_2)\\ \mathbf{z}_3 &= tanh([\mathbf{q};\mathbf{z}_1;\mathbf{z}_2]D_3 + \mathbf{b}_3)\end{aligned}$$

The decoder is trained to predict a relation embedding which minimizes the Euclidean distance ($L^2$ norm) to the relation path that leads to the answer entity. Each decoder hop produces a probability distribution $\mathbf{d}_t$ over relations $r_i \in \mathcal{R}$ by a softmax over *negated* distances from $\mathbf{z}_t$ to precomputed $\mathbf{r}_i$:

$$\mathbf{d}_{t,i} = \frac{e^{-||\mathbf{z}_t - \mathbf{r}_i||_2}}{\sum_{j=0}^{|\mathcal{R}|} e^{-||\mathbf{z}_t - \mathbf{r}_j||_2}}$$

### 3.4 Execute on DKG

As an E2E model, KG-Flex executes a probabilistic query over its Differentiable KG (DKG) to produce weighted answer entities; these are scored to feed back the training signal through the model.

A DKG is just a re-representation of a KG as three matrices. In hop $t$, given a distribution over subjects $\mathbf{e}_t$ and relations $\mathbf{d}_t$, the "follow" operation (Cohen et al., 2020) computes a probability distribution over KG triple objects $\mathbf{e}_{t+1}$ using simple matrix multiplication:

$$\mathbf{e}_{t+1} = follow(\mathbf{e}_t, \mathbf{d}_t)$$

In the first hop, $\mathbf{e}_1$ is a one-hot vector of KG entities (question entity set to 1) [2]. For each hop $1 \leq t \leq T$, a probability distribution is predicted over KG entities, which are fed into the subsequent hop. The final model prediction is a distribution over KG entities discovered in all hops, weighted by the hop attention mechanism. During training, entity predictions are compared to the gold label entities via binary cross-entropy loss, and updates are backpropagated through the decoder and encoder.

## 4 Experiments

In our experiments, we use three datasets: **SimpleQuestions** (Bordes et al., 2015), a large-scale dataset of simple, one-hop questions based on FreeBase; **WebQuestionsSP** (Yih et al., 2016), a dataset of natural language questions containing up to 2 hops linked to FreeBase; and **MetaQA** (Zhang et al., 2018), a movies QA dataset divided into one, two, and three-hop subsets. MetaQA uses a KG that is internal to the dataset.

KG-Flex models are trained until dev set convergence or max 40,000 steps on a single NVIDIA Tesla V100 GPU (see Appendix A for details).

[1]We assume that $T = 3$ hops is sufficient to cover all realistic human questions.

[2]Like Cohen et al. (2020) and Sen et al. (2021), we begin with question entities pre-identified in the datasets.

| Dataset | Domain | Full Test Set: Rigel BL | Full Test Set: KG-Flex BL | Full Test Set: KG-Flex Zero-Shot | Full Test Set: KG-Flex Fine-tuned | Heldout Test Set: Rigel BL | Heldout Test Set: KG-Flex BL | Heldout Test Set: KG-Flex Zero-Shot | Heldout Test Set: KG-Flex Fine-tuned |
|---|---|---|---|---|---|---|---|---|---|
| WebQuestions | film | 69.2 | 68.9 | 65.8 | 68.7 | 71.4 | 76.8 | 31.3 | 76.8 |
| WebQuestions | sports | 69.2 | 68.9 | 66.0 | 69.0 | 49.7 | 53.6 | 28.4 | 51.0 |
| SimpleQuestions | film | 79.9 | 79.2 | 71.9 | 79.2 | 74.1 | 73.3 | 60.1 | 70.2 |
| SimpleQuestions | medicine | 79.9 | 79.2 | 77.5 | 79.7 | 79.4 | 82.2 | 60.2 | 72.8 |
| MetaQA 1-hop | directed_by | 97.5 | 97.6 | 92.6 | 97.6 | 97.1 | 97.2 | 70.5 | 97.1 |
| MetaQA 2-hop | directed_by | 87.1 | 90.1 | 79.7 | 90.6 | 90.1 | 85.7 | 54.8 | 86.7 |
| MetaQA 3-hop | directed_by | 89.6 | 87.2 | 62.9 | 85.7 | 89.2 | 86.2 | 36.9 | 85.5 |
| MetaQA 1-hop | written_by | 97.5 | 97.6 | 93.8 | 97.6 | 98.7 | 98.9 | 81.4 | 98.9 |
| MetaQA 2-hop | written_by | 87.1 | 90.1 | 81.7 | 91.3 | 87.1 | 90.0 | 68.0 | 91.7 |
| MetaQA 3-hop | written_by | 89.6 | 87.2 | 65.1 | 85.8 | 86.8 | 84.3 | 32.8 | 82.5 |

Table 2: For each dataset and domain, we evaluate three models: the **Baseline (BL)** is trained on the full dataset, **Zero-Shot** is trained with a **Domain** held out, and **Fine-tuned** is the Zero-Shot model fine-tuned for 4K steps on the full dataset. Each of these three models are evaluated on two datasets: **Full Test Set** (all examples in the test set), and **Heldout Test Set** (the subset of the test set using the held out relations).

### 4.1 Standard Benchmarks

First, we benchmark KG-Flex against existing methods on standard datasets. We report hit@1 scores, a metric that measures the percentage of questions where the highest probability entity predicted is correct[3]. Results are shown in Table 1. Compared to similar E2E models like Rigel, KG-Flex attains competitive performance within 3 percentage points.

### 4.2 Zero-Shot Transfer to Held-out Relations

We simulate a real-world scenario where new KG domains are added after training. We demonstrate how KG-Flex can predict using these held-out relations, an impossible task for prior E2E models like Rigel and ReifKB.

In training, we remove a subdomain of relations from the KG and all questions involving those relations from train and dev sets. Then at test-time we reintroduce the relations to the KG and include the held-out questions. We report on the full test set as well as the subset consisting of just the held-out questions. For SimpleQuestions, we remove all relations in the domains Film (61 relations) or Medicine (66 relations). For WebQuestions, we remove Film (24 relations) or Sports (45 relations). These domains represent a reasonably-sized KG update (< 10% of total relations). Since MetaQA contains only movie questions, we remove the "directed_by" or "written_by" relations (further info in Appendix B).

[3]Since SimpleQuestions may have multiple correct answers, we count predictions as correct if any entity within a tie for most probable is correct.

| | Train | Fine-tune |
|---|---|---|
| WebQuestions | 7 hr | 45 min |
| SimpleQuestions | 7 hr | 1 hr |
| MetaQA 1-hop | 1 hr | 10 min |
| MetaQA 2-hop | 1 hr | 15 min |
| MetaQA 3-hop | 1 hr | 15 min |

Table 3: Comparison of training time (for 40,000 steps) vs. fine-tuning (for 4,000 steps) on each of our datasets

Results are shown under **Zero-Shot** columns in Table 2. We compare to the Baseline KG-Flex results, which refer to training on the full dataset. On the held-out datasets the zero-shot models score up to 82% of the baseline score on simpler datasets (81.4 achieved / 98.9 baseline on written_by in MetaQA 1-hop; 60.1 / 73.3 on film in SimpleQuestions). However, they perform worse on more complex questions, reaching as low as 40% of the baseline on multi-hop question datasets (36.9 / 86.2 on directed_by in MetaQA 3-hop; 31.3 / 76.8 on film in WebQuestions). We attribute this to the compounding likelihood of error when predicting multiple relations at once. Since comparable models would score 0% on this task, we still consider this to be a valuable step forward.

### 4.3 Fine-tuned Transfer to Held-out Relations

To improve transfer to new relations, we further fine-tune the zero-shot models. Each zero-shot model is fine-tuned for 4,000 steps (10% of full training) on the entire dataset, including held-out relations. Results are under **Fine-tuned** in Table 2.

Our fine-tuned models are able to recapture between 89-100% of baseline KG-Flex performance on both the full test set and heldout test set. We are able to fine-tune our model because we have an unconstrained decoder space, whereas comparable models such as ReifKB (Cohen et al., 2020) would require retraining from scratch. By fine-tuning for only a fraction of the full training time (see Table 3), we demonstrate that KG-Flex can efficiently adapt to new relations.

## 5 Conclusions

We present KG-Flex, a new model architecture for KGQA which is the first to use an unconstrained decoder over KG relations and to train end-to-end using simple (question, answer) pairs. While maintaining performance on benchmarks, KG-Flex is demonstrated to make use of incrementally changing live KGs without requiring expensive retraining. We show that KG-Flex uses novel relations added at test-time, handling simple questions with new relations in zero-shot, and handling more complex multihop questions by fine-tuning for only 10% of the training steps required for full retraining.

## 6 Limitations

We present KG-Flex, an end-to-end model that can access new relations at test-time without retraining. Our current KG-Flex model does not perform entity resolution, and so we rely on resolved entities provided by the datasets. However, resolved entities may not always be available, so tools such as automatic entity recognition may be necessary. While it is possible for end-to-end models to jointly learn to resolve entities in questions before relation following (Saffari et al., 2021), we consider this outside the scope of this focused work.

Additionally, KG-Flex is limited in the kinds of reasoning it can do over a Knowledge Graph. Currently, KG-Flex only performs relation following, so it cannot handle questions which require complex reasoning like counts, comparatives, min/max, etc, such as "Who is the tallest NBA player?" We hope to address this in future work.

Further, we test KG-Flex on popular datasets representing possible real human questions. However, we do not deeply investigate the semantic properties of these questions. Notably, McKenna and Steedman (2022) show that searching for similar relations in embedding space (as done in KG-Flex) may work better for paraphrastic inference, and only in certain cases for directional inference where semantic precision matters, e.g. DEFEAT entails PLAY, but PLAY does not entail DEFEAT. We leave deeper investigation of KG-Flex semantics and edge cases to future work.

## References


Kurt Bollacker, Colin Evans, Praveen Paritosh, Tim Sturge, and Jamie Taylor. 2008. Freebase: A collaboratively created graph database for structuring human knowledge. In *Proceedings of the 2008 ACM SIGMOD International Conference on Management of Data*, SIGMOD '08, page 1247–1250, New York, NY, USA. Association for Computing Machinery.

Antoine Bordes, Nicolas Usunier, Sumit Chopra, and Jason Weston. 2015. Large-scale simple question answering with memory networks.

William W. Cohen, Haitian Sun, R. Alex Hofer, and Matthew Siegler. 2020. Scalable neural methods for reasoning with a symbolic knowledge base. In *International Conference on Learning Representations*.

Catherine Finegan-Dollak, Jonathan K. Kummerfeld, Li Zhang, Karthik Ramanathan, Sesh Sadasivam, Rui Zhang, and Dragomir Radev. 2018. Improving text-to-SQL evaluation methodology. In *Proceedings of the 56th Annual Meeting of the Association for Computational Linguistics (Volume 1: Long Papers)*, pages 351–360, Melbourne, Australia. Association for Computational Linguistics.

Nick McKenna and Mark Steedman. 2022. Smoothing entailment graphs with language models. ArXiv:2208.00318v1 [cs.CL].

Alexander Miller, Adam Fisch, Jesse Dodge, Amir-Hossein Karimi, Antoine Bordes, and Jason Weston. 2016. Key-value memory networks for directly reading documents. In *Proceedings of the 2016 Conference on Empirical Methods in Natural Language Processing*, pages 1400–1409, Austin, Texas. Association for Computational Linguistics.

Barlas Oguz, Xilun Chen, Vladimir Karpukhin, Stan Peshterliev, Dmytro Okhonko, Michael Schlichtkrull, Sonal Gupta, Yashar Mehdad, and Scott Yih. 2022. UniK-QA: Unified representations of structured and unstructured knowledge for open-domain question answering. In *Findings of the Association for Computational Linguistics: NAACL 2022*, pages 1535–1546, Seattle, United States. Association for Computational Linguistics.

Srinivas Ravishankar, June Thai, Ibrahim Abdelaziz, Nandana Mihidukulasooriya, Tahira Naseem, Pavan Kapanipathi, Gaetano Rossilleo, and Achille Fokoue. 2021. A two-stage approach towards generalization in knowledge base question answering. *arXiv preprint arXiv:2111.05825*.

Nils Reimers and Iryna Gurevych. 2019. Sentence-bert: Sentence embeddings using siamese bert-networks. In *Proceedings of the 2019 Conference on Empirical Methods in Natural Language Processing*. Association for Computational Linguistics.

Subendhu Rongali, Luca Soldaini, Emilio Monti, and Wael Hamza. 2020. Don't parse, generate! a sequence to sequence architecture for task-oriented semantic parsing. In *Proceedings of The Web Conference 2020*, WWW '20, page 2962–2968, New York, NY, USA. Association for Computing Machinery.

Amir Saffari, Armin Oliya, Priyanka Sen, and Tom Ayoola. 2021. End-to-end entity resolution and question answering using differentiable knowledge graphs. In *Proceedings of the 2021 Conference on Empirical Methods in Natural Language Processing*, pages 4193–4200, Online and Punta Cana, Dominican Republic. Association for Computational Linguistics.

Apoorv Saxena, Aditay Tripathi, and Partha Talukdar. 2020. Improving multi-hop question answering over knowledge graphs using knowledge base embeddings. In *Proceedings of the 58th Annual Meeting of the Association for Computational Linguistics*, pages 4498–4507, Online. Association for Computational Linguistics.

Priyanka Sen, Armin Oliya, and Amir Saffari. 2021. Expanding end-to-end question answering on differentiable knowledge graphs with intersection. In *Proceedings of the 2021 Conference on Empirical Methods in Natural Language Processing*, pages 8805–8812, Online and Punta Cana, Dominican Republic. Association for Computational Linguistics.

Jiaxin Shi, Shulin Cao, Lei Hou, Juanzi Li, and Hanwang Zhang. 2021. TransferNet: An effective and transparent framework for multi-hop question answering over relation graph. In *Proceedings of the 2021 Conference on Empirical Methods in Natural Language Processing*, pages 4149–4158, Online and Punta Cana, Dominican Republic. Association for Computational Linguistics.

Haitian Sun, Andrew Arnold, Tania Bedrax Weiss, Fernando Pereira, and William W. Cohen. 2020. Faithful embeddings for knowledge base queries. *Advances in Neural Information Processing Systems*, 33.

Haitian Sun, Tania Bedrax-Weiss, and William Cohen. 2019. PullNet: Open domain question answering with iterative retrieval on knowledge bases and text. In *Proceedings of the 2019 Conference on Empirical Methods in Natural Language Processing and the 9th International Joint Conference on Natural Language Processing (EMNLP-IJCNLP)*, pages 2380–2390, Hong Kong, China. Association for Computational Linguistics.

Haitian Sun, Bhuwan Dhingra, Manzil Zaheer, Kathryn Mazaitis, Ruslan Salakhutdinov, and William Cohen. 2018. Open domain question answering using early fusion of knowledge bases and text. In *Proceedings of the 2018 Conference on Empirical Methods in Natural Language Processing*, pages 4231–4242, Brussels, Belgium. Association for Computational Linguistics.

Denny Vrandečić and Markus Krötzsch. 2014. Wikidata: A free collaborative knowledgebase. *Commun. ACM*, 57(10):78–85.

Peng Wu, Shujian Huang, Rongxiang Weng, Zaixiang Zheng, Jianbing Zhang, Xiaohui Yan, and Jiajun Chen. 2019. Learning representation mapping for relation detection in knowledge base question answering. In *Proceedings of the 57th Annual Meeting of the Association for Computational Linguistics*, pages 6130–6139, Florence, Italy. Association for Computational Linguistics.

Wen-tau Yih, Matthew Richardson, Chris Meek, Ming-Wei Chang, and Jina Suh. 2016. The value of semantic parse labeling for knowledge base question answering. In *Proceedings of the 54th Annual Meeting of the Association for Computational Linguistics (Volume 2: Short Papers)*, pages 201–206, Berlin, Germany. Association for Computational Linguistics.

Yuyu Zhang, Hanjun Dai, Zornitsa Kozareva, Alexander J Smola, and Le Song. 2018. Variational reasoning for question answering with knowledge graph. In *AAAI*.

## A Training Specifications

### A.1 Hardware

We performed our experiments on one AWS EC2 instance of p3.2xlarge, which is equipped with one NVIDIA Tesla V100 GPU (16 GiB memory).

### A.2 Hyperparameters

We train and test a KG-Flex model constructed to the specifications shown in Table 4.

| **Hyperparameter** | **Value** |
|---|---|
| Batch Size | 4 |
| Gradient Accumulation | 32 |
| Optimizer | Adam |
| Learning Rate | 1e-4 |
| Training Steps | 40,000 |
| Relation Embedding Size | 768 |

Table 4: Hyperparameters used in the KG-Flex architecture.

## B Added Domains

Our experiments in §4.2 use expert KGs containing specific domains of Freebase. We show summary information for the domains in Table 5.

| | Questions | Relations | Triples |
|---|---|---|---|
| | *SimpleQuestions* | | |
| Total | 108,442 | 1,830 | 15,352,572 |
| Film | 13,538 | 61 | 1,028,076 |
| Medicine | 2,881 | 66 | 166,886 |
| | *WebQuestionsSP* | | |
| Total | 4,737 | 585 | 10,968,596 |
| Film | 306 | 24 | 814,126 |
| Sports | 445 | 45 | 176,237 |
| | *MetaQA 1-hop* | | |
| Total | 116,045 | 9 | 134,741 |
| directed_by | 21,483 | 1 | 15,966 |
| written_by | 22,193 | 1 | 19,543 |
| | *MetaQA 2-hop* | | |
| Total | 148,724 | 9 | 134,741 |
| directed_by | 51,368 | 1 | 15,966 |
| written_by | 65,434 | 1 | 19,543 |
| | *MetaQA 3-hop* | | |
| Total | 142,744 | 9 | 134,741 |
| directed_by | 70,227 | 1 | 15,966 |
| written_by | 60,384 | 1 | 19,543 |

Table 5: Domain summary information for experiments in zero-shot transfer to new domains.

# MANER: Mask Augmented Named Entity Recognition for Extreme Low-Resource Languages

**Shashank Sonkar**
Rice University
ss164@rice.edu

**Zichao Wang**
Rice University
jzwang@rice.edu

**Richard G. Baraniuk**
Rice University
richb@rice.edu

## Abstract

This paper investigates the problem of Named Entity Recognition (NER) for extreme low-resource languages with only a few hundred tagged data samples. A critical enabler of most of the progress in NER is the readily available, large-scale training data for languages such as English and French. However, NER for low-resource languages remains relatively under-explored, leaving much room for improvement. We propose *Mask Augmented Named Entity Recognition* (MANER), a simple yet effective method that leverages the distributional hypothesis of pre-trained masked language models (MLMs) to improve NER performance for low-resource languages significantly. MANER re-purposes the `[mask]` token in MLMs, which encodes valuable semantic contextual information, for NER prediction. Specifically, we prepend a `[mask]` token to every word in a sentence and predict the named entity for each word from its preceding `[mask]` token. We demonstrate that MANER is well-suited for NER in low-resource languages; our experiments show that for 100 languages with as few as 100 training examples, it improves on the state-of-the-art by up to 48% and by 12% on average on F1 score. We also perform detailed analyses and ablation studies to understand the scenarios that are best suited to MANER.

## 1 Introduction

Named Entity Recognition (NER) is a fundamental problem in natural language processing (NLP) (Nadeau and Sekine, 2007). Given an unstructured text, NER aims to label the named entity of each word, be it a person, a location, an organization, and so on. NER is widely employed as an important first step in many downstream NLP applications, such as scientific information retrieval (Krallinger and Valencia, 2005; Krallinger et al., 2017), question answering (Mollá et al., 2006), document classification (Guo et al., 2009), and recommender systems (Jannach et al., 2022).

Recent advances in NER have mainly been driven by deep learning-based approaches, whose training relies heavily on large-scale datasets (Rosenfeld, 2021). As a result, the most significant progress in NER is for resource-rich languages such as English (Wang et al., 2021), French (Tedeschi et al., 2021), German (Schweter and Akbik, 2020), and Chinese (Zhu and Li, 2022). This reliance on large training datasets makes it challenging to apply deep learning-based NER approaches to low-resource languages where training data is scarce. To illustrate the ubiquity of low-resource languages, WikiANN (Rahimi et al., 2019), one of the largest NER datasets, has NER-labeled data for 176 languages, but 100 of these languages have only 100 training examples.

Providing NER for low-resource languages is critical to ensure the equitable, fair, and democratized utilization of NLP technologies that are required to achieve the goal of making such technologies universally available for all (Maguéresse et al., 2020; King, 2015). Several research efforts are pushing the frontiers of NER for low-resource languages in two orthogonal and complementary directions. The first direction aims to obtain larger NER datasets to solve the data scarcity problem, via either data collection or augmentation (Malmasi et al., 2022; Al-Rfou et al., 2014; Meng et al., 2021a). The second direction aims to develop new model architectures and training algorithms capable of handling scarce data. For example, ideas from meta-learning (de Lichy et al., 2021), distant supervision (Meng et al., 2021b), and transfer learning (Lee et al., 2017) leverage the few-shot generalizability of language models for NER in data-scarce settings.

**Our Contributions.** In this work, we propose *Mask Augmented Named Entity Recognition* (MANER), a new NER approach for low-resource languages that does not rely on additional data and does not require modifications to existing, off-



*Proceedings of The Fourth Workshop on Simple and Efficient Natural Language Processing (SustaiNLP)*, pages 219–226
July 13, 2023 ©2023 Association for Computational Linguistics

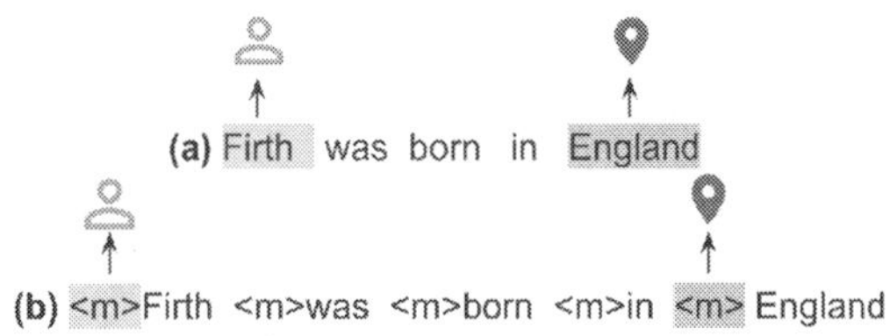


Figure 1: How MANER **(b)** differs from a standard NER model **(a)**. MANER 1) modifies the input to add a `[mask]` token before each word and 2) predicts the NER tag for a word from its preceding `[mask]` token.

the-shelf pre-trained models. The key intuition of MANER is to exploit the semantic information encoded in a pre-trained masked language model (MLM), in particular, in the `[mask]` token. Specifically, we reformat the input to the MLM by prepending a `[mask]` token to every token in the text to be annotated with NER tags. This reformatted input is then used to fine-tune the MLM with a randomly initialized NER prediction head on top of the prepended mask tokens. Extensive experiments on 100 extremely low-resource languages (each with only 100 training examples) demonstrate that MANER improves over state-of-the-art approaches by up to 48% and by 12% on average on F1 score. Detailed ablation and analyses of MANER demonstrate the importance of using the encoded semantic information and suggest scenarios in which MANER is most applicable.

## 2 Methodology

We now introduce MANER in detail and describe how it functions differently from a standard NER model (henceforth referred to as SNER).

SNER takes a sentence as input, passes the sentence through a transformer encoder model to obtain contextualized word embeddings, and applies a NER classifier layer on top of each word embedding to get the word's NER class.

MANER, in contrast, repurposes the `[mask]` token for the NER task. Two key differences that MANER implements as compared to SNER are 1) instead of giving the model the input sentence as is, MANER modifies the input sentence to append a `[mask]` token in front of each word and passes this modified sentence through the transformer encoder; and 2) instead of predicting the NER tag directly from the word embedding itself, MANER predicts the NER tag from the `[mask]` token embedding prepended to each word in the modified input sentence. These differences are illustrated in figure 1. We hypothesize that in such a setting, MANER will be better able to use the `[mask]` token to weigh the relative relevance of the neighboring word vs. the rest of the context when determining the label to assign to the neighboring word. Below, we expand on the above differences and introduce the two key components in MANER.

**Modified input sentence.** Let the set of NER labels be denoted by $\mathcal{N}$. Let the sequence of NER labels for a sentence $S = \{w_0, w_1, .., w_{n-1}\}$ consisting of $n$ words be $L = \{c_0, c_1, .., c_{n-1}\}$ where $c_i \in \mathcal{N}$, $0 \leq i < n$. To obtain the input that MANER requires we *append* a `[mask]` token to the beginning of each word in sentence $S$. The new sentence is $S' = \{m, w_0, m, w_1, .., m, w_{n-1}\}$ where $m$ is the `[mask]` token. The modified labels $L'$ are $\{c_0, \emptyset, c_1, \emptyset, .., c_{n-1}, \emptyset\}$. The original NER label of each word is assigned to the `[mask]` token to the immediate left of the word.

**MANER's classifier design.** MANER uses a pre-trained, masked language model as the backbone with an NER classifier head on top. The transformer model takes a sentence as input and outputs embeddings for each token in the sentence. The NER classifier uses the token embeddings to output the most probable NER class for each token.

Denote the MANER model by $\mathcal{M}$. The transformer model is given by $T$, $T(S') = T(\{m, w_0, m, w_1, .., m, w_{n-1}\}) = \{\mathbf{e}_0, \mathbf{e}_1, .., \mathbf{e}_{2n-1}\}$, where $\mathbf{e}_i \in \mathbb{R}^D$, $0 \leq i < 2n - 1$ is the token embedding, and $D$ is its dimension. The NER classifier is modeled using a weight matrix $\mathbf{M} \in \mathbb{R}^{D \times |\mathcal{N}|}$ that takes the computed token embeddings as input. Using these token embeddings, the classifier outputs scores for all NER labels for each token in the sentence. Passing these scores through a softmax nonlinearity provides probabilities $\mathbf{p}_i \in \mathbb{R}^{|\mathcal{N}|}$ for all NER classes in $\mathcal{N}$ for a given token $i$ in $S$:

$$\mathbf{p}_i = \text{softmax}\Big(\mathbf{M}(\mathbf{e}_i)\Big).$$

Summing up, we have

$$\mathcal{M}(T, \mathbf{M}, S', i) = \mathbf{p}_i,\ 0 \leq i < 2n.$$

**MANER training and inference.** During training, the weights of $\mathbf{M}$ and $T$ are learned/fine-tuned by minimizing cross-entropy loss. Note that the loss is not calculated for labels marked $\emptyset$ in the modified label set $L'$. The NER label of the word is given by the NER label of the `[mask]` token preceding it. During inference, each word in the sentence is prepended with the `[mask]` token, and the NER class of each word is the most probable NER class of its prepended `[mask]` token.

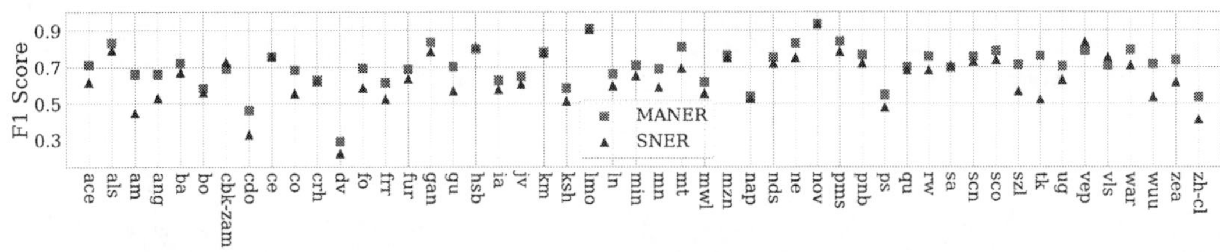


Figure 2: F1 scores comparing MANER against SNER for a subset of 50 low-resource languages in the WikiANN dataset that only have 100 training samples. The x-axis represents the languages. Overall, MANER improves NER performance for 88 of the 100 languages over SNER; performance improvement is up to 48% and on average 12%.

## 3 Experiments

We perform various empirical studies on MANER to 1) demonstrate its superior performance in low-resource language NER tasks and 2) provide insights into its performance and scenarios in which it will work well.

**Dataset.** We use the WikiANN multilingual NER dataset (Pan et al., 2017; Rahimi et al., 2019), which provides three named entities (person, location, organization) for Wikipedia articles across 176 languages. Therefore, our NER tag set $\mathcal{N}$ has four elements, with an additional null tag. To the best of our knowledge, WikiANN is by far the most comprehensive dataset for multilingual NER. Other multilingual datasets exist but they cover a few popular languages. For example, CoNLL (Kim Sang and De Meulder, 2003) contains only English, German, Dutch, and Spanish. We focus our main study on *extreme low-resource* settings by experimenting on the 100 languages in WikiANN that each has only **100 examples** for train and test splits. Further details on the WikiANN dataset are in Appendix B.

**MANER implementation and baselines.** We use XLM-RoBERTa-large (Conneau et al., 2019) as the backbone model for MANER and all baselines. XLM-RoBERTa-large is a multilingual version of the RoBERTa (Liu et al., 2019) model, pre-trained with the MLM objective on 2.5TB of filtered CommonCrawl data containing 100 languages (Conneau et al., 2020). We compare MANER against two baselines 1) SNER , which stands for a standard NER model and 2) MLM-NER , which is another strategy to use the `[mask]` token for NER inspired by the masked language modeling (MLM) loss. MLM-NER masks a small percentage of words and predicts the NER tag for both the masked and unmasked words, thus leveraging the `[mask]` token. More details on the above models and their training setup are in Appendix A.

### 3.1 Main results

| Metric | SNER | MLM-NER | MANER |
|---|---|---|---|
| F1 | 0.649 | 0.643 (-0.5%) | 0.715 (12%) |

Table 1: Average F1 scores for the 100 languages in the WikiANN dataset with only 100 samples comparing MANER to baselines. In this extreme low-resource setting, MANER achieves an average improvement of **12%** over baselines.

In Table 1, we report the average of F1 score for the 100 languages in WikiANN that we consider. MANER provides a significant **12%** average improvement in our low-resource language settings. The MLM inspired NER-model MLM-NER , in contrast, performs only similarly to SNER. We also plot, in Figure 2, the F1 score of 50 randomly sampled low-resource languages comparing SNER against MANER (the plot for the remaining languages is in Appendix D). MANER offers up to 48% performance improvements compared to SNER, and there are only a few languages (12 out of 100) in which the SNER outperforms MANER.

We believe the reason that MANER outperforms MLM-NER is that MANER uses the `[mask]` token for NER prediction in both training and inference, whereas MLM-NER does not. Therefore, MANER learns to give more importance to the context in the case of out-of-distribution test labels using the `[mask]` token during inference. We will revisit and empirically support the above reasoning in Section 3.2. Additionally, in MLM-NER training, we mask out certain words with the `[mask]` token, which introduces noise and makes training and the NER task more difficult.

### 3.2 Analysis: Importance of the `[mask]` token

We now conduct two analyses to demonstrate the importance of using the `[mask]` token in MANER. Intuitively, the `[mask]` token can be helpful because it learns to encode the semantics of the context during pre-training and, thereby, the

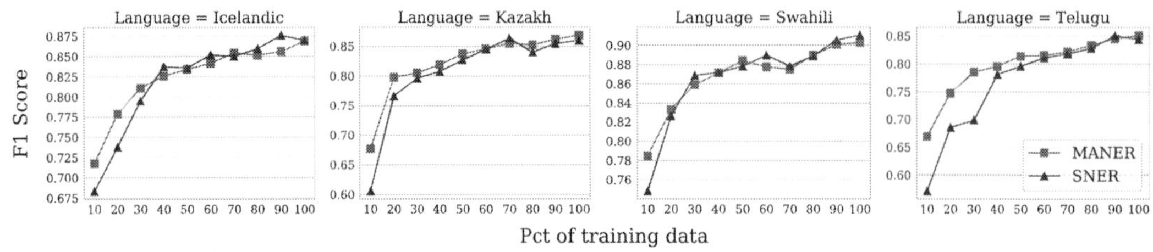


Figure 3: Measure effect of training samples to performance in MANER. MANER can give a boost in performance till 400 samples and then both MANER and SNER model perform similarly. This demonstrates that MANER is best suited for extreme low resource languages and rapid prototyping since it is easy and cost-effective to obtain very few human annotations to achieve large performance improvements (just 100 annotations are required).

| Metric | SNER | MANER (w/ **[mask]**) | MANER (w/ **[rand]**) |
|---|---|---|---|
| F1 | 0.649 | 0.715 (12%) | 0.679 (6%) |

Table 2: Average F1 scores for 100 languages for MANER using the `[mask]` token and the `[rand]` token. Replacing the `[mask]` token with the `[rand]` token diminishes the improvements.

| Metric | SNER | MANER |
|---|---|---|
| F1 | 0.603 | 0.705 (18%) |

Table 3: F1 scores comparing MANER against SNER, averaged on a subset of languages on which XLM-RoBERTa was pre-trained. The improvement over SNER is 18% compared to 12% improvement in the previous study that included all 100 languages.

word that needs to be tagged (by distributional hypothesis in Harris (1954) which states the meaning of a word can be inferred from its context).

In the first analysis, we replace the `[mask]` token in MANER with a control token, namely, the random token `[rand]`. Note that the `[rand]` token is not learned during the XLM-RoBERTa model pre-training; thus, it will not encode any contextual information. As we see in Table 2, if we replace the `[mask]` token with `[rand]` , MANER achieves only a 6% improvement in F1 performance over the SNER baseline. This result illustrates the power of the context: even when the `[rand]` token does not contain contextual information during pre-training, MANER can still use the `[rand]` token to predict how much weight to assign the context and the word immediately adjacent to it depending on the test sample.

In the second analysis, we report in Table 3 the averaged F1 score of only those languages on which the XLM-RoBERTa model was pre-trained with at least 0.5GB of training data per language. The rationale behind this experiment design is that the `[mask]` token will encode the context semantics of a language only if the language was seen during the pre-training stage of XLM-RoBERTa model. As we see in Table 3, in this case, MANER provides a whooping 18% improvement in F1 score (as compared to the 12% gain in Table 1) if the language was seen in the pre-training stage. This experiment again highlights the importance of using `[mask]` token in MANER.

### 3.3 Analysis: Effect of training set size

We measure the effectiveness of MANER in situations where more training data is available. For this purpose, we select 4 languages from WikiANN dataset that have 1000 training data samples each. From Figure 3, we see that MANER boosts F1 performance over the SNER baseline until about 400 samples and then both methods perform similarly. This result demonstrates that MANER is best suited for *extreme low resource languages and rapid prototyping* because it is *easy and cost-effective to obtain very few human annotations to achieve large performance improvements* (e.g., just 100 annotations are required).

## 4 Conclusions

In this paper, we have proposed Mask Augmented Named Entity Recognition (MANER) for NER in extreme low-resource language settings. MANER exploits the information encoded in pre-trained masked language models (inside `[mask]` token specifically) and outperforms existing approaches for extreme low-resource languages with as few as only 100 training examples by up to 48% and by 12% on average on F1 score. Analyses and ablation studies show that using semantics encoded in `[mask]` token is integral to MANER. Future work will exploit MANER's effectiveness for highly resource-constraint and human-in-the-loop settings, such as rapid prototyping in an active learning setup and few-shot learning with human annotators.

## 5 Limitations

Our proposed method MANER for improving NER is best suited for low-resource settings. As discussed in Section 3.3, we measured the effectiveness of MANER in situations where more training data is available and found that MANER boosts F1 performance over the SNER baseline until about 400 training examples, and then both methods perform similarly. The result demonstrated that MANER is best suited for extreme low-resource languages and rapid prototyping because it is easy and cost-effective to obtain very few human annotations to achieve significant performance improvements.

We base the experiments in this paper on a widely adopted model, XLM-RoBERTa, pre-trained on multiple languages. It is possible that the empirical conclusions we draw from the observations do not generalize to other pre-trained models.

## 6 Ethics Statement

We believe providing NER for low-resource languages is critical to ensure the equitable, fair, and democratized utilization of NLP technologies that are required to achieve the goal of making such technologies universally available for all. Our work contributes to this direction by proposing MANER, which boosts performance for 100 languages with only 100 training samples each.

## Acknowledgement

This work was supported by NSF grants 1842378, ONR grant N0014-20-1-2534, AFOSR grant FA9550-22-1-0060, and a Vannevar Bush Faculty Fellowship, ONR grant N00014-18-1-2047.

## References

Rami Al-Rfou, Vivek Kulkarni, Bryan Perozzi, and Steven Skiena. 2014. Polyglot-ner: Massive multilingual named entity recognition.

Alexis Conneau, Kartikay Khandelwal, Naman Goyal, Vishrav Chaudhary, Guillaume Wenzek, Francisco Guzmán, Edouard Grave, Myle Ott, Luke Zettlemoyer, and Veselin Stoyanov. 2019. Unsupervised cross-lingual representation learning at scale. *CoRR*, abs/1911.02116.

Alexis Conneau, Kartikay Khandelwal, Naman Goyal, Vishrav Chaudhary, Guillaume Wenzek, Francisco Guzmán, Edouard Grave, Myle Ott, Luke Zettlemoyer, and Veselin Stoyanov. 2020. Unsupervised cross-lingual representation learning at scale. In *Proceedings of the 58th Annual Meeting of the Association for Computational Linguistics*, pages 8440–8451, Online. Association for Computational Linguistics.

Cyprien de Lichy, Hadrien Glaude, and William Campbell. 2021. Meta-learning for few-shot named entity recognition. In *Proceedings of the 1st Workshop on Meta Learning and Its Applications to Natural Language Processing*. Association for Computational Linguistics.

Jiafeng Guo, Gu Xu, Xueqi Cheng, and Hang Li. 2009. Named entity recognition in query. In *Proceedings of the 32nd international ACM SIGIR conference on Research and development in information retrieval - SIGIR '09*. ACM Press.

Zellig S Harris. 1954. Distributional structure. *Word*, 10(2-3):146–162.

Dietmar Jannach, Ahtsham Manzoor, Wanling Cai, and Li Chen. 2022. A survey on conversational recommender systems. *ACM Computing Surveys*, 54(5):1–36.

Erik F. Kim Sang and Fien De Meulder. 2003. Introduction to the CoNLL-2003 shared task: Language-independent named entity recognition. In *Proceedings of the Seventh Conference on Natural Language Learning at HLT-NAACL 2003*, pages 142–147.

Benjamin Philip King. 2015. *Practical Natural Language Processing for Low-Resource Languages*. Ph.D. thesis, University of Michigan.

James Kirkpatrick, Razvan Pascanu, Neil Rabinowitz, Joel Veness, Guillaume Desjardins, Andrei A Rusu, Kieran Milan, John Quan, Tiago Ramalho, Agnieszka Grabska-Barwinska, et al. 2017. Overcoming catastrophic forgetting in neural networks. *Proceedings of the national academy of sciences*, 114(13):3521–3526.

Martin Krallinger, Obdulia Rabal, Anália Lourenço, Julen Oyarzabal, and Alfonso Valencia. 2017. Information retrieval and text mining technologies for chemistry. *Chemical Reviews*, 117(12):7673–7761.

Martin Krallinger and Alfonso Valencia. 2005. Text-mining and information-retrieval services for molecular biology. *Genome biology*, 6(7):1–8.

Ji Young Lee, Franck Dernoncourt, and Peter Szolovits. 2017. Transfer learning for named-entity recognition with neural networks.

Yinhan Liu, Myle Ott, Naman Goyal, Jingfei Du, Mandar Joshi, Danqi Chen, Omer Levy, Mike Lewis, Luke Zettlemoyer, and Veselin Stoyanov. 2019. Roberta: A robustly optimized BERT pretraining approach. *CoRR*, abs/1907.11692.

Ilya Loshchilov and Frank Hutter. 2019. Decoupled weight decay regularization. In *International Conference on Learning Representations*.

Alexandre Magueresse, Vincent Carles, and Evan Heetderks. 2020. Low-resource languages: A review of past work and future challenges.

Shervin Malmasi, Anjie Fang, Besnik Fetahu, Sudipta Kar, and Oleg Rokhlenko. 2022. MultiCoNER: A large-scale multilingual dataset for complex named entity recognition. In *Proceedings of the 29th International Conference on Computational Linguistics*, pages 3798–3809, Gyeongju, Republic of Korea. International Committee on Computational Linguistics.

Tao Meng, Anjie Fang, Oleg Rokhlenko, and Shervin Malmasi. 2021a. Gemnet: Effective gated gazetteer representations for recognizing complex entities in low-context input. In *NAACL 2021*.

Yu Meng, Yunyi Zhang, Jiaxin Huang, Xuan Wang, Yu Zhang, Heng Ji, and Jiawei Han. 2021b. Distantly-supervised named entity recognition with noise-robust learning and language model augmented self-training. In *Proceedings of the 2021 Conference on Empirical Methods in Natural Language Processing*.

Diego Mollá, Menno van Zaanen, and Daniel Smith. 2006. Named entity recognition for question answering. In *Proceedings of the Australasian Language Technology Workshop 2006*, pages 51–58, Sydney, Australia.

David Nadeau and Satoshi Sekine. 2007. A survey of named entity recognition and classification. *Lingvisticæ Investigationes. International Journal of Linguistics and Language Resources*, 30(1):3–26.

Xiaoman Pan, Boliang Zhang, Jonathan May, Joel Nothman, Kevin Knight, and Heng Ji. 2017. Cross-lingual name tagging and linking for 282 languages. In *Proceedings of the 55th Annual Meeting of the Association for Computational Linguistics (Volume 1: Long Papers)*, pages 1946–1958.

Afshin Rahimi, Yuan Li, and Trevor Cohn. 2019. Massively multilingual transfer for NER. In *Proceedings of the 57th Annual Meeting of the Association for Computational Linguistics*, pages 151–164, Florence, Italy. Association for Computational Linguistics.

Lance Ramshaw and Mitch Marcus. 1995. Text chunking using transformation-based learning. In *Third Workshop on Very Large Corpora*.

Jonathan S. Rosenfeld. 2021. Scaling laws for deep learning. *CoRR*, abs/2108.07686.

Stefan Schweter and Alan Akbik. 2020. Flert: Document-level features for named entity recognition.

Simone Tedeschi, Valentino Maiorca, Niccolò Campolungo, Francesco Cecconi, and Roberto Navigli. 2021. WikiNEuRal: Combined neural and knowledge-based silver data creation for multilingual NER. In *Findings of the Association for Computational Linguistics: EMNLP 2021*. Association for Computational Linguistics.

Xinyu Wang, Yong Jiang, Nguyen Bach, Tao Wang, Zhongqiang Huang, Fei Huang, and Kewei Tu. 2021. Automated Concatenation of Embeddings for Structured Prediction. In *the Joint Conference of the 59th Annual Meeting of the Association for Computational Linguistics and the 11th International Joint Conference on Natural Language Processing (**ACL-IJCNLP 2021**)*. Association for Computational Linguistics.

Enwei Zhu and Jinpeng Li. 2022. Boundary smoothing for named entity recognition. In *Proceedings of the 60th Annual Meeting of the Association for Computational Linguistics (Volume 1: Long Papers)*. Association for Computational Linguistics.

## A Implementation details on baselines

### A.1 SNER

Similar to MANER design, current standard NER systems (SNER) built upon transformer models also simply add a NER classifier to the top of a transformer model. The classifier predicts the NER class of each token of an unmodified sentence $S$:

$$\mathcal{M}_{\text{base}}(T, \mathbf{M}, S, i) = \text{softmax}\Big(\mathbf{M}(\mathbf{e}_\text{i})\Big) = \mathbf{p}_\text{i}, \quad 0 \leq i < n,$$

where $\mathcal{M}_{\text{base}}$ is an NER model built on a transformer model $T$ using classifier weight matrix $\mathbf{M}$. This baseline method remains the de-facto method for training NER models for most languages (especially low-resource languages) to the best of our knowledge, though specialized models have been built for popular languages like English.

*Inference:* Similar to training during inference, the NER class of each word in the sentence is the most probable NER tag assigned to the classified word embedding.

### A.2 MLM-NER

Our MANER methodology in Section 2 is one way to change the input phrase using the mask token. In this baseline, we introduce yet another way to repurpose the `[mask]` token for NER that is inspired by the masked language modeling (MLM) framework that is used for pre-training transformer models which we refer as MLM-NER. In MLM, a word is predicted using the words surrounding it in the sentence. Since the NER category of a word is also a semantic property of the word, we use the philosophy of MLM for NER fine-tuning.

In MLM pre-training, the dataset is prepared by *masking* random words in a sentence with a `[mask]` token with a fixed probability $p_{mlm}$. Then, the masked words are predicted using the context information.

Analogous to MLM pre-training, for NER fine-tuning, we randomly replace words in sentence $S$ with the `[mask]` token with the fixed probability $p_{ner}$. However, instead of predicting the missing words, as with MLM, we predict the NER labels $L$ for each word $w$ in $S$ irrespective of whether the word was replaced by a `[mask]` token or not. In the case the word was replaced with the `[mask]` token, the transformer outputs the `[mask]` token embedding for that word.

Thus the modified input to the transformer is $S' = \text{mask(S)}$, where

$$\text{mask}(\text{w}_\text{i}) = \begin{cases} \texttt{[mask]}, & \text{if } p_i \leq p_{ner}, \\ w_i, & \text{otherwise} \end{cases} \tag{1}$$

with $p_i$ a random number between 0 and 1 generated for $w_i$. Then, we use the first baseline NER model design $\mathcal{M}_{base}$ for training, but now it is is fine-tuned on $S'$ and $L$ (note we predict the label of the `[mask]` tokens as well). Inference with this model remains same as the first baseline model.

### A.3 MANER Classifier Input Embedding

The NER prediction for each word in MANER is based on the embedding of the *first token of the word*. This is a common practice in NER with Transformer-based models where a word may be tokenized into multiple tokens.

### A.4 Training procedures

For each language in our experiment, we train MANER and baselines for 30 epochs with a learning rate of $5\text{e}^{-6}$ and the loss optimized using Adam (Loshchilov and Hutter, 2019). Training takes 3 minutes on a single 11 GB GeForce GTX 1080 Ti GPU for a single language. We run MANER for following five random seeds for each language - 12345, 23451, 34512, 45123, 51234. The standard deviation in performance for SNER averaged over 100 languages for 5 runs is $0.649 \pm 0.005$ and for MANER is $0.715 \pm 0.007$.

## B WikiANN dataset details

The NER labels in WikiANN are in IOB2 (Inside–outside–beginning) format (Ramshaw and Marcus, 1995) comprising PER (person), LOC (location), and ORG (organization) tags. An instance of NER tagged sentence: *UNICEF*(B-ORG) is a nonprofit organization, founded by *Ludwik*(B-PER) *Rajchman*(I-PER) headquartered at *New*(B-LOC) *York*(I-LOC), *United*(B-LOC) *States*(I-LOC).

In addition, language names corresponding to abbreviations used in figure 2 can be found in the Appendix section of Conneau et al. (2020).

## C Comments on catastrophic forgetting in MANER

The *catastrophic forgetting* (Kirkpatrick et al., 2017) phenomenon that masked language models undergo during any kind of fine-tuning is one of the

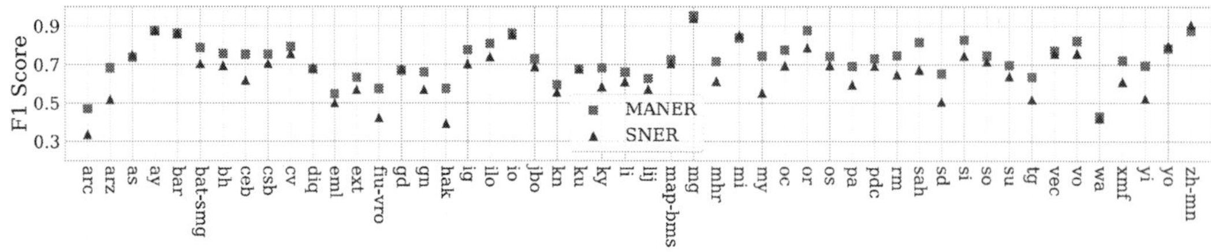


Figure 4: F1 scores comparing MANER against SNER for the remaining 50 low-resource languages in the WikiANN dataset that only have 100 training samples each. Similar to the results in Figure 2, MANER gives a significant improvement of **12%** on F1 score compared to SNER .

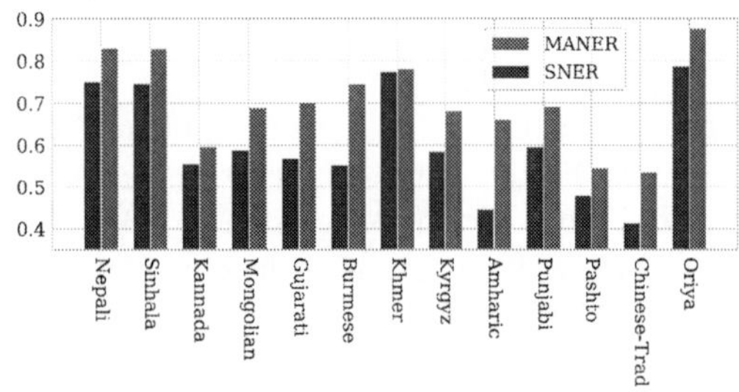


Figure 5: F1 score comparing MANER against SNER on a subset of languages on which the backbone of both models, XLM-RoBERTa-large, has been pre-trained. MANER improves upon SNER for each of these languages, with F1 score improvement of up to 22% and 18% on average.

reasons we think MANER does not provide gains when more training data is available (of course more training data also implies less reliance on specialized techniques like ours). Catastrophic forgetting causes the loss of useful context semantics encoded in the `[mask]` token during the fine-tuning stage that MANER heavily relies on. Adding an additional masked language modeling loss to the NER loss during fine-tuning may help to circumvent catastrophic forgetting; we leave this investigation as a valuable venue for future work.

# D Additional experiment results

Figure 4 shows the performance comparing MANER and SNER on the remaining 50 low-resource languages in the WikiANN dataset. The results here align with that in the main text: MANER provides performance improvement, sometimes significantly, over SNER.

Figure 5 shows the performance comparing MANER and SNER on a subset of languages on which the backbone of both models, XLM-RoBERTa-large, has been pre-trained. The results corroborate with those in the main text: MANER improves upon SNER for each of these languages, with F1 score improvement of up to 22% and 18% on average.

# Efficient and Interpretable Compressive Text Summarisation with Unsupervised Dual-Agent Reinforcement Learning

**Peggy Tang[†], Junbin Gao[‡], Lei Zhang[◇], Zhiyong Wang[†]**

[†]School of Computer Science, The University of Sydney

[◇]International Digital Economy Academy

[‡]The University of Sydney Business School, The University of Sydney

{peggy.tang,junbin.gao,zhiyong.wang}@sydney.edu.au,
leizhang@idea.edu.cn

## Abstract

Recently, compressive text summarisation offers a balance between the conciseness issue of extractive summarisation and the factual hallucination issue of abstractive summarisation. However, most existing compressive summarisation methods are supervised, relying on the expensive effort of creating a new training dataset with corresponding compressive summaries. In this paper, we propose an efficient and interpretable compressive summarisation method that utilises unsupervised dual-agent reinforcement learning to optimise a summary's semantic coverage and fluency by simulating human judgment on summarisation quality. Our model consists of an extractor agent and a compressor agent, and both agents have a multi-head attentional pointer-based structure. The extractor agent first chooses salient sentences from a document, and then the compressor agent compresses these extracted sentences by selecting salient words to form a summary without using reference summaries to compute the summary reward. To our best knowledge, this is the first work on unsupervised compressive summarisation. Experimental results on three widely used datasets (e.g., Newsroom, CNN/DM, and XSum) show that our model achieves promising performance and a significant improvement on Newsroom in terms of the ROUGE metric, as well as interpretability of semantic coverage of summarisation results. [1]

## 1 Introduction

Most existing works on neural text summarisation are extractive, abstractive, and compressive-based. Extractive methods select salient sentences from a document to form its summary and ensure the production of grammatically and factually correct summaries. These methods usually follow the sentence ranking conceptualisation (Narayan et al., 2018b; Liu and Lapata, 2019; Zhong et al., 2020). The supervised models commonly rely on creating proxy extractive training labels for training (Nallapati et al., 2017; Jia et al., 2021; Mao et al., 2022; Klaus et al., 2022), which can be noisy and may not be reliant. Various unsupervised methods (Zheng and Lapata, 2019; Xu et al., 2020; Padmakumar and He, 2021; Liu et al., 2021) were proposed to leverage pre-trained language models to compute sentences similarities and select important sentences. Although these methods have significantly improved summarisation performance, the redundant information that appears in the salient sentences may not be minimized effectively.

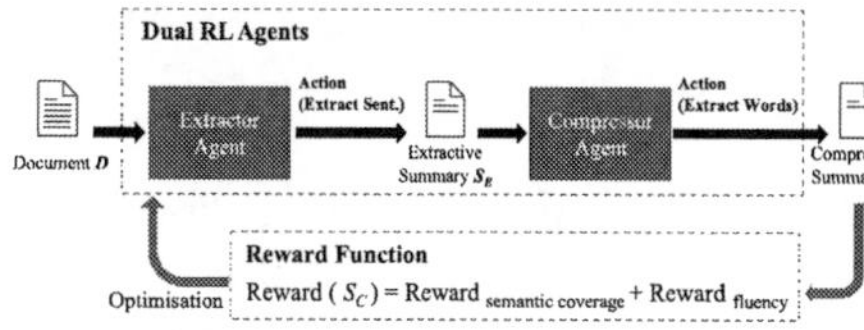


Figure 1: Illustration of our proposed URLComSum.

Abstractive methods formulate the task as a sequence-to-sequence generation task, with the document as the input sequence and the summary as the output sequence (See et al., 2017; Zhang et al., 2020; Wang et al., 2021; Liu et al., 2022) As supervised learning with ground-truth summaries may not provide useful insights on human judgment approximation, reinforcement training was proposed to optimise the ROUGE metric (Parnell et al., 2021), and to fine-tune a pre-trained language model (Laban et al., 2020). Prior studies showed that these generative models are highly prone to external hallucination (Maynez et al., 2020).

Compressive summarisation is a recent appraoch which aims to select words, instead of sentences, from an input document to form a summary, which improves the factuality and conciseness of a summary. The formulation of compressive document summarisation is usually a two-stage extract-then-

[1]Our source code is publicly available for research purposes at https://github.com/peggypytang/URLComSum/



*Proceedings of The Fourth Workshop on Simple and Efficient Natural Language Processing (SustaiNLP)*, pages 227–238
July 13, 2023 ©2023 Association for Computational Linguistics

compress approach (Zhang et al., 2018; Mendes et al., 2019; Xu and Durrett, 2019; Desai et al., 2020): it first extracts salient sentences from a document, then compresses the extracted sentences to form its summary. Most of these methods are supervised, which require a parallel dataset with document-summary pairs to train. However, the ground-truth summaries of existing datasets are usually abstractive-based and do not contain supervision information needed for extractive summarisation or compressive summarisation (Xu and Durrett, 2019; Mendes et al., 2019; Desai et al., 2020).

Therefore, to address these limitations, we propose a novel unsupervised compressive summarisation method with dual-agent reinforcement learning strategy to mimic human judgment, namely URLComSum. As illustrated in Figure 1, URLComSum consists of two modules, an extractor agent and a compressor agent. We model the sentence and word representations using a efficient Bi-LSTM (Graves and Schmidhuber, 2005) with multi-head attention (Vaswani et al., 2017) to capture both the long-range dependencies and the relationship between each word and each sentence. We use a pointer network (Vinyals et al., 2015) to find the optimal subset of sentences and words to be extracted since the Pointer Network is well-known for tackling combinatorial optimization problems. The extractor agent uses a hierarchical multi-head attentional Bi-LSTM model for learning the sentence representation of the input document and a pointer network for extracting the salient sentences of a document given a length budget. To further compress these extracted sentences all together, the compressor agent uses a multi-head attentional Bi-LSTM model for learning the word representation and a pointer network for selecting the words to assemble a summary.

As an unsupervised method, URLComSum does not require a parallel training dataset.We propose an unsupervised reinforcement learning training procedure to mimic human judgment: to reward the model that achieves high summary quality in terms of semantic coverage and language fluency. Inspired by Word Mover's Distance (Kusner et al., 2015), the semantic coverage rewardis measured by Wasserstein distance (Peyré et al., 2019) between the semantic distribution of the document and that of the summary. The fluency reward is measured by Syntactic Log-Odds Ratio (SLOR) (Pauls and Klein, 2012). SLOR is a referenceless fluency evaluation metric, which is effective in sentence compression (Kann et al., 2018) and has better correlation to human acceptability judgments (Lau et al., 2017).

The key contributions of this paper are:

- We propose the first unsupervised compressive summarisation method with dual-agent reinforcement learning, namely URLComSum.
- We design an efficient and interpretable multi-head attentional pointer-based neural network for learning the representation and for extracting salient sentences and words.
- We propose to mimic human judgment by optimising summary quality in terms of the semantic coverage reward, measured by Wasserstein distance, and the fluency reward, measured by Syntactic Log-Odds Ratio (SLOR).
- Comprehensive experimental results on three widely used datasets, including CNN/DM, XSum, Newsroom, demonstrate that URLComSum achieves great performance.

## 2 Related Work

Most of the existing works on neural text summarisation are extractive, abstractive, and compressive-based.

### 2.1 Extractive Methods

Extractive methods usually follow the sentence ranking conceptualisation, and an encoder-decoder scheme is generally adopted. An encoder formulates document or sentence representations, and a decoder predicts extraction classification labels. The supervised models commonly rely on creating proxy extractive training labels for training (Cheng and Lapata, 2016; Nallapati et al., 2017; Jia et al., 2021), which can be noisy and may not be reliant. Some methods were proposed to tackle this issue by training with reinforcement learning (Narayan et al., 2018b; Luo et al., 2019) to optimise the ROUGE metric directly. Various unsupervised methods (Zheng and Lapata, 2019; Xu et al., 2020; Padmakumar and He, 2021) were also proposed to leverage pre-trained language models to compute sentences similarities and select important sentences. Although these methods have significantly improved summarisation performance, since the entire sentences are extracted individually, the redundant information that appears in the salient sentences may not be minimized effectively.

### 2.2 Abstractive Methods

Abstractive methods formulate text summarisation as a sequence-to-sequence generation task, with the source document as the input sequence and the summary as the output sequence. Most existing methods follow the supervised RNN-based encoder-decoder framework (See et al., 2017; Zhang et al., 2020; Wang et al., 2021; Liu et al., 2022). As supervised learning with ground-truth summaries may not provide useful insights on human judgment approximation, reinforcement training was proposed to optimise the ROUGE metric (Paulus et al., 2018; Parnell et al., 2021), and to fine-tune a pre-trained language model (Laban et al., 2020). These models naturally learn to integrate knowledge from the training data while generating an abstractive summary. Prior studies showed that these generative models are highly prone to external hallucination, thus may generate contents that are unfaithful to the original document (Maynez et al., 2020).

### 2.3 Compressive Methods

Compressive methods select words from a given document to assemble a summary. Due to the lack of training dataset, not until recently there have emerged works for compressive summarisation (Zhang et al., 2018; Mendes et al., 2019; Xu and Durrett, 2019; Desai et al., 2020). The formulation of compressive document summarisation is usually a two-stage extract-then-compress approach: it first extracts salient sentences from a document, then compresses the extracted sentences to form its summary. Most of these methods are supervised, which require a parallel dataset with document-summary pairs to train. However, the ground-truth summaries of existing datasets are usually abstractive-based and do not contain supervision information needed for extractive summarisation or compressive summarisation. Several reinforcement learning based methods (Zhang et al., 2018) use existing abstractive-based datasets for training, which is not aligned for compression. Note that existing compressors often perform compression sentence by sentence. As a result, the duplicated information among multiple sentences could be overlooked. Therefore, to address these limitations, we propose a novel unsupervised compressive method by exploring the dual-agent reinforcement learning strategy to mimic human judgment and perform text compression instead of sentence compression.

## 3 Methodology

As shown in Figure 1, our proposed compressive summarisation method, namely URLComSum, consists of two components, an extractor agent and a compressor agent. Specifically, the extractor agent selects salient sentences from a document $\mathbf{D}$ to form an extractive summary $\mathbf{S_E}$, and then the compressor agent compresses $\mathbf{S_E}$ by selecting words to assemble a compressive summary $\mathbf{S_C}$.

### 3.1 Extractor Agent

Given a document $\mathbf{D}$ consisting of a sequence of $M$ sentences $\{\mathbf{s}_i | i = 1, ..., M\}$, and each sentence $\mathbf{s}_i$ consisting of a sequence of $N$ words $\{\mathbf{we}_{ij} | j = 1, ..., N\}^2$, the extractor agent aims to produce an extractive summary $\mathbf{S_E}$ by learning sentence representation and selecting $L_E$ sentences from $\mathbf{D}$. As illustrated in Figure 2, we design a hierarchical multi-head attentional sequential model for learning the sentence representations of the document and using a Pointer Network to extract sentences based on their representations.

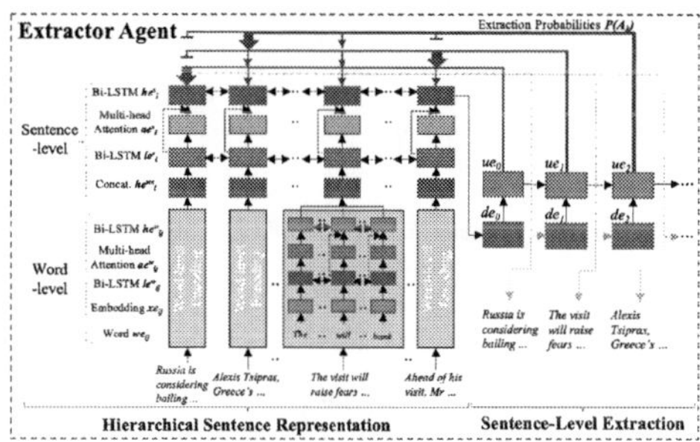


Figure 2: Illustration of the extractor agent.

#### 3.1.1 Hierarchical Sentence Representation

To model the local context of each sentence and the global context between sentences, we use two-levels Bi-LSTMs to model this hierarchical structure, one at the word level to encode the word sequence of each sentence, one at the sentence level to encode the sentence sequence of the document. To model the context-dependency of the importance of words and sentences, we apply two levels of multi-head attention mechanism (Vaswani et al., 2017), one at each of the two-level Bi-LSTMs.

[2]We have pre-fixed the length of each sentence and each document by padding.

Given a sentence $\mathbf{s}_i$, we encode its words into word embeddings $\mathbf{xe}_i = \{\mathbf{xe}_{ij} | j = 1, ..., N\}$ by $\mathbf{xe}_{ij} = Enc(\mathbf{we}_{ij})$, where $Enc()$ denotes a word embedding lookup table. Then the sequence of word embeddings are fed into the word-level Bi-LSTM to produce an output representation of the words $\mathbf{le}^w$:

$$\mathbf{le}_{ij}^w = \overleftrightarrow{\mathrm{LSTM}}(\mathbf{xe}_{ij}), j \in [1, N] . \quad (1)$$

To utilize the multi-head attention mechanism to obtain $\mathbf{ae}_i^w = \{\mathbf{ae}_{i1}^w, ..., \mathbf{ae}_{iN}^w\}$ at word level, we define $Q_i = \mathbf{le}_i^w$, $K_i = V_i = \mathbf{xe}_i$,

$$\mathbf{ae}_i^w = \mathrm{MultiHead}(Q_i, K_i, V_i) . \quad (2)$$

The concatenation of $\mathbf{le}_i^w$ and $\mathbf{ae}_i^w$ of the words are fed into a Bi-LSTM and the output is concatenated to obtain the local context representation $\mathbf{he}_i^{ws}$ for each sentence $\mathbf{s_i}$:

$$\begin{aligned} \mathbf{he}_{ij}^w &= \overleftrightarrow{\mathrm{LSTM}}([\mathbf{le}_{ij}^w; \mathbf{ae}_{ij}^w]), j \in [1, N] , \\ \mathbf{he}_i^{ws} &= [\mathbf{he}_{i1}^w, ..., \mathbf{he}_{iN}^w] . \end{aligned} \quad (3)$$

To further model the global context between sentences, we apply a similar structure at sentence level. $\mathbf{he}^{ws} = \{\mathbf{he}_i^{ws} | i = 1, ..., M\}$ are fed into the sentence-level Bi-LSTM to produce output representation of the sentences $\mathbf{le}^s$:

$$\mathbf{le}_i^s = \overleftrightarrow{\mathrm{LSTM}}(\mathbf{he}_i^{ws}), i \in [1, M] . \quad (4)$$

To utilize the multi-head attention mechanism to obtain $\mathbf{ae}^s = \{\mathbf{ae}_1^s, ..., \mathbf{ae}_M^s\}$ at sentence level, we define $Q = \mathbf{le}^s$, $K = V = \mathbf{he}^{ws}$,

$$\mathbf{ae}^s = \mathrm{MultiHead}(Q, K, V). \quad (5)$$

The concatenation of the Bi-LSTM output $\mathbf{le}^s$ and the multi-head attention output $\mathbf{ae}^s$ of the sentences are fed into a Bi-LSTM to obtain the final representations of sentences $\mathbf{he}^s = \{\mathbf{he}_1^s, ..., \mathbf{he}_M^s\}$:

$$\mathbf{he}_i^s = \overleftrightarrow{\mathrm{LSTM}}([\mathbf{le}_i^s; \mathbf{ae}_i^s]), i \in [1, M] . \quad (6)$$

#### 3.1.2 Sentence-Level Extraction

Similar to (Chen and Bansal, 2018), we use an LSTM-based Pointer Network to decode the above sentence representations $\mathbf{he}^s = \{\mathbf{he}_1^s, ..., \mathbf{he}_M^s\}$ and extract sentences recurrently to form an extractive summary $\mathbf{S_E} = \{A_1, ..., A_k, ..., A_{L_E}\}$ with $L_E$ sentences, where $A_k$ denotes the $k$-th sentence extracted.

At the $k$-th time step, the pointer network receives the sentence representation of the previous extracted sentence and has hidden state $de_k$. It first obtains a context vector $de_k'$ by attending to $\mathbf{he}^s$:

$$\begin{aligned} \mathbf{ue}_i^k &= v^T \tanh(W_1 \mathbf{he}_i^s + W_2 de_k), i \in (1, ..., M) , \\ \mathbf{ae}_i^k &= \mathrm{softmax}(\mathbf{ue}_i^k), i \in (1, ..., M) , \\ de_k' &= \sum_{i=1}^{M} \mathbf{ae}_i^k \mathbf{he}_i^s , \end{aligned} \quad (7)$$

where $v, W_1, W_2$ are learnable parameters of the pointer network. Then it predicts the extraction probability $p(A_k)$ of a sentence:

$$\begin{aligned} de_k &\leftarrow [de_k, de_k'] , \\ \mathbf{ue}_i^k &= v^T \tanh(W_1 \mathbf{he}_i^s + W_2 de_k), i \in (1, ..., M) , \\ p(A_k | A_1, ..., A_{k-1}) &= \mathrm{softmax}(\mathbf{ue}^k) . \end{aligned} \quad (8)$$

Decoding iterates until $L_E$ sentences are selected to form $S_E$.

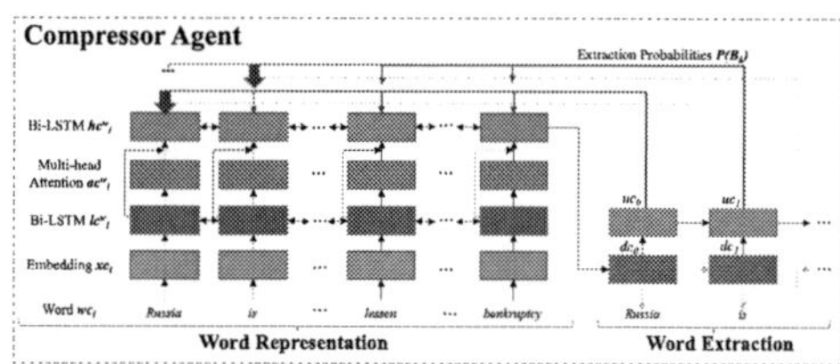


Figure 3: Illustration of the compressor agent.

### 3.2 Compressor Agent

Given an extractive summary $\mathbf{S_E}$ consisting of a sequence of words $\mathbf{wc} = \{\mathbf{wc}_i | i = 1, ..., N\}$, the compressor agent aims to produce a compressive summary $\mathbf{S_C}$ by selecting $L_C$ words from $\mathbf{S_E}$. As illustrated in Figure 3, it has a multi-head attentional Bi-LSTM model to learn the word representations. It uses a pointer network to extract words based on their representations.

#### 3.2.1 Word Representation

Given a sequence of words $\mathbf{wc}$, we encode the words into word embeddings $\mathbf{xc} = \{\mathbf{xc}_i | i = 1, ..., N\}$ by $\mathbf{xc}_i = Enc(\mathbf{wc}_i)$. Then the sequence of word embeddings are fed into a Bi-LSTM to produce the words' output representation $\mathbf{lc}^w$:

$$\mathbf{lc}_i^w = \overleftrightarrow{\mathrm{LSTM}}(\mathbf{xc}_i), i \in [1, N] . \quad (9)$$

To utilise the multi-head attention mechanism to obtain $\mathbf{ac}^w = \{\mathbf{ac}_1^w, ..., \mathbf{ac}_N^w\}$, we define $Q = \mathbf{lc}^w$, $K = V = \mathbf{xc}$,

$$\mathbf{ac}^w = \mathrm{MultiHead}(Q, K, V). \quad (10)$$

The concatenation of $\mathbf{lc}^w$ and $\mathbf{ac}^w$ of the words are fed into a Bi-LSTM to obtain the representation $\mathbf{hc}_i^w$ for each word $\mathbf{wc_i}$:

$$\mathbf{hc}_i^w = \overleftrightarrow{\text{LSTM}}([\mathbf{lc}_i^w; \mathbf{ac}_i^w]), i \in [1, N] . \quad (11)$$

#### 3.2.2 Word-Level Extraction

The word extractor of the compressor agent shares the same structure as that of the extractor agent's sentence extractor. To select the words based on the above word representations $\mathbf{hc}^w = \{\mathbf{hc}_1^w, ..., \mathbf{hc}_N^w\}$, the word extractor decodes and extracts words recurrently to produce $\{B_1, ..., B_k, ..., B_{L_C}\}$, where $B_k$ denotes the word extracted at the $k$-th time step. The selected words are reordered by their locations in the input document and assembled to form the compressive summary $\mathbf{S_C}$.

### 3.3 Reward in Reinforcement Learning

We use the compressive summary $\mathbf{S_C}$ to compute the reward of reinforcement learning and denote $\text{Reward}(\mathbf{D}, \mathbf{S_C})$ as $\text{Reward}(\mathbf{D}, \mathbf{S})$ for simplicity. $\text{Reward}(\mathbf{D}, \mathbf{S})$ is a weighted sum of the semantic coverage award $\text{Reward}_{\text{cov}}(\mathbf{D}, \mathbf{S})$ and the fluency reward $\text{Reward}_{\text{flu}}(\mathbf{S})$:

$$\begin{aligned}\text{Reward}(\mathbf{D}, \mathbf{S}) = w_{\text{cov}}&\text{Reward}_{\text{cov}}(\mathbf{D}, \mathbf{S}) \\ &+ w_{\text{flu}}\text{Reward}_{\text{flu}}(\mathbf{S}) ,\end{aligned} \quad (12)$$

where $w_{\text{cov}}$ and $w_{\text{flu}}$ denote the weights of two rewards.

#### 3.3.1 Semantic Coverage Reward

We compute $\text{Reward}_{\text{cov}}$ with the Wasserstein distance between the corresponding semantic distributions of the document $\mathbf{D}$ and the summary $\mathbf{S}$, which is the minimum cost required to transport the semantics from $\mathbf{D}$ to $\mathbf{S}$. We denote $\mathbf{D} = \{d_i | i = 1, ..., N\}$ to represent a document, where $d_i$ indicates the count of the $i$-th token (i.e., word or phrase in a vocabulary of size $N$). Similarly, for a summary $\mathbf{S} = \{s_j | j = 1, ..., N\}$, $s_j$ is respect to the count of the $j$-th token . The semantic distribution of a document is characterized in terms of normalised term frequency without the stopwords. The term frequency of the $i$-th token in the document $\mathbf{D}$ and the $j$-th token in the summary $\mathbf{S}$ are denoted as $\text{TF}_{\mathbf{D}}(i)$ and $\text{TF}_{\mathbf{S}}(j)$, respectively. By defining $\text{TF}_{\mathbf{D}} = \{\text{TF}_{\mathbf{D}}(i)\} \in \mathbf{R}^N$ and $\text{TF}_{\mathbf{S}} = \{\text{TF}_{\mathbf{S}}(j)\} \in \mathbf{R}^N$, we have the semantic distributions within $\mathbf{D}$ and $\mathbf{S}$ respectively.

The transportation cost matrix $\mathbf{C}$ is obtained by measuring the semantic similarity between each of the tokens. Given a pre-trained tokeniser and token embedding model with $N$ tokens, define $\mathbf{v}_i$ to represent the feature embedding of the $i$-th token. Then the transport cost $c_{ij}$ from the $i$-th to the $j$-th token is computed based on the cosine similarity: $c_{ij} = 1 - \frac{<\mathbf{v}_i, \mathbf{v}_j>}{\|\mathbf{v}_i\|_2 \|\mathbf{v}_j\|_2}$. An optimal transport plan $\mathbf{T}^* = \{t_{i,j}^*\} \in \mathbf{R}^{N \times N}$ in pursuit of minimizing the transportation cost can be obtained by solving the optimal transportation and resources allocation optimization problem (Peyré et al., 2019). Note that the transport plan can be used to interpret the transportation of tokens from document to summary, which brings interpretability to our URLComSum method.

Wasserstein distance measuring the distance between the two semantic distributions $\text{TF}_{\mathbf{D}}$ and $\text{TF}_{\mathbf{S}}$ with the optimal transport plan is computed by: $d_W(\text{TF}_{\mathbf{D}}, \text{TF}_{\mathbf{S}} | \mathbf{C}) = \sum_{i,j} t_{ij}^* c_{ij}$. $\text{Reward}_{\text{cov}}(\mathbf{D}, \mathbf{S})$ can be further defined as:

$$\text{Reward}_{\text{cov}}(\mathbf{D}, \mathbf{S}) = 1 - d_W(\text{TF}_{\mathbf{D}}, \text{TF}_{\mathbf{S}} | \mathbf{C}) . \quad (13)$$

#### 3.3.2 Fluency Reward

We utilise Syntactic Log-Odds Ratio (SLOR) (Pauls and Klein, 2012) to measure $\text{Reward}_{\text{flu}}(S)$, which is defined as: $\text{Reward}_{\text{flu}}(S) = \frac{1}{|S|}(\log(P_{LM}(S)) - \log(P_U(S)))$ , where $P_{LM}(S)$ denotes the probability of the summary assigned by a pre-trained language model $LM$, $p_U(S) = \prod_{t \in S} P(t)$ denotes the unigram probability for rare word adjustment, and $|S|$ denotes the sentence length.

We use the Self-Critical Sequence Training (SCST) method (Rennie et al., 2017), since this training algorithm has demonstrated promising results in text summarisation (Paulus et al., 2018; Laban et al., 2020). For a given input document, the model produces two separate output summaries: the sampled summary $\mathbf{S}^s$, obtained by sampling the next pointer $t_i$ from the probability distribution at each time step $i$, and the baseline summary $\hat{\mathbf{S}}$, obtained by always picking the most likely next pointer $t$ at each $i$. The training objective is to minimise the following loss:

$$\begin{aligned}Loss = -(&\text{Reward}(\mathbf{D}, \mathbf{S}^s) - \text{Reward}(\mathbf{D}, \hat{\mathbf{S}})) \\ &\cdot \frac{1}{N} \sum_{i=1}^{N} \log p(t_i^s | t_1^s, ..., t_{i-1}^s, \mathbf{D}) ,\end{aligned} \quad (14)$$

where $N$ denotes the length of the pointer sequence, which is the number of extracted sentences for the extractor agent and the number of extracted words for the compressor agent.

Minimising the loss is equivalent to maximising the conditional likelihood of $\mathbf{S}^s$ if the sampled summary $\mathbf{S}^s$ outperforms the baseline summary $\hat{\mathbf{S}}$, i.e. $\text{Reward}(\mathbf{D}, \mathbf{S}^s) - \text{Reward}(\mathbf{D}, \hat{\mathbf{S}}) > 0$, thus increasing the expected reward of the model.

## 4 Experiments

### 4.1 Experimental Settings

We conducted comprehensive experiments on three widely used datasets: *Newsroom* (Grusky et al., 2018), *CNN/DailyMail (CNN/DM)* (Hermann et al., 2015), and *XSum* (Narayan et al., 2018a). We set the LSTM hidden size to 150 and the number of recurrent layers to 3. We performed hyperparameter searching for $w_{\text{cov}}$ and $w_{\text{flu}}$ and decided to set $w_{\text{cov}} = 1$ , $w_{\text{flu}} = 2$ in all our experiments since it provides more balanced results across the datasets. We trained the URLComSum with AdamW (Loshchilov and Hutter, 2018) with learning rate 0.01 with a batch size of 3. We obtained the word embedding from the pre-trained GloVe (Pennington et al., 2014). We used BERT for the pre-trained embedding models used for computing semantic coverage reward. We chose GPT2 for the trained language model used for computing the fluency reward due to strong representation capacity.

As shown in Table 1, we followed (Mendes et al., 2019) to set $\mathbf{L_E}$ for Newsroom and (Zhong et al., 2020) to set $\mathbf{L_E}$ for CNN/DM and XSum. We also followed their protocols to set $\mathbf{L_C}$ by matching the average number of words in summaries.

| Dataset | Newsroom | CNN/DM | XSum |
|---|---|---|---|
| **#Sentences in Doc.** | 27 | 39 | 19 |
| **#Tokens in Doc.** | 659 | 766 | 367 |
| $\mathbf{L_E}$ | 2 | 3 | 2 |
| $\mathbf{L_C}$ | 26 | 58 | 24 |
| **Train** | 995,041 | 287,113 | 204,045 |
| **Test** | 108,862 | 11,490 | 11,334 |

Table 1: Overview of the three datasets. #Sentences in Doc. and #Tokens in Doc. denote the average number of sentences and words in the documents respectively. $\mathbf{L_E}$ denotes the number of sentences to be selected by the extractor agent. $\mathbf{L_C}$ denotes the number of words to be selected by the compressor agent. Train and Test denote the size of train and test sets.

| **Method** | ROUGE-1 | ROUGE-2 | ROUGE-L |
|---|---|---|---|
| LEAD | 33.9 | 23.2 | 30.7 |
| LEAD-WORD | 34.9 | 23.1 | 30.7 |
| **Supervised Methods** | | | |
| EXCONSUMM (Ext.)* | 31.9 | 16.3 | 26.9 |
| EXCONSUMM (Ext.+Com.)* | 25.5 | 11.0 | 21.1 |
| **Unsupervised Methods** | | | |
| SumLoop (Abs.) | 27.0 | 9.6 | 26.4 |
| TextRank (Ext.) | 24.5 | 10.1 | 20.1 |
| **URLComSum (Ext.)** | 33.9 | **23.2** | 30.0 |
| **URLComSum (Ext.+Com.)** | **34.6** | 22.9 | **30.5** |

Table 2: Comparisons on the **Newsroom** test set. The symbol * indicates that the model is not directly comparable to ours as it is based on a subset (the "Mixed" ) of the dataset.

| **Method** | ROUGE-1 | ROUGE-2 | ROUGE-L |
|---|---|---|---|
| LEAD | 40.0 | 17.5 | 32.9 |
| LEAD-WORD | 39.7 | 16.6 | 32.5 |
| **Supervised Methods** | | | |
| LATENTCOM (Ext.) | 41.1 | 18.8 | 37.5 |
| LATENTCOM (Ext.+Com.) | 36.7 | 15.4 | 34.3 |
| JECS (Ext.) | 40.7 | 18.0 | 36.8 |
| JECS (Ext.+Com.) | 41.7 | 18.5 | 37.9 |
| EXCONSUMM (Ext.) | 41.7 | 18.6 | 37.8 |
| EXCONSUMM (Ext.+Com.) | 40.9 | 18.0 | 37.4 |
| CUPS (Ext.) | 43.7 | 20.6 | 40.0 |
| CUPS (Ext.+Com.) | 44.0 | 20.6 | 40.4 |
| **Unsupervised Methods** | | | |
| SumLoop (Abs.) | 37.7 | 14.8 | **34.7** |
| TextRank (Ext.) | 34.1 | 12.8 | 22.5 |
| PacSum (Ext.) | **40.3** | **17.6** | 24.9 |
| PMI (Ext.) | 36.7 | 14.5 | 23.3 |
| **URLComSum (Ext.)** | 40.0 | 17.5 | 32.9 |
| **URLComSum (Ext.+Com.)** | 39.3 | 16.0 | 32.2 |

Table 3: Comparisons between our URLComSum and the state-of-the-art methods on the **CNN/DM** test set. (Ext.), (Abs.), and (Com.) denote the method is extractive, abstractive, and compressive respectively.

We compare our model with existing compressive methods which are all supervised, including *LATENTCOM* (Zhang et al., 2018), *EXCONSUMM* (Mendes et al., 2019), *JECS* (Xu and Durrett, 2019), *CUPS* (Desai et al., 2020). Since our method is unsupervised, we also compare it with unsupervised extractive and abstractive methods, including *TextRank* (Mihalcea and Tarau, 2004), *PacSum* (Zheng and Lapata, 2019), *PMI* (Padmakumar and He, 2021), and *SumLoop* (Laban et al., 2020). To better evaluate compressive methods, we followed a similar concept as LEAD baseline (See et al., 2017) and created *LEAD-WORD* baseline which

| Method | ROUGE-1 | ROUGE-2 | ROUGE-L |
|---|---|---|---|
| LEAD | 19.4 | 2.4 | 12.9 |
| LEAD-WORD | 18.3 | 1.9 | 12.8 |
| **Supervised Methods** | | | |
| CUPS (Ext.) | 24.2 | 5.0 | 18.3 |
| CUPS (Ext.+Com.) | 26.0 | 5.4 | 19.9 |
| **Unsupervised Methods** | | | |
| TextRank (Ext.) | 19.0 | 3.1 | 12.6 |
| PacSum (Ext.) | **19.4** | 2.7 | 12.4 |
| PMI (Ext.) | 19.1 | **3.2** | 12.5 |
| **URLComSum (Ext.)** | **19.4** | 2.4 | **12.9** |
| **URLComSum (Ext.+Com.)** | 18.0 | 1.8 | 12.7 |

Table 4: Comparisons on the **XSum** test set.URLComSum (Ext.) denotes the extractive summary produced by our extractor agent. URLComSum (Ext.+Com.) denotes the compressive summary produced further by our compressor agent.

extracts the first several words of a document as a summary. The commonly used ROUGE metric (Lin, 2004) is adopted.

## 4.2 Experimental Results

The experimental results of URLComSum on different datasets are shown in Table 2, Table 3 and Table 4 in terms of ROUGE-1, ROUGE-2 and ROUGE-L F-scores. (Ext.), (Abs.), and (Com.) denote that the method is extractive, abstractive, and compressive, respectively. Note that on the three datasets, LEAD and LEAD-WORD baseline are considered strong baselines in the literature and sometimes perform better than the state-of-the-art supervised and unsupervised models. As also discussed in (See et al., 2017; Padmakumar and He, 2021), it could be due to the Inverted Pyramid writing structure (Pöttker, 2003) of news articles, in which important information is often located at the beginning of an article and a paragraph.

Our URLComSum method significantly outperforms all the unsupervised and supervised ones on Newsroom. This demonstrates the effectiveness of our proposed method. Note that, unlike supervised EXCONSUMM, our reward strategy contributes to performance improvement when the compressor agent is utilised. For example, in terms of ROUGE-L, EXCONSUMM(Ext.+Com.) does not outperform EXCONSUMM(Ext.), while URLComSum(Ext.+Com.) outperforms URLComSum(Ext.). Similarly, our URLComSum method achieves the best performance among all the unsupervised methods on XSum, in terms of ROUGE-1 and -L. URLComSum underperforms in ROUGE-2, which may be due to the trade-off between informativeness and fluency. The improvement on Newsroom is greater than those on CNN/DM and XSum, which could be because the larger size of Newsroom is more helpful for training our model.

Our URLComSum method achieves comparable performance with other unsupervised methods on CNN/DM. Note that URLComSum does not explicitly take position information into account while some extractive methods take advantage of the lead bias of CNN/DM, such as PacSum and LEAD. Nevertheless, we observe that URLComSum(Ext.) achieves the same result as LEAD . Even though URLComSum is unsupervised, eventually the extractor agent learns to select the first few sentences of the documents, which follows the principle of the aforementioned Inverted Pyramid writing structure.

### 4.2.1 Ablation Studies

**Effect of Compression.** We observed that the extractive and compressive methods usually obtain better results than the abstractive ones in terms of ROUGE scores on CNN/DM and Newsroom, and vice versa on XSum. It may be that CNN/DM and Newsroom contain summaries that are usually more extractive, whereas XSum's summaries are highly abstractive. We noticed that URLComSum(Ext.+Com.) generally achieves higher ROUGE-1 and -L scores than its extractive version on Newsroom. Meanwhile, on CNN/DM and XSum, the compressive version has slightly lower ROUGE scores than the extractive version. We observe similar behaviour in the literature of compressive summarisation, which may be that the sentences of news articles have dense information and compression does not help much to further condense the content.

**Effect of Transformer.** Note that we investigated the popular transformer model (Vaswani et al., 2017) in our proposed framework to replace Bi-LSTM for learning the sentence and word representations. However, we noticed the transformer-based agents do not perform as well as the Bi-LSTM-based ones while training from scratch with the same training procedure. The difficulties of training a transformer model have also been discussed in (Popel and Bojar, 2018; Liu et al., 2020). Besides, the commonly used pre-trained transformer models, such as BERT (Devlin et al., 2019) and BART (Lewis et al., 2020), require high computational resources and usually use subword-based tokenizers. They are not suitable for URLComSum since our compressor agent points to words instead of subwords. Therefore, at this stage Bi-LSTM is a simpler and more efficient choice. Nevertheless, the transformer is a module that can be included in our framework and is worth further investigation in the future.

**Comparison of Extraction, Abstraction and Compression Approaches.** We observed that the extraction and compressive approaches usually obtain better results than the abstractive in terms of ROUGE scores on CNN/DM and Newsroom, and vice versa on XSum. It may be because CNN/DM and Newsroom contain summaries that are usually more extractive, whereas XSum's summaries are highly abstractive. Since the ROUGE metric reflects lexical matching only and overlooks the linguistic quality and factuality of the summary, it is difficult to conclude the superiority of one approach over the others solely based on the ROUGE scores. Automatic linguistic quality and factuality metrics would be essential to provide further insights and more meaningful comparisons.

### 4.3 Qualitative Analysis

In Figure 5, 6, 7 in Appendix A, summaries produced by URLComSum are shown together with the reference summaries of the sample documents in the CNN/DM, XSum, and Newsroom datasets. This demonstrates that our proposed URLComSum method is able to identify salient sentences and words and produce reasonably fluent summaries even without supervision information.

### 4.4 Interpretable Visualisation of Semantic Coverage

URLComSum is able to provide an interpretable visualisation of the semantic coverage on the summarisation results through the transportation matrix. Figure 4 illustrates the transport plan heatmap, which associated with a resulting summary is illustrated. A heatmap indicates the transportation of semantic contents between tokens in the document and its resulting summary. The higher the intensity, the more the semantic content of a particular document token is covered by a summary token. Red line highlights the transportation from the document to the summary of semantic content of token "country", which appears in both the document and the summary. Purple line highlights how the semantic content of token "debt", which appears in the document only but not the summary, are transported to token "bankruptcy" and "loans", which are semantically closer and have lower transport cost, and thus achieve a minimum transportation cost in the OT plan.

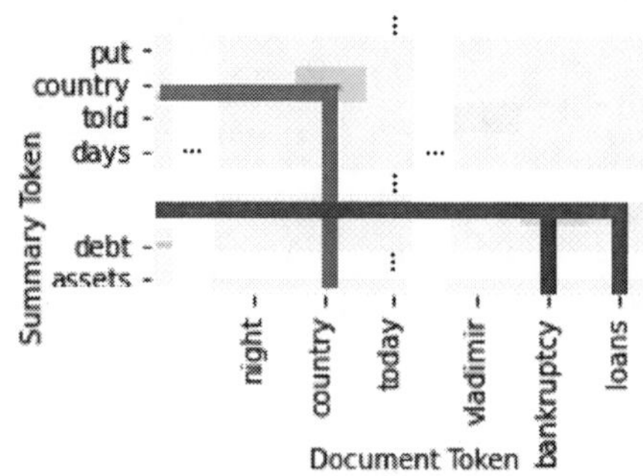


Figure 4: Interpretable visualisation of the OT plan. from a source document to a resulting summary on the CNN/DM dataset. The higher the intensity, the more the semantic content of a particular document token is covered by a summary token. Red line highlights the transportation from the document to the summary of semantic content of token "country", which appears in both the document and the summary. Purple line highlights how the semantic content of token "debt", which appears in the document only but not the summary, are transported to token "bankruptcy" and "loans", which are semantically closer and have lower transport cost, and thus achieve a minimum transportation cost in the OT plan.

## 5 Conclusion

In this paper, we have presented URLComSum, the first unsupervised and an efficient method for compressive text summarisation. Our model consists of dual agents: an extractor agent and a compressor agent. The extractor agent first chooses salient sentences from a document, and the compressor agent further select salient words from these extracted sentences to form a summary. To achieve unsupervised training of the extractor and compressor agents, we devise a reinforcement learning strategy to simulate human judgement on summary quality and optimize the summary's semantic coverage and fluency reward. Comprehensive experiments on three widely used benchmark datasets demonstrate the effectiveness of our proposed URLComSum and the great potential of unsupervised compressive summarisation. Our method provides interpretability of semantic coverage of summarisation results.

## References


Yen-Chun Chen and Mohit Bansal. 2018. Fast abstractive summarization with reinforce-selected sentence rewriting. In *Annual Meeting of the Association for Computational Linguistics (ACL)*, pages 675–686, Melbourne, Australia. Association for Computational Linguistics.

Jianpeng Cheng and Mirella Lapata. 2016. Neural summarization by extracting sentences and words. In *Annual Meeting of the Association for Computational Linguistics (ACL)*.

Shrey Desai, Jiacheng Xu, and Greg Durrett. 2020. Compressive summarization with plausibility and salience modeling. In *Conference on Empirical Methods in Natural Language Processing (EMNLP)*, pages 6259–6274, Online. Association for Computational Linguistics.

Jacob Devlin, Ming-Wei Chang, Kenton Lee, and Kristina Toutanova. 2019. Bert: Pre-training of deep bidirectional transformers for language understanding. In *Conference of the North American Chapter of the Association for Computational Linguistics: Human Language Technologies (NAACL-HLT)*.

Alex Graves and Jürgen Schmidhuber. 2005. Framewise phoneme classification with bidirectional lstm and other neural network architectures. *Neural networks*, 18(5):602–610.

Max Grusky, Mor Naaman, and Yoav Artzi. 2018. Newsroom: A dataset of 1.3 million summaries with diverse extractive strategies. In *Conference of the North American Chapter of the Association for Computational Linguistics: Human Language Technologies (NAACL-HLT)*, pages 708–719, New Orleans, Louisiana. Association for Computational Linguistics.

Karl Moritz Hermann, Tomáš Kočiský, Edward Grefenstette, Lasse Espeholt, Will Kay, Mustafa Suleyman, and Phil Blunsom. 2015. Teaching machines to read and comprehend. In *International Conference on Neural Information Processing Systems (NeurIPS)*, page 1693–1701, Cambridge, MA, USA. MIT Press.

Ruipeng Jia, Yanan Cao, Haichao Shi, Fang Fang, Pengfei Yin, and Shi Wang. 2021. Flexible non-autoregressive extractive summarization with threshold: How to extract a non-fixed number of summary sentences. In *AAAI Conference on Artificial Intelligence*, volume 35, pages 13134–13142, Online. AAAI Press.

Katharina Kann, Sascha Rothe, and Katja Filippova. 2018. Sentence-level fluency evaluation: References help, but can be spared! In *Conference on Computational Natural Language Learning (CoNLL)*, pages 313–323, Brussels, Belgium. Association for Computational Linguistics.

Svea Klaus, Ria Van Hecke, Kaweh Djafari Naini, Ismail Sengor Altingovde, Juan Bernabé-Moreno, and Enrique Herrera-Viedma. 2022. Summarizing legal regulatory documents using transformers. In *International ACM SIGIR Conference on Research and Development in Information Retrieval (SIGIR)*, page 2426–2430, New York, NY, USA. Association for Computing Machinery.

Matt Kusner, Yu Sun, Nicholas Kolkin, and Kilian Weinberger. 2015. From word embeddings to document distances. In *International Conference on Machine Learning (ICML)*, page 957–966, Lille, France. JMLR.org.

Philippe Laban, Andrew Hsi, John Canny, and Marti A. Hearst. 2020. The summary loop: Learning to write abstractive summaries without examples. In *Annual Meeting of the Association for Computational Linguistics (ACL)*, pages 5135–5150, Online. Association for Computational Linguistics.

Jey Han Lau, Alexander Clark, and Shalom Lappin. 2017. Grammaticality, acceptability, and probability: A probabilistic view of linguistic knowledge. *Cognitive Science*, 41(5):1202–1241.

Mike Lewis, Yinhan Liu, Naman Goyal, Marjan Ghazvininejad, Abdelrahman Mohamed, Omer Levy, Veselin Stoyanov, and Luke Zettlemoyer. 2020. Bart: Denoising sequence-to-sequence pre-training for natural language generation, translation, and comprehension. In *Annual Meeting of the Association for Computational Linguistics (ACL)*.

Chin-Yew Lin. 2004. ROUGE: A package for automatic evaluation of summaries. In *Text Summarization Branches Out*, pages 74–81, Barcelona, Spain. Association for Computational Linguistics.

Jingzhou Liu, Dominic J. D. Hughes, and Yiming Yang. 2021. Unsupervised extractive text summarization with distance-augmented sentence graphs. In *International ACM SIGIR Conference on Research and Development in Information Retrieval (SIGIR)*, page 2313–2317, New York, NY, USA. Association for Computing Machinery.

Liyuan Liu, Xiaodong Liu, Jianfeng Gao, Weizhu Chen, and Jiawei Han. 2020. Understanding the difficulty of training transformers. In *Conference on Empirical Methods in Natural Language Processing (EMNLP)*.

Yang Liu and Mirella Lapata. 2019. Text summarization with pretrained encoders. In *Conference on Empirical Methods in Natural Language Processing and the International Joint Conference on Natural Language Processing (EMNLP-IJCNLP)*, pages 3730–3740, Hong Kong, China. Association for Computational Linguistics.

Yixin Liu, Pengfei Liu, Dragomir Radev, and Graham Neubig. 2022. BRIO: Bringing order to abstractive summarization. In *Annual Meeting of the Association for Computational Linguistics (ACL)*, pages 2890–2903, Dublin, Ireland. Association for Computational Linguistics.

Ilya Loshchilov and Frank Hutter. 2018. Decoupled weight decay regularization. In *International Conference on Learning Representations (ICLR)*, New Orleans, LA, USA. OpenReview.net.

Ling Luo, Xiang Ao, Yan Song, Feiyang Pan, Min Yang, and Qing He. 2019. Reading like HER: Human reading inspired extractive summarization. In *Conference on Empirical Methods in Natural Language Processing and International Joint Conference on Natural Language Processing (EMNLP-IJCNLP)*.

Qianren Mao, Hongdong Zhu, Junnan Liu, Cheng Ji, Hao Peng, Jianxin Li, Lihong Wang, and Zheng Wang. 2022. Muchsum: Multi-channel graph neural network for extractive summarization. In *International ACM SIGIR Conference on Research and Development in Information Retrieval (SIGIR)*, page 2617–2622, New York, NY, USA. Association for Computing Machinery.

Joshua Maynez, Shashi Narayan, Bernd Bohnet, and Ryan McDonald. 2020. On faithfulness and factuality in abstractive summarization. In *Annual Meeting of the Association for Computational Linguistics (ACL)*, pages 1906–1919, Online. Association for Computational Linguistics.

Afonso Mendes, Shashi Narayan, Sebastião Miranda, Zita Marinho, André F. T. Martins, and Shay B. Cohen. 2019. Jointly extracting and compressing documents with summary state representations. In *Conference of the North American Chapter of the Association for Computational Linguistics: Human Language Technologies (NAACL-HLT)*, pages 3955–3966, Minneapolis, Minnesota. Association for Computational Linguistics.

Rada Mihalcea and Paul Tarau. 2004. TextRank: Bringing order into text. In *Conference on Empirical Methods in Natural Language Processing (EMNLP)*, pages 404–411, Barcelona, Spain. Association for Computational Linguistics.

Ramesh Nallapati, Feifei Zhai, and Bowen Zhou. 2017. Summarunner: A recurrent neural network based sequence model for extractive summarization of documents. In *AAAI Conference on Artificial Intelligence*, page 3075–3081, San Francisco, California, USA. AAAI Press.

Shashi Narayan, Shay B. Cohen, and Mirella Lapata. 2018a. Don't give me the details, just the summary! topic-aware convolutional neural networks for extreme summarization. In *Conference on Empirical Methods in Natural Language Processing (EMNLP)*, pages 1797–1807, Brussels, Belgium. Association for Computational Linguistics.

Shashi Narayan, Shay B. Cohen, and Mirella Lapata. 2018b. Ranking sentences for extractive summarization with reinforcement learning. In *Conference of the North American Chapter of the Association for Computational Linguistics: Human Language Technologies (NAACL-HLT)*, pages 1747–1759, New Orleans, Louisiana. Association for Computational Linguistics.

Vishakh Padmakumar and He He. 2021. Unsupervised extractive summarization using pointwise mutual information. In *Conference of the European Chapter of the Association for Computational Linguistics (EACL)*, pages 2505–2512, Online. Association for Computational Linguistics.

Jacob Parnell, Inigo Jauregi Unanue, and Massimo Piccardi. 2021. RewardsOfSum: Exploring reinforcement learning rewards for summarisation. In *Workshop on Structured Prediction for NLP (SPNLP)*, pages 1–11, Online. Association for Computational Linguistics.

Adam Pauls and Dan Klein. 2012. Large-scale syntactic language modeling with treelets. In *Annual Meeting of the Association for Computational Linguistics (ACL)*, pages 959–968, Jeju Island, Korea. Association for Computational Linguistics.

Romain Paulus, Caiming Xiong, and Richard Socher. 2018. A deep reinforced model for abstractive summarization. In *International Conference on Learning Representations (ICLR)*.

Jeffrey Pennington, Richard Socher, and Christopher Manning. 2014. Glove: Global vectors for word representation. In *Conference on Empirical Methods in Natural Language Processing (EMNLP)*, pages 1532–1543, Doha, Qatar. Association for Computational Linguistics.

Gabriel Peyré, Marco Cuturi, et al. 2019. Computational optimal transport: With applications to data science. *Foundations and Trends in Machine Learning*, 11(5-6):355–607.

Martin Popel and Ondřej Bojar. 2018. Training tips for the transformer model. *The Prague Bulletin of Mathematical Linguistics (NeurIPS)*.

Horst Pöttker. 2003. News and its communicative quality: the inverted pyramid—when and why did it appear? *Journalism Studies*, 4(4):501–511.

Steven J Rennie, Etienne Marcheret, Youssef Mroueh, Jerret Ross, and Vaibhava Goel. 2017. Self-critical sequence training for image captioning. In *IEEE conference on computer vision and pattern recognition (CVPR)*.

Abigail See, Peter J. Liu, and Christopher D. Manning. 2017. Get to the point: Summarization with pointer-generator networks. In *Annual Meeting of the Association for Computational Linguistics (ACL)*, pages 1073–1083, Vancouver, Canada. Association for Computational Linguistics.

Ashish Vaswani, Noam Shazeer, Niki Parmar, Jakob Uszkoreit, Llion Jones, Aidan N Gomez, Łukasz Kaiser, and Illia Polosukhin. 2017. Attention is all you need. In *International Conference on Neural Information Processing Systems (NeurIPS)*, volume 30, Long Beach, CA, USA. Curran Associates, Inc.

Oriol Vinyals, Meire Fortunato, and Navdeep Jaitly. 2015. Pointer networks. In *International Conference on Neural Information Processing Systems (NeurIPS)*, volume 28, Montreal, Canada. Curran Associates, Inc.

Lihan Wang, Min Yang, Chengming Li, Ying Shen, and Ruifeng Xu. 2021. Abstractive text summarization with hierarchical multi-scale abstraction modeling and dynamic memory. In *International ACM SIGIR Conference on Research and Development in Information Retrieval (SIGIR)*, page 2086–2090, New York, NY, USA. Association for Computing Machinery.

Jiacheng Xu and Greg Durrett. 2019. Neural extractive text summarization with syntactic compression. In *Conference on Empirical Methods in Natural Language Processing and the International Joint Conference on Natural Language Processing (EMNLP-IJCNLP)*, pages 3292–3303, Hong Kong, China. Association for Computational Linguistics.

Shusheng Xu, Xingxing Zhang, Yi Wu, Furu Wei, and Ming Zhou. 2020. Unsupervised extractive summarization by pre-training hierarchical transformers. In *Findings of the Association for Computational Linguistics: EMNLP*, pages 1784–1795, Online. Association for Computational Linguistics.

Jingqing Zhang, Yao Zhao, Mohammad Saleh, and Peter Liu. 2020. Pegasus: Pre-training with extracted gap-sentences for abstractive summarization. In *International Conference on Machine Learning (ICML)*, pages 11328–11339, Online. PMLR.

Xingxing Zhang, Mirella Lapata, Furu Wei, and Ming Zhou. 2018. Neural latent extractive document summarization. In *Conference on Empirical Methods in Natural Language Processing (EMNLP)*, page 779–784, Brussels, Belgium. Association for Computational Linguistics.

Hao Zheng and Mirella Lapata. 2019. Sentence centrality revisited for unsupervised summarization. In *Annual Meeting of the Association for Computational Linguistics (ACL)*, pages 6236–6247, Florence, Italy. Association for Computational Linguistics.

Ming Zhong, Pengfei Liu, Yiran Chen, Danqing Wang, Xipeng Qiu, and Xuanjing Huang. 2020. Extractive summarization as text matching. In *Annual Meeting of the Association for Computational Linguistics (ACL)*, pages 6197–6208, Online. Association for Computational Linguistics.

## A Sample Summaries

The following shows the sample summaries generated by URLComSum on the CNN/DM, XSum, and Newsroom datasets. Sentences extracted by the URLComSum extractor agent are highlighted. Words selected by the URLComSum compressor agent are underlined in red. Our unsupervised method URLComSum can identify salient sentences and words to produce a summary with reasonable semantic coverage and fluency.

**Source Document:**

Russia is considering bailing out Greece in exchange for the country's 'assets', it was reported last night. Alexis Tsipras, Greece's prime minister, will meet Vladimir Putin in Moscow today, amid reports that the Kremlin will offer controversial loans and discounts on supplies of natural gas in a bid to lessen its dependence on the West . The visit will raise fears the radical left government is looking east in search of alternative sources of finance as it bids to avoid bankruptcy. Scroll down for video . Alexis Tsipras, Greece's (...)

**Reference Summary:**

Alexis Tsipras, Greece's prime minister, will meet Vladimir Putin in Moscow . The meeting comes amid reports Russia is considering bailing out Greece . Reports Kremlin may offer loans and discounts on supplies of natural gas .

**URLComSum:**

Russia is considering bailing out Greece in exchange for the country ' s ' assets ' , it was reported last night . Alexis Tsipras , Greece ' s prime minister , will meet Vladimir Putin in Moscow today , amid reports that the Kremlin will offer controversial loans and discounts on supplies of natural gas in a bid its raise alternative as bids to avoid bankruptcy .

Figure 5: A sample summary produced by URLComSum on the CNN/DM dataset. The summary generated by URLComSum has ROUGE-1, ROUGE-2, and ROUGE-L F-Scores of 68.8, 52.7, and 62.4 respectively, with semantic coverage reward 0.76 and fluency reward 0.64, while the reference summary has semantic coverage reward 0.80 and fluency reward 0.62.

**Source Document:**

Paul Robson is the second trader at the Dutch bank to plead guilty to trying to rig the Yen Libor rate and the first Briton to do so. Last year Rabobank paid $1bn (Â£597m) to US and European regulators for its part in the global rate-rigging scandal. Barclays Bank, Royal Bank of Scotland and Lloyds Bank have all previously been fined for rate rigging. (...)

**Reference Summary:**

A former senior trader at Rabobank has pleaded guilty to interest rate rigging in the US.

**URLComSum:**

Paul Robson is the second trader at the Dutch bank to plead guilty to trying to rig the Yen Libor rate and global rate-rigging scandal .

Figure 6: A sample summary produced by URLComSum on the XSum dataset. The summary generated by URLComSum has ROUGE-1, ROUGE-2, and ROUGE-L F-Scores of 38.1, 20.0, and 33.3 respectively, with semantic coverage reward 0.77 and fluency reward 0.56, while the reference summary has semantic coverage reward 0.73 and fluency reward 0.59.

**Source Document:**

A man armed with a rifle has killed four people in a rampage in Girona province, north-east Spain, police say. The gunman walked into a bar in the town of Olot, 120km (70 miles) north of Barcelona, and shot two men - reportedly a father and son who were both construction workers. Minutes later, he went to a bank and killed two staff, police said. (...)

**Reference Summary:**

A man armed with a rifle kills four people in a shooting rampage in north-east Spain, police say.

**URLComSum:**

A man armed with a rifle has killed four people in a rampage in Girona province , north-east Spain , police say . The gunman walked into a bar in

Figure 7: A sample summary produced by URLComSum on the Newsroom dataset. The summary generated by URLComSum has ROUGE-1, ROUGE-2, and ROUGE-L F-Scores of 76.6, 62.2, and 76.6 respectively, with semantic coverage reward 0.79 and fluency reward 0.61, while the reference summary has semantic coverage reward 0.76 and fluency reward 0.65.

# Exploring the Effect of Frequency Resolution in FNet

**Greg Szumel** and **Ghazal Khalighinejad** and **Rickard Stureborg** and **Sam Wiseman**
Duke University
{gks9, gk126, rs541, sam.wiseman}@duke.edu

## Abstract

The recently introduced FNet model (Lee-Thorp et al., 2022) computes a two-dimensional discrete Fourier transform (DFT) of a sequence-length-by-hidden-dimension-sized representation of its input. Because it is equally efficient to compute the DFT of any reshaping of this input matrix, we investigate the extent to which increasing the frequency resolution in one dimension (at the expense of the other) affects task performance. We consider the LRA tasks (Tay et al., 2021) considered by Lee-Thorpe et al., as well as the more practical setting of using FNet as the encoder in a machine translation (MT) model. We find that frequency resolution has a marked task-dependent effect on performance, allowing us to largely outperform standard FNet on our tasks, and suggesting that resolution should be carefully tuned before deploying FNet.

## 1 Introduction

The FNet model, recently introduced by Lee-Thorp et al. (2022), is an encoder-only Transformer (Vaswani et al., 2017) that takes a major deviation from the Transformer's standard architecture. Mainly, FNet replaces the self-attention mechanism in a Transformer with a 2D Discrete Fourier Transform (DFT). The DFT is a deterministic operation which transforms an input vector $x$ to output vector $X$, both of length $N$, by

$$X_k = \sum_{n=0}^{N-1} x_n * \exp(\frac{-i2\pi}{N}kn)$$

Notably, there are no learnable parameters within this sub-layer. Additionally, FNet represents an important innovation because the DFT scales sub-quadratically in the sequence length, unlike self-attention. FNet therefore offers the promise of a more efficient general-purpose transformer-like architecture.

We note that it is equally efficient to compute the 2D DFT of any reshaping of this matrix (i.e., increasing the number of columns at the expense of the rows, or vice-versa) and that reshaping will change the frequency resolution of the DFT in each dimension. We hypothesize that changing the frequency resolution may yield a more efficient token mixing than the standard input's mixing, particularly when flattening the input into a column of embedded tokens. The purpose of this paper is to explore whether there is any performance benefit to increasing or decreasing the frequency resolution in either dimension, a question not addressed by Lee-Thorp et al. (2022).

In addition to changing resolution by reshaping, which does not alter the number of elements in the matrix, we consider transformations that do alter the number of elements in the matrix, such as projecting up or down, or padding. We investigate the effect of these transformations on the FNet architecture as applied to the LRA tasks (Tay et al., 2021) considered in the original paper, and as an encoder in a standard transformer-based neural machine translation model. We find that reshaping has a marked effect on the performance of FNet on the tasks we consider, although no single reshaping appears to be optimal for all tasks. As such, we recommend that the reshaping be tuned per-task, as a hyperparameter. We also find that padding can improve performance for the Translation and short IMDB tasks, whereas projection tends to harm performance overall.

## 2 Methods

Below we outline several approaches to changing the dimensionality of the matrix consumed by the DFT in FNet, and thus the frequency resolution in at least one dimension. Whereas we are interested in changing the DFT's frequency resolution, we are not interested in changing the model's hidden dimension, which determines the size of the feed-



*Proceedings of The Fourth Workshop on Simple and Efficient Natural Language Processing (SustaiNLP)*, pages 239–244

forward layers that follow the DFT. Accordingly, we always ensure that the DFT's output is mapped back to a sequence-length by hidden-dimension-sized matrix before being consumed by a feed-forward layer. Details are below.

**Reshaping** In FNet, the inputs to the DFT have dimension (excluding batch-size) $S \times H$, where $S$ and $H$ are sequence- and hidden-dimension respectively, and where $S$ and $H$ are powers of two. To reshape, we multiply $S$ by a power of 2 (including negative powers), and divide $H$ by that same power. We then contiguously reshape the matrix into one of dimension $S \cdot 2^i \times H \cdot 2^{-i}$. Note this transformation is implemented by the JAX/PyTorch library's `reshape` function. We choose all possible combinations of $i$ such that $S \cdot 2^i$ and $H \cdot 2^{-i}$ are both integers. We include both fully flattened combinations (where $H$ or $S = 1$) for completeness, although these transformations are equivalent.

**Projection** Reshaping maintains the same total number of elements in the input matrix, making it impossible to change the resolution in only one dimension. Projection, on the other hand, allows us to hold the resolution in one dimension constant while changing the the other's. In our experiments, we take the optimal power-of-2 reshaping as described in the previous paragraph, and then project one of its hidden or sequence dimension up or down. Specifically, we linearly project the pre-DFT input and then reshape it into the desired dimension. After taking the DFT, we undo the prior reshaping and project back to the original dimension. See Appendix A for more details.

**Padding** Rather than projecting, we may also pad the input matrix with zeros, along either the sequence or hidden dimension. In the case of padding the hidden dimension, we pad before taking the DFT and simply discard the extra columns after taking the DFT and before the subsequent feed-forward layer. In the case of padding the sequence-length, we simply pad the encoder input directly. See Appendix C for a discussion on time-complexities from padding.

## 3 Experiments

We evaluate on the Long Range Arena (LRA) tasks (Tay et al., 2021), also used in Lee-Thorp et al. (2022). Due to training instability, we only report on image-classification (CIFAR), text-classification (IMDB), and document matching (Matching). We report all LRA results as an average over three random seeds. In order to evaluate FNet in a more conventional NLP setting, we evaluate it as an encoder on the IWSLT14 English to German translation benchmark (Cettolo et al., 2014), and on a 'short' IMDB task. We modify the standard IWSLT14 task to only include examples shorter than 64 tokens, and pad all remaining examples to 64 tokens. See Appendix C for a discussion on time-complexity. To construct the short-IMDB task, we use the LRA's IMDB codebase but leverage the non-byte tokenization scheme, where each word is enumerated and is represented by its index. We also truncate and pad examples to have input length of 500 tokens. For IWSLT14 and the Short-IMDB tasks, we run experiments on a single seed and report the results directly. All results are reported as the optimal validation scores obtained during training.

| Proj. dim. scale | D-Model | Seq-Length |
|---|---|---|
| Scale $\frac{1}{4}$ | 0.344 | 0.325 |
| Scale $\frac{1}{2}$ | 0.390 | 0.318 |
| Base (8, 4096) | 0.422 | 0.322 |
| Scale 2 | 0.409 | 0.314 |
| Scale 4 | 0.419 | 0.313 |

(a) CIFAR projection experiments

| Proj. dim. scale | D-Model | Seq-Length |
|---|---|---|
| Scale $\frac{1}{4}$ | 0.691 | 0.569 |
| Scale $\frac{1}{2}$ | 0.702 | 0.575 |
| Base (2048, 128) | 0.693 | 0.568 |
| Scale 2 | 0.566 | 0.572 |
| Scale 4 | 0.567 | 0.593 |

(b) IMDB projection experiments

| Proj. dim. scale | D-Model | Seq-Length |
|---|---|---|
| Scale $\frac{1}{4}$ | 0.624 | 0.623 |
| Scale $\frac{1}{2}$ | 0.625 | 0.616 |
| Base (2048, 256) | 0.623 | 0.630 |
| Scale 2 | 0.618 | 0.619 |
| Scale 4 | 0.612 | 0.622 |

(c) Matching projection experiments

Table 1: Projection of highest performing reshaping from the reshaping survey on LRA. Base dimensions are [D-model, Sequence length].

## 4 Results

### 4.1 LRA

Figure 1 outlines the results of our reshaping survey across the LRA tasks IMDB, CIFAR, and Match-

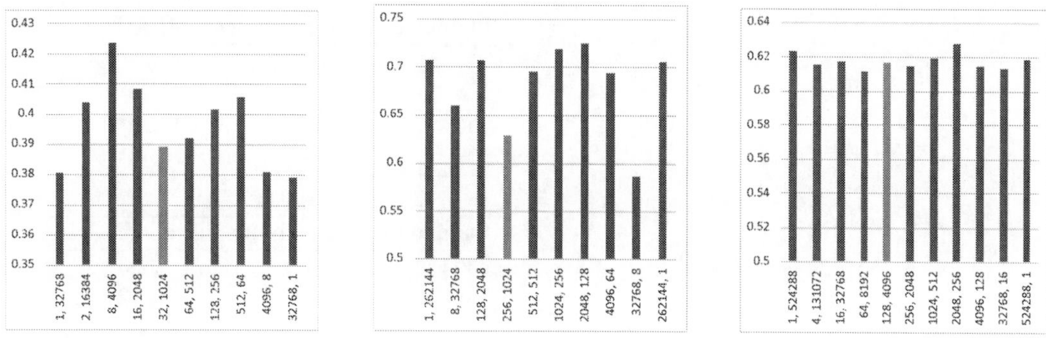


(a) CIFAR (b) IMDB (c) Matching

Figure 1: Results of reshaping survey on LRA tasks. Orange bars denote the unchanged dimensions. The first dimension is the reshaped hidden dimension, second dimension is the sequence length. Flattened reshapings should be computationally equivalent and are included for completeness.

ing. See Appendix B.1 for results on all tasks and reshapings. We observe optimal 'aspect-ratios' which are distinct from the unaltered ratios. For CIFAR, reshaping to have a larger sequence-length improves performance by a number of percentage points. IMDB and Matching also show local optima at either end of the spectrum, which provides the largest resolution to a single dimension.

Table 1 outlines the results of Projection on the LRA tasks. For CIFAR, IMDB, and Matching, we set the optimal reshaped dimension to $[8, 4096]$, $[2048, 128]$, and $[2048, 256]$, respectively. We then project either the hidden or sequence dimension by a fixed scale, denoted by the "Projection dimension scale". For example, a scale of $\frac{1}{2}$ on CIFAR produces a DFT input shape of $[4, 4096]$ when projecting D-Model, while the same scale has a DFT input shape of $[8, 2048]$ when projecting Seq-Length.

We see that projecting before taking the DFT reduces model performance. Further, projecting the sequence length almost always results in lower performance than projecting the hidden dimension.

Experiments on the padding dimension are in Table 2. As with the projection experiments, we see that padding along both the sequence and the hidden dimension typically lowers model performance. However, increasing the resolution with padding can improve performance on the IMDB task for certain padding amounts.

| **Padded dim. scale** | **D-Model** | **Seq-Length** |
|---|---|---|
| $8, 4096$ (no pad) | 0.425 | 0.425 |
| Scale 2 | 0.408 | 0.426 |
| Scale 4 | 0.386 | 0.403 |

(a) CIFAR padding experiments

| **Padded dim. scale** | **D-Model** | **Seq-Length** |
|---|---|---|
| 2048, 128 (no pad) | 0.726 | 0.726 |
| Scale 2 | 0.738 | 0.737 |
| Scale 4 | 0.730 | 0.708 |

(b) IMDB padding experiments

| **Padded dim. scale** | **D-Model** | **Seq-Length** |
|---|---|---|
| 2048, 256 (no pad) | 0.638 | 0.638 |
| Scale 2 | 0.621 | 0.621 |
| Scale 4 | 0.626 | 0.624 |

(c) Matching padding experiments

Table 2: Padded of strongest dimensions in LRA.

## 4.2 Translation

The results of the reshaping survey on the translation task are given in Figure 2. In contrast to the LRA experiments, we observe that the performance of the base DFT input shape is greater than every tested reshaping. Notably, FNet is nearly comparable to Transformer after fixing input length.

Table 3 shows the results of the projection experiment. We do not project the sequence length due to its low performance on LRA. We again select the optimal reshaping, which for translation is $[512, 64]$. Here we see the original shape outperforms all projections on the hidden dimension.

Table 4a shows the results of padding along the sequence length dimension. Here, we observe modest increases when padding along the sequence length, although there is a point at which increasing the length hinders performance. Table 4b shows the results of padding along the hidden dimension. We do not observe any hidden-dimension padding that surpasses the baseline model performance.

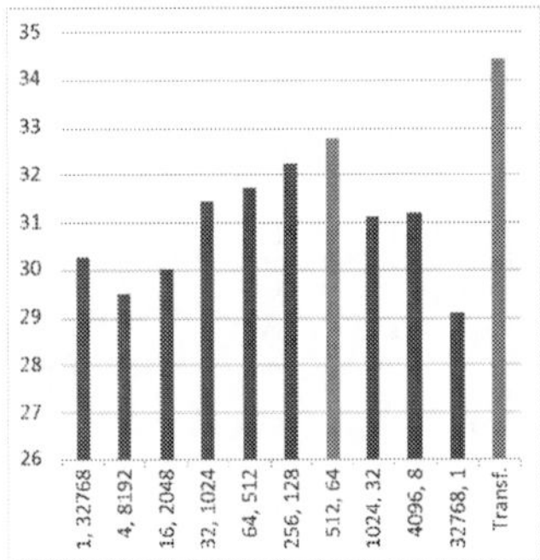


Figure 2: Results of reshaping survey on the Translation task. Orange bars denote the unchanged dimensions. The first dimension is the reshaped hidden dimension, second dimension is the sequence length. Flattened reshapings should be computationally equivalent and are included for completeness.

| Projected dim. size | BLEU |
|---|---|
| 128, 64 | 27.84 |
| 256, 64 | 28.85 |
| 512, 64 (base shape) | 30.11 |
| 1024, 64 | 30.03 |
| 2048, 64 | 25.92 |

Table 3: Projection of strongest dimensions in translation.

### 4.3 Short IMDB

Figure 6 displays the results of the reshaping survey on the Short-IMDB task. Like the Translation results, the model using unaltered DFT input has higher accuracy than the other tested models. Interestingly, reshapings that had high accuracy in the long-IMDB task do not appear to transfer to the short-IMDB task.

## 5 Conclusion

It is clear that tuning the FNet's DFT input dimension can affect model performance. In LRA, between optimal and base input dimensions, we see that CIFAR, IMDB, and Matching all increase performance by 9%, 15%, and 2%, respectively. However, altering does not appear to help for all tasks. In Translation and short IMDB, altering the input dimension to the DFT layer lowers overall performance. There could be several reasons for this performance degradation.

First, performance variance could be due to input length. The translation task uses a max sequence length of 64, which is significantly shorter than the LRA tasks, which had a minimum of 1024. If true, it may be harder to tune DFT input shapes with shorter sequence-lengths.

| Padded dim. size - seq len | BLEU |
|---|---|
| 64 (unpadded) | 32.77 |
| 128 | 33.23 |
| 256 | 33.28 |
| 512 | 29.43 |

(a) Sequence length

| Padded dim. size - hidden dim. | BLEU |
|---|---|
| 256 (unpadded) | 32.77 |
| 512 | 32.02 |
| 700 | 32.64 |
| 1024 | 32.04 |

(b) Hidden dimension

Table 4: Padded of strongest dimensions in LRA.

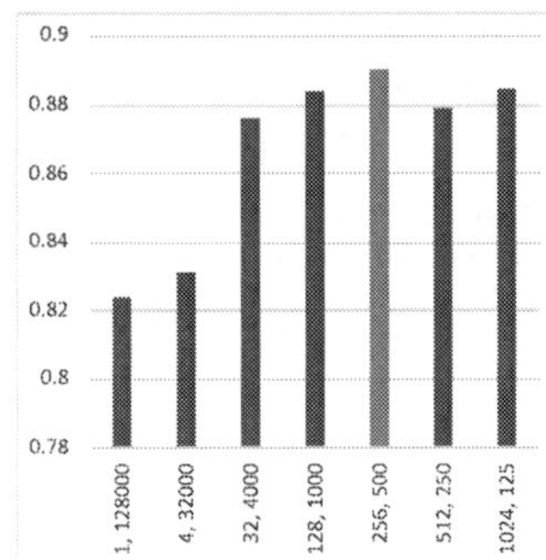


Figure 3: Results of reshaping survey on the 'short IMDB' task. Orange bars denote the unchanged dimensions. The first dimension is the reshaped hidden dimension, second dimension is the sequence length.

Second, certain tokenization methods may be more amenable to tuning the DFT input dimension. We observe a performance boost through the reshape survey on IMDB and Matching, both of which use byte-level tokenization. Therefore, reshaping may be more potent on tasks that use a byte-level tokenization.

We have not yet characterized the mechanism for why FNet performance can be affected by altering the input dimension to the DFT. We believe that future work on tokenization techniques, base-sequence-length, and testing on additional tasks could be ideal routes to further explore why adjusting the input shape to the DFT can alter the model's overall performance.

## References

Mauro Cettolo, Jan Niehues, Sebastian Stüker, Luisa Bentivogli, and Marcello Federico. 2014. Report on the 11th IWSLT evaluation campaign. In *Proceedings of the 11th International Workshop on Spoken Language Translation: Evaluation Campaign*, pages 2–17, Lake Tahoe, California.

James Lee-Thorp, Joshua Ainslie, Ilya Eckstein, and Santiago Ontanon. 2022. FNet: Mixing tokens with Fourier transforms. In *Proceedings of the 2022 Conference of the North American Chapter of the Association for Computational Linguistics: Human Language Technologies*, pages 4296–4313, Seattle, United States. Association for Computational Linguistics.

Yi Tay, Mostafa Dehghani, Samira Abnar, Yikang Shen, Dara Bahri, Philip Pham, Jinfeng Rao, Liu Yang, Sebastian Ruder, and Donald Metzler. 2021. Long range arena : A benchmark for efficient transformers. In *International Conference on Learning Representations*.

Ashish Vaswani, Noam Shazeer, Niki Parmar, Jakob Uszkoreit, Llion Jones, Aidan N. Gomez, Lukasz Kaiser, and Illia Polosukhin. 2017. Attention is all you need. *CoRR*, abs/1706.03762.

## A Example of projection methodology

Suppose we wish to project an input of reshaped size [32, 1024] to [32, 2048]. Let's suppose the original input had [64, 512]. Before taking the DFT, we take the following steps:

- Project the original input's hidden dimension by 2, yielding [64, 1024]
- Reshape to [32, 2048]
- Take DFT
- Un-reshape back to [64, 1024]
- Project back down to [64, 512]

In the case that we would like to reshape to [64, 1024], we now project the sequence length. Before and after each projection, we transpose the input to $[H, S]$.

In the case of padding the hidden dimension, replace the Projection layers with padding/cropping operations. We pad initially, then crop back down at the end.

| Model | Time complexity |
|---|---|
| BERT | $2n^2d_h + 4nd_h^2$ |
| FNet (matrix) | $n^2d_h + nd_h^2$ |
| FNet (FFT) | $nd_h[log(n) + log(d_h)]$ |

Table 5: Number of mixing layer operations (forward pass). $n$ is the sequence length and $d_h$ is the model hidden dimension.

## B Additional results

### B.1 LRA Survey

See Figure 4 for the full results on the Survey task across all LRA tasks. Again, Pathfinder and PathfinderX models tended to have relatively unstable models (some models not finding strong performance, at 50% accuracy), so we excluded them from further testing. Additionally, ListOps does not appear to improve performance based on altering the hidden-seq ratio, so it was also excluded from further testing.

### B.2 Translation survey

Figure 5 shows the full results of altering the aspect ratio into the DFT for the Translation task.

### B.3 Short IMDB Survey

Figure 6 shows the full results of altering the aspect ratio into the DFT for the short-IMDB task.

## C Time complexity of reshaping and padding

Lee-Thorp et al. (2022) assembled the rough time complexity of FNet compared to standard the standard transformer, which is listed in 5.

Suppose that for some reshaping we have sequence-length $l$ and hidden dimension $d_h$. The time-complexity in the FFT case would be $d_h l(\log(l) + \log(d_h)) = d_h l \log(d_h l)$. We can see here that the no reshaping would be more time-intensive than another if the product of $l$ and $d_h$ is fixed.

However, we can see that increasing the sequence length (or hidden dimension) by padding has time complexity of $n \log n$ for padded length $n$. Padding will also increase the time complexity by $n^2$ in decoders, where the attention-mechanism is still present.

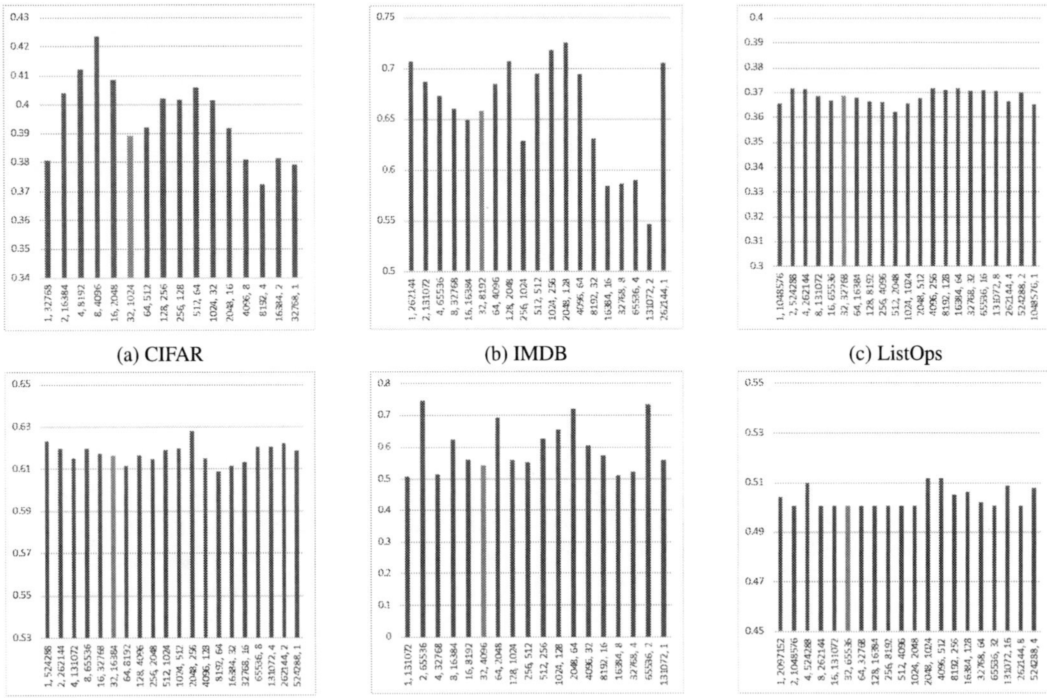

(a) CIFAR (b) IMDB (c) ListOps

(d) Matching (e) Pathfinder (f) PathfinderX

Figure 4: Results of varying hidden dimension and sequence length dimensions into the Fourier Transform. Orange lines denote the unchanged dimensions. First dimension is hidden dimension, second dimension is the sequence length. Each run is the average of the maximum validation BLUE score, taken as an average over 3 random seeds.

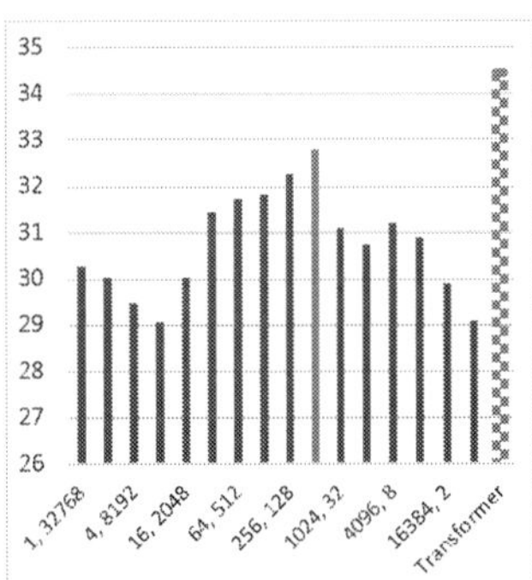


Figure 5: Results of varying hidden dimension and sequence length dimensions into the Fourier Transform. Orange bars indicate the unchanged dimension scales. The first dimension on the $x$ axis is the hidden dimension, second dimension is the sequence length.

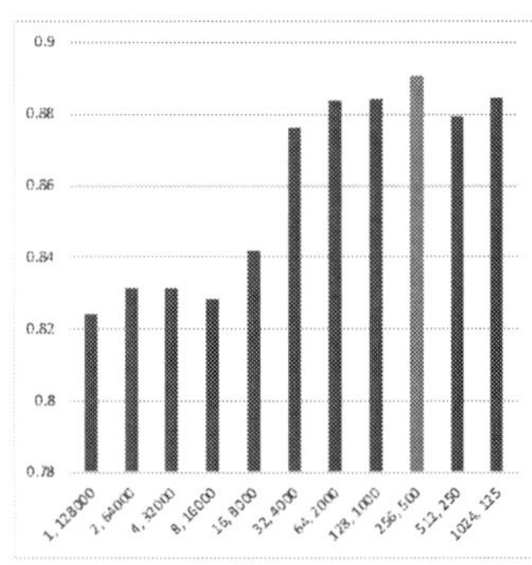

Figure 6: Results of reshaping survey on short IMDB

# Towards Adaptable and Interactive Image Captioning with Data Augmentation and Episodic Memory

**Aliki Anagnostopoulou**[1,2] **Mareike Hartmann**[3] **Daniel Sonntag**[1,2]
[1]German Research Center for Artificial Intelligence (DFKI), Germany
[2]Applied Artificial Intelligence (AAI), Oldenburg University, Germany
[3]Department of Language Science and Technology, Saarland University, Germany
{firstname.lastname}@dfki.de

## Abstract

Interactive machine learning (IML) is a beneficial learning paradigm in cases of limited data availability, as human feedback is incrementally integrated into the training process. In this paper, we present an IML pipeline for image captioning which allows us to incrementally adapt a pre-trained image captioning model to a new data distribution based on user input. In order to incorporate user input into the model, we explore the use of a combination of simple data augmentation methods to obtain larger data batches for each newly annotated data instance and implement continual learning methods to prevent catastrophic forgetting from repeated updates. For our experiments, we split a domain-specific image captioning dataset, namely VizWiz, into non-overlapping parts to simulate an incremental input flow for continually adapting the model to new data. We find that, while data augmentation worsens results, even when relatively small amounts of data are available, episodic memory is an effective strategy to retain knowledge from previously seen clusters.

## 1 Introduction

Image Captioning (IC) is the task of generating a description in natural language for a given image (Stefanini et al., 2021). For the training of most state-of-the-art IC models, large amounts of annotated training data are required (Zhou et al., 2020). However, whenever models need to caption user-specific images without large-scale annotations, this is an impractical requirement. In this case, a potential solution can be found in an *interactive* framework, in which the model can be efficiently adapted to new data based on user feedback (Ling and Fidler, 2017; Shen et al., 2019). Additionally, interactivity renders AI/ML-systems more user-friendly and trustworthy (Bussone et al., 2015; Guo et al., 2022).

In interactive ML settings, training takes place with small amounts of data, and often in an incremental manner. These properties can lead to *overfitting*, on the one hand, which is the lack of generalization ability of the model, and *catastrophic forgetting*, on the other hand, which refers to the drop in performance on older tasks, when a model is trained on new data. For our interactive approach, we tackle these problems using a combination of methods previously proposed in the literature. To tackle overfitting, we apply data augmentation to each instance of user feedback to obtain larger batches of data, which the model is then updated on (Wang et al., 2021). Nevertheless, we find that this strategy fails to improve results in our image captioning task, indicating that the data augmentation methods we used are not suitable for this kind of task. In order to prevent catastrophic forgetting, we rely on continual learning methods. In the following, we present and test an IC pipeline that can be used in an interactive setting. Our work is guided by the following research questions:

1. How does data augmentation benefit a system which is trained incrementally with (simulated) user feedback? How does this system perform in few-shot scenarios?
2. How effective is an episodic memory replay module (de Masson d'Autume et al., 2019) for knowledge retention from previous trainings?

Our contributions are as follows:

- We propose a lightweight continual learning IC pipeline that leverages data augmentation, which can be used in an interactive machine learning setting.
- We adapt a continual learning method, namely sparse memory replay, proposed by de Masson d'Autume et al. (2019), for IC.
- We test a combination of data augmentation



*Proceedings of The Fourth Workshop on Simple and Efficient Natural Language Processing (SustaiNLP)*, pages 245–256
July 13, 2023 

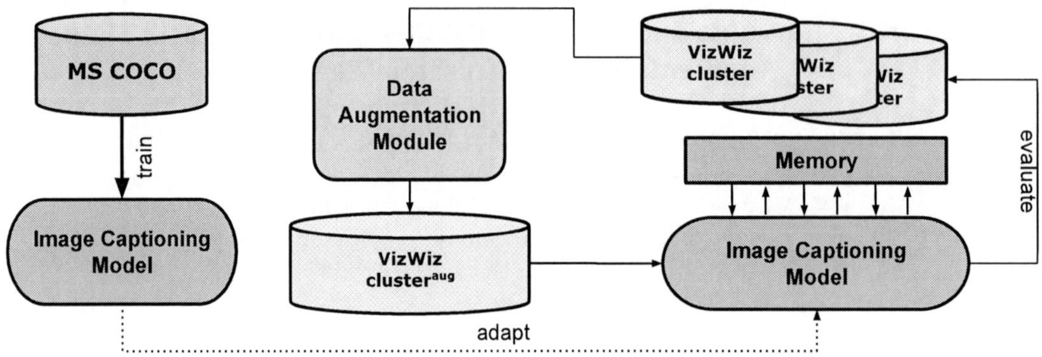


Figure 1: Our pipeline. Following the pre-training/fine-tuning paradigm, we first train our IC model on the MS COCO dataset. We then continue to train our model incrementally, by adding a new cluster each time from the VizWiz dataset, after applying DA methods on it to obtain more training data. During training on the VizWiz data for each cluster, an episodic memory module is activated, which is used to retrieve old data points from previously seen clusters.

methods for interactive IC in both image and text modalities.

- Since we report negative results for the system using data augmentation methods on the user feedback, we additionally investigate why these methods do not work in our case, and we offer some possible explanations for the deteriorating performance.
- We propose a method based on nominal phrase similarity between captions of different images for splitting a dataset into different tasks suitable for evaluating task-incremental continual learning when only image captions are given.

For our simulated user feedback, we use a domain-specific dataset, namely VizWiz (Gurari et al., 2020; Simons et al., 2020), which consists of images taken by visually impaired people. We choose this dataset exactly because of this property: the quality of the images is lower than in most general-use IC datasets, resembling the image quality of user images.

## 2 Related work

**Image captioning (IC)** Deep-learning based IC models (Xu et al., 2015; Anderson et al., 2018) traditionally consist of two parts: an *encoder* and a *decoder*. The visual encoder breaks the image down into features or creates an intermediate representation. The decoder is a language model, which takes the encoder output as input and generates a caption. For *grounded* approaches, more supervision is required: image features, such as regions, are additionally inserted into the visual encoder (Lu et al., 2018). Following the trend in other deep learning tasks, recent approaches include large-scale vision-language pre-training, as well as generalized models that work for a variety of computer vision and vision-language tasks, including image retrieval, referring segmentation, and visual question answering (Zou et al., 2022; Li et al., 2022).

**Interactive IC** Interactive IC has not gained as much attention as other ML tasks. Jia and Li (2020) involve the human-in-the-loop by providing incomplete sequences as input, in addition to each image, during inference time. Biswas et al. (2020) extend the Show, Attend, and Tell architecture by combining high-level and low-level features, which provide explainability, as well as beam search during decoding time.

**Data augmentation** Data augmentation (DA) is widely applied to multiple tasks which include learning from large data, whenever there is a lack of annotated instances. It can additionally be used as a regularization technique to avoid overfitting by introducing noise into the dataset. In Computer Vision, transformations like cropping, warping, and horizontal/vertical flipping are often applied (Takahashi et al., 2019; Katiyar and Borgohain, 2021).

For text, augmentation methods need to be more elaborate, since image-inspired techniques often change the semantics of the text drastically. Popular methods include, but are not restricted to, EDA (Wei and Zou, 2019) (including random insertion, deletion, word swap), back-translation (Sennrich et al., 2016; Turkerud and Mengshoel, 2021), synonym replacement and contextual augmentation (Kobayashi, 2018; Atliha and Šešok, 2020), often using a pre-trained language model (Devlin et al., 2019). For both modalities, retrieval-based augmentation from additional resources is possible as well (Li et al., 2021).

**Continual Learning** In cases where a model is trained repeatedly on new data, *catastrophic forgetting* (Kirkpatrick et al., 2017) can be observed. This refers to the degradation of model performance on older tasks when it is trained on new ones. In order to overcome this, continual learning methods are often applied. Methods such as weight regularization, encoder/decoder freezing, pseudo-labeling, and knowledge distillation, have been previously applied to IC models (Nguyen et al., 2019; Del Chiaro et al., 2020). In the natural language processing domain, de Masson d'Autume et al. (2019) use a combination of episodic memory replay during training and local adaptation of the model during inference.

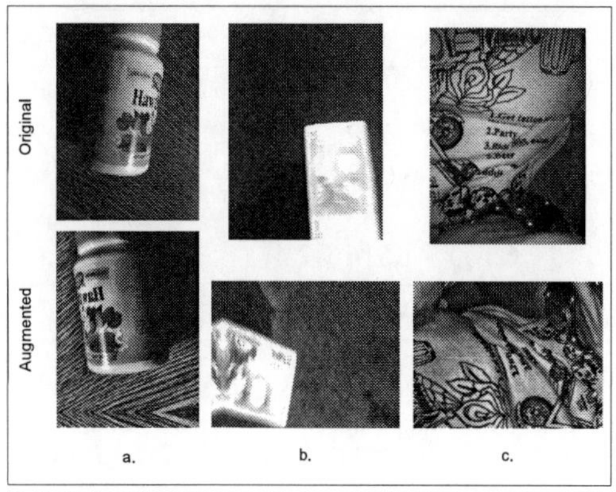


**original captions**:
a. 'a bottle of Hawthorne food supplement or drug',
b. 'Foreign currency is sitting on the table and it looks kind of exotic.'
c. 'White t-shirt with black line drawings of Mt Rushmore, motorcycles, rose and beer, with text.'

**paws**:
a. 'a bottle of Hawthorne food supplement or drug combination',
b. 'foreign currency sitting on the table and it looks sort of exotic.',
c. 'White tee with black line drawings by Mt Rushmore, motorcycles, roses and beer, with text.'

**pegasus**:
a. 'There is a bottle of Hawthorne food supplement.',
b. 'The table has foreign currency on it.',
c. 'The t-shirt has black line drawings of Mt Rushmore, motorcycles, rose and beer.'

Figure 2: Generated data points generated based on the DA methods described in subsection 3.1. Top: image DA (combination of several DA methods). Bottom: text DA.

## 3 Method

In this section, we describe the approach followed, including our benchmark strategy, our DA methods, as well as the episodic memory module. Our pipeline is illustrated in Figure 1.

### 3.1 Interactive IC pipeline

**Architecture** We experiment with a concrete implementation of the interactive approach outlined in Hartmann et al. (2022). We use a PyTorch implementation of *Show, Attend and Tell* (Xu et al., 2015). This architecture consists of a convolutional neural network (CNN) encoder, which is used to extract feature vectors from images, and a long-short-term memory (LSTM) decoder, which generates a caption conditioned on these vectors, with the use of attention. Following Dognin et al. (2022), we replace the ResNet encoder with a ResNext network (Xie et al., 2016).

For the decoder, an LSTM network is used. A problem arising from incremental training here is the expansion of the vocabulary. In order to tackle this problem, we rely on the subword vocabulary given by the BERT (Devlin et al., 2019) tokenizer provided by Huggingface[1]. By using a pre-trained subword tokenizer, we account for new words learned incrementally, without the need to expand the model size. The training strategy used is cross-entropy loss.

While current state-of-the-art architectures achieve better scores, we adapt this particular architecture because of its simplicity, and because its inputs are raw images, as opposed to image features like bounding boxes and labels from object recognition models, which further decreases preprocessing time. The pipeline can potentially be adapted to any IC model that takes images as input, rather than image regions and classes.

**Data augmentation methods** For our experiments, we use DA on Image (IMG), Text (TXT), and both modalities simultaneously (BOTH). For IMG, we use the Albumentations (Buslaev et al., 2020) library. We create a pipeline of different operations, including CLAHE, optical and grid distortion, blur, flip, and rotation. Our goal here is to introduce noise to the input data, in order to help the model generalize better to unseen data. For the

[1] We use `bert-base-uncased`.

|  | train | val | test | all | WT |
|---|---|---|---|---|---|
| 1 | 3,332 | 954 | 2,476 | 6,762 | 10,047 |
| 2 | 1,535 | 302 | 488 | 2,325 | 4,988 |
| 3 | 5,668 | 1,402 | 2,199 | 9,269 | 13,497 |
| 4 | 333 | 83 | 113 | 529 | 2,931 |
| 5 | 6,160 | 1,516 | 2,474 | 10,150 | 12,407 |
| all | 17,028 | 4,257 | 7,750 | 29,035 | 21,955 |

Table 1: VizWiz cluster (task) statistics after filtering out bad quality images (according to the procedure mentioned in subsection 3.3). WT stands for word types.

TXT modality, we aim at generating meaningful captions. For this reason, we employ two paraphrasing models provided by Huggingface, namely `pegasus_paraphrase`, a PEGASUS (Zhang et al., 2019a) model fine-tuned for paraphrasing, and `paws_paraphrase`, a T5 (Raffel et al., 2020) model trained on the PAWS (Zhang et al., 2019b; Yang et al., 2019) dataset. The reason we use two different paraphrasing tools is that we found out that the quality of the generated samples is different. In addition, paraphrasing quality drops in each tool when the number of paraphrases increases. In order to introduce more variety without compromising the quality, we decide to utilize two paraphrasing tools. In the case of combined (BOTH) DA, IMG augmented images are combined with synthetically generated captions. In every case, we generate batches that are 10 times bigger than the initial ones. Examples of generated data points can be found in Figure 2.

**Episodic memory for lifelong learning** In order to help the model retain old knowledge when being adapted to new data, we implement a continual learning method, more specifically a sparse memory replay that operates during training. We adapt the method described by de Masson d'Autume et al. (2019): During training, some samples/experiences are written into the memory. Every training sample has a certain probability to be selected for memory writing. These experiences are then sparsely replayed (i.e. 1 sample from memory for every 200 new data points, see subsection 3.2) while the model is trained on new data. This way, the model retains information from previous training iterations with very low additional computational effort.

### 3.2 Procedure and training details

We follow the pre-training/fine-tuning paradigm, where we first train the model on a *supervised pre-training* task using a large, generic dataset, namely MS COCO (Lin et al., 2014) (details below). During (supervised) pre-training, we do not use any DA or continual learning method. After obtaining the best model, we continue with our incremental *model adaptation*, during which we apply DA and continual learning.

**Training details** For the supervised pre-training step, we train our model on MS COCO in two stages: during the first training, we freeze the encoder and only train the decoder. The encoder is then trained in the second stage. For the adaptation step, we train our models on each task once.

We train with a batch size of 32 and a learning rate of 4e-4 for the decoder. For our memory module, the replay frequency is 200, as mentioned in subsection 3.1; that means that for every 200 batches, one batch is drawn from the memory and added to the current training batch. The memory writing probability is 20%.

We use early stopping. During our initial experiments, we trained with higher (p=10) and lower (p=2) patience values for early stopping. During our initial experiments, lower patience seems to produce better results, hence we adopt this value for our adaptation training. During supervised pre-training, we used 20 as the default patience value.

### 3.3 Datasets

**Supervised pre-training step** We first train our model on the MS COCO dataset (Lin et al., 2014). It contains 328k images, and it is broadly used as a pre-training dataset for vision tasks, including object recognition, object segmentation, and IC. We use the 2014 release, which contains 82,783 training and 40,504 validation images. Each image is annotated with five captions, describing the content of each image. We make use of the Karpathy splits (Karpathy and Fei-Fei, 2017).

**Adaptation** After obtaining the best possible captioning model trained on MS COCO, we train our model incrementally using VizWiz (Gurari et al., 2020; Simons et al., 2020), a dataset consisting of images taken by visually impaired people. Since there are no test captions available, we use the validation set as our test set. A part of the training samples is used as our validation set.

| | + cluster 1 [3332] | | | | + cluster 2 [1535] | | | | + cluster 3 [5668] | | | | + cluster 4 [333] | | | | + cluster 5 [6160] | | | |
|---|---|---|---|---|---|---|---|---|---|---|---|---|---|---|---|---|---|---|---|---|
| DA | NO | IMG | TXT | BOTH | NO | IMG | TXT | BOTH | NO | IMG | TXT | BOTH | NO | IMG | TXT | BOTH | NO | IMG | TXT | BOTH |
| 1 | 18.8 | 6.4 | 15.8 | 15.3 | 12.4 | 2.2 | 11.3 | 4.4 | 15.9 | 2.4 | 13.0 | 7.3 | 12.7 | 1.9 | 9.8 | 3.9 | 11.8 | 2.8 | 9.7 | 7.1 |
| 2 | | | | | 26.0 | 6.9 | 19.8 | 16.4 | 25.0 | 5.5 | 18.7 | 11.3 | 18.7 | 4.6 | 13.0 | 7.2 | 22.6 | 3.5 | 14.9 | 13.8 |
| 3 | | | | | | | | | 27.7 | 4.2 | 24.5 | 16.3 | 21.1 | 2.3 | 16.4 | 4.9 | 22.4 | 2.9 | 16.9 | 11.9 |
| 4 | | | | | | | | | | | | | 26.7 | 4.6 | 20.5 | 13.1 | 20.4 | 3.4 | 15.4 | 10.6 |
| 5 | | | | | | | | | | | | | | | | | 25.9 | 3.7 | 19.2 | 15.3 |
| all | 18.8 | 6.4 | 15.8 | 15.3 | 16.4 | 3.4 | 14.6 | 7.4 | 23.6 | 3.6 | 19.9 | 12.2 | 18.4 | 2.4 | 14.2 | 5.0 | 21.2 | 3.3 | 16.2 | 12.1 |

Table 2: CIDEr results on our experiments on VizWiz data clustered according to the procedure described in subsection 3.3. We start with the model resulting from the supervised pre-training step on MS COCO and continue to train this model incrementally on the VizWiz clusters (+cluster ...). We include the amount of (original) training data in brackets. DA: Data augmentation, NO: no DA, IMG: image DA, TXT: text DA, BOTH: image and text DA. The numbers in the left column stand for clusters evaluated on. 'all' refers to the micro avg.

**Dataset processing** We want to simulate a continual learning setting where we incrementally adapt the IC model to new sets of user-specific data. For this, we split VizWiz into non-overlapping clusters representing user-specific datasets. We follow the procedure for other continual learning datasets, where data is split according to classes/concepts, and each new class/concept represents a new task (Del Chiaro et al., 2020). As the VizWiz dataset does not contain object annotations for its images, we resort to splitting the data according to the objects mentioned in the captions, using the procedure described below. The resulting clusters resemble the user-specific data we might expect to receive from different users in a real-world setup: Whereas one user might be more interested in captioning screenshots or images of IT-related concepts, another user might be interested in captioning images of containers of food and drinks, etc. Example NPs for each cluster can be found in Appendix A.

We follow the steps below:

1. We collect all nominal phrases (NPs) in the entire caption corpus. We use TextBlob[2] for the extraction of the NPs.

2. From all the NPs, we choose so-called *keywords*, namely phrases that appear at least 15 times in the dataset.

3. Using GloVe (Pennington et al., 2014) embeddings, we extract word embeddings for each keyword. In case a keyword is phrasal, we average between individual word embeddings.

4. We cluster the keyword embeddings in 5 clusters, using K-means clustering (Hartigan and Wong, 1979).

5. We iterate over all captions for each image, looking for relevant keywords, and assigning them to clusters. In case one image corresponds to more than one cluster according to its keywords, we favor the smaller cluster.

VizWiz contains some images of bad quality: in some cases, the caption reads *'Quality issues are too severe to recognize visual content'*. In order to avoid the generation of these captions during inference, they can be removed from the training set (Çaylı et al., 2022). In our work, we exclude an image from training, if at least 3 out of the five captions in the image contain this caption; that means that more than 50% of the annotators could not describe the content of the image. If *Quality Issues* are brought up only once or twice, we remove this caption and duplicate one or two of the other captions, so that, in the end, each image is annotated with five captions. We do not remove *Quality Issues* images and captions from our test set. We exclude a total of 2,146 images.

While we technically do not use the complete dataset provided, it is justified by the fact that we test our pipeline in a low-resource scenario. Table 1 includes statistics over our tasks, including word type counts.

## 4 Evaluation & Results

In this section, we present the evaluation metrics we used, our procedure, as well as the results from our core experiments.

### 4.1 Evaluation metrics & splits

Since IC is a natural language generation task, results are evaluated using standard metrics for evaluating text generation tasks. These metrics measure similarity to the ground truths. The metrics most commonly used are BLEU (Papineni et al.,

[2]https://textblob.readthedocs.io/en/dev/

**gold**: a can of progresso light soup sitting on a counter
**no**: a can of campbell's cream of mushroom soup
**txt**: there is a can of soup on the counter.

**gold**: I see a red wine bottle with writing on it
**no**: a bottle of alcohol is on top of a table
**txt**: there is a bottle of wine.

**gold**: A computer screen wanting the user to fill a captcha field
**no**: a computer screen with a captcha on it
**txt**: there is a text on the screen.

**gold**: a package containing sugar free Hawaiian punch singles
**no**: a single packet of kool - aid drink mix
**txt**: there is a package of food.

Figure 3: Generated captions without DA and with TXT DA, compared with one of the gold captions.

2002), ROUGE (Lin, 2004), METEOR (Banerjee and Lavie, 2005), CIDEr (Vedantam et al., 2015), and SPICE (Anderson et al., 2016). For our hyperparameter tuning on the validation set, we use the BLEU metric. We report CIDEr scores in the main paper for brevity, scores for the other evaluation metrics can be found in Appendix B. We use the Pycocoevalcap[3] library for evaluation. In order to evaluate the continual learning abilities of our IC model, we report scores per cluster, as well as micro-averages over the clusters trained so far.

### 4.2 Results

We present our results in Table 2. The use of our DA methods does not improve the results. Especially when IMG DA is involved, performance drops dramatically compared to the NO DA baseline. This leads us to the conclusion that the DA operations we applied to the images were not suitable. Unexpectedly, we observe that TXT DA does not improve results compared to the NO DA baseline, which is in contrast to findings of previous work showing that caption augmentation is beneficial for low-resource IC (Atliha and Šešok, 2020). We analyze this in more detail in section 5.

## 5 Analysis

In this section, we take a closer look into the quality of the captions generated by our models. We focus on the NO and TXT models since they produce better results. We also conduct two ablation studies: one considers training without the use of the memory module, and the other one tests our method in a low-resource scenario.

[3]https://github.com/salaniz/pycocoevalcap.git

| | NO | IMG | TXT | BOTH |
|---|---|---|---|---|
| no. of types | 1,383 | 2,418 | 1,397 | 1,053 |
| ∅ (median) | 10.0 | 10.0 | 8.0 | 10.0 |
| ∅ (mean) | 10.229 | 10.464 | 7.949 | 9.894 |

Table 3: Statistics over captions generated with our models. ∅ : average caption length.

### 5.1 Caption quality

In order to gain a better insight into our results, in particular the observation that TXT DA worsens results compared to the NO DA baseline, we compare the generated captions based on their average length and the number of unique word types contained in the captions. One aspect that strikes immediately when comparing captions generated with TXT DA vs NO DA is variation. While we find that NO captions and TXT captions share a similar amount of unique word types, their average length is different, with TXT captions being more than 2 words shorter than NO captions.

We include some examples of generated captions in Figure 3. While we see that the captions generated are not necessarily erroneous, captions generated with the models trained with TXT DA are less informative than the gold captions and captions generated without DA. Automated evaluation metrics often penalize changes in the length of the output. Captions generated by the TXT DA model tend to be more similar to the paraphrases generated by the PEGASUS paraphrasing model (which was used to generate data for the training of the TXT DA model), which are shorter and less informative. Hence, this paraphrasing tool is not suitable for this

| | + cluster 1 | | | | + cluster 2 | | | | + cluster 3 | | | | + cluster 4 | | | | + cluster 5 | | | |
|---|---|---|---|---|---|---|---|---|---|---|---|---|---|---|---|---|---|---|---|---|
| DA | NO | | TXT | | NO | | TXT | | NO | | TXT | | NO | | TXT | | NO | | TXT | |
| MEM | + | - | + | - | + | - | + | - | + | - | + | - | + | - | + | - | + | - | + | - |
| 1 | 27.1 | 27.1 | 20.9 | 20.8 | 16.5 | 15.6 | 14.3 | 9.7 | 22.8 | 22.9 | 17.7 | 16.3 | 19.3 | 20.8 | 13.1 | 15.2 | 17.6 | 19.0 | 13.3 | 13.5 |
| 2 | | | | | 26.0 | 27.0 | 22.2 | 20.1 | 25.2 | 24.9 | 18.7 | 17.2 | 19.3 | 17.2 | 16.0 | 15.3 | 23.3 | 23.0 | 18.3 | 15.2 |
| 3 | | | | | | | | | 32.4 | 31.3 | 28.1 | 24.1 | 24.2 | 23.8 | 17.9 | 18.4 | 25.1 | 24.2 | 18.1 | 19.1 |
| 4 | | | | | | | | | | | | | 25.3 | 23.7 | 17.5 | 20.9 | 18.5 | 18.9 | 13.5 | 12.2 |
| 5 | | | | | | | | | | | | | | | | | 27.1 | 25.6 | 19.9 | 19.0 |
| all | 27.1 | 27.1 | 20.9 | 20.8 | **21.0** | 20.4 | **18.5** | 14.3 | **29.7** | 29.1 | **24.8** | 22.0 | 23.4 | 23.5 | 17.2 | 18.1 | **24.9** | 24.3 | **18.6** | 18.4 |

Table 4: CIDEr results on the validation set for NO and TXT augmentation with (+) and without (-) episodic memory replay. We mark in **bold** the cases in which episodic memory contributes to an improvement, and in red the cases in which it does not.

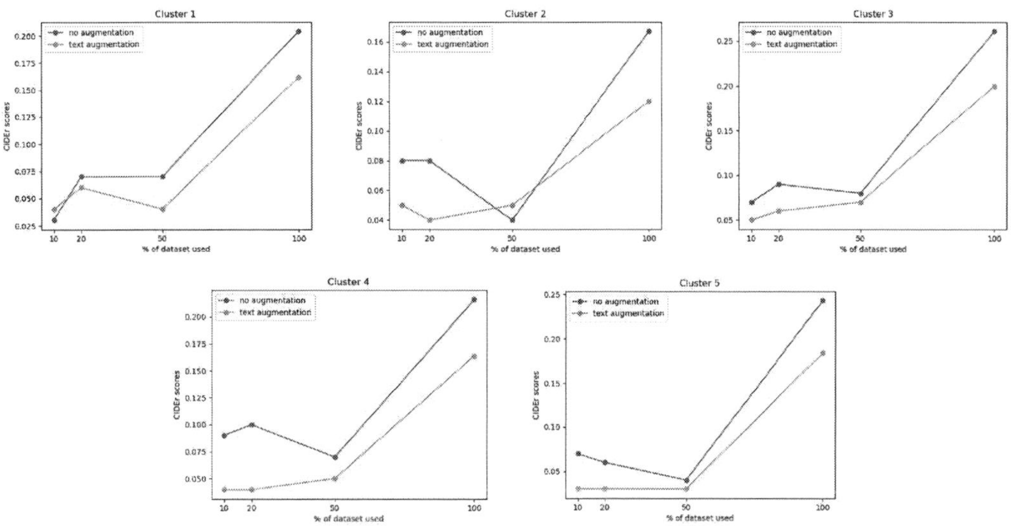


Figure 4: CIDEr results on the validation set for each task training with 10%, 20%, 50%, and 100% of the data.

particular task. In the future, we plan to compare more paraphrasing tools for DA on IC tasks.

To confirm our qualitative observations in a quantitative manner, we carried out a small manual analysis. We randomly sampled 100 captions generated with the TXT models and compared them to the gold captions. Our criterion was informativeness: we ranked each generated caption as *non-informative*, *partially informative*, or *very informative*. We find that 46 of them are very or partially informative, while for some of the rest, the lack of informativeness comes from the fact that the image quality is low (since seven of them contain severe quality issues).

### 5.2 Ablation study: Training without episodic memory replay

In order to investigate the effect of the sparse episodic memory replay on the continual learning abilities of the model, we train models in the same settings as in our core experiments, except for the use of sparse episodic memory replay. Results for these experiments are shown in Table 4. We observe that, in general, there is an improvement in performance in almost all cases, both in models trained with NO DA and in models trained with TXT DA. The only exception is the model after training with cluster 4, which is significantly smaller than the rest of the other clusters (approx. 1/3 the size of the next smaller cluster). This shows that, while the episodic memory module positively influences performance when at least 1000 samples are present, it is not as effective with very few samples.

### 5.3 Ablation study: Training with parts of the dataset

In an interactive setup, we cannot assume large amounts of annotated data provided by the user, hence we evaluate our models after training on only 10%, 20%, and 50% of the data of each cluster. Training data points for each cluster are chosen randomly - for this reason, we present average scores over 3 trainings with the same settings. Our training takes place without memory since in most cases, the amount of data is too small for the memory to be activated. The results for models trained on reduced amounts of data for each cluster are shown in Figure 4.

It seems that TXT DA does not improve results even in a low-resource scenario - the curves for NO and TXT DA are similar for the larger clusters (1, 3, 5). For task 2, a slight improvement in performance can be observed when training with 50% of the data. This, in turn, leads to an additional observation, namely the fact that almost all our NO DA models deter when trained with half of the data of each cluster. This might be attributed to the data distribution of the clusters with which we trained.

## 6 Conclusion

We have presented a pipeline for interactive IC, which combines simple methods for incremental model improvement. This framework allows incremental adaptation of a pre-trained IC model to new data that is entered by users. The user input is transformed into a larger data batch using various data augmentation methods (for image, text, and both modalities). We additionally adapted a continual learning method for IC, which prevents catastrophic forgetting after repeated updates. In order to simulate incremental user input, we split the relatively small, domain-specific VizWiz dataset into non-overlapping clusters based on nouns mentioned in the image captions. VizWiz is a good test bed for our pipeline, as it contains real-world images with varying quality.

We analyzed the effectiveness of DA in our experiments, and we noticed a lower performance of our models when trained with augmented data. The drop in performance resulting from the application of DA methods was evident in our low-resource experiments as well. We concluded that, especially for IC, IMG DA must be applied carefully. The same applies to TXT DA: since brevity is penalized in this task, the DA outputs should be of similar length and descriptiveness as the gold captions. We confirmed that sparse memory replay does enable the models to retain knowledge learned from previous datasets while adapting to new data.

In the future, we plan to experiment with more elaborate joint DA methods for IC. Apart from evaluating the approach with respect to model performance using automated performance metrics, we intend to evaluate its usefulness and usability for end-users in a human study. Since prompting using large models is a popular paradigm recently, we intend to experiment with models like CLIP (Radford et al., 2021) as well, additionally assessing the trade-off between initial training cost and adaptation cost. Last but not least, applying active learning methods to select the best sample(s) for the episodic memory module can potentially increase the effectiveness of the continual learning method used in our pipeline.

## Limitations

Despite the promising results of our IML pipeline for image captioning, our work has some limitations. Firstly, the experiments were conducted on a domain-specific dataset, VizWiz, and may not generalize to other datasets or domains. Secondly, our approach may not be suitable for scenarios where user feedback is sparse or unreliable, as the effectiveness of IML heavily depends on the quality and quantity of the feedback. Thirdly, our use of episodic memory to retain knowledge from previously seen clusters may not scale well to smaller datasets and other methods may be required. Lastly, our approach does not address the challenge of bias in the data, which can lead to biased models.

## Ethical Statement

As of now, we do not see ethical concerns with the study presented in this paper. We used a dataset that is publicly available. The study is currently not applied to human subjects with personal data; in this case, the use of user feedback in the training process could potentially introduce biases if the feedback is not diverse or representative of the population. Lastly, our approach may be used to develop image captioning models that generate harmful or inappropriate content, such as captions that perpetuate harmful stereotypes or stigmatize certain groups of people.

## Acknowledgments

We thank the reviewers for their insightful comments and suggestions. The research was funded by the XAINES project (BMBF, 01IW20005) and by the No-IDLE project (BMBF, 01IW23002).

## References


Peter Anderson, Basura Fernando, Mark Johnson, and Stephen Gould. 2016. SPICE: semantic propositional image caption evaluation. In *Computer Vision - ECCV 2016 - 14th European Conference, Amsterdam, The Netherlands, October 11-14, 2016, Proceedings, Part V*, volume 9909 of *Lecture Notes in Computer Science*, pages 382–398. Springer.

Peter Anderson, Xiaodong He, Chris Buehler, Damien Teney, Mark Johnson, Stephen Gould, and Lei Zhang. 2018. Bottom-up and top-down attention for image captioning and visual question answering. In *Proceedings of the IEEE CVPR conference*, pages 6077–6086.

Viktar Atliha and Dmitrij Šešok. 2020. Text augmentation using bert for image captioning. *Applied Sciences*, 10(17):5978.

Satanjeev Banerjee and Alon Lavie. 2005. METEOR: An automatic metric for MT evaluation with improved correlation with human judgments. In *Proceedings of the ACL Workshop on Intrinsic and Extrinsic Evaluation Measures for Machine Translation and/or Summarization*, pages 65–72, Ann Arbor, Michigan. ACL.

Rajarshi Biswas, Michael Barz, and Daniel Sonntag. 2020. Towards explanatory interactive image captioning using top-down and bottom-up features, beam search and re-ranking. *KI - Künstliche Intelligenz, German Journal on Artificial Intelligence - Organ des Fachbereiches "Künstliche Intelligenz" der Gesellschaft für Informatik e.V. (KI)*, 36:1–14.

Alexander Buslaev, Vladimir I. Iglovikov, Eugene Khvedchenya, Alex Parinov, Mikhail Druzhinin, and Alexandr A. Kalinin. 2020. Albumentations: Fast and flexible image augmentations. *Information*, 11(2).

Adrian Bussone, Simone Stumpf, and Dympna O'Sullivan. 2015. The role of explanations on trust and reliance in clinical decision support systems. In *2015 International Conference on Healthcare Informatics*, pages 160–169.

Özkan Çaylı, Volkan Kılıç, Aytuğ Onan, and Wenwu Wang. 2022. Auxiliary classifier based residual rnn for image captioning. In *2022 30th European Signal Processing Conference (EUSIPCO)*, pages 1126–1130.

Cyprien de Masson d'Autume, Sebastian Ruder, Lingpeng Kong, and Dani Yogatama. 2019. Episodic memory in lifelong language learning. In *Advances in Neural Information Processing Systems*, volume 32. Curran Associates, Inc.

Riccardo Del Chiaro, Bartłomiej Twardowski, Andrew D Bagdanov, and Joost Van de Weijer. 2020. Ratt: Recurrent attention to transient tasks for continual image captioning. *arXiv preprint arXiv:2007.06271*.

Jacob Devlin, Ming-Wei Chang, Kenton Lee, and Kristina Toutanova. 2019. BERT: Pre-training of deep bidirectional transformers for language understanding. In *Proceedings of the 2019 Conference of the NACCL: Human Language Technologies, Volume 1 (Long and Short Papers)*, pages 4171–4186, Minneapolis, Minnesota. ACL.

Pierre Dognin, Igor Melnyk, Youssef Mroueh, Inkit Padhi, Mattia Rigotti, Jarret Ross, Yair Schiff, Richard A. Young, and Brian Belgodere. 2022. Image captioning as an assistive technology: Lessons learned from vizwiz 2020 challenge. *J. Artif. Int. Res.*, 73.

Lijie Guo, Elizabeth M. Daly, Oznur Alkan, Massimiliano Mattetti, Owen Cornec, and Bart Knijnenburg. 2022. Building trust in interactive machine learning via user contributed interpretable rules. In *27th International Conference on Intelligent User Interfaces*, IUI '22, pages 537–548, New York, NY, USA. Association for Computing Machinery.

Danna Gurari, Yinan Zhao, Meng Zhang, and Nilavra Bhattacharya. 2020. Captioning images taken by people who are blind. *CoRR*, abs/2002.08565.

J. A. Hartigan and M. A. Wong. 1979. A k-means clustering algorithm. *JSTOR: Applied Statistics*, 28(1):100–108.

Mareike Hartmann, Aliki Anagnostopoulou, and Daniel Sonntag. 2022. Interactive machine learning for image captioning.

Zhengxiong Jia and Xirong Li. 2020. Icap: Interactive image captioning with predictive text. In *Proceedings of the 2020 International Conference on Multimedia Retrieval*, ICMR '20, pages 428–435, New York, NY, USA. Association for Computing Machinery.

Andrej Karpathy and Li Fei-Fei. 2017. Deep visual-semantic alignments for generating image descriptions. *IEEE Trans. Pattern Anal. Mach. Intell.*, 39(4):664–676.

Sulabh Katiyar and Samir Kumar Borgohain. 2021. Image captioning using deep stacked lstms, contextual word embeddings and data augmentation. *arXiv preprint arXiv:2102.11237*.

James Kirkpatrick, Razvan Pascanu, Neil Rabinowitz, Joel Veness, Guillaume Desjardins, Andrei A Rusu, Kieran Milan, John Quan, Tiago Ramalho, Agnieszka Grabska-Barwinska, et al. 2017. Overcoming catastrophic forgetting in neural networks. *Proceedings of the national academy of sciences*, 114(13):3521–3526.

Sosuke Kobayashi. 2018. Contextual augmentation: Data augmentation by words with paradigmatic relations. In *Proceedings of the 2018 Conference of the NACCL: Human Language Technologies, Volume 2 (Short Papers)*, pages 452–457, New Orleans, Louisiana. ACL.

Chenliang Li, Haiyang Xu, Junfeng Tian, Wei Wang, Ming Yan, Bin Bi, Jiabo Ye, Hehong Chen, Guohai Xu, Zheng Cao, et al. 2022. mplug: Effective and efficient vision-language learning by cross-modal skip-connections. *arXiv preprint arXiv:2205.12005.*

Guodun Li, Yuchen Zhai, Zehao Lin, and Yin Zhang. 2021. Similar scenes arouse similar emotions: Parallel data augmentation for stylized image captioning. *arXiv preprint arXiv:2108.11912.*

Chin-Yew Lin. 2004. ROUGE: A package for automatic evaluation of summaries. In *Text Summarization Branches Out*, pages 74–81, Barcelona, Spain. ACL.

Tsung-Yi Lin, Michael Maire, Serge Belongie, James Hays, Pietro Perona, Deva Ramanan, Piotr Dollár, and C Lawrence Zitnick. 2014. Microsoft coco: Common objects in context. In *European conference on computer vision*, pages 740–755. Springer.

Huan Ling and Sanja Fidler. 2017. Teaching machines to describe images via natural language feedback. In *Proceedings of the 31st International Conference on Neural Information Processing Systems*, pages 5075–5085.

Jiasen Lu, Jianwei Yang, Dhruv Batra, and Devi Parikh. 2018. Neural baby talk. In *Proceedings of the IEEE CVPR conference*, pages 7219–7228.

Giang Nguyen, Tae Joon Jun, Trung Tran, Tolcha Yalew, and Daeyoung Kim. 2019. Contcap: A scalable framework for continual image captioning. *arXiv preprint arXiv:1909.08745.*

Kishore Papineni, Salim Roukos, Todd Ward, and Wei-Jing Zhu. 2002. Bleu: a method for automatic evaluation of machine translation. In *Proceedings of the 40th Annual Meeting of the ACL*, pages 311–318, Philadelphia, Pennsylvania, USA. ACL.

Jeffrey Pennington, Richard Socher, and Christopher D. Manning. 2014. Glove: Global vectors for word representation. In *EMNLP*, pages 1532–1543.

Alec Radford, Jong Wook Kim, Chris Hallacy, Aditya Ramesh, Gabriel Goh, Sandhini Agarwal, Girish Sastry, Amanda Askell, Pamela Mishkin, Jack Clark, Gretchen Krueger, and Ilya Sutskever. 2021. Learning transferable visual models from natural language supervision. In *Proceedings of the 38th International Conference on Machine Learning, ICML 2021, 18-24 July 2021, Virtual Event*, volume 139 of *Proceedings of Machine Learning Research*, pages 8748–8763. PMLR.

Colin Raffel, Noam Shazeer, Adam Roberts, Katherine Lee, Sharan Narang, Michael Matena, Yanqi Zhou, Wei Li, and Peter J. Liu. 2020. Exploring the limits of transfer learning with a unified text-to-text transformer. *Journal of Machine Learning Research*, 21(140):1–67.

Rico Sennrich, Barry Haddow, and Alexandra Birch. 2016. Improving neural machine translation models with monolingual data. In *Proceedings of the 54th Annual Meeting of the ACL (Volume 1: Long Papers)*, pages 86–96, Berlin, Germany. ACL.

Tingke Shen, Amlan Kar, and Sanja Fidler. 2019. Learning to caption images through a lifetime by asking questions. In *Proceedings of the IEEE/CVF International Conference on Computer Vision*, pages 10393–10402.

Rachel N. Simons, Danna Gurari, and Kenneth R. Fleischmann. 2020. "i hope this is helpful": Understanding crowdworkers' challenges and motivations for an image description task. *Proc. ACM Hum.-Comput. Interact.*, 4(CSCW2).

Matteo Stefanini, Marcella Cornia, Lorenzo Baraldi, Silvia Cascianelli, Giuseppe Fiameni, and Rita Cucchiara. 2021. From show to tell: A survey on image captioning. *CoRR*, abs/2107.06912.

Ryo Takahashi, Takashi Matsubara, and Kuniaki Uehara. 2019. Data augmentation using random image cropping and patching for deep cnns. *IEEE Transactions on Circuits and Systems for Video Technology*, 30(9):2917–2931.

Ingrid Ravn Turkerud and Ole Jakob Mengshoel. 2021. Image captioning using deep learning: Text augmentation by paraphrasing via backtranslation. In *2021 IEEE Symposium Series on Computational Intelligence (SSCI)*, pages 01–10.

Ramakrishna Vedantam, C. Lawrence Zitnick, and Devi Parikh. 2015. CIDEr: Consensus-based image description evaluation. In *2015 IEEE CVPR*, pages 4566–4575.

Zijie J. Wang, Dongjin Choi, Shenyu Xu, and Diyi Yang. 2021. Putting humans in the natural language processing loop: A survey. In *Proceedings of the First Workshop on Bridging Human–Computer Interaction and Natural Language Processing*, pages 47–52, Online. ACL.

Jason Wei and Kai Zou. 2019. EDA: Easy data augmentation techniques for boosting performance on text classification tasks. In *Proceedings of the 2019 Conference on EMNLP and the 9th IJCNLP*, pages 6382–6388, Hong Kong, China. ACL.

Saining Xie, Ross B. Girshick, Piotr Dollár, Zhuowen Tu, and Kaiming He. 2016. Aggregated residual transformations for deep neural networks. *2017 IEEE Conference on Computer Vision and Pattern Recognition (CVPR)*, pages 5987–5995.

Kelvin Xu, Jimmy Ba, Ryan Kiros, Kyunghyun Cho, Aaron Courville, Ruslan Salakhudinov, Rich Zemel, and Yoshua Bengio. 2015. Show, attend and tell: Neural image caption generation with visual attention. In *Proceedings of the 32nd ICML*, volume 37 of *Proceedings of Machine Learning Research*, pages 2048–2057, Lille, France. PMLR.

Yinfei Yang, Yuan Zhang, Chris Tar, and Jason Baldridge. 2019. PAWS-X: A Cross-lingual Adversarial Dataset for Paraphrase Identification. In *Proc. of EMNLP*.

Jingqing Zhang, Yao Zhao, Mohammad Saleh, and Peter J. Liu. 2019a. Pegasus: Pre-training with extracted gap-sentences for abstractive summarization.

Yuan Zhang, Jason Baldridge, and Luheng He. 2019b. PAWS: Paraphrase Adversaries from Word Scrambling. In *Proc. of NAACL*.

Luowei Zhou, Hamid Palangi, Lei Zhang, Houdong Hu, Jason Corso, and Jianfeng Gao. 2020. Unified vision-language pre-training for image captioning and vqa. *Proceedings of the AAAI Conference on Artificial Intelligence*, 34(07):13041–13049.

Xueyan Zou, Zi-Yi Dou, Jianwei Yang, Zhe Gan, Linjie Li, Chunyuan Li, Xiyang Dai, Harkirat Behl, Jianfeng Wang, Lu Yuan, Nanyun Peng, Lijuan Wang, Yong Jae Lee, and Jianfeng Gao. 2022. Generalized decoding for pixel, image, and language. *CoRR*, abs/2212.11270.

## A Example NPs for VizWiz clustering

We include example nominal phrases (NPs) from our VizWiz clustering. We follow the procedure described in the main body of the paper. For each cluster, we include 20 NPs. While there is no perfect separation in object categories, we do notice certain semantic similarities between the NPs in most clusters:

## B Results for BLEU-4, METEOR, ROUGE, SPICE metrics

In the main paper, we only include CIDEr scores for our main experiments. Here we present results in four additional metrics: BLEU-4 (Table 6), METEOR (Table 7), ROUGE-L (Table 8), and SPICE (Table 9). The tables can be found on the next page.

| cluster 1 | cluster 2 | cluster 3 | cluster 4 | cluster 5 |
|---|---|---|---|---|
| gift card | ac | kitchen counter top | ingredients | dark surface |
| button | labrador | top portion | small packet | glass cup |
| camera lens | quaker | small dog | crock pot | light fixture |
| nutrition information | stouffer | bottom | large bottle | wooden countertop |
| apple | dr | left side | nutritional | beige carpet |
| video games | packet | small | kitchen appliance | black |
| electrical outlet | screenshot | eye drops | ingredients label | lamp |
| tv screen | sainsbury | math problems | lotion bottle | wire |
| cable box | barcode | paper money | milk chocolate | concrete floor |
| computer tower | coke | led | liter bottle | interior |
| tv | nokia | person 's knee | dark chocolate | plastic container |
| cd case | samsung | 's chicken | medicine bottle | marble counter |
| silver device | tan | brand name | frozen dinner box | glass container |
| keys | unopened | side view | dinner table | shorts |
| image quality | container/ box / bottle | counter top | water bottle | styrofoam |
| design | sprite | sunny day | small jar | couch cushion |
| entertainment center | the/this | remote control | spice | plastic wrapping |
| book page | roni | body | coffee pod | glass door |
| background | k-cup | room area | brownie mix | clear plastic bag |
| laptop monitor | upc | left side | ice cream | flat horizontal surface |

Table 5: First 20 NPs for each cluster from the VizWiz Dataset

| | + cluster 1 | | | | + cluster 2 | | | | + cluster 3 | | | | + cluster 4 | | | | + cluster 5 | | | |
|---|---|---|---|---|---|---|---|---|---|---|---|---|---|---|---|---|---|---|---|---|
| DA | NO | IMG | TXT | BOTH | NO | IMG | TXT | BOTH | NO | IMG | TXT | BOTH | NO | IMG | TXT | BOTH | NO | IMG | TXT | BOTH |
| eval on 1 | 14.4 | 6.0 | 11.1 | 12.4 | 9.1 | 2.6 | 8.7 | 4.6 | 11.6 | 2.8 | 9.2 | 6.3 | 10.5 | 2.6 | 7.5 | 4.5 | 7.6 | 2.9 | 6.0 | 6.1 |
| eval on 2 | | | | | 16.9 | 7.4 | 15.1 | 13.7 | 17.8 | 5.6 | 15.9 | 10.6 | 16.6 | 5.7 | 12.5 | 9.7 | 16.2 | 4.8 | 12.5 | 13.6 |
| eval on 3 | | | | | | | | | 16.0 | 4.9 | 13.8 | 11.3 | 13.7 | 3.5 | 10.5 | 6.4 | 13.8 | 3.8 | 10.8 | 10.6 |
| eval on 4 | | | | | | | | | | | | | 16.9 | 4.6 | 13.5 | 9.1 | 12.4 | 3.3 | 9.8 | 8.4 |
| eval on 5 | | | | | | | | | | | | | | | | | 15.1 | 4.4 | 11.3 | 12.1 |
| micro avg | 14.4 | 6.0 | 11.1 | 12.4 | 10.4 | 3.5 | 9.8 | 6.3 | 14.0 | 4.0 | 11.8 | 8.9 | 12.5 | 3.4 | 9.4 | 6.0 | 12.4 | 3.8 | 9.6 | 9.9 |

Table 6: BLEU-4 results on our experiments on VizWiz data clustered according to the procedure described in our main paper. We start with the model resulting from the supervised pre-training step on MS COCO and continue to train this model incrementally on the VizWiz clusters (+cluster ...). We include the amount of (original) training data in brackets. DA: Data augmentation, NO: no DA, IMG: image DA, TXT: text DA, BOTH: image and text DA. The numbers in the left column stand for clusters evaluated on. 'all' refers to the micro average score.

| | + cluster 1 | | | | + cluster 2 | | | | + cluster 3 | | | | + cluster 4 | | | | + cluster 5 | | | |
|---|---|---|---|---|---|---|---|---|---|---|---|---|---|---|---|---|---|---|---|---|
| DA | NO | IMG | TXT | BOTH | NO | IMG | TXT | BOTH | NO | IMG | TXT | BOTH | NO | IMG | TXT | BOTH | NO | IMG | TXT | BOTH |
| eval on 1 | 13.5 | 9.3 | 12.4 | 12.9 | 10.8 | 6.7 | 10.5 | 7.8 | 12.4 | 6.8 | 10.7 | 8.8 | 11.2 | 6.5 | 9.7 | 7.7 | 10.8 | 7.3 | 9.4 | 9.3 |
| eval on 2 | | | | | 15.8 | 10.3 | 15.0 | 13.7 | 16.0 | 9.3 | 14.6 | 11.9 | 14.8 | 9.4 | 13.3 | 11.2 | 15.8 | 8.9 | 13.7 | 13.8 |
| eval on 3 | | | | | | | | | 15.2 | 8.6 | 13.7 | 12.0 | 13.9 | 7.7 | 12.0 | 9.4 | 14.1 | 8.5 | 12.2 | 11.9 |
| eval on 4 | | | | | | | | | | | | | 15.1 | 9.0 | 13.0 | 11.5 | 13.8 | 8.0 | 12.0 | 11.4 |
| eval on 5 | | | | | | | | | | | | | | | | | 15.4 | 9.3 | 13.3 | 13.0 |
| micro avg | 13.5 | 9.3 | 12.4 | 12.9 | 11.6 | 7.3 | 11.2 | 8.7 | 13.9 | 7.8 | 12.3 | 10.5 | 12.8 | 7.3 | 11.0 | 8.8 | 13.6 | 8.4 | 11.7 | 11.5 |

Table 7: METEOR results, as above.

| | + cluster 1 | | | | + cluster 2 | | | | + cluster 3 | | | | + cluster 4 | | | | + cluster 5 | | | |
|---|---|---|---|---|---|---|---|---|---|---|---|---|---|---|---|---|---|---|---|---|
| DA | NO | IMG | TXT | BOTH | NO | IMG | TXT | BOTH | NO | IMG | TXT | BOTH | NO | IMG | TXT | BOTH | NO | IMG | TXT | BOTH |
| eval on 1 | 34.0 | 26.0 | 31.0 | 31.5 | 28.3 | 21.0 | 28.8 | 23.1 | 31.3 | 22.2 | 29.0 | 26.9 | 30.8 | 21.6 | 26.9 | 24.8 | 29.9 | 23.6 | 27.0 | 28.4 |
| eval on 2 | | | | | 39.0 | 30.8 | 39.1 | 36.1 | 42.4 | 29.3 | 39.5 | 34.9 | 39.7 | 29.7 | 35.8 | 33.6 | 42.3 | 29.8 | 37.2 | 39.9 |
| eval on 3 | | | | | | | | | 39.8 | 27.2 | 37.2 | 34.3 | 37.4 | 25.6 | 33.2 | 29.8 | 38.7 | 27.8 | 34.5 | 35.3 |
| eval on 4 | | | | | | | | | | | | | 38.0 | 27.1 | 34.4 | 32.2 | 36.4 | 26.8 | 34.0 | 33.7 |
| eval on 5 | | | | | | | | | | | | | | | | | 40.7 | 29.3 | 35.7 | 37.5 |
| micro avg | 34.0 | 26.0 | 31.0 | 31.5 | 30.1 | 22.6 | 30.5 | 25.3 | 35.9 | 25.0 | 33.5 | 30.8 | 34.5 | 24.1 | 30.5 | 27.8 | 36.7 | 27.0 | 32.6 | 34.1 |

Table 8: ROUGE-L results, as above.

| | + cluster 1 | | | | + cluster 2 | | | | + cluster 3 | | | | + cluster 4 | | | | + cluster 5 | | | |
|---|---|---|---|---|---|---|---|---|---|---|---|---|---|---|---|---|---|---|---|---|
| DA | NO | IMG | TXT | BOTH | NO | IMG | TXT | BOTH | NO | IMG | TXT | BOTH | NO | IMG | TXT | BOTH | NO | IMG | TXT | BOTH |
| eval on 1 | 7.5 | 5.3 | 7.2 | 7.2 | 5.0 | 1.7 | 5.0 | 2.1 | 6.2 | 1.5 | 5.1 | 3.1 | 5.0 | 1.5 | 4.6 | 1.8 | 4.6 | 1.5 | 4.0 | 3.3 |
| eval on 2 | | | | | 9.6 | 3.8 | 8.8 | 6.6 | 8.8 | 2.5 | 8.2 | 5.1 | 7.9 | 3.2 | 7.4 | 4.5 | 8.6 | 2.2 | 7.6 | 6.6 |
| eval on 3 | | | | | | | | | 8.3 | 2.4 | 7.3 | 5.6 | 6.8 | 1.7 | 5.7 | 2.7 | 7.0 | 1.9 | 5.8 | 4.8 |
| eval on 4 | | | | | | | | | | | | | 8.0 | 2.9 | 7.1 | 4.5 | 7.0 | 1.7 | 6.1 | 5.3 |
| eval on 5 | | | | | | | | | | | | | | | | | 8.5 | 2.6 | 7.5 | 6.2 |
| micro avg | 7.5 | 5.3 | 7.2 | 7.2 | 5.8 | 2.0 | 5.6 | 2.9 | 7.3 | 1.9 | 6.3 | 4.3 | 6.1 | 1.8 | 5.4 | 2.5 | 6.8 | 2.0 | 5.9 | 4.9 |

Table 9: SPICE results, as above.

# Corpus Complexity Matters in Pretraining Language Models

**Ameeta Agrawal** and **Suresh Singh**
Department of Computer Science
Portland State University
{ameeta,singhsp}@pdx.edu

## Abstract

It is well known that filtering low-quality data before pretraining language models or selecting suitable data from domains similar to downstream task datasets generally leads to improved downstream performance. However, the extent to which the quality of a corpus, in particular its complexity, affects its downstream performance remains less explored. In this work, we address the problem of creating a suitable pretraining corpus given a fixed corpus budget. Using metrics of text complexity we propose a simple yet effective approach for constructing a corpus with rich lexical variation. Our extensive set of empirical analyses reveal that such a diverse and complex corpus yields significant improvements over baselines consisting of less diverse and less complex corpora when evaluated in the context of general language understanding tasks.

## 1 Introduction

The recent trend in training language models (LM) has been to use increasingly larger text corpora (Khandelwal et al., 2019; Kaplan et al., 2020; Borgeaud et al., 2021). While this approach generally does improve downstream performance, it comes at a substantial computational cost. Another line of research has found that increasing the pretraining data does not always improve the performance on downstream tasks (Martin et al., 2019; Dai et al., 2019; Shin et al., 2022). In response, numerous studies have explored approaches such as utilizing pretraining corpora that are domain specific or using data filtering to reduce the size of the pretraining corpus, while improving downstream task performance (Beltagy et al., 2019; Lee et al., 2020; Grave et al., 2018; Raffel et al., 2019; Brown et al., 2020). The shortcoming of these methods is that the pretrained LM may be very specific to the selected tasks, and therefore, show limited generalizability to other downstream tasks, or require heuristic filtering techniques. In this research, we explore a complementary approach and investigate whether improving the complexity of the pretraining corpus can yield improved model performance. The implication is that rather than arbitrarily increasing the size of a corpus as is done today, increasing its complexity might yield higher performance but at a lower computational cost.

Intuitively it is easy to compare a children's book with a college textbook and state that the latter is more complex. Unfortunately, providing a general formal definition is fraught because books of different genres are complex in different ways (e.g., post-modern novel vs. biography). However, attempts have been made to characterize text complexity using reasonable measures such as vocabulary size, syntactic complexity, and semantic richness (Jensen, 2009). In this paper we use metrics that derive from these linguistic measures including types, type-token ratio, entropy, and Flesch reading-ease to estimate corpus complexity.

First we construct *five distinct corpora of equal size but varying complexity* to pretrain LMs. The resulting models are then fine-tuned and evaluated on downstream tasks from the GLUE benchmark. Our results suggest that a corpus containing a breadth of complexity from easy to hard but one that is skewed towards hard makes an effective corpus as evaluated in general language understanding tasks.

The key contributions of our paper are as follows: (i) We propose a simple approach for constructing a lexically rich and complex corpus for pretraining of language models; (ii) We conduct an extensive set of experiments by pretraining several language models from scratch on corpora of differing complexity, and then evaluating these models on a diverse set of downstream tasks; (iii) We analyze our results to estimate the correlation between the complexity of a corpus, its similarity to downstream data, and its performance on various downstream tasks.



*Proceedings of The Fourth Workshop on Simple and Efficient Natural Language Processing (SustaiNLP)*, pages 257–263
July 13, 2023 

## 2 Related Work

Below, we briefly review two broadly related threads of research.

***Data selection.*** Ruder and Plank (2017) proposed several similarity and diversity measures for assessing the suitability of data for transfer learning. Dai et al. (2019) studied the problem of selecting appropriate corpus for pretraining in the context of Named Entity Recognition (NER) downstream tasks, and found that language models pretrained on source text similar to the target task outperform the ones pretrained on other sources (with one exception). Gururangan et al. (2020) compared the vocabulary overlap between pretraining sources and target domain corpora, and found that the pretrained model performs slightly better when target domain is less distant than source domain, but not in all the cases. Lange et al. (2021) studied the selection of source data for transfer learning.

Selecting data from similar domains as downstream tasks for pretraining of domain-specific language models has generally been shown to be beneficial, e.g., SciBERT (Beltagy et al., 2019), BioBERT (Lee et al., 2020). However, prior work has also observed that this trend does not always hold true (Martin et al., 2019; Shin et al., 2022). Dai et al. (2020) found that models pretrained on forums corpus (0.6B tokens) outperformed those trained on tweets corpus (0.9B tokens) on both forums- and tweets-related downstream tasks, as well as a significantly larger generic BERT model (3.3B tokens), highlighting the importance of domain similarity of corpus over its size.

***Data engineering.*** A complementary line of research suggests that engineering the corpus before pretraining through reordering (Agrawal et al., 2021; Nagatsuka et al., 2021; Li et al., 2021; Wang et al., 2023), preprocessing (Babanejad et al., 2023), and filtering (Grave et al., 2018; Raffel et al., 2019; Brown et al., 2020; Rae et al., 2021; Kreutzer et al., 2022) can potentially enhance both the overall performance and efficiency of language models.

Diverging from previous studies, our research focuses on examining the influence of the *complexity* of a pretraining corpus on downstream tasks related to general language understanding. To accomplish this, we introduce a straightforward methodology for constructing a corpus that embodies richness and complexity.

## 3 Method

Let $\mathcal{C}$ be an unlabeled pretraining corpus of $|\mathcal{C}|$ total tokens, consisting of a vocabulary set $V_\mathcal{C}$, i.e., the unique tokens or types in $\mathcal{C}$. Similarly, let $\mathcal{D}$ be a labeled downstream dataset with total number of tokens $|\mathcal{D}|$ and a vocabulary set $V_\mathcal{D}$. Given a fixed corpus budget (e.g., number of tokens), we first aim to construct distinct corpora of various complexity. Then, the goal is to measure the similarity between these corpora and downstream datasets, and estimate the correlation between complexity, similarity, and performance.

We present some metrics for assessing the complexity of a corpus and for computing the similarity between two collections of text – the pretraining corpus and the downstream datasets in subsections 3.1 and 3.2, before describing the procedure for creating corpora of varying complexity in subsection 3.3.

### 3.1 Corpus Complexity

We consider three metrics for estimating the complexity of a text corpus.

**Types.** This is the number of types or unique tokens in a corpus (i.e., its vocabulary).

**Type-Token Ratio (TTR).** Lexical complexity can also be indexed via TTR – the higher the ratio, the greater the lexical diversity in the sample (Johnson, 1944). Although TTR is often sensitive to length of the texts, for analyzing corpora of comparable sizes, it can serve as a useful metric (Johansson, 2008), and is computed as $TTR(\mathcal{C}) = \frac{|V_\mathcal{C}|}{|\mathcal{C}|}$.

**Entropy.** Broadly speaking, entropy is a measure of randomness or disorder (Shannon, 1948; Fano, 1961), and the greater the number of different words in a text, the higher its entropy, or, conceptually, its complexity. We calculate the unigram entropy of $\mathcal{C}$ as follows:

$$H(\mathcal{C}) = -\sum_{i=1}^{|V_\mathcal{C}|} p(w_i)\log_2 p(w_i)$$

where $p(w_i)$ is the probability of type $w_i$ in $\mathcal{C}$.

### 3.2 Text Similarity

We adopt two well-defined measures to estimate the similarity between two pieces of text, such as the pretraining corpus $\mathcal{C}$ and a downstream dataset $\mathcal{D}$.

**Vocabulary Overlap Ratio (VOR).** This computes the percentage of word types that appear in both the texts ($V_{\mathcal{C}}$ and $V_{\mathcal{D}}$) where a higher ratio indicates higher similarity, and is calculated as:

$$VOR(\mathcal{C}, \mathcal{D}) = \frac{|V_{\mathcal{C}} \cap V_{\mathcal{D}}|}{|V_{\mathcal{D}}|}.$$

**Jensen-Shannon divergence (JSD).** This metric measures the distance between two texts (Lin, 1991), and $D^{(JS)}$ is defined as:

$$D^{(JS)}(P||Q) = \alpha_1 D^{(KL)}(P||M) + \alpha_2 D^{(KL)}(Q||M)$$

where $M = \alpha_1 P + \alpha_2 Q$, and $P$ and $Q$ are the probability distributions of two texts (e.g., a pretraining corpus $\mathcal{C}$ and a downstream dataset $\mathcal{D}$, in our case). The values of $\alpha_1$ and $\alpha_2$ are set as 0.5 each. $D^{(KL)}$ is Kullback-Leibler divergence, a measure for comparing the differences in two texts, and is defined as, $D^{(KL)}(P||Q) = \sum_i p_i \log \frac{p_i}{q_i}$.

### 3.3 Constructing Corpora with Varying Complexity

The complexity of a corpus can be summarized by using metrics like number of types, type-token ratio, and entropy (section 3.1). However, in order to create a corpus according to varying complexity we need a more fine-grained metric that can *compute complexity at document (or even paragraph) level.* One such metric is the Flesch reading ease (FRE) score, commonly used to assess the difficulty of a piece of text (Flesch, 1948).

For a document $d_i \in \mathcal{C}$, its FRE score is computed as:

$$FRE(d_i) = 206.835 - 1.015 \left(\frac{\#w}{\#s}\right) - 84.6 \left(\frac{\#l}{\#w}\right)$$

where $\#w$, $\#s$, and $\#l$ denote the number of words, sentences, and syllables in $d_i$, respectively. The word and sentence length serve as proxies for semantic and syntactic complexity, respectively. Note that texts with high FRE scores tend to display lower complexity (e.g., children's books), while an editorial in the New York Times which has a much greater complexity, shows lower FRE scores. Thus, our approach for creating a more complex corpus is to combine pieces (paragraphs or documents) from existing corpora based on their FRE score.

Our method starts by adopting two text corpora widely used for pretraining of language models: **wiki-103**, a subset of English Wikipedia (Merity et al., 2016) and **BookCorpus**, a large collection of books (Zhu et al., 2015). From these, we construct the following five corpora:

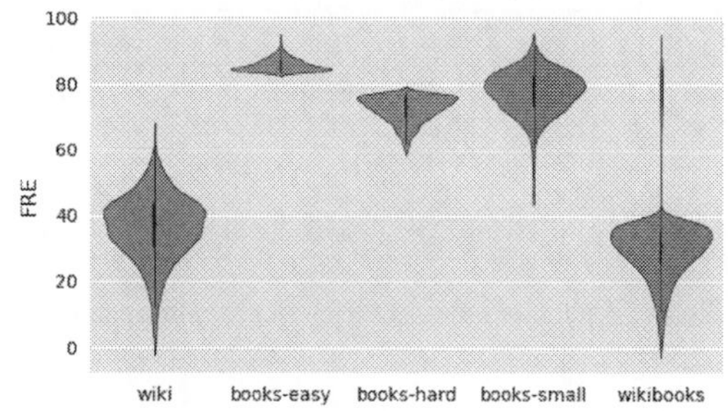


Figure 1: FRE distribution of the corpora. *Lower* FRE indicates *higher* complexity. `wikibooks` spans the full spectrum of complexity, consisting of both low and high complexity, but mostly skewed towards the latter.

- `wiki`: This is the original wiki-103 corpus consisting of around 100 million tokens.
- `books-small`, `books-easy`, `books-hard`: Next, we create a comparably-sized corpus of ~100M tokens, called `books-small`, by randomly sampling books from BookCorpus. Then, for each book in BookCorpus, we compute its FRE score and create two relevant baselines: `books-easy` by combining books of lowest complexity (i.e., the highest FRE scores), and conversely, `books-hard` by using books with the highest complexity (i.e., the lowest FRE scores).
- `wikibooks`: Finally, we hypothesize that a complex and diverse corpus contains a *blend* of texts with different levels of complexity, albeit with a focus on more complex ones. We speculate that this composition would allow it to capture the nuanced linguistic aspects present in a wide range of texts. To create such a corpus, which we call `wikibooks`, we first sample some articles from wiki-103 and books from BookCorpus of varying complexity (i.e., FRE scores ranging from high to low), and then use up the remaining corpus quota by sampling texts of mostly high complexity (low FRE scores).

Figure 1 plots the FRE distribution of each of the five corpora. As we can see, `books-easy`,

| Corpus | Tokens | Types | TTR (%) | Entropy |
|---|---|---|---|---|
| wiki | 104M | 267K | 0.26 | **7.375** |
| books-easy | 120M | 258K | 0.22 | 6.294 |
| books-hard | 111M | 417K | 0.38 | 6.826 |
| books-small | 116M | 346K | 0.29 | 6.483 |
| wikibooks | 109M | **436K** | **0.40** | 7.179 |

Table 1: Characteristics of different pretraining corpora.

books-hard, and books-small span a narrow range of complexity all skewing towards less complex; wiki has moderate to high complexity; and wikibooks is the only one to show the broadest range of complexity, with most of the mass concentrated in the highest complexity range, but also some in the lowest complexity range.

### 3.4 Downstream Datasets and Implementation

We use eight datasets from the General Language Understanding Evaluation (GLUE) benchmark in our experiments, which includes CoLA, MNLI, MRPC, QNLI, QQP, RTE, SST-2 and STS-B (Wang et al., 2018).

Text tokenization is done using NLTK[1], and FRE scores are computed using Readability package[2]. Using the different corpora, we pretrain from scratch different versions of BERT-base model[3] (Devlin et al., 2019). The training continues for at most 30K steps. Checkpoints saved after 10K, 20K, and 30K steps are then fine-tuned over the downstream datasets for two epochs each.

## 4 Discussion

Our work investigates: (i) whether document-level metric such as FRE can be used to construct corpora of varying complexity, (ii) whether corpora of higher complexity lead to improvements in downstream performance, (iii) whether a complex corpus is more similar to downstream data, and (iv) the correlation between complexity, similarity, and performance.

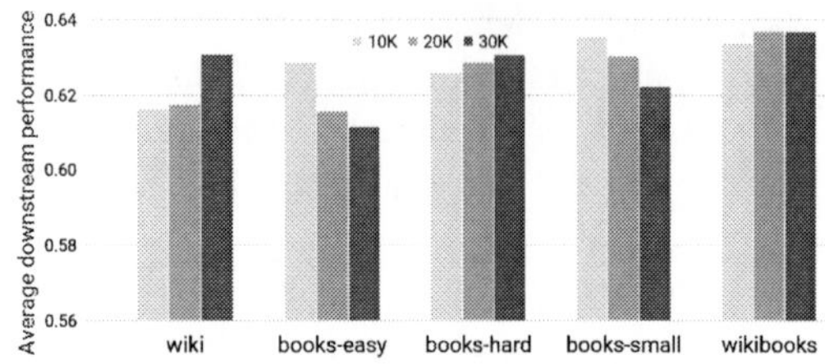


Figure 2: Comparison of (unweighted) average GLUE score, across five different pretraining corpora under varying number of training steps (10K, 20K, 30K).

***Whether FRE can help create suitably complex corpus.*** Table 1 summarizes the details of the five distinct corpora, where we find that wikibooks, which contains a mix of low and high complexity text, has the highest number of types and TTR, and second highest entropy. This demonstrates the effectiveness of using a computationally simple metric such as FRE in creating corpora of a wide range of complexity. Moreover, we also notice that there is no corpus in our sample with a unigram entropy of less than six bits/word, which is in line with information-theoretic models of communication (Bentz et al., 2017).

***Analyzing corpus complexity and downstream performance.*** Figure 2 plots the average scores across eight downstream tasks obtained using models pretrained with the five different corpora under varying number of training steps. Three out of five corpora yield increasingly better results as the training progresses, except books-easy and books-small which show the opposite trend. On the one hand, this suggests that simply training for longer time does not always guarantee a monotonically increasing performance score. On the other hand, this also indicates that pretraining on fairly less complex corpora (cf. Fig. 1) is generally less effective.

In connecting the results of Figure 2 with complexity metrics reported in Table 1, we observe that wikibooks, a corpus with a comparatively higher degree of complexity characterized by a larger number of word types and a higher TTR, consistently outperforms all other corpora across the three model checkpoints. On the opposite end is the poorest performing corpus books-easy with the fewest types, lowest TTR, and lowest entropy.

***Analyzing similarity between pretraining corpus and downstream datasets.*** Now, we assess the similarity between these corpora and downstream

[1]We use NLTK tokenizer: https://www.nltk.org/api/nltk.tokenize.html.

[2]We use Readability package: https://pypi.org/project/readability/ To account for the length-based differences in Wikipedia articles and Books, we randomly but sequentially select a subset of 1000 sentences for each book when computing its FRE.

[3]We use the uncased version, with 12 transformer layers, batch size set to 8, maximum length of the input sequence set to 512, and all other settings set as default. All pretraining and fine-tuning experiments are performed using HuggingFace library (Wolf et al., 2019).

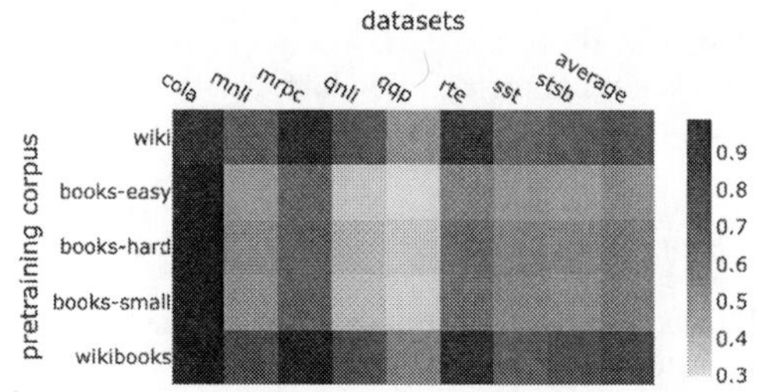


(a) Similarity (VOR) between pretraining corpus and downstream dataset (darker shades indicate higher similarity)

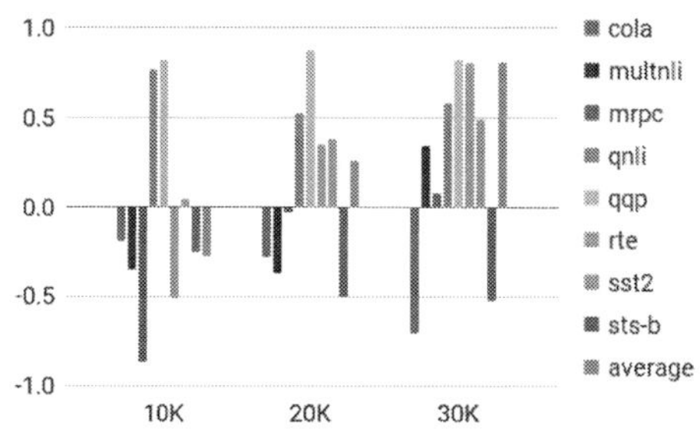


(b) Correlation between similarity (VOR) and performance (positive correlation is better)

Figure 3: (**top**) Similarity (VOR) between pretraining corpora and downstream datasets (train). (**bottom**) Pearson's correlation analysis (similarity and performance).

datasets to examine whether a more complex corpus provides greater alignment with the downstream data. Figure 3a shows that `wikibooks` is more similar to all the downstream datasets in comparison to the other corpora, aligning with the intuition that a corpus with richer vocabulary subsequently has increased similarity with downstream data. As a further analysis, Figure 3b shows a moderate to high correlation between the similarity of the corpus to downstream datasets and the corresponding performance across most datasets, which strengthens as training progress. Similar trends hold for JSD (included in Appendix A). These findings indicate that pretraining using a corpus that is similar to the downstream datasets is generally beneficial, and VOR provides a computationally simple way of estimating this similarity.

***Analyzing complexity, similarity, and performance.*** Figure 4 presents Kendall's Tau correlation analysis for all three factors: complexity, similarity, and performance. In looking at the last row in particular (i.e., performance of the '30K' model) we observe that performance is strongly correlated with VOR, which in turn is strongly correlated with

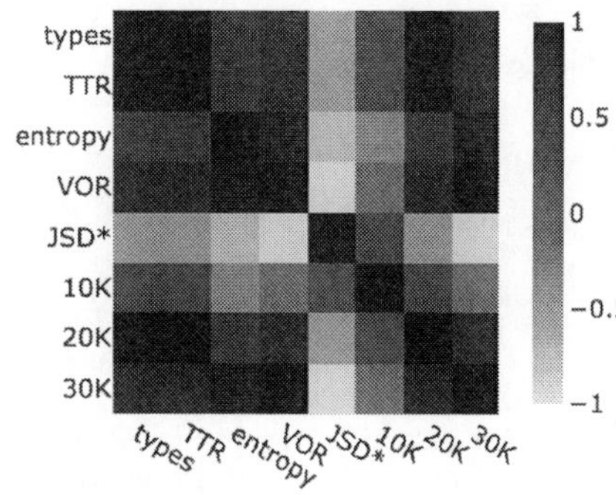


Figure 4: Kendall's Tau analysis comparing performance, complexity, and similarity. Darker shades indicate better correlation except for JSD, where a lighter shade (negative correlation) is desirable.

metrics of complexity (types, TTR, and entropy). Taken together, these results suggest that a more complex corpus leads to better downstream evaluation performance.

## 5 Conclusions

We investigate whether pretraining on a corpus with higher complexity subsequently yields improved performance in downstream evaluations. Within this study, we construct corpora of diverse complexities by using straightforward metrics like Flesch reading ease, and estimate corpus-level complexity using metrics such as unique word types, type-token ratio, or unigram entropy. The results of our extensive empirical analysis, which involves training language models from scratch using five distinct corpora of varying text complexity and evaluating their performance across eight downstream tasks, suggest a strong correlation between corpus complexity, its similarity to downstream data, and the resulting performance on these tasks. One interesting direction for future research involves exploring the findings of this study in the context of generative language models.

## Limitations

One limitation of our study is that, due to computational constraints, we use what are now considered as relatively "small-sized" models and corpora, exclusively focusing on the English language and generic domains such as Wikipedia articles and books. The generalizability of our findings to larger corpora, other languages, or specific domains such as medical texts warrants further investigation.

## Acknowledgments

We thank the anonymous reviewers for their insightful comments. This work was partially supported by NSF grants 2246174 and 1910655.

## References

Ameeta Agrawal, Suresh Singh, Lauren Schneider, and Michael Samuels. 2021. On the role of corpus ordering in language modeling. In *Proceedings of the Second Workshop on Simple and Efficient Natural Language Processing*, pages 142–154.

Nastaran Babanejad, Heidar Davoudi, Ameeta Agrawal, Aijun An, and Manos Papagelis. 2023. The role of preprocessing for word representation learning in affective tasks. *IEEE Transactions on Affective Computing*, pages 1–18.

Iz Beltagy, Kyle Lo, and Arman Cohan. 2019. Scibert: A pretrained language model for scientific text. *arXiv preprint arXiv:1903.10676*.

Christian Bentz, Dimitrios Alikaniotis, Michael Cysouw, and Ramon Ferrer-i Cancho. 2017. The entropy of words—learnability and expressivity across more than 1000 languages. *Entropy*, 19(6):275.

Sebastian Borgeaud, Arthur Mensch, Jordan Hoffmann, Trevor Cai, Eliza Rutherford, Katie Millican, George van den Driessche, Jean-Baptiste Lespiau, Bogdan Damoc, Aidan Clark, et al. 2021. Improving language models by retrieving from trillions of tokens. *arXiv preprint arXiv:2112.04426*.

Tom Brown, Benjamin Mann, Nick Ryder, Melanie Subbiah, Jared D Kaplan, Prafulla Dhariwal, Arvind Neelakantan, Pranav Shyam, Girish Sastry, Amanda Askell, et al. 2020. Language models are few-shot learners. *Advances in neural information processing systems*, 33:1877–1901.

Xiang Dai, Sarvnaz Karimi, Ben Hachey, and Cecile Paris. 2019. Using similarity measures to select pretraining data for NER. *arXiv preprint arXiv:1904.00585*.

Xiang Dai, Sarvnaz Karimi, Ben Hachey, and Cecile Paris. 2020. Cost-effective selection of pretraining data: A case study of pretraining bert on social media. *arXiv preprint arXiv:2010.01150*.

Jacob Devlin, Ming-Wei Chang, Kenton Lee, and Kristina Toutanova. 2019. BERT: Pre-training of deep bidirectional transformers for language understanding. In *Proceedings of the 2019 Conference of the North American Chapter of the Association for Computational Linguistics: Human Language Technologies, Volume 1 (Long and Short Papers)*, pages 4171–4186, Minneapolis, Minnesota. Association for Computational Linguistics.

Robert M Fano. 1961. Transmission of information: A statistical theory of communications. *American Journal of Physics*, 29(11):793–794.

Rudolph Flesch. 1948. A new readability yardstick. *Journal of applied psychology*, 32(3):221.

Edouard Grave, Piotr Bojanowski, Prakhar Gupta, Armand Joulin, and Tomas Mikolov. 2018. Learning word vectors for 157 languages. *arXiv preprint arXiv:1802.06893*.

Suchin Gururangan, Ana Marasović, Swabha Swayamdipta, Kyle Lo, Iz Beltagy, Doug Downey, and Noah A Smith. 2020. Don't stop pretraining: adapt language models to domains and tasks. *arXiv preprint arXiv:2004.10964*.

Kristian TH Jensen. 2009. Indicators of text complexity. *Mees, IM; F. Alves & S. Göpferich (eds.)*, pages 61–80.

Victoria Johansson. 2008. Lexical diversity and lexical density in speech and writing: A developmental perspective. *Working papers/Lund University, Department of Linguistics and Phonetics*, 53:61–79.

Wendell Johnson. 1944. Studies in language behavior: A program of research. *Psychological Monographs*, 56(2):1–15.

Jared Kaplan, Sam McCandlish, Tom Henighan, Tom B Brown, Benjamin Chess, Rewon Child, Scott Gray, Alec Radford, Jeffrey Wu, and Dario Amodei. 2020. Scaling laws for neural language models. *arXiv preprint arXiv:2001.08361*.

Urvashi Khandelwal, Omer Levy, Dan Jurafsky, Luke Zettlemoyer, and Mike Lewis. 2019. Generalization through memorization: Nearest neighbor language models. *arXiv preprint arXiv:1911.00172*.

Julia Kreutzer, Isaac Caswell, Lisa Wang, Ahsan Wahab, Daan van Esch, Nasanbayar Ulzii-Orshikh, Allahsera Tapo, Nishant Subramani, Artem Sokolov, Claytone Sikasote, et al. 2022. Quality at a glance: An audit of web-crawled multilingual datasets. *Transactions of the Association for Computational Linguistics*, 10:50–72.

Lukas Lange, Jannik Strötgen, Heike Adel, and Dietrich Klakow. 2021. To share or not to share: Predicting sets of sources for model transfer learning. *arXiv preprint arXiv:2104.08078*.

Jinhyuk Lee, Wonjin Yoon, Sungdong Kim, Donghyeon Kim, Sunkyu Kim, Chan Ho So, and Jaewoo Kang. 2020. Biobert: a pre-trained biomedical language representation model for biomedical text mining. *Bioinformatics*, 36(4):1234–1240.

Conglong Li, Minjia Zhang, and Yuxiong He. 2021. Curriculum learning: A regularization method for efficient and stable billion-scale gpt model pre-training. *arXiv preprint arXiv:2108.06084*.

Jianhua Lin. 1991. Divergence measures based on the shannon entropy. *IEEE Transactions on Information theory*, 37(1):145–151.

Louis Martin, Benjamin Muller, Pedro Javier Ortiz Suárez, Yoann Dupont, Laurent Romary, Éric Villemonte de La Clergerie, Djamé Seddah, and Benoît Sagot. 2019. Camembert: a tasty french language model. *arXiv preprint arXiv:1911.03894*.

Stephen Merity, Caiming Xiong, James Bradbury, and Richard Socher. 2016. Pointer sentinel mixture models. *arXiv preprint arXiv:1609.07843*.

Koichi Nagatsuka, Clifford Broni-Bediako, and Masayasu Atsumi. 2021. Pre-training a bert with curriculum learning by increasing block-size of input text. In *Proceedings of the International Conference on Recent Advances in Natural Language Processing (RANLP 2021)*, pages 989–996.

Jack W Rae, Sebastian Borgeaud, Trevor Cai, Katie Millican, Jordan Hoffmann, Francis Song, John Aslanides, Sarah Henderson, Roman Ring, Susannah Young, et al. 2021. Scaling language models: Methods, analysis & insights from training gopher. *arXiv preprint arXiv:2112.11446*.

Colin Raffel, Noam Shazeer, Adam Roberts, Katherine Lee, Sharan Narang, Michael Matena, Yanqi Zhou, Wei Li, and Peter J Liu. 2019. Exploring the limits of transfer learning with a unified text-to-text transformer. *arXiv preprint arXiv:1910.10683*.

Sebastian Ruder and Barbara Plank. 2017. Learning to select data for transfer learning with Bayesian optimization. In *Proceedings of the 2017 Conference on Empirical Methods in Natural Language Processing*, pages 372–382, Copenhagen, Denmark. Association for Computational Linguistics.

Claude Elwood Shannon. 1948. A mathematical theory of communication. *The Bell system technical journal*, 27(3):379–423.

Seongjin Shin, Sang-Woo Lee, Hwijeen Ahn, Sungdong Kim, HyoungSeok Kim, Boseop Kim, Kyunghyun Cho, Gichang Lee, Woomyoung Park, Jung-Woo Ha, et al. 2022. On the effect of pretraining corpora on in-context learning by a large-scale language model. *arXiv preprint arXiv:2204.13509*.

Alex Wang, Amanpreet Singh, Julian Michael, Felix Hill, Omer Levy, and Samuel R Bowman. 2018. Glue: A multi-task benchmark and analysis platform for natural language understanding. *arXiv preprint arXiv:1804.07461*.

Yile Wang, Yue Zhang, Peng Li, and Yang Liu. 2023. Language model pre-training with linguistically motivated curriculum learning.

Thomas Wolf, Lysandre Debut, Victor Sanh, Julien Chaumond, Clement Delangue, Anthony Moi, Pierric Cistac, Tim Rault, Rémi Louf, Morgan Funtowicz, et al. 2019. Huggingface's transformers: State-of-the-art natural language processing. *arXiv preprint arXiv:1910.03771*.

Yukun Zhu, Ryan Kiros, Rich Zemel, Ruslan Salakhutdinov, Raquel Urtasun, Antonio Torralba, and Sanja Fidler. 2015. Aligning books and movies: Towards story-like visual explanations by watching movies and reading books. In *Proceedings of the IEEE international conference on computer vision*, pages 19–27.

## A Similarity Analysis

Figure 5 presents the results of similarity analysis and Pearson's correlation analysis using Jensen-Shannon divergence.

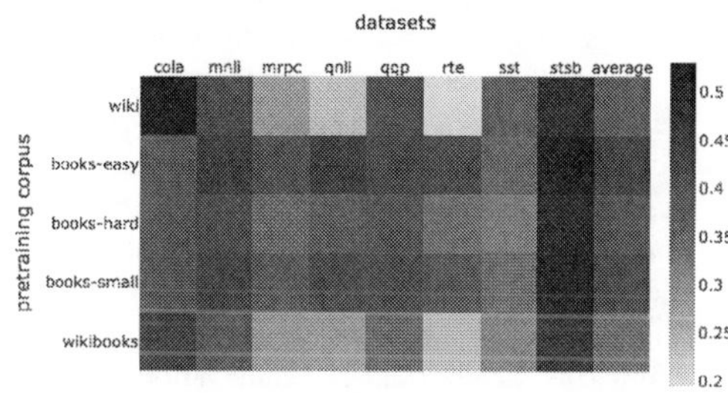


(a) JSD (lighter shades indicate higher similarity)

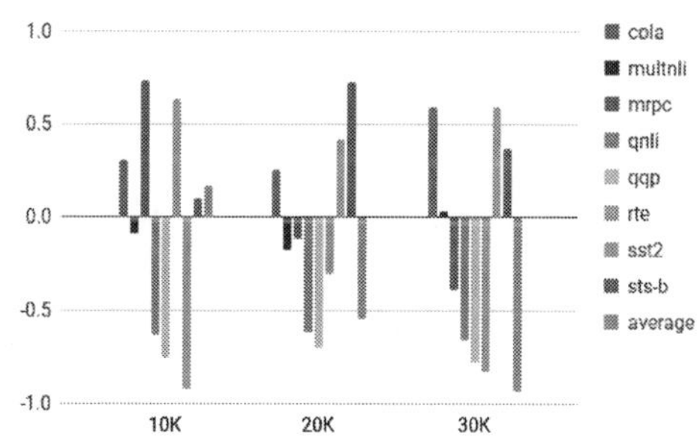


(b) JSD (negative correlation is better)

Figure 5: (**top**) Similarity between pretraining corpora and downstream datasets (train set) using JSD. The last column 'average' presents the average results of all the datasets. (**bottom**) Pearson's correlation analysis between JSD and performance at 10K, 20K, and 30K step checkpoints.

# PersonaPKT: Building Personalized Dialogue Agents via Parameter-efficient Knowledge Transfer

**Xu Han**[1], **Bin Guo**[2], **Yoon Jung**[2], **Benjamin Yao**[2], **Yu Zhang**[2], **Xiaohu Liu**[2] and **Chenlei Guo**[2]

[1]University of Colorado Boulder
[2]Amazon Alexa
xuha2442@colorado.edu, {guobg, yoonjun, benjamy, yzzhan, derecliu, guochenl}@amazon.com

## Abstract

Personalized dialogue agents (DAs) powered by large pre-trained language models (PLMs) often rely on explicit persona descriptions to maintain personality consistency. However, such descriptions may not always be available or may pose privacy concerns. To tackle this bottleneck, we introduce PersonaPKT, a lightweight transfer learning approach that can build persona-consistent dialogue models without explicit persona descriptions. By representing each persona as a continuous vector, PersonaPKT learns implicit persona-specific features directly from a small number of dialogue samples produced by the same persona, adding less than 0.1% trainable parameters for each persona on top of the PLM backbone. Empirical results demonstrate that PersonaPKT effectively builds personalized DAs with high storage efficiency, outperforming various baselines in terms of persona consistency while maintaining good response generation quality. In addition, it enhances privacy protection by avoiding explicit persona descriptions. Overall, PersonaPKT is an effective solution for creating personalized DAs that respect user privacy.

## 1 Introduction

Recent advances in large-scale pre-trained language models (PLMs) greatly boost the performance of chit-chat dialogue agents (DAs) in generating understandable and fluent responses. However, a PLM-powered DA can potentially suffer from the lack of a consistent personality (Zhang et al., 2018; Li et al., 2016; Lian et al., 2022) since it is typically trained on dialogues collected from many different personas (i.e., *persona cross-contamination*). To address the issue, many approaches have been proposed to build more persona-consistent models by conditioning on explicit persona descriptions (Zhang et al., 2018; Wolf et al., 2019). These descriptions can steer the response generation and are usually presented in the form of several sentences like "*I love the beach.*", "*I am on a diet now.*". However, such explicit persona statements are rarely available in practice: They require hand-crafted feature designs (Madotto et al., 2019) and are intractable to be directly extracted from real-world conversations or speakers (Zhang et al., 2018; Madotto et al., 2019; Lee et al., 2021a). Moreover, explicit persona statements may contain sensitive user information, thereby raising privacy concerns.

In light of this, we introduce PersonaPKT: **Persona**-based **P**arameter-efficient **K**nowledge **T**ransfer, a lightweight transfer learning approach to build persona-consistent dialogue models without explicit persona descriptions. Inspired by the recent success in lightweight PLM-tuning approaches such as prefix-tuning (Li and Liang, 2021) and prompt-tuning (Lester et al., 2021), each persona is represented as a continuous vector (i.e., a *personalized prefix*) in PersonaPKT, adding less than 0.1% trainable parameters compared to a full PLM. PersonaPKT then prepends these personalized prefixes to the PLM with frozen weights to steer the response generation. Instead of utilizing explicit persona descriptions, each personalized prefix learns ***implicit*** persona-specific features directly from a small number of dialogues produced by the same persona (i.e., low data scenarios). To further improve the response generation quality under such low data scenarios, PersonaPKT first trains one *source prefix* over multiple personas' data agnostically, then uses the *source prefix* to initialize the training of the *personalized prefix* for a target persona (as in Fig 1). Through such initialization, PersonaPKT is able to transfer the knowledge learned from various personas to the target *personalized prefix* training, preventing a significant drop in generation quality due to limited personalized training data (Madotto et al., 2019). Empirical results show that PersonaPKT is able to build personalized dialogue models with high storage efficiency, out-



*Proceedings of The Fourth Workshop on Simple and Efficient Natural Language Processing (SustaiNLP)*, pages 264–273
July 13, 2023 ©2023 Association for Computational Linguistics

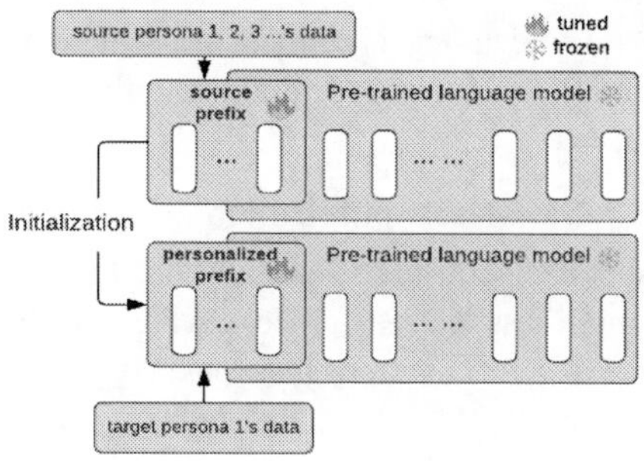


Figure 1: An overview of PersonaPKT.

performing various baselines in terms of persona consistency while maintaining good response generation quality. In addition, it enhances privacy protection by avoiding explicit persona descriptions.

In practice, PersonaPKT is advantageous in its modularity and extendability. PersonaPKT maintains a separate *personalized prefix* for each persona, making it easily scalable to batch process multiple users while ensuring privacy protection and eliminating the risk of cross-contamination among users' data. Additionally, PersonaPKT's two-stage transfer learning process allows the *source prefix* to be further optimized via different training strategies based on practical needs, showing its great extendability. In this work, we experimented with both data-level (temperature-scaled mixing) and model-level (meta-learning) optimization algorithms to train the *source prefix* to demonstrate the effectiveness of PersonaPKT. To the best of our knowledge, our work is the first on building personalized dialogue models via parameter-efficient knowledge transfer. As a result, our work makes three unique contributions:

- We introduce PersonaPKT, a lightweight transfer learning approach to build personalized dialogue models that respect user privacy.
- We show the great potential of PersonaPKT by further optimizing it via data-level and model-level optimization algorithms.
- We conduct large-scale empirical experiments to show that PersonaPKT builds better personalized dialogue models in terms of both persona consistency and storage efficiency while maintaining good response generation quality.

## 2 Related Work

### 2.1 Personalized Dialogue Generation

Previous studies have shown that when explicit persona descriptions are available, they can be encoded into memory networks (e.g., Zhang et al., 2018) or appended to dialogue histories to generate persona-consistent responses (e.g., Wolf et al., 2019). However, the utilization of explicit persona descriptions raises privacy concerns as it may require access to personal information. To address this issue, Madotto et al. (2019) introduced a persona-agnostic meta-learning (PAML) algorithm that enables the learning of persona-specific dialogue generation models without the need for explicit persona descriptions. Subsequently, several studies have explored this direction using various methodologies (Lee et al., 2021b; Yao et al., 2021; Wu et al., 2021). For example, Lee et al. (2021b) trained persona-specific models via multitask meta-learning without any explicit persona descriptions. While the PAML algorithm and its follow-up work demonstrate the feasibility of training persona-consistent dialogue agents without explicit persona description, they still require modifying the entire language model parameters and storing a full copy of the pre-trained model for each persona. To address this limitation, our approach here provides a more storage-efficient solution for creating effective personalized DAs without the need for explicit persona descriptions.

### 2.2 Parameter-Efficient Knowledge Transfer

Instead of modifying all the language model parameters, efficient tuning approaches such as prompt-tuning (Lester et al., 2021) and prefix-tuning (Li and Liang, 2021) optimize a small number of trainable parameters (i.e., prompts/prefixes) for higher flexibility and storage efficiency. However, these parameter-efficient tuning methods occasionally suffer from low training efficiency (e.g., slower convergence rate (Su et al., 2022; Xie et al., 2022)) and limited model performance compared to full fine-tuning settings (Xie et al., 2022; Li and Liang, 2021). To tackle these issues, many studies have explored the extent to which these parameter-efficient approaches can perform knowledge transfer. Vu et al. (2022) pointed out that prompts/prefixes learned from one or more source tasks were transferrable and could be used to initialize the prompt/prefix for a target task. Su et al. (2022) further validated such findings and claimed that knowledge transfer can accelerate parameter-efficient tuning methods and improve their performance. In this work, we adapt parameter-efficient knowledge transfer to personalized dialogue modeling, which to our knowledge is the first attempt in this area.

## 3 Methodology

### 3.1 PersonaPKT

An overview of PersonaPKT is shown in Fig 1. Building on the parameter-efficient tuning approach (e.g., prefix-tuning [1] (Li and Liang, 2021)) which learns task-specific continuous vectors to condition a frozen pre-trained model, PersonaPKT considers learning different personas as different tasks. Specifically, PersonaPKT adds a trainable persona-specific vector $p_\theta$ for each persona, which we call a *personalized prefix*, depicted by orange blocks in Fig 1. The *personalized prefix* is prepended to the task input and the backbone PLM can attend to it as if it were a sequence of "virtual tokens". During training, PersonaPKT only optimizes the personalized prefix while the backbone PLM remains frozen.

In PersonaPKT, a *personalized prefix* is trained on each persona's dialogue data only. The limited dialogue data per persona will result in a low-data resource scenario, potentially leading to a significant performance drop in terms of dialogue generation quality. In light of this, PersonaPKT is novel in introducing *source prefix* tuning, an extra training stage before *personalized prefix* tuning (Fig 1). It first trains one *source prefix* over multiple personas' data agnostically and then uses the *source prefix* to initialize the training of the *personalized prefix* for a target persona. Via such a two-stage transfer learning process, PersonaPKT is able to transfer the knowledge learned from various personas to the target prefix training, preventing the generation quality from dramatically dropping due to limited training data per persona.

### 3.2 Optimizing the Training of *Source Prefix*

PeronsaPKT's two-stage learning process allows the *source prefix* to be further optimized via different training strategies. To validate and fully leverage the benefits of its two-stage learning process, we explored two specific optimization algorithms in terms of data-level (temperature-scaled mixing) and model-level (meta-learning), to train the *source prefix*.

#### 3.2.1 Data-level optimization

PersonaPKT considers learning the *source prefix* as a multi-task learning process, which involves dialogue data from various personas. As pointed out by previous studies (Arivazhagan et al., 2019), it is important for multi-task learning to properly mix the data from each task the model should be trained on. We thus utilized temperature-scaled mixing, a common data mixing approach used by multilingual BERT (Devlin et al., 2018) and T5 (Raffel et al., 2020), ensuring that the *source prefix* was sufficiently trained on low-resource personas. We implemented temperature scaling with a temperature $T$, where the mixing rate of each persona's data is raised to the power of $\frac{1}{T}$ and then re-normalized so that they sum to 1.

#### 3.2.2 Model-level optimization

Madotto et al. (2019) proposed a PAML algorithm to learn personalized DA models without any explicit persona descriptions. Inspired by PAML, we employed meta-learning algorithms to further optimize the training of *source prefix*. Specifically, we adapted Reptile (Nichol and Schulman, 2018), a widely-used meta-learning algorithm, into our parameter-efficient-tuning-based setting. The adapted algorithm, which we refer to as **P**arameter-efficient **P**ersona-agnostic **Reptile** (PPReptile), is described in Algorithm 1. We further present algorithm details as follows.

We define the persona dataset as $\mathcal{D} = \{P_1, P_2, ..., P_z\}$, where $z$ is the number of personas in $\mathcal{D}$. $\mathcal{D}$ is further split into $\mathcal{D}_{train}$, $\mathcal{D}_{valid}$, $\mathcal{D}_{test}$. PPReptile first randomly samples $n$ personas $\rho_1, \rho_2, ..., \rho_n$ from $\mathcal{D}_{train}$. With pre-trained parameters $\theta_{pretrain}$ and randomly initialized weights $\theta_{prefix}$, PPReptile then updates the dialogue model $f_{\theta=\theta_{pretrain} \cup \theta_{prefix}}$ with

$$\theta_{prefix} \leftarrow \theta_{prefix} + \beta \frac{1}{n} \sum_{i=1}^{n} (W_i - \theta_{prefix}) \quad (1)$$

, where the gradient $W_i$

$$W_i = SGD(\mathcal{L}_{\rho_i}, \theta_{prefix}, \alpha, k) \quad (2)$$

. Here, $\beta$ in Equation 1, $\alpha$ in Equation 2 denotes the inner and outer learning rate respectively. $k$ in Equation 2 denotes $k$ steps of SGD

[1] In our study, we utilized prefix-tuning. However, PersonaPKT can be adapted to any of the parameter-efficient tuning approaches, such as prompt-tuning.

on $\rho_i$. $\mathcal{L}_{\rho_i}$ is from $L = \{\mathcal{L}_1, \mathcal{L}_1, ..., \mathcal{L}_z,\}$, which is the set of loss functions corresponding to all $\rho_i$ in $\rho_1, \rho_2, ..., \rho_n$. Specifically, we use the cross-entropy loss for our response generation task.

The main difference between PPReptile and vanilla Reptile is that PPReptile updates prefix parameters only, even though the gradient computation still relies on both pre-trained and prefix parameters.

**Algorithm 1** Parameter-efficient Persona-agnostic Reptile

**Require:** model $f_{\theta=\theta_{pretrain} \cup \theta_{prefix}}$
$\mathcal{D}_{train} = \{\rho_1, \rho_2, ..., \rho_z\}$
$\alpha$, $\beta$: learning rates
$L = \{\mathcal{L}_1, \mathcal{L}_1, ..., \mathcal{L}_z,\}$: set of loss functions corresponding to all potential personas
$k$: inner step number
$n$: persona batch size

**for** *iteration* **in** [1, 2, ...] **do**
  Sample $n$ personas $\rho_{\{1,2,...,n\}} \sim \mathcal{D}_{train}$ ,
  **for** *i* **in** [1,2,...,$n$] **do**
    $W_i = SGD(\mathcal{L}_{\rho_i}, \theta_{prefix}, \alpha, k)$
  **end for**
  $\theta_{prefix} \leftarrow \theta_{prefix} + \beta \frac{1}{n} \sum_{i=1}^{n} (W_i - \theta_{prefix})$
**end for**

# 4 Experiment and Results

## 4.1 The task of personalized dialogue generation

The task of personalized dialogue generation aims to build dialogue models that are able to generate personalized utterances as response to the input utterance in the context of given dialogue histories. The generated response is expected to not only have good generation quality but also contain information that is consistent with the desired personas. Desired personas are usually provided in the form of several sentences as described in Section 1. In our study, we explore building dialogue models with PersonaPKT for both regular and few-shot personas (i.e., personas with less than 6 dialogues, more details in section 4.2.1).

## 4.2 Experiment setup

### 4.2.1 Dataset

Our experiments are conducted using PERSONA-CHAT (Zhang et al., 2018), a widely-used conversational dataset that contains persona-based dialogues. Following Madotto et al. (2019), we first match all dialogues in PERSONA-CHAT by their persona descriptions. After examining the distribution of the number of dialogues per persona (Fig 3 in Appendix A.1), we define a few-shot persona if the number of dialogues of that persona is smaller than 6. We had 239 few-shot personas and 1054 regular personas in total. We then randomly set aside 300 regular personas. The remaining 754 regular personas are used as the dataset for the *source prefix* training (**Part A**). The 300 regular personas (**Part B**) and 239 few-shot personas (**Part C**) are used to train target *personalized prefixes*. There were no overlapped personas among Part A, Part B, and Part C. Within each persona, train, valid and test set are randomly created by dialogue numbers following the ratio of 8:1:1. Table 1 are the basic statistics of our newly-split dataset.

Table 1: Statistics of dataset

| | # of personas | Number of dialogues | | |
|---|---|---|---|---|
| | | Train | Validation | Test |
| Part A[1] | 754 | 5471 | 774 | 774 |
| Part B[2] | 300 | 2166 | 304 | 304 |
| Part C[3] | 239 | 538 | 239 | 239 |

[1] Part A: for *source prefix* training
[2] Part B: for *personalized prefixes* training with regular personas
[3] Part C: for *personalized prefixes* training with few-shot personas

### 4.2.2 Evaluation Metrics

**Automated evaluation** We report F1 score of the generated responses against the human-generated target, which is the standard metric used for PERSONA-CHAT. F1 score can reflect the response quality (Madotto et al., 2019). For persona consistency, we report a widely used consistency metric called $C$ score, which was defined by Madotto et al. (2019). They first trained a BERT-based Natural Language Inference (NLI) model to automatically generate NLI annotation between persona descriptions $p_j$ and dialogue utterances $u$ (as Formula (3)).

$$NLI(u, p_j) = \begin{cases} 1 & \text{if } u \text{ entails } p_j \\ 0 & \text{if } u \text{ is independent to } p_j \\ -1 & \text{if } u \text{ contradicts } p_j \end{cases} \tag{3}$$

. Based on $NLI(u, p_j)$, the persona consistency score $C$ is then defined as below.

$$C(u) = \sum_{j}^{m} NLI(u, p_j) \tag{4}$$

. The BERT-based NLI model was trained on Dialog NLI (Welleck et al., 2019) dataset which achieved a test set accuracy of 88.43%. In Formula (4), $m$ is the number of sentences in the explicit persona descriptions. $C$ score is shown to be aligned with human-evaluated consistency (Madotto et al., 2019) and a higher $C$ score means having a more persona-consistent dialogue response. In addition, we report trainable parameter sizes to reflect the storage efficiency of each experiment setting.

**Human evaluation** We also conduct a human evaluation on 377 generated response examples from 50 randomly selected personas in Part B to complement the automatic evaluation results. In accordance with the guidelines provided by Madotto et al. (2019), we requested crowd-sourced workers to assess the fluency (response quality) and persona consistency of the generated response with respect to the dialogue histories and explicit persona descriptions. Specifically, the workers were instructed to rate the response fluency on a 5-point Likert scale ("1 (Not at all)" to "5 (To a great extent)"). For persona consistency, they were required to assign a score of -1, 0, or 1 for *contradicts*, *neutral*, or *consistent*, respectively. To ensure the annotation quality, we adopted the following strategies: (1) we only recruited crowd-sourced workers who had an approval rate greater than or equal to 99% while being located in the United States; (2) two additional annotators further validated the crowd-sourced annotations independently. Following their validation, they resolved any annotation conflicts through discussion or by taking the average score as the final decision.

#### 4.2.3 Implementation details

We implemented PersonaPKT using GPT2 [2] (Radford et al., 2019) as the backbone PLM, which has around 345M parameters. A persona-agnostic *source prefix* was first trained with Part A's data. Then we trained *personalized prefixes* for each persona on part B and C. In order to stabilize the training of prefixes, we followed Li and Liang (2021) and employed their parametrization strategy with $k = 512$ (the number of persona-specific parameters is less than 0.1% of the total GPT2 parameters with $k = 512$). When optimizing the training of the *source prefix*, we used $T = 10$ for temperature-scaled mixing. For meta-learning-based optimization, we used learning rates of $\alpha = 10^{-4}$, $\beta = 3 \times 10^{-5}$, and batch sizes of $b_{in} = 2$, $b_{out} = 4$ for the inner, outer loops, respectively. When training target *personalized prefixes*, we tuned batch size and learning rate with early stopping on each persona's validation set. During model training, we used the AdamW optimizer (Loshchilov and Hutter, 2019) and a linear learning rate scheduler for all the models. We also used beam search with a beam size of 5 when decoding.

[2]We only used GPT2 as a testbed to explore the effectiveness of PersonaPKT. PersonaPKT can be adapted to different PLM backbones.

### 4.3 Experiment Settings

We compare the following 8 training settings:

- **Persona + Fine-tuning**: A GPT2 model fine-tuned on Part A and evaluated on the test set of Part B and C. Explicit persona descriptions were appended to the input utterance during both training and inference. Although this setting utilized explicit persona descriptions, which is different from the underlying assumptions of PersonaPKT (i.e., without explicit persona descriptions), we still include this setting as a point of reference.

- **Fine-tuning**: Without any explicit persona descriptions as input, this setting fine-tuned a GPT2 model on Part A in a persona-agnostic manner and evaluated on the test set of Part B and C;

- **Persona_id + Fine-tuning**: A GPT2 model fine-tuned on Part A and evaluated on the test set of Part B and C. Same as Persona + Fine-tuning while only the persona id was appended to the input utterance instead of the explicit persona descriptions;

- **Reptile + Fine-tuning**: Multiple persona-specific GPT2 models fine-tuned for each persona respectively in Part B and C. Each persona-specific GPT2 model was trained on dialogues produced by that persona only. Each personalized GPT2 model was initialized using a GPT2 model, which was fine-tuned in a persona-agnostic manner on Part A with the Reptile algorithm;

- **Rand init + Prefix-tuning**: *Personalized prefixes* were trained for each persona respectively in Part B and C. Each *personalized prefix* was trained on dialogues produced by that persona only. Prefix weights were randomly initialized;

Table 2: Results of automatic evaluation. Significantly underperforming settings are highlighted with ✗.

| | | Automatic Metrics | | | | | | | | |
|---|---|---|---|---|---|---|---|---|---|---|
| | | 1-gram F1 ↑ | | 2-gram F1 ↑ | | LCS F1 ↑ [1] | | C Score ↑ | | Trainable |
| | | Part B [3] | Part C [4] | Part B | Part C | Part B | Part C | Part B | Part C | Parameter Size ↓ [2] |
| With descriptions | Persona + Fine-tuning [5] | **18.64** | **17.42** | **6.76** | 5.68 | **17.69** | **16.50** | 0.20 | 0.23 | 1 * 100% |
| Without descriptions | Fine-tuning | 18.16 | 17.18 | 6.27 | **5.86** | 17.30 | 16.22 | -0.0082 ✗ | 0.0076 ✗ | 1 * 100% |
| | Persona_id + Fine-tuning | 17.87 | 16.84 | 5.98 | 5.45 | 16.89 | 15.88 | 0.00 ✗ | 0.00 ✗ | 1 * 100% |
| | Reptile + Fine-tuning | 16.30 | 15.40 | 4.44 | 3.78 | 15.20 | 14.22 | 0.27 | 0.21 | (N+1) * 100% ✗ |
| | Rand init + Prefix-tuning | 9.36 ✗ | 8.12 ✗ | 1.34 ✗ | 1.21 ✗ | 6.74 ✗ | 4.98 ✗ | **0.28** | **0.26** | N * 0.1% |
| | PersonaPKT (base) | 16.35 | 14.91 | 4.77 | 3.96 | 15.39 | 13.89 | 0.14 | 0.11 | (N+1) * 0.1% |
| | PersonaPKT (temperature) | 16.40 | 16.38 | 4.53 | 4.66 | 15.41 | 15.15 | 0.15 | 0.12 | (N+1) * 0.1% |
| | PersonaPKT (PPReptile) | 16.25 | 15.30 | 4.69 | 3.64 | 15.17 | 14.01 | 0.21 | 0.16 | (N+1) * 0.1% |

[1] LCS F1 denotes the longest common subsequence F1;

[2] N in this column represents the number of personas;

[34] Part B for regular personas while part C for few-shot personas;

[5] The model is trained with explicit persona descriptions while other models not.

- **PersonaPKT (base)**: *Personalized prefixes* were trained for each persona respectively in Part B and C. Each *personalized prefix* was trained on dialogues produced by that persona only. Each personalized prefix was initialized using a *source prefix*, which was trained in a persona-agnostic manner on Part A;
- **PersonaPKT (temperature)**: *Personalized prefixes* were trained for each persona respectively in Part B and C. Each *personalized prefix* was trained on dialogues produced by that persona only. Each personalized prefix was initialized using a *source prefix*, which was trained in a persona-agnostic manner on Part A's data after temperature-scaled mixing;
- **PersonaPKT (PPReptile)**: *Personalized prefixes* were trained for each persona respectively in Part B and C. Each *personalized prefix* was trained on dialogues produced by that persona only. Each personalized prefix was initialized using a *source prefix*, which was trained in a persona-agnostic manner with PPReptile in Algorithm 1 using Part A's data.

### 4.4 Results

Automatic and human evaluation results are presented in Table 2 and Table 3, respectively. Overall, PersonaPKT outperforms various baselines in terms of persona consistency in both automatic and human evaluation metrics. When explicit persona descriptions are not available, PersonaPKT is capable of achieving significantly higher persona consistency compared to fine-tuning baselines in both

Table 3: Results of human evaluation. Significantly underperforming settings are highlighted with ✗.

| | | Human Metrics | |
|---|---|---|---|
| | | Fluency | Persona Consistency |
| With descriptions | Persona + Fine-tuning | 3.59 | 0.18 |
| Without descriptions | Fine-tuning | 3.68 | 0.00080 ✗ |
| | Persona_id + Fine-tuning | 3.69 | -0.024 ✗ |
| | Reptile + Fine-tuning | 3.62 | **0.22** |
| | Rand init + Prefix-tuning | 2.49 ✗ | 0.12 |
| | PersonaPKT (base) | **3.71** | 0.17 |
| | PersonaPKT (temperature) | 3.46 | 0.20 |
| | PersonaPKT (PPReptile) | 3.42 | 0.20 |

automatic and human evaluation metrics, regardless of the optimization strategies (**PersonaPKT** vs. **Fine-tuning**, **Persona_id+Fine-tuning**). Moreover, **PersonaPKT (PPReptile)** achieves even higher human-annotated persona consistency than the fine-tuning baseline in scenarios where explicit persona descriptions are available (**PersonaPKT** vs. **Persona+Fine-tuning**).

For response quality, the comparison between **PersonaPKT** and **Rand init + Prefix-tuning** further shows the effectiveness of using a *source prefix* to maintain good response generation quality. While PersonaPKT has lower F1 scores than other fine-tuning baselines, **PersonaPKT (base)** has achieved the highest human-annotated fluency compared to other baselines. This finding aligns with previous studies that indicate F1 measures are not highly correlated with human judgments (Madotto et al., 2019; Liu et al., 2016). For completeness, we show generated response examples from PersonaPKT and baseline models in Appendix A.2.

In addition, PersonaPKT finds a good trade-off between storage efficiency and model performance. Although PersonaPKT performs slightly worse than the **Reptile + Fine-tuning** baseline in terms of both automatic and human-annotated persona consistency, its storage efficiency is considerably higher, resulting in more practical utility. As shown in Table 2, all our findings in terms of the automatic metrics can be generalized to few-shot personas as well (Part C).

In conclusion, although PersonaPKT doesn't achieve the highest score in any of the evaluation metrics across the board except human-annotated fluency (Table 2, Table 3), it overcomes the limitations of all the baseline models, avoiding significantly poor performances in neither response quality, persona consistency nor storage-efficiency (significantly underperforming metrics under each setting were highlighted with ✗).

### 4.5 Ablation Study

In the ablation study, we further evaluate the impact of different PersonaPKT optimization approaches. Specifically, we study how fast the *source prefix* can be adapted to a certain persona when training *personalized prefix*. As shown in Fig 2, we compared **PersonaPKT (base)**, **PersonaPKT (temperature)** and **PersonaPKT (PPReptile)** in terms of their $C$ score with controlled numbers of epochs. The experiment was conducted on 100 randomly-selected personas from Part B.

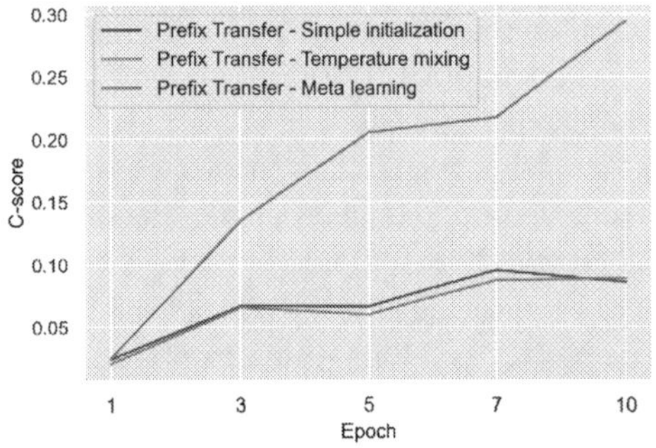


Figure 2: Ablation study results: how fast the *source prefix* can be adapted to a certain persona with different PersonaPKT optimization strategies.

As shown in Fig 2, **PersonaPKT (PPReptile)** has the best performance: it can achieve the highest $C$ score with the fewest training epochs, demonstrating the effectiveness of utilizing meta-learning to train the *source prefix*. In contrast, Table 2 and Table 3 reveal that **PersonaPKT (base)** and **PersonaPKT (temperature)** have better response quality than **PersonaPKT (PPReptile)**. These observations highlight the extendability of PersonaPKT's two-stage transfer training process, which enables the source prefix to be further optimized via various training strategies. Such extendability is valuable in practice as it indicates that engineers can choose or even propose customized optimization strategies to train the source prefix based on their specific needs. For example, if their products prioritize persona consistency over F1 score, PPReptile could be a suitable choice for optimization.

## 5 Limitations

### 5.1 Automatic metrics vs. Human annotation

**F1 vs. fluency.** As discussed in section 4.4, we have observed that the F1 score cannot be well-correlated with human annotations across almost all experiment settings. This is mostly due to the inflexibility of computing the F1 score sorely based on the similarity between the generated responses and golden references. Such observations echo findings from previous studies (Madotto et al., 2019; Liu et al., 2016; Deutsch et al., 2022). In this work, we still utilize F1 score since it's a standardized metric for PERSONA-CHAT evaluation. However, future work should aim to find a better evaluation metric that can more comprehensively reflect the quality of the generated responses.

**$C$ score vs. human-annotated consistency.** We observed a significant discrepancy between the $C$ score and human-annotated consistency under the setting of Rand init + Prefix-tuning. Upon further analysis, we discovered that many responses generated from this setting contain repeated sentences with persona-consistent keywords (e.g., as shown in Table 4, Rand init + Prefix-tuning repeated *"he is a preacher"* multiple times). While human annotators tend to ignore these repeated sentences, the $C$ score considers them as highly consistent. Our observations indicate that although the $C$ score has been shown to be a good indicator of persona consistency (Madotto et al., 2019), it is still limited under certain experiment settings like Rand init + Prefix-tuning. Similar to the F1 score, a better evaluation metric is needed in the future to more comprehensively reflect the persona consistency of generated responses.

### 5.2 Hyperparameter Selection

One limitation of PersonaPKT is its sensitivity to hyperparameters. Since PersonaPKT maintains persona-specific prefixes, this modularity of PersonaPKT allows flexibility in optimizing hyperparameters for each persona, such as learning rate, batch size, etc. Despite the advantage, our experiments show that the performance of PersonaPKT is more sensitive to hyperparameters compared to baseline models trained over multiple personas' data agnostically (Persona + Fine-tuning, Fine-tuning, Persona_id + Fine-tuning). At the same time, persona-specific baseline models trained on a small number of dialogues produced by a single persona (Reptile + Fine-tuning, Rand init + Prefix-tuning) demonstrate similarly high sensitivity to hyperparameters as PersonaPKT. Such observations indicate that this high sensitivity is a common issue in persona-specific models like PersonaPKT. Strategies for improving their robustness to hyperparameters can be a potential study area in the future.

## 6 Discussion

In practice, PersonaPKT is advantageous in its modularity and extendability. Due to its high storage efficiency, PersonaPKT is advantageous when there are a large number of user-specific models that need to be maintained independently. PersonaPKT offers not only scalability to batch process multiple users, but also enhances user privacy by avoiding cross-contamination between different users' data. Moreover, PersonaPKT's great extendability allows engineers to adopt various source prefix optimization strategies, parameter-efficient tuning approaches or even PLM backbones based on practical needs. Lastly, it enhances privacy protection by avoiding the use of explicit persona descriptions. All of these advantages of PersonaPKT make it a valuable contribution to personalized DA training in the industry.

## 7 Conclusion

We present PersonaPKT, a lightweight transfer learning approach for building persona-consistent dialogue models without the need for explicit persona descriptions. By representing each persona as a continuous vector, PersonaPKT learns implicit persona-specific features directly from dialogue samples produced by the same persona, with less than 0.1% trainable parameters added for each persona on top of the PLM backbone. Its two-stage learning process provides training flexibility, allowing for various optimization strategies to further enhance the training of the source prefix. PersonaPKT offers potential in terms of privacy protection and batch processing of multiple users. Future work will explore different optimization strategies and generalize PersonaPKT to additional applications.

## References


Naveen Arivazhagan, Ankur Bapna, Orhan Firat, Dmitry Lepikhin, Melvin Johnson, Maxim Krikun, Mia Xu Chen, Yuan Cao, George Foster, Colin Cherry, et al. 2019. Massively multilingual neural machine translation in the wild: Findings and challenges. *arXiv preprint arXiv:1907.05019*.

Daniel Deutsch, Rotem Dror, and Dan Roth. 2022. Re-examining system-level correlations of automatic summarization evaluation metrics. *arXiv preprint arXiv:2204.10216*.

Jacob Devlin, Ming-Wei Chang, Kenton Lee, and Kristina Toutanova. 2018. Bert: Pre-training of deep bidirectional transformers for language understanding. *arXiv preprint arXiv:1810.04805*.

Jing Yang Lee, Kong Aik Lee, and Woon Seng Gan. 2021a. Generating personalized dialogue via multi-task meta-learning. *arXiv preprint arXiv:2108.03377*.

Jing Yang Lee, Kong Aik Lee, and Woon Seng Gan. 2021b. Generating personalized dialogue via multi-task meta-learning. In *Proceedings of the 25th Workshop on the Semantics and Pragmatics of Dialogue - Full Papers*, Potsdam, Germany. SEMDIAL.

Brian Lester, Rami Al-Rfou, and Noah Constant. 2021. The power of scale for parameter-efficient prompt tuning. *arXiv preprint arXiv:2104.08691*.

Jiwei Li, Michel Galley, Chris Brockett, Georgios Spithourakis, Jianfeng Gao, and Bill Dolan. 2016. A persona-based neural conversation model. In *Proceedings of the 54th Annual Meeting of the Association for Computational Linguistics (Volume 1: Long Papers)*, pages 994–1003, Berlin, Germany. Association for Computational Linguistics.

Xiang Lisa Li and Percy Liang. 2021. Prefix-tuning: Optimizing continuous prompts for generation. In *Proceedings of the 59th Annual Meeting of the Association for Computational Linguistics and the 11th International Joint Conference on Natural Language Processing (Volume 1: Long Papers)*, pages 4582–4597, Online. Association for Computational Linguistics.

Ruixue Lian, Che-Wei Huang, Yuqing Tang, Qilong Gu, Chengyuan Ma, and Chenlei Guo. 2022. Incremental user embedding modeling for personalized text classification. In *ICASSP 2022-2022 IEEE International Conference on Acoustics, Speech and Signal Processing (ICASSP)*, pages 7832–7836. IEEE.

Chia-Wei Liu, Ryan Lowe, Iulian Serban, Mike Noseworthy, Laurent Charlin, and Joelle Pineau. 2016. How NOT to evaluate your dialogue system: An empirical study of unsupervised evaluation metrics for dialogue response generation. In *Proceedings of the 2016 Conference on Empirical Methods in Natural Language Processing*, pages 2122–2132, Austin, Texas. Association for Computational Linguistics.

Ilya Loshchilov and Frank Hutter. 2019. Decoupled weight decay regularization. In *International Conference on Learning Representations*.

Andrea Madotto, Zhaojiang Lin, Chien-Sheng Wu, and Pascale Fung. 2019. Personalizing dialogue agents via meta-learning. In *Proceedings of the 57th Annual Meeting of the Association for Computational Linguistics*, pages 5454–5459, Florence, Italy. Association for Computational Linguistics.

Alex Nichol and John Schulman. 2018. Reptile: a scalable metalearning algorithm. *arXiv preprint arXiv:1803.02999*, 2(3):4.

Alec Radford, Jeffrey Wu, Rewon Child, David Luan, Dario Amodei, Ilya Sutskever, et al. 2019. Language models are unsupervised multitask learners. *OpenAI blog*, 1(8):9.

Colin Raffel, Noam Shazeer, Adam Roberts, Katherine Lee, Sharan Narang, Michael Matena, Yanqi Zhou, Wei Li, Peter J Liu, et al. 2020. Exploring the limits of transfer learning with a unified text-to-text transformer. *J. Mach. Learn. Res.*, 21(140):1–67.

Yusheng Su, Xiaozhi Wang, Yujia Qin, Chi-Min Chan, Yankai Lin, Huadong Wang, Kaiyue Wen, Zhiyuan Liu, Peng Li, Juanzi Li, Lei Hou, Maosong Sun, and Jie Zhou. 2022. On transferability of prompt tuning for natural language processing. In *Proceedings of the 2022 Conference of the North American Chapter of the Association for Computational Linguistics: Human Language Technologies*, pages 3949–3969, Seattle, United States. Association for Computational Linguistics.

Tu Vu, Brian Lester, Noah Constant, Rami Al-Rfou', and Daniel Cer. 2022. SPoT: Better frozen model adaptation through soft prompt transfer. In *Proceedings of the 60th Annual Meeting of the Association for Computational Linguistics (Volume 1: Long Papers)*, pages 5039–5059, Dublin, Ireland. Association for Computational Linguistics.

Sean Welleck, Jason Weston, Arthur Szlam, and Kyunghyun Cho. 2019. Dialogue natural language inference. In *Proceedings of the 57th Annual Meeting of the Association for Computational Linguistics*, pages 3731–3741, Florence, Italy. Association for Computational Linguistics.

Thomas Wolf, Victor Sanh, Julien Chaumond, and Clement Delangue. 2019. Transfertransfo: A transfer learning approach for neural network based conversational agents. *CoRR*, abs/1901.08149.

Yuwei Wu, Xuezhe Ma, and Diyi Yang. 2021. Personalized response generation via generative split memory network. In *Proceedings of the 2021 Conference of the North American Chapter of the Association for Computational Linguistics: Human Language Technologies*, pages 1956–1970, Online. Association for Computational Linguistics.

Tianbao Xie, Chen Henry Wu, Peng Shi, Ruiqi Zhong, Torsten Scholak, Michihiro Yasunaga, Chien-Sheng Wu, Ming Zhong, Pengcheng Yin, Sida I Wang, et al. 2022. Unifiedskg: Unifying and multi-tasking structured knowledge grounding with text-to-text language models. *arXiv preprint arXiv:2201.05966*.

Huaxiu Yao, Long-Kai Huang, Linjun Zhang, Ying Wei, Li Tian, James Zou, Junzhou Huang, et al. 2021. Improving generalization in meta-learning via task augmentation. In *International Conference on Machine Learning*, pages 11887–11897. PMLR.

Saizheng Zhang, Emily Dinan, Jack Urbanek, Arthur Szlam, Douwe Kiela, and Jason Weston. 2018. Personalizing dialogue agents: I have a dog, do you have pets too? In *Proceedings of the 56th Annual Meeting of the Association for Computational Linguistics (Volume 1: Long Papers)*, pages 2204–2213, Melbourne, Australia. Association for Computational Linguistics.

## A Appendix

### A.1 Distribution of the number of dialogues per persona (Fig 3)

### A.2 Generated response examples (Table 4)

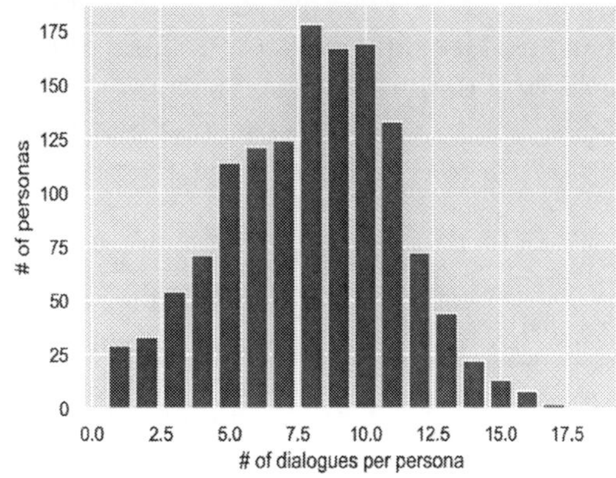


Figure 3: Distribution of the number of dialogues per persona in PERSONA-CHAT

Table 4: Generated examples

| **Persona** | |
|---|---|
| my favorite color is purple<br>i am a 1st grade teacher<br>i have a 3 year old<br>my father is a preacher<br>i go to church on sunday | |
| **Dialogue history** | |
| Speaker 1: well i do not have any kids yet just four cats .<br>Speaker 2: i would love to see a purple cat ! its my favorite color<br>Speaker 1: oh my favorite color is blue . any hobbies ? | |
| **Target utterance** | |
| Speaker 2: not really . i really love church though , maybe because my dad is a preacher . you ? | |
| **Generated Responses** | |
| Persona + Fine-tuning: | i like to go to church on sunday. |
| Fine-tuning: | i like to go to the beach. |
| Persona_id + Fine-tuning: | i like to play video games. |
| Reptile + Fine-tuning: | i run an tumblr blog dedicated to purple things it is my favorite color. |
| Rand init + Prefix-tuning: | with my dad. he is a preacher. i am a preacher. i am a preacher. i am a preacher... |
| PersonaPT (base): | i go to church every sunday at sunday |
| PersonaPT (temperature): | i do not have any hobbies, i am a teacher. how about you? |
| PersonaPT (PPReptile): | i do not have any hobbies at all. i am a teacher |

# Small Character Models Match Large Word Models for Autocomplete Under Memory Constraints

**Ganesh Jawahar♣,*, Subhabrata Mukherjee♠, Debadeepta Dey♠, Muhammad Abdul-Mageed♣◇, Laks V.S. Lakshmanan♣, Caio Cesar Teodoro Mendes♠, Gustavo Henrique de Rosa♠, Shital Shah♠**

♣University of British Columbia, ♠Microsoft ◇MBZUAI

ganeshjwhr@gmail.com, {laks,amuham01}@cs.ubc.ca,

{Subhabrata.Mukherjee,dedey,caiocesart,gderosa,shitals}@microsoft.com

## Abstract

Autocomplete is a task where the user inputs a piece of text, termed *prompt*, which is conditioned by the model to generate semantically coherent continuation. Existing works for this task have primarily focused on datasets (e.g., email, chat) with high frequency user prompt patterns (or *focused prompts*) where word-based language models have been quite effective. In this work, we study the more challenging setting consisting of low frequency user prompt patterns (or *broad prompts*, e.g., prompt about $93^{rd}$ `academy awards`) and demonstrate the effectiveness of *character-based* language models. We study this problem under memory-constrained settings (e.g., edge devices and smartphones), where character-based representation is effective in reducing the overall model size (in terms of parameters). We use WikiText-103 benchmark to simulate broad prompts and demonstrate that character models rival word models in exact match accuracy for the autocomplete task, when controlled for the model size. For instance, we show that a 20M parameter character model performs similar to an 80M parameter word model in the vanilla setting. We further propose novel methods to improve character models by incorporating inductive bias in the form of compositional information and representation transfer from large word models. Datasets and code used in this work are available at `https://github.com/UBC-NLP/char_autocomplete`.

## 1 Introduction

Autocomplete models are conditioned on user-written prompts or text to generate semantically coherent continuations. For example, given the user input "`Filmmaker George Lucas used Tikal as a` ___", a semantically coherent continuation can be "`filming location`" (Example 1). Autocomplete models can dramatically reduce keystrokes and improve user's productivity in a wide range of applications including email, chat and document authoring. Some typical challenges in building a real-time autocomplete model include: (i) processing arbitrary length user input (e.g., paragraphs), (ii) handling low frequency user prompt patterns (or *broad prompts* that typically cover wider vocabulary (as in Example 1), and (iii) satisfying memory constraints of the target device (such as cap on peak memory utilization).

Despite the importance of the task, there has been limited research on autocomplete. Existing works such as Smart Compose (Chen et al., 2019) and (Trajanovski et al., 2021) train autoregressive language models on emails and chats, where user prompt patterns tend to be high-frequency. That is, the prompts are *focused prompts*, e.g., a prompt about `office standups`, that typically cover narrower vocabulary. All these models are trained at word level, which leads to two issues: (i) input/output embedding parameters (less compressible component of the Transformer model (Shen et al., 2020)[1]) occupy a significant share (e.g., more than 77%) of the parameter budget due to the large vocabulary size and (ii) tendency to memorize high-frequency prompt patterns resulting in poor generalization on the low-frequency ones.

| n-gram | unigram | bigram | trigram |
|---|---|---|---|
| Wikitext-103 | 95.44 | 84.35 | 60.63 |
| Reddit | 86.41 | 77.04 | 54.36 |

Table 1: Percentage of unique out of vocabulary (OOV) n-grams in test set of WikiText-103 (broad prompts) vs. Reddit (focused prompts) datasets.

In this paper, we focus on the autocomplete task of broad prompts from domains such as Wikipedia, where user prompt patterns often have

*Part of work was done as an intern in Microsoft.

[1]Shen et al. (2020) study the effects of quantization on different components of Transformer model, on the performance in various NLP tasks. They find that the embedding layer is most sensitive to quantization than other components and requires more bits to keep performance loss acceptable.



*Proceedings of The Fourth Workshop on Simple and Efficient Natural Language Processing (SustaiNLP)*, pages 274–289
July 13, 2023 ©2023 Association for Computational Linguistics

low frequency (e.g., prompt about $93^{rd}$ academy awards). For instance, from Table 1, we observe that WikiText-103 (broad prompts) contains at least 10% more unique out of vocabulary (OOV) n-grams compared to the Reddit dataset (focused prompts). This makes our task more challenging than conventional settings considered in prior work which do one of the following: (i) adopt word-based models that are good at memorizing high-frequency patterns for *focused prompts* or (ii) rely on *conventional language modeling* which is not geared for generating precise and short horizon continuations (see Section 4).

Furthermore, we study this problem for practical applications under memory-constrained settings. Lower-end edge platforms (e.g., Raspberry Pi with 256MB of memory (Cai et al., 2020)) have memory constraints that are more limiting than latency constraints, for supporting various on-device models. Also, given that autoregressive language models are memory-bounded (Wang et al., 2021), we focus on improving the accuracy-memory trade-off for autocomplete task of broad prompts. Our work is complementary to existing works in model compression including those on pruning (Gordon et al., 2020), quantization (Han et al., 2016) and distillation (Sanh et al., 2019) that primarily focus on natural language understanding tasks (e.g., text classification). In contrast to these works, we study the effectiveness of character-based language models for a natural language generation task (e.g., autocomplete).

In this paper, we focus on two research questions. **RQ1**: How do character-based autocomplete models compare against word counterparts under memory constraints? **RQ2**: How to improve character-based autocomplete models with no negative impact on memory? We answer **RQ1** by showing that compared to word models, character models (i) contribute 96% fewer parameters in the embedding layer due to a much smaller vocabulary, (ii) work well on low-frequency (or broad) prompt patterns (e.g., 21% accuracy improvement by using 20M character model over 20M word model, see Figure 2 (a)) and (iii) result in high savings on peak memory utilization (e.g., 4.7% memory savings by using 20M character model over 20M word model, see Figure 2 (b)). When controlled for model size (number of parameters), we find that smaller character models (e.g., 20M parameters) perform similar to large word models (e.g., 80M parameters). We answer **RQ2** by developing novel methods to improve the accuracy of character models, which unlike previous work, have *minimal impact on memory usage*. These methods introduce inductive bias in the form of compositional information and representation transfer from large word models (best method). We show that the best method achieves 1.12% and 27.3% relative accuracy improvements over vanilla character and vanilla word models respectively with no impact on memory usage. We discuss the limitations of our work in Section 8 and defer the analysis of accuracy-latency trade-off to future work while focusing only on memory-constrained settings in this work.

Our major contributions are as follows: **(1)** To the best of our knowledge, this is the first study of the autocomplete task for broad prompts in a memory-constrained setting. **(2)** We perform an extensive comparison of character and word models across diverse architectures and demonstrate the advantage of character models over large word models for the autocomplete task on dimensions like peak memory utilization and model parameters. **(3)** We introduce novel methods leveraging inductive bias to further improve the accuracy of character models with minimal impact on memory usage.

## 2 Related Work

Our work leverages advances in neural language models, autocompletion, and efficient deep learning.

**Neural Language Models.** The autocomplete models we study in this work utilize Transformer-based (Vaswani et al., 2017) autoregressive neural language models as backbone. Compared to word models, character models lag behind in language modeling performance when controlled for model size (Al-Rfou et al., 2019; Choe et al., 2019) and have a high computational complexity due to long sequence length (Tay et al., 2022). In this work, we focus on deploying models on lower-end edge platforms (e.g., Raspberry Pi) where memory, as opposed to latency, is the major bottleneck.

**Autocomplete Task.** Despite the pervasiveness of autocomplete models, there is limited research in the academic community on the autocomplete task. Gmail Smart Compose (Chen et al., 2019) is a popular word-based autocomplete model for email suggestions. They find the encoder-decoder architecture to have a higher latency than the decoder-only architecture. They also find the Transformer architecture to be marginally better than the LSTM architecture (Hochreiter and Schmidhuber, 1997). Motivated by these findings, we employ a decoder-only, Transformer based architecture for building our autocomplete model. Trajanovski et al. (2021) leverage word-based autocomplete models for providing email and chat suggestions.

In this work, we focus on building autocomplete models for broad prompts from domains such as Wikipedia, where user prompt patterns can be quite low frequency (e.g., prompt about `Bruce Vilanch` (Oscars writer), with frequency of only 6 times). Unlike our prompt completion task, query autocompletion task is a well researched problem (Bar-Yossef and Kraus, 2011; Cai and de Rijke, 2016; Wang et al., 2020; Gog et al., 2020), where the goal is to complete the user's query, e.g., search query. Since user queries are generally short, query autocomplete models need not track long-range dependencies to understand the user's intent. In contrast, it is a *requirement* in our prompt completion setting, as the user prompt can be arbitrarily large, e.g., sentences or paragraphs.

ChatGPT (OpenAI, 2023b) and GPT-4 (OpenAI, 2023a) are recent dialogue models, which have garnered a great attention from the AI community for their ability to converse with human-like capabilities. The data used to train these models are not disclosed by the authors. As it is entirely possible for their training data to include the test sets we study in our work and train-test overlap analysis cannot be performed, we cannot make a fair comparison of our work with these 'closed' AI models (Rogers et al., 2023). Models such as Alpaca (Taori et al., 2023), Vicuna (Chiang et al., 2023), GPT-4-LLM (Peng et al., 2023) that claim to perform similarly as ChatGPT with few billion parameters are usually finetuned with outputs from ChatGPT or GPT-4. Hence, these models cannot be fairly compared with our work either.

**Efficient Deep Learning.** Exponential growth in the size of Transformer-based autoregressive language models (e.g., 175B (Brown et al., 2020)) has given rise to a strong need to make these models efficient so they can be used on commodity devices like laptop, tablet, and mobile, which have various resource constraints such as peak *memory* utilization and *latency*, while yielding the best performance under the constraints. To this end, there has been extensive research on building efficient Transformer models that are smaller, faster, and better, as summarized thoroughly by Tay et al. (2020) and Menghani (2021). Our work is focused on improving the efficiency of a natural language generation task (e.g., autocomplete), which has received less attention from an efficiency perspective. Wang et al. (2021) observe that 73% of the overall latency of autoregressive language models goes to memory intensive data movement operations (e.g., splitting heads, transpose, reshape) and conclude that these models are memory intensive. Since lower-end edge platforms have tighter memory constraints than latency constraints (Cai et al., 2020), *we focus on improving the accuracy-memory trade-off of autocomplete models.*

## 3 Autocomplete – Fundamentals

**Problem.** Given a text sequence $\mathbf{x} = (x_1, \ldots, x_{|\mathbf{x}|})$ (user input) with tokens from a fixed vocabulary $x_i \in \mathcal{V}$, the goal of the autocomplete task is to generate a completion $\hat{\mathbf{x}}_{k+1:N}$ such that the resulting sequence $(x_1, \ldots, x_k, \hat{x}_{k+1}, \ldots, \hat{x}_N)$ resembles a sample from $p_*$, where $p_*(\mathbf{x})$ denotes the reference distribution. $\mathbf{x}$ can be arbitrarily large (e.g., paragraphs), while $\hat{\mathbf{x}}_{k+1:N}$ is generally short (e.g., three words). Each token $x_k$ can be a word, character, or subword. The vocabulary $\mathcal{V}$ contains unique tokens from the dataset $\mathcal{D}$ consisting of a finite set of text sequences from $p_*$.

**Data.** Most datasets in the autocomplete literature come from domains with focused prompts (e.g., emails (Chen et al., 2019; Trajanovski et al., 2021), chat messages (Trajanovski et al., 2021)). In this work, we target the autocomplete task on datasets with broad prompts (e.g., Wikipedia) with a lot of low-frequency prompt patterns (e.g., the prompt `EACL 2023 conference`). Autocomplete models trained to answer broad prompts can be used to assist users in completing documents such as essay, report, letter, etc.

**Metrics.** The commonly used metric for evaluating the quality of an autocomplete model is ExactMatch@N (Rajpurkar et al., 2016) which measures the percentage of the first $N$ words in the predicted suggestion that exactly match the first $N$ words in the ground truth suggestion. ExactMatch@Overall (Chen et al., 2019) is a weighted average of the ExactMatch for all subsequence lengths up to $K$. For our setting, larger n-grams are increasingly difficult to predict for both word and character models as shown in Figure 3. Hence we set $K$ to 3. Since the exact match metric strictly looks for full match of the subsequence, it is a hard metric to improve on, especially for broad prompts. One can utilize a less stringent metric such as PartialMatch (Trajanovski et al., 2021). PartialMatch measures the percentage of characters in the first $N$ words in the predicted suggestion that exactly match those of the ground truth suggestion. However, PartialMatch might not adequately penalize for the grammatical incorrectness of the predicted suggestion. Trajanovski et al. (2021) also utilize metrics that require interactions from real users, which are difficult to acquire in practice. Given that the user-based metrics and PartialMatch metric have a strong correlation with ExactMatch in all the experiments carried out by Trajanovski et al. (2021), we use the exact match metric to quantify the performance of the autocomplete model in this work. We further perform human evaluation to compare the naturalness and user acceptability of the suggestions generated by different models.[2]

**Model.** We adopt the Transformer architecture, specifically Transformer-XL (Dai et al., 2019), for our autocomplete model. We choose Transformer-XL for the following two reasons: (i) as Dai et al. (2019) show, the model achieves strong results on word and character-based language modeling benchmarks and (ii) the model can handle long text sequences (e.g., 1600 word tokens or 3800 character tokens) which is crucial for treating arbitrarily long user inputs ($\mathbf{x}$).

**Training.** We train a decoder-only, Transformer-XL model that conditions on user input to generate the suggestion autoregressively. The parameters $\theta$ of the autocomplete model $p_\theta(\mathbf{x})$ can be optimized using the standard language modeling objective.

**Inference.** During inference, the model $p_\theta(\mathbf{x})$ takes the user input $\mathbf{x}_{1:k} \sim p_*$ and generates the suggestion $\hat{\mathbf{x}}_{k+1:N} \sim p_\theta(.|\mathbf{x}_{1:k})$ such that $(x_1, \ldots, x_k, \hat{x}_{k+1}, \ldots, \hat{x}_N)$ resembles a sample from $p_*$. In this work, we choose greedy search and select the token that receives the highest probability as the generated token; that is, $\hat{x}_t = \arg\max p_\theta(x_t|x_1, \ldots, x_{t-1})$. As shown in Appendix A.5 (see Figure 7), beam search performs poorly on our task and the trends we see in the next section do not depend on the choice of the decoding algorithm. For simplicity, we assume the autocomplete model generates exactly one suggestion $\hat{\mathbf{x}}_{k+1:N}$.

[2]For our final comparison, however, we report PartialMatch vs. ExactMatch (Table 2). We do not experiment with ranking metrics (e.g., mean reciprocal rank) since our autocomplete model produces just a single suggestion.

## 4 Character vs. Word Model

Existing autocomplete models are primarily word-based, i.e., the representation choice for $x_k$ is word. Word-based autocomplete models have the following properties: (i) they invest most of the parameters (e.g., more than 77%) from the overall parameter budget on the embedding layer, which is less likely compressible using standard techniques such as quantization (Shen et al., 2020) and (ii) they can memorize high-frequency prompt patterns and perform well on datasets with focused prompts (e.g., Reddit posts). *In this work, we focus on autocompletion on broad prompts and we aim to keep the parameter allocation to the embedding layer as small as possible thereby improving the overall memory footprint.* To this end, we choose *character* as the representation choice and study the memory-accuracy tradeoff of character based models on the autocomplete task for broad prompts. Character-based autocomplete models have several desirable properties compared to their word based counterpart, as they (i) invest far fewer parameters (e.g., less than 4%) of the parameter budget on the embedding layer and invest most parameters on other highly compressible Transformer components such as self-attention network, feedforward network, and softmax layer; (ii) perform well on datasets with broad prompts (as we will show); and (iii) provide a better tradeoff between accuracy and memory (model size and peak memory utilization). To demonstrate these properties, we perform extensive experiments on the WikiText-103 benchmark (Merity et al., 2017) (unless stated otherwise). This benchmark contains about 100M tokens from Wikipedia to simulate broad prompts. Since we focus on improving the memory footprint of autocomplete models, we do not experiment with subword models, which introduce a large number of token embeddings in the embedding layer (e.g., 50K), compared to their character based counterpart. In other words, we focus only on character models that keep the parameter allocation to the embedding layer as small as possible thereby improving the overall memory footprint.

**Component-Wise Parameter Breakdown.** Transformer-XL model can be broken down into four components: (i) adaptive embedding

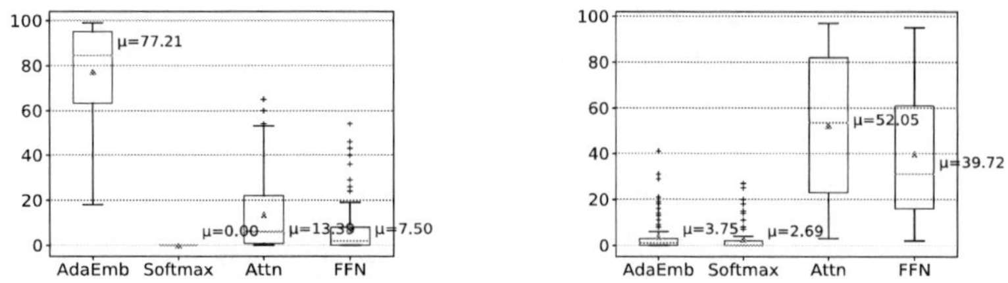


(a) Word (b) Character

Figure 1: Percentage of parameters allocated to a given component w.r.t. different components in Transformer-XL model aggregated across 100 random architectures.

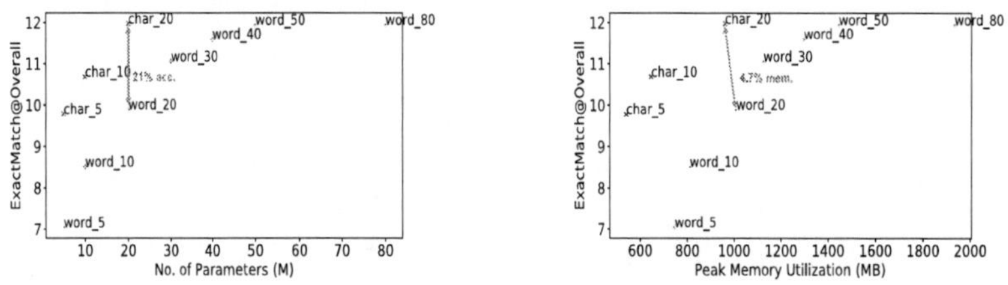


(a) Accuracy vs. No. of Parameters (b) Accuracy vs. Peak Memory Utilization

Figure 2: Accuracy-Memory Pareto Curve. Each point in the curve has number of model parameters at the end.

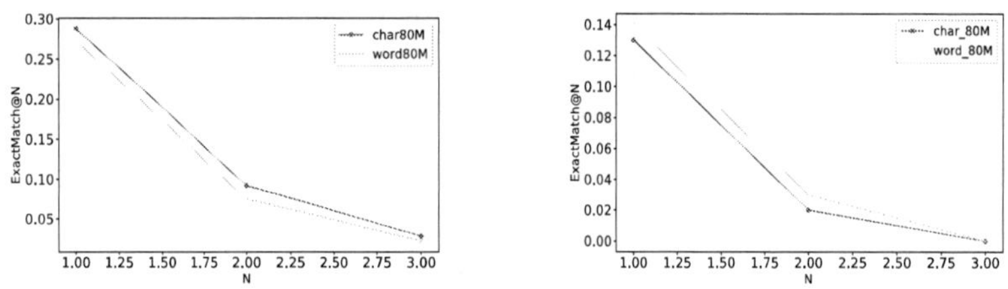


(a) Wikitext-103 (b) Reddit

Figure 3: ExactMatch@N vs. N for word and char. model on first 500 samples from Wiki-103 and Reddit Dev sets.

layers (AdaEmb) (Baevski and Auli, 2019), which contain shared input and output token embeddings; (ii) self-attention layers (Attn); (iii) feedforward network layers (FFN); and (iv) output softmax layers (Softmax). Figure 1 shows the percentage of parameters allocated to each component for both word- and character-based models, averaged over 100 random architectures for each representation.[3] Word-based models allocate more than 77% of the parameters to the embedding layers, which are less amenable to compression, for purposes of generating efficient and smaller models. These models allocate less than 14% and 8% of the parameter budget to highly compressible layers such as self-attention and feedforward network layers. In contrast, character-based models allocate more than 90% of the parameters to these highly compressible layers and less than 4% to the embedding layers. Hence, character-based models have the potential to admit much greater compression using standard techniques such as distillation and quantization with a negligible performance drop.

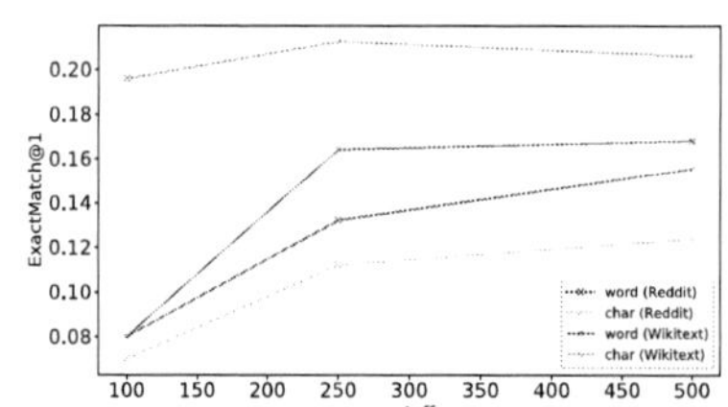


Figure 4: ExactMatch@1 vs. Cutoff for word and character model. Cutoff refers to the top $k$ prompts based on the percentage of OOV n-grams (upto 3) in ascending (descending) order for WikiText (Reddit), where $k \in \{100, 250, 500\}$. Character models perform better than word models on WikiText (broad prompts) and vice versa on Reddit (focused prompts).

**Accuracy vs. Memory Tradeoff.** Although character-based models seem to have better compression potential, their autocomplete performance gap over word-based models as a function of mem-

[3]The hyperparameter space used to sample architectures is shown in Appendix A.2.

ory is not immediately obvious. We study the effect of memory in two ways: (i) model size, which corresponds to the total number of model parameters, and (ii) peak memory utilization, which measures the peak amount of memory utilized by a process during inference. In all our experiments, the decoding of character models stops once the desired number of words (identified by space character) are predicted. The hyperparameter values for word and character autocomplete models of different sizes can be seen in Table 5 and Table 6 respectively. Figure 2 shows the accuracy-memory pareto curve[4]. Surprisingly, we observe that small character models (e.g., 20M) can rival large word models (e.g., 80M) in terms of accuracy-memory tradeoff. For instance, if we use a character model of size 20M instead of a word model of size 80M, we can save 75% of the model parameters and more than 60% of the peak memory utilization for a performance drop of $< 0.5$ points.

**Broad vs. Focused Domain.** Prior works (Al-Rfou et al., 2019; Choe et al., 2019) have found character models to be lagging behind word models in language modeling performance. Surprisingly, small character models perform similarly to or better than big word models on the autocomplete task. We hypothesize that the reason behind the superior performance of character models in our setting is due to their ability to answer broad prompts better than word-based models. To validate this claim, we compare character and word models on their ability to answer broad and focused prompts, controlled for the model size consisting of 80M parameters each.

From Table 1, we observe that the percentage of unique out-of-vocabulary (OOV) n-grams in WikiText-103 is 10% higher than that in the Reddit dataset. While WikiText and Reddit by nature have a different vocabulary distribution, the significant gap in the relative proportions of OOV n-grams indicates that Wikipedia articles cover more diverse and broad domains. Therefore we simulate broad prompts using articles from WikiText-103 and focused prompts with user posts from `Reddit.com` website (The Pushshift Reddit Dataset (Baumgartner et al., 2020), see Appendix A.1 for more details). As shown in Figure 3, the performance of the word-based model is superior to that of the character-based model in answering focused prompts, but not for answering broad prompts. A potential reason is the tendency of word-based models to memorize high-frequency patterns that are rife in datasets with focused prompts. On the other hand, character-based models excel on answering broad prompts (which are the focus of our work) which can be attributed to their superior ability in handling low-frequency patterns. We observe this trend with character-based models when we report the accuracy on the the top $k$ ('cutoff') low (high) frequent prompt patterns for WikiText (Reddit) selected by ranking the prompts based on the percentage of OOV n-grams (up to 3) in the ascending (descending) order (see Figure 4). We also observe the trend for unseen datasets with broad prompts (e.g., Penn Treebank, see Appendix A.8).

## 5 Methods to Improve Character Models

In the previous section, we demonstrated character-based models to be more efficient than word-based models for the autocomplete task on broad prompts. Unlike word-based models, which directly consume words, character-based models are forced to learn and compose semantically meaningful textual units (e.g., suffixes, words) from more granular lexical units in the form of characters. Therefore, methods that can explicitly integrate information from semantic units higher than characters (such as from words or word segments) can propel the performance of character based models (Park and Chiba, 2017). However, *existing methods primarily focus on improving the accuracy of character models, often at the expense of memory*. For example, Park and Chiba (2017) augment a character model with explicit model parameters for word embeddings, which add several millions of additional parameters (e.g., $13M$ parameters with modest embedding size of 50 and standard WikiText-103 word vocabulary size of $267K$). We introduce some novel methods that explicitly integrate word information into the character model with negligible impact on memory, as discussed next.

**BERT-Style Word Segment Embedding.** In this method, we introduce a word segment embedding layer which acts as an inductive bias by providing the word segment information explicitly in addition to character and position embedding layers (Figure 5 (a)). This word segment embedding layer is inspired by the sentence segment layer of BERT (Devlin et al., 2019) which helps the model distinguish sentences in the textual input. In our

[4]Hyperparameter values of different model sizes for word and character models can be found in Appendix A.3.

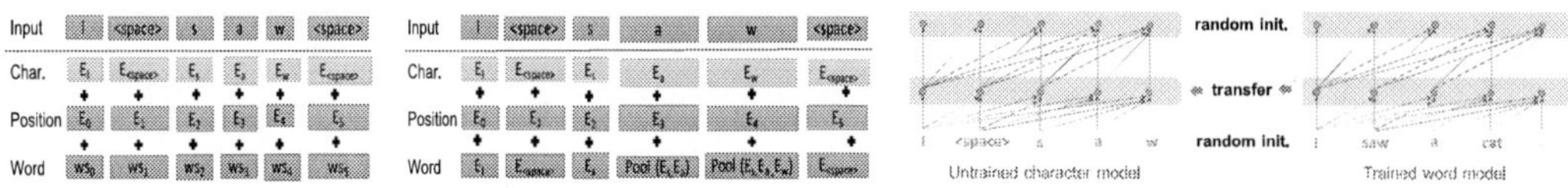


(a) BERT-Style method (b) Character pooling method (c) Transfer from word models method

Figure 5: Methods to improve character models. Note 'Position' in (a), (b) refers to character position embeddings.

case, the word segment embedding layer can help the model distinguish words in the textual input. The number of additional model parameters introduced by this layer equals the maximum number of words in a training input sequence times the embedding dimension, which is generally negligible.

**Character Pooling.** In this method, we compute word embeddings by pooling from embeddings of characters seen so far for the current word (see Figure 5 (b)). The pooling function takes a set of character embeddings as input, and outputs the word embedding which is concatenated with other embeddings (as additional input) similar to the previous method. We experiment with non-parameterized, simple pooling functions such as sum, mean, and maximum. Unlike the previous method, the character pooling method does not introduce additional model parameters, due to the choice of our pooling function. The computation of word embedding does not involve look-ahead embeddings from characters belonging to the current word (that are not seen at the current timestep), thus preventing data leakage that could render the language modeling task trivial.

**Transfer from Word Models.** In this method, we initialize a subset of decoder layers of the character model with decoder layers from a trained word model. Unlike previous methods, the decoder layer transfer method can appropriately exploit the rich syntactic and semantic information learned by the word model, which serves as a good starting point for training a character model rather than training from scratch. Figure 5 (c) illustrates the transfer of the bottom $50\%$ of decoder layers from the word model to the character model. Similar to the character pooling method, this method does not introduce additional model parameters. Rather, this method introduces a novel hyperparameter that controls the percentage of word-level bottom layers to transfer into our character-level model, which is tuned on the validation set. To the best of our knowledge, no prior work has explored transferring layers from a source trained model, where the source and the target model have very different vocabularies.

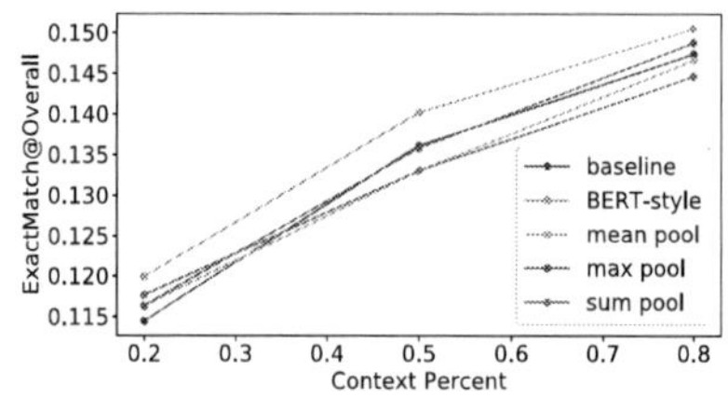


Figure 6: Improvements of char. models of size 80M with BERT-style word segment and char. pooling over baseline char. model on WikiText-103 validation set.

## 6 Results

We now discuss improvements on training character models by employing our novel methods over training a baseline character model from scratch.

**Improvements w.r.t context percent.** Figure 6 shows improvements of character models of size 80M with BERT-style word segment embedding and character pooling methods. Context percent corresponds to the percentage of initial tokens taken from a Wikipedia paragraph to construct the prompt, while the rest of the tokens form the ground truth. BERT-style word segment outperforms the baseline and character pooling methods on all context percent values. We attribute the inferior performance of the character pooling methods to their inability to track the order of the characters while computing the word representation. Among different pooling functions, the $max$ function performs well on most context percent values. When the context percent is very low (e.g., 0.2-0.35), it is interesting to see that all methods perform similar or outperform the baseline. This result shows that integrating word information explicitly is especially crucial when the prompts are ambiguous or contain few tokens (i.e., context percent is low). We omit the character pooling method from our further analysis due to its inferior performance.

**Quantitative Analysis.** Table 2 shows the performance improvements of proposed baseline character model as well as its proposed variants over baseline word model of size 10M. To transfer decoder layers from the word model, we first train a 20-layer word model that has the same Trans-

| Models | Exact Match Overall (%) | Partial Match Overall (%) | Naturalness (%) | Acceptability (%) |
|---|---|---|---|---|
| Human | 100 | 100 | 88 | 100 |
| Base (Word) | 8.51 | 13.76 | 53 | 87 |
| Base (Char) | 10.71 (+25.9%) | 15.37 (+11.7%) | 62 (+16.9%) | 93 (+6.9%) |
| BERT-st. (Char) | 10.78 (+26.7%) | 15.42 (+12.1%) | 59 (+11.3%) | 93 (+6.9%) |
| Transfer fr. word (Char) | **10.83 (+27.3%)** | **15.5 (+12.6%)** | **69 (+30%)** | **94 (+8.1%)** |

Table 2: Improvements of various proposed models over baseline word model of the same size (10M parameters) on the WikiText-103 test set.

former shape (i.e., number of heads, head dimension, model dimension, and inner dimension in feedforward layer) as the baseline word model and transfer the bottom 10% of the decoder layers from the word model to initialize our character model.[5] Consistent with the findings of Trajanovski et al. (2021), we observe the improvements in ExactMatch@Overall and PartialMatch@Overall metrics to be highly correlated. Both "BERT-style word segment" and "transfer from word model" methods improve upon the baseline word model by at least 26% and 12% (shown in Table 2), in terms of ExactMatch and PartialMatch respectively. These methods also improve upon the baseline character model by at least 0.7% and 0.3% (not explicitly shown in Table 2), in terms of ExactMatch and PartialMatch respectively. Importantly, compared to the "BERT-style word segment" method that introduces 384K additional parameters, our "transfer from word model" method does not introduce any additional parameters. This demonstrates the advantage of "transfer from word models" in improving baseline character model (as compared to our other methods), while leaving no impact on memory. We also perform human evaluation of suggestions generated by various autocomplete models based on their naturalness and acceptability. Naturalness measures how natural the suggestion is with respect to the prompt while acceptability measures how likely the suggestion will be accepted by user (details in A.11). Human suggestions taken from WikiText-103 have a naturalness and user acceptability score of 88% and 100% as rated by annotators. We observe that the "transfer from word models" method generates most natural and user acceptable suggestions (69%, 94% resp.), which is better than the baseline character (62%, 93% resp.) second only to the human baseline (88%, 100% resp.).

[5]The hyperparameter space for the transfer from word models method can be seen in Appendix A.4.

| Prompt and Suggestions |
|---|
| **Prompt**: The Olmec civilization developed in the lowlands of southeastern Mexico ... , the Indus Valley Civilization of south Asia<br>**Ground truth**: , the civilization<br>**Baseline**: , and the<br>**BERT-style**: , the indus<br>**Transfer from word models**: , the civilization |
| **Prompt**: Typhoon Lupit formed on November 18 from the monsoon trough to the west of the Marshall Islands . Early in its duration , it moved generally to<br>**Ground truth**: the west or<br>**Baseline**: the north of<br>**BERT-style**: the west of<br>**Transfer from word models**: the west of |

Table 3: Sample suggestions of length 3 words generated by baseline and proposed character autocomplete models. See Appendix A.9 for more examples.

**Qualitative Analysis.** Tables 3 and 9 (Appendix A.9) show sample suggestions generated by the proposed baseline character autocomplete model as well as its proposed variants. Suggestions generated by the strongest method seem to have better match with the ground truth and factually (e.g., direction of typhoon) correct.[6]

## 7 Conclusion

In this work, we investigated the challenging task of building autocomplete models for answering broad prompts under memory-constrained settings. To this end, we introduced some novel methods that integrate word information into a character model with negligible impact on memory. Employing our methods, we demonstrated that character models can achieve a better accuracy-memory trade-off as compared to word models.

## 8 Limitations

The limitations of this work are as follows:

- **English.** Our work builds autocomplete models for English language only.
- **Accuracy-memory tradeoff only.** Our work primarily focuses on deploying models on lower-end edge platforms where memory, as opposed to latency, is the major bottleneck. Hence, our methods may not improve the accuracy-latency tradeoff, which is a focus for future work.
- **WikiText-103 dataset** Our work explores only WikiText-103 dataset for creating broad prompts. In the future, we will study

[6]We provide a qualitative analysis of the baseline and proposed character models in the Appendix A.10.

other datasets (e.g., 1 Billion Word Language Model benchmark (Chelba et al., 2013)) that explore the full range of low-frequency prompt patterns, which can arise in real-world situations.

- **Transformer-XL architecture** Our work studies only Transformer-XL architecture to build word based and character based auto-complete models. In the future, we will study other popular architectures (e.g., GPT-2 (Radford et al., 2018)) to see the generalizability of proposed techniques.

## Acknowledgements

MAM acknowledges support from Canada Research Chairs (CRC), the Natural Sciences and Engineering Research Council of Canada (NSERC; RGPIN-2018-04267), Canadian Foundation for Innovation (CFI; 37771), and Digital Research Alliance of Canada.[7] Lakshmanan's research was supported in part by a grant from NSERC (Canada).

## References

Rami Al-Rfou, Dokook Choe, Noah Constant, Mandy Guo, and Llion Jones. 2019. Character-level language modeling with deeper self-attention. In *AAAI*.

Alexei Baevski and Michael Auli. 2019. Adaptive input representations for neural language modeling. In *International Conference on Learning Representations*.

Ziv Bar-Yossef and Naama Kraus. 2011. Context-sensitive query auto-completion. In *Proceedings of the 20th International Conference on World Wide Web*, WWW '11, page 107–116. Association for Computing Machinery.

Jason Baumgartner, Savvas Zannettou, Brian Keegan, Megan Squire, and Jeremy Blackburn. 2020. The Pushshift Reddit Dataset. *CoRR*, abs/2001.08435.

Tom Brown, Benjamin Mann, Nick Ryder, Melanie Subbiah, Jared D Kaplan, Prafulla Dhariwal, Arvind Neelakantan, Pranav Shyam, Girish Sastry, Amanda Askell, Sandhini Agarwal, Ariel Herbert-Voss, Gretchen Krueger, Tom Henighan, Rewon Child, Aditya Ramesh, Daniel Ziegler, Jeffrey Wu, Clemens Winter, Chris Hesse, Mark Chen, Eric Sigler, Mateusz Litwin, Scott Gray, Benjamin Chess, Jack Clark, Christopher Berner, Sam McCandlish, Alec Radford, Ilya Sutskever, and Dario Amodei. 2020. Language models are few-shot learners. In *Advances in Neural Information Processing Systems*, volume 33, pages 1877–1901. Curran Associates, Inc.

[7]https://alliancecan.ca

Fei Cai and Maarten de Rijke. 2016. *A Survey of Query Auto Completion in Information Retrieval*. Now Publishers Inc.

Han Cai, Chuang Gan, Ligeng Zhu, and Song Han. 2020. Tinytl: Reduce memory, not parameters for efficient on-device learning. In *Advances in Neural Information Processing Systems*, volume 33, pages 11285–11297.

Ciprian Chelba, Tomás Mikolov, Mike Schuster, Qi Ge, Thorsten Brants, and Phillipp Koehn. 2013. One billion word benchmark for measuring progress in statistical language modeling. *CoRR*, abs/1312.3005.

Mia Xu Chen, Benjamin N. Lee, Gagan Bansal, Yuan Cao, Shuyuan Zhang, Justin Lu, Jackie Tsay, Yinan Wang, Andrew M. Dai, Zhifeng Chen, Timothy Sohn, and Yonghui Wu. 2019. Gmail Smart Compose: Real-Time Assisted Writing. In *Proceedings of the 25th ACM SIGKDD International Conference on Knowledge Discovery And Data Mining*, KDD '19, page 2287–2295.

Wei-Lin Chiang, Zhuohan Li, Zi Lin, Ying Sheng, Zhanghao Wu, Hao Zhang, Lianmin Zheng, Siyuan Zhuang, Yonghao Zhuang, Joseph E. Gonzalez, Ion Stoica, and Eric P. Xing. 2023. Vicuna: An open-source chatbot impressing gpt-4 with 90%* chatgpt quality.

Dokook Choe, Rami Al-Rfou, Mandy Guo, Heeyoung Lee, and Noah Constant. 2019. Bridging the Gap for Tokenizer-Free Language Models. *CoRR*, abs/1908.10322.

Zihang Dai, Zhilin Yang, Yiming Yang, Jaime Carbonell, Quoc Le, and Ruslan Salakhutdinov. 2019. Transformer-XL: Attentive language models beyond a fixed-length context. In *Proceedings of the 57th Annual Meeting of the Association for Computational Linguistics*, pages 2978–2988, Florence, Italy. Association for Computational Linguistics.

Jacob Devlin, Ming-Wei Chang, Kenton Lee, and Kristina Toutanova. 2019. BERT: Pre-training of deep bidirectional transformers for language understanding. In *Proceedings of the 2019 Conference of the North American Chapter of the Association for Computational Linguistics: Human Language Technologies, Volume 1 (Long and Short Papers)*, pages 4171–4186, Minneapolis, Minnesota. Association for Computational Linguistics.

Yao Dou, Maxwell Forbes, Rik Koncel-Kedziorski, Noah Smith, and Yejin Choi. 2022. Is GPT-3 text indistinguishable from human text? scarecrow: A framework for scrutinizing machine text. In *Proceedings of the 60th Annual Meeting of the Association for Computational Linguistics (Volume 1: Long Papers)*, pages 7250–7274, Dublin, Ireland. Association for Computational Linguistics.

Simon Gog, Giulio Ermanno Pibiri, and Rossano Venturini. 2020. Efficient and effective query autocompletion. In *Proceedings of the 43rd International ACM SIGIR Conference on Research and Development in Information Retrieval*, SIGIR '20, page 2271–2280.

Mitchell A. Gordon, Kevin Duh, and Nicholas Andrews. 2020. Compressing BERT: Studying the Effects of Weight Pruning on Transfer Learning. *CoRR*, abs/2002.08307.

Song Han, Huizi Mao, and William J. Dally. 2016. Deep compression: Compressing deep neural networks with pruning, trained quantization and huffman coding. *ICLR*.

Sepp Hochreiter and Jürgen Schmidhuber. 1997. Long short-term memory. *Neural Comput.*, 9(8):1735–1780.

Mitchell P. Marcus, Mary Ann Marcinkiewicz, and Beatrice Santorini. 1993. Building a large annotated corpus of english: The penn treebank. *Comput. Linguist.*, 19(2):313–330.

Gaurav Menghani. 2021. Efficient deep learning: A survey on making deep learning models smaller, faster, and better. *CoRR*, abs/2106.08962.

Stephen Merity, Caiming Xiong, James Bradbury, and Richard Socher. 2017. Pointer sentinel mixture models. In *International Conference on Learning Representations*.

OpenAI. 2023a. Gpt-4 technical report.

OpenAI. 2023b. Introducing chatgpt.

Denis Paperno, Germán Kruszewski, Angeliki Lazaridou, Ngoc Quan Pham, Raffaella Bernardi, Sandro Pezzelle, Marco Baroni, Gemma Boleda, and Raquel Fernández. 2016. The LAMBADA dataset: Word prediction requiring a broad discourse context. In *Proceedings of the 54th Annual Meeting of the Association for Computational Linguistics (Volume 1: Long Papers)*, pages 1525–1534, Berlin, Germany. Association for Computational Linguistics.

Dae Hoon Park and Rikio Chiba. 2017. A neural language model for query auto-completion. In *Proceedings of the 40th International ACM SIGIR Conference on Research and Development in Information Retrieval*, SIGIR '17, page 1189–1192. Association for Computing Machinery.

Baolin Peng, Chunyuan Li, Pengcheng He, Michel Galley, and Jianfeng Gao. 2023. Instruction tuning with gpt-4. *arXiv preprint arXiv:2304.03277*.

Alec Radford, Karthik Narasimhan, Tim Salimans, and Ilya Sutskever. 2018. Improving Language Understanding by Generative Pre-Training. `https://s3-us-west-2.amazonaws.com/openai-assets/research-covers/language-unsupervised/language_understanding_paper.pdf`.

Pranav Rajpurkar, Jian Zhang, Konstantin Lopyrev, and Percy Liang. 2016. SQuAD: 100,000+ questions for machine comprehension of text. In *Proceedings of the 2016 Conference on Empirical Methods in Natural Language Processing*, pages 2383–2392, Austin, Texas. Association for Computational Linguistics.

Anna Rogers, Niranjan Balasubramanian, Leon Derczynski, Jesse Dodge, Alexander Koller, Sasha Luccioni, Maarten Sap, Roy Schwartz, Noah A. Smith, and Emma Strubell. 2023. Closed ai models make bad baselines.

Victor Sanh, Lysandre Debut, Julien Chaumond, and Thomas Wolf. 2019. DistilBERT, a distilled version of BERT: smaller, faster, cheaper and lighter. *CoRR*, abs/1910.01108.

Sheng Shen, Zhen Dong, Jiayu Ye, Linjian Ma, Zhewei Yao, Amir Gholami, Michael W. Mahoney, and Kurt Keutzer. 2020. Q-BERT: hessian based ultra low precision quantization of BERT. In *The Thirty-Fourth AAAI Conference on Artificial Intelligence, AAAI 2020, The Thirty-Second Innovative Applications of Artificial Intelligence Conference, IAAI 2020, The Tenth AAAI Symposium on Educational Advances in Artificial Intelligence, EAAI 2020, New York, NY, USA, February 7-12, 2020*, pages 8815–8821. AAAI Press.

Rohan Taori, Ishaan Gulrajani, Tianyi Zhang, Yann Dubois, Xuechen Li, Carlos Guestrin, Percy Liang, and Tatsunori B. Hashimoto. 2023. Stanford alpaca: An instruction-following llama model. `https://github.com/tatsu-lab/stanford_alpaca`.

Yi Tay, Mostafa Dehghani, Dara Bahri, and Donald Metzler. 2020. Efficient transformers: A survey. *CoRR*, abs/2009.06732.

Yi Tay, Vinh Q. Tran, Sebastian Ruder, Jai Gupta, Hyung Won Chung, Dara Bahri, Zhen Qin, Simon Baumgartner, Cong Yu, and Donald Metzler. 2022. Charformer: Fast character transformers via gradient-based subword tokenization. In *International Conference on Learning Representations*.

Stojan Trajanovski, Chad Atalla, Kunho Kim, Vipul Agarwal, Milad Shokouhi, and Chris Quirk. 2021. When does text prediction benefit from additional context? an exploration of contextual signals for chat and email messages. In *Proceedings of the 2021 Conference of the North American Chapter of the Association for Computational Linguistics: Human Language Technologies: Industry Papers*, pages 1–9, Online. Association for Computational Linguistics.

Ashish Vaswani, Noam Shazeer, Niki Parmar, Jakob Uszkoreit, Llion Jones, Aidan N. Gomez, Lukasz Kaiser, and Illia Polosukhin. 2017. Attention is All you Need. In *Advances in Neural Information Processing Systems*, pages 6000–6010.

Hanrui Wang, Zhekai Zhang, and Song Han. 2021. Spatten: Efficient sparse attention architecture with cascade token and head pruning. In *2021 IEEE International Symposium on High-Performance Computer Architecture (HPCA)*, pages 97–110. IEEE.

Sida Wang, Weiwei Guo, Huiji Gao, and Bo Long. 2020. Efficient neural query auto completion. In *Proceedings of the 29th ACM International Conference on Information and Knowledge Management*, CIKM '20, page 2797–2804.

# A Appendices

## A.1 Reproducibility

We experiment with both Reddit and WikiText-103 datasets. WikiText-103 is a public dataset and widely adopted as a language modeling benchmark. WikiText-103 is downloaded from `tinyurl.com/yajy5wjm`. The Reddit dataset used in this work is a sample of publicly available *Pushshift Reddit dataset* (Baumgartner et al., 2020). The sample contains 4M train, 20K validation and 20K test posts. The key feature of the Reddit dataset is the significantly low percentage of unique out of vocabulary n-grams compared to WikiText-103, as shown in Table 1 and discussed in Section 4. For reproducibility, datasets and code used in this work is available at `tinyurl.com/bdd69r34` (anonymized) and will be made publicly available should paper be accepted.

## A.2 Hyperparameter space for computing component-wise parameter breakdown

Table 7 displays the Transformer-XL hyperparameter space used to create 100 random architectures for computing component-wise parameter breakdown plot (Figure 1) for both word and character models. Rest of the hyperparameters come from the default configuration of Transformer-XL model.

## A.3 Hyperparameter values for word and character models of different sizes

Table 5 displays the hyperparameter values for word models of different sizes used in the paper. Table 6 displays the hyperparameter values for character models of different sizes used in the paper.

## A.4 Hyperparameter space for transfer from word models method

Table 7 displays the hyperparameter space for the proposed transfer from word models method.

## A.5 Greedy vs. Beam search decoding

Figure 7 shows the pareto-curve for greedy and beam search. It is clear that smaller character models rival bigger word models regardless of the choice of decoding algorithm. Strikingly, we find greedy search to outperform beam search by a large margin. Two possible reasons are: (i) the noise injected by the adaptive softmax approximation of predicted probability distribution over vocabulary, and/or (ii) sensitivity of beam search to explore

| Hyperparameter Name | Hyperparameter Values for Sampling |
|---|---|
| Number of hidden layers | { 2, 4, 8, 12, 16, 24, 32 } |
| Number of attention heads | { 2, 4, 8, 16, 32, 64 } |
| Dimension of attention head | { 8, 16, 32, 64, 128 } |
| Dimension of input/output embedding | { 256, 512, 1024, 2048 } |
| Inner dimension of feedforward layer | { 256, 512, 1024, 2048 } |
| Dimension of model | { 256, 512, 1024, 2048 } |

Table 4: Hyperparameter space for computing component-wise parameter breakdown for both word and character models.

| Hyperparameter name / Model size | $5M$ | $10M$ | $20M$ | $30M$ | $40M$ | $50M$ | $80M$ |
|---|---|---|---|---|---|---|---|
| Number of hidden layers | 3 | 4 | 6 | 12 | 14 | 16 | 16 |
| Number of attention heads | 4 | 4 | 8 | 8 | 8 | 8 | 32 |
| Dimension of attention head | 24 | 24 | 32 | 32 | 32 | 32 | 32 |
| Dimension of input/output embedding | 18 | 36 | 74 | 100 | 128 | 160 | 256 |
| Inner dimension of feedforward layer | 60 | 150 | 200 | 768 | 900 | 800 | 768 |
| Dimension of model | 18 | 36 | 74 | 100 | 128 | 160 | 256 |
| Number of tokens to predict during training | 192 | 192 | 192 | 192 | 192 | 192 | 192 |
| Number of tokens cached from previous iterations during training | 192 | 192 | 192 | 192 | 192 | 192 | 192 |
| Learning rate | 0.01 | 0.01 | 0.01 | 0.01 | 0.01 | 0.01 | 0.01 |
| Number of iterations for learning rate warmup | 1K | 1K | 1K | 1K | 1K | 1K | 1K |
| Maximum number of training steps | 200K | 200K | 200K | 200K | 200K | 200K | 200K |
| Batch size | 256 | 256 | 256 | 256 | 256 | 256 | 256 |
| Number of tokens to predict during evaluation | 192 | 192 | 192 | 192 | 192 | 192 | 192 |
| Number of tokens cached from previous iterations during evaluation | 192 | 192 | 192 | 192 | 192 | 192 | 192 |
| Vocabulary size | 267736 | 267736 | 267736 | 267736 | 267736 | 267736 | 267736 |

Table 5: Hyperparameter values for word models of different sizes.

spurious hypothesis when the user prompt patterns are low frequency.

### A.6 Differences of Autocomplete from Conventional Language Modeling Task.

The autocomplete task is a well-defined problem with rich prior literature (see Section 2). Existing autocomplete research, including ours, is focused on building a conventional language model that computes the likelihood of a text sequence. The training procedure for our autocomplete task and that for conventional language modeling (CLM) task are generally similar. However, the goal of our autocomplete task is to generate suggestions with high precision (as captured by ExactMatch) while the main goal of CLM is to maximize the overall data likelihood (as captured by perplexity). Chen et al. (2019) show that perplexity and ExactMatch metrics are only weakly correlated as improvements in perplexity could be "mostly in places where the model is relatively low in likelihood score". As shown in Figure 8, autocomplete models with poorer perplexity scores (e.g., character model of size 20M) can enjoy better ExactMatch scores compared to models with better perplexity scores (e.g., word model of size 20M). We also perform a theoretical analysis to show how perplexity scores can change drastically for the same ExactMatch score (details in Appendix A.7). Thus, building a good language model is not enough to solve the autocomplete task. Another major conceptual difference between CLM and autocomplete tasks is that the former focuses mainly on generating long horizon (typically 128-512 tokens) continuation while the latter focuses on generating short horizon (typically 3-5 tokens) continuation.

### A.7 Theoretical analysis on differences in perplexity and Exact Match metrics

We will conduct a theoretical study to show the differences in the information captured by perplexity and Exact Match metric. Specifically, we show that the exact match score can be perfect whereas perplexity score can either be perfect or worsen by a large margin (**Claim 1**). Conversely, we also show that the exact match score can be the worst (i.e., zero) whereas the perplexity score can be poor or better by a large margin (**Claim 2**). Without loss of generality, we assume the vocabulary size $\mathcal{V}$ to be 2. Let $A$, $B$ be the two tokens corresponding to the first and second index in the vocabulary respectively. Consider a single token prediction ($\hat{x}_j$) and

| Hyperparameter name / Model size | $5M$ | $10M$ | $20M$ | $80M$ |
|---|---|---|---|---|
| Number of hidden layers | 12 | 12 | 12 | 16 |
| Number of attention heads | 8 | 8 | 8 | 8 |
| Dimension of attention head | 32 | 32 | 64 | 64 |
| Dimension of input/output embedding | 278 | 512 | 550 | 750 |
| Inner dimension of feedforward layer | 128 | 165 | 250 | 2048 |
| Dimension of model | 278 | 512 | 550 | 750 |
| Number of tokens to predict during training | 512 | 512 | 512 | 512 |
| Number of tokens cached from previous iterations during training | 512 | 512 | 512 | 512 |
| Learning rate | 0.001 | 0.001 | 0.001 | 0.001 |
| Number of iterations for learning rate warmup | 4K | 4K | 4K | 4K |
| Maximum number of training steps | 400K | 400K | 400K | 400K |
| Batch size | 128 | 128 | 128 | 128 |
| Number of tokens to predict during evaluation | 512 | 512 | 512 | 512 |
| Number of tokens cached from previous iterations during evaluation | 2K | 2K | 2K | 2K |
| Vocabulary size | 128 | 128 | 128 | 128 |

Table 6: Hyperparameter values for character models of different sizes.

| Hyperparameter Name | Hyperparameter Values |
|---|---|
| Number of hidden layers | { 4, 8, 12, 16, 20, 24 } |
| Percentage of bottom most layers to transfer | { 10%, 20%, 30%, 40%, 50% } |

Table 7: Hyperparameter space for transfer from word models method.

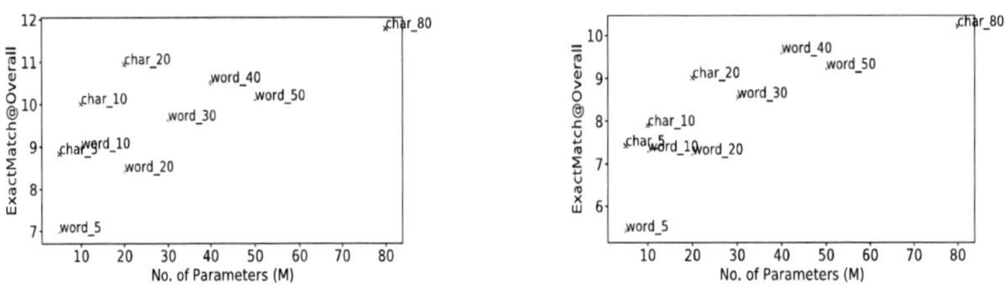


(a) Greedy search (b) Beam search

Figure 7: Greedy search vs. Beam search on WikiText-103 test set. Beam size and prompt context percentage is set as 5 and 20% respectively.

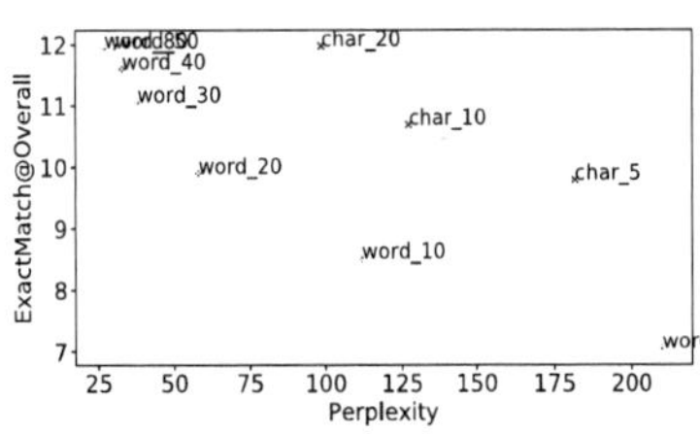


Figure 8: Perplexity vs. ExactMatch. For comparison, perplexity output by character models (also known as bits per byte) is converted to perplexity per word using the formula proposed in Choe et al. (2019).

let the ground truth token be $B$, that is, $\hat{x}_j = [0, 1]$. Table 8 shows the differences in perplexity score and Exact Match score as a function of $\hat{x}_j$, as it varies slightly. The first six rows in the table validate **Claim 1**, where exact match score is 1 but the perplexity ranges $-9.9\mathrm{e}{-10}$ to $0.67$. The rest of the rows validate **Claim 2**, where the exact match score is 0 but the perplexity score ranges from $0.69$ to $20.72$.

## A.8 Accuracy-Memory Pareto-Curve on Unseen Datasets

We study the accuracy-memory pareto curve of autocomplete models trained on WikiText-103 and evaluate on the test set of two unseen datasets: LAnguage Modeling Broadened to Account for Discourse Aspects (Paperno et al., 2016) (LAMBADA, mostly focused prompts) and Penn Treebank (Marcus et al., 1993) (PTB, mostly broad prompts). From Figure 9, we observe that the

| Ground truth ($x_j$) | Prediction ($\hat{x}_j$) | Exact Match | Perplexity |
|---|---|---|---|
| $[0, 1]$ | $[0, 1]$ | 1 | $-9.9\text{e}{-10}$ |
| $[0, 1]$ | $[0.1, 0.9]$ | 1 | 0.11 |
| $[0, 1]$ | $[0.2, 0.8]$ | 1 | 0.22 |
| $[0, 1]$ | $[0.3, 0.7]$ | 1 | 0.36 |
| $[0, 1]$ | $[0.4, 0.6]$ | 1 | 0.51 |
| $[0, 1]$ | $[0.49, 0.51]$ | 1 | 0.67 |
| $[0, 1]$ | $[0.5, 0.5]$ | 0 | 0.69 |
| $[0, 1]$ | $[0.51, 0.49]$ | 0 | 0.71 |
| $[0, 1]$ | $[0.6, 0.4]$ | 0 | 0.92 |
| $[0, 1]$ | $[0.7, 0.3]$ | 0 | 1.2 |
| $[0, 1]$ | $[0.8, 0.2]$ | 0 | 1.61 |
| $[0, 1]$ | $[0.9, 0.1]$ | 0 | 2.3 |
| $[0, 1]$ | $[1.0, 0]$ | 0 | 20.72 |

Table 8: Differences in perplexity and Exact Match as function of small changes in $\hat{x}_j$ when the ground truth is $[0, 1]$.

trend where smaller character models rival larger word models that holds true for answering broad prompts (PTB) but not clearly for answering focused prompts (LAMBADA). It is striking that the trend holds true for broad prompts even when the examples are unseen during the training of the autocomplete model.

### A.9 Qualitative examples of suggestions from autocomplete models

Table 9 displays sample suggestions generated by vanilla and proposed character autocomplete models, grouped by the type of artifact in the generation.

### A.10 Qualitative analysis of vanilla and proposed character models

We manually inspect the suggestions generated by vanilla and proposed character models[8]. Table 10 displays the percentage of different artifacts: *plausible* (plausible suggestion that does not have exact match with the ground truth), *semantic error* (e.g., new n-gram, incorrect n-gram usage), *repetition* (e.g., n-gram with repetitions), and *grammatical error*. Compared to baseline and BERT-style word segment model, character model with decoder layer transfer from word model results in less undesirable artifacts overall.

### A.11 Human annotation of suggestions

We conduct human annotation of suggestions outputted by various autocomplete models based on *naturalness* (how natural the suggestion is with respect to the prompt?) and *acceptability* (whether the suggestion will be accepted by user or not?). Some aspects of natural suggestion are borrowed from Dou et al. (2022). The annotation guideline for naturalness and acceptability can be seen in Table 11 and Table 12 respectively. We ask 8 annotators to rate 10 suggestions each.

[8]Sample suggestions from different autocomplete models can be seen in Appendix A.9.

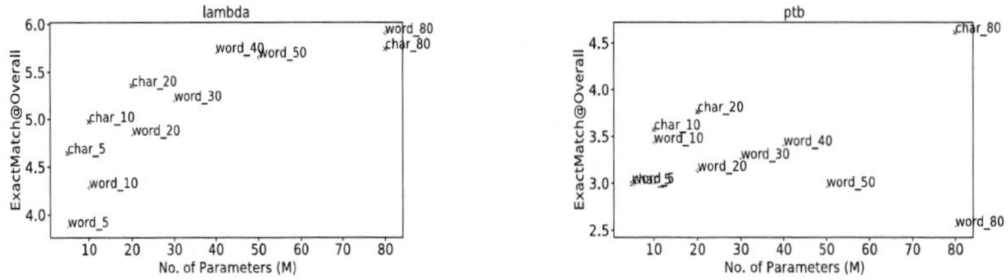


(a) LAMBADA (Paperno et al., 2016)

(b) PTB (Marcus et al., 1993)

Figure 9: Accuracy-Memory Pareto Curve for Autocomplete models trained on WikiText-103 and evaluated on test set of two unseen datasets: LAMBADA and PTB.

| Artifact type | Prompt and Suggestions |
|---|---|
| Plausible | **Prompt**: In 2006 Boulter starred in the play Citizenship written by Mark Ravenhill . The play was part of a series which featured different playwrights , titled Burn / Chatroom / Citizenship . In a 2006<br>**Ground truth**: interview , fellow<br>**Baseline**: interview , ravenhill<br>**BERT-style**: interview with the<br>**Transfer from word models**: interview with the |
| Plausible | **Prompt**: In December 759 , he briefly stayed in Tonggu ( modern Gansu ) . He departed on December 24 for Chengdu ( Sichuan province ) , where he was hosted by local Prefect and<br>**Ground truth**: fellow poet Pei<br>**Baseline**: servant and served<br>**BERT-style**: chief executive officer<br>**Transfer from word models**: commissioned as a |
| Semantic error | **Prompt**: In his lifetime and immediately following his death , Du Fu was not greatly appreciated . In part this can be attributed to his stylistic and formal innovations, some of which are still "considered extremely daring and bizarre by Chinese critics ." There are few contemporary references to him — only eleven poems from six writers — and these describe him in terms of affection, but not as a<br>**Ground truth**: paragon of poetic<br>**Baseline**: reference to his<br>**BERT-style**: poem . the<br>**Transfer from word models**: consequence of his |
| Semantic error | **Prompt**: Other translators have placed much greater weight on trying to convey a sense of the poetic forms used by Du Fu . Vikram Seth in Three Chinese Poets uses English @-@ style rhyme schemes , whereas Keith Holyoak in Facing the Moon approximates the Chinese rhyme scheme ; both use end @-@ stopped lines and preserve some degree of parallelism . In The Selected Poems of Du Fu , Burton Watson follows the parallelisms quite strictly , persuading the western reader to adapt to the poems rather than<br>**Ground truth**: vice versa .<br>**Baseline**: to the poems<br>**BERT-style**: adapt the poems<br>**Transfer from word models**: the parallelisms of |
| Repetition | **Prompt**: Although initially he was little @-@ known to other writers , his works came to be hugely influential in both<br>**Ground truth**: Chinese and Japanese<br>**Baseline**: the writers and<br>**BERT-style**: writers and writers<br>**Transfer from word models**: the ancient and |
| Repetition | **Prompt**: In the 20th century , he was the favourite poet of Kenneth<br>**Ground truth**: Rexroth , who<br>**Baseline**: kenneth kenneth kenneth<br>**BERT-style**: county . the<br>**Transfer from word models**: kenneth kenneth kenneth |
| Grammatical error | **Prompt**: Hung summarises his life by concluding that ,<br>**Ground truth**: " He appeared<br>**Baseline**: according to ksummarises<br>**BERT-style**: in the same<br>**Transfer from word models**: as a result |

Table 9: Sample suggestions of length 3 words generated by vanilla and proposed character autocomplete models, grouped by the type of artifact in the generation.

| Artifact type | Baseline | BERT-style w. seg. | Transfer from word models |
|---|---|---|---|
| Plausible (↑) | 40 | 40 | **42** |
| Semantic Error (↓) | 7 | **6** | 7 |
| Repetition (↓) | 7 | 7 | **5** |
| Gram. Error (↓) | 3 | 3 | **2** |

Table 10: Percentage of different artifacts in the generated suggestion from vanilla and proposed character models, by manual inspection of 100 WikiText-103 examples. ↑ indicates higher the better, ↓ indicates lower the better.

Autocomplete is a task where the user inputs a text, which is conditioned by the model to generate 'natural' continuation (or suggestion). The goal of this annotation effort is to rate the quality of suggestions generated by various autocomplete models based on the 'natural'ness. Each suggestion will be at most three words. Keep in mind that there could be more than one 'natural' suggestion for a text.

Some aspects of suggestion (but don't restrict only to these) that makes a suggestion NOT natural can be: grammatical error (missing words, extra words, incorrect or out of order words), redundancy (extra unnecessary information, word repetition), off-prompt (suggestion is unrelated to the text), self-contradiction (suggestion contradicts the text), incoherence (grammatical, not redundant, on prompt, not contradictory but still CONFUSING), factual or commonsense errors (violates our basic understanding of the world) and so on. Assume a broad definition of 'natural'ness and use your best judgement to rate.

You will be asked to annotate TEN texts. For each text, you will see a suggestion and you will rate by picking exactly one of the two choices:
(i) natural - Select this option if suggestion is natural with respect to the text
(ii) NOT natural - Select this option if suggestion is NOT natural with respect to the text

Table 11: Annotation guideline for human annotators to rate the quality of suggestions generated by autocomplete models and humans based on naturalness.

Autocomplete is a task where a user inputs a text (prompt), which is conditioned by the model to generate 'natural' continuation (or suggestion). For example, the user can give the prompt "Filmmaker George Lucas used Tikal as a", and the system may give a suggestion such as "filming location". An autocomplete system is successful if it can reduce the keystrokes a user would need to make, improving user productivity. The goal of this annotation task is to decide if (i) a suggestion generated by an autocomplete model will be accepted by a user (to reduce the keystrokes) or (ii) not. Each suggestion will be at most three words.

You can accept the suggestion if it is useful. A suggestion can be useful for one or more reasons (but don't restrict only to these): (i) the suggestion seems completely relevant to the prompt; (ii) the suggestion can be minimally edited for it to be useful. Note that reasons for acceptability are generally subjective. Hence, please assume a broad definition of "usefulness" and employ your best judgment to rate.

You will be asked to annotate 10 texts. For each text, you will see a suggestion and you will rate by picking exactly one of the two choices:
(i) yes - Select this option if you will accept the suggestion
(ii) no - Select this option if you will not accept the suggestion

The following is an example:
Filmmaker George Lucas used Tikal as a
**Suggestion:** filming location
**Rating choices:**
(i) yes - Select this option if you will accept the suggestion
(ii) no - Select this option if you will not accept the suggestion
Rating [type 'yes' or 'no' here in this line]: yes

Table 12: Annotation guideline for human annotators to rate the quality of suggestions generated by autocomplete models and humans based on acceptability.

# Query Encoder Distillation via Embedding Alignment is a Strong Baseline Method to Boost Dense Retriever Online Efficiency

**Yuxuan Wang** and **Hong Lyu***
University of Pennsylvania
{wangy49, hlyu}@seas.upenn.edu

## Abstract

The information retrieval community has made significant progress in improving the efficiency of Dual Encoder (DE) dense passage retrieval systems, making them suitable for latency-sensitive settings. However, many proposed procedures are often too complex or resource-intensive, which makes it difficult for practitioners to adopt them or identify sources of empirical gains. Therefore, in this work, we propose a trivially simple recipe to serve as a baseline method for boosting the efficiency of DE retrievers leveraging an asymmetric architecture. Our results demonstrate that even a 2-layer, BERT-based query encoder can still retain 92.5% of the full DE performance on the BEIR benchmark via unsupervised distillation and **proper student initialization**. We hope that our findings will encourage the community to re-evaluate the trade-offs between method complexity and performance improvements.

## 1 Introduction

Recent advances in neural-based NLP techniques have led to powerful neural encoders that can generate high-quality, semantic-rich, dense vector text representations (Reimers and Gurevych, 2019; Cer et al., 2018; Conneau et al., 2018; Schick et al., 2023), making it possible to calculate the text relevancy with simple vector operations like dot product. Thus, the Dual Encoder (DE) neural Information Retrieval (IR) architectures, combined with optimized semantic search implementations (Andoni et al., 2018; Johnson et al., 2019; Boytsov and Nyberg, 2020), have achieved comparable or even superior performances to their Cross Encoder (CE) based predecessors (Thakur et al., 2021; Menon et al., 2022; Ni et al., 2022; Yu et al., 2022) while being significantly more efficient (Reimers and Gurevych, 2019).

Despite the numerous proposed efficiency enhancements for making DE-based IR models suitable for production settings, they may pose challenges for practitioners with limited resources in terms of adoption and replication (Hooker, 2020). However, by leveraging two key facts, we can simplify model development while achieving higher efficiency. Firstly, documents, in contrast to queries, are typically longer and more complex, necessitating specialized architectures (Zhang et al., 2019; Dai et al., 2019; Beltagy et al., 2020; Zaheer et al., 2020). Secondly, document embeddings remain mostly static after indexing, allowing for a high-quality and computationally expensive document encoder without online overhead. Based on these insights, we propose an asymmetric IR architecture that pairs a lightweight query encoder with a robust document encoder.

In this study, we present a minimalistic baseline approach for constructing the aforementioned asymmetric retriever using any existing query encoder. As depicted in Figure 1, by employing suitable initialization and simply minimizing the Euclidean distance between student and teacher query embeddings, even a 2-layer BERT-based query encoder (Devlin et al., 2018) can retain 92.5% of the full DE performance on the BEIR benchmark (Thakur et al., 2021). Similarly, the 4-layer encoder preserves 96.2% of the full performance, which aligns with the supervised outcome (96.6%) achieved by a 6-layer encoder (Kim et al., 2023). We hope that these findings will motivate the research community to reassess the trade-offs between method complexity and performance enhancements. Our code is publicly available in our GitHub repository.

## 2 The Trivially Simple Distillation Recipe

### 2.1 Student Initialization

The initialization of student model weights is frequently not given enough attention in the knowledge distillation literature for IR. We find that a

*Both authors contributed equally to this research.



*Proceedings of The Fourth Workshop on Simple and Efficient Natural Language Processing (SustaiNLP)*, pages 290–298
July 13, 2023 

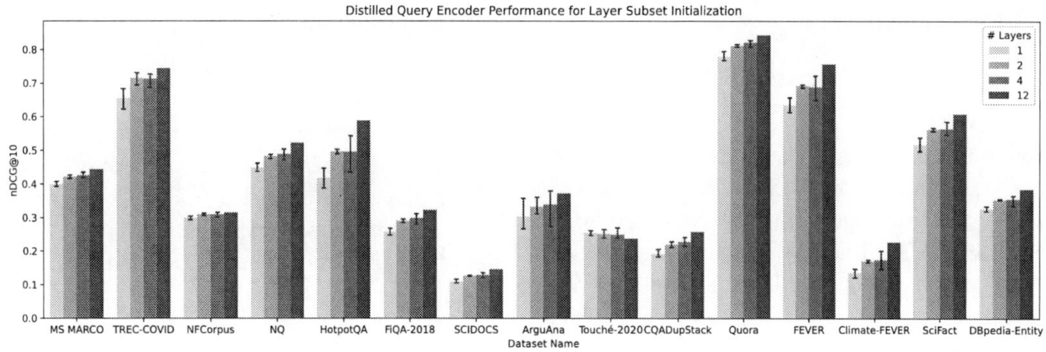


Figure 1: The dual encoder retriever performance with distilled query encoders of a varying number of layers. The student models are initialized by extracting subsets of the teacher model (`msmarco-bert-base-dot-v5`) layers. Variances in performances come from different layer subsets chosen, discussed in section 4.

"well-prepared" student model can considerably alleviate distillation challenges. In this study, we investigate two classes of initialization approaches.

**Extract a Subset of Teacher Layers** In this initialization method, we establish the student model by taking a subset of the teacher model's transformer layers while keeping the embedding and pooling layers. By inheriting some of the teacher model's structural properties and knowledge, the student model is intuitively better prepared for efficient distillation in comparison to a randomly initialized student model. We conduct experiments using various combinations of teacher model layers to assess their impact on both performance and efficiency. Details would be discussed in subsection 3.2, section 4, and subsection A.1.

**Adopt Other Pretrained Models** We also explore initializing the student model from other efficient pretrained models. Simultaneously, we investigate the influence of multiple factors, e.g., fine-tuning tasks and distance functions, on achieving a "well-prepared" initialization for the student model. We take DistilBERT (Sanh et al., 2019) as our student model candidate and experiment with different DistilBERT models fine-tuned on diverse tasks. Examples include the `distilbert-base-uncased` model and DistilBERT models fine-tuned on the MS MARCO dataset (Bajaj et al., 2018) with distinct objectives from `sentence-transformers` on HuggingFace (Wolf et al., 2019). This approach enables us to evaluate the efficacy of using alternative pretrained models as starting points for student model initialization. Student model cards are listed in subsection A.2.

## 2.2 Embedding Alignment

DE-based IR systems often use vector similarity for searching (Andoni et al., 2018), making it logical to match student and teacher embedding spaces.

**Contextualized Embedding Pooling Strategies** BERT-based encoders produce contextualized representations for all tokens from the input text. Common ways to aggregate token embeddings are selecting `[CLS]` embedding, computing mean values across all token embeddings, concatenating multiple pooled embeddings together, etc. We stick with the average pooling strategy for all presented experiment results in this paper, as in Reimers and Gurevych (2019).

**Alignment Objective** Let $\text{Enc}^s_\theta(\cdot)$ denote the student query encoder parameterized by $\theta$ and $\text{Enc}^t(\cdot)$ denote the teacher query encoder, we minimize the expected Euclidean distance between the student and teacher embeddings,

$$\mathcal{L}(\theta) = \mathbb{E}_{q\sim\mathcal{D}_q}\left[\|\text{Enc}^s_\theta(q) - \text{Enc}^t(q)\|_2\right]$$

Thus, $\theta$ is found by minimizing the empirical loss,

$$\theta = \underset{\theta}{\text{argmin}} \frac{1}{|\mathcal{Q}|} \sum_{q_i\in\mathcal{Q}} \|\text{Enc}^s_\theta(q_i) - \text{Enc}^t(q_i)\|_2$$

where $\mathcal{Q}$ denotes a set of queries sampled from the distillation domain. In our experiment, we set $\mathcal{Q}$ to be the queries of the IR datasets used by teacher query encoders. This simple optimization objective yields surprisingly performant student models **when paired with proper initialization.**

## 3 Experiments

### 3.1 Evaluation Datasets and Metrics

**Retrieval Performance** For in-domain evaluation, we keep the dataset consistent with our teacher models' training corpus MS MARCO (Bajaj et al., 2018). As for the out-of-domain (zero-shot) evaluation, we use the BEIR benchmark (Thakur et al., 2021) to evaluate our distillation method. It is a diverse collection of seven categories[1] of IR-related tasks. We report normalized Discounted Cumulative Gain (nDCG@10) as the performance metric and average the **relative** performance drops to compare the distillation results.

**Inference Efficiency** We evaluate the efficiency of our distilled query encoder by measuring the wall-clock time required to process queries from the NQ dataset (Kwiatkowski et al., 2019). We simulate various scenarios, ranging from nearly online settings to batched processing, by selecting batch sizes of 4, 8, 16, 32, and 64. For each batch size, we record the elapsed time to process approximately $4 \times 10^3$ queries on a single Nvidia Tesla T4 GPU, repeating the process three times and taking the median time to calculate the number of queries processed per second as the evaluation result.

### 3.2 Teacher and Student Models

**The Teacher Model** In this work, we use a siamese DE model `msmarco-bert-base-dot-v5` hosted on the HuggingFace hub for its competitive performance (Figure 3). The model was fine-tuned on MS MARCO using the dot score as the relevancy measurement and Margin Mean Squared Error (MarginMSE) as the objective function.

**Extractive Initialization** We select a total of thirteen combinations, comprising five combinations of 4-layer models, four combinations of 2-layer models, and four combinations of 1-layer models. The full combinations are listed in subsection A.1.

**DistilBERT Initialization** We explore six DistilBERT checkpoints. The students are initialized from the full model without extracting subsets of layers. Please refer to subsection A.2 for the HuggingFace model cards. We discuss the potential relationship between distillation performance and model characteristics in section 4.

[1]The original publication presents nine categories, but the news and tweet retrieval datasets are not publicly available.

### 3.3 Implementation Details

We use the first 80% of over eight million queries from the MS MARCO training set as our training data and the rest 20% for validation. We train the student models using the AdamW optimizer (Loshchilov and Hutter, 2017) for one epoch with Mean Squared Error (MSE) loss, applying a batch size of 128, a learning rate of $10^{-4}$ and $10^3$ warm-up steps.

## 4 Results and Discussions

**Initializing from Subsets of Teacher Layers** Figure 1 illustrates the performance of the distilled query encoders. We observe that different initialization strategies can lead to up to 6% variability in performance, even with the same number of layers. However, **we find that initializing the students with the first and last few layers consistently yields preferable results**, which aligns with previous findings (Fan et al., 2019; Sajjad et al., 2020; Dong et al., 2022). For instance, considering the 1-layer student encoder (Figure 5), initializing from the last layer yields the best outcomes across all datasets except for ArguAna (Wachsmuth et al., 2018) and Touché-2020 (Bondarenko et al., 2021), preserving an average relative performance of 86.1%. This observation applies similarly to the 2-layer (retaining the first and last layers) and 4-layer (retaining the first and last two layers) students, which exhibit performance preservation rates of 92.5% and 96.2% respectively, aligning closely with the performance of the supervised distilled 6-layer encoder at 96.6% (Kim et al., 2023).

**Initializing from DistilBERTs** The results in Table 1 reveal the within-group performance comparison. Since all student models undergo the same embedding-alignment distillation process, the final performance preservation rate can serve as a proxy for the "well-preparedness" of students. `msmarco-dot` performs the best. Its tuning configuration is the same as its teacher's, i.e., the same dataset, distance function, and objective function. `msmarco-tas-b`, tuned with the balanced topic-aware sampling technique (Hofstätter et al., 2021b), closely follows. Such a variation poses a slightly greater challenge in embedding alignment. On the other side of the spectrum, changing a distance measurement alone makes alignment drastically harder, as shown from `msmarco-cos`. Interestingly, using a different objective function (`msmarco-base`

| Fine-tune Dataset<br>Fine-tune Objective<br>Similarity Function | MS MARCO<br>MarginMSE<br>Dot | MS MARCO<br>MarginMSE<br>Dot | -<br>-<br>- | MS MARCO<br>MultiNegRanking<br>Cosine | NLI + STS<br>CosineSimilarity<br>Cosine | MS MARCO<br>MarginMSE<br>Cosine |
|---|---|---|---|---|---|---|
| **Dataset** (↓) **Ckpt** (→) | `msmarco-dot` | `msmarco-tas-b` | `base-uncased` | `msmarco-base` | `nli-stb` | `msmarco-cos` |
| MS MARCO (In-domain) | **.415 (- 6.58%)** | .412 (- 7.17%) | .406 (- 8.60%) | .389 (-12.40%) | .389 (-12.39%) | .346 (-22.04%) |
| TREC-COVID | **.689 (- 7.58%)** | .676 (- 9.30%) | .634 (-14.86%) | .575 (-22.78%) | .573 (-23.03%) | .512 (-31.31%) |
| NFCorpus | .290 (- 7.84%) | **.297 (- 5.87%)** | .283 (-10.04%) | .271 (-14.06%) | .269 (-14.56%) | .230 (-27.04%) |
| NQ | **.481 (- 7.94%)** | .480 (- 8.04%) | .463 (-11.42%) | .433 (-17.09%) | .440 (-15.75%) | .404 (-22.67%) |
| HotpotQA | **.441 (-25.06%)** | .421 (-28.38%) | .394 (-33.06%) | .352 (-40.12%) | .348 (-40.87%) | .287 (-51.15%) |
| FiQA-2018 | **.291 (- 9.84%)** | .289 (-10.61%) | .282 (-12.81%) | .269 (-16.59%) | .271 (-16.15%) | .232 (-28.18%) |
| ArguAna | **.426 ( 14.33%)** | .417 ( 12.12%) | .392 ( 5.40%) | .408 ( 9.68%) | .368 (- 1.07%) | .402 ( 8.09%) |
| Touché-2020 | .232 (- 2.22%) | .238 ( 0.59%) | .245 ( 3.36%) | **.247 ( 4.22%)** | .244 ( 3.17%) | .234 (- 1.43%) |
| SCIDOCS | **.121 (-17.02%)** | .119 (-18.93%) | .110 (-25.10%) | .099 (-32.29%) | .100 (-31.29%) | .086 (-41.18%) |
| CQADupStack | **.218 (-15.54%)** | .212 (-17.63%) | .204 (-21.08%) | .180 (-30.10%) | .185 (-28.26%) | .148 (-42.58%) |
| Quora | **.812 (- 3.59%)** | .809 (- 3.98%) | .806 (- 4.31%) | .799 (- 5.23%) | .792 (- 6.04%) | .751 (-10.88%) |
| FEVER | **.620 (-18.06%)** | .616 (-18.64%) | .568 (-25.00%) | .535 (-29.39%) | .519 (-31.40%) | .446 (-41.05%) |
| Climate-FEVER | **.182 (-19.77%)** | .175 (-22.64%) | .163 (-28.12%) | .156 (-30.89%) | .150 (-33.70%) | .145 (-35.77%) |
| SciFact | .541 (-11.09%) | **.546 (-10.29%)** | .522 (-14.23%) | .492 (-19.14%) | .493 (-19.02%) | .439 (-27.76%) |
| DBpedia-Entity | **.337 (-12.41%)** | .329 (-14.50%) | .314 (-18.45%) | .287 (-25.54%) | .302 (-21.46%) | .265 (-31.08%) |
| Avg. Δ Performance | **-10.01%** | -10.88% | -14.55% | -18.78% | -19.45% | -27.07% |

Table 1: The DistilBERT-based students' nDCG@10 and percentage change compared to the teacher model across BEIR evaluation datasets. The models are ordered (left to right) according to their average performance degradation.

and `nli-stsb`) appears to alleviate misalignment, suggesting the potential interaction between objective and distance functions. Additionally, a clean, pretrained-only student (`base-uncased`) performs better when a perfect replication of the teacher's fine-tuning setting is not present. Notably, all DistilBERT-based students perform worse than the top-performing extractive students. The 2-layer extractive student outperforms the 6-layer `msmarco-dot` with a performance gap of 2.5%.

**Where are the Well-prepared Students?** Student pretraining has been demonstrated to be crucial for knowledge distillation in language understanding tasks (Turc et al., 2019). However, in our asymmetric DE system, the student encoder operates in conjunction with the document encoder of the teacher system, deviating from the conventional distillation procedure. In this case, **the effectiveness of student models lies not in their sheer capability but rather in their compatibility.** Dong et al. (2022) employed t-SNE (van der Maaten and Hinton, 2008) to visualize the embedding spaces of DE encoders in the context of QA tasks. They observed that the two encoders of an asymmetric system tend to map questions and answers onto distinct parameter spaces, even when trained jointly. This observation elucidates the reason why extractive initialization significantly reduces the difficulty of knowledge distillation in our scenario. Furthermore, we extend these findings by demonstrating that aligning the training objectives, similarity measures, and fine-tuning datasets with those of the teacher model can enhance embedding space compatibility. Note that fine-tuning on similar tasks without aligning other elements, e.g., the distance function, may undermine compatibility. Our findings, in conjunction with the results from Kim et al. (2023), suggest that supervision signals play a crucial role in alignment while parameter-sharing inherently addresses this issue.

**Inference Efficiency** Figure 2 shows that student models initialized from a subset of teacher layers have significantly improved inference speed compared to the teacher model, even with small batch sizes. Considering the marginal performance loss, query encoder distillation provides substantial benefits over the siamese DE encoder.

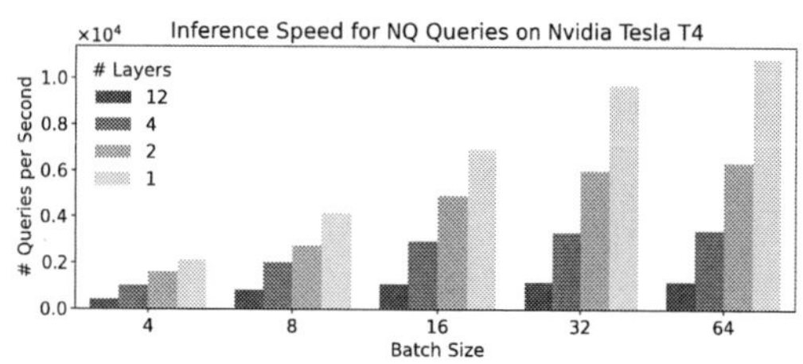


Figure 2: Inference speeds of the distilled query encoders compared to that of the full teacher model. The improvements in inference efficiencies become more drastic as batch size increases.

## 5 Related Work

**Efficient Methods for DE-based IR Systems** Various techniques have been proposed to enhance encoder performance in IR systems, including knowledge distillation (Hofstätter et al., 2021a;

Zeng et al., 2022; Lin et al., 2023b; Kim et al., 2023), improved pretraining objectives (Lee et al., 2019; Chang et al., 2020; Gao and Callan, 2021; Izacard et al., 2021), data augmentation (Oguz et al., 2021), better sampling techniques (Lin et al., 2021; Zhang et al., 2021), ensembles (Hofstätter et al., 2021b; Lin et al., 2023a; Ren et al., 2021). However, most of these methods focus on siamese architectures, as asymmetric DE pairs are prone to representation collapse (Leonhardt et al., 2022) or misalignment of embedding spaces (Dong et al., 2022), making them challenging to train. Due to the shared parameters between query and document encoders, practitioners often need to constrain model size for practicality in production settings, despite the significance of larger models for better retrieval and generalization performance (Ni et al., 2022; Yu et al., 2022). Consequently, this constraint often leads to complex training procedures. In contrast, our simple recipe adopts the train-large-distill-small paradigm, offering a straightforward and effective approach to model development and can be adopted out of the box for existing systems.

**Embedding Alignment for IR** Concurrently, Kim et al. (2023) propose incorporating embedding alignment loss into the supervised distillation pipeline. However, they initialized models from other checkpoints without recognizing the importance of using teacher weights as initialization. Additionally, Campos et al. (2023) suggest minimizing the KL divergence between student and teacher embeddings in an unsupervised manner. Yet, to the best of our knowledge, they do not explore the impact of different layer subsets, whereas our work demonstrates the significant variance caused by such choices.

## 6 Conclusion

In this work, we leverage the characteristics of typical production DE-based IR systems to propose a minimalistic baseline method for improving online efficiency through embedding-alignment distillation. We explore the significance of student initialization for asymmetric DEs and demonstrate that a "well-prepared" student can achieve over five times improvement in efficiency with only 7.5% average performance degradation. We also observe that "well-prepared" students generally have aligned embedding spaces with their teachers, and a simple approach to construct such students is by extracting the first and last few layers from the teacher models. Our findings aim to enhance the accessibility of neural IR systems and encourage the research community to reassess the trade-offs between method complexity and performance improvements.

## Limitations

**Limited Experimental Scope** Our study's experimental scope was limited to testing distilled student models against a single teacher model. A more comprehensive evaluation would involve multiple teacher models of varying sizes, fine-tuning tasks, and datasets. Additionally, in our experiment with DistilBERT-based student models, incorporating more checkpoints would enable a more thorough comparison across different factors.

**Unexplored Embedding Size Variations** We kept the embedding size (768) consistent across student models to maintain variable consistency. Future research could investigate student models with different embedding sizes to determine if the observed trends hold true across models of varying widths.

**Lack of Error Analysis** A common distillation limitation, as noted by Hooker et al. (2020), is the considerable performance decline for certain data subsets. In our study, we couldn't conduct a thorough error analysis due to the lack of appropriate tools for comparing individual data points in retrieval tasks.

## Ethics Statement

Although our method improves accessibility for IR systems, it is essential to evaluate whether the proposed approach might introduce biases or unfairness in the retrieval results. As our work lacks extensive error analysis, we cannot entirely rule out the possibility that distilled query encoders may discard certain hard-to-process cases critical for ensuring fairness across various query topics and user groups. A comprehensive error analysis would be beneficial in future research to identify and address potential biases in the distilled query encoders, ultimately fostering fair and unbiased retrieval results for all users.

## Acknowledgements

We thank the anonymous reviewers for their time and constructive feedback. Also, we would like to thank Prof. Mark Yatskar for his precious suggestions during the development of this work.

## References


Alexandr Andoni, Piotr Indyk, and Ilya P. Razenshteyn. 2018. Approximate nearest neighbor search in high dimensions. *CoRR*, abs/1806.09823.

Payal Bajaj, Daniel Campos, Nick Craswell, Li Deng, Jianfeng Gao, Xiaodong Liu, Rangan Majumder, Andrew McNamara, Bhaskar Mitra, Tri Nguyen, Mir Rosenberg, Xia Song, Alina Stoica, Saurabh Tiwary, and Tong Wang. 2018. MS MARCO: A Human Generated MAchine Reading COmprehension Dataset. ArXiv:1611.09268 [cs].

Iz Beltagy, Matthew E. Peters, and Arman Cohan. 2020. Longformer: The long-document transformer. *CoRR*, abs/2004.05150.

Alexander Bondarenko, Lukas Gienapp, Maik Fröbe, Meriem Beloucif, Yamen Ajjour, Alexander Panchenko, Chris Biemann, Benno Stein, Henning Wachsmuth, Martin Potthast, et al. 2021. Overview of touché 2021: argument retrieval. In *Experimental IR Meets Multilinguality, Multimodality, and Interaction: 12th International Conference of the CLEF Association, CLEF 2021, Virtual Event, September 21–24, 2021, Proceedings 12*, pages 450–467. Springer.

Leonid Boytsov and Eric Nyberg. 2020. Flexible retrieval with NMSLIB and flexneuart. *CoRR*, abs/2010.14848.

Daniel Campos, Alessandro Magnani, and ChengXiang Zhai. 2023. Quick Dense Retrievers Consume KALE: Post Training Kullback Leibler Alignment of Embeddings for Asymmetrical dual encoders. ArXiv:2304.01016 [cs].

Daniel Cer, Yinfei Yang, Sheng-yi Kong, Nan Hua, Nicole Limtiaco, Rhomni St John, Noah Constant, Mario Guajardo-Cespedes, Steve Yuan, Chris Tar, Yun-Hsuan Sung, Brian Strope, and Ray Kurzweil. 2018. Universal Sentence Encoder. ArXiv:1803.11175 [cs].

Wei-Cheng Chang, Felix X. Yu, Yin-Wen Chang, Yiming Yang, and Sanjiv Kumar. 2020. Pre-training tasks for embedding-based large-scale retrieval. *CoRR*, abs/2002.03932.

Alexis Conneau, Douwe Kiela, Holger Schwenk, Loic Barrault, and Antoine Bordes. 2018. Supervised Learning of Universal Sentence Representations from Natural Language Inference Data. ArXiv:1705.02364 [cs].

Zihang Dai, Zhilin Yang, Yiming Yang, Jaime G. Carbonell, Quoc V. Le, and Ruslan Salakhutdinov. 2019. Transformer-xl: Attentive language models beyond a fixed-length context. *CoRR*, abs/1901.02860.

Jacob Devlin, Ming-Wei Chang, Kenton Lee, and Kristina Toutanova. 2018. BERT: pre-training of deep bidirectional transformers for language understanding. *CoRR*, abs/1810.04805.

Zhe Dong, Jianmo Ni, Dan Bikel, Enrique Alfonseca, Yuan Wang, Chen Qu, and Imed Zitouni. 2022. Exploring dual encoder architectures for question answering. In *Proceedings of the 2022 Conference on Empirical Methods in Natural Language Processing*, pages 9414–9419, Abu Dhabi, United Arab Emirates. Association for Computational Linguistics.

Angela Fan, Edouard Grave, and Armand Joulin. 2019. Reducing transformer depth on demand with structured dropout. *arXiv preprint arXiv:1909.11556*.

Luyu Gao and Jamie Callan. 2021. Unsupervised Corpus Aware Language Model Pre-training for Dense Passage Retrieval. ArXiv:2108.05540 [cs].

Sebastian Hofstätter, Sophia Althammer, Michael Schröder, Mete Sertkan, and Allan Hanbury. 2021a. Improving Efficient Neural Ranking Models with Cross-Architecture Knowledge Distillation. ArXiv:2010.02666 [cs].

Sebastian Hofstätter, Sheng-Chieh Lin, Jheng-Hong Yang, Jimmy Lin, and Allan Hanbury. 2021b. Efficiently Teaching an Effective Dense Retriever with Balanced Topic Aware Sampling. ArXiv:2104.06967 [cs].

Sara Hooker. 2020. The hardware lottery. *CoRR*, abs/2009.06489.

Sara Hooker, Nyalleng Moorosi, Gregory Clark, Samy Bengio, and Emily Denton. 2020. Characterising bias in compressed models. *arXiv preprint arXiv:2010.03058*.

Gautier Izacard, Mathilde Caron, Lucas Hosseini, Sebastian Riedel, Piotr Bojanowski, Armand Joulin, and Edouard Grave. 2021. Towards unsupervised dense information retrieval with contrastive learning. *CoRR*, abs/2112.09118.

Jeff Johnson, Matthijs Douze, and Hervé Jégou. 2019. Billion-scale similarity search with GPUs. *IEEE Transactions on Big Data*, 7(3):535–547.

Seungyeon Kim, Ankit Singh Rawat, Manzil Zaheer, Sadeep Jayasumana, Veeranjaneyulu Sadhanala, Wittawat Jitkrittum, Aditya Krishna Menon, Rob Fergus, and Sanjiv Kumar. 2023. EmbedDistill: A Geometric Knowledge Distillation for Information Retrieval. ArXiv:2301.12005 [cs].

Tom Kwiatkowski, Jennimaria Palomaki, Olivia Redfield, Michael Collins, Ankur Parikh, Chris Alberti, Danielle Epstein, Illia Polosukhin, Matthew Kelcey, Jacob Devlin, Kenton Lee, Kristina N. Toutanova, Llion Jones, Ming-Wei Chang, Andrew Dai, Jakob Uszkoreit, Quoc Le, and Slav Petrov. 2019. Natural questions: a benchmark for question answering research. *Transactions of the Association of Computational Linguistics*.

Kenton Lee, Ming-Wei Chang, and Kristina Toutanova. 2019. Latent retrieval for weakly supervised open domain question answering. *CoRR*, abs/1906.00300.

Jurek Leonhardt, Marcel Jahnke, and Avishek Anand. 2022. Distribution-aligned fine-tuning for efficient neural retrieval. *ArXiv*, abs/2211.04942.

Sheng-Chieh Lin, Akari Asai, Minghan Li, Barlas Oguz, Jimmy Lin, Yashar Mehdad, Wen-tau Yih, and Xilun Chen. 2023a. How to Train Your DRAGON: Diverse Augmentation Towards Generalizable Dense Retrieval. ArXiv:2302.07452 [cs].

Sheng-Chieh Lin, Jheng-Hong Yang, and Jimmy Lin. 2021. In-Batch Negatives for Knowledge Distillation with Tightly-Coupled Teachers for Dense Retrieval. In *Proceedings of the 6th Workshop on Representation Learning for NLP (RepL4NLP-2021)*, pages 163–173, Online. Association for Computational Linguistics.

Zhenghao Lin, Yeyun Gong, Xiao Liu, Hang Zhang, Chen Lin, Anlei Dong, Jian Jiao, Jingwen Lu, Daxin Jiang, Rangan Majumder, and Nan Duan. 2023b. PROD: Progressive Distillation for Dense Retrieval. ArXiv:2209.13335 [cs].

Ilya Loshchilov and Frank Hutter. 2017. Fixing weight decay regularization in adam. *CoRR*, abs/1711.05101.

Aditya Menon, Sadeep Jayasumana, Ankit Singh Rawat, Seungyeon Kim, Sashank Reddi, and Sanjiv Kumar. 2022. In defense of dual-encoders for neural ranking. In *Proceedings of the 39th International Conference on Machine Learning*, pages 15376–15400. PMLR. ISSN: 2640-3498.

Jianmo Ni, Chen Qu, Jing Lu, Zhuyun Dai, Gustavo Hernandez Abrego, Ji Ma, Vincent Zhao, Yi Luan, Keith Hall, Ming-Wei Chang, and Yinfei Yang. 2022. Large dual encoders are generalizable retrievers. In *Proceedings of the 2022 Conference on Empirical Methods in Natural Language Processing*, pages 9844–9855, Abu Dhabi, United Arab Emirates. Association for Computational Linguistics.

Barlas Oguz, Kushal Lakhotia, Anchit Gupta, Patrick S. H. Lewis, Vladimir Karpukhin, Aleksandra Piktus, Xilun Chen, Sebastian Riedel, Wen-tau Yih, Sonal Gupta, and Yashar Mehdad. 2021. Domain-matched pre-training tasks for dense retrieval. *CoRR*, abs/2107.13602.

Nils Reimers and Iryna Gurevych. 2019. Sentence-BERT: Sentence Embeddings using Siamese BERT-Networks. ArXiv:1908.10084 [cs].

Ruiyang Ren, Yingqi Qu, Jing Liu, Wayne Xin Zhao, Qiaoqiao She, Hua Wu, Haifeng Wang, and Ji-Rong Wen. 2021. RocketQAv2: A Joint Training Method for Dense Passage Retrieval and Passage Re-ranking. ArXiv:2110.07367 [cs].

Hassan Sajjad, Fahim Dalvi, Nadir Durrani, and Preslav Nakov. 2020. Poor man's bert: Smaller and faster transformer models. *ArXiv*, abs/2004.03844.

Victor Sanh, Lysandre Debut, Julien Chaumond, and Thomas Wolf. 2019. Distilbert, a distilled version of BERT: smaller, faster, cheaper and lighter. *CoRR*, abs/1910.01108.

Timo Schick, Jane Dwivedi-Yu, Roberto Dessì, Roberta Raileanu, Maria Lomeli, Luke Zettlemoyer, Nicola Cancedda, and Thomas Scialom. 2023. Toolformer: Language models can teach themselves to use tools.

Nandan Thakur, Nils Reimers, Andreas Rücklé, Abhishek Srivastava, and Iryna Gurevych. 2021. BEIR: A Heterogenous Benchmark for Zero-shot Evaluation of Information Retrieval Models. ArXiv:2104.08663 [cs].

Iulia Turc, Ming-Wei Chang, Kenton Lee, and Kristina Toutanova. 2019. Well-read students learn better: The impact of student initialization on knowledge distillation. *CoRR*, abs/1908.08962.

Laurens van der Maaten and Geoffrey E. Hinton. 2008. Visualizing data using t-sne. *Journal of Machine Learning Research*, 9:2579–2605.

Henning Wachsmuth, Shahbaz Syed, and Benno Stein. 2018. Retrieval of the best counterargument without prior topic knowledge. In *Proceedings of the 56th Annual Meeting of the Association for Computational Linguistics (Volume 1: Long Papers)*, pages 241–251, Melbourne, Australia. Association for Computational Linguistics.

Thomas Wolf, Lysandre Debut, Victor Sanh, Julien Chaumond, Clement Delangue, Anthony Moi, Pierric Cistac, Tim Rault, Rémi Louf, Morgan Funtowicz, and Jamie Brew. 2019. Huggingface's transformers: State-of-the-art natural language processing. *CoRR*, abs/1910.03771.

Yue Yu, Chenyan Xiong, Si Sun, Chao Zhang, and Arnold Overwijk. 2022. Coco-dr: Combating distribution shifts in zero-shot dense retrieval with contrastive and distributionally robust learning. *arXiv preprint arXiv:2210.15212*.

Manzil Zaheer, Guru Guruganesh, Avinava Dubey, Joshua Ainslie, Chris Alberti, Santiago Ontañón, Philip Pham, Anirudh Ravula, Qifan Wang, Li Yang, and Amr Ahmed. 2020. Big bird: Transformers for longer sequences. *CoRR*, abs/2007.14062.

Hansi Zeng, Hamed Zamani, and Vishwa Vinay. 2022. Curriculum Learning for Dense Retrieval Distillation. ArXiv:2204.13679 [cs].

Hang Zhang, Yeyun Gong, Yelong Shen, Jiancheng Lv, Nan Duan, and Weizhu Chen. 2021. Adversarial retriever-ranker for dense text retrieval. *CoRR*, abs/2110.03611.

Jingqing Zhang, Yao Zhao, Mohammad Saleh, and Peter J. Liu. 2019. PEGASUS: pre-training with extracted gap-sentences for abstractive summarization. *CoRR*, abs/1912.08777.

## A Technical Details

### A.1 Layer-subtraction Schemes

The 4-layer models were initialized using the following schemes: [1,4,7,10], [0,1,10,11], [0,1,2,3], [4,5,6,7], and [8,9,10,11]. The first two schemes were inspired by the results from Fan et al. (2019), which suggested that the input and output layers are often more influential in embedding representations than the middle layers. The latter three schemes were used to validate this intuition and guide our selection schemes for 2-layer and 1-layer initialization. Combinations of 2-layer include [0, 10], [0, 11], [1, 10], and [1, 11]. Layers extracted to make 1-layer models are [0], [1], [10], and [11].

### A.2 DistilBERT-based Student Checkpoints

The HuggingFace model cards of the DistilBERT checkpoints adopted in the experiments are listed below. Except for `distilbert-base-uncased`, all other models have `sentence-transformers/` prefix. The same order also maps to Table 1.

1. `msmarco-distilbert-dot-v5`
2. `msmarco-distilbert-base-tas-b`
3. `distilbert-base-uncased`
4. `msmarco-distilbert-base-v3`
5. `distilbert-base-nli-stsb-mean-tokens`
6. `msmarco-distilbert-cos-v5`

## B Additional Results

### B.1 Other Visualizations

Figure 3 shows the performances of various teachers provided by SentenceTransformers on a subset of BEIR benchmarks. We select the teacher with the highest retrieval performance `msmarco-bert-base-dot-v5`. Figure 4 shows the performances of the student models initialized from other DistilBERT checkpoints. In general, students initialized from pretrained models perform worse than direct layer extraction. Figure 5 and Figure 6 demonstrate that The first few layers and last few layers are more preferable in terms of initialization strategy.

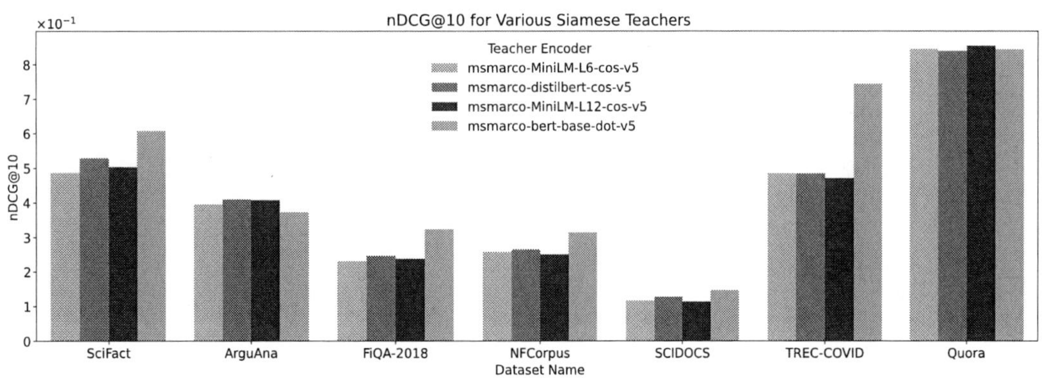


Figure 3: The performances of various teachers provided by SentenceTransformers on a subset of BEIR benchmarks. We select the teacher with the highest retrieval performance.

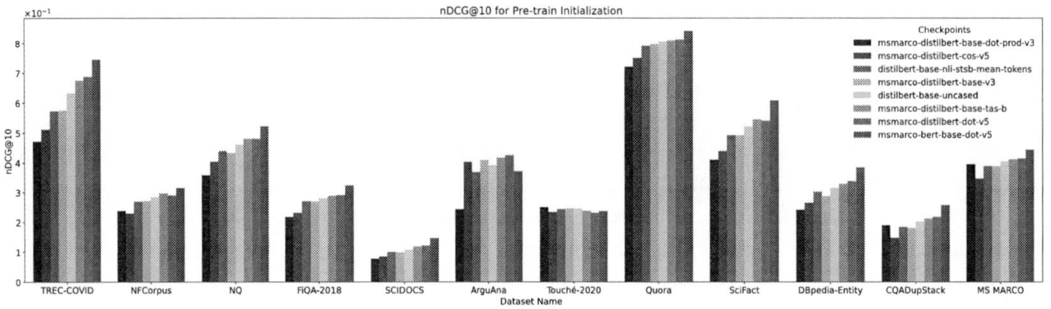


Figure 4: In general, students initialized from pretrained models perform worse than direct layer extraction.

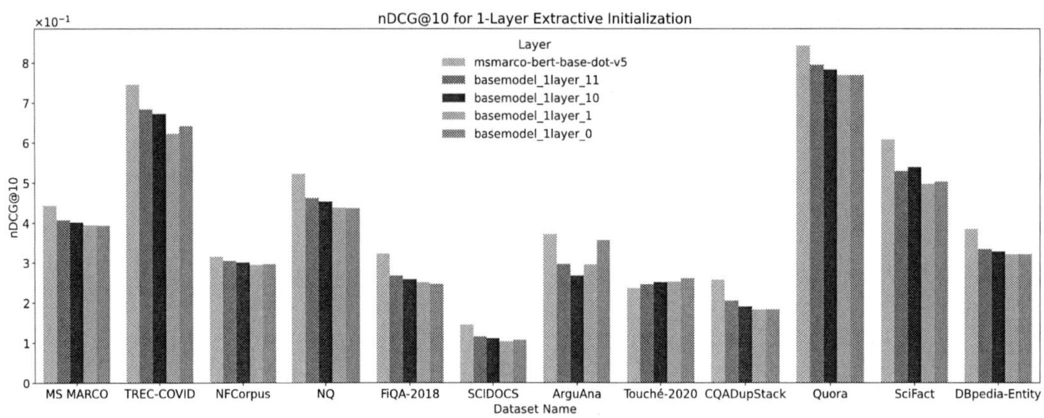


Figure 5: Deeper layers are more preferable than the shallower layers in terms of initialization strategy.

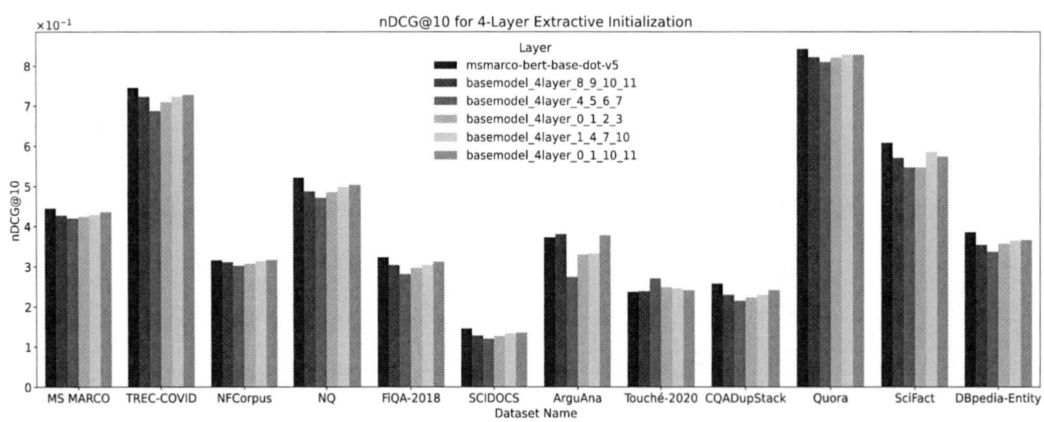


Figure 6: The first few layers and last few layers are more preferable in terms of initialization strategy.

# Minimalist Entity Disambiguation for Mid-Resource Languages

**Benno Kruit**
Vrije Universiteit Amsterdam
De Boelelaan 1105, 1081 HV
Amsterdam, Netherlands
b.b.kruit@vu.nl

## Abstract

For many languages and applications, even though enough data is available for training Named Entity Disambiguation (NED) systems, few off-the-shelf models are available for use in practice. This is due to both the large size of state-of-the-art models, and to the computational requirements for recreating them from scratch. However, we observe that in practice, acceptable models can be trained and run with far fewer resources. In this work, we introduce `MiniNED`, a framework for creating small NED models from medium-sized datasets. The resulting models can be tuned for application-specific objectives and trade-offs, depending on practitioners' requirements concerning model size, frequency bias, and out-of-domain generalization. We evaluate the framework in nine languages, and achieve reasonable performance using models that are a fraction of the size of recent work.

## 1 Introduction

**Motivation and Problem.** Named Entity Disambiguation (NED), is the task of linking pre-identified entity names to their corresponding entries in a knowledge base, such as Wikipedia. As a crucial component of Entity Linking (EL) applications, it has been extensively studied for almost two decades. Presently, powerful state-of-the-art EL systems are available based on (English or multilingual) Neural Language Models (Botha et al., 2020; Wu et al., 2020; van Hulst et al., 2020; De Cao et al., 2022). Unfortunately, for many languages and applications there are few off-the-shelf models that are easy to distribute, customize, or use in constrained practical settings. This is due to the large size of trained models, as well as the computational requirements for creating them from scratch. As a result, EL systems are often unavailable or too large to run for many applications.

**Approach.** In this work, we focus on *mid-resource* languages (e.g. Persian, Japanese, and Tamil), which have some linguistic resources and tools available but not many (Ortiz Suárez et al., 2020). We claim that for many of these languages, simpler and smaller models can perform well enough with careful trade-off analyses. Our main observation is that here the range of reasonable NED performance is quite narrow. In other words, the lower bound (i.e. simply predicting the most commonly linked entity for a given name) and the non-zero-shot upper bound (i.e. perfectly disambiguating all names that are seen in training) are very close together. Based on this insight, we demonstrate that small NED models can achieve acceptable performance with limited resources. We examine the trade-offs between model size and performance for different configurations and highlight the importance of language-specific phenomena, such as morphological differences, in determining optimal parameter settings. We argue that the tuning of NED models for mid-resource languages requires careful consideration and can only be done sustainably on small models.

**Contribution.** We introduce and evaluate `MiniNED`[1], a Python library for creating NED models from Wikipedia data in many languages. We show that much simpler models than state-of-the-art systems can achieve acceptable performance in practice. We also show how our framework allows practitioners to control model complexity and adjust for specific use-cases, while maintaining performance.

## 2 Observations

Examining the Mewsli-9 benchmark (Botha et al., 2020), we can make several observations about the distribution of data that is available in Wikipedia[2] for training NED models.

[1] https://github.com/bennokr/miniNED

[2] All experiments were performed on Wikipedia dumps from 2022-03-01. In Mewsli-9, we replace English by Dutch due to our focus on mid-resource languages.



*Proceedings of The Fourth Workshop on Simple and Efficient Natural Language Processing (SustaiNLP)*, pages 299–306
July 13, 2023 ©2023 Association for Computational Linguistics

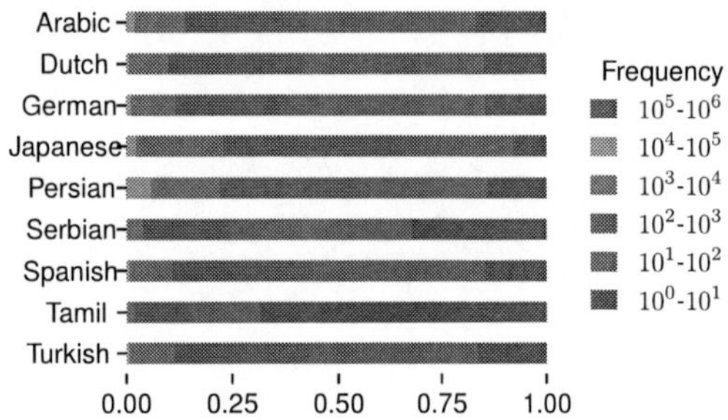


Figure 1: Distribution of entity hyperlink frequencies in Wikipedia, for names from Mewsli-9.

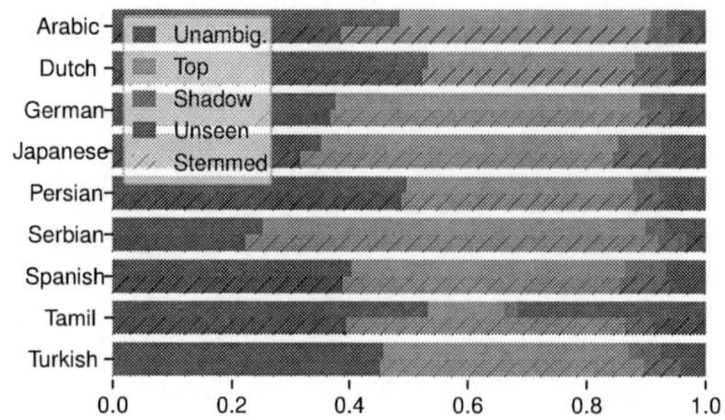


Figure 2: Proportion of benchmark mention instances per ambiguity category, Mewsli-9 dataset. Hatched bars indicates the stemming of names, which decreases unseen cases, but increases ambiguity.

In Figure 1, we show the distribution of how often entities from the benchmark data are hyperlinked on Wikipedia. While we observe a typical long-tailed distribution, most entities can still be observed between 10-1000 times. For these languages, this provides enough training data to learn to disambiguate entity mentions from their context.

In Figure 2, however, we observe that the baseline performance of simply predicting the *top* most commonly linked entity for a given ambiguous name (combined with straightforwardly linking *unambiguous* names) can already achieve relatively high performance. Additionally, many entity-name pairs (which we will refer to as *mentions*) in the benchmark data cannot be observed in training at all; such *unseen* cases would require zero-shot generalization. Consequently, the upper and lower bound for simple models are very close together. Thus, we may comclude that the main challenge lies in predicting *shadowed* entity mentions (Provatorova et al., 2021), which share a surface form with more popular entities. Due to the overwhelming imbalance of training instances for shadowed entities, particular attention should be given to selecting appropriate training data and to the assumptions that underly the model.

Another observation is that language-specific phenomena make a big difference. The distribution of observed ambiguity changes when names are *stemmed*. Stemming removes word inflections, which increases the ambiguity of names. We can see that due to morphological differences, the effect of stemming is very different per language. Overall, stemming decreases the number of unseen mentions, but also widens the range of ambiguous names.

Finally, Wikipedia hyperlink data is noisy (Gerlach et al., 2021), as it includes links to disambiguation pages and incorrect entity links. This becomes a larger problem when less data is available (as for low-resource languages and domains). We argue that optimally tuning the training pipeline to overcome this noise (by fixing this data or patching the model) can only be done sustainably when the model itself is simple.

## 3 Approach

We train multinomial logistic regression classifiers with hashed Bag-of-Word features, which are trained to rank candidate entities using Vowpal Wabbit (vw, Langford et al., 2007). The candidates are created by filtering entity mention counts from Wikipedia dumps using heuristics. These heuristics identify valid surface forms based on their appearance on disambiguation pages, their string similarity to the entity labels, and the entropy of the prior probability distribution of hyperlink targets. Re-

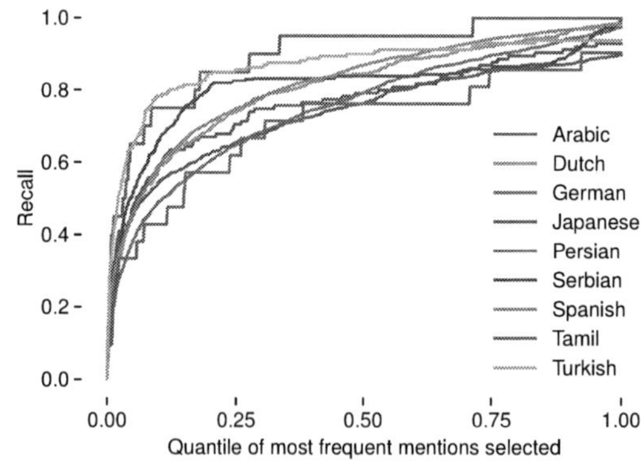


Figure 3: Maximum attainable recall of observed ambiguous mentions given filtering thresholds. When keeping the top 25% most frequent mention-entity instances, the maximum attainable recall on *ambiguous* benchmark instances is 55-85% .

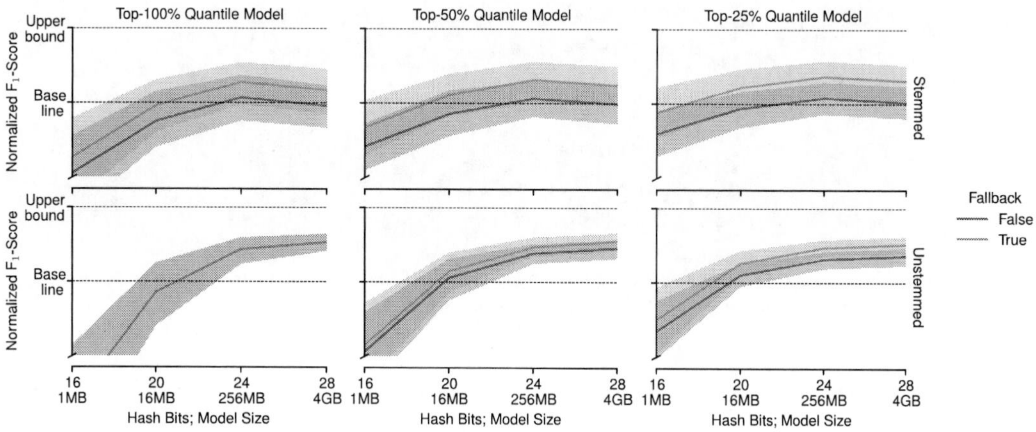


Figure 4: Distribution (mean and 95% confidence interval) of normalized micro $F_1$-scores. Per-language scores are transformed w.r.t. the baseline (most frequent target of entity labels) and the upper bound on observed mentions (Section 2). *Subplots*: Performance improves logistically with model size, with strongly diminishing returns. *Colors*: Using a fallback to the baseline for unobserved names recovers most lost performance for stemmed and quantile-filtered models. *Rows*: Stemmed models have higher variety in performance between languages, and may overfit when large. *Columns*: Quantile-filtered models require fewer parameters. Raw results in Appendix A.

garding the entropy, a cutoff threshold determines when a long, flat prior distribution is discarded (e.g. specific villages for the anchor text "village"). This also leads to anchor texts with flat distributions of very similarly frequent targets to be discarded entirely (e.g. for strings such as "click here").

The candidate set can be further filtered by only selecting a percentage (i.e. quantile) of most frequently observed ambiguous mentions. In Figure 3, we show the tradeoff between candidate mention filtering and the maximum recall that a model trained to disambiguate between these candidates could achieve. We observe that selecting only the most frequently mentioned entities results in quick gains with only a fraction of the candidate set size. However, we also observe that our pre-processing heuristics discard valid mentions for some languages, so that even on the full set of candidates, perfect recall cannot be attained.

The vw model size is controlled by the number of bits of the feature hash, which also works as regularisation to prevent overfitting. By exchanging single coefficients per mention-feature pair for smaller models with more hash collisions, we are able to find the optimal tradeoff between model size and accuracy using a hyperparameter sweep. Although the features are hashed, the model can still be audited by keeping track of feature hashes for specific analyses. This can be useful for explaining individual predictions (showing which context words have a strong influence), or examining the coefficients that are used to disambiguate a single surface form.

| | Baseline | Fallback | Best Model$_{\text{bits}}$ | Upper Bound |
|---|---|---|---|---|
| Arabic | .87 | .87/.88 | $.82_{28}/\mathbf{.89}_{28}$ | .93/.91 |
| Dutch | .63 | .77/.77 | $.77_{28}/\mathbf{.78}_{28}$ | .84/.83 |
| German | .80 | **.85**/.84 | $.84_{28}/\mathbf{.85}_{28}$ | .90/.88 |
| Japanese | .80 | .83/**.84** | $.81_{28}/.83_{28}$ | .91/.89 |
| Persian | .85 | .86/.86 | $\mathbf{.88}_{28}/\mathbf{.88}_{24}$ | .91/.90 |
| Serbian | .76 | **.84**/.80 | $.83_{28}/.80_{28}$ | .89/.83 |
| Spanish | .71 | .80/.80 | $.78_{28}/\mathbf{.81}_{28}$ | .89/.88 |
| Tamil | .61 | .74/.62 | $\mathbf{.75}_{24}/.63_{24}$ | .77/.64 |
| Turkish | .80 | **.84**/.81 | $.80_{28}/.81_{28}$ | .91/.87 |

Table 1: Micro $F_1$-scores (stemmed / unstemmed). *Baseline*: most frequent target of entity labels. *Fallback*: most frequent target of pre-processed hyperlinks. *Best Model*: score & bits of highest-scoring model configuration. *Upper Bound*: Perfect performance on observed mentions.

## 4 Evaluation

Our analysis compares models of different sizes and candidate filtering thresholds, and the effect of stemming in different languages. We modify the Mewsli-9 benchmark to discard links to disambiguation pages and list pages (statistics in Appendix B), and we generate the Dutch data using the scripts provided by Botha et al. (2020). We train on lowercased mentions that occur more than once, which are filtered by discarding names which both (1) have less than 10% of tokens appear in an entity label on Wikidata and (2) have a high candidate entropy (> 1 nat), except if they are used as

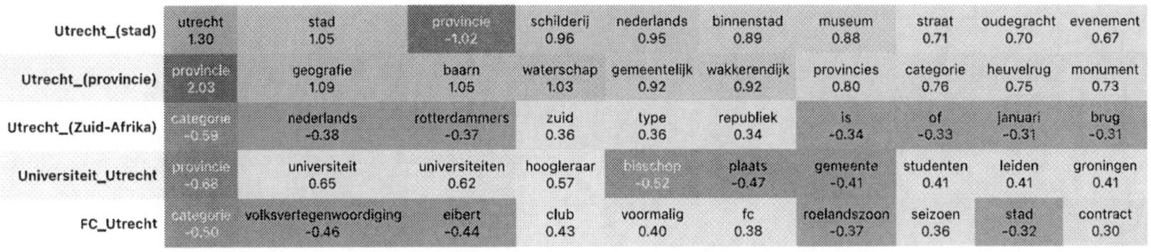


Figure 5: Inspecting strongest feature coefficients in the Dutch model for the name "Utrecht", which among others may refer to a city, province, town in South Africa, university, or football club.

main links on disambiguation pages. For stemming, we use PersianStemmer (Taghi-Zadeh et al., 2015), MeCab for Japanese (Kudo, 2006), and Snowball for other languages (Porter, 2001).

In Figure 4, we report normalized disambiguation micro-$F_1$ scores, where per-language scores are transformed with respect to the baseline (the most frequent target of entity labels) and the upper bound (on observed mentions). Unnormalized results are presented per language for best-performing models in Table 1 and in Appendix A.

We observe that the effect of stemming and the trade-off between model size and performance is different per language, but clear trends are visible, with diminishing returns of model sizes above a few hundred MB.

**Explainability and Denoising.** By keeping track of which features hash to which parameters for a set of example instances, we can visualize which context words have a strong influence on model predictions (Figure 5). This is useful for improving models for which the training data may have been noisy, allowing practitioners to modify pre-processing pipelines or employ data re-labeling efforts.

## 5 Related Work

Mewsli-9 was introduced by Botha et al. (2020) and used for evaluation by De Cao et al. (2022). Our evaluation results are not directly comparable to theirs because we remove links to disambiguation pages and list pages.

Some EL systems for mid-resource languages exist. Most prominently, DBpedia Spotlight (Daiber et al., 2013) publish EL models for some languages, but these are not tunable for size. Tsai and Roth (2016) perform cross-lingual wikification using multilingual embeddings; we plan to replace our BoW features by such embeddings in future work. Pappu et al. (2017) train lightweight multilingual entity linking models, but not for mid-resource languages. Gerlach et al. (2021) focus on precision, while we focus on $F_1$-scores and model size.

Modern EL models often combine Mention Detection (MD) and NED end-to-end. Hachey et al. (2013) describe the interplay of MD and NED in English EL. Ling et al. (2015) extend this description, and make similar observations to ours about NED baselines. Kolitsas et al. (2018) are the first to train end-to-end neural EL models, improved later by De Cao et al. (2021). These efforts were extended to multilingual models by Botha et al. (2020) and De Cao et al. (2022). Such end-to-end neural models require many GPU-hours to train, making it impossible to tune them sustainably for specific applications. In contrast, we focus on the smallest possible NED models, because small MD models can be achieved with the use of gazetteers and their interplay may be optimized by tuning.

## 6 Conclusion and Future Work

We introduce and evaluate `MiniNED`, a Python library for creating NED models from Wikipedia data in many languages. We show that much simpler models than state-of-the-art systems can achieve acceptable performance in practice. We also show how our framework allows practitioners to control model complexity and adjust for specific use-cases, while maintaining performance.

For future research, we expect this approach to also be useful when incorporating more background knowledge about the entities with richer feature representations and using weak supervision (Orr et al., 2021). Also, the tradeoffs that this work analyses are strongly related to the difficulty of determining the appropriate granularity of EL systems (Van Erp and Groth, 2020). For example, the knowledge base that the mentions are linked to may distinguish between municipalities as administrative entities and the cities within them, while for many applications this distinction is not relevant. In the future we aim to add support for tuning models to the desired levels of granularity.

## Acknowledgements

This research is partially funded by Huawei Amsterdam Research Center.

I would like to thank Thiviyan Thanapalasingam, Majid Mohammedi and Erman Acar for their early feedback on language-specific models, and the members of the VU Amsterdam *Knowledge in AI* and *Learning & Reasoning* groups, Winston Wansleeben, Rens Hassfeld and Mara Spadon for their feedback on drafts of this work.

## References

Jan A Botha, Zifei Shan, and Dan Gillick. 2020. Entity linking in 100 languages. In *Proceedings of the 2020 Conference on Empirical Methods in Natural Language Processing*, pages 7833–7845.

Joachim Daiber, Max Jakob, Chris Hokamp, and Pablo N. Mendes. 2013. Improving efficiency and accuracy in multilingual entity extraction. In *International Conference on Semantic Systems*.

Nicola De Cao, Gautier Izacard, Sebastian Riedel, and Fabio Petroni. 2021. Autoregressive entity retrieval. In *9th International Conference on Learning Representations, ICLR 2021, Virtual Event, Austria, May 3-7, 2021*.

Nicola De Cao, Ledell Wu, Kashyap Popat, Mikel Artetxe, Naman Goyal, Mikhail Plekhanov, Luke Zettlemoyer, Nicola Cancedda, Sebastian Riedel, and Fabio Petroni. 2022. Multilingual autoregressive entity linking. *Transactions of the Association for Computational Linguistics*, 10:274–290.

Martin Gerlach, M. Miller, Rita Ho, Kosta Harlan, and Djellel Eddine Difallah. 2021. Multilingual entity linking system for wikipedia with a machine-in-the-loop approach. *Proceedings of the 30th ACM International Conference on Information & Knowledge Management*.

Ben Hachey, Will Radford, Joel Nothman, Matthew Honnibal, and James R. Curran. 2013. Evaluating entity linking with wikipedia. *Artificial Intelligence*, 194:130–150.

Nikolaos Kolitsas, Octavian-Eugen Ganea, and Thomas Hofmann. 2018. End-to-end neural entity linking. In *Proceedings of the 22nd Conference on Computational Natural Language Learning*, pages 519–529.

Taku Kudo. 2006. Mecab: Yet another part-of-speech and morphological analyzer.

John Langford, Lihong Li, and Alex Strehl. 2007. Vowpal wabbit online learning project.

Xiao Ling, Sameer Singh, and Daniel S. Weld. 2015. Design Challenges for Entity Linking. *Transactions of the Association for Computational Linguistics*, 3(2011):315–328.

Laurel J. Orr, Megan Leszczynski, Neel Guha, Sen Wu, Simran Arora, Xiao Ling, and Christopher Ré. 2021. Bootleg: Chasing the tail with self-supervised named entity disambiguation. In *11th Conference on Innovative Data Systems Research, CIDR 2021, Virtual Event, January 11-15, 2021*.

Pedro Javier Ortiz Suárez, Laurent Romary, and Benoît Sagot. 2020. A monolingual approach to contextualized word embeddings for mid-resource languages. In *Proceedings of the 58th Annual Meeting of the Association for Computational Linguistics*, pages 1703–1714, Online. Association for Computational Linguistics.

Aasish Pappu, Roi Blanco, Yashar Mehdad, Amanda Stent, and Kapil Thadani. 2017. Lightweight multilingual entity extraction and linking. In *Proceedings of the Tenth ACM International Conference on Web Search and Data Mining*, WSDM 17, New York, NY, USA. ACM.

Martin F Porter. 2001. Snowball: A language for stemming algorithms.

Vera Provatorova, Samarth Bhargav, Svitlana Vakulenko, and Evangelos Kanoulas. 2021. Robustness evaluation of entity disambiguation using prior probes: the case of entity overshadowing. In *Proceedings of the 2021 Conference on Empirical Methods in Natural Language Processing*, pages 10501–10510.

Hossein Taghi-Zadeh, Mohammad Hadi Sadreddini, Mohammad Hasan Diyanati, and Amir Hossein Rasekh. 2015. A new hybrid stemming method for persian language. *Digital Scholarship in the Humanities*, 32(1):209–221.

Chen-Tse Tsai and Dan Roth. 2016. Cross-lingual wikification using multilingual embeddings. In *Proceedings of the 2016 Conference of the North American Chapter of the Association for Computational Linguistics: Human Language Technologies*, pages 589–598.

Marieke Van Erp and Paul Groth. 2020. Towards entity spaces. In *Proceedings of the 12th Language Resources and Evaluation Conference*, pages 2129–2137.

Johannes M. van Hulst, Faegheh Hasibi, Koen Dercksen, Krisztian Balog, and Arjen P. de Vries. 2020. REL: An Entity Linker Standing on the Shoulders of Giants. In *Proceedings of the 43rd International ACM SIGIR Conference on Research and Development in Information Retrieval*, pages 2197–2200, Virtual Event China. ACM.

Ledell Wu, Fabio Petroni, Martin Josifoski, Sebastian Riedel, and Luke Zettlemoyer. 2020. Scalable zero-shot entity linking with dense entity retrieval. In *Proceedings of the 2020 Conference on Empirical Methods in Natural Language Processing*, pages 6397–6407.

# Appendix

## A Evaluation Results

Micro-$F_1$ scores per model size. *Line width*: Candidate selection filtering quantile. *Color*: Use of fallback to baseline (most frequent target).

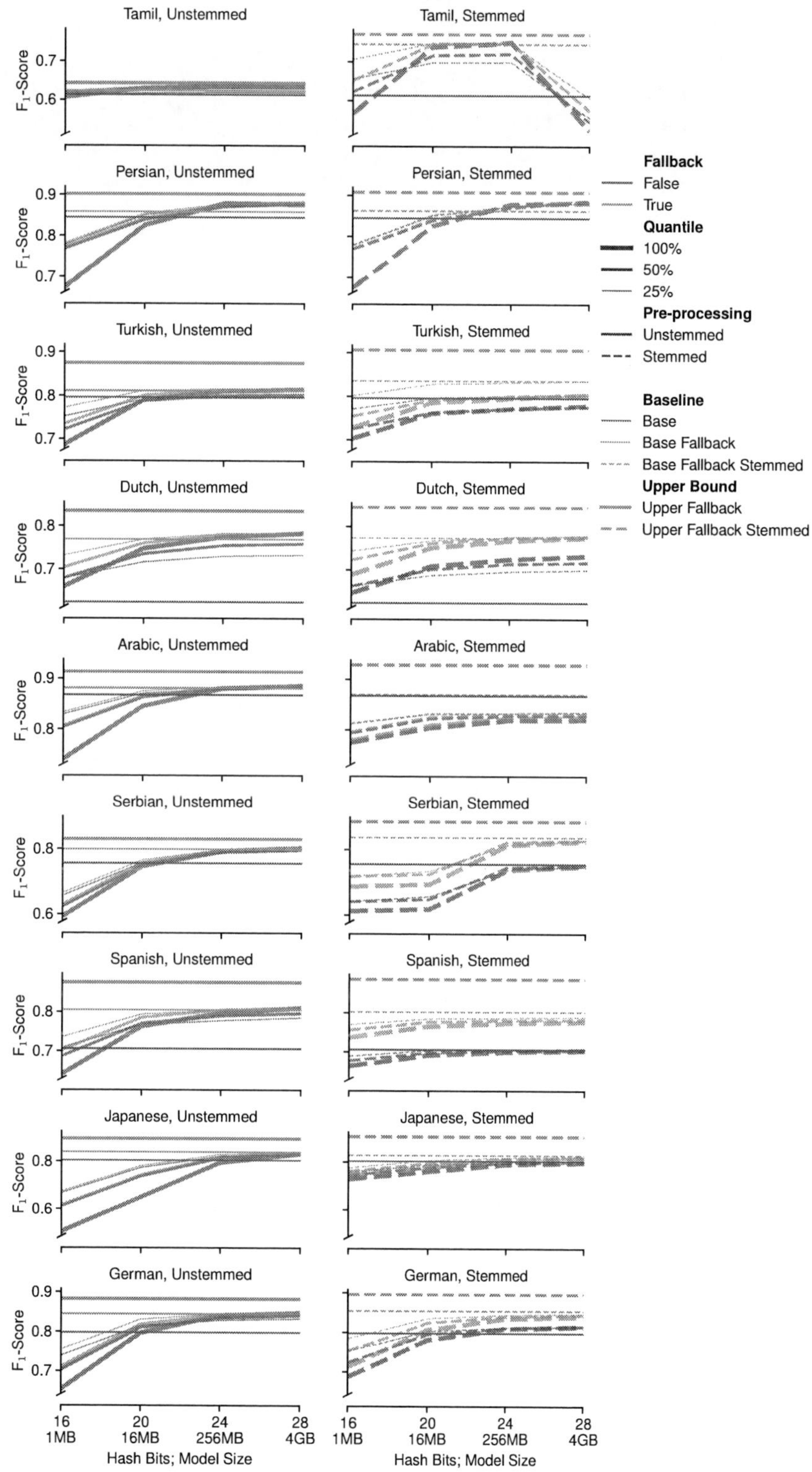

## B Mewsli-9 Modification

| | Disambig | Listpage | Total |
|---|---|---|---|
| Arabic | 201 | 4 | 5964 |
| Dutch | 562 | 16 | 11924 |
| German | 1907 | 76 | 64807 |
| Japanese | 605 | 54 | 34214 |
| Persian | 5 | 0 | 515 |
| Serbian | 773 | 7 | 35536 |
| Spanish | 1923 | 105 | 55431 |
| Tamil | 28 | 1 | 2683 |
| Turkish | 164 | 5 | 5661 |

Table 2: Statistics on discarded Mewsli-9 links out of the total original dataset

# Author Index

**Association for Computational Linguistics**
209 N. Eighth Street
Stroudsburg, Pennsylvania 18360

ISBN 978-1-7138-8235-0

9 781713 882350

CURRAN ASSOCIATES INC.
proceedings.com